The Shaker Spiritual

"The Final Procession," from *The Graphic*, Vol. 1, no. 24, May 1870

THE SHAKER
✳ SPIRITUAL ✳

By Daniel W. Patterson

PRINCETON UNIVERSITY PRESS

PRINCETON, NEW JERSEY

Contents

List of Illustrations

List of Tables and Diagrams

A Note on Abbreviations and Symbols

Many of the sources cited throughout this book are manuscripts. Each such citation is prefaced by a symbol (e.g., NHCb, OCWR, DWt, etc.) showing the location of the manuscript. A key to all of these source abbreviations is on pages 483 and 484, below.

Symbols used for dance steps in some tunes are as follows:

B—back toward the starting place
Bw—moving backwards toward the starting place without turning
F—forward
L—left foot
R—right foot
Shf—shuffle
Sk—skip
St—step
TnL—turn to the left
TnR—turn to the right

Preface

Many a year has passed since I started down this path. I first glimpsed it in a chance reading of Edward D. Andrews' *The Gift to be Simple.* The Shaker way appeared narrow, but the beauty of some of the melodies Andrews printed promised rewards enough for a brief excursion. Further browsing disclosed other Shaker tunes equally good in two slight articles that Phillips Barry wrote in the 1930s, and ones handsomer yet in Clara Endicott Sears' *Gleanings from Old Shaker Journals.* Hers were printed as facsimiles of manuscript pages and roused my curiosity to know just what might survive in such records. My random inquiries brought a scattering of answers from libraries with manuscripts not mentioned in Andrews' book and led me to Harold Cook's then unpublished dissertation, "Shaker Music: A Manifestation of American Folk Culture."[1] This study contained a checklist of 354 Shaker music manuscripts held by the Western Reserve Historical Society. Clearly the number as well as the quality of the Shaker songs made the path worth serious exploration.

At this time Andrews had projected, and he eventually nearly completed, a sequel to *The Gift to be Simple,* but he was unfamiliar with other Anglo-American secular and religious folk songs. Cook's interest in Shaker song had been exhausted by the writing of his dissertation. There was room, then, for a third student, but I had an even better reason for entering the field. In my search I had discovered a major document unknown to either Cook or Andrews, Elder Russel Haskell's manuscript "A Record of Spiritual Songs."[2] Perhaps other equally important ones could yet be found. I therefore resolved to find and study every surviving Shaker song book. No doubt I failed, but I did track down nearly eight hundred manuscripts. They are rich in possibilities for research, and in hopes of helping later students I have prepared an appendix listing all those I have seen. It describes 371 not known to Cook and departs from his format in presenting the entries by, so far as possible, community of origin and author, and in summarizing the contents of each song book.

These collections hold a prodigious number of songs. Haskell's great manuscript alone is a compendium of nearly 2,400 tunes, and it covers only ones used in the small community at Enfield, Connecticut, between 1780 and 1854. The entire body of surviving manuscripts must preserve 8,000 to 10,000 songs.[3] One object of my research has therefore been to gather the best of these for publication. My selection forms, I believe, one of the most varied and distinguished tune collections yet harvested from Anglo-American tradition; but this is a matter I must leave the reader to judge.

Happily, Russel Haskell showed a way of rising above subjective judgments in selecting the songs. He in fact offered two useful coordinates for mapping the Shaker repertory. First, he grouped his songs by genre. Each type proves to have its own distinctive melodic and textual models. From secular tradition the Shaker singer could expropriate only tunes compatible with these models, but a model might itself also encourage him to recast a ballad melody into dance-tune form, or to clip and piece out its phrases to make it fit an untraditional stanza, or to cap one tune with another of equal length, or simply to elaborate a fresh tune from familiar turns and phrases. In short, analysis of the Shaker genres has enabled me to document the singers' use of traditional song as a musical language with which to create new tunes.

The second coordinate established in Haskell's manuscript was chronological. He arranged the genres, and the songs within them, roughly by the date of their entry into the repertory at Enfield. Other documents helped to show how both the life span and the aesthetic form of each of the song types derived from its function in Shaker life. Text and tune were affected by whether the author sat down to compose a song or "received" it spontaneously in a "spiritual impression" or in a dream, trance, or possession state. From decade to decade first one and then the other of these two modes of composition would predominate in Shaker song. Moreover, whole classes of songs came into and passed out of use following changes in the size and composition of the membership, or shifts in Shaker beliefs, attitudes, and imaginative interests.

The structure that Haskell gave his collection proved, in short, so revealing that I have followed it on my own, though with many adjustments. While I cannot claim to give each phase or genre a number of pages directly proportional to its weight in the total song repertory, I do offer at least one example of each genre and roughly approximate the contour of the surviving repertory. My collection is in consequence a better representation of Shaker song than those of Andrews and Cook, which grossly overemphasize the Gift Songs of the years 1837 to 1850.

What I have in fact tried to do is to seize an exciting opportunity offered by the Shaker manuscripts: a chance to study the complete life history of a well-documented folk-song repertory created by one distinctly bounded group. I do not know of another branch of American folk song for which this would be possible. The Shaker song manuscripts, however, record the group's singing from the 1780s into the twentieth century, and thousands of other documents richly supplement them. These include letters, diaries, journals, and histories, and the accounts of outsiders as well. Shaker oral tradition preserves additional songs and information. Taken together, these compose a surprisingly full, if by no means complete, record of Shaker song and its context.

The interplay between the songs and the beliefs and practices of the Shakers inevitably drew my attention past the spirituals to the institution itself, and in the works that others have written about it I looked for insights into the nature of Shakerism. The greater number of these writings are chapter-length treatments in books dealing with millennialism, exotic sects, or utopian and communitarian enterprises. They range from the shoddy (Ronald Knox's *Enthusiasm: A Chapter in the History of Religion*) to the stolidly adequate (John Whitworth's *God's Blueprints: A Sociological Study of Three Utopian Sects*). As a body, these writings show no advance over the pioneering studies from the end of the nineteenth century, John Humphrey Noyes' *History of American Socialisms*, Charles Nordhoff's *The Communistic Societies of the United States*, and William Hinds' *American Communities.*[4]

The early years also produced the most useful book focused solely on the Shakers, Eldress Anna White and Leila S. Taylor's *Shakerism: Its Meaning and Message.*[5] Andrews' *The People Called Shakers* is of course a deft, methodical, and objective account of Shaker history, and the community histories written by Caroline Piercy and Julia Neal are solid and intensive within their range.[6] White and Taylor, however, reveal much more of how Shakerism was felt and understood by the participants. The chief weaknesses of their book are that it lacks perspective on the context within which Shakerism developed and that its Shaker authors naturally omit issues they felt improper for general review.

The one full-length sociological study of Shakerism, Henri Desroche's *Les Shakers Américains*, is weak, but requires comment, since the book has been translated into English, published by an American university press, and endorsed by the director of one of the leading Shaker museums. The book suffers from two methodological flaws. First, the author confined his research solely to published sources. As a result he wandered often into erroneous suppositions that a deeper knowledge of the Shaker literature would have corrected. Since his book, moreover, rests chiefly on the writings of Shaker apologists, Desroche looked mainly at the face that the Shakers' intellectual leaders wished to present to the World. Sometimes he recognized the stratagems these writers knowingly or unconsciously used in dealing with outsiders or with crises in the inner life of the sect, but he was equally likely to accept their statements uncritically. To take but one example, he followed an account of the French Prophets that Benjamin S. Youngs presented in *The Testimony of Christ's Second Appearing* (1808). Andrews and others read the account equally uncritically, but Desroche built an entire chapter upon it, using it to theorize upon the sources of important ideas and attitudes of the Shakers. Youngs, however, made no claim to be recording traditions learned from the English Shakers. He was quoting, with an acknowledgement of his source, from Hannah Adams' *Views of Religion*, a handbook of popularized religious history.[7] As a Believer, he regarded the Pentecostalism of the French Prophets as proceeding from the same Spirit as that of the Shakers. His was a familiar exercise in legitimation of his faith. Any direct historical relationship between Shakerism and the French Prophets is doubtful and is certainly yet to be proved.

Desroche's second methodological error is more serious. Like the Shaker author, Desroche himself was presenting a pious interpretation of history. He was less eager to explore the actual theological and social milieu within which Shaker men and women moved and had their being than to burnish the glory of twentieth-century "self-conscious class struggle."[8] He conceived himself to be documenting the grand evolution of society. Although he deplored the "undisciplined and disappointing social content of the Shakers' class consciousness," he found the group worth note as "a catalyst, facilitating the passage" of society from dark ages into the dazzling brilliance of socialism. Working from this doctrinal premise, he not surprisingly arrived by subtle shifts at the views that for the Shakers "the only real resurrection is an earthly experience of angelic life" and that the Shakers wanted in effect to substitute for the Eucharist "the immanent reality of transubstantiation."[9] In this way he could present Shakerism as a half-way house to Marxian materialism. Even a Transcendentalist music critic could see more clearly than that, though he lived in a misty age and lacked training in the rigors of "scientific" social analysis. The Shakers, said John Sullivan Dwight in 1847, wanted "the spiritual *without* the material, not the spiritual *in* the material."[10]

More serious than such errors of interpretation are the questions left unasked. New ground is broken not in the works just cited but in several less-pretending studies, F. Gerald Ham's doctoral dissertation on the Western Shakers, Robley E. Whitson's booklet on Shaker theology, Thomas Swain's article on the editing of the *Testimonies*, and several pieces by Theodore Johnson.[11] I have profited from all of these, as well as from a number of suggestive writings on psychology, sociology, anthropology, and American social and religious history that mention Shakerism only briefly, if at all. Although my most intensive reading has been in the Shaker documents themselves, these scholarly writings encouraged me to look for the interplay between the Shaker song tradition and the social world outside the villages or between the spirituals and the ways the Shakers structured and experienced their lives. Into my song collection I weave many previously unpublished materials that throw light on these topics.

Such insights as I have gained I present as background for the songs rather than as a systematic ethnographic study. Even if the songs were not my primary concern, I would find the latter approach unwise, and not solely for the reason that I lack the requisite training. At any moment in its history Shakerism was a complex movement, and it passed through many phases across the years. Even painting with very broad strokes the sociologist Bryan Wilson was forced to admit complexity into his characterization of the Shakers. His typology of "deviant religious responses" to the world includes seven categories of sects, and he concedes that the Shakers blend traits of three of these.[12] The Shakers brought seekers to a realization of their own sinfulness, he says, "in a way that might be found in a conversionist sect, but the consequence was a life of separation that was thoroughly introversionist." The Shaker leader Frederick Evans shows, in Wilson's terminology, "essentially a utopian response to the world." Wilson might have gone further. Shaker spiritualism and faith healing were traits he would normally call those of a "thaumaturgical sect."

Another reason for caution is that the Shaker documents do not permit the extraction of much "hard" data. One example will illustrate the problem. To establish the motivations of the converts who came to Shakerism in the 1780s one has little evidence beyond the collections of testimonies first written down thirty years after the death of Ann Lee. Although the members doubtless tried to state the facts truthfully, their memories seem to have settled into formulas. Both the content of their statements and the editing of successive collections of testimonies were also shaped by immediate concerns of the Society in the years when they were gathered.[13] Even the *Testimonies* of 1827, which most nearly attain a full narrative form, often fail to include such crucial information as the Believer's age at the time of his conversion, whether he had been orphaned or married, and whether his family and friends opposed or supported his conversion. Moreover, many early converts had died before the compilations were made. These included all persons of advanced years at the time of their conversion; their motivations probably differed from those of converts who joined as adolescents. We have almost no information about members who later dropped into apostasy or about persons who from the first rejected Shakerism. In short, we cannot determine in precise percentages just what factors counted most with Shaker converts or how Believers differed in temperament or experience from people who took other courses.

The songs themselves do, however, provide a way through these methodological morasses. Since the basis of my selection was musical, the texts form a reasonably unbiased survey of Shaker sentiments. Moreover, as I worked with the Shaker manuscripts, I found that to a surprising extent I was able to establish the authorship of songs attracting my attention and that other Shaker documents yielded much information about the lives of these singers. Although I cannot prove the songsters completely typical of the membership at large, the patterns that emerge in their stories do appear also in the biographies of less-musical Shakers. The information at any rate bears directly on the songs, and I incorporate it in my headnotes, as I do other materials needed to explain the origins, themes, and functions of the songs.

I believe that my glosses have some validity as a picture of Shakerism, but they are subject to one serious distortion. The spirituals—and often the passages with which I clarify them—voice an ideal Shakerism and mostly record only by implication the singers' daily world of toil and mortal stumblings. This limitation is at least fairly novel among current studies of religious sects, and Peter Berger, for one, has urged that "the scientific study of religion return to a perspective on the phenomenon 'from within,' that is, to viewing it in terms of the meanings intended by the religious consciousness."[14] I hope my song selection and commentaries will enable the reader sometimes to penetrate the thin and outward rind of facts and to enter and apprehend the world of Shaker feeling and aspiration. Such a goal accords with the Shakers' own insistence that their spirituals be regarded not as songs but literally as "deep feelings from the soul."[15]

In closing this preface I have a deep feeling of my own to share: my gratitude to the many people from whom I received kindness during my research and the writing of this book. The work proved an ordeal for relatives, friends, colleagues, students, and even, I fear, a few wedding guests, who involuntarily heard more than they wished about Shaker songs. I shall not forget their forebearance.

To the staffs of the following libraries I tender my thanks for more than merely professional help, and also to the directors and trustees of these institutions my appreciation for kind permission to consult and quote from their manuscript holdings: the American Antiquarian Society; the American Society for Psychical Research; the Berkshire Athenaeum; the Buffalo and Erie County Public Library in Buffalo, N. Y.; the Connecticut State Library; the Darrow School; the Dayton and Montgomery County Public Library of Dayton, Ohio; the Duke University Library; the Filson Club; the Manuscript and Music Divisions of the Library of Congress; the New Hampshire Historical Society; the New-York Historical Society; the Manuscript and Music Divisions of the New York Public Library; the New York State Library; the New York State Museum; the Ohio State Museum; the Philadelphia Museum of Art; Shaker Community, Inc., of Hancock, Mass.; the Shaker Historical Society of Shaker Heights, Ohio; Shakertown at Pleasant Hill, Ky.; the University of Michigan Library; the Warren County Historical Society in Lebanon, Ohio; the Williams College Library; and the School of Music at Yale University. The Smith Fund and the University Research Council of the University of North Carolina at Chapel Hill provided numerous grants enabling me to carry on my research in these collections.

I owe thanks for extraordinary kindness to Mr. William Henry Harrison and the Fruitlands Museum, to Mrs. Elizabeth H. Hill and Dr. Frank H. Sommer, III, of the

Henry Francis du Pont Winterthur Museum, and especially to Mr. Robert F. W. Meader of The Shaker Museum in Old Chatham, N. Y. He has been an obliging and helpful correspondent over many years. Most of all I am indebted to the Western Reserve Historical Society in Cleveland. Its director, Mr. Meredith B. Colket, Jr., and its staff have given me on many visits a warm welcome and indispensable aid.

Many private collectors have also shared both their homes, their manuscripts, and their knowledge of Shaker history and culture with me. I am much in the debt of Professor Raymond Adams of Chapel Hill, N. C., the late Dr. Edward Deming Andrews and Mrs. Andrews of Pittsfield (to whom I owe both personal and scholarly debts), Mr. and Mrs. R. W. Belfit of Watertown, Conn., Mrs. James H. Bissland of Charlemont, Mass., the late Mrs. Clarice Carr of Lebanon, N. H., the late Professor Harold E. Cook of Lewisburg, Pa., the late Mr. H. Phelps Clawson of Old Chatham, N. Y., the late Mr. Jerome Count of Mount Lebanon, N. Y., Dr. Bailey F. Davis of Lynchburg, Va., the hospitable Mr. William L. Lassiter of Albany, N. Y., Mr. Robert Temple of North Chatham, N. Y., and the dedicated and kindly Mr. Charles H. Thompson of Canterbury, N. H.

Others have given special help along the way, and I wish to express my gratitude to them: Professor Walter Brumm of Notre Dame, Ind.; Professor Faith Clark of Macomb, Ill.; Mr. Donald E. Christenson of Columbus, Ohio; Mrs. Mary Lou Conlin, Mr. Roger L. Hall, Mr. Frank A. Myers, the late Mrs. Herman J. Nord, Mr. Bill Randle, Mrs. Arthur Sherburn, and Ms. Susanne Toomey of Cleveland, Ohio; my friend Tom Davenport of Delaplane, Va.; Miss Ruth von Euw of Rockville, Conn.; Professor Wilton E. Mason of Chapel Hill, N. C.; the late Margot Mayo of New York City; Professor Julia Neal and Ms. Vicky Middleswarth of Bowling Green, Ky.; Mr. Vincent Newton of Los Angeles, Cal.; my friends Professor and Mrs. Robert E. Stipe of Chapel Hill; and those generous photographers, Professor Elmer R. Pearson of Chicago, Ill., and Mr. John V. Goff. For help in proofreading, my special thanks to my ever-reliable students, Mr. Joel Brett Sutton and Ms. Mary Lee, and to a generous friend, Mr. David G. Morrow. To Ms. Margot Cutter, Mr. Robert E. Brown, and others at Princeton University Press and William Clowes and Sons, Ltd., I'm deeply grateful for suggestions, support, and professional excellence. They spared neither expense nor pains to turn my manuscript into exactly the book for which I had hoped.

Above all, I wish to express my thanks to those willing to share with me their personal experience of Shakerism. At her home in Gloucester, Mass., Miss Florence Phelps gave lively views of her days at Canterbury and cleared up points in correspondence. I recall with genuine pleasure several visits to the home of Olive Hayden (Mrs. Morris E.) Austin in Clinton, Conn., and her warm recollections of her youth at Hancock. The Canterbury Shakers have welcomed me many times for visits all too brief. I am particularly grateful to Eldress Bertha Lindsay for opening the library of the society to me, and to Eldress Gertrude Soule, whose singing of "Where is the gem" first disclosed to me that early songs remained alive in Shaker memories. The late Eldress Marguerite Frost spent many hours with me singing and discussing the songs and Shakerism. Like all who knew her, I remember Eldress Marguerite with respect and affection. Hers was a gentle spirit, but one that feebleness of body could not dim.

Without the friendship and help of the family at Sabbathday Lake this would have been a far different book, and I want to thank each member for all services great and small. Brother David Serette has frequently benefited me with his photographic expertise and his knowledge as a bibliophile. Brother Theodore Johnson shared his deep knowledge of Shaker history, both in conversation and writings and through his valuable service as editor of *The Shaker Quarterly*. Sisters Marie Burgess and the late Eleanor Philbrook were always ready with a room for the traveler, and Sisters Elsie McCool, Frances Carr, Elizabeth Dunn, and Minnie Green always happy to lay the table with another plate or to make time for a chat—as were those two bright spirits, the late Sisters Ethel Peacock and Della Haskell.

Most of all, I am indebted to Sister R. Mildred Barker, who in a difficult period in Shaker history has striven to bear witness to her faith and to the consecrated lives of generations of Believers by gathering and preserving the historical records of the society. She has generously opened the rich manuscript collections at Sabbathday Lake to me and other students and without stint given of her own time and energy and knowledge. Many a page of this book benefited from her suggestions, the faithfulness of her memory, and her love of song. In past years I have tried to be an instrument through whom others could share my appreciation of the purity and beauty of Sister Mildred's own singing. With the present collection of spirituals I try to open to the reader not only the range of the Shaker song tradition, but also a glimpse of the singers' consecration and their humanness. I dedicate the volume to Sister Mildred Barker, in gratefulness for her warm friendship and encouragement and with the hope that she will find it a worthy presentation of the tradition in and for which she worthily stands.

Daniel W. Patterson
Chapel Hill, North Carolina

The Shaker Spiritual

CHAPTER I

Early Forms of British and American
Religious Folk Song

In 1805 Jeremiah Ingalls, New England farmer, cooper, tavern keeper, and tunesmith, sounded a battle cry for the American folk-hymn movement. He exhorted the Godly to plunder the "carnal lover" of his songs:

> Strip him of every moving strain,
>   Of every melting measure;
> Music in virtue's cause retain,
>   Risk the holy pleasure.

As good as his word, he fitted these lines to a reworking of the tune "The Devil's Nine Questions," which he gave a three-voice setting and printed in his hymnal *The Christian Harmony*.[1] This tunebook was praised by George Pullen Jackson, the rediscoverer of the white spiritual, as a "veritable Comstock Lode of religious folk song," the first of the singing-school publications to draw on the spirituals that had for at least a generation been developing in New England.[2] It was Jackson's theory, set forth in its fullest form in *White and Negro Spirituals*, that those backwoods New Englanders stirred up by the Great Awakening of the 1740s began to venture forth from psalmody into the singing of hymns set to folk tunes. He believed that after 1770 this new religious music was a significant feature in their landscape and that it spread west, south, and even across the Atlantic to England. Reaching its fullest growth between 1800 and 1860, it flowered into camp-meeting songs, black spirituals, and the shape-note settings.

Jackson's position is strengthened by the discovery of a few folk-tune settings earlier than those of Ingalls—"Kedron" in Amos Pilsbury's *The United States Sacred Harmony* (Boston, 1799) and William Billings' folkish setting of the carol text "A virgin unspotted" in *The Singing Master's Assistant* (Boston, 1778)—for these pieces are exceptional in the collections in which they are found.[3] Jackson himself, however, drastically amended his own theory on the origin of the folk spiritual in a terse one-page discussion in *Down-East Spirituals and Others*.[4] There he stated a belief that "of the many dissenting groups in Albion" the Baptists were the denomination "chiefly responsible for the importation" of religious folk song into the colonies. He offered no elaboration on this statement. His next and last book, *Another Sheaf of White Spirituals*, was silent on the matter.

The implication of Jackson's words is that England had a native tradition of religious folk song to which the American spiritual is directly indebted. The suggestion has not aroused the interest of British folklorists. The songs of the Ranting Methodists did receive a nod from Reginald Nettel, and A. L. Lloyd granted that their hymn texts had been "lightly folklorized" through the use of refrains.[5] But English discussions continue to range safely within the bounds posted by *The Oxford Book of Carols* in 1928: The one glory of English religious folk song is the body of "old carols . . . made during the two centuries and a half between the death of Chaucer in 1400 and the ejection of the Rev. Robert Herrick from his parish by Oliver Cromwell's men in 1647."[6] In a veritable Cock Robin chorus, Nettel, Lloyd, Douglas Brice, Erik Routley, Elizabeth Poston, and Frank Howes—all the recent British commentators except Maud Karpeles—continue to chant over the bones of the folk carol, shot low by the Puritan. Not all have the political bias of A. L. Lloyd, who blames "bourgeois Nonconformism" and "the sober burgess," or the religious bias of Father Douglas Brice, who regards the Reformation as a cataclysmic "death blow to all that the nation had ever held dear," but these writers, like the great genteel collectors of fifty years ago, show a distaste for the Dissenting tradition.[7]

The term *carol*, when literary historians use it, is clear and precise. Rossel H. Robbins or Richard L. Greene will reserve it for a body of some five hundred art poems preserved in manuscripts written between the fourteenth and sixteenth centuries; the poems deal with diverse topics, but take a stanza-and-burden form and served for ceremonial song.[8] As canonized, however, in *The Oxford Book of Carols* and as used in most discussions of folk song, the word *carol* is not susceptible of a consistent definition on the basis of either form, theme, origin, or known life and function in oral tradition. Writers apply it both to songs that have refrains and to ones that lack them. They use it to label a traditional ballad like "The Cherry-Tree Carol," a Christmas hymn like "A Virgin Most Pure," a forfeit-game song like "The Twelve Days of Christmas,"[9] a *quête* song like "Here We Come A-Wassailing," as well as a processional song like "Oss Oss Wee Oss" in the Padstow May Day celebration. This diversity can be encompassed only by a very loose definition such as the one formulated in 1865 by H. R. Bramley and endorsed by Maud Karpeles: "A kind of popular song appropriated to some special season of the ecclesiastical or natural year."[10] This wording neatly avoids the sentimental error of using *carol* to denote religious songs acceptable because of their tastefulness and presumed origin in a folk or medieval community.

Ballads, like carols, long charmed folklorists by their supposed medieval graces, but confidence in the antiquity of the surviving ballad *corpus* has dwindled. "Anyone may declare, if he likes, that the fifteenth century was a Golden Age of balladry," writes Bertrand Bronson, but "to support the assertion, setting inferences aside, three or four Robin Hood ballads, and the *Gest*, are all that survives in English."[11] Bronson even asserts that "the best texts in Child's great collection date from near the close of the eighteenth century."[12] The role played in carol theory by the destructive Puritan has in ballad histories been given to the printers and vendors of broadsides. Sheets printed with the verse of England's worst scribblers began by 1520 to be hawked in street and hedgerow lane; for three centuries English presses ground them forth relentlessly, serving up song texts that rarely rise above the execrable. It was for years an axiom that a surfeit of this broadside verse eventually choked the ballad muse. By the late nineteenth century the song repertories of English rustics contained more sub-literary verse than simple and seemingly immemorial folk poetry. Their ballad tunes, sheltered by the singers' musical illiteracy, were less contaminated than their texts.[13]

As successive generations of scholars have inched nearer to an accurate understanding of the two kinds of ballad verse, however, the question of the origins of folk song has declined in importance. Many of the best ballads not only owe their preservation to broadside printings, but even originated as broadside hackwork and were worn to a smooth and classic form by the flow of oral tradition. "The corpus of balladry," says A. B. Friedman, "is the result of a process capable of remaking to pattern verse of diverse sorts and sources, adapting it to the needs of an oral art."[14] Of all the factors in this process the most important, as Bertrand Bronson has shown, is the inevitable paring of a flowery or awkward text to make its syntax conform to the musical phrase and its narrative units to each turn of the tune.[15]

What has been said of the history of balladry may be said of the carol. One may postulate a Golden Age of folk caroling in the fifteenth century, but few songs survive to support the theory. Only three "folk carols" can be traced back so far. "The Corpus Christi Carol," which Bronson believes to be a pious reworking of some early variant of "The Three Ravens,"[16] and "Joys Seven" were recorded in a sixteenth-century manuscript—but in stanza forms unlike those of versions collected from oral tradition, and less folklike. "The Boar's Head Carol" was printed by Wynkyn de Worde in 1521, but it has a Latin burden and survived in a community of scholars. Other early manuscript poems prized as carols have beauty, but their diction and syntax are not those of verse from oral tradition.

In *The Oxford Book of Carols* those songs marked "traditional" are a mixed lot, but as many as fourteen may be genuine folk verse. One of these, "As I Sat on a Sunny Bank," was printed at Aberdeen in 1666. The second oldest is "The Holly and the Ivy," traced to a broadside of about 1710. Eighteenth-century broadsides carried "The Cherry-Tree Carol" and "Joys Seven."[17] "Wassail, Wassail, All over the Town" can be taken back to about 1800. All the rest were gathered, beginning in 1822, from oral tradition and printed sources. The remainder of the "traditional" carols in the Oxford collection are actually broadside and hymn verse in varying stages of recomposition into folk poetry. "Dives and Lazarus" was licensed for printing in 1557. "The Carnal and the Crane," "A Virgin Most Pure," and "God Rest You Merry Gentlemen" have broadside histories documented as far back as the eighteenth century. Of other carols not included in this collection much the same could be said. One collected by Ralph Vaughan Williams, for example—"Awake, Awake Sweet England"—was composed in 1580 by Thomas Deloney; originally a broadside poem upon an earthquake, the verses were reworked and reprinted many times in later centuries.[18]

In short, the process of remaking "verse of diverse sorts and sources, adapting it to the needs of an oral art," took place in the history of the carol as in that of the ballad. From the second half of the sixteenth century until nearly the twentieth, raw material for this recomposition was supplied by a stream of broadsides and chapbooks. Puritans did not extirpate the carol. Most of the songs usually called carols either survived, or originated after, the Puritan era. Indeed, the evidence suggests that for the carol as for the ballad the eighteenth century may well have been a period of fruition. But the carols were less fortunate in the response of the educated. The songs that would be lovingly gathered into *The Oxford Book of Carols* in 1928 were dismissed by Thomas Wharton in 1781 as inventions of "those enemies of innocent and useful mirth, the puritans."[19] He was correct in at least one respect. Insofar as the Reformation affected the folk carol, it must have increased the common man's desire to voice in song his deepening Christian commitment.

Christmas songs alone could not satisfy that desire, and they doubtless comprised only a small fraction of the English religious folk songs. Many of the songs that the folklorist and the commercial publisher have crowded under the label *carol* are actually from a sizable repertory of religious ballads, which includes "The Cherry-Tree Carol," "King Herod and the Cock," "The Miraculous Harvest," "The Bitter Withy," "The Holy Well," "Dives and Lazarus," "The Carnal and the Crane," "The Romish Lady," and for that matter, "The Wife of Usher's Well," "The Cruel Mother," and others in the Child canon. Pious folk singers have also long had a weakness for the repentance of condemned criminals and took up numerous "farewells" from broadsides into oral tradition. Collectors have sought them for their topical contents, overlooking as far as possible their function as religious expression and moral instruction.[20]

Oral tradition so thoroughly absorbed some of the religious broadsides that their influence has gone generally unsuspected. One of these, whose history has been studied by Katherine Susan Barks, is "The Great Messenger of Mortality; Or, A dialogue betwixt Death and a Lady."[21] The original poem, which survives on a blackletter broadside of the seventeenth century, was written in sluggish pentameter couplets. Death opens the dialogue, commanding the Fair Lady to lay her costly robes aside and take leave of carnal vain delights. In the eighty-nine lines that follow, the Lady first haughtily rebuffs this pale-faced visage, then exhibits the imagination of disaster. Crying "spare my life to have a longer date," she offers gold and other victims, begs a reprieve until her daughter's wedding, and finally calls on learned doctors to display their skill. Death, unmoved, proceeds to exercise his alarming sway. The final lines bristle with a moral condemnatory of the privileged orders: "Great men submit to Death as well as we."

Unpromising matter, the broadside. But Mrs. Barks shows that reprintings not only kept the original verse alive in oral tradition for centuries (in 1908 Lucy Broadwood heard a quite faithful rendition by Henry Burstow, the remarkable illiterate ballad singer of Horsham), but also begot a number of quite different songs. Most of these appear to be recompositions of the poem to fit some different tune and attitude. They betray their indebtedness to the broadside, however, not only in their subject, but usually also in their use of certain striking images from the original, of the dialogue form, and often even of rhyming couplets.

One of these collected in England relates the untimely encounter of a Maid with an "aged man"—"His head was bald, his beard was grey, / His clothing made of the cold earthen clay." After attempting to bargain for her life with "costly rich robes," she submits to his summons, though not without first making her moan:

> Let this be put on my tomb-stone, she cried:
> Here lies a poor, distress-ed maid;
> Just in her bloom she was snatch-ed away.
> Her clothing made of the cold earthen clay.

In America, where it was also reprinted, the broadside has more numerous progeny, to all of which Evangelical Protestantism has lent its tone. Some singers in the Southern white tradition know a song that proceeds along the lines of the original broadside, but closes with the grim words:

> Too late, too late, to all farewell,
> My doom is fixed, I'm summonsed to hell
> As long as God in heaven shall dwell,
> My soul, my soul, shall scream in hell.

This unfortunate character is no longer the object of class resentment, but like Wicked Polly a warning to the spiritually unconcerned. Some white singers know a shorter, more lyrical piece that focuses instead on the numbing clutch of Death's cold icy hand, each stanza rounded off with the refrain,

> O death, O death
> Can't you spare me over for another year.

American black singers more frequently develop the pathos of the death-bed scene:

> Oh, mother standin' by the bed
> With a aching heart and a hung down head
> And the doctor looked around very sad
> Say its the worst old case I ever had.

But in black tradition the songs generally exult in the vanquishing of death by those that "have that true religion, hallelu, hallelu."

Religious broadsides and most of the pieces that derive from them were everyday songs. Another class of folk songs cropped up in the aftermath of the Reformation as music for the worship service. This development took place of course outside the Church of England, which patronized art music and across the years turned increasingly to foreign fashions. Somewhat more egalitarian, the Kirk in Scotland and the English Presbyterians and Puritans did eject the professional musician and reclaim song for the worshiping congregation. Their music, however, was not folk song but psalmody. Learned poetasters provided them metrical versions of the Psalms of David, and accidents of history caused them largely to borrow and imitate the staid Genevan psalm tunes. Possibly some rustic adherents, as the Clown alleges in *The Winter's Tale* (act 4, scene 3), sang these versified psalm texts to hornpipe tunes, but this was not the normal practice.

Native folk music probably did, however, influence the style in which Dissenters performed the psalm tunes. When their leaders sought guidance in reforming worship, they threaded through a mazeway of conflicting passages to just those scriptures that accorded best with the preferences of traditional song. Thus they took a strong stand in favor of performing (like most folk singers in the British Isles) without instrumental accompaniment. In areas the Bible left cloudy they also tended to follow folk tradition. They sang loudly and with a stringent vocal tone. Even in those denominations that condoned part-singing, early congregations seldom practiced it. Though an ability to read music was rare among them, musical illiteracy would have been no bar to these strenuous Christians had they conceived part-singing to be necessary for the glorification of the Lord. Instead, they most commonly printed their psalm tunes without harmonic settings and until the rise of the village-choir movement early in the eighteenth century, most congregations resisted the efforts of reformers to introduce the use of harmony.[22]

The most unusual feature of their psalm singing—an extraordinary indulgence in melismatic embellishment—bears a more complex relationship to British folk singing. According to the seventeenth-century treatise *A New and Easie Method to Learn to Sing by Book*, the psalm singer did not render a tune as plainly as it was written. Instead, the author says, the notes of a tune "are usually broken or divided, and they are better so sung."[23] In actual fact, the ornamentation with which early Dissenters sang their psalm tunes must have been quite florid, resembling in some degree what one hears in recent sound recordings of psalmody from the Hebrides.[24] These performances are not simply an *outré* Gaelic development exhibiting, as James Porter suggests, "the favorite Celtic device of multiple variation within a strict framework or conceptual pattern."[25] In America many blacks still sing hymns in a related style, and early accounts of psalmody describe just such singing in nineteenth-century Scotland, in eighteenth-century America, and in seventeenth-century England.[26] The singers took up much time, complained Thomas Walter of Massachusetts in 1721, "shaking out these Turns and Quavers," leaving the tunes "miserably tortured, and twisted, and quavered."[27]

Probably this melismatic style developed from an attempt to mediate the frequently awkward intervals of the psalm tunes and to compensate for their boring uniformity of time values and for the dragging tempos at which the congregations sang. But the embellishments are quite different from the instrumentally influenced vocal acrobatics fashionable in contemporaneous Baroque art music. While psalmody differed also from the more straightforward rendition that now characterizes most folk-song performances in the British Isles, it does seem to have carried to an extreme some latent folk-song conventions that emerge whenever the tempo is sufficiently slow.[28] On nineteenth-century sailing ships, for example, the nature of the tasks required that most of the work shanties be sung very deliberately, and the seamen performed them with a high degree of melodic embellishment. The British ship's officer W. B. Whall, in fact, specifically compared the ornamented singing of seamen he had heard in the years before 1870 to that of "the old school of parish clerks." But Whall—who said, "I have often been struck by the apparent ignorance of writers on 'folk-songs' of the music of those songs as they used to be sung"—also believed that British folk-singing style had undergone a change in the last half of the nineteenth century. He thought that no one born after 1840 or so had ever heard "the old style of singing amongst 'the people'; this was full of such airs and graces. Hymn tunes were no exception to the rule."[29]

Although the original goal of the congregations seems to have been unison song, their embellishment of the tunes produced heterophonic performances rather than the merely "unblended unison" that Alan Lomax defined as a characteristic of Western European group folk singing.[30] No two men in the congregations, said Thomas Walter, "quaver alike, or together." If this grumpy reformer can be believed, such ornamentation had the effect of encouraging melodic variation similar to that found in secular folk tradition: "Yea, I have my self heard," he complained, *"Oxford* Tune sung in *three* Churches . . . with as much difference as there can possibly be between *York* and *Oxford*, or any two other different Tunes."[31]

One might have expected native folk melody to enter the congregational singing of British Dissenters through the hymnody of Isaac Watts or of the Methodists or, as Jackson suggested, of the Baptists. All these played an important part in the development of the folk spiritual in America. In Britain, singers may have put hymn texts to folk tunes in daily life, but seldom in Sabbath worship. Those who sought to use congregational song to reach the common people gave them tunes along with texts for their hymnody. Dr. Watts himself apparently intended his hymn verses to be sung to the conventional psalm tunes.[32] Wesley's melodic sources were various—psalmody, the German chorale tune, the Anglican hymn tune, art and popular song—but when folk song finally entered Methodist singing in England in the early nineteenth century, it was brought over by American evangelists and affected only the schismatic Primitive or Ranting Methodists.[33]

In the first century of their history in England the Baptists were more reluctant than most other Dissenters to sing during worship, but after some years of debate over the "lawfulness" of meter and rhyme, of nonscriptural texts, and of "conjoint" or congregational singing, both the General and the Particular Baptists adopted first psalmody and then hymnody. No Baptist tune collection was printed until 1791, when John Rippon edited *A Selection of Psalm and Hymn Tunes*. Robert H. Young, however, presents evidence that for more than a century prior to this time they had continuously sung the conventional psalm tunes. Significantly, the rough Baptist farmers who composed the Deign Layrocks of Rossendale in the mid-eighteenth century were enamored not of folk melody but of the music of Handel. One who ventured to play a hornpipe upon his cello in the church vestibule after services drew a rebuke from a fellow member, who came in exclaiming, "Hush, hush Robert, you are playing an idle tune."[34]

Native folk song could enter worship in Britain only in dissenting sects that were congregational in polity, found their adherents among such as were, in the words of one enemy, "by their trades Coblers, Tinkers, Pedlers, Weavers, Sowgelders, and Chymney Sweepers," and were sufficiently free from the direction of an educated leadership to follow the musical preferences of the congregation.[35] The earliest evidence for the use of folk tunes by such groups appears to be the Diggers' song "Stand Up Now, Diggers All," dating from about the year 1650. From its peculiar stanza form Bertrand Bronson deduced that the text must have been sung to the durable tune of the ballad "Samuel Hall":

> To conquer them by love, come in now, come in now,
> To conquer them by love, come in now,
> To conquer them by love, as it does you behove,
> For He is King above; no power like to love.
> Glory here, Diggers all.[36]

Documentation of a significant use of folk and popular tunes by a mid-eighteenth-century sect appears in a tune list appended to the Glassite hymnal *Christian Songs*. The author expects the singer to be at no loss for psalm tunes for the common- and long-meter hymns, but he says that "some of the Scots Song Tunes answer a few of them well."[37] He thereupon recommends thirty-three popular and folk tunes—among them "Gilderoy," "Roslin Castle," "Gaberlunzie Man," "Galashiels," and "Gypsy Laddie"—for use with specific texts in his book. Jackson for some reason discounted the folk influence in this tune list, but a selection of these melodies published in a Glassite pamphlet in 1875 includes some that are clearly traditional.[38]

The preface to the ninth edition of *Christian Songs*, published in Edinburgh in 1805, states that when the first edition of these hymn texts appeared "many were much scandalized, by some of them being adapted to what are called profane tunes."[39] The statement corroborates other evidence that the pairing of hymn text and folk tune was not a widespread practice in British churches. Glassites were also clearly not a major influence upon American folk hymnody. Although Glas's son-in-law, Robert Sandeman, brought the Glassite singing tradition to America, his followers were too few to have much effect on American practices. Jackson was probably correct in his original view that the American folk hymn was not an imported but an indigenous form of congregational song.[40]

There was, however, yet another tradition of British songs of worship that demonstrably influenced Americans, that of Pentecostal song. The doctrinal premise out of which this tradition grew was that "all worship of the new testament properly so called is spirituall, proceeding originally from the hart." Set forms of worship quench the spirit, because "the Spirit is not then at liberty to utter itself, but is bounded *in*."[41] The little recorded about the music of this tradition makes one thing clear: In an attempt to purify song, to make it what they felt to be more truly of the Spirit, some of the radical Dissenting groups not only reverted to traditional melodies but developed new forms of song rooted in traditional music.

Already in 1608 John Smyth was insisting that any singing in the services be done "in the Spirit" by the one singer receiving the gift. He was not to hobble the Spirit with rhyme and meter or to "have the booke before the eye in time of singing a psalm." His position may, however, have been purely theoretical, for Henry Ainsworth charged that song was not used at all in the Separatist assemblies.[42] Whatever these early Baptists may have done, the Quakers were singing in the gift by the middle of the seventeenth century. George Fox tells, for example, of being "made to sing in the Lord's power" as a jailer in Carlisle was beating him with a great staff:

> and that made him rage the more. Then he fetched a fiddler and brought him
> into the dungeon and set him to play thinking to cross me; and when he played
> I was moved in the everlasting power of the Lord God to sing; and my voice
> drowned them and struck them and confounded them and made the fiddler
> sigh and give over his fiddling; and so he passed away with shame.[43]

The state of exaltation is even more explicitly described in a letter in which Fox's follower Thomas Holme tells of being filled, as he lay on a prison floor, with sweet melody and the power of the Lord, which compelled him to sing:

> And the power was so great it made all my fellow-prisoners amazed, and some
> were shaken, for the power was exceeding great, and I scarcely know whether
> I was in the body, yea or no, and there appeared light in the prison and aston-

ished me, and I was afraid, and trembled at the appearance of the light and wondered, and the light was so glorious it dazzled my eyes.[44]

In such a burst of Pentecostal fervor the singers likely abandoned rule and pale forethought, but descriptions leave in mystery the nature of the songs thus produced. Several accounts suggest that they sang prose texts from the Scriptures, as when a small party of Friends trudging through the mud into Bristol sang the words "'Holy, holy, holy, Lord God of Israel' with a buzzing melodious noise, not easy to understand."[45] Fox himself wrote in 1658 that such as "are moved to sing with understanding, making melody to the Lord in their hearts we own; *if it be in meeter*, we own it."[46] The conclusion of his statement is ambiguous but presumably means that singing was acceptable even if the words were those of versified psalms rather than of the unaltered Biblical text. A more detailed, if not entirely clear, account published by an outsider in 1696 suggests that Friends may even have sung without either words or conventional melodies. Sometimes, according to this author, they would sing one by one, sometimes simultaneously:

> They sing and praise, not by a regular pronunciation of words or musical melody, far less by the numbers of metre or verse (which sort of singing is never lawful with them, but when one of 'em has an extemporary faculty to compose) but in the collision, sound, and stretching of the voice, almost as the Spaniards, or Moors in Afric, if you have ever heard 'em, as I have heard 'em both, frequently singing in their own countries. And thus not only one or two, but all that are present, do sing with a sweet and pleasant voice.[47]

The drift of Quaker singing was from outbursts of improvised solo song toward more subdued group performance and soon to a preference for silent worship. Other groups in the seventeenth and eighteenth centuries surpassed them in liveliness. George Fox himself tells of challenging the Ranters to "come forth and try their God, and there came abundance who were rude . . . and sung and whistled and danced."[48] Other groups, such as the revivalists stirred up by the French Prophet refugees in 1706, may have voiced inspired song in their Pentecostal worship, but the best documented instance of it is the singing of the "Shaking Quakers" of Manchester, who in 1747 began to hold meetings in which they "were occasionally exercised in singing, shouting, or walking the floor, under the influence of spiritual signs, swiftly passing and repassing each other, like clouds agitated by a mighty cloud."[49] Within this group arose a leader, the blacksmith's daughter Ann Lee, who was to found the American religious order commonly called Shakerism. When she and a band of followers crossed the ocean in 1774, they did not change songs with the change of skies. Manuscript records of what they sang probably hold the only surviving musical examples from a long tradition of Pentecostal song among radical Dissenting sects in England—and reveal the seedbed of the American Shaker spiritual.

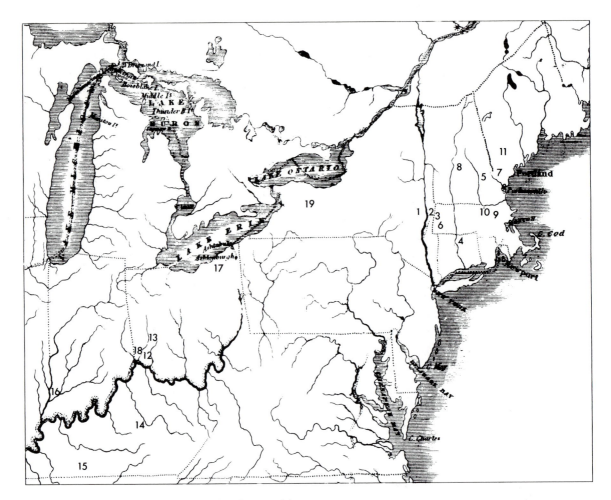

Fig. 1. The Locations of the Chief Shaker Communities

1 Watervliet, N. Y., 1787–1938.
2 Lebanon, N. Y., 1787–1947.
3 Hancock, Mass., 1790–1960.
4 Enfield, Conn., 1790–1917.
5 Canterbury, N. H., 1792–.
6 Tyringham, Mass., 1792–1875.
7 Alfred, Me., 1793–1932.
8 Enfield, N. H., 1793–1923.
9 Harvard, Mass., 1793–1918.
10 Shirley, Mass., 1793–1908.

11 Gloucester (Sabbathday Lake), Me., 1794–.
12 Union Village, Ohio, 1806–1912.
13 Watervliet, Ohio, 1806–1910.
14 Pleasant Hill, Ky., 1806–1910.
15 South Union, Ky., 1807–1922.
16 West Union, Ind., 1810–1827.
17 North Union, Ohio, 1822–1889.
18 Whitewater, Ohio, 1824–1907.
19 Groveland, N. Y., 1826–1895.

CHAPTER II

The Institutional Background
of Shaker Song

"We must remember that these were not just songs," wrote Eldress Marguerite Frost of Canterbury, "but deep feelings from the soul."[1] These spirituals served to voice both the most private of the Shaker's experiences and those all Believers unitedly shared. Through the songs one accordingly enters the Believers' inner life. But that life was sustained within the body of a Church. For readers unfamiliar with the history, structures, and beliefs of that Church the following résumé will offer a framework for an understanding of the Shaker songs.

The Shaker faith grew from the personality and teachings of an obscure woman born in eighteenth-century England, but the institution of Shakerism, like its first official name, "The United Society of Believers in Christ's Second Appearing," was the creation of American converts won by Ann Lee. Two in particular were influential: Joseph Meacham, a Baptist preacher from Connecticut, and Lucy Wright, a woman of good family from western Massachusetts. Between them they headed the Believers from 1787 until 1821, the formative years of American Shakerism.

Father Joseph's major contribution was to devise the economic and social structure within which the faith could prosper. He gathered the Believers into villages, of which there were eventually nineteen of importance, stretching from Maine to Kentucky. During the mid-nineteenth century, when the Shaker membership fluctuated between 4,000 and 6,000 persons, a village held from 100 to 600 Believers. The larger societies were divided into at least three branches or orders: a church family for covenanting Believers, a junior order for persons advanced in the faith who had not yet made a final commitment, and a novitiate. These families lived in dormitorylike dwellings, each with its own large room for family worship and its cluster of barns and workshops. At the center of a Shaker village stood a central meetinghouse, and on either side of it the several families were scattered a half mile or more along a road.

Except when afflicted by a disaster such as fire or drought, each village, or society, was largely self-sustaining. It constructed its own buildings, grew its own food, made its own clothing and furniture, and carried on some commercial ventures, selling agricultural products such as seeds, herbal medicines, and cattle, or handicrafts such as baskets, wooden boxes, and furniture. Each person signing the church covenant contributed to the society all he owned, after settling just debts, and all that was produced by the society was held to be used for the good of the united body and for charity.

Shaker societies were celibate as well as communitarian and communistic. All the physical and social structures of the Shakers separated the sexes. The Believers not

Shaker Village, Mount Lebanon, N.Y.

Fig. 2. The Parent Society at Lebanon, N. Y.

Fig. 3. The Church Family at Enfield, N. H.

Fig. 4. Shaker Meetinghouse, Gloucester (Sabbathday Lake), Me.

Fig. 5. Shaker Meetinghouse, South Union, Ky.

only maintained traditional sexual distinctions in dress and work assignments, but in their dwellings and meetinghouses provided one door, one stairwell, one side of the building for men and the other for women. Brethren's and sisters' workshop buildings were also separated to the right or left of the dwelling.

The Shaker brethren and sisters, however, stood equal. In the daily business of the families, deacons supervised the work of the brethren and deaconesses that of the sisters. All temporal and more particularly all spiritual activities in each family were under the care of a first and second elder and a corresponding first and second eldress. These family leaders were responsible to a ministry, also composed of two leaders of each sex, who had the oversight of several villages. Governance of the entire Church lay with the four members of a divinely guided central ministry at Lebanon on the slopes of the Berkshires in eastern New York.[2]

The Shakers were, then, a theocratic society, but they were also a covenanting body. Membership in the society was voluntary and the ministry might seek the willing concurrence of the entire group in major decisions. The ministry was also responsive to "gifts" and "spiritual impressions" of individual members when these seemed in harmony with the common good of the Society. In the 1840s the ministry even employed gifted persons as mediums or "instruments" to gain divine direction.

The formulation of these social arrangements took many years of experiment, but grew from the vision of Father Joseph. He also began the task of ordering Shaker beliefs, writing a concise statement for publication in 1791. It was during the ministry of Mother Lucy, however, that the Shakers began—a decade after Father Joseph's death in 1796—to work out and write down full statements of their theology. None of the many volumes they printed over the next century holds a definitive Shaker creed, for the writers wished never "to bind the faith and conscience of any."[3] Less ready to govern belief than behavior, they nevertheless reached fair agreement on the following points: that mankind fell into "loss" and "separation" through lust of the flesh; that restoration is attained through man's moral choices and works rather than through the atonement of Christ; that the first step in regeneration is to make honest confession of all sins and renounce the World, the Flesh, and the Devil; that salvation is offered to all, even those dead before the opening of the gospel; that revelation is progressive, its fourth and millennial dispensation having begun in Ann Lee; that the resurrection is not of the body but the spirit, a gradual and increasing work in the heart and in the Church; and that the fruits of this work are seen in the unity, love, and peace manifested by the faithful Believers.

In their day the Shakers were less unusual for having such beliefs than for carrying so many of them to their logical extremes and attempting to live by them. Secular reformers like Robert Owen shared to a degree the Shaker positions on ownership of property and separation into communities. Christians and transcendentalists alike exalted the supernal over the sensual and earthly. Quakers were pacifists and favored equality for women. Most heirs of the dissenting tradition—whether Baptist revivalist or chilly Unitarian—rejected the Calvinist belief in limited atonement and proclaimed some form of universalism and salvation through works. Millerites and less spectacular sects thrilled with millennial hopes. Mormons and others received new revelations or still insisted, as the Shakers did, on a church of visible saints.

With this variety of alternatives, one may wonder why so many people sought satisfaction in Shakerism. All the converts had, of course, some purely personal reasons. These were varied. Harvey Eades, Isaac Youngs, O. C. Hampton, Betsey Bates, and many others came as children with their converted parents or were taken in as wards, learned to love the people, and accepted their faith. Mary Antoinette Doolittle sensed an affinity with the Shakers and entered the Society even before gaining much understanding of its beliefs. The sight of a company of brethren and sisters living in equality and peace convinced Daniel Sizer that the faith must be as good as its fruits. To John Lockwood—an energetic, practical man—the logic of Shaker theology looked inescapable, and he liked the notion of "doing the work." Eunice Bathrick weighed the passing sacrifice the Shakers asked against their promise of eternal bliss and prudently deferred her pleasures. Eunice Wyeth was unhappily married to a drunkard and discovered in Shakerism a source of strength and solace. Issachar Bates found Shakerism his only escape from a tormenting sense of guilt.

Even these purely private crises, however, were aggravated by disturbances in American life. In the collapse of colonial Calvinism Issachar Bates, Richard McNemar, and Eunice Bathrick wandered through several churches in search of a more satisfying faith. Bates's autobiography shows clearly that the social turmoil accompanying the Revolution had heightened his religious anxieties. Three decades later the new textile mills prevented the widow Blake from continuing to support her children by her weaving. In the West, Indian warfare left Lydia Flynn in need of a physical and emotional refuge, and economic stresses and temptations of the raw new society appalled others like Charles Hampton, causing them to turn to Shakerism for a more meaningful life.[4]

Embuing all the theological, social, and personal motives for entering Shakerism was the craving of troubled spirits for order. They found an abundance of it on every level of Shaker life. Shaker writings provided the convert an intellectual system harmonizing his life with the Bible through a typological reading of its text. This theology stressed a flexible acceptance of changes inspired by an unfolding revelation, but the ministry provided at any one moment a clear definition of the light that already had been received. The Shaker's daily life was as secure as the world of his thoughts. Old age and illness were no threats; he was assured of the loving care of his brethren. The group asked of his daily work only that he give his best effort, so that he did not need to feel shame for having a small talent. Separation from the World protected him from the temptations of commerce and the passions of politics. The mild persecution the Shakers suffered only caused them to unite more firmly, and even this harrassment passed away as courts and legislatures defined the legal status of the Society.

Within the Shaker villages, each year rolled quietly past in rhythms founded on the patterns of worship and on the daily and seasonal tasks of a farming community. After 1821 the Believer heard periodic readings of Millennial Laws that gave him a clear understanding of his duties and their relation to the principles of the Faith. Nothing in his life was meaningless or trivial. When he mended a fence, retrieved a button from the floor, or danced, the Believer served God and supported the material or spiritual welfare of his brethren and sisters. When he failed his faith in thought, word, or deed, an honest confession to the Shaker "Lead" restored him into harmonious union and peace of conscience.

Fig. 6. Dwelling Room at Hancock, Mass.   Fig. 7. Dwelling Room at Hancock, Mass.

Secular communities of the era—though they might be founded on applied rationalism or on some moral vision—collapsed of boredom, ineptitude, and dissension. Nashoba, New Harmony, Fruitlands, Brook Farm, each had but a short day. Equally ephemeral were most of the sects that gathered about a magnetic leader like Isaac Bullard or Shadrack Ireland. When the leader's light flickered or his prophecies failed, his flock scattered. Shaker communities have survived for nearly two hundred years.

Their vitality at first came from the fact that Ann Lee won not merely the belief but also the love of those she converted. These "first born" carried to their graves a deep devotion to her. Joseph Main, for example, visited Watervliet in 1780; on seeing Ann Lee, he straightway experienced conversion. The testimony he wrote forty-five years later shows the moment still vivid in his mind. He was passing through a room where Mother Ann was, he said, and saw her

> sitting in a chair, and singing very melodiously, with her hands in motion; and her whole soul and body seemed to be in exercise. I felt, as it were, a stream of divine power and love flow into my soul, and was convinced at once that it came from Heaven, the source and fountain of all good. I immediately acknowledged my faith, and went and confessed my sins.[5]

For those converted after the death of Ann Lee, the power of Shakerism derived less from such testimonials or from the organizational skill of Father Joseph than from the success of the Society in finding other symbols of "Spiritual Motherhood" to call forth devotion. Shakerism owed much, for example, to the important standing it gave other women. The Shakers institutionalized roles for women at every level of leadership. A few like Mother Lucy came to head the entire Society.

In other structures, too, the Shakers exalted the feminine principle. They formulated a theology that recognized feminine attributes in deity itself. They found in godhead "the likeness of male and female, forming the unity of that creative and good principle from which proceeds the work of *Father and Mother*, manifested in *Power* to create, and *Wisdom* to bring forth into proper order, all the works of God."[6] In their theology as in their social order, Father and Mother stood equal, but in fact the Believers responded less deeply to fatherhood than to motherhood in God. Their list of maternal attributes manifested in all God's work—"beauty, order, harmony and perfection"[7]— is a catalogue of the virtues on which they based the social order of Shakerism. As faithful members of a Shaker community the Believers in effect felt themselves at one with the maternal principle in deity. It naturally followed that the slackness and infidelity and dissension which grew within the Society during the 1830s would be purged through a renewed assertion of the feminine principle, in a revival often called "Mother's Work." At its climactic moments Holy Mother Wisdom, the feminine aspect of the Godhead, manifested Herself and with admonitions and encouragements restored the Society to order and harmony.

Holy Mother Wisdom's power over Believers, like that of Mother Ann, was proportional to the love felt by each member. Ann Lee had taught that love was the divine Christ Spirit which opened the millennium in any heart prepared to receive it. This spirit entered only after one had renounced the World and the Flesh in all their allures— lust, wealth, status, fame, power—and all their consequences, such as pride, anger, guilt, and indifference. But even then the Believers had one further preparation to make, that of "waking up, and laboring" to "feel the life of God" in their souls.

The craving for this inward sense of life and love provided the most persistent theme and many of the most characteristic metaphors of Shaker speech and song. The Believers wanted to escape "death," "bondage," "stupidity," and a "bound-up," "starched," "stiff," or "scattered sense." They longed to feel "quickened," "limber," and "free." They craved the "holy fire" of "heavenly love."

More than anyone the Shakers ever knew, Ann Lee had been able to awaken in others this liberating love. At the final step, she took them across the threshold not with words but with a gesture, a smile, or a song. Many converts treasured the memory of experiences such as Elizabeth Johnson described in her testimony. Ann Lee, she said,

> came singing into the room where I was sitting, and I felt an inward evidence that her singing was in the gift and power of God. She came and sat down by my side, and put her hand upon my arm. Instantly I felt the power of God flow from her and run through my whole body. I was then convinced beyond a doubt that she had the power of God, and that I had received it from her.[8]

The Shakers recalled such times as a "happy season." Through Mother Ann they had learned to "love the operation of the Power of God among the people" and to share in the tradition of Pentecostal song into which this Power overflowed.

CHAPTER III

The Relation of the Shaker Spiritual to Traditional Song

During Ann Lee's lifetime and for the rest of the eighteenth century the Shaker song repertory probably numbered fewer than two hundred tunes, most sung without words. The Believers' acceptance of worded songs in 1805, however, started an outpouring of new songs that would flow for more than a century. In the early decades Shakers traveling from one community to another were expected to teach and memorize as many songs as possible. But the communities were widely scattered and the travelers few. Some of the songs—anthems in particular—were long, irregular, and hard to learn. Depending on the ear and memory alone then, the Shakers could retain or exchange relatively few songs. In consequence, leading singers began about 1815 to propose a study of the "rules of music."

Few of the Shakers converted prior to 1820 had ever had musical training. I know of only two, Issachar Bates and Abraham Whitney. Bates played no role in the development of Shaker musical theory or notation. He was sent west as a missionary in 1805 and gave his energies to building the Ohio societies. Whitney had been a singing master before he was admitted to the Shirley society, and he lost little time in recommending music classes.[1] The ministry was at first wary of his efforts to introduce a worldly science, but by 1821 or 1822 had sent him to give lessons at Canterbury, where a few were permitted to study music "with reserve."[2] Meanwhile Russel Haskell at Enfield, Connecticut, and Isaac N. Youngs and others at Lebanon were beginning to probe its mysteries. All were probably largely self-taught. D. A. Buckingham of Watervliet, Abraham Perkins of Enfield, New Hampshire, and Harvey L. Eades of South Union later joined the circle. The thinking of these men is recorded in their letters and treatises, which were surveyed by Harold Cook in the chapters "Shaker Notation" and "Shaker Theory and American Tune-Book Theory" of his book *Shaker Music: A Manifestation of American Folk Culture*. Here I shall repeat or extend chiefly those parts of his discussion that bear on the relation of the Shaker spirituals to Anglo-American folk song.

Cook shows that the first Shaker musicians derived some knowledge of musical terminology and theory from the shape-note tunebooks then in use among rural singing masters. We do not know what book Whitney had employed in his teaching or what Haskell had at his disposal. But as early as 1818 the Watervliet Shakers were writing shape-notes,[3] very likely deriving them from a recent edition of Little and Smith's *Easy Instructor*. At Lebanon someone made a hand copy of this book in 1823,[4] and Youngs echoed some of its wording in the glossary of his earliest surviving treatise, "The Rudiments of Music," dated 1833.[5]

This essay, which Cook saw but did not examine, is less indebted to Little and Smith than to more approved urban authors of the day. In a number of passages Youngs cited *The Musical Reader* of Thomas Hastings,[6] and he relied quite heavily on *A Musical Grammar* by Dr. John W. Callcott, "Organist of Covent-Garden Church."[7] Youngs closely followed the organization of Callcott's manual and quoted and paraphrased it extensively, with acknowledgement of his source.

A comparison of Youngs' "Rudiments" with Callcott's book, however, also shows great differences between them. The most obvious is that Youngs was teaching a form of notation that dispensed with fixed pitch and key signatures and substituted letters of the alphabet for conventional notes. The authority for this departure was the spirit of Mother Ann, who had revealed it to Abraham Whitney about the year 1824.[8] Most other Shaker musicians soon recognized the handiness of this innovation. Making occasional refinements, they used it for the next fifty years.

Their adoption of "letteral" notation is emblematic of the Shakers' relation to the musical practices of the educated. The radical sectarianism of Youngs and his colleagues safeguarded their folk-song heritage. When they found a discrepancy between their own music and that described by genteel musicians like Hastings and Callcott, they assumed their own to be proper for themselves. As Shakers, they disapproved of the values of the upper class, did not want to climb into its ranks, and refused to copy the musical trappings that symbolized its status and attitudes.

This outlook enabled Youngs, as he studied the books by Hastings and Callcott, to analyze in some measure the actual nature of the tunes he knew. He saw, for example, that Callcott's definition of the *tonic* as "that chief sound upon which all regular Melodies depend, and with which they all terminate"[9] did not match the use of the tonic in Shaker tunes. In his "Rudiments" Youngs rephrased the definition to read "upon which all regular melodies depend, on which they *frequently* begin, & on which they *generally incline* to terminate."[10] Youngs was also puzzled to find that authorities called the leading tone the "master note." He confessed he did not understand their reason. He thought the seventh tone of the major scale "not apt to occur frequently." When it is used, he said, it "seldom receives much accent" and is in fact "remarkable for its having a kind of narrowly contracted, faint sound."[11] The forty-two Shaker tunes in Youngs' treatise prove his point. In his examples the gapped scales CDEFGA-C and CDE-GA-C are twice as frequent as the diatonic major. Even in the major or in the hexatonic scale CDE-GABC the leading tone is used infrequently and almost never on a down-beat. The tendencies in Youngs' examples are paralleled by what Harold Cook found when he analyzed a body of Shaker tunes. Sixteen percent of Cook's sample used the hexatonic scale CDEFGA-C and eleven percent the pentatonic scale CDE-GA-C.[12]

Youngs was also dubious of other aspects of the conventional presentation of the scales. He copied Callcott's statement that all music uses either the major or the minor scale, but qualified it in a footnote, saying that this may be true of the harmonized tunes sung by "the common order of mankind," but that Shakers compose "more by the impulse of sensation than by rule" and have tunes which are "a mixture of both modes."[13] His statement is supported by his Example no. 41. Mode changes were in fact sufficiently frequent in Shaker singing to cause the musicians to invent a symbol (called the *enclosure*) enabling them to write such tunes without accidentals.

Since all Youngs' musical sources taught the use of the harmonic minor, he reproduced it in his own treatise. But Youngs cautioned that when the notes occur in a promiscuous position rather than ascend in a regular succession through the scale—meaning, I take it, when they occur in a melody rather than an exercise—the sixth and seventh steps are not necessarily raised. Illustrating with the A minor scale, he says that the seventh is not likely to be raised in tunes "where A does not immediately succeed G" or "when G receives the strongest accent of the two."[14] Sometimes F is to be raised and not G. Russel Haskell went even further. On reading Youngs' words he wrote that the sharping of F and G in an ascending minor scale is "altogether an artificial intrusion." The "natural flow of the voice," he says, does require the raising of F in both the ascending and descending forms of the scale, but as for the sharping of G, he "never knew the instance in any song from first to last."[15] Both authors were struggling to reconcile the unfamiliar harmonic minor prescribed by Hastings and Callcott with the Shaker use of both Dorian and Aeolian modes. Characteristically, the two Shakers gave their allegiance not to learned doctrine but to traditional practices. In Young's words, "there can be no positive rule given" concerning the position of semitones in the minor scale; "a critical ear alone must determine."[16]

These attempts of Shaker musicians to square classical notation with their own traditional song raise a crucial question: Do their transcriptions accurately record what they sang and heard? Clearly they were less biased by preconceptions than either shape-note singing masters or the sophisticated musicians of their day. Their transcriptions are sufficiently accurate to be presented to a modern reader with few editorial alterations. But the reader needs a warning about the quirks and failings of the Shaker scribes.

One problem area has already been mentioned, the treatment of what the Shakers called the minor. Haskell held the conviction that it could be written without accidentals only if D were made the governing tone, and he was emphatic on the matter: "I certainly know it to be the only right method, whatever may be said to the contrary." His conviction seems to grow from both a theoretical belief that "it is an invariable rule" for semitones to occur "between B and C and E and F" and from his experience that these are "the natural places" for them.[17] I take the last phrase to mean that his ear was accustomed to Dorian tunes. In any case, he almost invariably took D for the root tone when writing any tune having a minor third.[18] He followed this practice in setting down a tune in 1830, he prescribed it in his treatise *A Musical Expositor* in 1847, and he was still using it in his manuscript songbooks in the 1870s. Since Haskell was the dominant musician at Enfield, Connecticut, all other scribes in that society followed his method. It is likely that Haskell even managed to train many in the Enfield community to sing all "minor" tunes in the Dorian mode.

Outside this society his practice was resisted. The other Shaker theorists regarded A as the governing tone of the minor. Buckingham at Watervliet wrote that Haskell was contradicted by "the universal opinion of Music writers, both ancient & modern," adding that to take D as the governing tone "gives the notes or sounds an unnatural air . . . destroying the beauty & melody of the tune."[19] Eades at South Union must have agreed. In one manuscript he wrote a tune in the Dorian form and added the note, "Br Russell Haskells order of noting the minor key—seems awkward."[20] Youngs was long familiar with Haskell's theory but never succumbed to it. Neither the 1843 nor the 1846 edition of his *Short Abridgement of the Rules of Music* even mentions Haskell's position. The minor scale, they state, "commences on A."[21] Youngs took this as the rule for his own transcriptions.

I believe that Youngs laid down this rule simply because he thought it the prudent course. He could not discover any logic in the variability of the sixth step of the "minor" tunes and must have felt that he could minimize the errors of others by ignoring a distinction for which he could give them no rule of thumb. Youngs, after all, intended his *Short Abridgement* as a very simple statement for beginners.

Even in its pages, however, he hints of greater complexity. The tones of the minor scale, he admits, are "more uncertain than those of the major."[22] A decade earlier, when writing "The Rudiments of Music," Youngs was much more explicit: "in many tunes, if we key them on A, we are obliged to sharp the F to represent its true sound, which would be prevented by keying, or begining on D."[23] His musical examples in this manuscript make clear what he sang. All his eight minor tunes are keyed on A, but in five of them Youngs inserted a sharp before every F. The year after he wrote this manuscript Youngs entered one of these very tunes in a song collection, still keying it on A but omitting the sharps.[24] Henceforth for the rest of his career he wrote all his "minor" tunes on A. Most other Shaker scribes united with this respected brother in the practice.

Two forms of evidence show that they were nevertheless continuing to sing frequently in the Dorian mode. One is the emergence, as Youngs fell ill and inactive in the late 1850s, of scribes who keyed minor tunes on both A and D in the course of the same manuscript. At Lebanon, for example, Anna White filled one notebook with 486 songs as she learned them at the North Family between April 1858 and July 1863. These were new songs, a great many of them received in the family in which she lived. Fifty-eight of the songs are keyed on A and twenty-one on D. Most of the Dorian tunes were entered before 1862, but they alternate irregularly in the pages with the Aeolian ones.

The singing of present-day Shakers also confirms the use of both modes. Sister R. Mildred Barker of Sabbathday Lake has sung me fourteen tunes that Youngs or Haskell would have considered to be in the diatonic minor. In numerous performances she always sang four of these in the Aeolian mode and eight others in the Dorian. In the remaining two, the sixth degree was variable, though she rendered the tunes the same way in every performance. She also used both the major and the minor sixth in one hexatonic tune and sang two others with the major. I have found all but two of these songs in nineteenth-century transcriptions; sixteen of the seventeen key the songs on A and use no accidentals.[25]

Sister Mildred's renditions cannot, of course, be taken as the only way the songs were ever performed. In Shaker singing, though more rarely than elsewhere in folk practice, songs sometimes drifted from one mode to another. The manuscripts in fact record both major and modal variants of a few Shaker songs.[26] Singing for me, Eldress Marguerite Frost at Canterbury used the Aeolian mode for "I never did believe," which Sister Mildred sings in the Dorian. Sister Mildred herself uses a hexatonic scale for one song that the scribes set down in the Aeolian mode and for another that they transcribed as Dorian.[27] Conversely, she sings one Dorian tune that the manuscripts record as hexatonic, and she alters the sixth in other hexatonic melodies.[28] Nevertheless, for scales (if not tempos) her singing must be a more reliable guide to nineteenth-century practice than are the manuscripts. A number of songs in which her Dorian performance contradicts an early Aeolian transcription originated in the Maine societies, were used there for group singing, and came down to Sister Mildred through unbroken oral tradition. In the present collection I therefore often follow her singing rather than the manuscripts when I print these songs. Elsewhere the reader must allow for the Enfield scribes' insistence on forcing all minor tunes into the Dorian mode and for the other scribes' habit of recording them all as Aeolian. The reader should also assume that many tunes transcribed in the major were actually sung with an ambiguous or unstable leading tone. Haskell alone regularly attempted to show the pitches actually sung in the course of such songs.[29]

Misbarring of tunes is a second problem—and a very common one—in the Shaker transcriptions. Some of the errors resulted from the haste of a scribe; some were the blunders of beginners. But even highly competent writers had trouble reconciling what they learned from textbooks with the singing they actually heard. "The timeing and barring of our tunes," wrote Isaac Youngs, "is a more difficult part to learn, & to perform to perfection, than any other branch of music," for Shaker songs were often "considerably irregular."[30]

Outside the Shaker communities, the rural musicians who compiled the shape-note hymnals faced the same problem. They had learned that rhythm is composed of but three modes of time—common, triple, and compound—and that a tune is sung in the same mode from beginning to end. To transcribe a tune they sang in 5/4 time, they might force the melody into the 4/4 mold or bar it in 4/4 despite its actual meter. The Shakers, by contrast, at times wrote such a tune in 4/4 time, but sprinkled it with fermatas. Sometimes they set down the actual time values of the notes and omitted the time signature and barring. After the 1830s they generally made a literal transcription of the tune, changing time signatures from measure to measure.[31] But they did not always take these wiser options.

Like the shape-note editors, the Shaker scribes also often smoothed out lesser rhythmic irregularities in their tunes. In singing common-time hymns, for example, the Shakers must often have elided a beat at the beginning of a phrase. In triple-time hymns they at times added a beat at the same point. But it was unusual for the early scribes to record the practice.[32] Until the 1840s they must often have lengthened or shortened notes to get a regular number of beats in a bar. Many of the scribal errors resulted from the difficulty of recording folk performances that made free use of rubato, particularly in tunes having an underlying 3/4 rhythm. Some of these melodies were apparently sung with accenting so light that even the better scribes might fail to perceive the downbeat.[33]

Around 1840 the scribes became much more skilled and literal in their work. They had strong incentive to do so. The revival called Mother's Work brought an outpouring of new songs often quite irregular in structure. How complex such gift songs might be, both in inspiration and in form, is shown by a note accompanying a transcription in one Pleasant Hill manuscript:

This song was sung by an angel to Z. P. April 22nd 1839. George Washington was present & said, if he had heard it sung at that day, he should have bowed his heart in thankfulness to God. The angel had a very singular trumpet with two branches curled one under each wing; & the mouth of it, from whence the sound issued, was in front of the breast, & by pressing the branches it caused it to sound. Z. P. did not retain the words nor the song when she heard it sung. But on [Thursday] the 25th the words were revealed to her; and she was told she would receive the song in a dream. On Monday the 29th, feeling unwell, she laid herself down and fell asleep, and in her sleep the song was given to her. Where I have made capitals, the Angel brought down his wings upon the trumpet & made very long sounds, longer than a semibreve. You can sound them longer or shorter just as you like best. I have not barred it at all, as we have no mood for it.[34]

Shaker scribes felt challenged to capture such songs exactly as they were sung, for these were divine gifts. From this time forth, the writers appear to accept any rhythmic vagary without cavil, and the work of many is without doubt reasonably faithful to the living performance.

A related difficulty was also solved in these years. The role of dance in the Shaker services had made tempo markings a matter of importance to the scribes. For guidance they first turned to shape-note song books for tables of the "moods of time," but these led the musicians into many difficulties. Since these bear directly on songs printed in this collection, I reserve a detailed discussion of the problems for my next section, "A Note on Shaker Notation and My Tune Transcriptions." Here I may in summary state that in 1840 the Shaker scribes worked out an entirely new schedule of tempos. From this date on, their tempo markings are reliable, but those set down in earlier manuscripts are not.[35]

Tunes in the "compound mode" posed another problem. Youngs was dissatisfied with the "general opinion" that in 6/8 time all the eighth notes of a triplet are of the same length, and he spent nine pages of his "Rudiments" presenting his view.[36] He had observed that Shaker singers sometimes rendered the triplets in "two distinct ways . . . insomuch that there will be a kind of clash among the singers, some inclining to sing them in the equal, even manner, and others in what is . . . vulgarly called the jumping manner." He thought it even "rather difficult" to perform shuffling tunes with triplet notes "just of a length" because this would be "so contrary to the natural motion" of the melodies and of the dance. In these tunes, Youngs said, the first note of a triplet was held longer as well as accented more heavily than the other two, a fact he could demonstrate with "machines, such as chime clocks, music boxes &c." He suggested writing such tunes in 7/8 measures and "pointing" notes as in the following example:

Haskell agreed that some classes of compound tunes were performed unlike each other, but thought differences in tempo the reason. "A horse is a horse, let him go fast or slow," he said, "but he changes his gait something according to the speed of his traveling." Haskell would not unite with Youngs' proposal. Pointing the shorter note of a couplet made it three-quarters as long as the longer note, a proportion existing only in the quickest shuffling tunes. Moreover, in these tunes the first note of a triplet might be longer than the others but the second was also shorter than the third. Haskell thought it simpler to continue transcribing all compound tunes in the old way, leaving the singers to be guided by their sense of style.[37]

One last aspect of Shaker singing only partially recorded in the manuscripts is that of vocal embellishments. The Shakers went much further in this effort than the shape-note musicians, who offer little guidance beyond an occasional "passing tone." The Shakers also showed complete independence from the definitions, if not the terminology, of classical musicians like Callcott. Youngs borrows the term *trill*, but calls it "a kind of shake of the voice" usually consisting of two "diminutive notes" and a longer one. He says that the first and third notes have the same pitch, the middle note being a step above or below them. The diminutive notes may either precede or follow the long note. Unfortunately, he directs the scribes to write the symbol *tr* over the long note, leaving the singer "to take that form of the trill that feels the most familiar."[38] The Shakers also picked up the term *appoggiatura*, but they defined it as "a short graceful slide of the voice" made in approaching a longer note from either above or below. Shaker notation generally shows the direction of the approach and gives a rough idea of the size of the interval covered by the slide. A third embellishment, the *roll*, appears to overlap with the appoggiatura, but is not defined or illustrated in the treatises. The word seems mainly to refer to two diminutive notes used in ascending to a longer one or gliding away from it.

The treatises do not explain when to use these embellishments. Indeed, the practice within the Society must have been far from uniform. In his "Rudiments" Youngs complains that some singers "will croud in trills, & apoggiaturas, slides, shakes & slurrs as thick as they can get them!"[39] He thinks it better to be sparing, but both he and Haskell sprinkle appoggiaturas through their transcriptions fairly freely. This embellishment is common in slow tunes when a half note follows another on the same pitch or when the voice approaches the tonic from a fourth below at the beginning of a phrase. Most scribes can probably be relied upon to have recorded any marked use of the appoggiatura.

The trill is less common, and Youngs warns that in most tunes its use would be "unnatural."[40] In the forty-two melodic examples he included in this manuscript, Youngs set down only one trill, though he says a second might also be sung in the same tune. Haskell's practice can be defined more clearly. He uses the trill as seldom as Youngs, but the 459 hymn tunes in his manuscript "A Record of Spiritual Songs" at least offer a larger sample. In thirty-one of these tunes he inserts the symbol *tr* a total of forty-eight times. Eleven times the trill occurs on D before a cadence on C, and ten on E before a cadence on D. Haskell also restricts the symbol *tr* to the figure

. In *A Musical Expositor* he says this is the "manner trill notes should always be sung,"[41] and in "A Record of Spiritual Songs" he twice wrote out this figure in the first phrase of a tune but substituted *tr* for it in a repetition of the phrase. By contrast, he writes out the figure fourteen times in these tunes. It occurs only five times in cadences like those where he uses *tr*. No rule seems to govern the other situations in which he uses these two embellishments.

From the pens of Haskell and Youngs come other comments that may follow Shaker practices less closely. It is likely that Haskell states a general Shaker preference when he says, "a trembling in the voice is to be carefully avoided";[42] and in cautioning his readers that "constant indulgence" in the habit of "harsh, or very loud singing" has ruined many good voices, he is merely offering the advice of an experienced teacher.[43] But both he and Youngs go further, tacitly admitting the possibility of making expressive use of dynamics. In their tables of musical characters they include conventional symbols for the crescendo and diminuendo. Haskell does not elaborate on them, but Youngs says that while in hymn tunes "these marks may seldom be applicable," in anthems they "might sometimes be used with propriety." Indeed, he says, "singing would sound better if something similar was observed thro' the whole, that is not to begin and end words & sentences in an abrupt or blunt manner but go on and off smooth & soft."[44]

Some of Haskell's views on dynamics are more idiosyncratic. He contrasts the performance of major and minor (i.e., Dorian) melodies. In minor tunes, he says, "the voice seems to be more shrill, . . . more smooth and solid." In these melodies it is possible for the voice to be "so modified" as to be "mournful and pathetic"; but minor tunes generally are "the most favorable to shrill singing, which also has its peculiar force and beauty." His usual term for the minor is in fact "the shrill air of melody." By contrast, he calls the major the "soft air," and he describes it as "an air mixed or softened with a whisper." In the "soft air" the voice is "not generally so clear and solid." The major is therefore the "most favorable to soft singing, which makes the sweetest melody."[45]

In Shaker singing all such theoretical niceties must actually have gone ignored. I cannot recall a single instance of the use of dynamic markings in any early Shaker song manuscript, even those written by Youngs or Haskell. The comments of both the Shakers and the World's people show that in the first half of the nineteenth century Shaker singing was usually "strong, with a high pitch and great volume." One elder at Union Village explained that "in those days there was war, in heaven, and the Musicians beat a charge, to stimulate and arouse the warriors to an onset against the foe."[46] Even without this incentive, however, the Shakers would have preferred strength to delicacy: in Anglo-American folk culture group singing is normally loud and full.[47] In other respects as well the early Shaker singers—like those at Sabbathday Lake today—must have remained faithful to the traditions of Anglo-American folk singing, using neither vibrato nor covered tone, avoiding "expressive" devices such as ritards, diminuendos, or crescendos, and making no effort to play up winsomely to their listeners.[48]

From a reading of the song transcriptions alone one would never suspect that Shaker performances also included one untraditional element, the pantomiming of songs. This practice—"motioning," as it was called—was taken up about 1815 for use with laboring songs and soon spread to anthems, hymns, and Extra Songs.[49] Motioning must have been quite common between the years 1820 and 1870, yet the song manuscripts rarely mention it.

Apostates often thought motioning a fit subject for their satire, however, and gave some idea of these "most ridiculous gestures and motions."[50] William J. Haskett, who had lived at Hancock, told how the singers bowed their heads, stamped, grinned, or made "a violent motion similar to a man mowing" in one song or another. He even described the performance of one song, stanza by stanza:

> 1   The devil in walking the earth to and fro,
>   Has stamped the whole human race;
> This awful impression believers do know,
>   Great I in the front of the face.

When they come to the last line, they put their hands up to their foreheads, as it were, pointing to the impression alluded to in this verse.

> 2   Since Mother has taught me that this is the case,
>   No more I'll be deceived with a lie,
> But now from my forehead I'll quickly erase
>   The stamp of the devil's great I.

In singing the third line of this verse, as it were in a rage, they all put their hands up to their foreheads, and give a violent pluck, and then proceed to the next verse.

> 3   Come brethren and sisters, pull low and pull high
>   Pull away with a free heart and hand;
> O pull away, pull away, pull down great I,
>   Then we who are little may stand.

In singing this verse, they perform the contents of it in a nautical manner, with great zeal and ease.[51]

Another full description was given by the anonymous author of *Extracts from an Unpublished Manuscript on Shaker History*. The writer quotes "a very solemn song in 'Unknown Tongues' and English, called Vicalun's prayer":

> Hark! hark!! my holy, holy,
> Vicalun seelun voo,
> I have come to mourn
> And weep with you,
> In low humiliation,
> Pray to the vilun sool
> Whose hand can stay the billows,
> And save si ree lu nvool.

This account says the words were accompanied by the following gestures:

> At the first line the head is inclined forward, with the fore finger pointing to the right ear, as in the act of listening. At the third line, the hands are brought

Fig. 8. Ritual Motion: "Supposed to suggest the free flight of an eagle and the general effect was one of considerable abandon as the enthusiasts lifted themselves on tiptoe and fluttered about the great hall. A single figure gives a faint idea of the impressiveness of the dance as done by fifty or more trained Shakers" —Emily Williams, 1905.

Fig. 9. Ritual Motion: "Represents the strife of the faithful against sin and satan. It is called a 'warring song,' and the attitudes throughout are not unlike those of the conventional pugilist"—Emily Williams, 1905.

forward with an earnest beckoning motion. At the fourth line the hands are carried to the eyes, as in the act of weeping, the body is gradually bending till it sinks on the knees, and the face touches the floor at the close of the fifth line. At the commencement of the sixth line both hands are brought up at the side of the head as in prayer.—At the seventh the right hand is thrown convulsively upward. At the word billows, both hands are extended wide. At the last line, and at the last word, they are clasped over the heart.[52]

I know of only one Shaker document—a letter written by Isaac N. Youngs concerning "Our support we'll gather in"—that gives a description equally detailed.[53] Motions are recalled for a few other songs, however, by persons raised in the Shaker communities. Though Mrs. Olive H. Austin learned none during her childhood at Hancock, Sister Mildred Barker performs two—"With a new tongue" and "Let me have Mother's gospel"—that she was taught at Alfred. Eldress Marguerite Frost showed me motions for "To a fullness" and "Yielding and simple may I be." (They sing three of these with the motions in Tom Davenport's film "The Shakers.") Miss Florence Phelps also talked with me about motioning as it was practiced at Canterbury in the 1890s.

By her account, the singers united less strictly than in earlier years, each spontaneously motioning "whatever in the emotion came . . . as long as it was in harmony" with the sentiments of the song.[54]

The practice of motioning seems to explain one other unusual feature that I first noticed in the singing of Mrs. Austin. In the song "I will be a living soul, free from all that's evil," she delivered the words "Yea, I will!" very forcefully. This was appropriate to the text, but unlike the customary restraint of her singing. I suspect that the words were once performed with emphatic gestures, for in the song "With a new tongue" Sister Mildred gives similar emphasis to the words *cross* and *crabbed*, which she pantomimes with a stamp, a shake of her head, and a spurning gesture with her hands.[55] One might expect this performance to have a theatrical effect, yet the gestures do not violate the restraint and inwardness of the singing. The Shaker "motions" the song without thought of his listener. Indeed, the reason for motioning was to enable the singer to enter "into the spirit of the Sentiments contained in the songs."[56] The practice is thus consonant with Anglo-American folk-song tradition, which values text above tune and renders a song impersonally.

Shaker music was shaped by the conscious and unconscious preferences of the Anglo-American folk singer. These were powerful enough at times to override even Biblical precedents. The first Shakers, for example, often likened their singing to that of the virgin company of the Lamb which John saw in vision standing on Mount Zion singing a new song with the voice of harpers harping on their harps. The Shakers went so far as to sing new songs in tongues no man could learn, but they did not become harpers harping. Instead they held fast to traditional unaccompanied song. Their stated reasons were that the World had used instruments "to excite lasciviousness, and to invite and stimulate men to destroy each others lives,"[57] but the Shakers did not even permit the most blameless instruments within their villages; an elder at Enfield, New Hampshire, once in a meeting gave a severe rebuke to a boy who had brought a jews' harp into the family and "played upon it some tunes."[58] The Shakers might sing about harps and timbrels, trumps and organs, but they chose to sing without them. They were convinced that "the best and in fact the only proper instrument is the human voice wholly devoted to God in sounding forth prayer and praise."[59]

Anglo-American folk tradition preferred not only unaccompanied but also monophonic song, and the Shakers, too, insisted on singing in unison. This was common practice among folky groups like the Shakers, Baptists, and Methodists. They could hardly countenance musical literacy as a prerequisite for salvation. But as other churches crept gradually into more elegant musical tastes, the Shakers came to regard their own monophonic song as a badge of their separation from the World. During the 1840s divine injunctions were even received against "picking up the songs of the World, and singing after their manner, carrying the parts."[60] As long as the Shakers held an essentially folk outlook they resisted part-song. It was not until the 1870s that the Shakers began to purchase organs and pianos, get music teachers from the World, study the songbooks of other denominations, and regularly compose hymns with four-part harmony.

The Shakers had another, deeper reason for resisting the use of instruments and part-singing. They believed the direct result of introducing elaborate instrumental

Fig. 10. A "Tone-ometer" Invented by Isaac N. Youngs
This instructional monochord, photographed at Shaker Community, Inc., of Hancock, was probably made at Harvard, Mass., modifying specifications given by Youngs in his "Rudiments" (1833), pp. 58–61. In MS. ENH–3, p. [67], Timothy Randlett of Enfield, N. H., directs the student to "set it upon some hollow thing such as a chest or a box or even upon a table it sound very well, place the little square block to the line of the letter you wish the sound of with your finger on the wire press it snugly, with the other hand you can touch the wire giving it a quick motion and it will give you the correct sound."

music into a church had always been to "induce a lifeless form."[61] They wanted no class of professional performers usurping the Believer's musical expression of his devotion, for in a Shaker service "each one for one" sought "that power of God that alone saves the soul from sin." They needed songs that even indifferently gifted singers could "unite in," ones "substantial, not given to great extreems, forcible, clear & plain."[62]

For good reason the Shakers took many tunes directly from secular folk song, a fact sophisticated visitors rarely failed to notice. One dance tune, said an English gentleman who attended a service at Lebanon in 1838, was a song "I had not heard for thirty years at least," though it was popular "in my boyhood, among sailors especially."[63] A high-toned Virginian wrote that at Pleasant Hill he heard such tunes as "Fire in the Mountains" and others "made use of among the vulgar class at their frolicks."[64] Many of the early Shakers were well supplied with such tunes. By his own word Elder Issachar Bates could in his youth sing "about every song that was going, whether civil, military, sacred or profane."[65] The Shakers rarely borrowed or made over the words of one of the World's songs, but they were quite conscious in the early years of making use of common tunes. One writer sent a hymn from Union Village to Lebanon in 1808 saying it had been composed by Richard McNemar "to the Tune that was formerly cauld Black Joke," and adding "we begin upon the low part of the tune."[66] Clearly, he expected those at Lebanon to know the melody.

Later generations of Shakers came to regard their songs as wholly unique, tunes and all. Increasing numbers were raised in the Society from childhood, either because their parents were converts or after 1834 because they were orphans accepted as wards. These members found the Society possessed of a body of songs and had little knowledge of their background or of the World's music. Their understanding of the songs was bolstered on occasions, as when a spirit testified through one Shaker medium in 1839 that "the manner in which believer's have always sung" was not "picked up and stolen from the world" but was given by "the Angels in heaven" that there might be a "distinction" between the Shakers and the World.[67] The Shakers could not believe that the melodies which voiced their deepest love, joy, penitence, or reverence could have served the World merely as toys.

The Shaker view also held an important truth: As a corollary of their doctrine of continuing revelation, the Shakers prized songs that bore the "feeling" of being "given or matured under a heavenly sensation or spiritual impulse"—in other words, ones "received" by divine inspiration.[68] They believed that the Spirit flowed forth in songs as in other impulses of the regenerate Believer and that new songs were unceasingly provided. For this reason the editors of *Millennial Praises*, the first printed collection of Shaker hymn texts, stated in 1813 that "these hymns, wherever they may be sung by Believers, must be limited to the period of their usefulness: for no gift or order of God can be binding on Believers for a longer term of time than it can be profitable to their travel in the gospel."[69] As early as 1827 a Shaker diarist could call a meeting noteworthy when Believers "brought forth out of our treasure" songs "that had not been sung nor scarcely thought of these sixteen or seventeen years."[70] The song manuscripts themselves were rarely intended as historical compilations. They are usually commonplace books where the singer entered songs newly received by himself or others. They are proof of the scribes' openness to spiritual direction.

We have many accounts of how the inspired received their songs, and the headnotes for songs in this collection quote extensively from them. Here one may say in summary that the Shaker might sometimes feel his soul overflow with music, sometimes hear supernatural singing, sometimes in dream or vision learn the song from a heavenly spirit, or sometimes become an instrument through whom a spirit sang a new song. Records tell even of a Shaker's learning both the words and music of a song from a written copy presented to his spiritual eye.[71]

Accounts rarely show what circumstances or states of mind prepared the way for inspiration, but these seem to have been varied. Issachar Bates once burst into a new song of thanksgiving as he reached a familiar hilltop after a long and painful winter journey (see "The sixteenth day of January"). As a young girl, Eldress Bertha Lindsay received the words and music of a song when she had gone off by herself "feeling bad" about something she had done; the song warned that she should resist temptation.[72] The apostate David Lamson charged that during the Era of Spirit Manifestations the ministry played on the suggestibility of the members, prompting them to become inspired with song during the exciting meetings of those years. Awakening into a Pentecostal gift was the goal, however, of most Shaker worship. The Believer "labored" spiritually to attain this state, and since it often overflowed into songs, he valued and craved them as evidence of this blessing.

Having such a powerful desire to receive new songs, the singers brought forth enormous numbers of them. I have recorded on tape nearly 200 from oral tradition, and these make only a tiny fraction of those contained in the some 800 surviving Shaker tune manuscripts. These notebooks hold, I believe, between 8,000 and 10,000 different songs, some in as many as 40 variants.

From 1820 on, the Shaker song repertory bore a much closer relation to written record than is sanctioned by conventional definitions of *folk song*. The texts are almost always of Believers' making. Recognizable variants of traditional tunes do appear in the manuscripts, but many Shaker melodies seem not to have been passed down from misty ages. They originated within the sect, with persons whose names we often know. Moreover, after 1840 the Shaker songs usually underwent relatively little change in oral tradition. Scribes fixed them too soon in writing, or new songs crowded them from the repertory.

Inspiration, however, often had an effect upon song materials similar to that of oral transmission. The inspired melodies, according to Isaac Youngs, differed significantly from consciously composed ones. The "made" songs, he said, usually seemed "hammered out to suit some taste for musical crooks & turns, & airy fleety sounds." But those "given as it were without the author's exertion of art" were "the easiest to prick down & to learn" and seemed "more like fresh roses & matchless blossoms."[73] Youngs appears to be making two points: that the inspired songs sounded more natural to an ear accustomed to folk melody, and that they conformed to the taste of the community instead of exploiting idiosyncracies of the individual Shaker.

The singer, moreover, drew his melodic formulas and structures from the communal stock. His inventiveness played over the musical material best known to the early Shakers, traditional song. The Shaker spirituals in consequence have a stronger claim to the name *folk song* than many a piece collected from oral tradition but modeled on the hit tunes of the music hall or phonograph.

It does not follow, however, that the Shakers simply borrowed the structures of earlier folk song or even that one can draw a sharp profile of a Shaker folk-song model, though Harold Cook attempted to do so in his posthumously published doctoral dissertation.[74] Surveying two hundred Shaker melodies, he tabulated their tonalities, interval preferences, tonal ranges, recurrent rhythmic patterns, and habitual cadences and openings. Cook found half his tunes to have a range of either an octave or a ninth and another thirty-five percent that of an eleventh. Sixty-eight percent of the successive tones were either unisons or major seconds. He reported the dominant mode in his tunes to be Ionian (thirty-five percent), followed by various hexatonic (thirty-four percent) and pentatonic scales (seventeen percent). Aeolian and Dorian modes together occurred in only twelve percent of his tune sample.

Of the two hundred randomly chosen tunes in Cook's sample, half had the rhythmic signature 2/4 and a third had 6/8. Ten percent were in 4/4 time, and three percent were too free to classify, being unbarred or changing signature often. Cook summarized his lengthy tables of rhythmic patterns by saying that "parallel rhythms occupy the first

seven or eight places of prominence (♩♩♩♩ – ♫♫; ♩♩♩ – ♩♫; and so on)" and

that in 6/8 time there are "no dotted eighth notes" or eighth notes preceding quarters in triple groups.[75] The songs tended to begin on the weak beat before a bar line and to end in the middle of a measure after reaching their final pitch level or keynote on its first beat. From all these tabulations Cook's chief inference was that dance strongly influenced the Shaker melodies, causing the use of narrow intervals suiting the worshipers' quick, regular pacing and of cadences that allowed the repetition of a tune without a break in its momentum.

I fear that Cook's tables conceal more than they reveal, for Shaker spirituals fall into many distinct genres, no one of them the "typical" Shaker song. Decade by decade not only individual songs but also song types succeeded each other in popularity and use. The congregational song of the 1790s consisted of wordless "Solemn Songs." Long doctrinal hymns displaced them in 1805, and about 1820 these in turn were followed by shorter hymns of sentiment. Concurrent with this congregational singing, the Shakers also had vocal bands to perform tunes for the "exercises." Dancing held a formal place in Shaker worship from 1790 until the 1880s. Marching, which was adopted in 1822, persisted until nearly 1930 in a few societies. During all these years many forms of dancing and marching—each with its own set of tunes—came into use and were discarded. Meantime, the Shakers began in 1809 to sing Extra Songs during the intervals of rest between the exercises. "Gift Songs," a specialized branch of Extra Song, developed during the revivals of the 1840s. It was these Gift Songs that probably formed most of Cook's tune sample; from this group came most of the songs he transcribed in his collection.

Each of these genres of Shaker songs differed from the others not only in function and period of use, but also in what it selected from traditional song stock. Both dancing and marching songs drew on the fiddle and fife repertory, but with a difference. Marching songs could use the secular tune without alteration; the restrictive figures of the Shaker dances, however, prevented the use of some secular tunes and caused a recasting of others. Extra Songs might adapt ballad-tune material to the secular dance-tune structure. Gift Songs often took phrases from secular song but spun them into anomalous forms.

Haskell's manuscript "A Record of Spiritual Songs" permits a detailed comparison of the musical features of each of the Shaker song types, for it documents the repertory of a single village, offers large numbers of tunes of every kind, and carefully distinguishes between the genres. Cook's profile of Shaker song corresponds to none of them. In writing down hymn tunes, for example, Haskell recorded only four percent in 2/4 time. Sixty percent of the hymns have 4/4 as the time signature, and twelve percent have 6/8. Twenty-two percent are rhythmically quite free. By contrast, forty-four percent of his early Extra Songs are recorded in 4/4 time, and thirty-eight in 6/8. Twelve percent are too free to classify. The time signature of all the Holy Order shuffling tunes is 6/8. That of all Regular Step tunes is 2/4.[76]

Even the average tonal compass of the Shaker tunes differed from genre to genre. In Haskell's collection the range of the Gift Songs of the early 1840s is usually between an octave and a tenth. Two thirds of the hymn tunes that Haskell recorded as in use at Enfield between 1805 and 1813 had a compass of from a tenth to a thirteenth. One-third of his early dance tunes had a range of a ninth, but slightly more than one-third ranged from a tenth to a thirteenth.

Preferred tonalities also change from genre to genre. In Haskell's manuscript diatonic "minor" tunes outnumber the major by two to one and form more than a third of the total repertory of the Turning Shuffle tunes, a mortification exercise from the 1790s. His early Holy Order tunes—most of them from the years 1800 to 1820—use the major and minor scales about equally and these comprise half the total number. The hymn tunes Haskell recorded for the years 1805 to 1813 are quite different. In them the major tunes slightly outnumber the minor, but gapped scales are much more numerous. They are used in nearly sixty percent of the hymn tunes. By contrast, hexatonic and pentatonic tunes make up only a third of the Holy Order and only forty-five percent of the Turning Shuffle tunes, a fact that suggests a degree of affinity between diatonic scales and the narrow pacing of the exercises. The Shaker singers, in short, consciously or unknowingly made a different selection and adaptation from traditional melody for each genre of Shaker songs. For this reason, my collection groups the songs by type and introduces each genre with a discussion of its history, form, and function.

A wider context for interpreting the melodic characteristics of the Shaker song types is hard to establish. We have no comparable record of songs from any other American folk community. None is so sharply bounded, so copious, or so richly documented. The most closely related repertory is that which George Pullen Jackson collected from religious tunebooks for his *Down-East Spirituals and Others.* The three hundred songs in his book come from Northern as well as Southern evangelical tradition of the first half of the nineteenth century. They roughly parallel at least the hymn-tune branch of Shaker song.

Jackson found some differences between the modes used in the Southern and the Northern books. The former more frequently printed Mixolydian and Dorian modes; the latter had more minorized tunes. Jackson believed that this difference did not represent contrasting performance styles so much as the Northern editors' greater penchant for dressing up the folk tunes before presenting them in print.[77] The Shaker records support his surmise. Jackson's findings in turn support my own conclusion that Isaac Youngs and scribes influenced by him transcribed many Dorian tunes as Aeolian. Jackson shows that Southern shape-note singers often by tradition unconsciously reinstate the Dorian in songs that the tunebooks print as Aeolian.

The tonal range of the tunes in *Down-East Spirituals and Others* underscores the importance of analyzing this feature in conjunction with the song type. Jackson divides the collection into "Religious Ballads," "Folk Hymns," and "Revival Spirituals." In the religious ballads a melodic range of a tenth or an eleventh predominates. This range is but slightly narrower than that of the Shaker hymn tunes. Jackson's folk hymns are more contracted. A third have a compass like that of the religious ballads, but another third measure a ninth. Significantly the folk hymns include many short-phrase tunes. As in the Shaker hymn-tune repertory (where they make only a fourth of the total number), the short-phrase tunes show a marked correlation with narrow range. Jackson's revival spirituals typically have a range of an octave. As many are narrower as wider than this norm. It appears that the melody as well as the message of these songs was adjusted to serve the humblest convert. For a parallel in the Shaker spirituals one must turn from the hymns to the one-stanza Gift Songs of the 1840s. These too had a narrow melodic range and were to a large extent the contributions of members regarded as "not much natural singers."[78]

The white spirituals that Jackson collected from the shape-note and revival tune-books overlap very little with those in the Shaker manuscripts. Other denominations had no wordless Solemn Songs to record, no tunes for dancing. The Shakers knew the hymnbooks of the day and often took their verse as a model, but doctrinal concerns ruled out their using the hymns themselves.[79] For the same reason the World borrowed very few of the Shaker hymns.[80] More surprisingly, the Shakers contributed nothing at all to the repertory of revival spirituals and did not even employ the characteristic form of these songs—one whose repeated lines, incremental stanzas, and rousing choruses made it extremely useful in backwoods services.

The few revival spirituals that appear in the Shaker manuscripts clearly were set down as curiosities. Haskell, for example, preserved the following one, but tucked it away at the end of a manuscript following a stretch of blank pages:[81]

Harvey Eades recorded another revival spiritual at South Union, but with the explanation that it was "A Methodist farewell, sung by some Negroes in Ky on leaving for Liberia":[82]

THE PROMISED LAND

Most of the revival spirituals in the Shaker song manuscripts were brought in by disillusioned Adventists in the 1840s and are distinctly labeled "Adventist" or "Advent Song."[83]

Many Shaker songs differed from the folk hymns and revival spirituals almost as much in text as in musical features. There is nothing in Jackson's collections at all comparable to the Shaker Gift Songs of the 1840s, the Era of Spirit Manifestations. In the Gift Songs key words may be spelled rather than spoken. If brought by the spirits of Indians or other "natives," the songs may use pidgin English. They may even be partly or wholly in unknown tongues. Many of the songs bring warnings or words of comfort from heavenly spirits. Others describe the wonders visible in Shaker meetings—the turning wheels of the marches, the Believers dancing like living sparks, the pretty angels and all their gifts. Often the words of these songs are metaphors for spiritual states, vowing and calling others to shake out the starch and stiffening, wake up and be a living soul, be little and low, come into the narrow way, and travel home for Mother's blessing. Adolescent girls produced many of the songs of the decade, pushing to its farthest extreme the Shaker longing for a childlike spirit and acting out their own symbolism.

Better educated older Shaker men, on the other hand, had composed most of the earlier hymns. While they openly copied the stilted diction of eighteenth-century English hymnody, they were after all farmers and now and then broke out with homely phrases. They made as little use of standard evangelical imagery as of ballad tags, indifferent both to "milk-white steeds" and to "fountains filled with blood." The Shaker hymn writers, however, gave currency in the Society to certain images from folk song and the Bible and began to define their symbolic value for Shakers.

Over the years the Shakers gradually gathered these symbols and stamped them with the mark of Shakerism. Their songs about vines illustrate the process. Like other Christians the Shakers were much moved by the beautiful verses from John 15 in which Christ declares himself the "true vine," His Father the watchful husbandman, and His followers the fruitful branches set in Him. The passage had already inspired the Baptist folk hymn "Lovely Vine" (see page 205). Like it, the early Shaker hymn "Christ is the true and living vine" (see Hymn no. 2) is a straightforward adaptation of the Biblical text, altered only enough to accommodate the Second Appearing. In contrast, the Extra Song "O we have found a lovely vine" (see page 205) does not mention Christ. This piece, which dates from 1829, implies rather that the vine is the Shaker faith, a sheltering vine of dazzling brightness blooming in Zion's vale. Such later songs as "O heres a beautiful spreading vine" (Gift Song no. 21) and "O heres a lovely creeping vine" (Gift Song no. 22), both of them received in 1849, define the vine as Shaker humility and the safety it brings. Other vine songs usually stress humility. In "Humble Heart," a hymn from the 1820s, the Lord Jehovah declares he has chosen from all the trees one vine, from all the sects one little band:

> The meek and low are nigh to God
> The humble heart is mine.

Two other songs from the 1850s (Later Songs nos. 11 and 12) seemingly return to John 15 for their wording, but actually use its imagery to stand for the humble Believer. They ring, however, with a new tone. Their message is that the humble Believer must attain a state of spiritual purity meriting the Father's favor. In both songs the viewpoint is that of the singer himself. One of them opens, "Ive come into my vineyard to prune each growing vine," and the other, "I am the true vine, which my father has set in his lovely kingdom fair." That the speaker is the faithful Christian, not Christ himself, is implied in the latter song, which says that the Father will shake off the withered branches "that in me there be found no decay." It is made explicit in the other song, for after four stanzas descriptive of the pruning of the vineyard, the song concludes:

> My Father then can glory / In such a lovely sight
> And Wisdom too can view it / With joy & sweet delight
> The Bride & Groom can bless it / And watch it with great care
> That no destructive insect / Its precious fruit impair.

In sum, for his song the Believer took Christ's words as his own, just as in his life he took Christ as the pattern of perfection.

Other images as well as the vine are given a distinctive interpretation in Shaker song. Oak no longer symbolizes strength but overweening pride. Willows do not weep but bend to God's will. The valley is not the valley of the shadow of death or the lonesome valley where the penitent has got to go by himself, but the low vale of humility. Jordan has cleansing waters, not stormy banks and mortal tides. The dove is no longer an emblem of the Holy Ghost but of the gentle and peaceful soul. The Shaker lamb is rarely the Lamb of God, but instead the humble follower of the Good Shepherd.

Shaker theology also molded the themes of Shaker song. Like other Christians, the Shakers had songs of prayer and praise to God, of admonition to the sinner and exhortation to the faltering saint. Like others with a millennial faith, they had songs of Jubilee, but of Jubilee arrived, not longed for. They sang not of Christ's atonement but of themselves taking up a full cross against the World, the Flesh, and the Devil. Their imaginations turned not to the Calvinist God, the fearsome regal Father, nor to the redeeming Son, whose sacrifice set other revivalists a-shouting, but instead to the maternal principle in the Godhead, now newly revealed in and through Mother Ann.

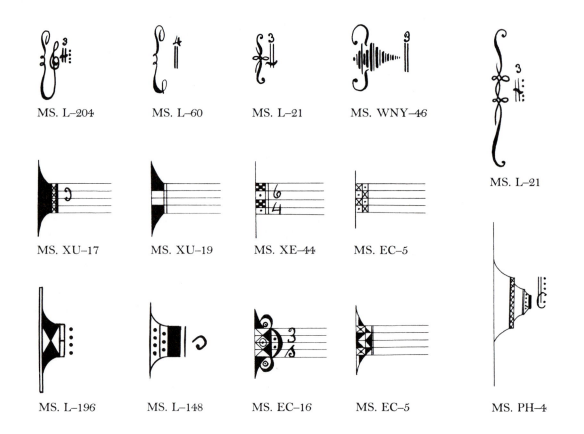

Fig. 11. Decorative "Initials" (*After Scribal Designs*)
Having no need for a key signature, the Shaker scribe either omitted the clef or lifted it to a decorative design at the opening of the tune transcription.

CHAPTER IV

A Note on Shaker Notation and
My Tune Transcriptions

In my research for this song collection I tape-recorded some two hundred early songs from the lips of Shakers and of former members of the communities. My transcriptions of twelve of their performances are included in this book, all of them corrected and verified by my colleague Professor Wilton E. Mason of the University of North Carolina Department of Music. Most of the songs I print, however, are taken from manuscripts written between the years 1825 and 1870. Each is a faithful copy of a variant one scribe set down, my manuscript source being indicated by symbols at the upper right of the tune. (The symbols are keyed to the 798 manuscripts listed in an appendix to the collection.) In the few cases where a song branched into markedly contrasting forms, I print more than one variant. Notes at the rear of the book cite manuscripts and published books holding other variants, provide references to melodic analogues outside Shaker tradition, and document information given in the headnotes to the songs.

Although I have taken an extremely conservative course in editing the songs for presentation, the differences between standard musical notation and the various Shaker systems require a degree of editorial intrusion. To make my procedures clear—and to offer a guide to others who may wish to read the manuscripts—I present the following brief survey of Shaker notation and its problem areas.

A. The Representation of Time Duration and Pitch

1. *Standard Musical Notation* (See Figure 12)

After 1870, when most Shaker communities began to introduce organs, pianos, musical primers, and teachers from the outside world, their song manuscripts use standard notation with increasing frequency and correctness. Prior to that date, however, few Shakers followed the World's system. The exceptions were an occasional convert with prior musical training—like John Wood of Lebanon, the author of MS L–129— and the members selected in the years around 1820 to invest time in studying the rudiments of music. Manuscripts recording tunes in "round notes" at this earliest stage (see MSS L–34, L–55, XU–3, and XU–19) were usually the work of beginners who failed to bar their tunes or to provide clef signs or time and key signatures. Occasionally the scribes designated the position of the leading tone by means of a diamond-shaped "mi," but to decipher their tunes the reader must usually be familiar with the traits of Anglo-American folk song.

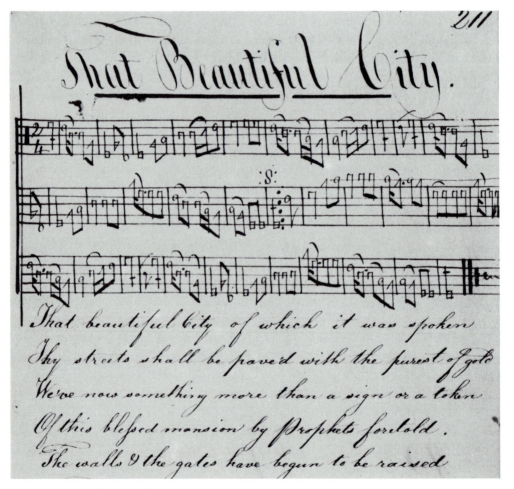

Fig. 12. Shaker Use of Standard Notation
From MS L–136, written by Isaac N. Youngs.

Fig. 13. Shaker Form of Patent Notes
Detail from MS WNY–16, p. 211, written by D. A. Buckingham.

2. *Patent or Shape-Note Notation* (See Figure 13)

Some of the early Shaker musicians studied the shape-note notation introduced into the rural singing-school tradition by William Little and William Smith's *The Easy Instructor* (1801). This notation appears in several Shaker song collections written in the 1820s at Enfield, Conn. (MS EC–24), at Lebanon (MSS L–34, L–55, and L–266), and at Watervliet, N. Y. (MSS WNY–11 and WNY–13). It was used in the 1840s in Kentucky (MSS PH–7 and SU–2) and at Hancock (MS HN–5). Most examples, however, were written in the 1830s at Watervliet (MSS WNY–10, WNY–13, WNY–14, WNY–16, and others).

In one collection he wrote in 1873 (MS WNY–17) D. A. Buckingham of Watervliet showed familiarity with the seven-shape system introduced in 1846 by the singing master Jesse B. Aiken of Philadelphia.[1] Other Shaker song manuscripts employing patent notes draw, however, on the older four-shape notation, the basis of which was an old-fashioned set of syllabic names that early nineteenth-century singing masters still taught for the notes of the scale. In a major scale ascending from the tonic these were: *faw, sol, law, faw, sol, law,* and *mi*. To each of the four names *The Easy Instructor* assigned a distinctive head shape (reproduced here from page 9 of an edition printed in Albany in 1812):

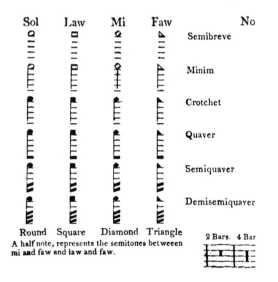

Second, taking their hint from the shape-note system itself, they concerned themselves only with the relative pitch of the notes. Rarely did they use key signatures. They keyed major tunes on *faw* and the modal tunes they called "minor" on *law*, placing

In adopting these shapes the Shaker scribes at Watervliet made two changes. First, to write the notes more conveniently with pen and ink they generally outlined the shapes of the heads but did not black them in, distinguishing between a quarter and a half note by drawing a horizontal line through the stem of the latter:

Second, taking their hint from the shape-note system itself, they concerned themselves only with the relative pitch of the notes. Rarely did they use key signatures. They keyed major tunes on *faw* and the modal tunes they called "minor" on *law*, placing

these governing tones on any line or space that permitted the tune to be written without many leger lines. In singing, they pitched a tune wherever it suited their voices.

3. *Letteral Notation, Capital* (See Figure 14)

About the year 1824 Abraham Whitney of Shirley was inspired with the idea of
using the letters of the alphabet in place of the heads of the musical notes. In contrast
to the two *faw*'s, two *sol*'s, and two *law*'s of the shape-note scale, Whitney's system

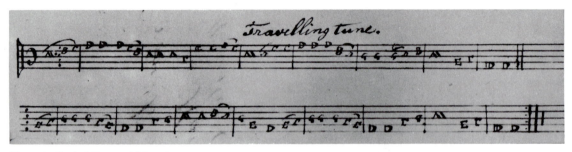

Fig. 14. Capital Letteral Notation
From a letter written by Russel Haskell (OCWR, iv.A.9, Feb. 11, 1830).

gave each degree of the scale a different name and appearance. Whitney also discarded
stems and flags. The printed form of the capital letter stood for the quarter note. Adding
a vertical line to the letter changed it to a half note. Slanting the letter to the right
made it an eighth note and to the left a sixteenth, though the scribes also often simpli-
fied the formation of the letters for these shorter time values:

So long as the scribe was careful about the tilt of his letters, the reader has no trouble
in correctly determining the time values. As in the shape-note system, the note desig-
nates relative rather than fixed pitch. The scribes wrote on a staff, but without using
a clef sign or key signature. They placed the key note at any convenient position on the
staff. They used *C* for the governing tone of all major tunes and *A* for all that they
identified as minor. In theory the position of the semitones was the same in these scales
as in the C major and A minor scales in standard notation, but Shaker singing actually
employed a greater number of scales. (See pages 22–24 for a discussion of modes ob-
scured by Shaker notation.)

A number of Shaker scribes accepted this system—doubtless impressed both by its
practicality and by Whitney's report that the spirit of Mother Ann had revealed it
to him. It appears in manuscripts from the hand of Lucy Williams of Canterbury
(MSS CB–25 and CB–26), of Elder Abraham Perkins of Enfield (MS ENH–2), of
Sally Loomis and Thomas Hammond of Harvard (MSS HD–15, HD–18, HD–20),
of Russel Haskell (his correspondence only), and of other scribes who did not sign
their work. Between the years 1825 and 1830 it was the most commonly used nota-

tion, but by 1835 had everywhere yielded before the superiority of the small letteral system.

4. *Letteral Notation, Small* (See Figure 15)

Russel Haskell labored to gain general acceptance for Whitney's innovation, but said that within a year he had also begun to improve this system.[2] Haskell reserved the clumsy capital letters for the seldom-used whole notes. For other time values he

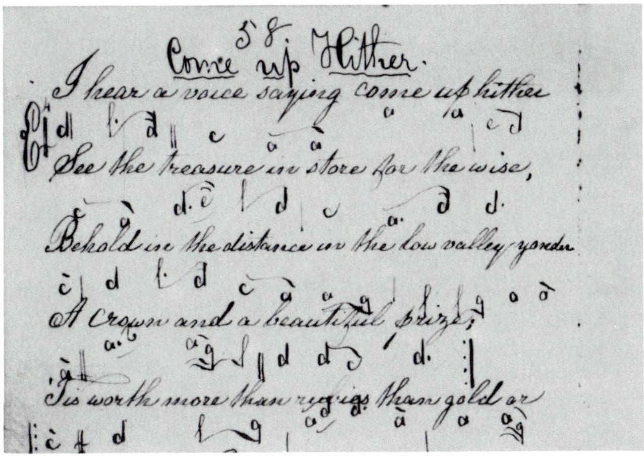

Fig. 15. Small Letteral Notation
Detail from MS HD–38, p. 58.

wrote letters in a modified form of minuscule script, making his upward and downward strokes like stems rather than loops. He could then add flags to the stem to indicate eighth or sixteenth notes. To convert the quarter into a half note he added a vertical stroke to the stem or head:[3]

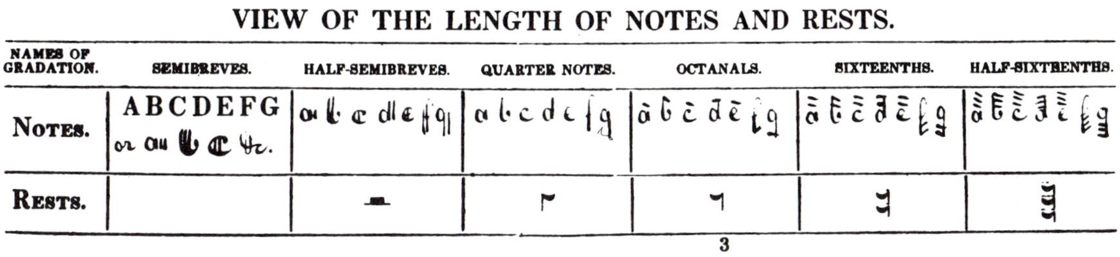

VIEW OF THE LENGTH OF NOTES AND RESTS.

NAMES OF GRADATION.	SEMIBREVES.	HALF-SEMIBREVES.	QUARTER NOTES.	OCTANALS.	SIXTEENTHS.	HALF-SIXTEENTHS.
NOTES.	ABCDEFG or au 𝕭 ℭ 𝔥c.	a b c d e f g	a b c d e f g	a b c d e f g	a b c d e f g	a b c d e f g
RESTS.		▬	⌐	⌐	⌐⌐	⌐⌐⌐

3

At first the scribes set these letters on a five-line staff, but by the late 1830s they realized that a single horizontal line representing the median tone of a tune sufficed to clarify whether a particular note was in the upper or lower octave. Soon they substituted writing paper manufactured with guidelines, either binding it into small blank song books or buying blank notebooks from a nearby stationer. The books were easily obtainable and the notational system simple and clear. From the mid-1830s until the 1880s it was by far the most common form of Shaker notation, and some scribes were still setting down tunes in the small letteral style as late as 1904.

5. *Letteral Notation, Linear* (See Figure 16)

For a few years around 1835 the musicians at South Union sometimes committed a variation on the small letteral system. They separated the text (if any) from the tune

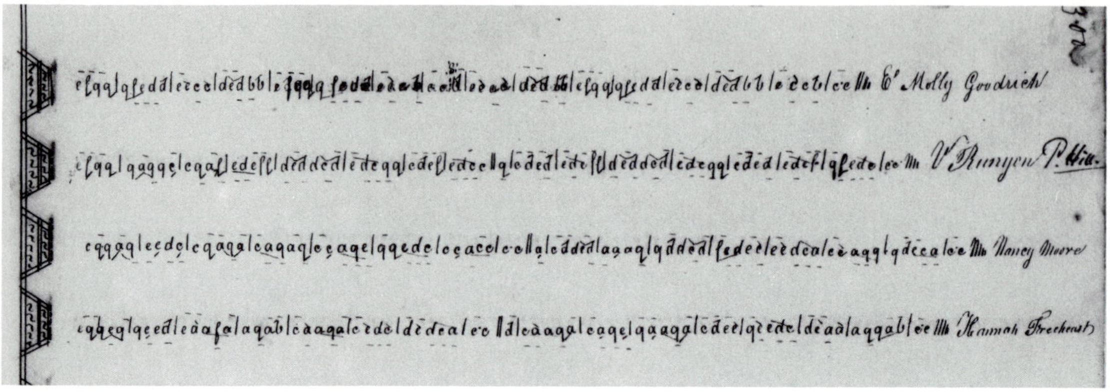

Fig. 16. Linear Letteral Notation
Detail from MS SU–1, p. 300, written by Harvey L. Eades.

and wrote the music in a straight line in a monstrous small hand. To show that a note was higher or lower than the one preceding it they made a small horizontal pen stroke above or below the letter. Since in hastily written transcriptions it was easy to confuse these lines with stems and flags, they sometimes omitted the latter, leaving the reader to guess which notes in a particular bar were crochets and which quavers. The experiment appealed to the South Union scribes because of its economy and neatness, but its result was ambiguity and eyestrain.

6. *Letteral Notation, Cursive* (See Figure 17)

Shortly after publishing directions for writing the small letteral notation in *A Musical Expositor* (1847), Haskell began to experiment with improvements in it for his private use. One of these is preserved on a leaf dated September 1852 laid into the manuscript of another scribe (DWt, SA1211). Haskell seems not to have employed the system often in the next twenty years, but in the early 1870s he began again to dabble with it. In August 1871 he set down some tunes in this notation in MS EC–20. During that same year he entered two different keys to it in another notebook (MS EC–12), once with the note "Perfected in Feb. 1871." (A facsimile of pages from this

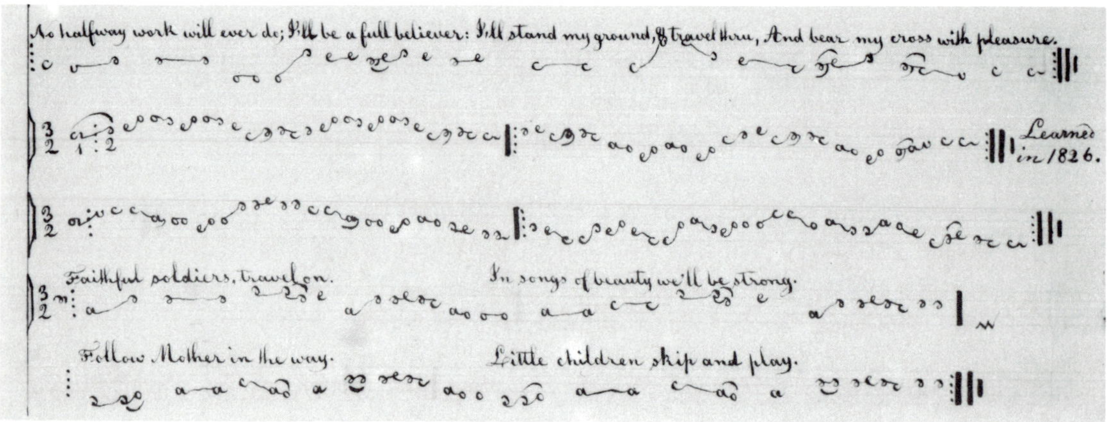

Fig. 17. Cursive Letteral Notation
Detail from MS EC–11, p. 556, written by Russel Haskell.

song book is reproduced on page 121 of Harold Cook's *Shaker Music*.) At this stage of his experimentation, Haskell seems to have been trying to simplify the letteral system by omitting bar lines and forming the letters with fewer strokes, using forms that in fact resemble the capital letters devised in the 1820s:

Latest improved Musical Notes.

Half-semibreves, ♪ ∨ ⊄ ⊅ ⅇ ⅊ ⊙
Quarter notes, ⅰ ∨ c ⅆ ⅇ ⊃ ⊙
Transition notes. ~ ⅼ ⅽ ⅆ ⅼ ℘ ,
October, 1871.

To these note heads Haskell added flags, but not stems, to indicate eighth or sixteenth notes. He omitted even the flags in the final form of this notation, one appearing in some sixty pages scattered through his major song collection, MS EC–11 (especially pages 553 to 592 of its "Marching Songs" section). Here Haskell wrote his new notes in a cursive style, recording each beat (a quarter note, a dotted quarter, or all the notes that made up one of these time values) with a single run of the pen. Unfortunately, his cursive notes, like those of the South Union linear style, leave to the reader the problem of interpreting some of the time values. In duple time, for example, Haskell may write three linked notes for one beat, failing to show whether the intended rhythmic figure was ♫♩ or ♩♫ . Haskell's last notational system was his least clear, and no other scribe employed it.

7. *Numerical Notation* (See Figure 18)

D. A. Buckingham of Watervliet was less happy with letteral notation than any other major Shaker musician. He frequently recorded his tunes in shape-notes and played at times with numeral systems. His earliest experiment in the latter form is recorded in MS WNY–13, a collection he began in 1830. He was probably the author of MS WNY–43, a compilation dating from 1838–1842, in which a second form of numeral notation appears. In 1873, late in his life, Buckingham tried numerals a third time in MS WNY–12. These experiments appear not to derive from those of the

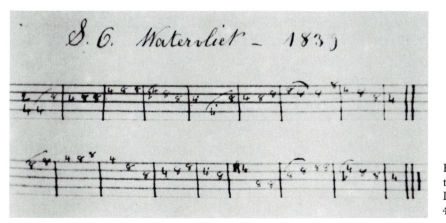

Fig. 18. Numeral Notation
Detail from MS WNY–43, p. 47.

non-Shaker musicians discussed by George P. Jackson on pages 338–342 of his *White Spirituals in the Southern Uplands.* MS WNY–13 antedates Thomas Harrison's *Sacred Harmonicon* (1839), believed to be the first American singing-school publication to employ numerals for notes. Shaker MS WNY–43 uses numbers to stand for time values (a figure 4 for a quarter note, an 8 for an eighth note), rather than for the degrees of the scale, as in the systems of Harrison and of A. D. and J. H. Fillmore. In 1873 Buckingham did use numbers to represent the scale, but instead of adding stems and flags to them, he let the unadorned numeral stand for an eighth note and added superscriptions to represent other time values—a circumflex for a quarter note and two *x*'s for a half note. These experiments, however, amount to only a few pages in Buckingham's manuscripts, and he seems not to have taken them very seriously. One other scribe, James G. Russell, left a treatise entitled "Numeral System of Music Writing" (DWt, SA1211), but apparently wrote no song manuscript in the system.

8. *Shorthand Notation* (See Figure 19)

Shaker manuscripts reveal that several scribes learned or invented systems of shorthand (cf. OCWR, xxii.13 and 14, and WLCMs, nos. 138 and 198). In song collections a scribe occasionally used shorthand to name the Believer who received or composed

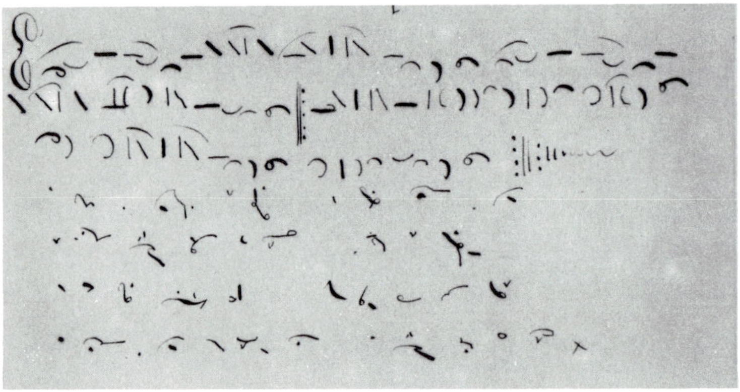

Fig. 19. Shorthand Notation
From the anonymous MS XU–7, p. 14; tune and second stanza of "The Humble Heart."

a particular song, as if torn between a desire to record an association of interest to him and a typically Shaker wish to "hide the giver in the gift" (cf. MS ENH–2, p. [57]). One anonymous scribe, however, apparently spent twenty years making a shorthand copy of hymn texts, some with their tunes also recorded in shorthand. The following unshaded pen strokes represent the letters of the scale in their eighth-note time values:

$$\underline{\quad} \qquad \backslash \qquad | \qquad (\qquad) \qquad \frown \qquad \smile$$
$$\text{C} \qquad \text{D} \qquad \text{E} \qquad \text{F} \qquad \text{G} \qquad \text{A} \qquad \text{B}$$

When the note was of longer duration, the scribe either shaded the stroke or added a loop. To turn *A*, for example, from an eighth to a quarter note, he made a heavier line. To convert the note into a dotted quarter, he added a loop on its right end. To turn it into a half note, he put the loop on its left:

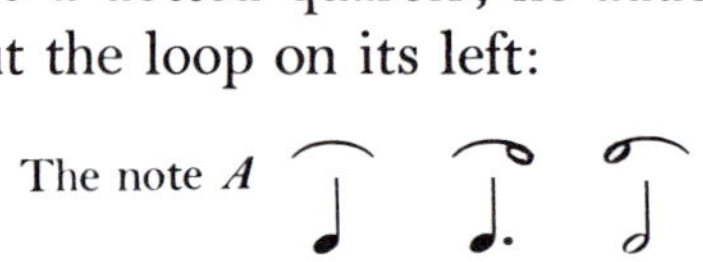

The note *A*

The shorthand system was no improvement over Shaker small letteral notation, and I have seen it used only in MS XU–7.

9. *Native Notation* (See Figure 20)

The most unusual Shaker notation is that used in a single piece in MS L–260, a gift song "Learned by Scetteque Petwait on de great da while sailin on de sea ob de fate in de canoe. Nov. 6th 1842." This Indian spirit apparently communicated the song visually to the scribe, who set it down in a system resembling pictographs. Each of

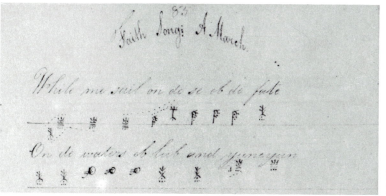

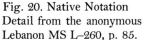
Fig. 20. Native Notation
Detail from the anonymous
Lebanon MS L–260, p. 85.

the symbols, however, stands for one letter of the alphabet. Judging from their relative heights and from the patterns of other Shaker melodies, I believe their equivalents in the English alphabet are as follows:

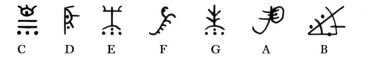

C   D   E   F   G   A   B

A line of small dots between two notes indicates a flag, but the time values appear to have been imperfectly recorded in Scetteque Petwait's song.

B. Time Signatures and Tempo Markings

Shaker scribes usually made an effort to record the tempos proper for the performance of their songs. They found many problems in this side of musical notation, however, as they struggled to reconcile long-standing Shaker practices with the instructions they found in singing-school manuals. In 1839 or 1840, after more than a decade of confusion, the musicians at Lebanon began to work out a uniform and satisfactory system. They scrapped the time and tempo signatures they had inherited from the World's notation and devised symbols of their own to stand for a new schedule of tempos. (They may at this time also have altered some of their performance speeds but seem chiefly to have striven to change their conceptions to fit their practices.) After a session with the Watervliet musicians in September 1840 Isaac N. Youngs sent a letter containing their proposals to scribes at other societies, some of whom copied it into song books (see MSS HD–17 and SU–15).[4] During the next year the musicians amended the system until they found a plan that met fairly general approval, though Youngs himself still saw such weaknesses in it as a failure to provide a tempo marking for the fastest 6/8 dancing tunes.[5] For the musicians at Lebanon he constructed a pendulum he called a "mode-ometer," which had a movable stop that could be slid to positions along a color-coded scale marked for the newly agreed upon tempos. (Figure 21 shows

Fig. 21. Shaker Instruments for Musical Instruction
At the top is a "violin-piano," a monochord constructed in 1869 by Elisha Blakeman of Lebanon. Its metal keys depress against a wire stroked across the neck by the bow at the lower right. Beneath this "violin-piano" is a "mode-ometer," a color-coded pendulum made about the year 1841 by Isaac N. Youngs. These instruments and Daniel Boler's baton at the lower left are preserved in the Shaker Museum at Old Chatham, N. Y.

a mode-ometer made by Youngs about 1841, now preserved in the Shaker Museum at Old Chatham, N. Y.) To help the other societies unite in the new tempo system, Youngs in 1843 published his *A Short Abridgement of the Rules of Music*, in which he provided a table of moods of time, complete with pendulum lengths for each tempo.

There was, however, one dissenting voice, that of Russel Haskell at Enfield. He liked the general design of Youngs' plan, but thought its tempos too slow. He accordingly prepared a table of his own in which he advanced the speed of most of the moods of time and added one for the fastest tunes in compound time. It was probably to gain support for these tempos that Haskell in 1847 published a treatise of his own, *A Musical Expositor*. A digest of Youngs' and Haskell's plans appears below in Table 1. Its bracketed figures show the beats per minute computed from Haskell's pendulum lengths and corrections of small errors in Youngs' calculations. I also adjust the tempos in his compound modes—Youngs made two downward beats in each bar of 6/8 time, but followed singing-school practice in counting the top and bottom of each swing of the hand as a separate beat; the modern equivalents of his figures are accordingly half the number of beats printed in his book.

The tempos given in Table 1 can be relied upon in reading manuscripts written after 1839. Haskell, however, by the year 1850 modified his symbols for time signatures.[6] Ceasing to use bar lines except at the end of the strains, he began to present his time and tempo signatures in a form resembling fractions. The numerator denotes the degree of speed and the denominator the number of "octanals" in a beat.[7] In his later transcriptions, then, the figure 3/2 means that each quarter note gets one beat and that the piece is performed in the third mood of time. A 5/3 signature means that a dotted quarter note gets one beat and that the tempo is that of the fifth degree of speed.

TABLE 1. The Schedule of Tempos Established about 1840

Name of the Mood	Signature	Modern Equivalent	*Youngs*, Abridgement (*1843*), *pp. 30–32*: Seconds per Measure	Beats per Measure	String Length	MM. ♩ =	*Haskell*, Expositor (*1847*), *pp. 23–27*: Beats per Measure	String Length	MM. ♩ or ♩. =
					Common Time				
Adagio	$\|^{1}$	4/4	3	4	22″	80	4	22″	[80]
Largo	$\|^{2}$	4/4	$2\frac{5}{8}$	4	17″	91 [92]	4	$15\frac{1}{4}$″	[96]
Allegro	$\|^{3}$	4/4	$2\frac{1}{4}$	4	$12\frac{1}{2}$″	106	4	11″	[113]
Presto	$\|^{4}$	4/4	$1\frac{7}{8}$–$1\frac{1}{2}$	4	$8\frac{3}{4}$–$5\frac{1}{2}$″	128 [127] –160	4	$7\frac{1}{2}$″	[138]
					Sub-Measures				
Sub-adagio, etc.	$\#^{1}$ etc.	2/4	half the above	2	same as the above		2	same as the above	
					Triple Mode				
Adagio triple, etc.	$\#^{1}$,	3/4	three-fourths the above	3	same as the above		3	same as the above	
					Compound Mode				
First	$¢\|^{1}$	6/8	$2\frac{1}{4}$	4 [2]	$12\frac{1}{2}$″	106 [53]	4 [2]	11″	[113 = 56]
Second	$¢\|^{2}$	6/8	$1\frac{7}{8}$	4 [2]	$9\frac{1}{2}$″	122 [61]	4 [2]	$7\frac{1}{2}$″	[138 = 69]
Third	$¢\|^{3}$	6/8	$1\frac{5}{8}$	4 [2]	7″	142 [71]	2	22″	[80]
Fourth	$¢\|^{4}$	6/8	$1\frac{3}{8}$–$1\frac{1}{8}$	4 [2]	$4\frac{3}{4}$–$3\frac{1}{8}$″	170 [85] –213 [106]	2	$15\frac{1}{4}$″	[96]
Fifth	$¢\|^{5}$	6/8	$1\frac{1}{8}$	4 [2]	$3\frac{1}{8}$″	213 [106]	2	11″	[113]
Sixth	$¢\|^{6}$	6/8	$\frac{7}{8}$–$\frac{3}{4}$	4 [2]	$2\frac{1}{4}$–$1\frac{1}{2}$″	250 [125] –300 [154]	2	$7\frac{1}{2}$″	[138]
Seventh	$¢\|^{7}$	6/8	—	—	—	—	2	$4\frac{3}{8}$″	[180]

Another set of time signatures also keyed to Table 1 was in use at Lebanon and some other societies during the transitional phase in 1840 and 1841.[8] These symbols somewhat resemble those later developed by Haskell, having the appearance of fractions. Their numerators, as in his system, signify the mood of time. These scribes still used bar lines, however, and their denominators represent the number of eighth notes in a measure. Accordingly 4/4 time is symbolized by the denominator 8; 2/4 by the denominator 4; and 3/4 by the denominator 6. For 6/8 time Youngs must have briefly secured the assent of other musicians to use the denominator 7—basing the figure on his belief that 6/8 measures actually hold the equivalent of seven eighth notes (see page 25, where I discuss his view). Other scribes soon rejected the notion, insisting instead on the denominator 6; this caused 3/4 and 6/8 time to be indistinguishable and forced the abandonment of this set of symbols in favor of those shown in Table 1.

If the tempos of songs written down after 1839 are easy to determine, those of songs transcribed in the earlier years are not. During the 1820s many scribes provided no guidance at all, and the tempo markings used in the 1830s are full of difficulties. In this phase the scribes got their knowledge of tempos and time signatures from such singing-school books as Little and Smith's *The Easy Instructor*. They learned:

1. a set of symbols (C, ₵, Ɔ, 2/4, etc.) that were at once time signatures and indications of tempo;
2. divergent interpretations of the tempos represented by these symbols, since Shaker musicians either used several books that were not in agreement or had differing understandings of the vague directives they found in them (e.g., "half as quick again," or "$\frac{1}{4}$ faster");[9]
3. a set of tempos that were both at variance with long-established Shaker practices and too few to accommodate the many Shaker dances and song types; and
4. the notion that the semibreve has a fixed time duration and that all other note values should derive proportionately from this "measure note"— a conception that inhibited their making needful alterations in the systems they inherited from the World.

The resulting confusion of the scribes is evident in the various systems of modes recorded in their manuscripts in the 1830s. Youngs himself set down two different tables in a single manuscript, the "Rudiments of Music" he wrote in 1833.[10] One, labeled "Plan of Improved Modes," he tucked into an appendix to the work (see Table 2). Whether he or any other scribe actually followed its tempos is uncertain. His other plan (see Table 3) is presented under the title "Modes of Time" in the body of his treatise. It omits both pendulum lengths and a computation of the beats per minute. Its very incompleteness suggests that this table may already have had currency among Shaker musicians in the 1830s, but several other manuscripts recommend tempos different from those given by Youngs. For example, an early draft of "A Musical Expositor" completed by Haskell in 1831 discards altogether the adagio mode of common time as a tempo slower than Believers sang. Both this manuscript and CB–36, written at Canterbury in 1832, give one second rather than a second and a half as the proper duration of a measure of 6/8 time.

TABLE 2. THE "PLAN OF IMPROVED MODES" IN YOUNGS' "THE RUDIMENTS OF MUSIC" (1833)

Name of the Mode	Signature	Modern Equivalent	Seconds per Measure	Beats per Measure	String Length	M.M. ♩, ♩, or ♩. =
Common Time						
Adagio	c	4/4	$3\frac{1}{2}$	4	$30\frac{1}{2}''$	68
Largo	¢	4/4	3	4	22''	80
Allegro	Ɔ	2/2	$2\frac{1}{4}$	2	$48\frac{1}{4}''$	54
Presto	♪	2/2	$1\frac{3}{4}$	2	$30\frac{1}{2}''$	68
2/4 or Submovements						
Sub-adagio	2/4	2/4	$1\frac{3}{4}$	2	$30\frac{1}{2}''$	68
Sub-largo	2/4	2/4	$1\frac{1}{2}$	2	22''	80
Sub-allegro	2/4	2/4	$1\frac{1}{8}$	2	12''	108
Sub-presto	2/4	2/4	$\frac{7}{8}$	2	$7\frac{5}{8}''$	136
Triple Time Modes						
Adagio triple	3/4	3/4	$2\frac{5}{8}$	3	$69\frac{1}{2}''$	45
Largo triple	3/4	3/4	$2\frac{1}{4}$	3	$48\frac{1}{4}''$	54
Allegro triple	3/4	3/4	$1\frac{3}{4}$	3	28''	71
Presto triple	3/4	3/4	$1\frac{3}{8}$	3	$17\frac{3}{8}''$	90
Compound Time Modes						
1st	7/8	6/8	2	2	$39\frac{1}{4}''$	60
2nd	7/8	6/8	$1\frac{3}{4}$	2	$30\frac{1}{2}''$	68
3rd	7/8	6/8	$1\frac{3}{8}$	2	$18\frac{1}{2}''$	87
4th	7/8	6/8	1	2	$9\frac{3}{4}''$	120

TABLE 3. THE "MODES OF TIME" IN YOUNGS' "THE RUDIMENTS OF MUSIC" (1833)

Name of the Mode	Signature	Modern Equivalent	Beats per Measure	Seconds per Measure	MM.
Common Time Modes					
Adagio	c	4/4	4	4	[♩ = 60]
Largo	¢	4/4	4	3	[♩ = 80]
Allegro	Ɔ	2/2	2	2	[♩ = 60]
Presto	2/4	2/4	2	$1\frac{1}{2}$	[♩ = 160]
Triple Time Modes					
First	3/2	3/2	3	3	[♩ = 60]
Second	3/4	3/4	3	2	[♩ = 90]
Third	3/8	3/8	3	$1\frac{1}{2}$	[♪ = 120]
Compound Time Modes					
First	6/4	6/4	2	2	[♩. = 60]
Second	6/8	6/8	2	$1\frac{1}{2}$	[♩. = 80]

But none of these tables accurately reflects the tempos that those who recorded them actually sang. Youngs closed Table 3 with an admission that the modes were defective in not providing "a sufficient variety to apply to all the different speeds of tunes."[11] Haskell in his "Expositor" manuscript evades the problem by suggesting that the reader regard the figures in his table as the median speed in each mode, feeling free to vary each one as far as half way to the next tempo. The most revealing criticism, however, was set down by Harvey Eades in a letter he wrote to Youngs in 1833. He had observed, he said, that some tunes written with the signature Ɔ for the third mode of common time were hymn tunes performed at the tempo of ♩ = 60; other tunes with the very same signature were marching tunes "sung with us nearly as fast again." Youngs had sent South Union, Eades continued, some tunes for the "circular dance" marked for the "4th mood of common time, or the 2nd mood of compound time; that is, a half second to the beat, which is a great deal slower than we sing them."[12] These discrepancies led Eades in 1834 to work out a new set of tempos (see Table 4).[13] Eades, Betsy Smith, and other South Union scribes sometimes used these time signatures, but they were not taken up by scribes in the other societies.

TABLE 4.   "Moods of Time" from Eades' "Letter Music," MS SU–8 (1834)

Name of the Mode	Signature	Modern Equivalent	Beats per Measure	Seconds per Measure	MM.
Common Time Modes					
First	ɔ	2/2	2	2	[♩ = 60]
Second	2/4	2/4	2	1	[♩ = 120]
Third	2/8	2/8	2	½	[♪ = 240]
Triple Time Modes					
First	3/2	3/2	3	3	[♩ = 60]
Second	3/4	3/4	3	1½	[♩ = 120]
Third	3/8	3/8	3	3/4	[♪ = 240]
Compound Time Modes					
First	6/4	6/4	2	3	[♩. = 40]
Second	6/8	6/8	2	1½	[♩. = 80]
Third	6/16	6/16	2	3/4	[♪. = 160]

In short, the uncertainties surrounding the early tempo markings are so great that in presenting the tunes transcribed prior to 1840 I refrain from translating the time signatures into the metronome equivalents implied by Shaker treatises. For these songs I enter on the staff the closest modern approximation of the scribe's time signature and above it record his original symbol in parentheses. Where I can, I provide in brackets a reliable tempo marking for the song from manuscripts written after the 1830s. Otherwise, I leave the reader to be guided by the tempos of other songs belonging to the same genre. For tunes taken from manuscripts written after the Shaker musicians had worked out satisfactory tables of the modes of time I give metronome markings calculated from the system within which the scribe worked. If other writers who set down the same tune showed a marked preference for a different tempo, I include it in brackets after the tempo given in the manuscript from which I copy the tune.

C. Repeat Signs

Since Shakers normally sang as members of a congregation or of a vocal band performing while others danced or marched, they necessarily followed strict conventions concerning the repetition of sections of their tunes. Like secular musicians they rendered each half of most of their dance tunes two times, but the Shaker singers broke with this pattern in their Holy Order tunes, singing the set strain only once. They repeated both parts of an Extra Song, but only the second half of a hymn tune. The Shaker scribes were so familiar with these practices that although they employed standard repeat signs they often neglected to use them with precision. They might enter a repeat sign only at the start of a section, or only at the end of it, or might omit the symbols altogether. Some writers followed their private notions; others were simply careless. In my copies I refrain from bewildering the reader with these vagaries. Having established (from the work of careful scribes and from secondary documents) the singing practice for each genre, I silently regularize the repeat signs in the songs I print. Where I feel any suspicion, however, that a song may have been an exception to the general practice or that I may be placing it in the wrong genre, I enter a statement of my misgivings in a note or refrain from altering the scribe's presentation.

The habit of repeating sections of a tune caused problems in one other area of transcription, that of recording the alternate openings and closings of the strains. Haskell and a few other scribes may scrupulously count beats and write out the gathering tone at the start of a tune and the first and second cadences at the close of each strain. Most Shaker scribes, however, simply leave the singer to make these minor adjustments in the tune. I present whatever they set down, believing it will cause no serious confusion for any reader.

D. Barring

Shaker scribes made frequent errors in barring tunes. They regularly failed to recognize 3/2 time in their singing and were often confused by 5/4 time, by rubato in 3/4 tunes, and by other irregular measures. Sometimes even highly competent scribes abandoned bar lines in bewilderment; most beginners did not attempt barring at all. Where I can, I offer help to the reader by choosing the most competently written variant of several having equal musical interest. I also insert on the staff a bracketed time signature, if the tune is regular enough to admit one. But aside from correcting (and acknowledging in my notes) a few blunders obviously resulting from scribal haste, I do not alter the barring given in the original manuscript. The scribe's perception of the rhythm is not likely to give serious trouble to a reader, and it has its own interest.

E. Embellishments

Some Shaker singers enjoyed ornamenting a vocal line, and the scribes at times attempted to record the practice. Their most common symbols were the "trill" and the "appoggiatura." The former was represented by a *tr* inscribed over the note; I reproduce the symbol, leaving the reader to be guided toward an interpretation of it by my discussion of it on pages 26–27. The "appoggiatura," or slide toward or away from a note, is set down with clarity in the manuscripts of the 1830s. In those years the scribes used a tiny letter placed on the appropriate line or space to record the note on which a slide began and tied it by a slur to the letter representing the weightier tone. After 1840 the scribes usually gave a less precise idea of the interval covered by the slide. By that time they were no longer using a full staff, and they now often represented the slide by a figure resembling a reversed or inverted comma. The distance of the head of this comma from the main note suggests the width of the slide; in standard notation this necessarily appears more precise than in the Shaker system.

F. Vocables

Many Shaker manuscripts hold songs that Believers performed with vocables instead of English texts. Scribes recorded these vocables when they wrote down some of the songs that Mother Ann had sung in the 1780s or those learned in the 1840s from the spirits. They understood these texts to be in unknown tongues. The Solemn Songs of the 1780s and 1790s probably were sung with similar syllables, but the scribes failed to set down any of these texts. Wordless laboring songs were performed differently. For these the vocal bands used a few simple syllables. They commonly sang "lo" or "do" for each quarter note. A pair of eighth notes they might render as "do-dle", "lo-dle," "lo-rel," "lul-ly," or "dul-ly." For triplets they sang "lo-dle-lo" or "lo-rel-lo." In cadences they usually closed off the vowel with an *m*, as in "lo lo lum" or "lum-de-um dum."[14]

Although the scribes usually did not record the syllables they used in singing laboring songs, they were careful to insert slurs to show when two notes were to be sung to the same syllable. A statement by Haskell discloses why the scribes thought this important. Tunes in 2/4 time, he wrote, could be sung for both the Regular Step and the Quick Dance. But in the Regular Step the laborers took only one step for each quarter note; they took one for every eighth note in the Quick Dance. In performance the two classes of tunes accordingly differed perceptibly in accenting, and the singers exaggerated the difference by singing "lo" for each eighth note in the Quick Dance but "lo-dle" for a pair of eighth notes in the Regular Step. In the latter (as also in the Walking Tunes and the Marches) sixteenth notes were either "sounded liquid on the syllable lul or dul [*sic*]" or "*articulated*, on the syllables dully or lully."[15]

For further guidance in the use of vocables in the wordless, or "noted," songs, the reader may consult March no. 2, Extra Song no. 23, and Gift Song no. 57.

G. Song Titles

When a particular song has no title in any manuscript that records it, I take its first line for my title. Often, however, the manuscripts will hold many different ones for the same song, for the scribes often invented names at whim. This resulted in many songs sharing the same title. In such cases I avoid duplication by picking some suitable one from among those set down in the various song collections.

Shaker Spirituals

PART I

Songs of the Gospel Parents

In 1816 the Shakers issued a small volume entitled *Testimonies of the Life, Character, Revelations and Doctrines of our Ever Blessed Mother Ann Lee and the Elders with Her*. It set down memories "collected from living witnesses" who had themselves been converted by these "gospel parents." Again and again these testimonies describe occasions when the English Shakers "broke forth in heavenly songs" and "sounded the gospel trumpet with singing."[1]

The songs themselves could not be collected in 1816. The Shakers were then first learning to prick notes. Fifteen years would pass before many could transcribe a melody, and not until the late 1830s did it apparently occur to them to gather these earliest songs. By this time Mother Ann had been dead nearly fifty years. Many of her converts had also passed away. At Lebanon or Harvard or Enfield the songs had branched into contrasting variants. The musicians were able, however, to recover fifty melodies attributed to one or another of the English Shakers.[2] Nine of these had been sung by Mother Ann herself, fifteen by her brother William, twenty-three by James Whittaker, and two by John Hocknell. A last song is reported to have been "Learned of the Angels by James and Jane Wardley," leaders of the Manchester worshipers when Ann Lee first came among them in 1758—they remained behind when the others came to America.[3] These fifty songs may well be the only surviving musical record of the tradition of Pentecostal singing among early English Dissenting sects.

As one would expect, these fifty early Shaker tunes include some borrowed from ballads or similar to ballad tunes. Father James's Song no. 3 in the collection that follows is composed, for example, of four phrases in an ABCB[1] pattern. The tune survives in three different transcriptions. One variant has a text in rough accentual meter. All three are incorrectly barred, apparently because a rubato style of performance blurred the scribes' perception of the ternary rhythm of the tune. All these characteristics—the rubato song style, the text, and the melodic structure—imply the tune's kinship with balladry. But in two of the transcriptions, repeat signs are inserted at the midpoint of the melody, as if it were a dance tune. This feature is in keeping with the greater number of the tunes of Ann Lee and the English elders. At least half of their songs are dance tunes. Not all are composed of the two balancing eight-bar sections characteristic of much British and American folk dance, but they do divide near the middle, have repeat signs at that point, and show phrase patterns typical of dancing songs.

This high proportion of dance tunes among the earliest Shaker spirituals bears out what we are told in Shaker historical records and in the comments of outsiders. Many passages in the *Testimonies* tell how they "went forth in the dance." A newspaper account written five years before Ann Lee and her English followers emigrated described the Shaking Quakers of Manchester as singing and dancing to the "pious tunes of Nancy Dawson, Bobbin Joan, Hie thee Jemmy home again, &c."[4] To the community at large this seemed a matter of wonder, if not shocking. In both New and Old England the Shakers' dancing provoked protest from unruly mobs, but it was a feature recurrent in radical Dissenting worship. In England, as George Fox's account showed, the Ranters had danced to the annoyance of Quakers. New Lights in the American Great Awakening had also broken into the exercise. In 1746, for example, a woman named Hannah Huckins "fell to dancing round the room" at a meeting in Durham, New Hampshire, "singing some dancing-tunes, jiggs, minuets, and kept the time exactly with her feet."[5] Later, in the Kentucky Revival of 1800, many were to be taken with the "dancing exercise," which Barton W. Stone described as "heavenly to the spectators." There was "nothing in it like levity," he said. "The smile of heaven shone on the countenance of the subject, and assimilated to angels appeared the whole person. Sometimes the motion was quick and sometimes slow. Thus they continued to move forward and backward in the same track or alley till nature seemed exhausted."[6] Probably no sect, however, turned so deliberately to dancing as did the Shakers.

The dance background suggests one explanation for the fact that some of the tunes of the first elders appear in the manuscripts with texts composed of meaningless syllables. The use of such vocables must have been familiar to the early Shakers from British folk-song tradition, in which a solo singer may make "mouth music" for dancing as a substitute for a fiddler or piper. (The practice was common at dances in Newfoundland as late as the 1930s, and it has been recorded in recent years in Scotland and Ireland.)[7] Mother Ann was probably continuing a custom long familiar to her when Angell Matthewson heard her singing "with much glee & politeness" for a group of dancing children.[8] Mother Ann's Song no. 2 is the kind of song she would have been singing them.

Other factors also reinforced the early Shakers' tendency to use vocables in their singing. Neither psalmody nor the hymnody of the Baptists and Methodists was in harmony with the spirit of their new faith. The Scriptures seem occasionally to have provided them texts, as when William Plummer in 1782 heard Shakers singing "words out of the Psalms . . . but not in rhyme."[9] One of the surviving early songs, Father James's "In yonder's valley," illustrates this practice. It is in fact the only early song with a fully developed lyric. Half of the other songs by Father James and two of those attributed to Father William also have words, but the texts are simply ejaculations in prose. The tunes of many seem equally improvised. Father William's "O will I love" is typical of them:[10]

O   will I love, O my love? Come my love, my dove,   O pret-ty love, my

joy.   Come, lit-tle love, my   joy.

Such inchoate songs are explained only in part, however, by the fact that they were produced at a time when Shaker tradition was still largely unformed. Another explanation is that the early Shakers might sing while in a trance state. In such moments song must rarely have been tidily squared off into balanced tunes. While the converts would have been unable to remember lengthy rhapsodic songs, some tunes they preserved do suggest such an origin. The following one by Mother Ann, for example, exhibits in its second strain a teasing of the leading tone very unlike the patterns of traditional English folk melody:[11]

Of the three English leaders, Mother Ann is the one most often and explicitly described as singing extemporaneously in a gift. Timothy Hubbard, for example, told of once seeing her stand "for the space of an hour" noticing nothing of "the things of time" and all the while singing "chiefly in unknown tongues." On another occasion he saw her "sit in her chair, from early in the morning until afternoon, under great operations and power of God. She sung in unknown tongues, the whole of the time; and . . . all her sensations appeared to be engaged in the spiritual world."[12]

It is not surprising that the manuscripts hold fewer songs by Mother Ann than by Father William and Father James. They ministered very differently with song. William is usually described as singing for laboring exercises. One typical account tells how Believers

> all assembled in the meadow, near the house. Father William sung for them, and they all went forth, with great power, in the worship of God, and danced till they trod the grass into the earth, and even trod down the earth, so that it was like an earthen threshingfloor, with scarcely the appearance of grass upon it.[13]

Although Father James at times sang for the dancers, he seems customarily to have used song in yet another way. He was a man of words and served the group as its public speaker. It is no accident that many of his songs have English texts, for his singing was often an extension of his preaching. In one song that Haskell preserves Father James frequently varied the words "according as the occasion or circumstance might require." Addressing young Believers he sang, "How can you refuse me, how can you deny me, when I plead for your souls!" Turning to Ann Lee, he might change the closing words to "when I plead for my soul!" To the people of the World he would sing "when I humbly do come!"[14] Father James, Father William, and Mother Ann in short offered their converts models for three uses of song. Their followers would later devise still others, but for a hundred years Shaker song would continue to serve for public testimony, for the dance, and for the voicing of Pentecostal exaltation.

Mother Ann Lee

Even in childhood Ann Lee had visions of heaven, where she observed the prophets and apostles looking so "wishfully" after her that she "wondered at it." She saw "heavenly things" and "beautiful colors" and dreaded to have her mother get up in the morning "lest she should open the window and let them out."[15] The everyday world to which Ann returned was that of the Manchester slums, where she was born in 1736, one of eight children of a blacksmith. Her parents were very poor and put her to work, while still a young girl, in a cotton mill. She later earned a living as a fur cutter and as an infirmary cook; her husband Abraham Standerin was a blacksmith. The memory of deprivation never left her. Years afterwards when her followers at Watervliet finished a meal she would eat their leavings, saying, "The American people are so full fed, that they have not learned to pick their bones, and clean up their plates as we English people have."[16]

Mother Ann came slowly to her calling. She did not receive her crucial revelation until the age of thirty-four. She had reached the lowest point of her life. For nine years, her marriage bed had increasingly filled her with loathing and guilt. She had borne four children, and the last of them had just died at the age of six. She had a tormenting fear of eternal damnation. Shaker tradition says that in her travail and tribulation her flesh "consumed" upon her bones and "bloody sweat pressed through the pores of her skin." Miraculously she was "brought through" and reborn into the "spiritual kingdom." She herself said of the experience, "I was like an infant just born into the world; they see colours and objects; but they know not what they see; and so it was with me, when I was born into the spiritual world. But before I was twenty-four hours old, I saw, and knew what I saw."[17] She had earlier sought comfort in the small group of Shaking Quakers in Manchester. Her new understanding filled her with power that now made her the center toward whom the others turned. The group began to witness strongly, provoking harrassments which caused Ann Lee and her closest supporters to look for asylum in America.

The exact nature of what Mother Ann taught is irretrievably lost. The only writings known to survive from the hands of the English Shakers are two letters by James Whittaker, neither of them intended as a doctrinal statement. Early accounts of Ann Lee by outsiders are sketchy and filled with patent absurdities. Village gossips delighted themselves and travelers with tales that Ann Lee had been the mistress of a British officer, that she and William swigged gin till they fell to brawling or dancing naked.[18] A more reliable source of knowledge is the body of anecdotes and aphorisms recollected by the early converts and gathered many years later in the *Testimonies*. But Thomas Swain has shown that successive versions of this collection alter the wording, the arrangement, and the repertory itself.[19] Even the earliest accounts were set down thirty years after the events, when the passage of time must have left a blurred memory of Ann Lee's exact phrasing and of the contexts within which she spoke. The core of her teaching, however, is clear: that "lust of the flesh" is the cause of man's "loss" and "separation," that "God does not look upon creatures according to their lost natures but according to their desires after God," and that by taking up a "full cross" one can attain baptism into the Spirit.[20]

The universalism and Arminianism implicit in this message were already proving highly attractive to backwoods revivalists in New England. These plain farming people must have also felt comfortable with the practical godliness Ann Lee urged. She reproved them for having both too much and too little pride—for laying their tables with silver spoons while leaving filth in their dooryards—and she counseled that they "set out apple-trees, and raise calves, and make provision as though they were to live a thousand years, and gather something to do good with."[21]

Some of her converts, however, were already prepared to expect not merely spiritual teachings, but the manifestation of divinity in a woman. Louis Burch, for one, said that shortly before he heard of Ann Lee, he had a vision in which he suddenly saw a great light, and angels coming forward in that light, and Christ with a woman walking by his side. "In that woman's face," said Louis, "I saw faces of all the Saints from the foundation of the world to the last age of man. Yet her face was no larger than any common woman's face, and in her face I saw my face. But I never saw the face of that woman till I saw Mother Ann's face."[22]

The words that report Mother Ann's own sense of her relation to the Holy Spirit are her most difficult sayings. She speaks of herself variously as "your fellow servant," "the first Elder in the Church," "the second Eve," and "the bride of Christ." She speaks both of feeling "the blood of Christ" running through her soul and washing her, and of conversing with Christ or with God "as one friend converses with another, face to face."[23] Some of her words are scriptural allusions, others describe visions, and yet others are metaphors for the state of her feelings. Her converts may often have imperfectly grasped her meaning.

They at the least regarded her as a woman of impressive righteousness and spiritual understanding. She could not read the written word, but they felt she read character with penetration. Their accounts say that events bore her out when she charged Tryphena Perkins with whoredom and accused certain men of buggery.[24] Jemima Blanchard and Sarah Robbins, two of her converts, testified that Mother Ann was very "tender and loving" to the one and "talked sharp" to the other. If she had dealt evenly with them, she would have frightened away Jemima at once or "made but little impression" on Sarah.[25]

Mother Ann seems, however, to have impressed her converts chiefly through the intensity of her own emotional life. She touched their sympathy and gratitude by her frequent periods of deep suffering, when she "labored" for the lost state of their souls. At other times she overawed them when her spirits rose in visions and exaltation and she cried, "I see the glory of God, as bright as the sun!—I see multitudes of the dead, that were slain in battle, arise and come into the first resurrection!—I see Christ put crowns on their heads, of bright, glorious, and changeable colours!"[26]

Yet it was not through words that she most often manifested her power. Father James witnessed in that mode. Jemima Blanchard said he and William would "labor in the worship with great power and zeal," but Jemima never saw Mother Ann "under

Mother Ann's Song No. 1

A song remembered only at Enfield, Connecticut.

MS EC–11, p. [1].

Mother Ann's Song No. 2

A song learned by James Bishop of Lebanon as a child of four.

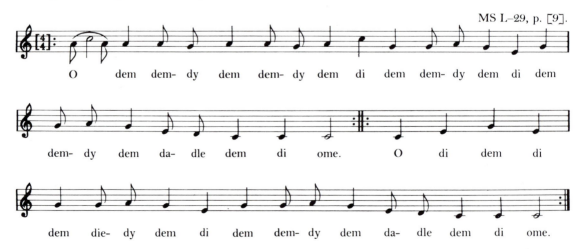

MS L–29, p. [9].

Mother Ann's Song No. 3

A second song learned by James Bishop. He died in the faith in 1868, at the age of eighty-nine.

MS L–29, p. [9].

O   bem   bem   bem   O   wip- py   bem   bem

bem- by em   bem- by bem   O   wip- py   bem   bem

bem- by em;   O   wip- py   bem   bem   bem   bem

any violent operation of the power of God." Ann was "the supporter of all their gifts and the centre of their influence." When she was "under the immediate influence of the spirit of God," the mere sound of her voice or movement of her hand was far more potent than "the united gifts of all others." At these moments she broke into song. Thankful Goodrich remembered a characteristic scene in which Mother Ann walked through the worshipers saying, "Be joyful Brethren & Sisters!—Be joyful! Joy away! Rejoice in the God of your salvation." She then sang "the most melodious & heavenly song" that Thankful ever heard, "which raised the assembly of 300 or more into rejoicing, leaping & shouting." At the sound of her voice the Pentecostal fire swept the hearts of the congregation, and "the spacious apartment would ring with beautiful songs which no man could learn."[27]

Father William Lee

Before his conversion Father William Lee was very much of the World. He was married and had a son. A "thick set, strong built" young fellow with an unusually powerful voice, he had entered the army, where Shaker tradition says he served as "an officer of the highest company in the regiment of grenadiers." He wore his "scarlet colored clothes, and long hair down to the waistband" of his trousers, and walked the streets with his cane. "I always meant to treat mankind well," he said, "but I would not take a misbeholden word from any man."

His older sister Ann, who had already emerged as the leader of the Shaking Quakers, sent for him, "spoke the word of God" to him, and convinced him that he was "a lost soul." He asked, "Mother, what shall I do?" "Go and throw up your commission," she answered; "settle up your affairs—strip off your pride, and then come to me."

William did as she said. He dressed in "mean low apparel" and took work in a blacksmith shop. When people saw what an alteration there was in him, they ridiculed him: "Yea, little boys not more than seven years old would throw dirt at me, and abuse me, and I dare not speak one word. Was not this enough to kill old Adam?" William found he had been a wicked man, and now during the daytime he "put his hands sharp to work," fearing God every time he set his foot down and chastizing every member of his body that had sinned against God. In the night season he labored to God for His gifts and power. He washed his face with tears till he felt God "speak peace" to his soul.[28] After this turning point in his life he said, "Once I served God out of fear; but now I serve him out of pure love."[29] William readily bore more than his share of the abuse of mobs in Manchester and New England and of the hardships at Niskeyuna. He seemed under continual suffering, and was only forty-four when he died in 1784.

Father William "labored but little in public word and doctrine," but touched seekers by acts and words that showed his warmth and tenderness. When a crowd of Believers arrived at Watervliet, he would meet them at the door crying, "Come in, brethren and sisters, come in; we have but little room in our house; but we have a great deal of room in our hearts."[30] To the young converts he would declare, "I love you so well, that I should be willing to give you every gift of God that I have, and then set out anew to labor for more."[31] They were moved by the gratitude he felt for even the smallest of God's gifts. So "feelingly alive" was his soul that they sometimes observed him, when going to wash himself, to weep and say, "I thank Heaven for this water; for it is the blessing of Heaven."[32] Comparing him with Father James, Joseph Bennett said that William had a greater "gift of sorrow." "That he has," answered Mother Ann, marking the differing roles of the two men: "James plants and William waters."[33]

Father William's Song No. 1

Father William's Song No. 2

A.

MS GME–3, no. 237.

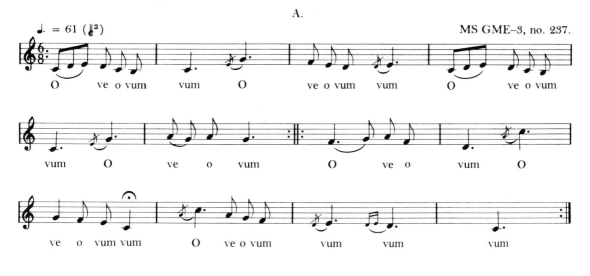

O ve o vum vum O ve o vum vum O ve o vum

vum O ve o vum O ve o vum O

ve o vum vum O ve o vum vum vum vum

B.

This manuscript names Father James as the singer of the song.

(c)

MS XE–49, p. [3].

MS EC–11, p. 8.

Father William's Song No. 3

MS XU–36, p. [11].

Father William's Song No. 4

Attributed to Father William in one of the two manuscripts preserving the song.

♩ = 92 (‖²)   MS L–244, p. [131].

Father James Whittaker

At Father William's funeral James Whittaker praised him as "the most violent man against sin that ever my eyes beheld,"[34] but James surpassed him. He was only twenty-three when he came to America and even less ready than most young idealists to temporize with error. When mild means failed to convert Sarah Robbins, James suddenly threw a candle-stub into the fire, exclaiming, "Thus, will your soul drop into hell, if you obey not this gospel."[35]

James served as public speaker for the first Shakers, and accounts say that he could preach powerfully. His words set down in the *Testimonies* are rather bland and probably show less of his tone than does one letter he wrote to an erring brother in Hancock:

> Thou art idle and slothful, whereby thy land lies unimproved, & pretty much waste, from whence arises want; & is a great burden to the poor man that dwells in the house not far from thee. . . . Thy women with thee are also idle, hatchers of cockatrices eggs, & breeders of lust & abominable filthiness, as well as covenant breakers. What mean ye by these cursed ways & works? Will you bring yourselves not only to want & poverty, but distress those connected with thee in this life, rendering yourselves incapable of doing deeds of charity which are blessed before God. . . . I charge thee before God to mend thy ways. First rouse up thy senses; shake off thy sloth & idleness. And as the time of plowing & seeding is approaching, get thy farm in readiness, neglect no means. . . . And all things do to the glory of God, in all readiness, cheerfulness, & faithfulness. . . . He that is slothful in business, is brother to him that is a great waster, & such God hates. And know this that if thou dost not obey, not only willt thou be obnoxious to the wrath of God, but thou wilt have no land to improve long; for God is able, in the workings of his providence to take it from thee.[36]

Father James's contribution to early Shakerism, however, went beyond "the searching testimony" he delivered against evil. He was not only Mother Ann's principal support, but seems to have sensed and clarified some of the later directions of Shakerism. The departure from England followed a vision in which he saw America and the church of Christ to be established there represented by a tree whereof every leaf "shone with such brightness as made it appear like a burning torch."[37] After the English Shakers had begun to win converts in New England, Mother Ann predicted another opening in the Southwest, and James had a gift confirming this, saying that he heard singing there, sometimes very near and again a thousand miles off.[38] Shortly before his death in 1787 he told of a vision predictive of the gathering of the Church. "I saw all the Believers travel," he said, "and then come to a stop, as up against a wall; and then they were brought into order; after which, I saw the old men and women travelling, and bearing their own burdens."[39]

Father James also enunciated many of the attitudes that would later become characteristic of Shakerism. His expectation of a gathering of the Church grew from his own sense of the necessity for severing all ties with the World. To his parents, who raised him as a Shaking Quaker but drew back from Mother Ann's doctrine of celibacy, he wrote, "As therefore you have forsaken God, so I also forsake you."[40] For the same reason he counseled Believers to disengage themselves from the "party spirit," the political contentions of the World.[41] Father James stressed the hopefulness of the Shaker message. Having a great sense of "the worth of souls," he urged Believers to "Remember this thing and lay it up: never throw yourselves away: tho' you be fallen ever so low it is never too late to cry to God."[42] As a means to spiritual growth he also greatly valued simple gifts. Speaking of some new converts, he said, "Let them be never so uncultivated, never so untaught in their gifts, don't you strike at those things; for if you do, you will take away their gifts, and then they will be lean and barren. . . . But you must teach them how to improve the gifts of God, and let the power of God work inwardly upon their souls."[43] To such of the young as would prove faithful in the new order of the gospel, he gave a promise that they would "be full of the gifts of God" and—in a phrase that Eleazer Rand would echo in a song to Father James—"feed on every lilly, and suck at every flower."[44]

Father James's Song No. 1

This is Haskell's version of the most widely remembered of the early songs.

$\quad$ = 96 ($\|^2$)   MS EC–11, p. 3.

In yon- der's val- ley there grows sweet un- ion. Let us a-
rise, and take our fill. The win- ter's past, and the

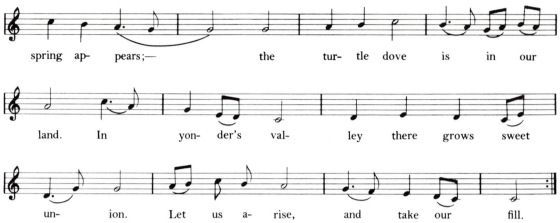

spring ap- pears;— the tur- tle dove is in our

land. In yon- der's val- ley there grows sweet

un- ion. Let us a- rise, and take our fill.

Father James's Song No. 2

A song attributed to both Father James and Father Elizur Goodrich.

(‖) [♩ = 80 (‖¹)]   MS XU–36, p. [24].

Father James's Song No. 3

A.

♩ = 80 (‖¹)   MS GME–1, no. 135.

B.

A related melody preserved in the tradition at Canterbury.

MS CB–25, p. 15.

Father James's Song No. 4

A song remembered only at Enfield, Connecticut.

MS EC–11, p. 4.

The way lies o-pen; we will run, Un- til we come to the mount Zi- on. Our

harps & our or- gans we will play, As we go a- march-ing on our way.

Father James's Song No. 5

MS XU–36, p. [14].

Fare- well un- to this world for I'm bound to Mount Zi- on Fare-

well un- to this world for I'm bound to Mount Zi- on.

PART II

Solemn Songs

In June 1780 the Baptist church in Pittsfield heard of the "strange work above Albany" and sent its minister, Valentine Rathbun, to investigate. He returned from Niskeyuna proclaiming, "I would as quick speak against the Holy Ghost, as to speak against that people; they sing the song of the redeemed, they sing the song of the hundred and forty and four thousand, which were redeemed from the earth; they sing the song that no man can learn; I could not learn their song any more than I could track the birds in the air; they seemed like an innumerable company of Angels, and Church of the first born, singing praises to the Heavenly Host."[1]

The songs that so impressed him may have been those sung by Ann Lee herself under the "operations of the Spirit." But we know that very shortly the entire company of her followers had taken up the singing of some of these songs. As early as 1783 Timothy Dwight encountered a group of Shaker travelers at an inn and heard them sing together "in what they called an *unknown language*." He described it as a "succession of unmeaning sounds, frequently repeated, half articulated, and plainly gotten by heart; for they all uttered the same sounds in succession."[2] Three years later Ezra Stiles recorded in his diary a similar account of the congregational song in a Shaker service. After dancing, the worshipers stood in a semicircle and "sang in a mixture of words & unknown sounds as of words, in a pretty solemn & melodious Tone for five Minutes."[3]

These songs were in fact called by the Shakers "Solemn Songs." Since the Shakers understood them to be the new song of the virgin company of the Lamb (Rev. 14), they had incentive to memorize the language of the songs along with the melodies. In worship, however, Solemn Songs would soon take on a new function contrasting with the private gift in which they were originally sung—namely, helping to draw the body of Believers into union.

It was the American-born Father Joseph Meacham who established this use for song. Mother Ann had taught that Believers should seek union, or general conformity of behavior, mind, and heart, with the leading gift. But in her day fresh converts could hardly think of themselves in united order. Their minds were aflame with millennial prospects, while their bodies were still bound to their scattered farms and families. When their duties at home could safely be laid aside, young Believers traveled to Niskeyuna to spend a few days or flocked to some neighboring house where Ann Lee was visiting. There for a brief time they could listen to her teachings and enjoy her presence. Worship was not confined to stated hours or days. Mother Ann spent most of her time in witness or devotions, and converts partook of these as they could. One who visited Niskeyuna for eight days in 1782 said they "attended meeting every night, which lasted till cock crowd for day" and then "retired for rest till the sun arose, then took breakfast."[4]

The meetings themselves had little formal order, except that "previous to assembling they generally sat in silence fifteen or twenty minutes to prepare their minds for devotion." The service might begin with shaking or a song or a "violent quick exercise." During the service the men and women stayed separate, but otherwise each labored "according to the impulse which he or she felt," receiving "Spiritual gifts of Tongues and signs, shaking, turning, bowing, rolling on the floor," and diverse other operations felt to be "simplifying, mortifying, and debasing." They had prayer, exhortation, and "a searching testimony against evil."[5]

Upon the death of the English leaders the center of this worship was lost. Their successor, Father Joseph, realized that if the Believers were not to scatter back to the World, they must draw together in communities where, through mutual support, they could sustain both body and the inner life. After the "gathering" of the churches, which began in 1788, both worship and workaday business were assigned a place in the round of daily life.

This step would lead eventually to the creation of various kinds of services and meetings: union meetings, in which small groups of brethren and sisters gathered for singing, refreshments, and social conversation; singing meetings for the practice and learning of songs; family meetings in the dwellinghouse for worship in song and dance; and church worship in the meetinghouse. These meetings came eventually to be arranged in a schedule that was followed, as circumstances allowed, during much of the nineteenth century. Family meetings for singing were held on Monday and Wednesday evenings and on Sunday mornings at nine; family meetings for "exercising" in the dance on Thursday and Saturday evenings. Union meetings fell on Tuesday and Friday evenings and on Sunday mornings at ten. A public testimony was given in the meetinghouse on Sunday at eleven. In some periods this service was held by the junior orders, and the senior order or Church Family attended service there at one or at half past two, a meeting to which unbelievers were not admitted. Large singing meetings were held once a month on Sunday evenings.[6]

Along with beginning this ordering of services, Father Joseph also initiated the development of a more regular order of worship within the meetings. The Spirit would still lead a Believer into spontaneous acts of devotion, but such moments occurred within a framework in which all Believers acted in union. This union was to them both the symbol of a consecrated life and a means of attaining it. Emotionally the Shakers had the gratification of being at one with a body of fellow Believers and with the will of God. In practice, this union meant that Believers wearing uniform attire entered the meetinghouse at given hours through designated doors, drew themselves into ranks and followed a familiar order in the service. The usual Shaker worship throughout most of the nineteenth century included silent prayer, brief exhortations, several forms of congregational song, laboring exercises, testimonies, and in seasons of revival, spontaneous gifts.[7]

The full development of this schedule of meetings and of these modes of worship took place only gradually over many years, but Father Joseph himself had the Believers unite in orderly laboring and in the singing of congregational Solemn Songs in the services. During his ministry, and afterwards until about 1807, Solemn Songs opened the meeting and were sung several times in its course. The repertory included songs learned from the English leaders and others which the American converts added. How many Solemn Songs there were cannot be known. Haskell transcribed twenty-six, exclusive of the thirty-one songs he attributed to the English leaders. His manuscript preserves the Connecticut tradition as it was retained in 1845. A half-dozen other manuscripts dating from the late 1830s through the 1850s record somewhat different traditions preserved in Canterbury, Harvard and Shirley, and the Maine societies.[8] The scribes who wrote these manuscripts generally lumped all the "ancient noted songs" together, and they commonly managed to gather between thirty and sixty. Members at Hancock, Lebanon, and Watervliet must have remembered the early songs long after the noting of music had become common, but unless the Sabbathday Lake manuscript "The Songs of Blessed Mother Ann" was written in Lebanon, only a few songs survive from those communities.

Unlike some of the songs of the English Shakers, the Solemn Songs are always recorded bare of any text. Elder Henry Blinn says that occasionally singers took the liberty of using "some select sentence"—presumably from the Scriptures—as "special to themselves." But singing without words was deliberately instituted, he explains, to "wean the Believers from that class of songs which they had formerly used, and which were surcharged with a mixture of theological doctrines that could not be made to harmonize with the testimony of the cross of Christ."[9]

The Solemn Songs also differ from those attributed to the English Shakers in being derived almost exclusively from ballads. Many are recognizable variants of tunes sung for such ballads as "Clerk Saunders," "Lady Isabel and the Elf Knight," and "High Barbary." Others that seem not to have specific secular analogues still show affinities with the tune stock of balladry. In Haskell's collection Solemn Songs rarely have two balancing sections, each marked for repetition. Five of his twenty-six are to be sung straight through, and fifteen more have repeat signs for only the second half. The songs also exhibit a rhythmic freedom not permissible in dance tunes. Fifteen of Haskell's tunes show some change in meter. Rubato was in fact probably more characteristic of the singing of the Solemn Songs than most of the manuscripts show, for Haskell was the only scribe who seriously aimed at presenting literal transcriptions.

Whether because they lacked the stabilizing influence of a text or because they circulated widely and then fell into disuse years before they were recorded, the Solemn Songs show more divergent variants than do other melodies set down in the Shaker manuscripts. It is not uncommon to find variants of a tune differing as greatly in mode and curve of phrase as those of Solemn Song no. 16. The relationship between no. 4 and no. 5 is more teasing; they may be forms of the same tune, but one cannot be sure. The three tunes grouped under Solemn Song no. 2 seem to exhibit the creation of a new tune from portions of older ones. The B variant is related to both the A and C variants, which do not seem at all related to each other.

Many of the melodies make rather free, however, with the ballad-tune model. Some are eleven or thirteen or twenty bars long, rather than the eight or sixteen typical of balladry. They often have phrases and sections of unequal length. In some of the songs, three rather than the customary four phrases make up the complete tune. The least conventional of the melodies is no. 7. Its extended structure and irregular phrasing probably carry us close to what the inspired sang in their trances. Song no. 2A is a more classic folk tune, but Solemn Song no. 7 haunts the ear.

The most surprising thing about the Solemn Songs is the rapidity with which they were discarded. Despite their beauty, the authority from which they came, and the sharpness with which they divided Shaker singing from that of the World, they dropped from the Shaker services in the space of two years. The Solemn Songs had in their day served well enough to gather the feelings of the faithful, but the hymn was a form more useful in a time when the Shakers were thinking through their doctrines and propounding them to those they hoped to convert. By 1807 hymns had crowded the older songs from the services, though from time to time even as late as 1868 one might be revived or received.[10] Probably the Solemn Songs were heard a little more often in union meetings, during the exchange of reminiscences.

Shaker scribes rarely name the singer from whom a Solemn Song was learned or describe occasions when Believers sang it. For this reason I can give little background information about specific songs. Early documents do tell much, however, of the world of feeling, belief, and practice within which the singers lived. These writings reveal that the first Shaker converts had shared in the social and religious unrest that swirled through backwoods New England in the years around the Revolution, their disquiet finding expression in rumors and revivals, in visionary signs and millennial expectations. The arrival of the English Shakers powerfully impressed many of those already caught up in the ferment of these years. Accounts show that the converts found healing powers in the Shakers' strange new ordinances of celibacy, separation from the World, confession of sins, bearing for the dead, and the various exercises induced by gifts of the Spirit. In their progress toward conversion they shared certain paradigms of experience, ones derived from their New England religious heritage or shaped by the mood of the times or the bias of their temperaments. As a background for the songs, I explore such topics in a series of brief essays interleaved among the following examples of the "Ancient Solemn Songs."

A Time of Signs

When news of the Elect Lady at Niskeyuna began in 1780 to attract inquirers, they came mostly from the Berkshires. She and her company passed through that country in 1781 and traveled on to Enfield in north-central Connecticut and up to the town of Harvard, thirty miles northwest of Boston. They gathered followers in all these places, and others came to them from Vermont, New Hampshire, and Maine. The early Shaker converts, then, were from inland New England, a region where commerce and colleges had not yet extinguished the embers of the Great Awakening. They also came from the class that had chiefly supported the revivals. They were of farming stock. Most had reached adulthood during the Revolution.

To judge from the autobiography left by Elder Issachar Bates, the unsettled times had bred disquietude in many of them, and they framed their expectations in terms provided by their training. Issachar had as a child been taught to fear Judgment, and he watched for signs and wonders. When he was eleven, a few years before the Revolution, "frightful signs" began to appear. First the northern lights flashed for weeks across the sky, spreading one night over the horizon until "the whole heavens appeared to me like a flaming Brushheap." Next came a comet, "bell muzzled, in perfect shape of a trumpet," some nights as red as blood. Even more frightening was an apparition seen by his family as they sat at sunset in the dooryard. It was a "black vane" in the air, "about the size of a common Stove pipe . . . about 5 rods long and crooked like a black Snake." It drew up like a horse leech into a round ball and then exploded, and "the fire blew in every direction," in one moment turning the sky as red as blood. His family all thought it was a sign of Judgment.

About this time too a man named Green had a vision of things shortly to come. He saw an angel, who cried to another with a loud voice, "Watchman! what of the night? What of the night?" The other answered, "Midnight! Midnight!" And the first one called, "What of the times? what of the times?" To which the other replied, "Doleful times! for the judgments of God shall begin in Old England; and shall spread into New England—and there shall be wars and great calamities—and darkness shall cover the whole face of the land." Soon after this, two men watching through the night with a sick person heard the seventh chapter of Ezekiel read in the air, with the words, "An end is come—the end is come—it watcheth for thee." Part of "the sharp edge" of Issachar's horror was taken off by the mockery of a Deist, but still he "kept a sharp lookout." Then the War did come, and afterwards the Dark Day over all New England, when "no work could be done in any house, without a candle" and the neighbors went out wringing their hands and howling, "The day of judgment is come!" "And," says Issachar, "what next!—Right on the back of this—On came the Shakers! and that made it darker yet—for they came forth to fulfill the VII chapt of Ezekiel that was read in the open air—Yea! and I am a witness that they did fulfill it . . . for they testified, that an end was come on them; and proved it, by their life of seperation from the course of this world; and by the wicked persecutions they endured, from this adulterous generation."[11]

Solemn Song No. 1

A melody sung at Enfield, Connecticut, as early as 1780 or 1781.

Solemn Song No. 2

In these three tunes one seems to see evidence of new melodies made from elements of older ones. Version C, recorded by Elder Otis Sawyer of Maine in the 1840s, is closely related throughout to the tune "Lame Dermot" printed by Patrick Joyce from an Irish manuscript compiled in the same years. Version B, which was remembered at Canterbury as having been sung by the blacksmith Thomas Wright prior to 1800, opens with the second half of the "Lame Dermot" tune. He seems, however, to have confused the opening section of the original with one strain of Variant A, a Solemn Song known at both Canterbury and Enfield, Connecticut. In the form sung at Enfield in the 1780s this strain serves as a refrain—a fact that may explain the reversing of the strains in Thomas Wright's tune. The refrain itself, however, may not even have been part of the secular original of the Enfield tune. The closest analogue of the melody, an Appalachian variant of "Lady Isabel and the Elf Knight," lacks the refrain. The additional phrases in the Shaker tune seem suspiciously similar to ones in a Scots version of "The Famous Flower of Serving-Men." Whether a composite or not, the Enfield melody is one of the loveliest ever recorded by the Shakers.

MS EC–11, p. 9.

B.

MS CB–25, p. 16, no. 57.

C.

Solemn Song No. 3

The opening phrase of this melody is a modal form of the middle section of Father James's Song no. 1, "In yonder's valley." Similar material also serves for the opening of one branch of tunes for "The Bailiff's Daughter of Islington," for "Gilderoy," and for many later Shaker songs. The present melody is one recalled at Enfield.

And Rumour Shall be Upon Rumour

Tales that flooded the countryside around Niskeyuna are a measure of the anger and uneasiness roused by the strange work of the English Shakers. Some of the stories were satiric. Stopping in Albany in 1784 the Marquis de Barbé-Marbois was told, for example, that the "Holy Matron" gathered a crowd to witness her raise a man from the dead but was challenged by an American officer. This rival miracle worker drew his sword, according to the yarn, crying in a terrible voice, "Come to life, come to life, or I will kill you!" and rushed at the corpse, which nimbly scampered away.[12]

Some of the tales were less jocular. Many of the country people were outraged or alarmed by the Shakers. According to one rumor they spread, the English law had cropped Ann Lee's ears, branded her forehead, and bored her tongue through for blasphemy. Near Ashfield, Massachusetts, a mob stormed a house where she was staying, demanding to see if this was true.[13] Stories of her power to read thoughts and of astonishing changes in people who had visited her caused one young man to run off to sea when she passed through his neighborhood. Another tucked a coin in his mouth to ward off witchcraft when he went to take a look at her.[14]

Persons more friendly also had their tales. Sarah Thomas, who years later became a Believer at Harvard, told of a strange happening at Wenham in the winter of 1784. After buttoning the shutters one dark evening she sat down in a room with her cousin William and their grandmother. William fell to talking of the Shaking Quakers "in such a strain of wickedness and abuse" as Sarah at fifteen had never heard before. The grandmother's rebukes only excited him to say worse. Just as he was declaring that "the Elect Lady was an old bitch," they were startled by the sound of a horse's feet "which came rushing with great violence directly up to the door." All three distinctly heard (though they could later find no hoof prints in the snow, and no one else in the house heard or felt anything unusual) his shoes strike upon the door stone. Instantly a "mighty rushing wind" shook the house, flung open the shutters, extinguishing the candles, and shaking open the inner doors of the room. Sarah felt "this alarming concussion" strike with "a sensible impression" upon her own body. Her grandmother and William sat terrified, looking like corpses in their chairs. Sarah rose and turned toward the west window, where she beheld a woman standing within the window with her hands folded before her. Sarah said, "She first eyed William with a look of severe rebuke; Then turning her eyes on me she looked very mild and pleasant." Sarah fell back into her chair, powerless to stand, and the woman disappeared.

Her description of the woman matched that of Ann Lee, and forty-seven years later she could still see and describe the image distinctly:

> a shortish thick set person with a very bright countenance; light complexion with bright mild looking blue eyes. Her dress appeared to be a camlet gown, the color a reddish brown nearly resembling the color now worn by the sisters a checkered apron, a white handkerchief with a kented tinted border and a white cap something of the mob fashion so called all her dress appeared to be perfectly clean and neat.[15]

Solemn Song No. 4

An early song preserved in manuscripts written in Alfred in the mid-nineteenth century.

Solemn Song No. 5

Transcribed from a manuscript of uncertain origin, possibly the work of Thomas Hammond, Jr., at Harvard. Haskell also knew the tune and said that it was "frequently sung by the Believers at funerals in the first of the faith."

(c)   MS XE–47, p. [2].

The Opening of Minds

When Valentine Rathbun returned to Pittsfield from Niskeyuna and reported on the Elect Lady to a crowd gathered in the largest barn, a man named Walter Cook leapt upon a bench and cried out, "I know it is the way of God, but if it is, I hope I shall die before the week is out." He roared this over and over, bowing with all his might, until friends carried him home and chained him to the floor to keep him from killing himself. He was buried six days later. In a vision Mother Ann saw him "in the same hell with murderers, as hot as a glowing oven, for defiling his own body, and going to dumb beasts."[16] But she maintained if they had not chained the man "he would have fought his way thro' and got to her and been released."[17]

He would have attained his releasement by the instrument of confession, the most useful of the Shaker ordinances. It gave hope and help to seekers who, especially in the early years, often arrived in terror of Judgment and condemnation. The day that Walter Cook's funeral was held, the neighbors and kin gathered at his house in grief and consternation. In one room Amos Rathbun lay rolling from side to side upon a bed, repeating in "a mournfull song" the words, "I have lost my day, there is no mercy now for me." Mother Ann told him that he could find a release if he confessed his sins "before God and his witnesses." This he was thankful to do, and said, "O the forgiving love I felt, I found the healing morning ray. I felt my soul baptized with repentance, and washed from guilt and despair."[18]

Believing Father William's words that one sin, wilfully covered, will be "like mountains of lead upon the soul, to sink it from the presence of God,"[19] the Shaker ministry taught all elders that no duty or consideration was so important as attending the "opening" of a soul that desired to confess. To underscore the point, they told the story of Samuel Fitch. Building a chimney one day, he was interrupted by a man who came up from Lebanon asking the privilege of confessing. Samuel told him to come back after the work was done. As he was shaving later in the day, Samuel felt an unaccountable temptation to cut his throat. Shortly afterwards he understood why: the man had gone home "with a heart full of sorrow" and killed himself in that way. For eight years Samuel's own throat bore a red scar "giving it the appearance of having been cut."[20]

Solemn Song No. 6

The Canterbury scribe who recorded this tune must have learned his "moods of time" from tables that included the signature 3/2, but like other Shaker musicians he failed to recognize it in his singing. The meter occurs chiefly in songs in which the rhythmic figure ♩♩ ♩♩ — derived from earlier hymn and psalm tunes—is superimposed on ballad airs.

MS CB–25, p. 15.

A Gospel Relation

"Do not go away and report that we forbid to marry," Mother Ann told Daniel Moseley; "for unless you are able to take up a full cross, and part with every gratification of the flesh, for the Kingdom of God, I would counsel you . . . to take wives in a lawful manner, and cleave to them only, and raise up a lawful posterity, and be perpetual servants to your families."[21] The thrust of her testimony, however, favored the full cross, and the forsaking of those who could not do the same. Ann Lee and her small band were consequently mobbed and beaten in many towns for "going around breaking up churches and families."

In the country around Hancock the Rathbun family was bitterly divided. The elder Valentine Rathbun and his son Daniel were adherents for a time, but fell back to the World and wrote savage tracts against the Shakers. When Ann Lee came to Hancock in 1783, Valentine led a mob against her. The old man was severely reproved by his son Valentine, a faithful Believer, and in a rage struck his son several blows with a hickory staff, laying his skull bare for nearly three inches.[22]

On their side, the Shakers maintained that if the selfish nature is entirely rooted out of a man and the seed of God planted in his soul, "he will then love all that God loves, and hate all that God hates." Then his closest relations will not be his blood kin but those who "come nearest to God by their faith & obedience."[23] Thus when Amos Rathbun broke through his guilty bonds, he took father, mother, wife and children, house and land, and all that was dear in the world and put them into one scale and his soul in the other and "quick found out which ballanced." He took up a full cross, joined his gospel relations, and would sooner have filled his bosom with "glowing embers" than look back.[24]

Solemn Song No. 7

Russel Haskell alone recorded this most unusual of Solemn Songs, but left no comment on its origin or use.

Bearing for the Dead

Hannah Kendall came to Mother Ann one day saying she felt very unwell. "I do not wonder that you feel as you do," said Mother Ann; "for you have been bearing for the dead. I see a tall soul right behind you now."[25] One whole chapter of *Testimonies* is a record of similar incidents. When dark presences were felt among the Believers, Ann Lee rarely identified them as spirits or devils. They were the suffering dead, and she felt great compassion for them. In several visions she even saw herself fly down a deep gulf and with the tips of her wings uncover the dead, where they lay on the banks of the gulf, and give them the gospel.[26]

The scriptural foundation for this belief lies in three passages in the New Testament: Matt. 12:40, which foretells that the Son of Man will be three days and three nights in the heart of the earth; 1 Pet. 3:18–20, in which Christ is described as having preached to spirits in prison, who had been disobedient in the days of Noah; and 1 Pet. 4:6, which says the gospel was preached "also to them that are dead, that they might be judged according to men in the flesh, but live according to God in the spirit." Ann Lee's interest in these passages is one expression of her challenge to the Calvinist doctrines of total depravity and election. Even those already dead and in hell were not to be denied a chance to change their state.

Still, Ann Lee did not present herself as a Biblical exegete. She normally spoke not from obscure texts but from inspiration, and she addressed the immediate spiritual condition of her hearers. What this condition was is revealed in significant features of these tales. They describe the young Believer coming to her "under great weight of body and spirit"; she diagnoses his state as that of "bearing the pains of death and hell" for a relative who died out of the faith. For when the convert broke off his ties with those he left behind in the World, he often felt not only hurt, anger, guilt, or concern, but also alarm at the lost condition of persons he had loved. He dreaded lest they suffer in hell, that bottomless pit in which souls felt the extreme horror of "continually sinking, further and further from God."[27] Entrammeled in such worries, the Believer could find no healing or joy in the gospel.

Such was the case with the Mathewsons. Philip's father Thomas, who had died some years earlier, was "a very senseless man, as to the things of God," and Philip and Lydia were in tribulation on his account. Hearing of Thomas, Mother Ann also "felt his lost state." One night while the others went to meeting she stayed behind laboring for him. The power of God came upon her and began to move her hands up and down. She felt and saw them covered with wings as bright as gold, and the power moved them to part the darkness to where souls lay in the ditch of hell. As sounds of Father James's preaching came trumpeting down, many of the dead arose and ascended to the meetinghouse. Thomas was in their number. Coming out of her trance, Mother Ann went into the meetingroom and found Philip lying as if dead upon the floor. "He is bearing the last pains of death and hell for his father," she said, "he is now released." And as she went from the room she continued to exclaim, "He is released! He is released!"[28]

In these stories Ann Lee often herself undertakes to bear for the dead and witness to them, but she gives relief to her followers, telling them of the conversion and re-

Solemn Song No. 8

A song preserved at Enfield.

Solemn Song No. 9

This song from Enfield is perhaps related to the preceding one. In the second section of each there may be an echo of a phrase from the ballad tune "Hughie Grame."

leasement of souls dear to them. The next generation of Shaker leaders apparently feared even this much entanglement with the suffering dead. Elder Henry Clough felt that "if souls who had left the body, came and hung on to their relations and acquaintances among Believers, it was liable to draw such to an untimely death." When a recently dead girl came swiftly into a meeting and caught hold of her sister exclaiming, "There is great war among the spirits tonight," Elder Henry immediately directed, "Shake off the dead!"[29]

Love the Power

The name "Shaker" was given in derision, but accepted in pride. It denoted one who yielded to an "operation of the spirit" the most careful description of which was written by the Marquis de Barbé-Marbois after his visit to Niskeyuna in 1784. The exercise was a convulsive shaking, he said, during which

> the most usual movement is to turn the head from left to right, with eyes closed or raised towards the sky, with an expression which proclaims ecstasy, anguish, and pain. We noticed that the women shed tears, were pale and downcast, and that their face reanimated itself only when the convulsion was at an end. The men raised their arms, trembling; their knees gave way and knocked together. Often while all their members shook, they would seem to have a seizure under which they would succumb, but it was the end of the ecstasy. The head turned less rapidly, and when the crisis was over, they sighed deeply, like people relieved at length of excessive anxiety, or coming out of a painful swoon.[30]

The operation might be a brief jolt which scarcely interrupted an activity like plowing or chopping wood, but it was sometimes of long duration. In services it sometimes swept over Believer and unbeliever alike.

The Shaker experienced this operation as "a shock of spiritual Power." Calvin Green, who had held the gift from his earliest years—he was in fact born while his mother was under operations—usually perceived it as coming upon him from without. Once as he was turning his sense to prayer and thanks he heard a "sound like a rushing

Fig. 22. Ritual Motion: Shaking

The involuntary shaking seizures described by Calvin Green came to be stylized and practiced as a group ritual. Illustrating "the attitude of 'shaking'" in her photograph, Emily Williams wrote, "In the early days of the faith the 'shake' was composed of three simultaneous movements, shaking, whirling, and stamping; but in this exaggerated form it caused so much ridicule from outsiders that the Elders modified it to 'mother's shake' which is shown here."

wind strike the north end of the house," causing it to creak. The sound "rolled on" and quickly struck him with "such a violent shock as raised me considerably from the floor." On another occasion, just as he was pitching a song for dancing, he heard over his head a sound of water "pouring down from a large vessel." Instantly "a power fell upon me," he said, "with great force & run all over & thro my whole system."

The Shaker valued these operations not only because he felt them to be divine gifts, but also for their effects. Sometimes they healed bodily illness. When he was eleven, Green suffered an injury to his back that left him unable to stand, walk, or lie down without severe pain. When meeting time came, he felt unable to join in the laboring, but undertook it. "As the exercise closed," he said, "I felt three forcible shocks of power in succession, run thro my whole system & it completely relieved me, so that I did not again have a turn of lame back in six years." More commonly the power "dispelled weakness of soul and body" and filled him with "devotional energy." He found the greatest benefit, however, in his youth, when struggling with "propensities of a worldly life in every sense." Turning his sense to prayer, he would be "met with a shock of power both internal & external." It would run all through him and "take the feeling all away." Thus he regarded it as a source of "much strength & protection."

These sudden accesses of power were not without their price, especially to one's pride. Kneeling in prayer before one meal, Calvin Green was struck with a sudden shock that jarred a table at which there were thirty or forty other persons. He was the youngest—only eighteen, "when the natural pride of youth is strongest"—and naturally bashful. It mortified him, and he "gave away to feel ashamed of the operation." As a consequence he felt no further operations for several weeks and feared he had lost the gift.

When he confessed to John Farrington, Elder John smiled and said he too "got served just so once." Traveling with Father James, he had a sharp knock of power when they knelt in a tavern before eating. A member of the World was present, and John felt ashamed. After eating, he felt no shock when they knelt. As they rode away, Father James kept his horse back a little for a time, then rode up beside him and said, "John, you must not *do so*, if you are ashamed of the gifts of God they will be taken away from you." This was also Mother Ann's advice. Once while Abijah Worster was under operations she cried, "Love that power, & it will save your soul."[31]

Solemn Song No. 10

A tune recorded by Elder Otis Sawyer at Gloucester.

By This Sign

Before his conversion, the early Shaker studied the face of nature for signs, the hints and threats of divine intentions. After receiving the faith, he discovered the portents or "gifts" within himself. Often he was compelled to enact symbolic scenes he had not planned and could not halt. This is the key to much that genteel observers reported as unaccountable frenzy. Sometimes the message was private and disclosed its meaning only after thought and consultation. At times it was addressed to the outsider, but in a language more forcible than he was accustomed to hear.

In one characteristic instance, Angell Matthewson, a sometime Shaker, saw Aaron Wood leap into the air during a meeting in 1783 and fall upon the floor ("j thought hard anof to have killed a man that was not under the operation of the spirit"). Aaron then began to roll swiftly from one side of the room to the other, screaming and crying "marcy" and at times making signs calling for "one drop of water to cool his tongue." After an hour in which he was "an estonishing object of agony & dispare & torment," there was not a dry spot in his shirt and trousers. He at length began to recover and crept on hands and knees to one Dr. Catlin, an aged man wearing "a pare of buckskin britchis," and began to pat him on the thigh and in a voice so "horce & feeble he could but jest be hered" said,

> com com the gospil feest is opn com bye milk bye wine without money with-
> out price now all things are reddy the Spirit sais com—now god has shoed
> you by this sine the awful seens of the damned & will you not try to escape the
> torments of hell whilst free grace is offered.[32]

Solemn Song No. 11

Lucy Williams at Canterbury set down this handsome melody as one of a group "sung by Mother Ann and the first Elders while on earth." In the 1820s the tune would serve as the basis of an equally fine marching song (no. 26).

MS CB–25, p. 14, no. 35.

A Beautiful Messenger

Ann Lee died in 1784 at the age of forty-eight, and the following song was sung at her funeral. The Marquis de Barbé-Marbois, who visited Niskeyuna a short time later, believed that her followers had not expected the event and were cast into doctrinal confusion.[33] Almost certainly he was wrong. They were instead staggered by their sense of personal loss. Jemima Blanchard, for one, said that when she heard of Mother Ann's death she felt so distressed and sorrow-stricken that she "retired in secret and lay prostrate upon the floor," expecting to breathe out her soul in sorrow. The more she tried to refrain, the deeper her sorrow became. "This continued," she said, "untill I saw the appearance of Mother Ann, about the size of a child 3 years old. This beautiful messenger held something in each hand that appeared like a wing, which she waved inward, and advansing towards me, said, 'Hush, hush.' This took away my sorrow, so that I was able to attend to my duty."[34]

Jemima and many others among the "first born" had been swayed toward conversion less by their prior unhappiness or by the Shaker teachings than by the deep attachment that Ann Lee evoked from them. Jemima herself lived on until 1847, and as long as "reason and health would admit," she liked to tell young Believers about Mother Ann and the divine influence that she "shed upon all around." Often they could discover from her expression alone "that she was thinking of Mother—before she uttered a word."[35]

Solemn Song No. 12

Haskell recorded this melody with the note, "This is one of the songs that were sung at Mother Ann's funeral." The strong tune has also served for such ballads as "Clerk Saunders" and "Pretty Polly," and Jackson found it sung as a spiritual in both Pennsylvania and Virginia.

The Altar of Love

At the climax of a service at Niskeyuna in 1785 the brethren "got together in a cluster holding out both hands, as if supporting something." One of them spoke—and the others repeated "as by way of response"—the words, "This is our altar &

our altar is love & none can build this altar or sacrifice upon it but the pure in heart & such are we;—therefore we will sacrifice on our altar & we will love one another.'' The entire congregation responded with a shout, clapped hands, and broke into dancing, after which the brethren gathered once again, lifting their hands and saying, "The dead should be buried, yes we will bury the dead, but we are alive & we will sacrifice on our altar, communion, union, love, we will love one another."[36]

Observers had just been instructed by a "decent & sensible man" that Christ's Second Coming was "manifested in the flesh" in the Believers. Their enactment of this ritual—like their singing in tongues, their dancing, their bodily operations—expressed the converts' sense of embodying the Millennium. At this point in their history Believers understood the Millennium as having begun in Ann Lee and as expanding its work as it entered each new heart. The regenerative Christ Spirit was Love. The Devil, said Father Joseph, "could do anything to appearance that a christian could do, but to love: this he could not do because it was not in his power to love. So he may transform himself into an angel of light, but not into an angel of love."[37]

Solemn Song No. 13

This song was remembered at Enfield as one sung by Childs Hamblin and Jethro Turner "in the time of their being here, to finish off some part of the first meeting house." The building was raised and covered and the inside work nearly completed in 1786. The two brethren came from Lebanon to help with the work near the beginning of 1787. Later in that year the funeral of Father James was held in this building.

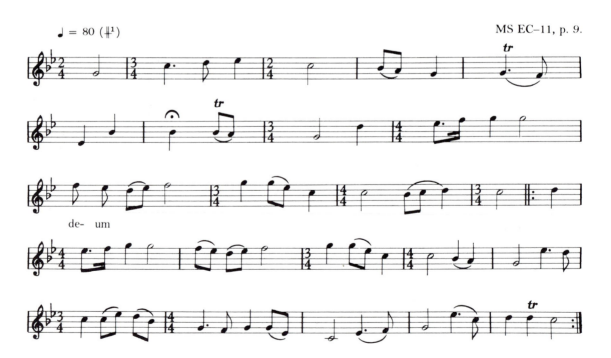

Solemn Song No. 14

A song known at Enfield. Its place in Haskell's manuscript suggests that he believed it to have been introduced after 1787.

Working on a Building

Observers in the decades following the gathering of the Church often commented on the pallor and emaciation of the Shakers, which they believed to result from excesses in worship. Another cause is more likely. Most of the early converts were young and poor.[38] They brought little to the support of the Society except their zeal in its behalf. Rebecca Clark, for example, was only twenty-one when she entered Hancock in 1791. Such clothing and bedding as she and others came with they divided "as equally as could be." In her family the sisters slept fourteen to a room, and many three to a bed, on straw pallets laid on the floor. The sisters were diligent at their own tasks of spinning and weaving, and also "worked much out of doors" to help the brethren raise buildings.

To support these labors, they ate for breakfast and supper "bean porridge and water porridge." Monday mornings they had a little weak tea, and "once in a week a small piece of cheese." Wheat bread was very scarce, theirs chiefly of "rye and indian meal mixed." The dinners were "generally boiled." Once in a while they had a little milk, but that was a great rarity. "Our food was very scanty," said Rebecca, "but what we had we eat with thankful hearts."[39]

Solemn Song No. 15

In 1805 Jeremiah Ingalls printed this tune in his *Christian Harmony* songbook under the title "Rejoice in Thy Youth," but the Canterbury Shakers had already for twenty years been using it in their worship as a Solemn Song.

Solemn Song No. 16

The ballad "Johnie Cock" may have been the source of this melody, but the Shaker song is twice as long as that short-phrase tune. Believers at Enfield, Connecticut, who preserved Variant A, associated the song with their early leader from New Jersey, Father Calvin Harlow. Elijah Brown, the leading singer at Canterbury and later its teacher of "the rules of music," taught Variant B to the elders from Poland Hill in 1822.

Elijah had probably learned it quite early. He embraced the faith while in his teens, many times walking the thirty miles from his home in Weare to "enjoy the company of his brethren and sisters" in Canterbury before the gathering of the Church. Elder Henry Blinn recalled him as a "tall & spare" man with "straight, black hair, black eyes, and a pleasant and agreeable disposition," though he had the "peculiarity of soliciting a favor, without directly asking to have it conferred." Elijah was "an excellent wood workman, a good shoemaker & tanner & currier," and in 1809 invented a mill for the grinding of bark for tanning. He wished to patent it, but the ministry at Lebanon forbade this. It was, Elder Henry said, "too early in the history of the church, to enter so fully into relations with the world after the severe struggle of the Believers to get out."

B.

MS XE–46, p. [23].

Solemn Song No. 17

A tune from the tradition at Enfield.

MS EC–11, p. 10.

A Prodigal's Path

"Never a soul went to heaven," Father William once said, "but what went right thru hell first."[40] In the early years at least, this was a paradigm of the Believer's experience. A man like Elder Issachar Bates, whose neighbors thought him in his youth "a clever, jolly, honest fellow," was inwardly full of increasingly troubled thoughts. He dreaded and resisted conviction, but by the time he was thirty-seven, a father with seven children, he acknowledged that his heart was diseased with sin. He prayed for convicting power to "burst it asunder like marsh-mud before the cannon ball." He asked for judgment, being unworthy of mercy. His anguish grew so great that for six weeks he bore a great lump of soreness in his heart. The Baptists at a meeting one evening strove powerfully with him, but he could not accept their belief in original sin, election, and perseverance. So he started home with his heart in "tormenting pain" and in desperation concluded that he must finally ask for mercy. Right there, Issachar wrote,

> in the middle of the road, a hot flash like lightning struck me through the neck and shoulders, into my heart; and drove out the sore lump, and every weight about me; and left me feeling as light as nothing; with my hands stretched, on my tip-toes, expecting every step to leave the earth, and step into the air. . . . My happiness was truly unspeakable; for I could not utter the half of it then, neither can I describe the half of it now.

Arriving at home, he astonished his family by "skipping across the floor, singing psalms, and hymns" until one o'clock, and then lay down "in perfect peace." In the morning he went to the meetinghouse and poured out a testimony that "threw them all into tears." At the burying ground, which had always filled him with dread, he stretched his hand over the fence and "bid defiance to the grave, to death, and to hell" and never feared them again.[41]

Issachar's light was still flickering and unsteady. When he came up out of the waters at his baptism, "Lo! the spirit of death came upon me! and I was as dark as ever." He later realized that his faith was with the Shakers, his union with the World, and he "a tormented Baptist preacher." From childhood on he had played the prodigal with his portion from God, and now, he said, "I had to go through dreadful sufferings to get back to my Fathers house. . . , but the Father knew, I was on the way. And it was 7 years, before I got stripped & found admittance into the house."[42]

Solemn Song No. 18

Elder Henry Clough, to whom two New Hampshire manuscripts attribute this song, is described as being of medium height, very well proportioned, with auburn hair, hazel-gray eyes, and a sandy complexion. He was born in 1754 to a farming family of "character and wealth" in Concord, New Hampshire, and was raised a Congregationalist. During the Revolution a New Light or Free Will Baptist revival broke out in Canterbury, and Henry became zealous in the movement. In the 1780s some of the New Lights, with Henry in their number, converted to Shakerism. He was about thirty and owned some 400 acres of land "with commodious Buildings attached" when he "set out to obey the Gospel." The heaviest cross he had to bear for his faith was to forgo delving with his hands and become a preacher of the gospel. He thought this more than he could do, but submitted to Father James's direction and proved "truly blessed of God in that calling." Elder Henry's Shaker biographer called him "a frugal, honest, moral, commonsensed plain-hearted sturdy yeoman; one of a class who could meet difficulties and overcome them, and face danger with the firmness of the granite hills upon which he was reared."

(ɔ)   MS ENH–2, p. [64].

A Wise Virgin

In the early eighteenth century even the mind of young Jonathan Edwards had been "full of objections" against the doctrine of God's sovereignty in leaving whom He pleased "eternally to perish, and be everlastingly tormented in Hell." Only by some incomprehensible operation did he come to accept the orthodox stand and view the doctrine as "exceeding pleasant, bright, and sweet."[43] Seventy years later the generation of the first Shaker converts came of age in a New England where religious opinion spoke with more varied voices. Eunice Bathrick of Harvard remembered listening once to a dispute between her father and a strict Calvinist. "This man's side," she said, "was horrifying to me." Even as one of the elect, she thought, she could not love a creator who doomed the greater portion of His children to eternal misery. She wrote of the experience, saying,

> I can never describe the sufferings I passed thru in consequence of that conversation. . . . My distress at length became so intense that I felt that I could endure it no longer. I arose & went into the garden, where I kneeled & laid my face in the dust & implored Divine aid. I had scarcely began my invocation, when I felt as tho' a large body of cold water was dashed all over me, & I was filled with ineffable love. Tears gushed forth, my sorrow vanished & I now wept for joy. While still kneeling, I was impressed that I had received a shower of love from that Being whom man had so falsely represented, & that if I would obey the voice of conscience, I had nothing to fear. I arose comforted and refreshed, & felt that I was in the keeping of a kind Father, whom, if I obeyed, it would be well with me.

She soon began to attend Methodist meetings, where she "felt more of the true spirit" than she did listening to any of the Congregational preachers. One night, however, as Eunice was walking alone down a road, returning from a Methodist meeting and making plans to offer herself as a "candidate," she became "impressed" that a spirit was following her. It gave her to understand that if she wanted salvation, she must join the Shakers. Although she heard no audible voice, the words were as strongly impressed upon her as if they had been "trumpeted by a voice of thunder."

She thought the prospect repugnant, like entering a convent, but dared not disobey. Thus she entered on her

> pilgrimage without a tho't of ever taking any more pleasure in this life, but as it was of short duration in comparison with eternity, I concluded to forego it, & began my uphill journey. . . . Instead of the life of pain & sorrow which I anticipated, I have experienced far more pleasure than I could, had I pursued the common course of the world, if I may judge by the portion of those I left behind.[44]

Solemn Song No. 19

About the year 1834 a scribe at Canterbury wrote down this tune under the title "Hannah Brownson's Visionary Song." Hannah, who was born at Norwich, Vermont, in 1781, must however have grown up hearing the melody. A variant turned up in 1942 in Colebrook, New Hampshire, with the ballad text of "The Famous Flower of Serving-Men," and it serves "Kedron" and other Southern shape-note hymns. Both earlier Shaker hymns and later Gift Songs also drew upon the tune.

MS CB–36, p. 78.

Healing Gifts

Editing the testimonies of Mother Ann's first converts, Seth Wells gave an entire chapter to stories of miraculous healings. There were "but few persons who had much opportunity with her," he said, "who were not able to relate something of the kind."[45] Similar tales are frequent in later testimonies and spiritual autobiographies and must often have been heard in workshop and worship service. They served of course to assert the truth and power of the gospel, but had other implications as well.

In tales presenting the narrator as the object of the healing gift, an affliction usually appears as akin to a spiritual failure that must be mastered. Jemima Blanchard, for example, told of once finding her feet so lame and sore and her legs so swollen that she could not take a step. Others went off to services, leaving her behind "crying over my feet, because I could not come to meeting and dance." When Mother Ann learned of it, she sent a carriage to fetch Jemima, questioned her to make sure that her faith was strong, and had Father William "labor for a healing gift." He stroked Jemima's feet three or four times and told her to "go and labor for the power of God, and be joyful." This took place, she says, in the forenoon, and

> I went to laboring, and I never stoped for dinner nor supper, for I felt perfect heaven, being carried by the power of God, and my feet scarcely touched the floor. I often leaped so high that my head struck the top of the room, and I wished it was out of the way, that I might see how far I could go. My feet and legs were perfectly well.[46]

The narrator in another set of tales is the agent of the healing. Calvin Green, for one, left detailed descriptions of times when the power operated through himself. One occasion was when he first saw Olive Fairbanks. Her widowed mother had in desperation come to Lebanon with her six children begging admission. Olive—then a child of two—was covered with sores, which had been doctored skillfully but "with little gain." "I was struck with a powerful impression," says Elder Calvin, "that the good spirit had a gift of healing for the little innocent, & that I was the agent to administer it. On making this feeling known to Elder Ebenezer, he felt a gift in it & gave me his union." Calvin went to where the mother sat holding Olive and reached his hands toward the child. Olive

> seemed anxious to move towards me. I took her in my arms & stroked the sores on her head, neck & arms. Her Mother said they were so all over her body. The child seemed pleased, & endeavored to turn that I might stroke them, to the surprise of her Mother, who said 'I cant touch them without her squalling.' It was the spirit operating upon the little one that made the difference. I signified that she would get well, & left her. About 48 hours after, on being set on the floor, she got up & walked. As this was the first time she ever walked a step, it surprised her Mother very much, who took her up, & on examination found that every sore was healed. She was well, & grew up smart & healthy, bright & intellectual. . . . I have reason to believe this gift implanted faith that brot forth fruit.[47]

These tales concern, in short, an outward work growing from two cardinal tenets of Shakerism: the healing to be found in personal efforts inspired by love and faith, and the curative powers held by the supportive body of the faithful.

Solemn Song No. 20

Someone at Hancock transcribed this tune, using shape-notes and a tempo system with which Isaac Youngs briefly experimented in 1840. By this year Solemn Songs were rarely received, but the Shaker repertory does not hold one more lovely.

Original key
♩ = 80 (111/684)

MS HN–5, p. 41.

PART III

Early Laboring Songs

Shaker dance began as one of the gestures of transport. The individual worshiper erupted into bodily expression of his joy in salvation—leaping, shuffling, whirling as the spirit moved. Even when many danced simultaneously and a singer raised a tune for them, each dancer followed his own bent, and Mother Ann "wisely refrained" from teaching any regular form for the dance. It was Father Joseph Meacham who by the revelation of God transformed this "promiscuous dance" into the ordered ceremony called "laboring." In one or another variation of its two forms—the dance and the march—laboring was practiced in Shaker worship from 1788 until nearly 1930.

In introducing laboring Father Joseph at a stroke created the feature of Shaker life that most provoked curiosity and ridicule. A celibate religious order was no great novelty in the world. Pentecostal worship often broke out in Methodist camp meetings on a scale that the Shakers could not equal. Other revivalists occasionally bounded and danced as they shouted their joy. In Ohio in the wake of the Kentucky Revival one group, the Schismatics, even parted company with their fellow New Lights in order to have freedom to "praise God in the dance."[1] But disciplined dance as a form of worship seemed shocking or risible. It was chiefly the amusement of watching the dance that on the Sabbath brought fashionable carriages rolling out from towns to the Shaker villages, where they "tumbled into the temple a herd of young blades with their ladies accompanied by the uproar common to this group the world over."[2] It was the dance that also attracted foreign travelers. Rare was the touring Briton who could resist penning for his Gentle Readers a record of his disdain: "The scene was very absurd, and I could have laughed had I not felt disgusted at such a degradation of rational and immortal beings."[3] Rarer still was the commentator like Frederick von Raumer, who was shocked that a people "noted for cleanliness, industry, honesty, regularity, and benevolence" should be "especially held up to censure and ridicule, because they *dance* to the honor of God!" In his view the Shaker might well have rejoined, "If it is esteemed pleasing to God . . . to raise the arms, clasp the hands, or (as in the silent mass) to perform countless unintelligible motions in his honor, why should our mode be alone thought offensive and irrational?"[4] However their worship might appear to outsiders, the Shakers' eyes saw it as "very solemn & heavenly." Of one dance they wrote that it "generally made believers weep at the first sight of it, & the world to hang their heads."[5]

The Shakers used the Scriptures to defend their practice. Miriam the sister of Moses danced in triumph on the banks of the Red Sea (Exod. 15:20) and the women of the cities of Israel at the slaying of Goliath (1 Sam. 18:6). David and all Israel had danced as the Ark was removed from the city of Shiloh (1 Chron. 15:29).[6] In the Shaker view, moreover, these passages "expressly signified" that dance was the "peculiar manner of worship to be established in the latter day." Filled with millennial hopes and steeped in a heritage of typology, the Shakers pondered correspondences between the Old Heavens and the New. The safe passage of the Children of Israel through the Red Sea they regarded as "a striking figure of the day of full redemption from the bondage and dominion of sin," and they compared it with John's vision of "them that had gotten the victory over the beast" standing on the "sea of glass mingled with fire" singing the "song of Moses" (Rev. 15:2–3). The removal of the Ark from Shiloh to the City of David was typical of the "final establishment of the Ark of God and His Testament." Prodigal souls were right, then, to return to their Father's house and enter in to celebrate with music and with dancing (Luke 15:25).[7]

The meaning of the dance and the march to the Shakers, however, is hardly explained by these scriptural defenses. Had the Shakers merely been Biblical literalists, they might easily instead have worshiped God with harps and timbrels. As if anticipating fashionable twentieth-century theories, the apostate John Woods charged that the vigorous dancing was intended to "keep down the lustful propensities of our nature."[8] The Shakers recognized this as one legitimate aim of the exercises, though their phrasing of the idea differed; Father James commended dancing as "the greatest gift of God that ever was made known to man for the purification of the soul."[9] At times the dancing was also clearly intended and felt to be an act of mortification. Calvin Green said that from about 1793 to 1796 the exercises consisted chiefly of a heavy shuffle which "grew slower & slower until it became almost impossible to exercise it at all. I scarcely ever felt so distressing a cross as to attempt it."[10]

Another apostate, John Whitbey, charged that singing and dancing were among the ministry's "most powerful means of uniting" the flock and "leading them on to a state of complete order and tranquility."[11] The Shakers would have agreed with this analysis, but where Whitbey saw dance as the tool of a subtle priestcraft, the Believers regarded it as "beautiful and glorious" because its "unity and harmony" were "emblematical of the *one spirit* by which the people of God are led."[12] To them, laboring was "mighty through God, joyful as heaven, and solemn as eternity," and they therefore eagerly "united in the dance."

That the Shakers called these joyful exercises "laboring" relates this mode of worship also to the Believers' view of their whole lives as consecrated endeavor. In repudiating the Calvinist doctrine of Election, they believed that salvation was offered to all who earnestly sought to pattern their lives after that of Christ. Salvation was thus a wondrous gift that both rewarded and required faithful labor. The Believer labored in field or workshop for the temporal welfare of the Society. In worship he labored to awaken his feelings to spiritual gifts. Thus when Daniel Rathbun, who for a brief while united with the Shakers in the 1780s, at times unaccountably felt all his efforts "gendering to bondage" and became filled with much "trouble and distress," Mother Ann would send him dancing to "labour it off" and "resume great cheerfulness again."[13] Her teaching underlay the pattern of worship frequently described in the next century by such observers as Horace Greeley: the "measured dance" that opened the Shaker service tended to quicken into what Greeley called a "wild, discordant

Fig. 23. An Early Dance
This lithograph entitled "SHAKERS near LEBANON, state of N YORK, their mode of Worship" claims to be "Drawn from life." A Worldly Lady, however, has usurped the eldress's seat, if we view the scene from the ranks of the vocal band. The brethren and sisters also more commonly danced facing the singers.

frenzy."[14] The Shakers on such occasions felt their exertions in the dance had helped to raise them from dull spirits into "life and power."

Having a desire to keep all alive, the ministry recognized the need for "a diversity of spiritual gifts" suited to the "great difference or variety in the ages, travel & experience of the believers."[15] A variety of forms of laboring was accordingly devised and taught with all the authority of the ministry itself. But spontaneous gifts were also encouraged in others. Isaac Youngs, while still one of the lesser brethren, "had a feeling" during the laboring of one exercise song "to have the inside rank of the circle turn their faces the other way, for he wanted to see the faces of the Brethren and sisters as he was going round." The suggestion was accepted, "and every wheel was in motion."[16]

The meaningfulness and the pleasure that the Shakers found in laboring provoked their imaginations into creating many forms. In these they unselfconsciously continued habits from British and American folk dancing. Even more than in the case of folk melody, however, it was imperative that they remodel their borrowings. A celibate order could hardly employ country dance unchanged, for "flirtation or coquetry lies at the root of nearly all its figures and evolutions."[17] Its manifold patterns present, as Curt Sachs phrased it, inexhaustible "combinations of the finding and losing of partners."[18] The sailor's hornpipe and the buck dance of the American backwoods were solo exhibitions of prowess equally inappropriate for a people wishing to unite as a body in the celebration of humility. What the Shakers could do was to draw upon a traditional manner of carrying the body, upon a step or two, upon a hint from familiar dance figures, and with these simple elements work out forms suitable for use in their worship.

Common to all the Shakers' dancing and marching was an easy bearing, with the trunk erect or bent only slightly forward. In other exercises the worshipers might bow and bend and twist and reel, but in the dance they were admonished to keep the "body right erect with every joint unbound" and not to make "unbecoming motions or jestures."[19] This is the normal posture of British and American folk dance, a trait as characteristic and as quintessential as the self-effacement with which a traditional singer performs a song.

The footwork in the Shaker dances consisted of two forms, the step and the shuffle. The latter was used whenever the laborer remained in one spot. Execution of the shuffle required considerable practice because it had "a particular hitch, difficult for some to learn."[20] One was supposed to "strike the shuffle little back, make the solid sound," bending the knees twice, apparently, in each shuffle, though without great vertical motion of the body.[21] The speed with which it was performed depended upon the tempo of the tune. In the Turning Shuffle dance of the mid-1790s the shuffling grew so slow as to be hard for the sisters, and for them a half-shuffle was introduced. Other variations were also practiced. Aurelia Mace said that the brethren at Gloucester commonly took a "back-step" shuffle and the sisters a single shuffle. With other children she was taught both of these steps and also a double and a "treble" shuffle. Their teacher wanted them to take the double shuffle to show their "activity." They were unable to "go the treble shuffle on any song."[22] The step used when the dancers advanced across the floor was simpler. It was "a kind of double hop, or a little slip of the foot on the floor"[23]—in other words, a skip. The beat of the music was timed with hands as well as feet. The dancers carried their forearms horizontal, their hands "gently beating like the wings of a bird."[24]

The absence of physical contact between the worshipers in these hand movements points toward the chief way in which Shaker dance differed from secular group folk dancing. The sexes kept apart on the floor, the brethren taking the left side as they entered the meetinghouse and the sisters the right. At a time when Congregationalists and Baptists were abandoning their earlier colonial practice of separating the sexes in worship, the celibate Shakers held fast to it. No country dance figures that intermixed the sexes could be employed in a Shaker service, but the "longways" set, familiar from such dances as the Virginia Reel, may have provided a hint for the earliest of the Shaker dance forms. In these the laborers stood in ranks, facing sometimes each other but more often the band of singers on the other side of the room. The ranks alternately advanced, retreated, and shuffled in place. These simple elements were elaborated into at least seven different dances before 1800 and into a few later ones.

The longest lived of these dances, the two for which by far the greatest numbers of tunes are preserved, were the Holy Order (frequently called the Square Order Shuffle) and the Regular Step (the name of which suggests that it may have been performed with something closer to a trotting step than to a skip).[25] Each heads a family of dances. The Holy Order group includes the Skipping Manner and the Hollow Square. The Regular Step family is made up of the Drumming Manner, the Walking Manner, and the Square Step. (Two other early dances, the Back Manner and the Turning Shuffle, stand somewhat apart.) The two groupings can be differentiated on the basis of both tune and dance pattern. Tunes for the Holy Order class are always in 6/8 time, those of the Regular Step type in 2/4. All the dances open with a section in which the laborers advance and withdraw two times. The Holy Order dance family, however, requires some manner of shuffle in place during the second section of the tune. In the Regular Step group the dancers continue moving back and forth across the floor during the second strain, though they omit some of the flourishes in that part.

The tunes for these dances, as early visitors generally noted with surprise, were related to dance, fiddle, and fife tunes popular at that or an earlier day in New England and the British Isles. Many were directly appropriated from this secular tune stock, but the nature of the Shaker dances determined just which tunes could be borrowed and also required many to be remodeled. Whether it belonged to the Holy Order or to the Regular Step family, a Shaker dance presented but two physical events—the movement across the floor and the spell of dancing in place. This dance pattern may derive from the two-strain structure of most Anglo-American folk-dance tunes, but it also required that all Shaker dance tunes be exactly two strains long. To use any of the secular dance tunes having three or more sections, the Shakers would have had to clip them short to fit the Shaker dance.

In a secular dance tune of two strains one often lies higher than the other in range, and the tune may open with either the high or the low strain. Samuel P. Bayard's Pennsylvania collection, *Hill Country Tunes*, is significantly weighted with tunes opening with the low section.[26] Nearly seventy of his one hundred tunes have this pattern, and in some twenty more the two sections do not have contrasting ranges. Shaker dance tunes, however, conform with great regularity to the following tune model:[27]

As the example shows, a Shaker dance tune has distinctly contrasting sections and begins with the high part of the tune. (Shaker terminology distinguishes between the two—the high section being called the "turn" and the low the "set" part of the tune.) In a sampling of one hundred Holy Order and Regular Step songs I found that four-fifths of the tunes of each class were composed of a high section followed by a low one.[28]

In no tune of either class did the second section extend higher in range than the first. In half the Regular Step tunes even the compass of the second section is narrower than that of the first. The explanation for these characteristics of the Shaker tunes is that the high sections correspond to the dancers' energetic movement across the floor. The more subdued set strain of the melodies matches the quieter movements of the second part of the Shaker dances.

But the dance movements may be impressed upon even subtler aspects of the tunes. Like most secular dancing songs, these melodies are sixteen bars long, and each section of a tune contains two four-bar phrases. However, the actual building blocks of the Shaker tunes are units two measures long. Two of these join together to make one of the long phrases, and the patterns these small melodic motifs form also tend to reflect the action on the floor. The forceful movements of the first section of the dance compel greater uniformity in the turn part of the tune than one finds in the set part. The opening sections of the Regular Step tunes, for example, employ the two-phrase building blocks in only one-sixth the number of combinations used in the second strains. Moreover, four-fifths of these opening sections show melodic contours in which ascending figures parallel the dancers' forward motion and descending ones accompany their return to their original places on the floor. Holy Order tunes are more varied, but—as the example above shows—their most frequent pattern does alternate rising and falling figures twice in each phrase. Since a continuous shuffling was performed through the set section of the Holy Order, it is not surprising that in half these tunes the units composing a phrase in this section have the same tonal range rather than contrasting ones.

Having such specialized requirements for their dance tunes and a need for large numbers of them, the Shaker singers went beyond merely borrowing secular dance tunes. They invented many suitable new ones of their own. One of their techniques seems to have been to shuffle about the two-bar motifs, arranging them in fresh combinations and varying their repetition patterns. But when they knew a secular tune that served their purposes well, they might use it as a model in the creation of new melodies. One tune pattern which fitted the Holy Order, for example, was that of the English song, "Oh, Dear, What Can the Matter Be?" [29] The rapid triplets of the second half of the song were ideal for the continuous shuffling in the set section of the Holy Order dance. The dotted quarter notes in the first half of the secular tune fell at the points where the Shaker laborers were stepping out in a new direction. The triplet preceding these dotted quarter notes matched the quick shuffle taken as the dancers made an about-face. In Haskell's collection of 188 Holy Order tunes some seventeen have exactly this rhythmic scaffolding or vary it only slightly. Many others use it in some looser pattern, as for example, introducing bars of dotted quarter notes into the second half of the tune. Often—as in the example that follows—the melodic contours are wholly different from those of the original English song, the rhythmic structure alone disclosing the kinship: [30]

The Shakers drew some of their melodic ideas for laboring songs from other branches of secular folk song. This required an even greater alteration of the traditional tunes. In the present collection, for example, both Walking Manner Tune no. 2 and the melody for the hymn "Voyage to Canaan" derive from an older English song, "You Gentlemen of England."[31] The hymn faithfully preserves the contour of the original tune, an AABA structure in which the B phrase climbs higher than the others. This is contrary to the patterns favored by Shaker dance. Accordingly, the Walking Manner tune uses only the A phrase and adds wholly different material to it to build the lower set strain.

Other examples among the songs that follow will make more clear the relation of the Shaker dance tunes to the figures and footwork of the laboring exercises, for in addition to a brief history and description of each dance I also provide an annotation of the first tune in a section to show the action performed in each beat of the melody. I do this to illuminate the intimate relation between the tune structures and the physical movements of the dance, not to offer a recipe for performances. Both the early and the present-day Shakers have rightly resented parodies of their mode of worship by persons not in union with the gift.

The Back Manner

Most references to the earliest Shaker laboring exercise call it "promiscuous dancing," meaning "the irregular manner in which, without any particular form, the believers danced, before the first gathering of the church at New Lebanon" in 1788. A Believer was generally led into this dance by "supernatural power," but accounts show that when a dance tune was struck up, many of those nearby "went forth in the dance." Probably men tended to dance on one side of a room or clearing and women on the other, but each person must have danced more or less alone and with his own steps and figures.

Russel Haskell calls this dance the "Back Manner" and says that as early as 1788 it was made "partly regular." The dance was then performed in ranks. During the first half of the tune the laborers, in a "kind of hitching step," went forward, turned, came back, and turned. The action was apparently repeated. In the second half of the tune the dancers either shuffled "some kind of shuffle" standing in their ranks or skipped forward and back without turning. In this form the Back Manner was practiced, at Enfield at least, until 1791. Other forms of dance then replaced it. The Back Manner had by that time already ceased at Lebanon "except on special occasions, accompanied with warring against evil &c., as it was felt necessary by the Lead."[32] The promiscuous form of the Back Manner was revived at Enfield in December 1807 during a powerful revival that lasted four weeks. After that time a partly regular Back Manner was sometimes labored at Enfield for a "quick manner," until the introduction of the Quick Dance in 1811.

Haskell says that the tunes for the Back Manner were of differing tempos and meters, but that all served well for the Quick Dance and some could be used for the Round Dance and others for the Heavenly March.[33]

Back Manner Tune No. 1

A.

Russel Haskell reports this tune in use among the converts at Enfield, Connecticut, as early as 1781.

Back Manner Tune No. 2

Haskell says Eunice Goodrich sang this tune before the first gathering of the Church. She was then in her mid-twenties, one of a numerous family attracted to the Shakers. She died at Lebanon in 1820.

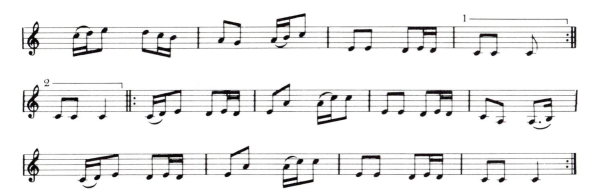

Back Manner Tune No. 3

Recorded by Haskell from the tradition at Enfield.

MS EC–11, p. 13.

The Holy Order

In 1787 or 1788 Father Joseph Meacham taught the Holy Order to the newly gathered Church, saying, "I received this manner of worship by the 'Revelation of God' & it must be handed down through you from generation to generation."[34] Holy Order was, in fact, one of only two early laboring manners to be long used in worship. Under one name or another—it was also called Square Order Shuffle, Step Manner, Shuffling Manner, Regular Shuffle, and Step and Shuffle—Holy Order was known from South Union to Gloucester. For years it opened the Sunday afternoon services at Lebanon. As late as 1868 a writer at Union Village called it the Church's "most solemn & beautiful order of worship."[35]

To execute the dance the worshipers formed into ranks on one side of the meeting room, the brethren and sisters in separate bodies. The two groups faced the band of singers standing in a line along the opposite wall. During the first half of the tune, which was sung twice, the laborers alternately advanced and retreated three steps, turning (brethren to the right and sisters to the left) and shuffling after the third and sixth steps and shuffling without turning after the ninth and twelfth steps. During the second half of the tune, which was sung only once, the dancers shuffled in their places, facing the singers.[36]

From time to time short-lived variations were introduced. Russel Haskell says that between 1798 and 1830 it was sometimes the custom at Enfield to advance and retreat during the first and third quarters of the tune and to shuffle during the second and fourth quarters. In this form both halves of the tune were sung twice.[37] At Lebanon the laborers experimented in May 1821 with raising their hands about as high as their heads, "with motions like waving."[38] They had heard that this was done in the Western societies. In 1852 the Lebanon ministry showed the worshipers at Union Village "some about clapping hands" in the Holy Order, "as it is something new to them."[39] A few undesired variations also appeared in the worship. One common failing was to take only two steps when advancing and returning, and to begin the turn carelessly after the second step. The ministry fretted over the problem, but Isaac Youngs wrote, "I scruple whether our assembly will ever take three whole steps, or set their feet straight forward, for after all our labour there is not more than four or five that do either."[40] A song with instructions on these points was received "by a perticular gift of Inspiration" at Watervliet in 1841.[41] The "Millennial Laws" of 1845 addressed a paragraph to the problem.[42] Doubtless it was never solved.

For a dance so long in practice a large number of tunes accumulated. Haskell collected 188 in use at Enfield. All are 6/8 tunes. He says the tempo in the early years was Shaker mode 4. After 1810 or 1815, the tunes were performed at a faster speed, always either mode 5 or 6.[43]

Holy Order Tune No. 1

Haskell says this was one of the first tunes learned at Enfield for the Holy Order. Daniel Tiffany and Daniel Goodrich sang it there when they came bringing instructions for the dance about the year 1790.

1 L   2 R   3   4   5   6   7   8
Stand and shuffle facing singers

9   10   11   12   13   14   15   16
                                    lum de um   dum

Holy Order Tune No. 2

The Phrygian mode is so rare in Shaker tune transcriptions that one would suspect an error if this song had been set down by any scribe other than Russel Haskell. He entered it without comment among tunes learned in 1791.

♩. = 113 (♩⁵)   MS EC–11, p. 70.

Holy Order Tune No. 3

Haskell says the Shakers at Enfield learned this tune from Hannah Kendall when she came on a visit in the autumn of 1791. She was then a young woman of thirty-one but would shortly be chosen to stand with Father Eleazer Rand in the Harvard ministry and bear the title Mother. Of all the American converts she had been Mother Ann's closest companion, traveling with her and sharing the abuse in many scenes of mob violence. For her spirit the English Shakers named her "Valiant."

♩. = 96 (♩⁴)   MS EC–11, p. 71.

Holy Order Tune No. 4

Haskell recorded the A variant of this song as a Holy Order tune from the early 1790s. The B variant comes from a manuscript—possibly written at Lebanon—entitled "The Songs of Blessed Mother Ann." There the song is one of a group labeled "slow shuffling tunes." Others in the same class are related to Haskell's tunes for the Turning Shuffle. Probably his groupings are too strict. With some change of tempo, many a shuffling tune must have been suitable for use with a number of related dances. Beginning in the 1820s they would also serve for the marches.

Holy Order Tune No. 5

"This is the first song that was sung and danced by believers in the western Country," says a note in the only manuscript preserving the tune. The scene was a noon meeting on May 23,

1805, when three Shaker missionaries from the East preached to a gathering of some forty persons fresh from the Kentucky Revival. The singing of the hymn lines,

> With him in praises we'll advance
> And join the Virgins in the dance

excited Jane McNemar, who "got exercised in dancing." Elder Issachar Bates immediately pitched a laboring song, and the other two missionaries began a Shaker dance in the presence of the congregation. Some converts joined them, but they were so little schooled in Shakerism and wrought to so high a pitch that their exercise was "like the carnal Dances of the World." At successive meetings over the next months they began to fall into the more orderly manner of the Shaker exercise. By December, when Polly Kimball "had a gift of song" during a service and leaned back on some who held her up and, without moving her lips, sang a Solemn Song which "turned into a perfect laboring tune," the people could labor "with great comfort & power."

MS L–105, p. [213].

Holy Order Tune No. 6

A Mixolydian tune in the rhythmic pattern of "O Dear, What Can the Matter Be?" Haskell claims the song for the Church Family at Enfield and places it with ones learned around 1822.

♩. = 113 (𝄵⁵)   MS EC–11, p. 86.

Holy Order Tune No. 7

Joshua Bennet of Enfield had this tune in 1825. He was then a man of twenty-six and, according to Haskell, so "young in the faith" that he had not yet moved from his home in Rhode Island to the Shaker village.

Holy Order Tune No. 8

In the 1840s Giles Avery recorded this song at Lebanon with the note, "An ancient shuffling tune sung by Betty Babbet while here—1826." Betty, a native of Hardwick, Massachusetts, had only the year before been called into the Harvard ministry at the age of forty-four. For twenty-two years she would carry the burdens of that lot.

Holy Order Tune No. 9

The phrase patterns of this tune seem too irregular to match the tight figures of the Holy Order dance, but Abraham Perkins placed it among the "shuffling songs" in a collection he wrote in

1832. He ascribed the song to Oliver Holmes of Gloucester. A man of small stature with jet-black eyes and black hair "always smooth and glossy," Elder Oliver was much admired for his "clear and melodious" voice. His singing and the songs he composed while about his work of making flax wheels were so much spoken of that the other societies asked for him to make a singing tour. The small, poor, out-of-the way village at Gloucester, greatly pleased "to see her idolized son honored in this way," sent Oliver on a six weeks' journey through the Eastern communities in the summer of 1808. Few of the songs he sang were recorded at Gloucester, for Oliver died of consumption in 1841, the year before Otis Sawyer began what he claimed to be the first music manuscript ever written in the Maine societies. Oliver himself, however, was long remembered at Gloucester for having a spirit as pure "as the finest gold from the crucible." "But Oliver Holmes stands not alone," wrote Aurelia Mace: "This is a clean spot in the wilderness of the world."

MS ENH–2, p. [1].

Holy Order Tune No. 10

In a collection of "shuffling songs" Elder Abraham Perkins set this tune down with the note, "Sung by Elder Br. Daniel Clark (deceased) Enfield Con. to one of the brethren." The song seems to date from 1837, the year of Daniel Clark's death at the age of sixty-one.

MS ENH–2, p. [28].

Holy Order Tune No. 11

FATHER JOSEPH'S SOLID STEP SONG

A manuscript written at Watervliet, New York, where this song originated about 1840, places it with shuffling tunes. Probably the title refers to Father Joseph's instructions that in laboring a song the dancers should "take some solid steps."

Holy Order Tune No. 12

Harvey L. Eades recorded this tune at South Union, dating it "Sept. 1840."

Holy Order Tune No. 13

Russel Haskells' terse note on this song reads "H. Ch. Joshua G."—Joshua Goodrich of Hancock—a son of one of the three Goodrich couples converted by Mother Ann. Elizur and his wife Mother Lucy Wright, Daniel, Mother Hannah, Thankful, Hortense, Molly, a roster of the members of this family is a roll call of many of the early Shaker leaders. Aside from word that he was one of the best singers at Hancock, Joshua's career, however, went mostly unrecorded. He had this song when he was fifty-nine, in 1841.

Holy Order Tune No. 14

A tune introduced at Enfield, Connecticut, in 1842.

The Skipping Manner

Russel Haskell says that the Skipping Manner was introduced at Enfield in 1789 as the second regular form of dance. The laborers were placed in ranks facing the singers. For the first step the brethren skipped out on the left foot (sisters used the right). They advanced three steps, turned without shuffling, returned the three steps, wheeled again without drumming, and, beginning on the left foot, finished out the section with the single shuffle, facing the singers. The same action accompanied the repetition of this first half of the tune and both singings of the other section of the tune.

Writing in 1845, Haskell was not entirely confident of the descriptions given him by elderly Believers or of the four Skipping Manner tunes he was able to assemble. All these were 6/8 melodies performed in Shaker mode 6, but one tune was composed of a four- and an eight-bar section, and the other three tunes of two six-bar sections. Perhaps because of the anomalous length of these tunes the Skipping Manner did not prove satisfactory. It was discontinued after a few months and was never revived.[44]

Skipping Manner Tune No. 1

Sung at Enfield, Connecticut, about 1789.

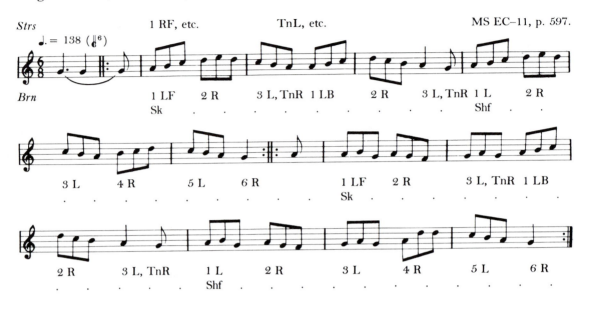

The Turning Shuffle

The Turning Shuffle was introduced about the year 1790. This was a period when Father Joseph Meacham wanted to prune out from the Church all the dead branches and the fruit that would not set. He accomplished this by causing the members to "labor down into mortification & into as deep and heavy bearing for the loss of man, as any body of people was able to endure, even deeper than any would ever hereafter be required to descend." Members were "plainly taught" the orders of the Church, "pressingly admonished" to obey them, and "severely reproved for any disorder." Father Joseph refrained from all gifts "tending to raise the feelings from the heft of mortification."[45] In 1796, the culminating year of this work, Lebanon did not admit a single member and twenty left. Not until the 1860s did that society again lose so many persons in a single year.[46]

The Turning Shuffle was intended to further this mortification. In it, dance was reduced to footwork alone. Standing in their ranks, the laborers for the first part of the tune performed the "proper single shuffle" turning around twice in place. Haskell says that "in making one shuffle with each foot, they turned one eighth of a circle," the brethren to the right and the sisters to the left. Those who were "limber jointed, would bend their knees in the exercise, till their fingers would almost or quite touch the floor." During the second half of the tune the laborers shuffled in their ranks, facing the singers. It was a very slow shuffle; in Haskell's manuscript all the thirty-one tunes for the Turning Shuffle are either 3/4 tunes performed at Shaker mode 2 or 3, or 6/8 tunes sung at mode 1.[47]

In the latter part of 1796 Father Joseph discontinued all exercises in the meetings, and when they were reintroduced a year and a half later, the Turning Shuffle was apparently not revived. Prior to this the Enfield ministry had made the Turning Shuffle a little less difficult by "hastening the speed to nearly twice as fast" and teaching the sisters a "half shuffle." But at Lebanon from 1793 until the cessation of exercises in 1796 the laboring was a "heavy shuffle" which grew slower and slower "until it became almost impossible to exercise it at all." Calvin Green said, "I scarcely ever felt so distressing a cross as to attempt it."[48]

Turning Shuffle Tune No. 1

A tune preserved at Enfield, Connecticut. The AAAB phrasal structure of the turn section would have made it inappropriate for use in any of the shuffling dances requiring movement across the floor.

Turning Shuffle Tune No. 2

The singers at Enfield recalled this as a tune sung by Father Calvin Harlow. It probably dates between 1792, when he was appointed Lead over the societies at Hancock, Tyringham, and Enfield, and 1795, when he died at the age of forty-one.

Turning Shuffle Tune No. 3

An Enfield tune from the early 1790s.

♩. = 56 (𝄵¹)   MS EC–11, p. 66.

Turning Shuffle Tune No. 4

Jeremiah and Daniel Goodrich sang this tune at David Meacham's house in Enfield when they visited there a number of times between 1790 and 1793. Song was the instrument of Daniel's own conversion during a visit to Watervliet a decade earlier. His feelings had not been affected by the elders' preaching "a faithful and sound testimony against all sin of every name and nature." But when Mother Ann and "her little family" sat down that afternoon and sang in "a solemn and heavenly manner," Daniel said, "I felt as tho I had got among the heavenly hosts, and had no right there; for I had neither part nor lot in it. I cried aloud, in distress of soul; for I believed it to be the worship of the living God, such as my ears had never heard, nor my soul ever felt before."

♩ = 113 (𝄵³)   MS EC–11, p. 68.

Turning Shuffle Tune No. 5

The opening phrase of the tune of the ballad "One Morning in May" or "The Nightingale" probably was the seed from which this Enfield dance tune grew.

MS EC–11, p. 68.

Turning Shuffle Tune No. 6

This second dance melody deriving from "The Nightingale" was preserved in the tradition at Harvard. Betty Babbit learned it there in 1791, when she was ten, from the singing of a brother visiting from Lebanon.

MS HD–16, p. 69.

Turning Shuffle Tune No. 7

A third tune related to that of "The Nightingale." Daniel Tiffany was remembered as having sung it at Harvard when the church was first gathering in 1793. He died in the same year, a young man of twenty-five. It is said that he and his brother Nathan worked together "& were very frolicsome." Their father, a Believer, at last persuaded Nathan to go to see Ann Lee. He returned greatly changed and also a Believer. Daniel "stood out for a while & resisted conviction" and even tried to turn Nathan back. According to one Harvard journal,

> At last Nathan said to him, If you had one drop of the blood of Christ in you, you would not act as you do. This struck him with some feeling. A woman by the name of Billings had a great feeling for Daniel, & invited him to a meeting. While there, she spoke to him & said, Daniel, bow the knee & God will bow your heart. He kneeled, & . . . cried out like a calf. Ever after this, he was a very zealous & faithful believer.

MS HD–16, pp. 91–92.

Turning Shuffle Tune No. 8

This tune survives in one manuscript from Harvard and another written possibly at Lebanon. In the latter it is placed among the "slow shuffling tunes," some of which are variants of Haskell's Turning Shuffles. Neither manuscript comments on the song.

MS XU–36, p. [28].

Turning Shuffle Tune No. 9

Another "slow shuffling tune" probably from Lebanon.

MS XU–36, p. [31].

Turning Shuffle Tune No. 10

A third "slow shuffling tune."

MS XU–36, p. [31].

The Regular Step

In 1789, about two years after introducing the Holy Order or Square Order Shuffle, Father Joseph taught the worshipers at Lebanon a new manner he had learned by inspiration, the Square Step or Square Order Step. The name implies a relation between the two dances. Indeed the first half of the Square Order Step was identical with the dance for the opening section of the Square Order Shuffle. In the Square Step, however, the second section of the tune was sung twice, and instead of shuffling throughout, the laborers took three paces forward, shuffled, retreated three paces without turning, shuffled again, and continued in this way until the return of the first part of the melody. The name Square Step and the fact that the tunes for this manner are in 2/4 time suggest that the dancers may also have "stepped" rather than skipped. But on this the early descriptions are unclear.[49]

The manner was discontinued in 1794, when only the slowest shuffling was permitted. In 1798 the Square Step was revived at Lebanon because "dullness and lack of devotion pervaded the meetings."[50] Haskell says that the manner was first learned and brought into use at Enfield in this year. He calls it the Regular Step, and I use his term, to distinguish between this dance and a later one generally called the Square Step.

Under whatever name, the Regular Step was one of the most durable of the dances. It was practiced continuously until past the middle of the nineteenth century. Haskell collected sixty-three tunes sung for the Regular Step before 1825 and thirty-two more used for both it and the related Square Step manner between 1825 and 1848.[51] Occasionally in a footnote on one of these tunes he commented that the song "is probably not so suitable for the regular step as it is for marching."[52] Except that the tempo of these tunes is always mode 3 rather than 3q, I do not see the basis for his distinction. The melodies that other scribes label "Step Song" are, however, sometimes quite different in phrasal contour or length from the Regular Step tunes of Haskell and clearly ill suited for the dance that he describes. These tunes I place in the marching song section.

The Regular Step was one of the few early dances learned in the Western societies. Laboring manners that fell into disuse before 1805 never reached the West, and others still practiced were introduced slowly to the new converts. It was not until 1812 that those at Union Village saw the Regular Step. That it made a deep impression on them is proved by the following deposition taken on July 21, 1813, from the mouth of a young sister at Union Village:

> I Martha Dragoo was in a trance (or extacy) as the Greek word may be rendered, being in the proper exercise of my senses and judgment and in open day light—
>
> Saw heaven opened to my view towards the south—Brethren and sisters in great Multitudes extending from the house to the grave yard—praising the Lord with songs—and mooving in perfect order in the step dance—the brethren on the west, the sisters on the east—a small space between—Jethro & Caleb ware singers and sang so loud and heavenly that they ware heard distinctly to the extreme of this vast assembly—They ware all clothed in white bright and glitering and in the dance appeared to advance and step back the distance of three or four poles—nor were they impeded by houses fences hills or vallies—but like lightning passed through every thing—None of this vast multitude ware distinctly recognized by the beholder; save Jethro and Caleb singers
>
> But Jethro was so distinctly seen that his dimple on his chin was minutely marked with his black eyes blazing like comets or stars—Also Calebs countenance was bright his teeth white as ivory his black eyebrows meeting over his nose—
>
> The singers sat on the top of the kitchin as she understood to be distinctly heard and seen by all—During this vision Martha was spoken to by Nancy once or twice to rise to the fire but her reply was that she could not yet— having a desire to gaze upon this wonderful sight a little longer—Viz the saints in their stately stepings—[53]

Regular Step Tune No. 1

A tune in use at Enfield about 1792.

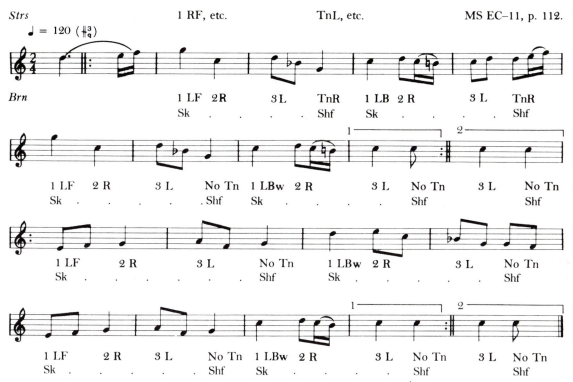

Strs   1 RF, etc.   TnL, etc.   MS EC–11, p. 112.

$\quad = 120\ (\sharp\frac{3}{q})$

Regular Step Tune No. 2

The Enfield Shakers got this tune in the early 1790s from one Rebecca Gillet. In 1959 the melody was still sung in the Hebrides as a Gaelic love song.

$\quad = 120\ (\sharp\frac{3}{q})$ MS EC–11 p. 112.

Regular Step Tune No. 3

Haskell says the Enfield Shakers used this song "in the early days" for the Drumming Manner and later adapted it for the Regular Step.

Regular Step Tune No. 4

A song that came into the Enfield repertory about 1810.

Regular Step Tune No. 5

The Enfield Shakers were using this tune by 1825.

Regular Step Tune No. 6

Haskell dates this tune Feb. 23, 1846. For twenty years, however, Believers had been singing a variant of the melody as the marching song "Faithful Soldiers Travel On." The Step Tune alters the second halves of the first and third phrases to make them parallel a little more clearly the retreating movements of the dancers. The ultimate source of both these songs—as also of Walking Manner Tune no. 2 and the Round Dance "Living Souls"—is the first half of the ballad tune "You Gentlemen of England" or "Gilderoy." The Shakers used the melody intact for "Voyage to Canaan" and other hymns.

MS EC–11, p. 122.

Regular Step Tune No. 7

This song and many others in the same Lebanon manuscript of the early 1840s bear the attribution "E. B." These initials probably stand for the name of Emily Babcock, a young sister who had come to the Society from Ashford, Connecticut, with her four older brothers. She was musically gifted. Isaac Youngs wrote in 1838 that she was having "new songs, *every night.*" Three years earlier, at the age of twelve, she had inscribed an impeccable example of her musical skill and penmanship in the songbook of a South Union visitor. She probably also executed the beautifully written manuscript holding this Step Song. The name of the scribe was cut off the title page, a fact that takes on significance in the light of one journal entry: in October 1846 Emily Babcock "obsequatilated" to seek her fortune in New York City.

MS L–170, p. 227.

Regular Step Tune No. 8

"First part Moses Thayer's & last part Oliver Hampton's" says a note in a manuscript written by Moses himself in 1852. A tunesmith and a versifier often collaborated in writing a hymn, but evidence of joint authorship of a melody is extremely rare in Shaker manuscripts. Elder Oliver for one had little need to borrow anyone else's inspiration. He had made up many tunes for hymns. In the 1840s he also served as an instrument for musical spirits, as when a French fiddler appeared and spoke through him, "stepping around for some time very politely & playing some pretty lively airs" on his violin. Shaker journals tell less of Moses Thayer. He had entered North Union at the age of seventeen. Six years later, in 1845, he came to Union Village. Later in the year that he wrote his songbook Moses turned back to the World.

MS UV–17, p. 280.

Regular Step Tune No. 9

Phidelio Collins had this "quick tune" early in 1858, shortly before he entered the "Elder's lot." He was born in Chenango, Massachusetts, in 1813 and at the age of seven was "received into the family" at Hancock. Upon his death sixty-four years later, a memorial would call Phidelio's life "one of faithfulness and Christian kindness, which gave him universal love and respect."

The Drumming Manner

Russel Haskell believed the Drumming Manner to be "the first regular dance," and wrote that it was performed much like the Regular Step. The only differences were a "more forcible drumming of the feet" after the third step forward or back and a change of tempo during the course of the performance. The tunes were sung twice through in "regular step time" (2/4 at Shaker mode 1) and then changed to "shuffle time" (6/8 at mode 6q) with no alteration of the dance figure.[54]

Believers at Enfield learned the dance in 1788 from Elizur Goodrich, Daniel Goodrich, and Daniel Tiffany, three brethren sent out from Lebanon by Father Joseph as "messengers of spiritual gifts and as counselors." They taught the Square Order Shuffle, the Regular Step, and the Drumming Manner. Unlike the other two, the Drumming Manner was practiced only a short time. A letter written from Enfield in 1830 mentions a brief revival of the dance,[55] but Haskell preserves only seven tunes used for the Drumming Manner, and all of them are very early ones.

Drumming Manner Tune No. 1

A tune labored at Enfield, Connecticut, in 1788.

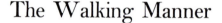

The Walking Manner

The Walking Manner was another variation on the Regular Step. It differed chiefly in the omission of shuffles following the third step forward and back and in being much slower—Shaker mode 1 is the tempo of the eleven tunes Haskell gathered, all of them in 2/4 time and sixteen bars long. The dance was introduced at the Connecticut society in 1797 and was practiced only a short time.[56] How many other communities used this exercise the records do not make clear, but I think it likely that Elder Henry Blinn was referring to the Walking Manner when he wrote that Believers at Enfield, New Hampshire, learned the Slow March in 1798.[57] His confusion of the two forms implies that the laborers paced in the Walking Manner, rather than using a skipping step.

Walking Manner Tune No. 1

From the tradition at Enfield, Connecticut.

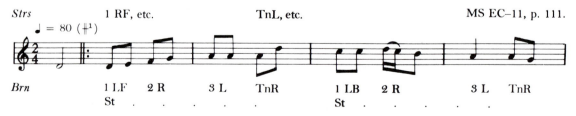

Walking Manner Tune No. 2

Another Enfield tune. The turn section derives from "You Gentlemen of England."

Walking Manner Tune No. 3

Solomon King, whom Haskell named as the author of this tune, was raised from childhood at Lebanon. He was twenty-two in 1797, when Believers used his song for the Walking Manner. Eight years later the Lead would send him to help establish Union Village, where Solomon served thirty years, for the last ten standing first in the ministry. Oliver Hampton says that he unfortunately lacked "that peculiar genius" for exacting "straight going" and allowed the society to drift into "many loose and derelict ways." Oliver, however, called him a "thoroughly good man, even exceedingly upright and pious." Solomon seems in fact to have been generally liked. A writer at Lebanon pronounced him "a very plain, simple, substantial man," and upon meeting him in 1846, Thomas Hammond of Harvard straight off "loved him much." He knew Solomon's tune, sang it to him, and reported that "it seemed rather to please him to be remembered so long by that song."

PART IV

Ballads

During one meeting at Harvard in the early 1780s Mother Ann went to the south door of the house and, extending her arm, declared, "The next opening of the gospel will be in the *South West*." Father James then joined her at the door and said, "I hear singing . . . in the *South West*, and sometimes it seemes very near, and again it seemes a thousand miles off."[1] Fifteen years later the Western frontier was indeed the scene of a new opening of the spirit—and of a new phase of Shaker song.

For eight years the excitement of the Kentucky Revival swept the backwoods, enveloping the pious and the ungodly alike. When word of it reached Lebanon, the ministry took the revival to be a confirmation of the Shaker prophecy. Even while Mother Ann spoke, events were preparing the fulfillment of her words. Settlers—and some in their number who would later enter Shakerism—had begun their great migration through the mountain gaps into the Western lands.

How this new world looked to their eyes was vividly recorded by one who came as a boy to the new Shaker settlement at West Union, Indiana:

> Prairies I had never seen before; some, as level as the Ocean, with nothing only the etherial *blue* to bound the sight; the prairies covered with a thick coat of Grass, of a *new kind*, peculiar to that Country: On this the Cattle of the Inhabitants fed promiscuously, as there was *plenty* for all, and the whole pasture belonging to "Uncle Sam"
>
> Here, for weeks & months, the Indians were our nearest neighbors, enjoying themselves in hunting, fishing, horse-racing, running foot-races, wrestling, jumping, &c &c. Also, at the same time keeping up, a little *domestic Commerce*, having for Barter deer skins, dressed & raw, mockasins, some of them tastefully wrought with porcupine Quills, and other articles peculiar to them. At that time they were perfectly innocent & harmless. When Melon-Time, & the fruit season came on, they came down the Waubash by hundreds to *enjoy* the Good things of the Land: Canoe loads of these copper-colored, semi-barbarian Brethren came down the Wabash River, and *encamped* in our neighborhood. The Males in a perfect state of nudity, excepting the figleaf-locality, their whole bodies greased & painted to the very nose: and yet they were a very modest, well-behaved people; especially the squaws, who were decently clad, in cloth coat, & calico frock: when the infant was nursed, he was introduced under it, mostly out of sight. These Sons of the forest enjoyed the melon-season to the *Nines*; visiting the saints daily, from house to house, feasting on the Melons and everything else, they could get; *never refusing to*

eat, at all times and hours: *Begging was now the Mode*: Melons they considered as Water, not to be paid for. As the season passed away, they gradually moved off west & North, into their accustomed Winter Quarters; where wild Game were more abundant. For singing & dancing, the males, exclusively excelled all people: their exercises were peculiar; the accented notes were touched, not with a fantastic toe, but with a laborious, active motion, accompanied, in beating time, with the hands, the rattling of Bear's claws, Deer's hoofs, stones in a gourd, a one-stick Drum &c. &c. This feast dance terminated in the *War Dance*; the Indians being *painted* in the most hiddeous manner; exercising vehemently, and vociferating, & screeching like so many panthers & demons; at the same time wielding their war clubs and hatchets; Some tho't these were Religious Dances; but aged John Slover said they might have religion, but it was of the same kind, as practiced when they had him at the stake to be *burnt*, and some were now engaged, who were present, at that awful scene! Slover moved his all, on the next Monday towards South Union. Of the Inhabitants of the Wabash Country I must say a word; the Males were clad in Buckskin pants, suspended by a leather thong; shirts, if they had any, were French check, with a coarse Blanket Chappeau; the coronet, a Raccoon's cap. This Habiliament was well calculated to shield their bodies, from the everlasting piercing Winds of the Prairies. You must recollect that, these Inhabitants were on the extreme frontier of Indiana Territory; only one family between them, & St. Louis, Missouri, and that was killed by Indians, the first winter after our arrival. The Prairies, rivers, ponds, bayous &c. abounded with birds, fishes, fowls & game of all kinds, peculiar to that country: wild geese, swans, pellicans, brants, cranes, ducks &c. fishes astonishingly plenty, of strange kinds, & enormous in size. Among the numerous Birds, Paroquets, as mischievous as beautiful; Black Birds by millions; Prairy-Hens by the thousands they rose from the fields as a cloud, making a noise like thunder. But I must not be tedious, for it would require a Book to hint at all the peculiarities of this New World; as seen by my juvenile eyes.[2]

Contemporaries recognized how many changes life in this new world worked in the settlers. The superficial observer, like one British traveler stopping at a log tavern in southern Ohio in 1816, saw the frontiersman as "coarse, large, and strong, vulgar, sturdy, and impudent." These "vulgar Democrats," complained the English gentleman, "hold in supreme contempt everything like, refinement, or neatness."[3] American religious leaders had a more serious concern, the social and moral degeneration taking place on the frontier. "Rogues' harbor" was Peter Cartwright's name for one Kentucky county.[4] When the Kentucky Revival broke out, some could see that its excesses were not merely an expression of the Western spirit, but a measure of the strength of disruptive forces the revival sought to curb.[5] Like the Methodist bishops, the Shaker ministry wanted contact with the Western revivalists and in 1805 sent out three missionaries to carry the gospel West. Their 1200-mile journey on foot led to the winning of important converts, notably the New Light leader Richard McNemar, and to the founding of Shaker communities in Kentucky, Ohio, and Indiana.

Extending their work into the backwoods brought important structural changes to denominations like Methodism, which was led to institutionalize circuit riding and the camp meeting. Similar effects might have been expected to follow from the Shakers' expansion into the West. Their earlier removal from England to America had transformed the Believers from a handful of followers clustered about a magnetic leader into a highly disciplined religious order. Whether because this discipline prevented any drastic reorientation or because the order itself was less deeply expressive of Western culture than of that of New England (where it still survives a half century after the closing of the last Western community), the new colonies replicated the Eastern societies in their economy, social arrangements, beliefs, and modes of worship.[6]

The Western converts did, however, bring about one development in Shaker song. As long as their faith was still tender, the missionaries had been wary of shocking them with such practices as laboring or the singing of wordless Solemn Songs. Converts like Richard McNemar accordingly began to state their new beliefs in verses and to sing them, in the manner to which they had been accustomed, as hymns with folk-tune settings. The Easterners quickly fell in with this practice, and soon all the Shaker communities were incorporating the singing of hymns into their worship.

Some of those who had passed through physical or spiritual adventures in the West were also excited to tell their tales in song. Clearly they were already familiar with the tradition of broadside verse. The missionary Issachar Bates, for example, had before his own conversion written and published a ballad entitled "Lines composed on the death of Mr. Isaac Orcutt, who was killed by the fall of a tree in Hartford, State of New York."[7] From Bates, McNemar, and a few of their Western associates we have some ten narrative and quasi-narrative songs. After the first decade of the century, this kind of composition virtually disappeared from the Shaker repertory. Rarely again did the outward life of the Shakers contain the conflict and incident which are the stuff of balladry.[8]

Ballad No. 1

THE HAPPY VOYAGE

"An Allegorical Detail of the entrance of Mother's Gospel in the West, in the year 1805. This Poem is still entertaining to those who understand its sublime imagery."

Richard McNemar's "The Happy Voyage" shows how the Western convert had fared in the choppy seas of the Kentucky Revival. McNemar knew them well. Although the basic stance of the New Lights had been struck sixty years earlier during the Great Awakening, McNemar himself believed that one new circumstance important to the rise of the revival party was the defection of Kentucky settlers to Deism in the aftermath of the Revolution. Many held Christianity itself to blame for abuses committed in its name by power-hungry kings and prelates. The apostasy deeply troubled devout Christians and turned them back to a reconsideration of their beliefs. This, McNemar felt, was the cause of the renewal of experiential religion among some in the Calvinist party. They were no longer satisfied that "the scriptures, explained according to sound reason and philosophy, was light sufficient." They craved instead to know the will of God "by an inward light which shone into the heart." They took the Kentucky Revival to be not "a day of small things," but "nothing less than an *introduction* to that work of *final redemption*, which God had promised." It was this millennial hope that "drew out the multitudes to encamp for days and nights in the wilderness" and prepared McNemar and his followers to accept the testimony of the Shakers. They wanted neither Calvinist nor Arminian doctrine, but some new word.

McNemar cast this account of his search for a new faith, however, into traditional forms. The underlying structure of the "Happy Voyage" seems indebted to that of the nautical ballad "The Bold Princess Royal." The tunes also are distantly related. McNemar was deeply enough rooted in Calvinist tradition to like an account of spiritual progress cast in the allegorical mode.

Text: *A Selection of Hymns and Poems*, pp. 136–137.

Tune: MS EC–11, p. 234.

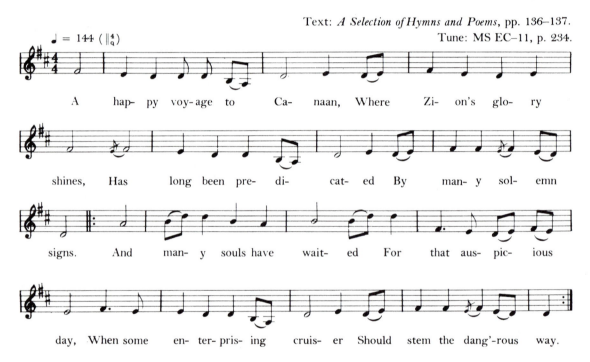

A hap-py voy-age to Ca-naan, Where Zi-on's glo-ry shines, Has long been pre-di-cat-ed By man-y sol-emn signs. And man-y souls have wait-ed For that aus-pic-ious day, When some en-ter-pris-ing cruis-er Should stem the dang'-rous way.

2 Deceiv'd by wicked pilots, who always led them wrong,
   They rais'd their cries to heaven—O mighty God how long!
   Their fervent aspirations, kind heaven did fulfil,
   And the Lord prepar'd a vessel, by his unerring skill.

3 He launch'd the royal New-light, in 18 hundred one,
   Commanded by Elijah, and the good boatswain John;
   The solemn trump was sounded—'Ye men of ev'ry kin,
   You may now obtain a passage, from this vain world of sin.'

4 Along the crouded harbor, we coasted to and fro,
   With this kind invitation—'O sinners will you go?'
   Can we forget that solemn day she first began to move,
   With all her flowing sails expanded with pure impartial love!

5 With our New-light colors flying, we had not sailed far,
   Till we spi'd upon our larboard a gallant man of war;
   'Reef up your sails (her boatswain cries) you shall not cross this sea,
   Unless you've been elected from all eternity.

6 We found it was bold Calvin, & to the right
  we steer'd,
  When just upon our starboard Arminus next
  appear'd;
  We gave them each a broadside, but would
  not stand to fite,
  And the wind being in our favor, we soon got
  out of sight.

7 4 years we plow'd the ocean, and o'er the
  waves did ride
  With mighty thunders roaring, and storms on
  ev'ry side;
  Sometimes we soar'd to heaven, upon a
  tow'ring wave,
  Then down we sink as low again, into the
  opening grave.

8 The marriners impatient to reach the happy
  ground—
  And sick of these sad changes, still tossing up
  and down—
  How oft the longing passengers look o'er the
  rolling seas,
  Crying surely yonder's Canaan, I think I see
  the trees!

9 At length a blessed convoy, on board the
  Royal Ann,
  Came forth to meet the New-light, & bring her
  safe to land,
  From such intervening dangers, the king of
  Zion knew
  We could never reach the harbor unless they
  brought us to.

10 About the first of April, this vessel we did spy,
  And our good boatswain hail'd her, "Aho the
  ship ahoy!
  To what empire do you belong, what is your
  captain's name?
  Let us know where you go & likewise from
  whence you came.

11 Our captain is Emanuel, to Canaan we pertain,
  & we're come to help you forward, across the
  rolling main,
  We bade her kindly welcome, and Leeward we
  did steer,
  Till a lying spirit enter'd, and some were
  struck with fear.

12 They are pirates, cries a sailor, from the high
  gallant-top
  They do not seem to know me, I think we'd
  better stop.
  They're deceivers cries another, they surely
  mean to kill,
  For if they belong'd to Canaan, they would
  not be so still.

13 What infinite confusion did instantly ensue;
  Our officers abus'd and insulted by the crew;
  Some crying, Lord have mercy, we're surely all
  deceiv'd,
  And our pilot's been a traitor, as some at first
  believ'd.

14 At length those wicked sailors concluded to
  divide,
  And down they let the long boat into the
  foaming tide;
  The fearful knew not what to do, but into it they
  ran,
  Crying here's a place of safety, we must not
  follow man.

15 The few that proved faithful & to the New-light
  cleav'd
  Were sure the honest pilot had not the crew
  deceiv'd;
  & such clamors from the longboat 'you must
  not follow man'
  Only urg'd them on the faster toward the royal
  Ann.

16 The Convoy we approach'd, thro' a little
  narrow pass,
  Between the infernal ocean, and the bright sea
  of glass,
  Where we receiv'd high orders, to cast out
  ev'ry sin:
  And when we had unloaded, they kindly took
  us in.

17 The crew that man'd the long-boat, recov'ring
  from their fright,
  Came veering on toward us, determin'd for a
  fight;
  Well charg'd with pride & envy, they let off
  many lies,
  While the R. Ann mov'd off, with the N. light
  as her prize.

18 Now under a good convoy and blest with a
  fresh gale,
  Thro' the sea of self-denial, we joyfully did sail:
  And in ev'ry scene of trial, our union did
  increase,
  Till we enter'd Salem's harbor, & found the
  land of peace.

Ballad No. 2

THE MOLES LITTLE PATHWAY

This second song by Richard McNemar was sent to the Eastern ministry in a letter dated 1807. It treats the events of the Kentucky Revival in a somewhat more autobiographical way, but reveals his inner experience rather than the outward facts. McNemar was born in 1770 in the Allegheny Mountains of central Pennsylvania. For one in his time and place he was an exceptional student. At fifteen he was teaching school. When he was twenty-one he joined a Methodist church and was soon studying Latin, Greek, and Hebrew. Before he was twenty-six he had married, fathered children, and left the Methodists for the Presbyterians. Two years later he was an ordained minister and had awakened to the excitement of the Kentucky Revival. Looking back on this period of his life he later wrote,

> As full of zeal and pure desire
> As e'er a coal was full of fire
> I flash'd & blazed by day and night
> A burning & a shining light.

When schism split the Western Presbyterians he was one of the leaders of the reform party and was ripe for the arrival of the Shaker missionaries in the spring of 1805. In September of that year he was able to write to Lebanon,

> For upwards of 15 years my soul has been on the wheel, forming into union with professed followers of the Lamb, but never did I find my mate, until I found the spirit from New Lebanon. Now I can say with the prophet, "This is my God, I have waited for him!"

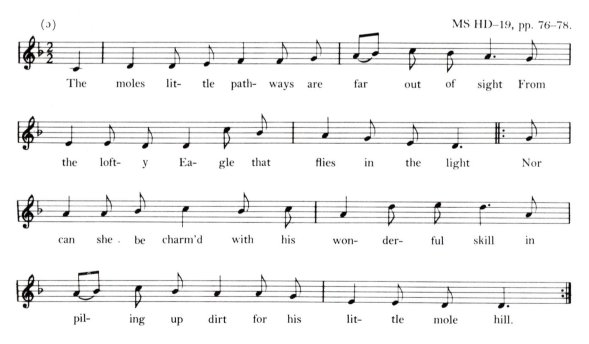

MS HD–19, pp. 76–78.

The moles lit-tle path-ways are far out of sight From the loft-y Ea-gle that flies in the light Nor can she be charm'd with his won-der-ful skill in pil-ing up dirt for his lit-tle mole hill.

2 A thousand reformers like so many moles,
   Have plow'd all the bible & cut it in holes
   And each has his church at the end of his trace
   Built up as he thinks of the subjects of grace

3 Through all their dark mole paths for more than
      ten years
   I sought for salvation with groaning & tears
   Their courses of duty did faithfully run
   But never could come to the light of the sun

4 At length I grew weary of such fruitless toil
  And pray'd for an earthquake to shake up the soil
  And God in his mercy did answer my prayer
  And let in more light than my vessel could bear

5 I look'd toward heaven & raised a shout
  And all that could hear it began to dig out
  The new light was precious & each that came in
  Cried Glory to God theres salvation from sin

6 The flaming scismatics a while did unite
  To tear down the mole hill & let in the light
  For this is the work of the light loving soul
  So long as its bound to the earth diging mole.

7 At length came the shakers to teach the new birth
  How souls might get loose from the moles of the
    earth
  They look'd like the Eagles that fly in the air
  And O how my spirit did long to be there

8 The last little mole hill that mortals have plan'd
  Is built of new christians but this cannot stand
  The name will not answer in this mighty shake
  Nor Christ spare the sinner just for his name sake

9 I know all the systems in antichrists plot
  And what the scismatics & christians have got
  Been born & converted & true to their cause
  Was never accused of a breach of their laws.

10 I've hear'd & believ'd what the gospel declares
   And strictly obey'd it for more than two years
   And yet you may see after all that is done
   My name is McNemar or nobody's son.

Ballad No. 3

NO ESCAPE FROM JUDGMENT

For this as for many other early song texts there are several tunes, the result of the words'
having been sent East by letter. The first tune printed here, which is kin to the old Scottish
melody "Ladie Cassilles Lilt" and to the Appalachian fiddle tune "Calico," is the one known
at Pleasant Hill and Union Village. The second tune, only distantly if at all related, was in use
by 1809 at Enfield, Connecticut, and Harvard.

Elder Issachar Bates wrote the song in the first flush of exhilaration as a successful missionary to the West. Stanzas three, four, and five allude to places in Kentucky, Ohio, and Indiana
where the Shakers won converts or opponents. Among the latter was Barton W. Stone of Cane
Ridge, one of the ministers who had joined with McNemar in setting up the schismatic Springfield Presbytery. He was soon to found the Christian Church. A country-bred evangelist like
Bates felt the full force of a phrase like "fisher of men." As Seth Wells wrote a Western leader,
if the catch is

> taken from the waters of trouble, and don't want to flounce back again before they
> are half scaled, (for there is but little danger after they are well scaled & gutted,)
> then I think you are in a very good work—It is an occupation of great antiquity,
> and very honorable, having been long ago followed by great and good men—tho'
> oftentimes attended with much trouble and affliction, and frequently with danger to
> the health and lives of the fishermen, especially in launching very far into the deep
> and grappling GREAT FISH, such as *whales*, *grampuses* and the like. But a good
> fisherman will never flinch from danger, not even in grappling a *whale*, tho' sharks &
> sea serpents should make their appearance & strive to thwart him & prevent his
> success. But in bobbing for trout or scooping for suckers or the like, in our small
> streams there is not much danger to be apprehended—and these, if well dressed,
> are very good fish in their place—But it frequently happens that even in our shallow
> waters there are many toad-fish, mud-turtles, bull-frogs & water-snakes & such like
> that sometimes give the fisherman much trouble—and I presume you find it so—
> But comparisons aside. The true work of God is, beyond all comparison, great
> and glorious—

A.

MS PH–4, pp. [23–28].

The proph- ets of old by the spir- it have fore- told Of a

time when the saints should be- gin The king- dom to pos-

sess and in truth and right- eous- ness Bring the world in- to

judg- ment for sin. And the na- tions should rise and the

judg- ment dis- pise And should gath- er a- round them to

fight But no weap- en they could form should pros- per in the

storm For the work should be out of their sight.

B.

MS EC–11, p. 218.

♩ = 113 (‖³)

2 This work it has begun And has gathered one
   by one
   Till Zion's foundation is laid
But fishers must be sent And hunters that can
   scent
   To their holes as the prophets have said
Tho' thousands of late Have lamented their state
   And prayed for the son to appear
Yet when he is revealed They lie closely
   concealed
   Or fly from his presence with fear.

3 God's fishers are come And the net has gather'd
   some
   While others escape in their sins
But his hunters are out And they'll chase them
   about
   While they cleave to their old heaven friends.
But tho' you should fly like a bird into the sky
   Or leap like a buck in affright
Tho' you hide like a fox In the holes of the rock,
   Your deeds you shall bring to the light.

4 Your mad river flight Has not been out of sight
   Nor your stantown battery of scorn
Your White Water Plot Will burn you so hot,
   You will wish you had never been born.
Your Springfield strong hold With her warriors
   so bold
   In the regions of darkness are cast
You may fortify Caneridge And lay Stone for
   your bridge
   But your mortar's untempered at last.

5 If Kentucky grows too hot You may hunt
   another spot
   For a season to cover your sins
But it is a poor relief To be running like a thief
   With a conscience tormented within.
You may go to the Wabash To find ease to the
   But Busrow is all in a flame   [flesh
You may flee to Elk or Duck Or tarry in
   Kentuck
   But the gospel will bring you to shame.

6 If you hide in Tennessee We shall find you
   where you be,
   For the Lord has a sacrifice there
And the shakers are not slack But as true upon
   As a hunter in chace of hare.   [the track
And tho' you should boast Of the strength of
   your host
   And forbid us to pass thro' your land
When once you get a sight Of a true Israelite
   Your spirit no longer can stand.

7 Tho' you dig into hell And say you're doing well
   The arrows of vengence are there
Tho' in Carmal you hide And have Baal on your
   side
   You just flee from a lion to a bear.
If to heaven you climb To find ease for a time
   From thence you shall surely be cast
And tho' you should flee To the bottom of the
   sea
   Theres a serpent shall bite you at last.

8 There is no other way Of escape in this day
   Where the gospel is open so clear
But to part with your lust And be honest and
   just
   And to such will the Savior appear.
But those that stand out will be driven about
   Till the saints in full order shall stand
Then the end will come about And transgressors
   And the meek shall inherit the land. [rooted out

9 The work has just begun And men begin to run
   To hide from the wrath of the Lamb.
But the work will still increase Till there will
   be not a place
   On the globe for a sinner to stand
Tho' the wicked scoff and say This can never be
   Tis a plan of the shakers tis clear   [the way
Well it is a shaker's plan But the shaker's not a
   But God the Eternal is here.   [man

10 Now my song I'll conclude Lest I'm judged to be rude
    In a fit of fanatic display
But it truly is not so For its not the half I know
    Of the end of the world in this day.
But now as I close One thing I'll purpose
    To the soul that salvation would find
No longer put your trust In a man that lives in lust
    For how can the blind lead the blind.

Ballad No. 4

A DIALOGUE BETWEEN JACOB & ESAU

Both the theme and the form of this song are rooted in the "doctrine of the two natures or two spirits held forth in the Kentucky Revival." Richard McNemar enumerates the figures in which the doctrine was symbolized: "As long as the world and the church exist we will have the old and New man, the first & second Adam, Cain and Abel, Esau & Jacob, Judas and Jesus, or in more intelligent terms, the temporal & spiritual gifts contending for the mastery." The song expresses the contrast with two voices and two well-chosen folk tunes, Jacob's having a close secular analogue in "Jock of Hazelgreen" and Esau's in "The Maid I Left Behind Me."

The song is probably considerably older than 1836, the date of the earlier of the two manuscripts in which it is found. Not only the theme but also the harshness of spirit exhibited by Jacob suggest the atmosphere of contention bred by the Kentucky revival. Shaker missionaries entering these fields found themselves bitterly attacked, as when "a great body of blazing hot Newlights" interrupted one of Elder Issachar Bates's addresses and, as he recorded, ordered him "back to hell from whence I came." The harshness was evident even within the newly formed Western Shaker societies. The following scene, for example, entitled in a South Union journal "Humbling of Doctors and Divines," would have been unthinkable at the time in the Eastern societies, or even in the West in later years:

> In the evening meeting Dr. Calvin Morrell & Rev. R. McNemar underwent the following: The Dr. was first laid on the floor & made to lick the dust & lie as one dead—putting dust on him thus settling the Doctors. They, the chief actors, David Carey & Saml Rollins, next went mockingly to R. McNemar, saying: How do you do Rev. Sir? This is the great Rev. Mr. McNemar, your vain philosophy and systems of divinity shall be brot down into the dust—they then brot him down & put his head with the Doctors & both their faces in the dust; then dragged him over the floor— rolled him over & over—S. Rollins kicked the dust over him—danced around him putting his foot on his head—D. Carey also put dust on him, in a sign of burying the Dr. & Divine—after this scene of mortification—the Rev. began to use scripture in his defence—They silenced him saying, "Not a word out of your mouth—you have explained away the sense of scripture long enough—your head knowledge, shall have an end—Not a sentence out of your mouth." & took him down & humbled him a second time—after this the sign of Esau & Jacob closed the scene.

> 1 Come all who hate old Esau & Jacobs cause defend
> See Jacobs faithful struggles on Esau dont depend
> Poor Esau's weak & feeble his armour & his shield
> Is sure to fall in battle and he will have to yield

MS PH–4, pp. [110–113].

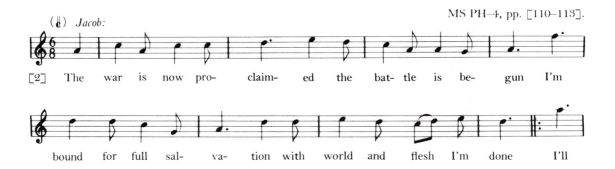

(𝄵) *Jacob:*

[2] The war is now pro- claim- ed the bat- tle is be- gun I'm

bound for full sal- va- tion with world and flesh I'm done I'll

keep you at a dis- tance to die it is your doom I'll

Esau:

nev- er shed a tear for you but lay you in the tomb [3] My

state is tru- ly aw- ful 'tis more than I can bear You

doom me to de- struc- tion I'm al- most in de- spair I

want to have sal- va- tion and go to heav- en too But

by your cru- el lan- guage my hopes you would un- do.

4 *Jacob*
Heaven is not intended for such a wretch as you
There is a place prepared for all old Adam's crew
I want none of your snuffles your talk will all be vain
I doom you to destruction with your old Brother Cain.

6 *Jacob*
Your race will soon be ended Salvation's not for you
For death it is your portion my strength I will renew
I'll slay you in the battle your torment I'll increase
Now give up for you're undone you never shall have peace.

8 *Jacob*
Pity is not intended for any of your race
Destruction is determined to meet you in the face
You need not plead your sorrow nor tell of my hard heart
I'm hard enough to tell you from me you shall depart.

5 *Esau*
O listen to my story and hear me plead my right
See what I've suffered with dont bring me to the light
I want to be concealed dont bring me to disgrace,
I want to have salvation when I have run my race.

7 *Esau*
You treat me more than cruel in anguish I lament
You will not have compassion altho' I do repent.
If I pour out my sorrow and tell you of my pain
I find you're so hard hearted your pity I cant gain

9 *Esau*
I'm troubled to the centre I wont consent to die
It looks like cruel murder you set me in a fry.
I have been your companion and led you at my will
And now you're so hard hearted my blood you want to spill.

10 *Jacob*
    Your blood it shall be spilled the least and last
        remains
    Now you may give the ghost up you surely
        shall be slain
    This is not all your portion to hell you've got
        to go
    With all your generation your doom'd to
        endless wo

11 *Esau*
    My troubles are enlarged forever I'm undone
    I'll plead no more for favor I'm done I'm done
        I'm done,
    I ask no more salvation I yield I yield I yield
    I'm sure to have damnation for I have left the
        field.

12 *Jacob*
    The battle is decided Old Esau's left the field
    No thanks for your surrender you was obliged
        to yield
    Now I'll go on to conquer dont think to rise
        again
    I have got on the armour and I intend to reign.

Ballad No. 5

THE SIXTEENTH DAY OF JANUARY

The temper of the men who established Shakerism in the Western lands is shown in this ballad by Elder Issachar Bates. In the summer of 1808 the missionaries returned to Ohio from Busro on the Wabash in Indiana Territory. They left behind them a community of seventy converts, but a "wicked set of priests," including the Methodist Peter Cartwright, began to prowl around the flock. By January it was clear that another visit was imperative despite flooding so severe that only the first thirty-five miles could be made on horseback. Three men—Bates himself, Elder Benjamin Youngs, and Richard McNemar—set out from Union Village and traveled westward for sixteen days the breadth of southern Indiana, a distance they estimated at 235 miles. Part of their route lay through pathless wilderness, part along the Vincennes road, which had been cut only the summer before. After leaving the settlement they passed only a few solitary cabins and three Indian encampments before they reached their friends. For much of their journey, and their return as well, they slogged across lowlands flooded with icy waters and poled themselves across rivers on old logs—but the ballad tells its own story.

Richard McNemar was apparently inured to frontier life, and Elder Issachar, a swarthy man of medium height, had "a firm close made body and a strong hardy constitution, well calculated in his physical make, to bear fatigue and hardship." The journey must have been hardest for Elder Benjamin, "apparently a delicate, as he was a small man" of "fine texture & rather feminine features."

The tune for the song was as common on the frontier as the hardships. It is related to ones used to tell of hard-hearted Barbara Allan and was widely sung as the shape-note hymn "Judgment." Later it was to be used for the spiritual "The Wayfaring Stranger."

MS EC–11, pp. 281–283.

The six-teen day of Jan-u-a-ry, Thru storm-y rains, thru ice and snow, From Tur-tle Creek we took our

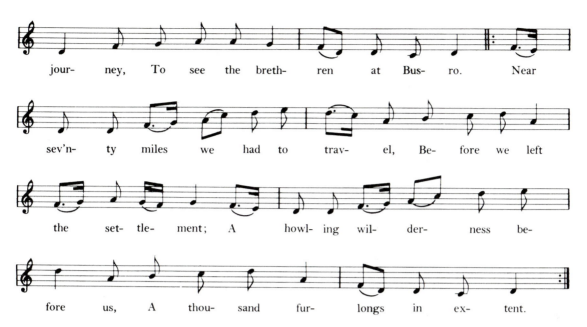

jour- ney, To see the breth- ren at Bus- ro. Near

sev'n- ty miles we had to trav- el, Be- fore we left

the set- tle- ment; A howl- ing wil- der- ness be-

fore us, A thou- sand fur- longs in ex- tent.

2 The way block'd up with floods of water;
  The land with ice was overlaid;
  On broken ice for miles we travel,
  And thru the chilling waters wade,
  On the third day, tho cold & stormy,
  It thunder'd, lighten'd, and it rain'd,
  Till by a foaming branch of Lockry
  One day and night we were detain'd.

3 Now here we left the last plantation,
  And pass'd the ground thus overflow'd,
  Prepar'd to tread the extensive desert,
  A new and unfrequented road:
  Each furnish'd with his staff & napsack,
  And some provision for the way,
  We ventur'd on, without conceiving
  What trials yet before us lay.

4 The heavy rains had loos'd the rivers,
  And set the ice all in a float.
  And tho we hop'd a raft would answer,
  In place of a canoe or boat,
  Yet bottom lands, for miles together,
  We knew were in one overflow
  With broken ice & floating timber,
  That there we knew not how to go.

5 Now for a sudden change of weather
  We pray'd upon our bended knees;
  That violent cold might fill the ether,
  And all these mighty waters freeze.
  The weather chang'd, the freeze commenced,
  And we desir'd it might not slack,
  Until it form'd a solid passage,
  Each side of the Muskaketac.

6 This low flat river at length obstructed,
  And mighty waters standing there,
  Six miles at least, all like an ocean,
  With ice too thin our weight to bear.
  By various means we sought a passage;
  But finding it could not be cross'd,
  In patient hope we there encamped,
  To wait the issue of the frost.

7 A while the country we explored,
  In hopes to find a passage round;
  And there a fox had kill'd a turkey,
  The leg and breast of which we found.
  These little fragments well dress'd and smoked,
  Did furnish one delicious meal;
  And for provision so unexpected,
  How glad and thankful did we feel!

8 Two days and nights we there remained,
  With hunger pinch'd, and freezing cold,
  While the majestic current flowed
  O'er all its banks so high & bold.
  On the third morn we ventur'd forward,
  However dang'rous it might seem;
  Wet to the loins, and in a snow storm,
  We built a raft, and cross'd the stream.

9 Six miles we trod the icy pavement,
  Like roaring thunder cracking round;
  And as the shades of night o'erspread us,
  We safely reach'd the solid ground.
  While frozen trees were loudly cracking,
  And whistling winds severely blow,
  Our most refreshing entertainment
  Was a good fire and melted snow.

10 This unknown flood we safely passed;
Yet still retain'd our former dread,
And we suppos'd the Muskaketac
Was at least ten miles ahead;
Till the next morning, a nob appeared,
Which show'd how far we had got along.
And on its top with joy we shouted,
And labor'd one thanksgiving song.

11 These nobs are high, the air most piercing,
And the north wind severely blows.
We ran and stamp'd till quite exhausted,
With swelled feet and frozen toes:
So swell'd and blister'd, so pinch'd and bruised,
We had to walk in our stocking soles,
Till two days travel thru snags and bushes,
Had worn them into fifty holes.

12 Our bed was brush; and in the morning
We strip'd, and bath'd in the cold snow.
We dress'd, and kneel'd, and ate our morsel;
And when we had prepar'd to go,
Our little comforts seem'd so endearing,
Tho joints were stiff and bellies lank,
We own'd kind Heaven's safe protection,
And kindly there each other thank.

13 The walnut, oak, and chesnut timber,
On ev'ry side the forest lin'd;
And tho their fruit we much desired,
No nut or acorn could we find.
Thus over hills and creeks and vallies
We marched thru the desert land,
Till early on the fourteenth morning,
White river brought us to a stand.

14 With floating ice the current rolled,
So that we knew not what to do,
Till far beyond our expectation,
We spied a house and good canoe,
A friendly hand convey'd us over,
With cold benum'd, with hunger faint;
And the refreshment we there received,
The strongest language cannot paint.

15 Now with renewed animation
The hopeful journey we pursue,
Till the next fork of the same river,
On the next morning, came in view.
There twenty furlongs of ice and water
Were mingling in one great uproar;
But being set across the current,
We forc'd our passage to the shore.

16 Our greatest suff'rings now were over,
And ev'ry danger left behind;
Scarce thirty miles remain'd to travel,
Where entertainment we could find.
Our weary limbs renew'd their vigor,
Until we reach'd the Busro soil;
And the kind welcome we received,
Made rich amends for all our toil.

Ballad No. 6

WE'VE SEEN SOME OLD BELIEVERS

The Eastern Shaker societies, which endured bitter poverty in their first decade or two, had attained by 1805 a degree of comfort that seemed remarkable to the converts on the Ohio frontier. One of these, John Wallace, was sent on a mission to Lebanon about the year 1808 and recorded his impressions of its order and abundance in the lengthy ballad that follows. John Wallace had been gathered to the faith in 1805 at the age of twenty-six. He was made a trustee at Union Village, but a passion for travel and money drew him from union. In 1818 he apostasized and began a career of harrassment of the Believers. His progress in these activities is shown in the series of journal entries transcribed below:

February 25, 1814—John Wallace returns from a long wandering trip.
February 1, 1818—John Wallace returns home from Dayton with a large black horse!!
February 14, 1818—John Wallace left home, under pretext of going to Columbus, to settle some business respecting Benjamin Cox's land; but turned his course to Cincinnati; and on the 16th he borrowed $3000 out of the United States'

Bank, for 60 days & signed the note Wallace & Sharpe; & left the Chh. the debt to pay & cleared out.

February 22, 1832—John Wallace, & a company of his fellow apostates, take possession of our Gristmill this evening, and try to hold possession, but were all dislodged. John presented the Brethren to the Grand-jury for dislodgment from the mill; but no bill was found.

Text: OCWR, SM276, pp. 42–50.
Tune: MS EC–11, p. 217.

2 The streams that comes from Zion My soul
   has often feed
Which gave me great desier To see the
   fountain head
At length on last December To Lebanon I
   steard
The 28th of the same month The lovely place
   appear'd

3 What feelings were excited As I approach'd
   the town
What scenes I recollected Transacted on the
   ground
While ore the vales and mountains My anxious
   eyes were cast
What objects were presented The present and
   the past

4 There Elder James and William With Mother
   at their head
Did blow the gospel trumpet And wak'd the
   sleeping dead
Here living crouds have started Up from old
   Adams fall
While the old earth and heavens Were burning
   like a scroll

5 Twas here that Father Joseph And Mother
   first believ'd
And here our Elder Brethren The holy Ghost
   receiv'd
And with our Elder Sisters All labor'd night
   and day
Preparing for to show us The true and living
   way

6 I cant express my feeling While thus I pass'd
   along
But now I am call'd to enter And meet the
   shining throng
At every recollection It fills me with amaze
To think what I discover'd In sixteen happy
   days

7 At Lebanon and hancock And lovely Watervliet
I pass'd thro rooms and chambers Thro every
   lane and street
While every lovely object Both outward and
   within
All testified together Here is no room for sin

8 The blessed love and union That flow'd in
        every face
   Proclaimed thro all my senses The Lord is in
        this place
   But nothing struck my passions With so sub-
        lime a sense
   To see the old believers Move in the solemn
        dance

9 Grave as the host of heaven They tim'd the
        solemn song
   And not one jaring motion In all the united
        throng
   The scene surpass'd discription And truly I can
        say
   I never saw such glory Displayed in human clay

10 The solemn house of worship Did not contain
        the whole
   Theres glory for the body As well as for the
        soul
   Their stores of food and raiment They did not
        all unfold
   But such is the abundance The half cannot be
        told

11 Their universal order Appeard a perfect charm
   Both in the house and garden The work-shop
        and the farm
   In pastures too and stables Some glory I could
        trace
   Where each inferior creature Was happy in its
        place

12 Here every upright feeling Must meet with
        pure delight
   Heres perfect entertainment For hearing and
        for sight
   In all that happy region Where the believers
        dwell
   Theres nothing offensive To either taste or
        smell

13 Upon their love and union I feasted every day
   But what a store they gave me Just as I came
        away
   If their eternal treasure I only could unfold
   You'd say it was more precious Than bags
        of purest gold

14 So many ardent wishes I never can relate
   Were breath'd from every quarter To the
        Ohio State
   And all their love and union They charged me
        to bear
   And give to Elder David and all thats in his
        care

15 From Mother and the Elders From brethren
        old and young
   From all the lovely sisters The salutation rung
   My love to Elder David My love to Eldress
        Ruth
   And to all good believers That will obey the
        truth

16 That zeal for gospel purity Can never be
        express'd
   That burns thro all Mount Zion And flows
        towards the west
   Then in this stream of glory With Turtle
        Creek in view
   I clos'd this heavenly vision And bid them all
        adieu

SECOND PART

17 Then what is all my journey A vision at the
        best
   The east affords the vision Our work is in the
        west
   The call is not from Zion You all may come
        and see
   But every old believer Says rise and follow me

18 They did their work in season Where they
        reciev'd the call
   Nor slack'd till they had finished Their part of
        Zion wall
   Our work is here before us That we are call'd
        to do
   Then let us all be faithful And we'll have Zion
        too

Ballad No. 7

SAMUEL HOOSER'S HYMN

A ballad, "The Famous Flower of Serving-Men," provided the tune for this account of Samuel Hooser's conversion, and a letter sent to the Lebanon Ministry from Union Village in 1808 rounds out his story:

> In the Month of January we were visited by one Samuel Hooser a Methodist preacher from Kentucky, he had lately moved from N. Carolina where he had heard many frightful reports respecting the believers in these parts: he opened his mind and went away very strong and zealous. He appears to be a man of talents, and one, who, if he abides faithful, may be proffitable to himself and others. While he tarried here he composed the following Hymn for the purpose of sending it in a letter to his brother, another Methodist preacher in N. C. . . .

> A few days after Hooser went from here another Methodist preacher attended our meeting and hearing the . . . song sung in publick received such a wound as will never be healed but by obeying the truth. He came again in a few days to enquire further into these things, and received full satisfaction: and went away with a feeling to sell all his land and property where he lives and to come & obey the Gospel.

Samuel Hooser too returned, and abided faithful. Among Believers he continued to serve more or less as a "public Minister . . . with singular ability, till the day of his death" in 1854.

Text: MS PH–1, pp. 25–26.
Tune: MS EC–11, p. 217.

I of- ten heard of Shak- ers while in my na- tive land That they were a de- lud- ed a blind be- witch- ed band Such aw- ful news was spread- ing, too hor- rid to re- late How wick- ed they were act- ing in the O- hi- o State

2 At length I went amongst them to see how they
went on
I quickly was convinced that those reports were
wrong.
I found they were a people such as I'd never
seen
So bright so pure so holy so much opposed to
sin.

3 I often heard of Zion but now I've found the
place
The City that's adorned with truth and love and
grace
My heart was struck with wonder to find such
glory there
Where all was peace and glory without a
single jar.

4 I found I'd got to Zion where saints and angels
   dwelt
  Such piercing streams of glory my heart had
   never felt
  This is no place of darkness but one eternal day
  Here doubts and fears are banish'd and satan
   cannot stay

6 Here is the holy fire that burns all sin and
   shame
  The guilty sons of babel cannot endure the
   flame
  I'll shout eternal praises to Jacobs awful King
  That I have found such glory as saves the soul
   from sin.

8 Salvation here is flowing from sin and dross
   refign'd
  I'm willing here to tarry and leave my lust
   behind
  I feel my soul united to this despised flock
  Let death and hell [oppose] us we are safe
   upon the rock.

10 Sweet union here is rolling all thro' this happy
   place
  Here flows the crystal fountain and God unveils
   his face
  Fair lillies here are growing that never fade nor
   die
  No other ground produces such fruits of peace
   and joy

5 I cried adieu to pleasure of every other kind
  I'll give up all my Idols and leave the world
   behind.
  I found the blessed people with whom I'll bear
   the cross
  And count all earthly glory but vanity and
   dross.

7 O why was I so stupid to stay away so long
  And labor in confusion with babel's mixed
   throng
  But since I've found the city where God in
   glory reigns
  I'll bid adieu to Sodom and all its dismal plains.

9 Though persecution rages we'll boldly shout
   and sing
  We shall be safely guarded by Salem's
   conquering King,
  Amidst all tribulation we feel our love increase
  Altho' the world doth hate us in Zion we have
   peace.

11 How blessed are the people who are admitted in
  And dwell secure in Zion delivered from all sin
  Their joys are still increasing their songs are
   always new
  They love their great Creator and all their
   brethren too.

PART V

Hymns

When Western hymns began to reach the East, the societies there were ripe for them. Certainly Elder Issachar was not the only Easterner who had tried his hand at versifying before becoming a Believer. At Alfred, Elder Elisha Pote had already written a hymn by the year 1804.[1] But hymns were rarely used in services, and it was the circulation of songs from the West that "awakened the muse" in the older communities. At Lebanon hymns were first sung in union meetings in 1805, and the next year in worship.[2] Within two years other societies were both singing hymns and producing them. They began to "come so plenty"—one man at Enfield, Connecticut, composed five in fifteen days[3]—that by 1810 scribes could not make enough copies for use, and the Society undertook to print copies on loose leaves.[4] One hundred forty of the texts were selected for book publication in 1813 under the title *Millennial Praises*.

The word hymn was applied by Shakers to any of their songs having more than one stanza sung to a recurrent melody. Russel Haskell for this reason put "The Sixteenth Day of January," a ballad, in the hymn section of his manuscript. The exclusion of narrative songs from *Millennial Praises*, however, shows that a stricter interpretation limited the term to songs of two or more stanzas appropriate for use in services.

In some ways the hymns were ill suited for Shaker worship and could contribute little to its momentum. They were long, often having ten to fifteen stanzas, with the second half of each stanza sung two times. In practice the singing tended to "run down" during hymns.[5] A hymnal brought to meeting not only weighed down the spirit with the letter, but also became an encumbrance during the laboring exercises. To overcome these problems the elders posted or announced in advance the choice of hymns for the week's services.[6] Members were expected to refresh their memories before the meetings. Normally only a hymn or two would be used in a service. One was usually sung at the beginning, before the spirit of the service had warmed, and sometimes another closed the meeting. The function of the hymn was thus to provide a bridge between the common reality and the quickened life at the heart of the service and to focus the Believers' thoughts on some doctrine or duty.

An increased concern with doctrine is one explanation for the burst of Shaker hymn writing in the first two decades of the nineteenth century. The missionaries to the West had found a need for a systematic and thorough statement of Shaker beliefs, and at Union Village in the summer of 1806 Benjamin S. Youngs and David Darrow began to draft one. The Society published it two years later as *Testimonies of Christ's Second Appearing*. Other leaders back East carried this labor further, issuing a revised edition in 1810. By the summer of 1808 those like Calvin Green who served as speakers began to expound the doctrines for the first time in the public meetings. Their statements were new to the World and "mostly new" even to Believers, who found this presentation of the Gospel "clearer than they ever heard before, & were much edified."[7] Though the authorship of most of the hymns in *Millennial Praises* is unknown, Eastern leaders such as Calvin Green probably had a large role in their composition,[8] for many of the pieces are versified statements of the newly clarified doctrines.

For their verse models the hymn writers turned chiefly to eighteenth-century hymnody as practiced by the Wesleys and Isaac Watts. Mother Ann herself had once declared, "Dr. Watts is now in heaven!"[9] Many of the early Shakers doubtless shared the conviction and knew, even if they did not sing, his verses. Their hymns were often more blunt than those of the English divine, but as the following specimen shows, they often employed his manner:

1 Are these O God, the living stones?
  And is the place thy pure abode?
  Do these support thy holy Throne?
  Is this thy sacred house, O God?
  "These are," saith God, "the living stones;
  This is my holy house indeed;
  These Pillars do uphold my Throne;
  These are the woman's faithful seed.

2 Here does my Church, my Temple rest;
  This is the New Jerusalem;
  Here's mine anointed with their guests;
  My name is glorified in them.
  Thus saith the King, the Lord Most High
  In her I'll make my glory known
  For as the apple of mine eye
  I value my beloved One

3 She is a signet on my hand,
  Sealed on the table of my heart,
  Firm as the hills & mountains stand;
  My love from her shall not depart,
  I've placed my love upon this house
  That on my holy mountain stands
  She's like a youthful virgin spouse,
  Joined by an everlasting band."

4 What perfect beauty do I see
  What glory in this spacious room
  The Spirit & the Bride agree
  To call the thirsty stranger home.
  O Heaven raise your joyful voice
  Let all created substance join
  Mount Zion is Jehovah's choice,
  His glory makes her summit shine.

This hymn, like many by Isaac Watts and Charles Wesley, begins with an interrogative. It is shot through with archaisms and with Latinate diction. The lines are locked tight in an *a b a b c d c d* rhyme pattern. The feet march relentlessly in iambic tetrameter. Watts's verse technique weighs upon this hymn even though its author, Eunice Wyeth of Harvard, did not deliberately compose her hymns but *saw* the written texts in visions. "Living Stones" itself accompanied a vision in which she beheld

> the appearance of a large room, ceiled with beautiful colored wood, of very curious workmanship. The plates for the second story, or chamber, seemed to rest on women's heads, as close together as they could stand. Only their heads & tops of their shoulders were visible. The rest of their bodies seemed hid within the ceiling. All were young & very beautiful. Their caps & linnen were exceeding white, & their complexion & features of every one looked exactly alike.[10]

Whether "receiving" his verses or consciously composing them, the Shaker created his hymn by a process quite different from that of the nonliterate traditional singer. The Tennesse farmer Joseph Able Trivett, for example, said of his own ballads,

> I'd be maybe out in the mountains by myself a-digging ginseng. Just a-
> prowling around, knocking the weeds down, watching on one side for a rattle-
> snake and on the other side for a bunch of 'sang. This stuff'd get on my mind
> and I'd just keep *humming away* [italics mine] on it till after a while I'd have
> a song made out of it.[11]

In other words, when he made his ballad "The Rolling Store" about a comic neighborhood incident, he took the tune of "The Farmer's Curst Wife" and put new words
to it, humming and singing them until they fit smoothly.

The Shaker hymnodist often composed his verses without any thought of a melody.
Many times he afterwards took his poem to some more musical member of the community, asking for a tune. Thus Eunice Wyeth's hymns have tunes provided by Eunice
Bathrick or by Thomas Hammond. Susannie Brady gave Ezra Leggeth a melody for
his "Star of Purity." One Shaker letter even tells how Genny Badgett, an eighteen-
year-old sister, and a "goodly young man" named Maurice Thomas received the
text and the tune of a hymn in separate gifts. Genny had returned one night from a
meeting in which she was "taken under greate opperations of the power of God." When
she sat down in her room, she suddenly saw a vision:[12]

> an Elder Sister appeared to her, and sung the first virce of a hymn, several
> times over, and Genny sung with her; then the E. sister said to her, that is
> a good work to be in, and you must be faithful and prove it.—the next
> morning, She appeared to her again, and larnt her the other two virces. and
> She saw a large number of people, both Brethren and Sisters all standing in
> order, and the E. Sister standing between them: She then said to Genny,
> have them virces drawn off by the middle of the day, and give them to Maurice,
> for he has got the song for them; Genny felt some doubtful, whether he would
> have the song or not. the E. Sister then spoke very sharp to her, and repeated
> it again several times to her, to give them to Maurice, for he had the same
> song, that she had learnt to her.—Then the E. Sister repeated these words
> over three times, "It is mine, and it is thine." then the whole Assembly united
> with her, and sung it, timeing with their hands, & feet.—So accordingly she
> gave the Hymn to Maurice, and he had the same song; when Genny come to
> hear him sing the song, just as she had learn't it in her vision, and knowing
> that he never had learnt it, from any one in the body she burst into tears.

The Shaker hymns, then, were in most ways unlike folk song. Even the verses received
in visions usually had a literary model instead of being shaped to fit a tune. Scribes
quickly fixed them in writing. They customarily voice the doctrinal interests of the
Shaker leaders.

The only music that the Shakers knew, however, was traditional, and for their
hymns they plundered balladry. In consequence their hymnals are treasuries of strong
and beautiful melodies. Paradoxically, patterning their verse on literary models forced
the Shakers at times to deal creatively with the tunes they borrowed. Like other early
American authors of "folk hymns," they might discover they had composed verses
in a stanza form that no tune known to them would fit. The writers were then

compelled to trim or piece out some of the phrases of a traditional tune. This is one
explanation for the fact observed by Bronson, that the tunes of folk hymns and spirituals
do not necessarily come in "direct line of descent from the ballads" but instead take
"somewhat different" and "slightly more complex patterns."[13]

An example, a tune that drifted through the secular, shape-note, and Shaker repertories, will illustrate this cause of melodic variation. Under the title "Royal Proclamation" this tune appeared in a number of shape-note collections, the first, according
to George P. Jackson, being Ananias Davisson's *Supplement to the Kentucky Harmony*
in 1820:[14]

Jackson felt this tune had "all the earmarks of an eighteenth-century fife-and-drum-
corps tune"; I think it derived from a ballad-tune complex that includes "The Lowlands
of Holland" and "Rose Connoley"—and thus that it is related to the Shaker hymn
tunes for "The Humble Heart," "Samuel Hooser's Hymn," and "The Precious Jewel."
The "earmark" of either a fife-and-drum tune or the melody of such ballads as these,
however, is that it is composed of four long phrases of equal length. A stanza composed to fit this tune structure is a quatrain of fourteeners or an octave of alternating
four- and three-stress lines. Davisson—or his source—had a stanza of six and a half
lines and tailored a folk tune to fit it.

Once this new tune floated into oral tradition, other hymn writers might compose
new texts specifically for it. Shaker manuscripts in fact hold a hymn entitled "Glorious
Day" composed around 1853 for a variant of Davisson's tune:

MS UV–10, pp. 87–88.

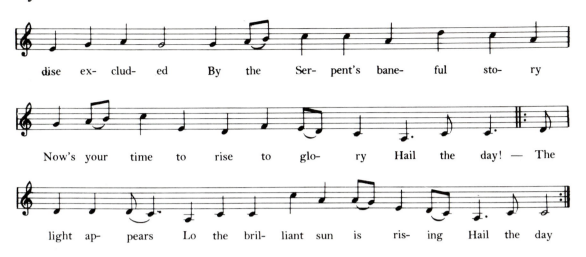

dise ex- clud- ed   By   the   Ser- pent's bane- ful   sto-   ry

Now's your   time   to   rise   to   glo-   ry   Hail   the   day! —   The

light ap-   pears   Lo   the   bril- liant   sun   is   ris- ing   Hail   the   day

Such a tune could also apparently breed further experimentation with both verse form
and melodic structure. Some twenty years before the composition of "Glorious Day"
another Shaker adapted a form of this melody closely resembling "The Lowlands of
Holland" to an octave stanza closing with four alternating tetrameter and dimeter
lines:

MS XU–40, pp. [14–15].

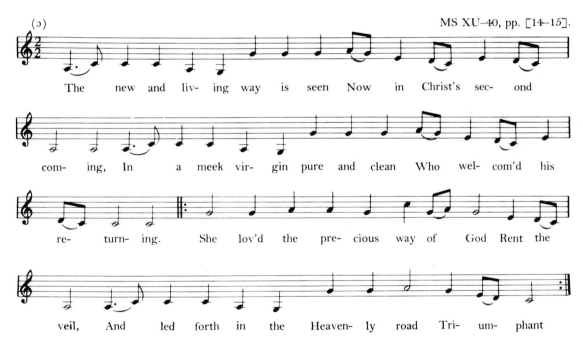

The   new   and   liv- ing   way   is   seen   Now   in   Christ's   sec-   ond

com- ing,   In   a   meek vir- gin pure and clean Who wel- com'd his

re-   turn- ing.   She lov'd   the   pre- cious way   of   God   Rent the

veil,   And   led   forth   in   the   Heaven- ly   road   Tri-   um-   phant

Even stripped of text and recast as a laboring tune this new melodic idea could maintain
a recognizable identity. In 1846 it appeared in a Shaker manuscript as a wordless
march with an eight-bar turn section and a set strain only six bars long:

MS WNY–29, p. [128].

A different manner of tailoring ballad-tune material to fit a nontraditional verse form can be seen in a hymn composed about 1845 by James McNemar of Union Village. For his text he chose an octave stanza suitable for use with a ballad tune, but wrote in pentameter lines. Another singer might simply have adapted the text to the tune, treating it as accentual verse with four-stress lines. James, however, took another course. He had in mind a tune that must have resembled, at least in its opening half, the following one collected in the 1930s with a text of the ballad "The Two Brothers":[15]

To make his tune fit his five-stress lines, James simply stretched the musical phrases with additional beats:

MS UV–12, pp. 37–41.

(‖)

I did set out while in my youth and prime

The way of ev-er-last-ing life to learn

For-sak-ing all the tran-sient joys of time

And heaven-ly things to la-bor to dis-cern

Tho there were paths which to my out-ward mind

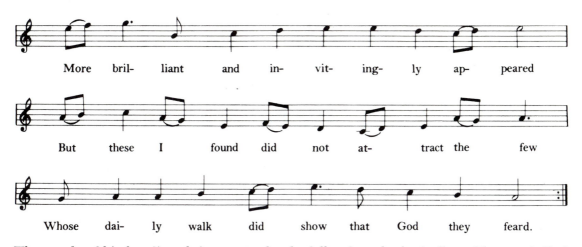

More bril- liant and in- vit- ing- ly ap- peared

But these I found did not at- tract the few

Whose dai- ly walk did show that God they feard.

The result of his handiwork is a tune clearly folky, but rhythmically unlike any ballad tune.

While a fair number of such anomalous tunes and stanzas are sprinkled through the Shaker hymn collections, most Shaker hymn tunes conform to the model of certain handsome tunes associated with broadside balladry. In American folk song the sixteen-bar long-phrase broadside tunes frequently have an ABBA structure in which the identical first and fourth phrases have a lower range than that of the identical second and third phrases. These rather dull tunes consort with "Come All Ye" texts brought by Irish immigrants in the middle of the nineteenth century. These singers carried the infestation into the Northern lumber camps, but not into the Shaker Zion. The tune pattern is rare in Shaker song.

The Shaker long-phrase hymn tunes generally derive instead from an earlier ballad-tune model in which only the third phrase ranges high:

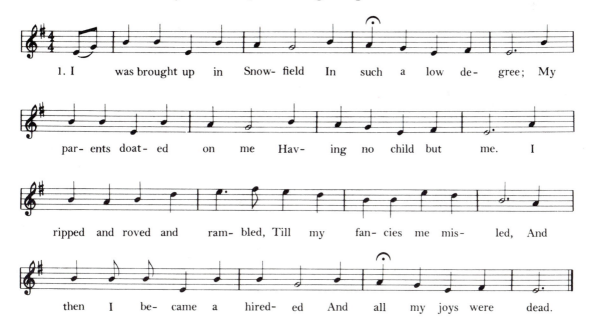

1. I was brought up in Snow- field In such a low de- gree; My

par- ents doat- ed on me Hav- ing no child but me. I

ripped and roved and ram- bled, Till my fan- cies me mis- led, And

then I be- came a hired- ed And all my joys were dead.

As this Appalachian variant of "The Sheffield Apprentice"[16] shows, the second tune model can result in an AABA pattern even more monotonous than that of the "Come

All Ye." By exploiting one peculiarity of the long-phrase melodies, however, the Shakers gave their tunes remarkable variety.

Although a traditional singer normally renders a long phrase in a single breath, the phrases actually are composed of two units of equal length. The dividing point in the melody is signaled by accent, pitch, and duration of certain notes, and also by syntactic units in the text. The entire musical phrase stands usually in exact alignment with a complete sentence of the text, but the caesura separates smaller grammatical units, setting off a prepositional or participial phrase, a dependent clause, or a predicate. In a Shaker hymn the half-phrase units, not the entire long phrases, form the building blocks of the melody. Most Shaker hymn tunes employ them in a much more subtle balancing of variation against repetition than "The Sheffield Apprentice" exhibits. The following Shaker hymn melody,[17] for example, might best be described as having the pattern *ab cd ef a^1d^1*:

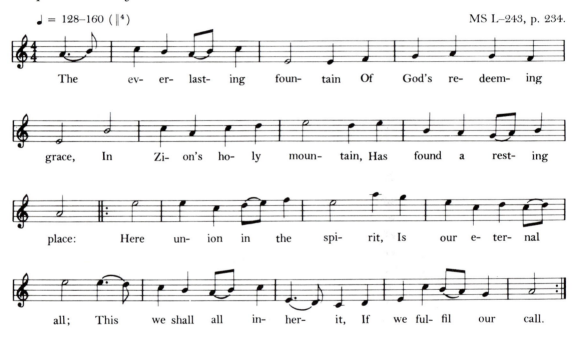

A random sample of sixty early hymn tunes taken from Haskell's collection exhibits twenty-four different arrangements of these half-phrase units, no one of the patterns predominant. In a few cases, as below, the units do not even fuse into long phrases, but form a tune of eight short phrases:[18]

He leads us to the foun- tain Where liv- ing wa- ters flow;

And we will drink our fill At the foun- tain where we go.

Lacking any accurate and extensive early record of secular folk singing, we cannot know whether the Shakers varied their long-phrase structures more creatively than ballad singers of their day. Shaker musicians did in any case record their melodies in forms demonstrably more interesting than those printed in the American nineteenth-century shape-note song books. The editors of these collections, needing to keep their printing costs low, frequently put three-part settings of two different tunes on a single oblong page. To accomplish this, they often distilled related phrases into a single form, cultivating repeat signs rather than subtle melodic variations. The Shakers succumbed to the influence of print when they wrote the words of their hymns, but in setting down their music they remained, to the very limit of their skill, faithful to traditional song.

Hymn No. 1

VOYAGE TO CANAAN

This hymn is one of the few that the Shakers shared with other denominations. The tune (a variant of "You Gentlemen of England") and four stanzas are still printed in the 1971 edition of *The Original Sacred Harp*, currently the most popular of the Southern shape-note songbooks. The hymn seems to have entered the shape-note tradition in 1835 through William Walker's *The Southern Harmony*. Walker had taken the words from the *Dover Selection*, where they are attributed to I. Neighbours. The text is virtually the same, however, as that printed in 1813 in the Shakers' first hymnal, *Millennial Praises*, except that stanzas four and five are—with some injury to the logic—reversed. Walker's tune is also close to the Shaker one, known at Enfield, Connecticut, by about 1810. It is likely, therefore, that the song originated among the Shakers and that Susan C. Liddil is correct when she names Richard McNemar as the author. In the period when the Western Shaker communities were forming, the Shakers had more contact with other denominations than they were ever again to have except for tentative encounters with the Adventists in the 1840s. An exchange of songs took place each time.

Text: *Millennial Praises*, pp. 26–27.
Tune: MS EC–11, p. 221.

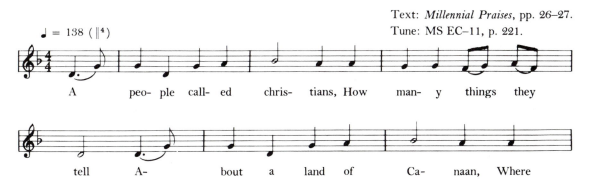

A peo- ple call- ed chris- tians, How man- y things they

tell A- bout a land of Ca- naan, Where

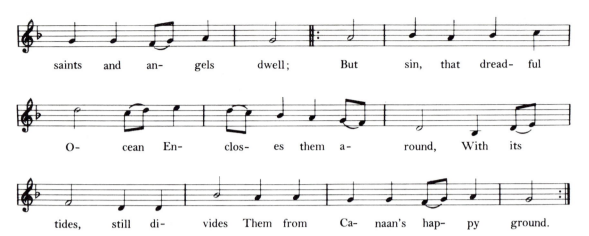

saints and an- gels dwell; But sin, that dread- ful

O- cean En- clos- es them a- round, With its

tides, still di- vides Them from Ca- naan's hap- py ground.

2 Thousands have been impatient
  To find a passage through,
And with united wisdom,
  Have try'd what they could do;
But vessels built by human skill,
  Have never sailed far,
Till we found them aground,
  On some dreadful sandy bar.

3 The everlasting gospel
  Has launch'd the deep at last;
Behold her sails extended
  Around the tow'ring mast!
Along the deck in order,
  The joyful sailors stand,
Crying, O! Here we go,
  To Emmanuel's happy land!

4 To those who stand spectators,
  What anguish must ensue,
To have their old companions
  Bid them a last adieu!
The pleasures of your paradise
  No longer can invite;
Here we sail, you may rail,
  But we'll soon be out of sight.

5 We're now on the wide ocean,
  We've bid the world farewell,
And where we shall cast anchor,
  No human tongue can tell:
About our future destiny,
  There need be no debate,
While we ride on the tide,
  With our captain and his mate.

6 The passengers united
  In order peace and love;
The wind all in our favour,
  How sweetly we do move!
Let tempests now assail us,
  And raging billows roar,
We will sweep thro' the deep,
  Till we reach the blessed shore.

Hymn No. 2

THE LIVING VINE

This hymn was composed by the year 1808, probably at Lebanon. The compilers of *Millennial Praises* did not choose to print the text, but its length, Biblical allusions, doctrinal message, and polemical tone make this a typical early Shaker hymn. It was moreover the first to use one of the Believers' favorite images, the vine. The melody—a variant of "The Braes of Yarrow"— is less characteristic, for only a fourth of the Shaker hymns are set to short-phrase ballad tunes. A later singer taking it for his Extra Song "Eternal Life" would lengthen the melody with a second strain, in keeping with Shaker preferences.

Text: DWt, SA1107, no. 19.
Tune: MS EC-11, p. 217.

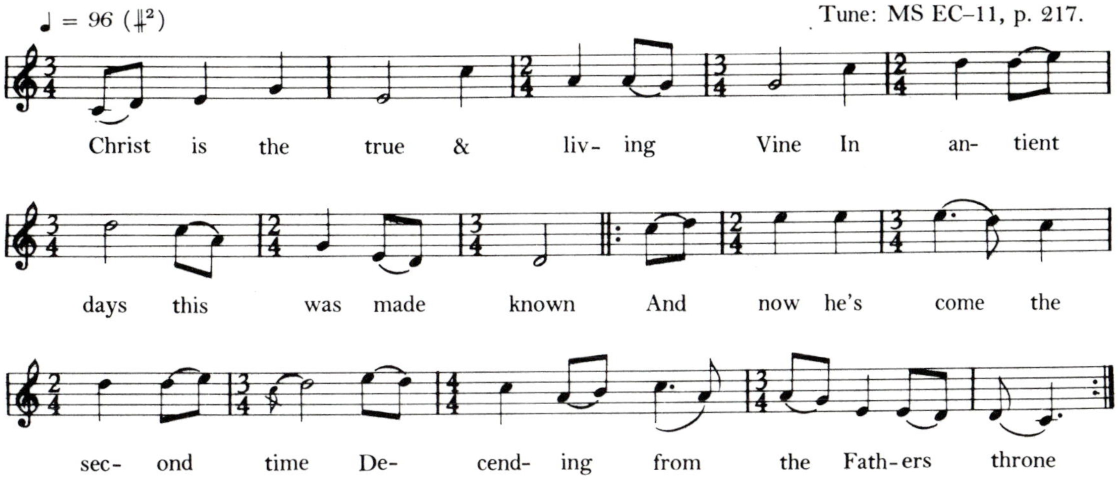
♩ = 96
Christ is the true & liv- ing Vine In an- tient
days this was made known And now he's come the
sec- ond time De- cend- ing from the Fath-ers throne

2 He first appeared in the male
There did Imman'els Glory shine
His second coming in Female
Is still the true and living Vine

3 This Beautiful and bearing Vine
Now flourishing on Zions hill
Is cultur'd by a hand devine
Whose Blessings on it do distill

4 Like gentle dews from heaven they fall
Upon the true and living Vine
Which makes true branches great & small
In harmony and beauty shine

5 This wonderful Almighty hand
Does prune the Vine from day to day
Adornd with fruit live branches stand
But wither'd ones he takes away.

6 The vine does spread far East & West
And yet the fruit is all the same
With which the upright Soul is blest
While sinners scorn the lowly name

7 The living Vine we know is good
We judge it by its precious fruit
The true Believers only food
That will his weary Soul recruit

8 Regenerating Souls they are
Thats joind unto the living Vine
Of them the Father does take care
And in his love they do combine

9 And those indeed who thus combine
Their faith will ever stedfast prove
In Christ the true and living Vine
The Vine of everlasting love

10 They are most blind who will not see
In scenes of sorrow they'll repine
While Souls in Gospel Liberty
Rejoice in Christ the living Vine

11 The vine does spread & spread it will
In vain does satans pow'r withstand
Thus Saith the Lord vain man be still
My Gospel shall go through the Land

12 And when the Gospel has gone thro'
And geather'd all true branches in
Amazing horror will persue
Souls thats left out all bound in sin

Hymn No. 3

SPIRITUAL RELATION

Abijah Worster, to whom manuscripts attribute this hymn, was a brother of marked character who had served as a fifer during the Revolution. One Shaker tradition says that he was wealthy and had been the captain of a whaler. He was born in the town of Harvard, Massachusetts, in 1745, and early launched himself into the religious currents that swirled in that time and place. His testimony says that at first he was so bold and confident in the Calvinist doctrine of imputed righteousness as to say "I would not accept of salvation in any other line. But wo to me, if God had taken me at my word!" He also maintained "that horrid and blasphemous doctrine of election and reprobation" but was never fully reconciled to it. Yet the "comfort and consolation" these beliefs brought him would at times leave him "like the morning cloud." He could find among the Presbyterians nothing but "leanness and barrenness," so he left them for the Baptists. They had a "degree of life and zeal, and a measure of love and union," but before long began to "settle down into a lifeless formality." Next he was swept into the wake of Shadrack Ireland, a New Light who prophesied his own resurrection three days after his death. Weeks after the failure of this prophesy, the melancholy duty of burying the man fell to Abijah. He says,

> after all my labor and tribulation in passing through these different denominations,
> like Noah's dove, I found no rest for the sole of my foot; and for a number of months,
> I was like a lone creature in the earth, not knowing a single soul on earth with whom I
> could unite in christian fellowship.

But he believed the day of redemption was at hand, and when Ann Lee entered New England, Abijah was convinced that this new day was revealed through her. He was one of the covenanting members when the Church was first gathered at Harvard. He was such an "incessant hard worker" for the Society that Father William worried that Abijah "might break down under the strain of his work and regret his liberality." Father William said to him, "Abijah, do you think that you can work as you now do through all your life and spend your strength and means for others. And when you have done it in most cases you will not be thanked for it." "Yea, Father," he replied, "I can endure all things for Mother's sake and the increase of the way of God revealed through her."

Text: MS HD–8, pp. 4–8.
Tune: MS EC–11, p. 215.

Not all the gar- dens here on earth, With eve- ry fra- grant
flow- er Such beau- ty shows as Shar- ons Rose That blooms in
Zi- ons tow- er The val- ley's lil- ly is com- bind To
feast each kind sen- sa- tion, And brings unto the labor- ing mind A spir- i- tual Re- la- tion.

2 With all our powers we'll sing the praise
  Of Judah's holy Lion;
  His power protects & still displays
  To shield the Mount of Zion.
  'Tis guarded with a Jasper wall,
  'Tis Angels admiration,
  To see poor souls raised from the fall,
  To Spiritual Relation.

3 How vain are all things here on earth!
  They're like the twinkling taper!
  They either languish in the birth
  Or vanish like a vapor.
  Let all the earth their joys resound
  In highest declamation,
  There are no comforts that are found
  Like Spiritual Relation.

4 Nothing on earth so meek & mild,
  Although so much a stranger;
  It personates the Virgin Child
  That slept in Bethlehem's manger.
  'Tis fill'd with purity and love,
  And every kind sensation;
  'Tis chaste as is the turtle Dove,
  'Tis Spiritual Relation.

5 There's nothing found in fleshly ways
  Nor natures path so flowery,
  That brings the soul such joyful days,
  Or yields so rich a dowery.
  Huge mounts of gold are but as dross,
  In Wisdom's estimation,
  To what we find who bear the cross
  In Spiritual Relation.

6 Since mercy hath our souls retrieved
  From the infernal Lion;
  We'll be no more by him deceived,
  We'll take the way to Zion.
  Sodom and Egypt we'll forsake,
  And Babylon's sensation;
  Our crosses we will joyful take,
  For Spiritual Relation.

7 The bands that male & female bind,
  Lead souls to desolation;
  Dividing joys distract the mind,
  And end in desparation.
  Male & female like one are known,
  In this blest restoration;
  Brethren & Sisters make but one,
  In Spiritual Relation.

8 Since God hath call'd us by the light,
  To this blest resurrection;
  We'll follow on with all our might
  Until we reach perfection.
  And when we quit this earthly stage
  And reach our destination
  We'll praise the Lamb thro' endless age,
  For Spiritual Relation.

Hymn No. 4

TRUTH

"The words of this hymn," says a note in the one manuscript preserving it, "were composed by Abijah Wooster, in the church at Harvard, as early as in the year 1807, and probably not earlier." Only one stanza is recorded, but there were probably many more, expressive of Abijah's strong convictions. These sometimes led him to lose his charity. He confessed that once when he met Ann Lee and the elders on the road to Harvard and went up to their sleigh, Mother Ann rebuked him, saying,

Abijah, you must not speak in hard, irritating language to the world; They are poor blind souls, and you should feel compassion for them; God has had compassion on you, & called you from among them, and you should feel a tender benevolence towards them, and labor to gather their feelings to the way of God. They are poor blind souls, groping along in death, and know not where they are going, and must all perish, if they are not saved by this gospel.

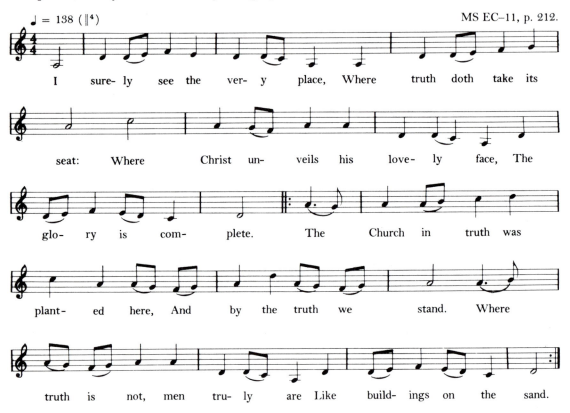

♩ = 138 (‖⁴)   MS EC–11, p. 212.

I sure-ly see the ver-y place, Where truth doth take its

seat: Where Christ un- veils his love- ly face, The

glo- ry is com- plete. The Church in truth was

plant- ed here, And by the truth we stand. Where

truth is not, men tru- ly are Like build- ings on the sand.

Hymn No. 5

THE HEAVENLY BRIDEGROOM AND BRIDE

The heightened imagery of this hymn is thoroughly characteristic of its author, Richard McNemar. Susan C. Liddil, on whose word this attribution is made, was awed by his forcefulness and appearance. She recalled him "in the form of the strong man he was" when she entered Union Village, a girl of ten. "To me," she said, "he looked tall, but he was hardly six feet in height . . . more spare than fleshy, but not showing bony in face nor form. His shoulders were square." She described him as having eyebrows "long and wider than usually seen, but not overhanging his eyes," a nose "long slim and somewhat Roman," and a chin "full and prominent" with "beard black and heavy but kept cleanly shaved." His lips were tightly closed and thin, but "ever wore a pleasing expression, though seldom diffusing noticeable smiles. And who ever heard him explode a loud laugh." At the first church meeting she attended he stepped out to speak, and

> his magnetic eloquence swayed and animated the audience by its power as I could see while I trembled under its *greatness*, as it felt to me. And I looked with wonder on his tall erect form, his hair black and strong as an Indians, forehead high and white, a raised vein along the center brought to the surface of the skin by the warming force of his testimony, large full eyes "blue as a Southern sky," which seemed to draw . . . the electric currents from the very heavens above.

Text: *Millennial Praises*, pp. 17–20.
Tune: MS PH–1, pp. 28–29.

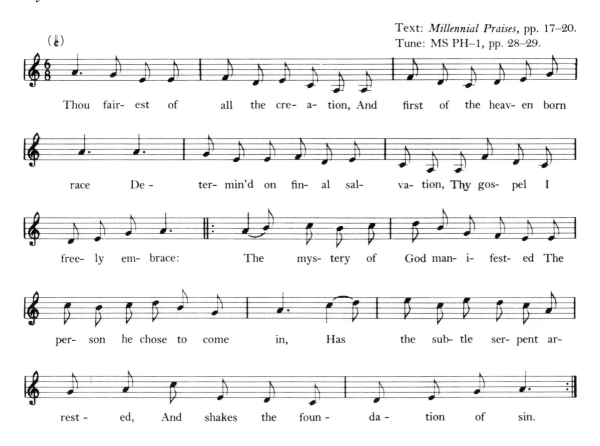

Thou fair- est of all the cre- a- tion, And first of the heav- en born race De- ter- min'd on fin- al sal- va- tion, Thy gos- pel I free- ly em- brace: The mys- tery of God man- i- fest- ed The per- son he chose to come in, Has the sub- tle ser- pent ar- rest- ed, And shakes the foun- da- tion of sin.

2 The mystery has long been concealed,
  Till wisdom unfolded the plan,
  And Christ in one part was revealed,
  And dwelt in a sin-hating man;
  His person was then a vexation,
  But O, how the wicked will rail,
  To see his last manifestation
  In female as well as in male!

3 The pride of all flesh must be stained,
  And satan no longer shall reign,
  Since Christ has a helper obtained,
  And God has united the twain:
  The types and the shadows are ended,
  The substance no longer we hide;
  For God from the first has intended
  A heavenly Bridegroom and Bride.

4 The law was by Moses engraved
  On two precious tables of stone,
  To shew that mankind must be saved
  By two dispensations in one:
  Two cherubs stood facing each other,
  This type was ordained until
  Our heavenly Father and Mother
  That same blessed law should fulfil.

5 Two lions so artfully raised,
  Stood facing king Solomon's throne,
  No wonder the world were amazed,
  The like in no kingdom was known:
  This ivory throne was erected
  On two mighty pillars and stays;
  How then could the Lord be expected
  For judgment in these latter days?

6 Tho' two rows of oxen were carved
  Around the bright laver of brass,
  The substance was never observed
  Until it came fully to pass:
  Of oxen and lions and pillars,
  The meaning no soul ever knew,
  Until we beheld the fulfillers,
  E'en Christ manifested in two.

7 The two olive trees we might mention,
  By good Zechariah once seen:
  Pray what was the Spirit's intention?
  And what could these olive trees mean?
  And who were the two that bore witness,
  In the revelation to John?
  Pray do they not show us the fitness
  Of male and the female in one?

8 Now Christ is reveal'd in the woman,
   And makes her as pure as the light;
   This sets the old serpent a foaming,
   But let him come on to the fight;
   We know he is justly alarmed,
   If only the scripture he'll read,
   He'll see that his doom is determin'd,
   His head must be bruis'd by her seed!

9 Ye rebels, who hate one another,
   With your vain objections begone!
   I know that my Father and Mother
   Are perfectly joined in one:
   The wicked may say I'm deceived,
   And not fit to live on the earth;
   But she that my soul has conceived,
   Will carry me safe thro' the birth.

10 Of Mother I am not ashamed,
   You may call her just what you please,
   My soul with her wine is inflamed,
   I now have it fresh from the Lees:
   Her wine is the life of my spirit,
   'Tis love well refin'd from all lust;
   But serpents who know not its merit,
   May take their contemptible dust.

Hymn No. 6

CHRIST & HEROD

Susan Liddil says that Richard McNemar composed this hymn on August 26, 1810, the day before the "great mob" of five hundred armed men marched on Union Village demanding that the Shakers release children they had allegedly imprisoned, abandon their beliefs and practices, and depart from the country. Similar scenes recurred at Union Village as late as 1824. On one such occasion Richard (who had taken the spiritual name of Eleazer Wright)

> quelled a furious wicked mob of three or four hundred men, by preaching poetry
> to them for two hours, from the house top of the old centre house, where he and a
> young brother were painting the eave troughs of the house. The young brother
> with him was the object of the mob. Some of his deluded kindred outside thought
> him too talented and "beautiful to look upon" to be a Shaker, & came to force him
> away, although his parents were living in the house with him, and he himself was
> perfectly satisfied. Eleazer bethought himself of the strategy . . . to give the young
> brother a chance to make good his escape unnoticed, by calling their attention to a
> peal of poetic scripture, an easy success for him as his voice was loud, clear and elec-
> tric, and he continued in his loud poetic stream until one after another, alighted from
> his horse, hitched it and came inside the gate, and sat down on the grassy sod to
> listen to him, and thus they continued, until the whole mob were seated in the door-
> yard listening to him and were so charmed and surprised at his genius, that they
> all became good humored and returned home peaceably.

Text: *Millennial Praises*, pp. 206–207.
Tune: MS L–136, p. 17.

The name of Her- od sig- ni- fies *The glo- ry of the skin;*

But Christ th'a- noint- ed pu- ri- fies The liv- ing soul from sin.

Thus Christ and Her- od plain- ly clash, And differ- ent points up-

hold; The one con- tend- ing for the flesh, The oth- er for the soul.

2 The fray with Christ did first commence,
About old Herod's wife;
"Depart, (say they,) and get thee hence,
"Or he will take thy life."
The Baptist had already fell
Beneath his fatal blow;
But all his threats could not compel
The Nazarene to go.

3 His answer was, "Go tell that fox,
That I have cures to do,
And I shall keep my present walks,
Till I have travel'd through;
My work on earth shall not be void,
But I shall reign within,
When gnawing worms shall have destroy'd
The glory of the skin."

4 This subtle fox, now grey with age,
Continues his command,
And threatens us with cruel rage,
Unless we quit the land;
But tho' in number, we are few,
We mean to turn the chase;
For God has many cures to do,
Among the fallen race.

5 He has salvation to present,
To all the souls of men;
And if the fox don't love the scent,
He's welcome to his den;
But if his rage should fly abroad,
And hunters get the smell,
Those civil pow'rs ordain'd of God,
Will chase him into hell.

6 The life of Christ we will adore,
And live as we are taught,
Tho' Herod with his men of war,
Should set the truth at naught;
We'll travel on in peace and love,
And keep our souls from sin,
And seek a glory far above
The glory of the skin.

Hymn No. 7

RIGHTS OF CONSCIENCE

In this hymn Issachar Bates sings the praises of George Washington to a fife tune called "The President's March," but his verses reveal mixed feelings toward even that "prudent man of blood." Similar ambivalence runs through all the Shakers' relations with the secular arm. They were thankful for freedom of worship, and many like Bates, who had been a fifer boy at the Battle of Bunker Hill, had helped to fight for it, yet they would not again serve in the American army. They declined to accept their military pensions from the Revolutionary War—and petitioned for relief from fines imposed when the brethren did not attend musters. They abstained from voting, but scrupulously observed any day of Thanksgiving or commemoration proclaimed by a president. They wished to give Caesar his due, but never when this would transgress the bounds of a truer liberty or higher union.

Text: *Millennial Praises*, pp. 281–285.
Tune: MS EC–11, p. 221.

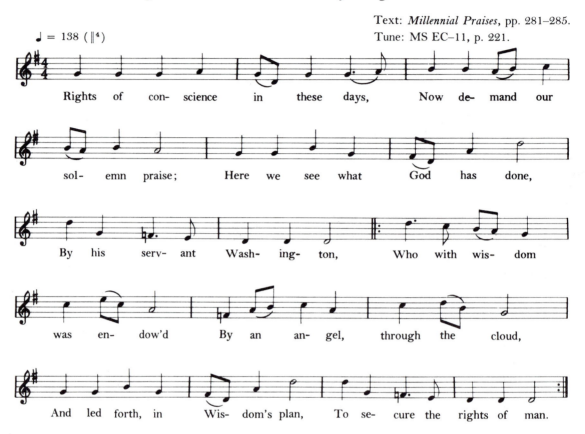

Rights of con- science in these days, Now de- mand our sol- emn praise; Here we see what God has done, By his serv- ant Wash- ing- ton, Who with wis- dom was en- dow'd By an an- gel, through the cloud, And led forth, in Wis- dom's plan, To se- cure the rights of man.

2 "Arm yourselves, unsheath the sword!
(Cries this servant of the Lord,)
Rights of freedom we'll maintain,
And our independence gain."
Fleets and armies he withstood,
In the strength of Jehu's God;
Proud Cornwallis and Burgoyne,
With their armies soon resign.

3 Thus the valiant conqu'ror stood
To defend his country's good,
Till a treaty he confirms,
Settling peace on his own terms.
Having clos'd these warlike scenes,
Chosen men he then convenes;
These a constitution plan'd,
To protect this ransom'd land.

4 Prince of all the host he stands,
Keeps the helm in his own hands,
Till a law stands to declare,
Bind the conscience if you dare!
Then he spreads the eagle's wings
(Signs of freedom) on all things,
Form'd an order to his mind,
Blest the earth and then resign'd.

5 When by precept he had shown
What kind heaven had made known,
By example aids the cause,
Forms his own domestic laws,
Breaks the yoke at his own door,
Clothes the naked, feeds the poor,
Bondage from his house he hurl'd,
Freed his slaves and left the world.

6 Cyrus-like, was Washington
Call'd to do what he has done;
We his noble acts record,
Tho' he did not know the Lord:
As a prudent man of blood,
He the hosts of earth withstood;
Nature's rights he did restore,
God from him requir'd no more.

7 Now we'll swell the joyful news,
With the glory that ensues;
God, thro' Christ, did then begin
To attack the man of sin;
By a woman struck the blow,
Broke the battle and the bow,
And in flaming fire reveal'd
What the beast had long conceal'd.

8 Carnal swords are laid aside,
  Every fleshly lust deny'd;
  Each one seeks his neighbour's good,
  No more shed each other's blood.
  Let the eyes of priests and kings
  View the eagle's spreading wings;
  These are to the woman given,
  Guard the place where she is driven.

9 Now the dragon's host may rage,
  His black bands of priests engage;
  While of freedom still he raves,
  All his subjects are his slaves;
  As his messengers, they rise,
  Forge and spread his sland'rous lies,
  Spew at us his foaming flood;
  Yet they dare not spill our blood.

10 Mighty Christians, stout and bold!
   Full of lust as you can hold,
   Fighting for religious rights!
   God has notic'd all such fights;
   Still your souls are not releas'd,
   Bound by sin and wicked priests:
   Tho' your country has been sav'd,
   You in bondage are enslav'd.

11 With all this you're not content;
   Still on bondage you are bent,
   Binding the poor negro too,
   He must be a slave to you!
   Yet of Washington you boast,
   Spread his fame thro' every coast,
   Bury him with great ado,
   Precepts and examples too!

12 Did you think in seventy five,
   When the states were all alive,
   When they did for freedom sue,
   God was deaf and blind like you?
   You were fighting on one side,
   To build up your lust and pride;
   God was bringing in a plan,
   To defeat the pride of man.

13 Liberty is but a sound,
   If the conscience still is bound;
   Could you but her reigns controul,
   You would creed-bind every soul.
   You, and when we say 'tis *you*,
   We've no respect to Greek or Jew;
   But boldly tell you that we mean,
   Your vile *Church* that lives in sin.

14 Now we mean to let you know,
   We've not treated freedom so;
   Since God's Kingdom has come in,
   We find freedom from all sin.
   O, ye priest-bound souls, come out!
   Help us raise the living shout;
   Never heed your former stuff,
   You have prov'd it long enough.

15 See the woman's seed advance,
   Glor'ous in Emmanuel's dance!
   At this strange victor'ous play,
   Earth and heavens flee away:
   Swift as light'ning see them move,
   Labouring in unfeigned love:
   God, thro' Mother we adore,
   Hate the flesh and sin no more.

Hymn No. 8

THE EARTHQUAKE

Susan C. Liddil of Union Village recorded a story about the origin of this hymn:

Sister Clarrissa Patterson tells me this morning March 12th 1877 that the following hymn was composed by elder Daniel Mosely in the year 1811 during a time of earthquake shocks which greatly alarmed him and moved by the impulse of fear or by the power of Inspiration more likely, he went to each family in the village singing his song and preaching in accordance with the views which his lines illustrate. Sister Clarrissa says that she was a child in the childrens order then and was in the room with her caretaker and the girls when the first shock of Earthquake came which frightened her caretaker thinking it was the boys out at play prying up the side of the house (hewed log set on stones at the corners) flying and throwing up one window after another and crying out "Boys what are you about there," meanwhile the childrens knitting baskets hanging on pegs in the beams over head were all on a violent swing and every door in the house opened. The fowls were shaken from their roosts and went sqwacking from place to place trying to hide themselves under woodpiles and elsewhere.

Elder Daniel was born at Norwich, Connecticut, in 1760 and received the gospel from Mother Ann herself. He called himself "God's Battle Ax," and others said of him, "What Elder Daniel Moseley did he did with his might." In addition to doing "much good to other souls," he worked for many years as a blacksmith. In 1805 he was sent from Lebanon to "assist in planting the gospel in the West" and labored there for seven years. Susan Liddil said that more anecdotes were told of him and more of his sayings remembered than of any other Eastern missionary except Issachar Bates. It would seem, she wrote, "that he had retained something of the boy, the big hearted, good hearted boy, ever ready and feeling himself sufficient for any undertaking to oblige and help along, either in a temporal or a spiritual direction."

A Sacred Repository of Anthems and Hymns, p. 14.

Lift your heads, ye once af-flict-ed! Let your eyes with joy be-hold,

What the proph-ets long pre-dict-ed, What the Song of God fore-told.

Now Je-ho-vah fills his tem-ple, Thence his glo-ry shines a-broad;

There his saints with rev'-rence trem-ble And con-fess that he is God.

2 Sacrifices of thanksgiving,
  To his courts they daily bring;
  Songs of joy among the living,
  Make his sacred temple ring.
  Through the ranks of vast creation,
  Nothing can be deaf or dumb,
  All must give their approbation,
  That the day of God is come.

4 While the judgment is advancing,
  Satan's kingdom to destroy,
  Fields and forests fall to dancing,
  Dwelling houses crack for joy;
  Rivers heave and swell like Jordan,
  Water fowls ascend the air;
  Soon this earth shall loose her burden,
  All creation does declare.

3 While his last loud call he utters,
  Nature can no more be still;
  All creation moves and flutters,
  In obedience to his will.
  When his power is to be proved,
  To convince the stupid soul,
  If he says, "O earth, be moved!"
  Lo, it rocks from pole to pole!

5 God will shake this old creation,
  Rocks and mountains overturn,
  Fill the world with consternation,
  Till the way of truth they learn.
  Those who will not be restored,
  Sink to their respective hells;
  But our God shall be adored,
  In his temple where he dwells.

Hymn No. 9

SPIRITUAL WINE

For this hymn Issachar Bates borrowed—and improved—the tune of an elegant song entitled "The Death of General Wolfe," and his refrain probably echoes that of the more plebeian ditty, "The Miller of Dee." A more important source of inspiration was Acts 1:13, to which his opening stanza alludes. This "new wine" of the Pentecost was long a theme for Shaker songs, but Issachar and others were at times uneasy lest their words be misunderstood. In the year of his death Issachar wrote, "I have never made use of any kind of spirits since I confessed my sins, for any other purpose than meaning it for my health. And I never drank a teaspoonful of raw spirits since the day I confessed my sins."

Elder Issachar may also have been defending himself against charges an apostate named John Woods made against his sobriety in a book called *Shakerism Unmasked*. Woods, who had been assigned to run the village distillery, carried a ten-gallon keg of his product to the ministry's shop. There, he says, it was "kindly received" by Bates and put away to mellow till they had used what they had on hand. The "good old Apostle" shocked sober young John by quipping, "John, this will give you a good chunk of union."

In 1828, two years after the book appeared, the Lebanon ministry sent all societies a statement on the use of alcohol:

> Old believers & young believers—*Ministry—Elders—Deacons*—Brethren & Sisters of every Society—Every family, every individual everywhere— . . . Ardent Spirits by any name—Whisky, Gin, Rum, Brandy, etc. are never more to be used by Believers—neither in the house nor out of the house—nor in the shops, nor in the fields, nor in Harvests, nor clearings, nor grubbings, nor House Raisings nor corn Huskings—neither in hot weather nor cold weather, neither in the water nor out—neither wet nor dry at home nor abroad, under any kind of exercise nor any occasion.

The new position implies that even the self-denying Shaker laboring man had earlier seen no harm in a moderate use of liquor for the health's sake. John Woods was probably less responsible for the letter than a changing national attitude toward drink.

Text: *Millennial Praises*, pp. 36–38.
Tune: MS EC–11, p. 225.

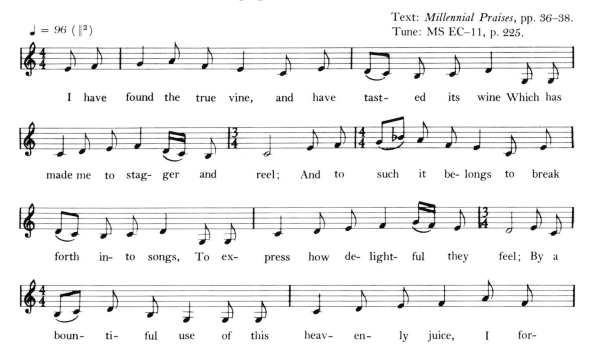

I have found the true vine, and have tast- ed its wine Which has made me to stag- ger and reel; And to such it be- longs to break forth in- to songs, To ex- press how de- light- ful they feel; By a boun- ti- ful use of this heav- en- ly juice, I for-

get all my sor- rows and woes; Give me plen- ty of this, I want

no oth- er bliss, And I care not much how the world goes goes

goes, And I care not much how the world goes.

2 I have shed many tears, and been harrass'd with
      fears,
   Lest the judgments of God should roll in,
   And this vain wicked world into ruin be hurl'd,
   For their horrid advances in sin;
   But let judgments come on, all my terror is gone,
   Since the pure gospel Church has arose;
   In her bosom I see, there's a mansion for me,
   And I care not much how the world goes———

4 Since my sins I confess'd, some are greatly
      distress'd,
   And lament how deluded I be;
   But at every fresh draught, I have heartily
      laugh'd,
   At their crocodile weeping for me.
   In my free happy choice, I can daily rejoice
   In this blest holy way that I've chose;
   If they will not pursue, I shall bid them adieu,
   And I care not much how the world goes———

6 Of their honors, I own, I desire to have none,
   For their titles are only a lie;
   When the bishop and squire are brought into
      the fire,
   They'll not be a whit greater than I:
   I should then be a fool if I wanted to rule,
   In a kingdom so near to a close;
   From such honor I fly, and myself I deny,
   And I care not much how the world goes———

3 I have settl'd my score with the beast & the
      whore
   And from them I have nothing to crave,
   And of all I possess, in my spirit'al dress,
   There is nothing the wicked will have;
   Then as we come out square, I'm releas'd from
      all care,
   And no matter how many oppose,
   I shall go on my way, and the gospel obey,
   And I care not much how the world goes———

5 All the pleasures they boast are but bubbles at
      most,
   And by heaven were never design'd,
   In their bondage to hold an enlightened soul,
   Or an honest believer to bind.
   As the mighty and rich have to fall in the ditch,
   Then let me have my victuals and clothes,
   And I ask not a cent, but shall still be content,
   And I care not much how the world goes———

7 To promote Adam's seed, for the flesh they may
      plead;
   But when they have said all that they can,
   As a true gospel heir, my full cross I will bear,
   And I'll put off the cursed old man:
   He may plead that he's bound to replenish the
      ground,
   But his lusts are his motive, he knows,
   Then I gladly retreat from this sink of deceit,
   And I care not much how the world goes———

8 With the saints I unite, and will do what is right,
   From the pure obligation of love,
   Till I've serv'd out my day, and put off this old
      clay
   To be cloth'd with my house from above:
   Then believe it or not, I shall stand in my lot,
   Where the fountain eternally flows,
   And I'll drink what I please, well refin'd on the
      lees
   And I'll care not much how the world goes———

Hymn No. 10

THE EXCELLENT GIFT

A song writer in England probably invented this melody by tailoring that of "Muirland Willie" to fit an untraditional six-line stanza. Set adrift in oral tradition, the tune would inspire many a new song text—in England "Jockie to the Fair" and in New England the hymn "Hope," in Jeremiah Ingalls' *Christian Harmony* of 1805. Some Shaker, most likely an Eastern leader, also fashioned this metrical paraphrase of 1 Cor. 15 expressly to fit the tune. The year was 1811 or 1812. At this time the book of Revelation was a more customary source of inspiration for Shaker hymns, and doctrinal apology their usual theme. "The Excellent Gift," however, draws closer to what most Believers would always seek in the faith.

Text: *Millennial Praises*, pp. 201–203.
Tune: MS EC–11, p. 229.

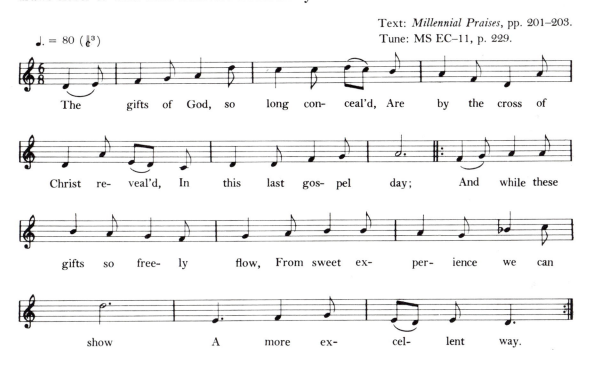

The gifts of God, so long con- ceal'd, Are by the cross of
Christ re- veal'd, In this last gos- pel day; And while these
gifts so free- ly flow, From sweet ex- per- ience we can
show A more ex- cel- lent way.

2 Tho' I could speak all human tongues,
  And those of the angelic throngs,
    And heaven and earth compass,
  Without the gift of charity,
  A tinkling cymbal I should be,
    Or like the sounding brass.

3 Tho' future things I could foretell,
  And understand all myst'ries well,
    And of deep knowledge boast;
  And tho' my faith could mountains move,
  Without the precious gift of love,
    All other gifts are lost.

4 Tho all my goods I should bestow,
  And to the stake a martyr go,
    It would no blessing prove;
  My works can no acceptance find,
  Unless they're of that noble kind,
    That flows from heavenly love.

5 Love suffers long, is kind to all,
  And envies not the great nor small,
    Nor will she vaunt herself;
  Unseemly she will not behave,
  Nor her own ways will strive to have,
    She seeks no sordid pelf.

6 Not soon provok'd, she thinks no ill,
  But in the truth rejoices still,
    Tho' satan's legions rail:
  She bears all things and standeth sure,
  Hopes and believes, and will endure,
    When other gifts all fail.

7 Tongues and the like are for a sign,
  And tho such gifts awhile may shine,
    They must at length decrease;
  But perfect love is come again,
  And on the earth shall ever reign,
    In righteousness and peace.

8 Great signs and wonders, we are told,
    Were given to the saints of old;
        But justly we reply,
    They ate their manna and are dead;
    But Lord, give us this living bread,
        And we shall never die.

Hymn No. 11

FLESH AND BLOOD CANNOT INHERIT
THE KINGDOM OF GOD

Susan Liddil says that Richard McNemar wrote this paraphrase of Eccles. 12:1–7. His text was published in *Millennial Praises*, and when singers in the far-flung branches of the Church could not learn the proper tune for a hymn like this from some traveling brother or sister, they had to supply their own. This was doubtless a matter of regret to all lovers of gospel union, but it left us with three good tunes for "Flesh and Blood Cannot Inherit the Kingdom of God." The first is attributed to Asa Tiffany of Enfield, Connecticut. The other two come from a manuscript that Isaac Youngs wrote at Lebanon. We have no record of Richard's own tune.

A.

Text: *Millennial Praises*, pp. 255–256.
Tune: MS EC–11, p. 251.

In vain we call on flesh and blood, To think on our Cre-
a- tor God, He nev- er rais'd his thoughts so high, But like a
beast does live and die. He nev- er did God's law o- bey, But
went his own self- pleas- ing way, And his mean pas- sions,
wrong or right, Were still the source of his de- light.

B.

MS L–136, p. 19.

C.

MS L–136, p. 19.

3 Yet has this beastly nature stole
   God's gracious promise to the soul,
   And fondly hopes, tho' he decay,
   To rise again at the last day.

4 But now the proper heir appears,
   And now begins his awful fears;
   His evil days come hast'ning on,
   And he must say, My joys are gone.

5 One cheerful smile he cannot raise,
   He has no pleasure in his days;
   His moon and stars, his light and sun,
   Have their contracted circles run.

6 The keepers of his house do shake,
   His strong men all their posts forsake;
   How dismal dark his windows grow!
   His grinding sounds exceeding low.

7 Afraid of that which is on high,
   His old desires must fail and die;
   Nor can his best musicians charm,
   Or drive away his dread alarm.

8 His silver cords are growing slack,
   His golden bowl begins to crack,
   His broken pitcher will not hold,
   His wheel is now exceeding old.

9 The spirit now to God returns,
   And he with disappointment burns;
   His suit has fail'd—he's lost the cause,
   And back he goes to where he was.

10 To his long home he must retreat,
   His mourners now may walk the street;
   Since God has settled up the score,
   The poor old man returns no more.

Hymn No. 12

THE TRUE BELIEVER'S TREASURE

The expressions of trust and conviction in this song were not empty rhetoric. Particularly in the West the Shakers had need of faith in a sure foundation. On May 11th, 1812—about the year when this hymn was composed—Father David Darrow wrote a grave letter from Union Village describing the "tormenting fear & restless anxiety" roused in the minds of the settlers by the Indian warfare:

the week before last—a few miles above us—a family were kill'd—& the house burnt down—last week a house opposite to us—on the other side of the river was plundered & burnt down—

the whole country in general are collected into forts—many families have left the country altogether & are gone—the governor & a number of the first characters have sent their families to Kentucky for refuge—The whole country is up in arms— we see none passing or repasing but such as are equipt for war—we Expect every day when a drafft will take place—& every believer capable of bearing arms will be called on to go—we are already find five hundred dollars. for last falls delinquency— the officer has allready been round demanding the money. if it is not paid the next time he comes—an Execution will be isued against any delinquent—in order to make sale of their property—

the legislature passed an act last sesion—to exonerate us from attending musters— by every man's paying five dollars per anum—yet it subjects us to stand our draft— & pay such fines as the court marshall shall levy on us—for our noncomplience with their fighting law—our situation in these respects is truly distressing—for from whence shall we get money to sattisfy so many demands—we have it not—they must take our property while we have any—until they get satisfied—or there is no more—for we are determined to live keep & obey our faith—let the consequencies be as they may—our greatest concern is, for some of the young believers—if it should be the case that the Indians should come in among us & commit any depredations— & the believers thereby be Influenced to act in contradiction to their own faith— & bring reproach on the Gospel—

Many cruel & bitter threats are thrown out against us by the world—such as this—they swear if we do not fort—& the indians do not kill us, they will—again they say—they will now show us indian play—

But in none of these things we feel mooved—being confident we are followers of that which is good—& who shall harm us—

Text: *Millennial Praises*, pp. 199–201.
Tune: MS EC–11, p. 252.

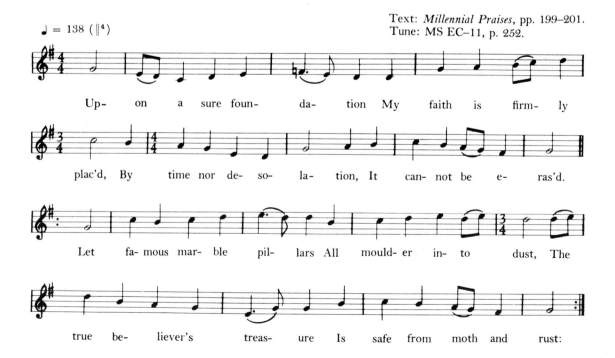

Up- on a sure foun- da- tion My faith is firm- ly plac'd, By time nor de- so- la- tion, It can- not be e- ras'd.

Let fa- mous mar- ble pil- lars All mould- er in- to dust, The

true be- liever's treas- ure Is safe from moth and rust:

2 With faith more firm and stable
  Than a stupendous mount,
  No human skill is able
  Its value to recount:
  The earth may reel and totter,
  And mountains pass away,
  The true believer's treasure,
  It never can decay.

3 The former earth and heavens
  No longer can abide;
  Behold the new is given,
  Adorned like a bride:
  This is our Father's pleasure,
  Then fear not, little flock,
  The true believer's treasure
  Is founded on a rock.

4 This is the new creation,
  The Kingdom of the Son,
  Whose subjects in relation,
  Are firmly join'd in one:
  The Spirit without measure,
  Our God does freely give,
  The true believer's treasure,
  Which causes souls to live.

5 Christ's marriage is performed,
  The Bride is pure and clean,
  The virgin guests adorned,
  And purify'd from sin.
  According to their measure,
  In union with the Bride,
  The true believer's treasure
  Forever will abide.

6 Christ comes in all his glory,
  God's promise to fulfil;
  His foll'wers must be holy,
  And do their Master's will,
  Forsake all carnal pleasure,
  And live upright and pure;
  The true believers treasure
  Forever will endure.

7 The sacred hosts of heaven
  Are in one union join'd,
  To whom all power is given,
  The man of sin to bind;
  His works we quit forever,
  Christ's Kingdom to obtain;
  The true believers treasure,
  Is holy pure and clean.

8 The greatest bliss and pleasure,
  That feeds a carnal mind,
  Is quickly gone forever,
  And leaves a sting behind;
  Then I'll pursue with pleasure,
  In union with the wise,
  The true believer's treasure,
  The pearl of greatest price.

Hymn No. 13

THE SOLDIERS OF CHRIST

Evangelical Protestants of nineteenth-century America were soldiers of the Church Militant, and this Shaker hymn rings with their martial spirit. But the song is also a distinctively Shaker expression of that spirit. Other denominations waged warfare not only against Satan but also against each other. A great champion like the Methodist circuit rider Peter Cartwright was as likely to boast of bodies saved from total immersion as about souls won from Hell, and after each skirmish he counted up his captives. The Shakers also mounted an occasional attack, but usually only after a likely convert had come scouting on Shaker ground. When Joseph Adams, for example, came to visit a friend living at Lebanon, Calvin Green "clearly saw that he was providentially called to the Gospel" and "determined to have him, for he was of the right sort." After Joseph had begun to think himself "about proof against Shakerism," Calvin delivered in public meeting an address "adapted to his state." The next day he followed this with an "arrowlike question." By this time Joseph "felt so worked" that he answered, "I see what you are at—I rather see a man with a pistol pointed at my breast than to see you." From that moment Green felt "sure of the prize." Then it became Joseph's turn to take up the Shaker arms. In a short time he came in saying, "I must confess my sins." Green cautioned him to "wait longer & labor upon it," to be "fully determined to be honest" before he attempted it "& then set out to be faithful forever." Joseph answered, "O but I must do it now, or I shall certainly die, & if it kills me I can but die."

Text: *Millennial Praises*, pp. 246–247.
Tune: MS L–136, p. 18.

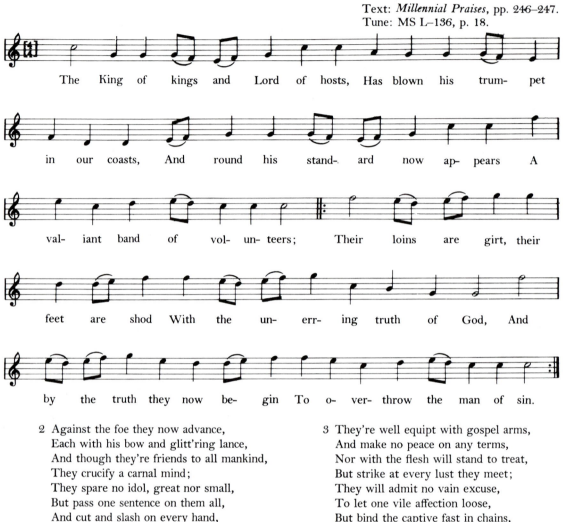

The King of kings and Lord of hosts, Has blown his trum- pet
in our coasts, And round his stand- ard now ap- pears A
val- iant band of vol- un- teers; Their loins are girt, their
feet are shod With the un- err- ing truth of God, And
by the truth they now be- gin To o- ver- throw the man of sin.

2 Against the foe they now advance,
   Each with his bow and glitt'ring lance,
   And though they're friends to all mankind,
   They crucify a carnal mind;
   They spare no idol, great nor small,
   But pass one sentence on them all,
   And cut and slash on every hand,
   To purge all evil from the land.

3 They're well equipt with gospel arms,
   And make no peace on any terms,
   Nor with the flesh will stand to treat,
   But strike at every lust they meet;
   They will admit no vain excuse,
   To let one vile affection loose,
   But bind the captive fast in chains,
   While one flesh-pleasing tie remains.

4 Now every soul that would do right,
   Is welcome to enlist and fight;
   These weapons of victorious truth,
   Are for the aged and the youth;
   No soul of man does God exclude
   From hating sin and doing good;
   And in such souls, we do maintain,
   The God of truth will ever reign.

5 While living truth, like burning coals,
   Is purging evil from our souls,
   We know we are in him that's true,
   And what he says we freely do:
   The empire of eternal bliss,
   Has its foundation laid in this,
   And all who gain this holy ground,
   With everlasting life are crown'd.

Hymn No. 14

HEAVENLY FEAST

Samuel Hooser of Pleasant Hill, who wrote this hymn about 1815, served faithfully for forty-seven years as one of the servants calling the rich and the poor to the banquet prepared by the

Lord. Few of the rich answered the call. According to Shaker records, one who did was Charles Wylling Byrd, a federal judge in Ohio who had been born in Virginia in the citadel of the Byrd clan, Westover on the James. But Judge Byrd died before removing to Pleasant Hill. Another patrician who actually entered the South Union community was Willie Jones of Halifax, whose father—landowner, politician, sportsman, and formidable Deist—was one of the most prominent North Carolinians of his day. Young Willie attended Princeton College and graduated from the University of North Carolina in 1804. A decade later he was in Kentucky. The South Union ministry thought him "a young man of a very noble mind—middling small, & very lively, of a strong & understanding faith; and a true cross-bearer." It was impressed by his acquaintance with the president and "many of the most respectable persons in the United States."

Willie posed, however, a serious problem for the ministry: he had inherited 107 slaves. Willie at first wished to bring them all out to Kentucky to "receive the gospel," but the ministry thought this imprudent. The country was already "full of jealousy & evil report against Believers." The ministry had also learned from experience that it was much more difficult to bring blacks than whites "into the mortification necessary for their protection." They were "much more averse to either receiving the gospel or bearing their cross." Though the Kentucky Shakers were then desperately poor and the sale of the slaves would have brought them twenty or thirty thousand dollars, it was, the ministry said, "not our faith that they should be sold and the money made use of among Believers." After instruction, Willie accordingly "directed his Attorney to dispose of them as a *free gift* to persons of their free choice," unless some chose to follow him into the Shaker faith. Four eventually joined him in Kentucky.

A year later the South Union ministry reported curtly to Lebanon that "some few are gone out from us since we wrote in May last—but more, & we hope better, are come in. Among those who went out, we reckon Willie. . . . It would seem he was too rich to abide in the self-denying path of the poor to the end." Willie died in North Carolina, unmarried, in 1837. Of his opinion of his experience with the Shakers we have two clues: his lawsuit against the Society for the recovery of $12,000, and a Jones family tradition that these were years when Willie took the Grand Tour and in the beautiful city of Constantinople kept a harem.

MS PH–1, p. 237.

O Zi- on thou beau- ti- ful Cit- y of peace Where

truth love and un- ion for- ev- er in- crease, Thy

glo- ry shall rise and e- ter- nal- ly blaze And

cause the dark na- tions to won- der and gaze. The

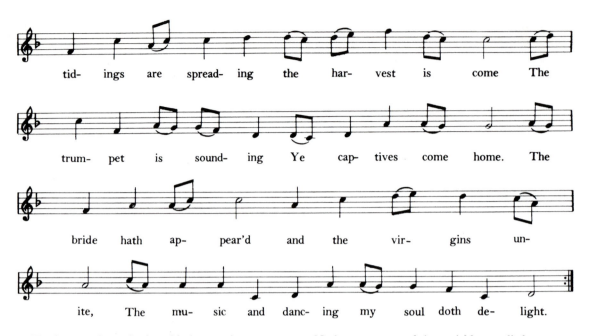

tid- ings are spread- ing the har- vest is come The

trum- pet is sound- ing Ye cap- tives come home. The

bride hath ap- pear'd and the vir- gins un-

ite, The mu- sic and danc- ing my soul doth de- light.

2 The banquet is ready the table is spread
  And all who are willing may come and be fed
  The Lord in his mercy hath open'd the door
  His servants are calling the rich and the poor
  The soul that is needy may come and secure
  The riches of heaven a robe that is pure
  With glory and comfort the feast doth abound
  No lack of one blessing hath ever been found.

3 No banquet on earth is so richly supplied
  The guests who are worthy no good are denied
  These glorified people shall never complain,
  Of bondage or darkness affliction or pain.
  It shall be my labor by night and by day
  To walk in obedience to watch and to pray
  That I may be able to enter the door,
  When I shall desire and ask for no more.

Hymn No. 15

EZEKIEL'S VISION

The Round Dance was introduced as a form of worship in 1823, and the rapture it roused flowed forth in this hymn. The inner and outer circles of dancers reminded the writer of passages in Ezek. 1:4–24, and he drew heavily upon them. This author was probably Richard McNemar. Anapestic meter, detailed Biblical allusions, and florid imagery are all characteristic of Richard's verse. The song, moreover, was brought east from Ohio in the year 1825. Only the year before McNemar had written from Union Village of his pleasure in

> some new gifts . . . to my sense, more heavenly than I ever saw before particularly
> what is called . . . the circular dance, that which the children of Israel danced after
> their three days march out of Egypt. To me it felt both awful & glorious to see such
> a vast body of well trained believers in a solid body of brethren & sisters alternately
> move round, like the rushing of a mighty wind.

Text. MS EC–6, pp. 54–55.
Tune: MS EC–11, p. 273.

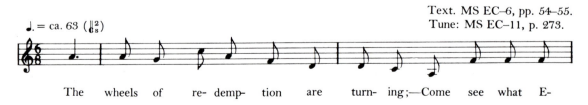

The wheels of re- demp- tion are turn- ing;—Come see what E-

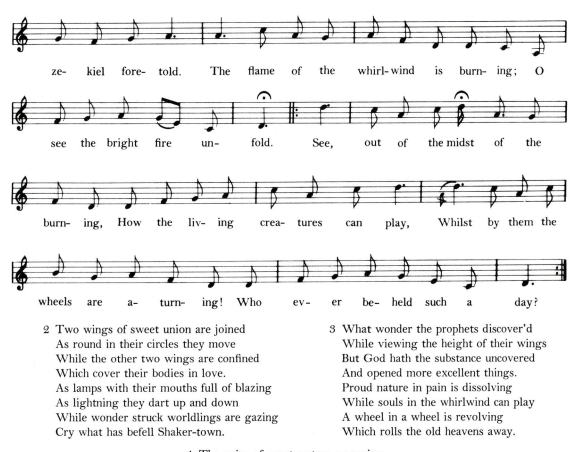

ze- kiel fore- told. The flame of the whirl-wind is burn- ing; O

see the bright fire un- fold. See, out of the midst of the

burn- ing, How the liv- ing crea- tures can play, Whilst by them the

wheels are a- turn- ing! Who ev- er be- held such a day?

2 Two wings of sweet union are joined
As round in their circles they move
While the other two wings are confined
Which cover their bodies in love.
As lamps with their mouths full of blazing
As lightning they dart up and down
While wonder struck worldlings are gazing
Cry what has befell Shaker-town.

3 What wonder the prophets discover'd
While viewing the height of their wings
But God hath the substance uncovered
And opened more excellent things.
Proud nature in pain is dissolving
While souls in the whirlwind can play
A wheel in a wheel is revolving
Which rolls the old heavens away.

4 The voice of great waters a-pouring
Is heard through the trembling coast
Its like the Almighty a roaring
It sounds like the voice of an host.
The world all amazed with wonder
At such unaccountable things
Are glad when the children of thunder
Are ready to let down their wings.

Hymn No. 16

THE HUMBLE HEART

This most beautiful of Shaker hymns was fashioned by Thomas Hammond, Jr., and Eunice Wyeth of the Harvard Shakers, probably about the year 1820. The more prominent of the two was Thomas, who served as an elder for forty-three years and was an active historian and copyist of music. His contribution to the song was its melody, for which he wisely went to the ballad "The Lowlands of Holland."

Eunice's words are worthy of this strong tune and are indeed a distillation of several of the images that most powerfully moved the Shaker imagination. Three other hymns composed by her are included in this book—from a total, it is said, of six hundred she wrote. That figure may well be too high, but one manuscript copy of her hymns contains eighty-two compositions and closes with the words "End of volume 1st." Her songs clearly had some reputation among the Shakers. "The Humble Heart" was copied in more than twenty manuscripts, and one letter writer at Lebanon praised another's hymns by saying they had "an Unction in them which came near the neighborhood of Eunice Wyeth."

Her niece and namesake Eunice Bathrick says in a biographical sketch that Eunice Wyeth

> has frequently told the writer, that she has seen Hymns in the darkest hours of the night suspended from the ceiling over her head, written in letters of gold; and she had arrisen at that hour and copied them. She did not give me the impression that the illumination which caused them to appear so vividly to her spiritual sight remained while she was writing, as she had to strike a light in order to see, but by having seen them, they became so firmly engraved on the mind, that they were like lessons learned by heart.

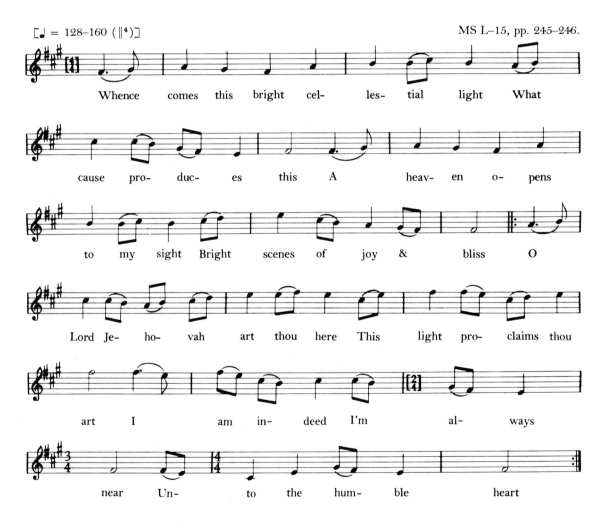

Whence comes this bright cel- les- tial light What cause pro- duc- es this A heav- en o- pens to my sight Bright scenes of joy & bliss O Lord Je- ho- vah art thou here This light pro- claims thou art I am in- deed I'm al- ways near Un- to the hum- ble heart

2 The proud & lofty I despise
But bless the meek & low
I hear the humble soul that cries
And comfort I bestow
Of all the trees among the wood
I've chose one little vine
The meek & low are nigh to me
The humble heart is mine

3 Tall cedars bow before the wind
The tempest breaks the Oak
While slender vines will bow & bend
And rise beneath the shock
I've chosen me one pleasant grove
And set my lovely vine
Here in my vineyard I will rove
The humble heart is mine

4 Of all the fowls that beat the air
I've chose one little dove
I'll make her spotless white & fair
The object of my love
Her feathers are like purest gold
With glory she does shine
She is a beauty to behold
The humble heart is mine

5 Of all the kinds that range at large
I've chose one little flock
And these I make my lovely charge
Before them I will walk
Their constant shepherd I will be
And all their ways refine
And they shall serve & reverance me
The humble heart is mine

6 Of all the sects that fill the land
One little band I've chose
And led them forth by my right hand
And placed my love on those
The lovely objects of my love
Around my heart shall twine
My flock my vineyard & my dove
The humble heart is mine

Hymn No. 17

WOLVES AMONG SHEEP

This hymn by Eunice Wyeth seems to grow from her own struggle to gain union with the Believers. Many members of her family—a brother, a sister, a brother-in-law, both her parents, as well as her husband and three children—traveled for a time with the Shakers. All of them except Eunice and her sister turned back to the World. Eunice was strong in the faith, and to attend meetings she frequently walked from her home in Cambridge six full miles to Woburn "carrying in her arms a heavy infant."

When Ann and William Lee first came to eastern Massachusetts, Eunice was thirty-four years old and a Baptist. Her parents, "though non-professors," were "moral people" and had striven to bring Eunice up "in the fear of God," not even letting her attend public schools for fear of bad influences. She had married Joseph Wyeth "in obedience to her mother" and had borne him four children, one of whom died in infancy. Both Eunice and Joseph became converts to the Lees' teachings and went to live at Harvard, but Joseph and the children "became uneasy, and wished for another home," and left the Shakers. According to Eunice Bathrick, Joseph "did not seem to lack faith, but strength to obey it." As he was unable by himself to maintain his own household and care for a crippled daughter, he began "to importune Eunice to come and live with him, promising her she should enjoy her faith unmolested, . . . which promise he faithfully kept." To avoid trouble, the Shaker elders counseled Eunice to go to her husband, "a severe trial to her, as she knew she must thereby be deprived of almost all her privilege of attending meetings." She also rightly feared many tribulations, for Joseph was a drunkard.

In 1808 Joseph again "set out to obey his faith," but the elders, doubting that Joseph could "bear the cross," did not permit the couple to move back to Harvard until 1825. From this time Eunice continued in a "calm, serene & joyful state of mind" until in 1830 at the age of seventy-four she went to unite with "her dear Mother, Elders and friends in happier spheres."

♩ = 106 (‖³)

MS HD–5, pp. 156–159.

Let the young & the old now cleave to the fold The

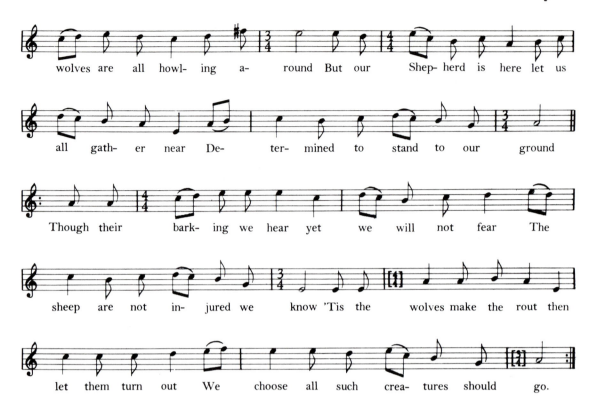

wolves are all howl- ing a- round But our Shep- herd is here let us

all gath- er near De- ter- mined to stand to our ground

Though their bark- ing we hear yet we will not fear The

sheep are not in- jured we know 'Tis the wolves make the rout then

let them turn out We choose all such crea- tures should go.

2 When the wolves are away like wild beasts of
     prey
   They make the most dreadful alarm
   But the faithful of choice will stay & rejoice
   The sheep have received no harm
   Though these wolves I suppose appeared in
     sheeps cloths
   So passed along with the rest
   Yet the good Shepherd's voice was never their
     choice
   And therefore they could not be blest.

3 Let the faithful be strong & travel along
   And leave all the rubbish behind
   Though lions do roar behind and before
   Their howling we never will mind
   For our Shepherd is true and we will pursue
   His footsteps we safely may tread
   He has fountains & springs & many good things
   With which all the faithful are fed.

4 Let the sheep be content to stay in their tent
     For this is a peaceable home
     But the goat that wont stay may try his own way
     Deserters are welcome to roam
     Let them take to their heels & see how it feels
     To roam in the Devil's broad way
     Let them sell their birthright for carnal delight
     We want no such creatures to stay.

Hymn No. 18

LOVELY LOVE

Eunice Bathrick, who provided the lovely melody for this hymn composed by Eunice Wyeth,
gave an account of the circumstances that fed her aunt's gift of song. She stated that in the winter
of 1807 a powerful revival swept through all the Shaker societies, bringing many Pentecostal

gifts, including "many Hymns & Spiritual songs." The elders at Harvard did not want Eunice Wyeth to carry copies of any of these new songs to her home for fear they might fall into the hands of her oldest daughter, a widow "opposed to the testimony of Believers." This restriction grieved her and became the subject of her prayers. She eventually "became inspired with a poetic spirit, and a Hymn was given her."

From this time on she was "ever blessed with the gift of poetry." When her husband Joseph reentered the faith "a great burden was removed from her mind," but "she still deeply felt her seperation from her Brethren and sisters, whose union to her was dearer than life. Therefore did she pour forth the efusions of her grief-stricken spirit in songs of prayer and lamentation as did David of old, and like him too, in times of refreshment did she tune her harp to praise and thanksgiving." When she was readmitted to the village at Harvard in 1825 "her songs of lamentation ceased," and for the last five years of her life she felt "a joy too deep to be expressed except in poetic strains." "Lovely Love" seems to date from these last years of Eunice Wyeth's life.

♩ = 106 (‖³)   MS HD–5, pp. 117–119.

Love- ly love is flow- ing sweet- ly From the love- ly
host a- bove What can fill the soul com- plete- ly
Like the love- ly gift of love Love- ly love is
my de- sire Heav- en fill me with the same
O thou love- ly pu- ri- fi- er Glow in- to a gen- tle flame

2 Lovely Parents, lovely children
Joined in union's lovely band
Lovely love from heaven descending
In the love of God they stand
Lovely near and [dear] communion
Nothing surely equals this
Everlasting love and union
Lovely pledge of heavenly bliss

3 How this lovely love advances
Springing from the lovely root
Love puts forth her lovely branches
Love produces lovely fruit
Lovely subjects shine with beauty
Every feature love has graced
Love has made them fair and lovely
Here the love of God is placed

4 Love's a robe prepared in heaven
  Love's the glory of the day
  Love's the mantle Mother's given
  Love has paved the lovely way
  Love's my comfort, love's my beauty
  Here my lovely treasure lies
  It is my important duty
  To obtain this lovely prize

5 Love's a gift of God approved
  Love is Mother's golden chain
  Let us love and be beloved
  Love's our everlasting gain
  Love has formed the New Creation
  Breathing life from breath to breath
  Love has brought our restoration
  Love complets the day of rest

Hymn No. 19

MY HEAVENLY KEEPER IS NEAR

A last hymn by Eunice Wyeth, with a tune by her niece. The hymn is not merely an elaboration upon the Twenty-third Psalm. To these Shakers heavenly guardians were literally real. Eunice Bathrick's account of Joseph Wyeth's last years offers an illustration of their belief. Joseph survived his wife, she says, by more than six years, but

> as he was a visionist he frequently saw and conversed with her. He would often say to me, "Eunice sent her love to you." But when I interrogated him concerning what she said to him, he would answer, "That is for me." It appears that she was permitted to be a ministering spirit to help him till he was called home.
>
> He likewise told of often seeing Father William, but would seldom tell any one what Father said to him.
>
> It was no uncommon occurrence for him to see disembodied spirits at any time of day. Soon after he embraced the gospel the second time, he said to the writer, "Father William came to me at noon day" (I think this was precisely the expression) "and told me to go and confess my sins; and I would rather have gone to hell than to do so; but for the love I bore to Father William I went in obedience to him and did as he told me." Said he, "Father William told me when he was in the body that he could not go to heaven without me."

MS HD–4, pp. [108–111].

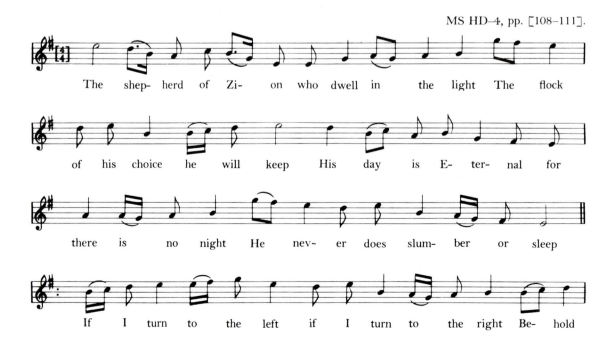

The shep-herd of Zi-on who dwell in the light The flock

of his choice he will keep His day is E-ter-nal for

there is no night He nev-er does slum-ber or sleep

If I turn to the left if I turn to the right Be-hold

my good shep- herd is here For sleep- ing or wak- ing by

day or by night My heav- en- ly keep- er is near

2 I never need look to the clouds of the sky
  To find out the place of His throne
  His presence is with me my Shepherd is nigh
  His voice to his sheep is well known
  I need not ascend to the mansions above
  For my precious Savior is here
  His hand doth support me with mercy & love
  My heavenly keeper is near

3 O why should we search to the ends of the Earth
  To find where the Savior does reign
  To follow his precepts to walk in his path
  His presence will with us remain
  Nor need we to dive in the depths of the sea
  To make his true wisdom appear
  He's opened the way of salvation & peace
  My heavenly helper is near

4 My Savior is nigh me my heaven's within
  Then why should I wander abroad
  To find my redemption the way out of sin
  I'll walk in the way of my God
  O Yea I will follow my heavenly lead
  Since Christ does in glory appear
  Let no filthy demon my travel impead
  My heavenly keeper is near

5 I never need look to the clouds or the sky
  To bring down the Savior from thence
  Remember the stable where Jesus did lie
  And search for the rock of offense
  Remember he comes as a thief in the night
  But mark where the star does appear
  Observe yonder mountain there shines a bright light
  My heavenly Comforter's here.

Hymn No. 20

MY ROBE IS NEW

One manuscript attributes this song, probably correctly, to Eunice Wyeth, but Susan Liddil believed it to be by Richard McNemar. She had a vivid memory from childhood of his singing it in a Union Village meeting. She says that when the circular dances and marches closed, the assembly would scatter to the seats that lined the walls and sit quietly to await any further discourse or gift a brother or sister might feel moved to offer. She remembered seeing Richard rise in one of these moments, step to the head of the aisle, and speak "at more or less length" and then—"clear voiced, musicle, and the sweetest of singers"—strike up this favorite song. He would start to march up and down the church aisle, his unbuttoned coat "hanging long and loose," disclosing his jacket and church meeting suit of homemade blue broadcloth, his "hands and his feet timing his voice . . . singing his song all alone." She remembered his face "in rapturous glow, his eyes upward raised . . . it verily seemed the heavens were opened to his survey."

Original key

$\left(\begin{smallmatrix}6\\8\end{smallmatrix}\right)$

MS L–129, p. 68.

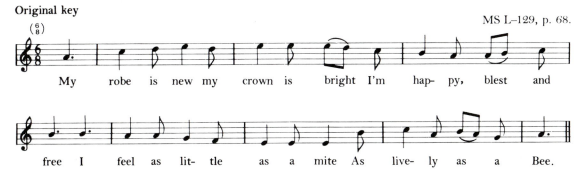

My robe is new my crown is bright I'm hap- py, blest and

free I feel as lit- tle as a mite As live- ly as a Bee.

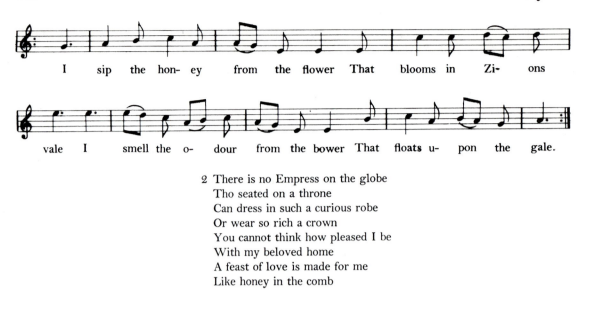

I sip the hon- ey from the flower That blooms in Zi- ons

vale I smell the o- dour from the bower That floats u- pon the gale.

> 2 There is no Empress on the globe
>   Tho seated on a throne
>   Can dress in such a curious robe
>   Or wear so rich a crown
>   You cannot think how pleased I be
>   With my beloved home
>   A feast of love is made for me
>   Like honey in the comb

Hymn No. 21

I BEG AND PRAY

"This little hymn composed by Susanna Barrett at Shirley seems to press upon my mind," wrote one scribe in 1835. The song must have been written not long before. Sister Susanna was then near the age of seventy and had been a Believer since the early 1780s. She said she first believed when she saw the English Shakers passing by, for she "felt convinced by their countenances that they were the people of God." After attending a meeting she "felt a full evidence" and spent the next week laboring to convert her husband. They joined the following Sabbath. She had, however, some reservations:

> I thought I would watch them & if they did any thing wrong I would leave them. Then I saw one of the Elders go forth in the dance. I thought that could not be the way to serve God, for it appeared to me to be carnal, but thought to keep it to myself. After meeting I went into a room to see Mother. She told one of the Elders to take the Bible and read to me, but did not tell him where to read; he read the sentence where David danced before the Lord and the damsel despised him in her heart, then shut the Book and said no more. Then I knew for truth they were of God, for they knew my thoughts, and I know all they said & did was right, and by following Mothers precepts and Example, I have been saved from the polutions that are in the world, and have found that comfort and peace of conscience, which the world knows not of, and I still find an increase in the Gospel.

Sister Susanna died at eighty-five and was memorialized as "one of the good ones if there is any such."

MS L–14, p. [42].

I beg & pray with heart sin- cere That

I may be so faith-ful here That when on earth

my work is done With you I then can have a home.

2 What love & union peace & rest
Is felt with you cant be express'd
O may I when with time I've done
Into the full enjoyment come.

Hymn No. *22*

ADIEU YE FADING THINGS OF TIME

In this hexatonic melody the reiteration of the sixth degree and the ways it is approached produce a peculiar mournfulness, one deep enough to express any grief. And there were those among the Shakers who had felt poignantly how much the world could take away. Of none was this more true than Mrs. Lydia Flinn, who died at Union Village in 1826, at the age of eighty-five. She had been married twice. Her first husband, a man named Pryor, was killed in battle by Indians. Her second, a widower with children of his own, was David Flinn, and by him she had children named Susanna and Stephen. During the Revolutionary War the family was living north of Cincinnati. Mrs. Flinn's grandson, a child of four or five, got out of a fort unobserved and was killed by Indians as he walked about. On the same day her son Andrew Pryor was found shot by Indians on the bank of the Big Miami River. Her oldest son, Moses Pryor, and her daughter Susanna's husband, Andrew Goeble, were also attacked as they returned from hauling flour to the army. They tried to reach Mrs. Flinn's house, but Moses got tangled in his gear at the barnyard gate and was shot from his horse. Andrew had stopped for him at the house door and was also shot down. Susanna

> hearing the Indian whoops, shooting, and horses' feet so near the house, went into the kitchen, raised a corner of a window curtain. . . . The first object she beheld was her husband . . . bloody and dead. . . . Susanna opened the barred door and drew in the ghastly blood-clotted corpse on the floor, straightened and put a stick of wood under his head, it being partly turned over on the face.
>
> Then starting out of doors and looking down the lane and in every direction and racing . . . tall and fleet, in search of her half brother, Moses Pryor. She found him in the dusty road, groaning at the barnyard gate, mortally wounded. Quickly returning to the house she spread a pallet and then grasping her crying boy brother's hand to go and help her bring their brother to the house. Faster and faster darted the Indian's bullets, while carrying in the tall heavy man, and closer and closer sounding their approaching horses' feet.
>
> Moses was still breathing when they came into the room where . . . she and Stephen carefully laid him down. . . . Then Susanna looked at her weeping mother moaning in her unutterable sorrow, so overcome and exhausted that she could not

speak. Neither could she be spoken to: was a well known sadness. And Susanna said to her brother Stephen, "Come help to take revenge. Poke up the fire," she getting a suitable kettle . . . for "running" bullets. So Susanna without her mother's permission though in her mother's sight went to the cupboard and made the first break into her mother's two sets of table dishes. . . . When the pewter was melted they two "run" the bullets. Then she poured the bullets into a sack and told Stephen to hurry off to the Fort . . . with them to shoot the Indians with. Stephen was afraid and strove against her. . . . But Susanna dragged him to a back window and lifted and pushed him outside telling him to run to the Fort with the sack of bullets. Indian bullets were whizzing about the boy's head on his way to the Fort, and when he arrived at the Fort and got inside the Fortification he was so overpowered with fright and fatigue that he fell on his sack of bullets, folding up unconscious before saying a word. The army were out of bullets and wanting them when Stephen came with his offering.

Susanna later married John Miller, a butcher, and had four sons and two daughters. They all eventually accepted the Shaker faith and entered Union Village, "where the whole family lived the remainder of their lives, and where they each and all departed this life."

MS HD–10, pp. 108–109.

A-dieu ye fad-ing things of time A-dieu all earth-ly pleas-ures I prise the Gos-pel far a-bove The worlds de-lu-sive treas-ures, Yea joy-ful-ly I leave be-hind Those car-nal vain en-joy-ments When I be-hold the glo-rious crown Pre-pared for faith-ful serv-ants.

2 O Lord thou art my only strength
  In trials and temptations
  Thou hast redeem'd my soul from death
  And crown'd me with Salvation
  All Earthly Glory now I see
  Like vanity appear
  Since thou, O God hath taught me how
  Thy holy name to fear

3 Harken ye gay and blooming youth,
  In follies wide domain
  O! turn from every earthly charm
  A heavenly prise to gain
  No lasting joys do they affoard
  No sollid peace of mind
  O! then obey the voice of God
  And comfort you will find

4 In this I find true Happiness
   True peace and consolation
   And here my soul can be at rest
   Tho' in deep tribulation.
   I pray O Lord protect my soul
   Here in the new creation
   That I may dwell when done with time
   Within thy blessed Mantion

Hymn No. *23*

CITY OF PEACE

This strong tune—known also in a Southern shape-note setting called "Redemption"—was borrowed from the ballad "The Grey Cock." Shakers from New Hampshire to Kentucky sang the hymn, but in the East usually without the "Scotch snap" probably used by its author, James McNemar of Union Village. He composed the hymn in 1836, and it is one of many songs credited to him or written in his own hand.

James was only nine when his father Richard McNemar accepted the faith in 1805. According to Susan Liddil, James himself unknowingly influenced his father's decision to become a Shaker. In early childhood he had been subject to "very violent fits" from the time his mother found him "by the spring being charmed by a large snake." One day, feeling symptoms of a fit coming on, he ran to his parents in the house. He entered at a crucial moment. The three Shaker missionaries, whom Richard had been avoiding and who had not been "content to let him off so easily," were reasoning with him "on the subject of salvation." They had fought to a stand-off when James ran in.

Richard's "heart was moved to 'tempt' the brethren." He spoke

> in a taunting ridiculing tone of voice saying to them, "My friends, if your doctrine be of God, arrest the paroxysm attacting that child." All was silent, and he observing the brethrens' confusion, smiled at them, repeating, "If your doctrine be of God give us a miracle, and stay the infirmity of that child, and I will believe that the doctrine you preach is of God. I will accept it, and be a worker with you." Again all was silent, the brethren did not feel that they had a gift of miracles although they knew beyond a doubt that the doctrine they preached was of God. Finanly [*sic*] Jenny the mother arose, looking at her husband and the brethren saying, "let us pray." Accordingly they all knelt down and prayed and the child's threatening affliction was arested.

James never again had another fit; "so you see," said Susan, "God had Eleazer in a 'strait' place, but his was a noble soul and he did not retreat, but accepted truth and was a devoted faithful worker therein to the end of his days, and Jenny his companion and all his family united with him."

♩ = 92 (‖²)   MS PH–1, p. 279.

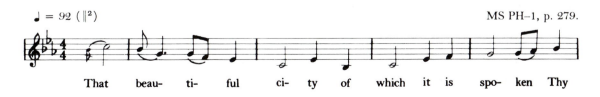

That beau- ti- ful ci- ty of which it is spo- ken Thy

street shall be paved with the pur- est of gold We've

now some- thing more than a sign or a to- ken Of

this bless- ed man- sion by proph- ets fore- told. The

walls and the gates have be- gun to be rais- ed, The

streets now with gold are be- gin- ning to shine Thy

name here O God will for- ev- er be prais- ed With

songs of thanks- giv- ing and an- thems di- vine.

2 And as this great building of God is erected
   Old Babylon towers to peices will fall
   The wicked from ruin cannot be protected
   Unless on this Zion of God they will call.
   In vain do they fly to their great splendid
      buildings
   To hide from the wrath of an Almighty God
   For down he will shake them with all their
      guildings
   And under the feet of the Lamb they'll be trod.

3 Then come up to Zion all you that desire
   To share in the treasures of heavenly things
   And likewise escape the unquenchable fire
   Which God in his wrath on old babylon brings
   While the ensign of freedom in mercy is waving
   In haste now repair to the city of peace
   For here is a refuge where souls can be saved
   A place where all troubles and sorrows will cease.

Hymn No. 24

THE BURNING DAY

John Lockwood composed this hymn in 1835 while at Sodus, New York. He was a man of
unusual ability and had been sent out from Lebanon to assist in "settling" this society, as he

was later to be moved on to serve as an elder at Groveland. In 1851 he was recalled to Lebanon, where he held posts first as elder of the East Family, and later as Deacon in the South Family. As he was an "ingenious mechanic & very industrious," he was felt to be indispensable in "that weak handed family."

Elder John came among the Shakers in 1815, when he was twenty-four, with his wife and two small children. Having gone west "on speculation," he had been "providentially led to believers at Union Village" and "received faith." Returning home to Poundridge, New York, he settled his business and moved with his family to Lebanon. In an autobiographical account he wrote,

> I never professed any religion before I came among Believers. I was a Rationalist, & when I heard the Gospel Testimony, it seemed like doing the *work*, & this is where I found a lack in all other Religions. Quakerism, Presbyterianism, Methodism, & all other isms, were nothing to me. They all seemed like chaff, for those that had them, did not lead any better lives than I did, & some of them not so good. Their Religion made them no better; they could be full of rascality & yet all carried away with Religion.
>
> But the Testimony of the Gospel showed me how to govern Nature's strongest propensity & travel away from it. I never had any particular work of the Spirit to prepare me for the Gospel that I know of, but I did feel condemned for the works of the flesh. I never had any confidence to plead in their defence, or to say the first word in their favor, for I was convicted of them from the first. I was damned already! And when I heard the Gospel Testimony & understood it, it looked so reasonable that I set out as a volunteer to obey it. I saw that if Christ was my Captain I must do as he said, & have nothing to do with the works of generation. If he was my Pattern, I must follow the Pattern & be like it, & my Faith has never wavered.

MS HD–8, p. 16.

Re-deem-ed souls your voic-es raise, And sing His won-ders o'er, In songs of ev-er-last-ing praise The great I Am a-dore On cher-ub's wings your flight be-gins, To leave this dark a-bode The cross will save us all from sin and bring us home to God.

2 To time and sense we'll bid adieu,
  Earth's glories we'll despise;
  Eternal treasure we'll pursue
  That everlasting prize.
  How fading are all earthly things!
  Like shadows flee away!
  The cross substantial treasure brings,
  That never will decay.

4 Gird on your sword ye valient band,
  Nor fear what hell can do!
  Devowering flames shall sweep the land,
  And mockers get their due!
  Like lightening on the wicked dart,
  While mighty thunders roll!
  Their terror strikes them to the heart
  But Glory to my soul.

3 I'll bid all carnal thoughts be gone!
  O Mother's spirit, come!
  In Father's love we'll travel on
  And all unite in one.
  By Love, we're known, by precious Love,
  To men did Jesus say;
  By love we're known in heaven above,
  Love bears the palm away.

5 Ye joyful mountains skip like rams
  While Edom melts away;
  And all the little hills like Lambs,
  Shall clap their hands and play!
  Join in their song ye virgin souls,
  For this great burning day!
  Now the old heavens away shall roll
  And earth no longer stay.

Hymn No. 25

TRIBULATION WORKETH PATIENCE

Elder Issachar Bates composed this song in 1835, two years before his death. The song openly expresses his mood during these last two years. He was filled with homesickness for the West, from which, after thirty years, he had been recalled to the parent society at Lebanon. A change of leadership had been needed in several Western societies still headed by elders appointed in the first years. Some through debility and impairment of judgment could no longer lead effectively. Friction grew. Richard McNemar, for one, had difficulty in bearing with Elder Issachar and was writing meanly of him in his journal.

When the summons came to Elder Issachar to return to the East, he tried to take joy in the "foundation laid in that Western world," but could not help feeling that he "brought more sorrow out of it than [he] took into it." He regarded the return as his "retreat," saying, "I had played it on a fife" many times as a soldier in the Revolution, "but I never had such a retreat as this before."

At seventy-seven, parting with dear friends was especially hard. In the East everyone was "full of loving kindness and tender compassion." Issachar wrote, "I believed that they loved me, and I knew that I loved them. But they almost provoked me to anger with their repeated saying, be comfortable, be comforted, &c, when they might as well have told a toad under a harrow to be comfortable, for I could not reach it."

When Issachar died in 1837, Isaac Youngs wrote tenderly of him,

> He was weary of this world and according to his wish, is now released. And we have good reason to believe that he was kindly attended by guardian spirits, who were prepared to attend him as soon as he left the body: For three bright lights were seen hovering over him, about three hours before his death from which time he was more calm and easy. . . . Even so beloved Issachar of thee it may well be said, "Well done thou good and faithful Servant, enter thou into the joy of thy Lord."

MS L–82, p. 206.

If trib-u- la-tion O my God Must be my por-tion here

I'll bear the stripes I'll kiss the rod Nor drop a
mur- m'ring tear. If I must suf- fer day and night
With cries and cease- less prayers While I have pa- tience
all is right How- ev- er hard to bear

2 And if my suffering hours increase
  And sleep forsake my eyes
  I'll charge my soul to hold her peace
  For murm'ring I despise
  Yet Lord in mercy give me strength
  To bear this heavy load
  That I may dwell with those at length
  Who trod the suffring road

3 If I with them may find a lot
  In mansions where they dwell
  I'll gladly leave this earthly spot
  And bid the dust farewell
  For earth with all its glittering hue
  Is but corrupting stuff
  To all her sweets I'll bid adieu
  I've used them long enough.

Hymn No. 26

SACRED TRUTH

When Frederick Wicker of Watervliet composed this song in the 1830s, he voiced the greatest fear of the Shaker: that pride and self-will might grow within him, costing him his union. No one could ever count the victory won, not even the seasoned veteran. In the very decade from which this song comes, the Lebanon ministry had to cope with the sad fall of Richard McNemar. Even more than Elder Issachar, Richard had found it difficult to accept the appointment of younger leaders. Through one of the visionists he received rebukes. Richard took great hurt, refused submission, and in 1839 was removed from the Society. He then set out from Ohio to present his grievances to the ministry in the East.

In the ministry's journal Elder Rufus Bishop assessed Richard's state on his arrival. "Richard," he wrote, "does not pretend to have denied the faith," but having "lost his union to his visible lead, of course he is like a wandering star." Richard looked "very feeble, . . . almost like a corpse" and seemed "to feel much tribulation" and "to weep considerable." Elder Rufus feared Richard was "bordering on insanity."

It was not Shaker practice to open such a matter for general review, but ripples of distress must have run throughout the village. How the community acted to restore harmony is revealed in a journal entry written six days later:

About the middle of this afternoon Samantha Fairbanks sat down to smoke her pipe, but was prevented by Father David Darrow who informed her that he had come from Ohoio [*sic*] with Richard McNamar for his protection, and that he now requested to speak to him. . . . Accordingly E[lder] Ebenezer and I went to his room and informed him that Father had come and wished to speak to him; whereupon he manifested much joy and surprize. Soon Elder Sister led Samantha Fairbanks into the room, whose eyes were closed, & every gesture plainly indicated that she was inspired. It was soon manifest that Mother Lucy was also there, and both of them gave him much good counsel. Father David acknowledged that he was one of the first who received and obeyed the gospel in the western country, and that he was one of its most able defenders. Mother's words were in accordance with what Father David had said, and all seemed well calculated to soothe and gather his feelings. Richard seemed to receive the whole with great reverence and thankfulness, and was much affected, even to tears.

The desire of the society to "gather" Richard's feelings back into union continued even after his death six months later. His funeral, we are told, was a solemn meeting and quite crowded, "altho very rainy." During the meeting a visionist saw the spirits of John Dunlavy and Richard McNemar "standing on the gate posts of the grave yard." She saw many more spirits in "a great retinue of loaded Chariots going in the procession to the Grave yard. She counted a while but gave it up. She also saw many on foot more than there were of us."

MS L–82, pp. 134–136.

My soul is fill'd with sor-row I free-ly do re-pent

What lan-guage shall I bor-row My heart to rep-re-sent

O pray for me kind Eld-ers That I may nev-er fall

For if I lose my un-ion I sure-ly do lose all

2 What pains there has been taken
   While in my days of youth
   My faith is now unshaken
   I will obey the truth
   For sure as there is heaven
   No soul can stand the test
   Unless they're strictly honest
   And every thing confessed

3 The way of God is pure
   I humbly will bow down
   I pray I may endure
   And gain a glorious crown
   It is my souls desire
   To be completely free
   Have nothing that is covered
   But all things plainly seen

Hymn No. 27

CONQUER OR DIE

Within himself the Shaker fought many battles; but the martial ring of this hymn echoes an earlier Protestant spirit. The tune is still sung by Orangemen of Ulster with equally militant words celebrating King Billy's defeat of the Papists at Boyne River in 1690. The song was doubtless brought over by ancestors of the Scotch-Irish pioneers who made up a large part of the membership of the Western Shaker societies, where this hymn was written.

How people of this stock harmonized their character with Shakerism is revealed in Eunice Patterson of Union Village. One diarist says her parents, John and Phoebe, had passed through the most "heart-rending scenes of the Pioneer Life" during Indian wars in Kentucky. Eunice's uncle Robert, who later founded Dayton, had barely escaped with his life from Blue Lick, and John may also have been in that disastrous battle. When the Kentucky legislature voted to permit slavery, the Pattersons removed to Ohio, where John and all his family were among the early Shaker converts.

Eunice herself was of such "sweeping executiveness" that Susan Liddil never met her on a walk without instinctively giving way "because she comes with such gliding force and haste." In 1874 this "aged Veteran" was finally forced to move into "the Nurse Department," and the ministry then wrote of her:

> she has braved the ills of Life, as long as a determined Will could animate and command the old Machinery; but it no longer obeying, she has yielded, perhaps for the final change. She walks still upright, and to the last, before leaving her room, performed the duties of House Work. No person has ever been more conscientious, in taking a full share of all the Duties of Life; not a deceitful, or a lazy particle in her Noble fabric!!

MS PH–1, pp. 125–126.

While march-ing up to Zi- ons mount What have we now to fear A

Cap- tain we have in our frount And one that's in the rear. With

ar- mour bright we all u- nite And move at his com- mand And

soon on Zi- on's glo- rious mount We joy- ful- ly shall stand

2 Our Captain is a valient man
  With courage bold he fights
  And now he calls for volunteers
  Who will maintain their rights
  True hearted souls we will enlist
  None others need apply
  For with such souls we will resist
  Our strongest enemy.

3 When once we've joined in the campaign
  We need not think to fly
  Our freedom then we have to gain
  Tis conquer then or die
  For if we should the cause desert
  Or yield unto the foe
  To endless shame we must depart
  Where all such cowards go.

4 Then let us boldly stand the test
  Still keeping in our view
  That glorious crown with which we're blest
  If we'll but stem it through.
  Our Captain has this crown obtain
  Christ Jesus is his name
  And if we will the cause maintain
  We'll truly wear the same.

5 Altho' we have a normous host
  Of devils to repel
  Yet if each one will keep his post
  The battle will go well
  If one true saint can put to flight
  A thousand of his crew
  Then if we all as one unite
  These fiends we will subdue.

Hymn No. 28

THE PLEASURES OF EARTH ARE FLEETING

Eunice Patterson composed the words of this hymn and Oliver C. Hampton the tune, not long before 1850. Like Eunice, Oliver Hampton was one of the stalwarts of Union Village, and like her he came into the Society as a child when his parents were converted. The story of his father, however, illustrates the experiences of a later wave of settlers.

Fig. 24. Susan C. Liddil 1824–
Union Village, Ohio.

Fig. 25. Oliver C. Hampton 1817–1901
Union Village, Ohio.

His father, Charles D. Hampton, was raised a Quaker in Philadelphia. Upon graduation from medical school, he decided to seek his fortune in the new Western lands with his wife and two small children. Most of his money he invested in a "neat little carriage" for the trip. He wrote that a few weeks after arriving in Ohio he attended a Quaker service and was impressed by the speaker's "pathetic appeal to the light within." It was "a quaint, simple, guileless looking man" with a "weak, childlike voice," whose "whole demeanor, betokened the most confiding, unsuspicious innocence & examplary meekness." The same afternoon this venerable Quaker called at Hampton's house offering to buy his carriage. "Poverty's cold wind & pinching rain, beat keen & heavy on our tender years," said Hampton, and he concluded the sale on the spot. The Quaker paid in notes on a bank that turned out to have failed only a few days before, and he refused to make good. "I was a stranger," said Hampton, "& he took me in. . . . From that moment my confidence failed, & gradually the least & last remains of dependance on man, went out forever."

Charles Hampton's first response was to adapt himself to Western cynicism. He determined to enrich himself as rapidly as possible. But he found this betrayal of his ideals filled him with self-contempt. He floundered blindly for a new belief, trying even Swedenborgianism before finally taking Shakerism as the rock on which to build. He came among the Believers at Union Village in 1822, bringing all his family.

No charms which this Earth can pro-duce Or pleas-ure which
na-ture a-dore Shall ev-er my spir-it se-duce Their
vain emp-ty scenes to ex-plore But here with my dear gos-pel
friends In my pret-ty home I'll re-main In-creas-ing in
vir-tue my days I will spend A treas-ure of love here to gain

2 Ther's naught which this world can bestow
That with Mother's love can compare
Then all its delights I'll forego
A treasure so precious to share
Time's bubbles fade fast from my sight
I'm seeking a treasure that's pure
Which yields to my spirit unfading delights
This my Mother's love will insure

Hymn No. 29

MOTHER'S INVITATION

This tune had earlier served "Henry Martyn," a tale of swaggering piracy poles away from this description of a Shaker meeting. The hymn resembles the ballad at least in illustrating a sexual role. Although in Shakerism all paths to intellectual and spiritual leadership were equally open to women and men, the sexes in actual fact tended to follow differing ones. The brother composed a doctrinal hymn; the sister was more likely to receive a gift song. A high proportion of the musical scribes were women; all the theorists were men. Mother Lucy might head the ministry and have the power to determine Shaker beliefs, but male leaders wrote all the volumes of theology. In meetings the expounding was done by an elder. An eldress instead, as the present song shows, exhorted Believers to good works and served as the fountain of their spiritual gifts.

MS HD–19, pp. 6–7.

2 Her kind invitation was young men be strong
  You'r called to overcom the wicked one
  She's anxious to show them the way that is new
  She loves her dear children thats faithful & true

3 And all our kind Elders how pleasant they feel
  Their cry is be good what can equal their zeal
  Their voice is so lovely & has such a seal
  That no human nature their birthright can steal

4 The Brethren and Sisters did bend like the trees
  When bowing in motion by a gentle breeze
  My soul was transported such beauty to see
  My tongue shall be loosed my voice shall be free

Hymn No. 30

THE PRECIOUS JEWEL

Some Shaker in the short-lived Port Bay colony composed this hymn about the year 1836. One secular branch of his strong tune comes equipped with a flowery street-ballad text lamenting a sweetheart, "my own dearest jewel." If the Shaker singer knew these words, he converted the image to spiritual purposes, inspired by Matt. 13:45–46. Like the merchant man of the parable, in seeking goodly pearls he had found "one pearl of great price," and he went and sacrificed all his worldly goods to buy it.

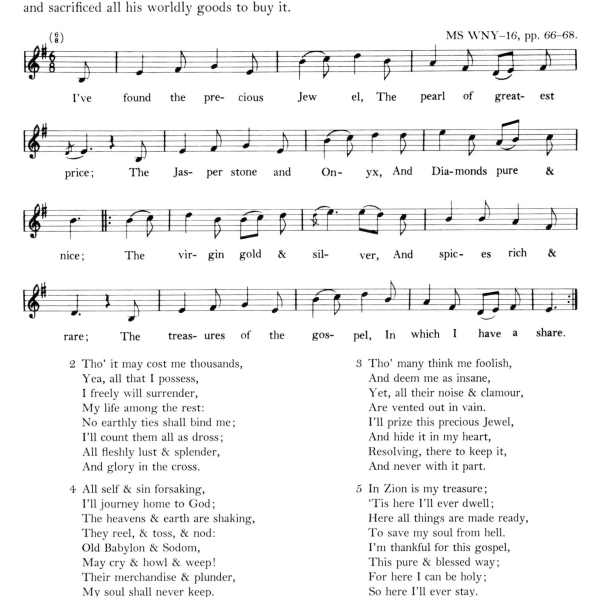

MS WNY–16, pp. 66–68.

(⁶⁄₈)

I've found the pre- cious Jew- el, The pearl of great- est

price; The Jas- per stone and On- yx, And Dia-monds pure &

nice; The vir- gin gold & sil- ver, And spic- es rich &

rare; The treas- ures of the gos- pel, In which I have a share.

2 Tho' it may cost me thousands,
Yea, all that I possess,
I freely will surrender,
My life among the rest:
No earthly ties shall bind me;
I'll count them all as dross;
All fleshly lust & splender,
And glory in the cross.

3 Tho' many think me foolish,
And deem me as insane,
Yet, all their noise & clamour,
Are vented out in vain.
I'll prize this precious Jewel,
And hide it in my heart,
Resolving, there to keep it,
And never with it part.

4 All self & sin forsaking,
I'll journey home to God;
The heavens & earth are shaking,
They reel, & toss, & nod:
Old Babylon & Sodom,
May cry & howl & weep!
Their merchandise & plunder,
My soul shall never keep.

5 In Zion is my treasure;
'Tis here I'll ever dwell;
Here all things are made ready,
To save my soul from hell.
I'm thankful for this gospel,
This pure & blessed way;
For here I can be holy;
So here I'll ever stay.

Hymn No. 31

VAIN WORLD

In May 1836 a party of Ohio Shakers sat at sunset on the deck of a canal boat traveling between Columbus and Cleveland. The evening was "still, & serenely calm." Most of their fellow travelers had gone off to bed, but they were still accompanied by "a grave old high Sherif" who had made it his aim to fall into their company whenever he "handsomely could." He at last "began to conclude he must hear a Shaker hymn, before he could go to rest" and asked that they sing one, "if it was agreeable" to their feelings. A brother struck up "Vain World." Immediately all the other travelers "came scampering out like so many mice," one poor old woman "so enamored, that she came with her night cap on!" After several hymns and an anthem or two, the Shakers went off to their own "little plank beds" with the cordial thanks of their audience.

From such chance meetings or from attending a service, Worldlings naturally picked up few Shaker songs, but it may seem surprising that songs were rarely taken into the World by people raised among the Shakers or resident for a time in one of the communities. Some, like Mary Dyer, left of course in bitterness and sang the songs, if at all, only to ridicule them. But many others probably refrained out of simple decency and a respect for religion in general or the Shakers themselves. The apostates from the community at Savoy, New York, for example, were never known to ridicule or speak against the Shakers. "Some of them," said Calvin Green, "when asked by the world to sing Shaker songs, would answer 'How shall I sing the Lord's songs in a strange land?'"

Text: *A Selection of Hymns and Poems*, pp. 174–175.
Tune: MS EC–11, p. 303.

2 Farewell, vain world! I say once more, I'm bound for Canaan's land.
I see a happy world before—prepar'd at God's right hand.
On life's tempestuous sea I sail, while countless billows roll;
But Christ my pilot will not fail, with him I trust my soul.

3 He can command the roaring tide, and silence all my foes:
With courage safely I can ride through ev'ry wind that blows;
Then as I daily homeward steer toward the land of peace,
This world does less and less appear and all its charms decrease.

4 The shining millions sail'd before, who gain'd the port above—
Found nothing in old Babel's store that they could prize or love.
That everlasting glory bright will tarnish all below,
Just as the sun's meridian light forbids the stars to glow.

PART VI

Extra Songs

Father James at times sang short worded songs, but after his death such songs dropped almost wholly out of Shaker singing. Manuscripts preserve no more than four composed by American converts during the next twenty years. The introduction of hymns about 1805, however, soon stimulated Believers once again to compose short worded songs. At Lebanon the first of these were the little anthemlike songs composed of words spoken by Mother Lucy Wright in meetings.[1] These were sung in 1810. Haskell recorded a stanza-length song brought to Enfield from Harvard a year earlier. Very shortly there was a full harvest of new short worded songs from every society.

Many of these songs were for the Quick Dance, and later for the Round Dance and the marches. A special need was found, however, for another kind of short song. The recently introduced Quick Dance was a strenuous exercise. The tempo of the Holy Order was also quickened about this time, and the amount of dancing performed in a service was increased.[2] The laborers needed a respite between dances, and short songs filled the purpose well. Haskell for this reason called them "one verse standing songs."

The name usually given at Lebanon was "Extra Songs," a more satisfactory term, for short worded songs were by no means limited to use while standing at rest between dances. In the services some were sung as prayers by the kneeling congregation. Most were doubtless often used outside the meetings, in hours when sisters worked together ironing or when a company at a union meeting shared songs and apples and the happenings of the day. A number of short songs were not intended for worship at all. They were used as New Year's greetings, or sung in the dooryard to welcome or bid farewell to Shaker travelers. (I gather such songs as these into a separate section labeled "Occasional Songs.") Others were addressed to some temporary concern, as when a drought threatened the crops. Some songs, like the one Marcia Hastings "breathed in anguish of spirit" when apostates worked up a Shaker dance routine for the theater, have the appearance of private prayer and may never have been sung to other Believers.[3]

The composition of hymns was limited to those few members sure of doctrine and meter, but most Shakers could put together a short song. They knew good tunes, shared the attitudes of the group, and had absorbed the verbal commonplaces and symbolism used in Shaker discourse. It is no surprise that the one-stanza songs far outnumber all others in the Shaker manuscripts, that they were created by all classes of Shakers, or that they are the ones in which the Shakers made their most creative use of their folk-song heritage.

Some of the stanza-length songs merely fit new words to a tune taken from a secular ballad like "Barbara Allan" or "Rose Connoley." Often, however, these songs are hybrids, crossings between ballad melody and dance-tune structure. Perhaps a single singing of a short-phrase ballad tune gave too short a pause between dances to be refreshing. Perhaps the singing of long-phrase hymn and dance tunes, with their repeated sections, had built a preference for longer melodies. In any case, the Shakers usually treated their one-stanza songs like dance tunes, dividing them in the middle and repeating each half.

Where the original melody was a short-phrase ballad tune, it would still, even with the repetitions, be shorter than most other Shaker songs. The repetition of each half from the mid-point of the tune might, moreover, destroy the logic of its phrases. Accordingly the Shakers sometimes took one of these tunes and capped it with another more or less related melody of equal length and sang each of these twice to make one complete melody. Examples of this are scattered through both the early and later Extra Songs in this collection. The second half of "Busy Bee" is a tune used with the ballad "Geordie." The melody usually used in lamenting "The Death of Queen Jane" makes a more joyful noise in the second half of "The World I Have Forsaken." In "Eternal Life" a variant of "The Braes of Yarrow" is sung complete for the first half of the song and then provides melodic elements for a closely related second section.

For a much larger number of Extra Songs—and short songs from the Era of Spirit Manifestations as well—the Shaker singer developed new melodies out of phrases or motifs in songs known to him. Sometimes he took a familiar cadential formula, such as the one from "Yankee Doodle" that closes each strain of "I'll Beat My Drum." More often his song began with the opening phrase of a secular tune but took some new and unexpected direction. In the present collection, for example, "I Beg and Pray" and "With Precious Gifts" flower very differently from an initial phrase borrowed from one family of "Barbara Allan" tunes.[4]

"O Ho the Pretty Chain" shows an even more complex indebtedness to traditional melodies. The piece is attributed to a sister at South Union, a community founded chiefly by settlers who, late in the eighteenth century, pushed their way into Kentucky from the mountains of Virginia, North Carolina, and Tennessee. In the regions from which they came, twentieth-century collectors have recorded tunes for the ballad "The Gypsy Laddie" clearly related to that of the Shaker song. The closest variant is one that Cecil Sharp recorded in 1915 at Flag Pond, Tennessee:[5]

The Shaker sister must have known a variant of the ballad closely resembling this, for the second phrase of the ballad tune (or third and fourth phrases, if Bertrand

Bronson is correct in regarding it as a tune of four short phrases with an external refrain[6]) is almost identical to the second phrase of the Shaker song:

The sister also used the same phrase to make the first and fourth phrases of her tune, slightly altering the closing and opening notes respectively. The third phrase of her song has a contrasting ascending line:

This closely parallels the beginning of a dance tune common in the Appalachians and the Midwest, "My Pretty Little Pink":[7]

[Original key: G]

The resulting Shaker song is treated as a dance tune, each half being sung twice:

O HO THE PRETTY CHAIN

MS SU–20, p. [106].

This new song is unlike either of its secular sources, and it differs from the typical patterns of the Shaker hymn and dance tunes. In "Oh Ho the Pretty Chain" the first, second, and fourth phrases lie high and the third low, a model not uncommon among the stanza-length songs, but the reverse of that of the hymns. How differently a dance tune would draw on the ballad melody can in fact be seen in a song written a decade earlier in another South Union manuscript. The "Gypsy Laddie" tune, shorn of its refrain but otherwise intact, serves as the high strain of the dancing song. The Shaker singer has invented a low strain, which characteristically closes with a reminiscence of the cadence of the first section:

MS SU–6, p. [155].

The single South Union manuscript preserving "O Ho the Pretty Chain" gives the date 1845 for its composition and identifies the singer as Martha Truesdale, who had entered the Society in 1817 at the age of ten. Whether Martha consciously borrowed from secular melodies to make her song, the manuscript does not tell. I think it unlikely. Patterns of association, however, may possibly underlie the songs. "The Gypsy Laddie" tells of a faithless wife who has left husband and babe to run off with a Gypsy; in this particular branch of the ballad the lady usually lives to lament,

> O once I had a house and land,
>   Feather-bed and money,
> But now I've come to an old straw pad
>   With the gypsens all around me.

The Shaker song, in contrast, promises joy and security to all who remain bound together in a chain of spiritual love. The Shaker's words "pretty chain whose links are love" may contain a reminiscence of the finery that the ballad lady "soon run through." The musical phrase to which Sharp's informant sang the words, "Her gold ring off her finger was gone, And the gold plate off her bosom" is the very one borrowed for the Shaker song.

A Shaker singer had less occasion to draw upon the words than the tunes of the World's songs. Most of the verbal commonplaces in ballads and love songs were alien to his themes. Even a phrase like "lily white" occurs, to my knowledge, only twice in all the Shaker songs.[8] The clichés of evangelical hymnody, which hymn writers among the Shakers often self-consciously borrowed, appear less frequently in the one-stanza songs. One notable exception proves the point. It is a little Extra Song that originated in 1829 at the North Family of Canterbury:

O WE HAVE FOUND A LOVELY VINE

(ɔ)   MS L–322, p. [11].

O we have found a love- ly vine In Zi- on's val- ley

bloom- ing Whose blos- soms shoot, and pro- mise fruit That's

beau- ti- ful and cheer- ing Whose ver- dant branch- es

spread so wide It shades the meek and low- ly Its

daz- zling light does shine so bright It tru- ly fills the val- ley

This song was woven together—probably in a spontaneous gift—from lines in a rambling Baptist hymn sometimes called "Lovely Vine." The wording and the order of the passages that I italicize demonstrate the indebtedness of the Shaker song:

1 Behold *a lovely vine*,
   Here in this desert ground;
   The *blossoms shoot and promise fruit*,
   And tender grapes are found.

2 Its circling *branches* rise,
   And *shade* the neighb'ring lands;
   With lovely charms she spreads her arms,
   With clusters in her hands.

3 This city can't be hid,
   It's built upon a hill;
   The *dazzling light* it *shines so bright*
   It doth the *vallies fill*.

4 Ye trees which lofty stand
  And stars with sparkling light;
  Ye christians hear, both far and near,
  'Tis joy to see the sight.

5 Ye insects, feeble race,
  And fish that glide the stream;
  Ye birds that fly secure on high,
  Repeat the joyful theme.

6 Ye beasts that feed at home,
  Or roam the vallies round,
  With lofty voice proclaim the joys,
  And join the pleasant sound.

7 Shall feeble nature sing,
  And man not join the lays?
  O may their throats be swell'd with noise,
  And fill'd with songs of praise.

8 Glory to God on high,
  For his redeeming grace;
  The blessed Dove came from above,
  To save our ruin'd race.

This hymn was long and widely sung in New England. As early as 1794 Joshua Smith published it in his *Divine Hymns, or Spiritual Songs*. Jeremiah Ingalls in 1805 printed a three-part setting of the text in his *Christian Harmony*, a songbook issued in Exeter, New Hampshire. The words were included in *Hymns and Spiritual Songs for the Use of Methodists and Free-Will Baptist Societies in New England*, published in 1811 in Concord, only twelve miles from Canterbury. The hymn was certainly known to many New Hampshire Shakers who had been raised in other denominations.

The Shaker singer ignored most of the images in the hymn: the city upon the hill, the "trees which lofty stand," the insects, fish, and beasts. They did not move him. From "Lovely Vine" only the vine, the valley, and the dazzling light rose into his mind.[9] He liked them not because they were startling and fresh, but because they were familiar to him from Shaker song and discourse. They were among the symbols that by 1820 the Shakers had accumulated for the expression of their faith and feelings. Most Shaker singers did not comb the hymns of other denominations for congenial phrases. They simply drew upon their Shaker formulas of word and tune and created new short songs that seemed, as Isaac Youngs said, "given as it were without the author's exertion of art." At their best, these songs were indeed like "fresh roses & matchless blossoms."

Extra Song No. 1

O DO YOU KNOW MY LOVEYER

One of the three manuscripts preserving this song adds the note, "Harvard. Ancient song of Father Elezer Rand to the memory of good Father James." It must have been sung in the years following James Whittaker's death in 1787. As late as 1846 a party of travelers leaving Enfield, Connecticut, for Harvard "stopped & went into the burying yard, & to Father James grave, Sung, O do you know my loveyer, & other songs, knelt around his grave."

Eleazer Rand knew Father James well, and all the English founders, having accepted the faith in 1781 together with the entire family of the farmer for whom he worked near Concord, Massachusetts. Eleazer was then eighteen and a youth of "medium height, light complexion, hair light brown, and eyes deep blue, mild, but bright & penetrating." In temperament he was "genial, kind, & affable, inclined to mirthfulness."

Eleazer's childhood had been hard, for his father, "a seafaring man," died in the West Indies before Eleazer's birth. His mother was a "high minded woman" who supported herself and the boy until he was eight, then found him a "place in a boarding house, to earn his own living untill he was fourteen." Perhaps as a result, Eleazer was a person of large sympathies, "ever seeming to realize the wants of others, more than his own." At twelve, when he saw the wounded brought in from the Battle of Bunker Hill, he took half his savings and bought supplies for them. As an elder at Harvard between 1790 and 1808 he showed "concern for the least child under his charge." He also showed the same tenderness in some of the early times of trial. Once he arrived on the scene just as a mob encircling James Shepherd had begun to whip him. "Eleazer, seeing these strokes, suddenly leaped on to James's back. This increased the rage of the mob to such a degree that they beat on with their clubs, canes, and whips." Maddened by Eleazer's praying under these blows, one man hurled him against a stone wall. Another called out, "Did you stop the little dog from praying?" "No," answered the first, "nor I could not unless I had killed him."

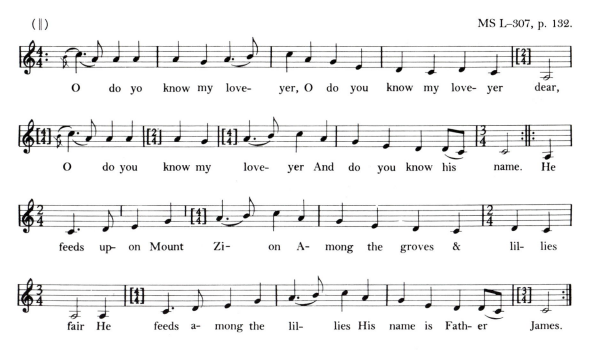

(∥)   MS L-307, p. 132.

O do yo know my love- yer, O do you know my love- yer dear, O do you know my love- yer And do you know his name. He feeds up- on Mount Zi- on A- mong the groves & lil- lies fair He feeds a- mong the lil- lies His name is Fath- er James.

Extra Song No. 2

A VISION

This song survives in two manuscripts, one of which states that it was sung to Reuben Cole in the year 1823 "by a spirit, whose name was Lydia Comstock." Of Reuben we know only that he was born in 1767 and lived many years at Hancock, dying there at the age of eighty-eight. Of his vision nothing more is known. In the 1820s visions were less frequently recorded, and probably less frequent in occurrence, than in the 1840s and 1850s. Typically those of the early period presented their instruction with a smaller admixture of the marvellous, as can be seen in an account of one of Richard McNemar's visions. Richard was "a swift mechanical worker" and kept a loom where he "put in and wove out many webs of cloth along from time to time in what would otherwise have been his leisure hours." One evening when it had grown too dark to see to guide his shuttle and he sat "regulating his quill box" before leaving, he suddenly

> heard singing off in the room in the sweetest voice that he had ever listened to in song. The singing continuing for three quarters of an hour, song after song. The singer stepped forth as through a parting vail. And there stood Sarah Coulter in the aspect of early womanhood—her face "like the face of an angel" and a signal light in the perfect form revealing "All glorious within"—then vanished out of sight.

> Richard said that he counted this vision one of the greatest lessons of his life: considering the lowliness and humble, quiet and retiring manner of Sarah Coulter as a sojourner in life, seldom spoken of and little thought about.

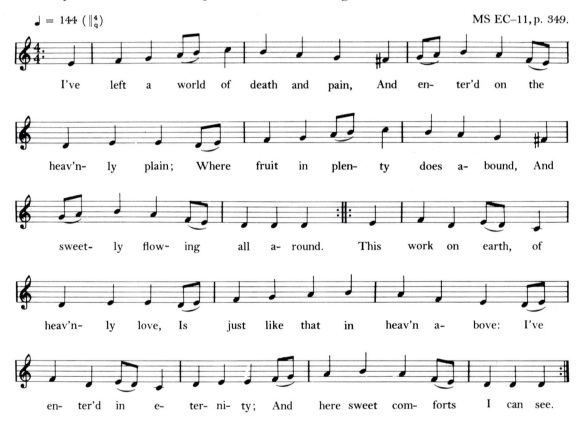

♩ = 144 (‖ 4/4)

MS EC–11, p. 349.

I've left a world of death and pain, And en- ter'd on the heav'n- ly plain; Where fruit in plen- ty does a- bound, And sweet- ly flow- ing all a- round. This work on earth, of heav'n- ly love, Is just like that in heav'n a- bove: I've en- ter'd in e- ter- ni- ty; And here sweet com- forts I can see.

Extra Song No. 3

STUBBORN OAK

In secular folk tradition this strong tune serves the ballad "Geordie" and other songs. As "Stubborn Oak" it occurs three times in Shaker manuscripts. One ascribes it to Susanna

Barrett of the Shirley community. The song dates from about 1823. Twelve years later it was still being improved in worship, for Giles Avery recorded in his journal that

> We have a very cheerful meeting for brother Issachar makes a very nice display of gestures added to the remoddling of the tune called the stubborn oak & we think the handle to it is very smoothe we try to learn to motion it after seeing him sing dance & motion it all alone to show us how & in the course of the meeting the family get the order of it nicely and perform it all together.

Extra Song No. 4

MOTHERS LOVE IS LIKE AN OCEAN

The only copy of this song is written in "round head" notation on a small slip of paper bearing the inscription "To Polly Davis with a goodly portion of my best love, Asenath Wilhite." It was probably enclosed in a letter mailed from South Union in the 1820s. Such mementos were often sent from society to society, and the songs seemed "to operate like the magnetic telegraph to convey love and union from one branch of Zion to another."

Original key: A minor   MS XM–4, no. 230604

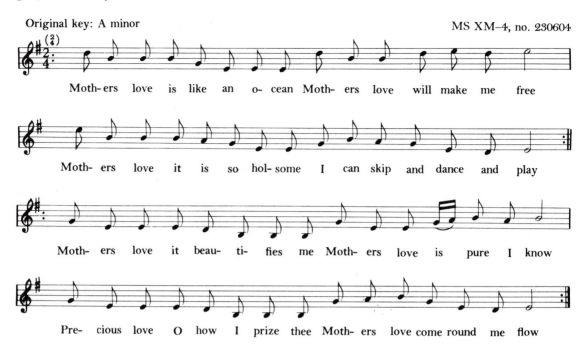

Moth- ers love is like an o- cean Moth- ers love will make me free

Moth- ers love it is so hol- some I can skip and dance and play

Moth- ers love it beau- ti- fies me Moth- ers love is pure I know

Pre- cious love O how I prize thee Moth- ers love come round me flow

Extra Song No. 5

BEAUTIFUL VALLEY

John Whitbey composed this humility song at Pleasant Hill in 1825. At the risk of swamping the song in a sea of ironies, I introduce an extended account of the man, who illustrates both the links between Shakerism and other communitarian groups and what the ministry feared as the libertine spirit of the West.

Whitbey came to Pleasant Hill in 1818 thinking to pay a brief visit to his brother Richesson, a member. John was at that time "disgusted with the world, sickened with the ways of men, and wearied with society." He found the quiet harmony of the Shaker village appealing, and made it his haven for seven years. Given his temperament, John could hardly have refrained from troubling the waters. His mother had died when he was quite small, and he was raised by a father "whose religious restrictions on the conduct of his children were far more than common." Instead of indulging the "vain and frivolous" fancies of youth, John "acquired the habit of observation and reflection; especially as it related to the ways and dispositions of men."

His first exercise of his powers had been in publicly charging a Methodist minister with falsehood, an act that resulted in his loss of membership in the church. Subsequently his mind ranged freely over such points of doctrine as atonement, resurrection of the body, and the existence of heaven. He regarded Shaker beliefs on such points as more sensible than those of other sects and found "the visible effects of their system . . . very delightful." But from the first he "felt shy in placing himself any more under the control of ecclesiastical power."

In Richard McNemar's view, the inexperience of the elders who had recently succeeded the venerable Father John Dunlavy to the Lead left Pleasant Hill exposed to a person like Whitbey, "of an insinuating turn, but volatile & unsteady, & from long habit, much given to fruitless speculations." John grew interested in Robert Owen and his plan of society and introduced Owens' writings among young Believers. This brought "a necessary check" from the elders, which only fired his ambition. "As disputation is ever the bane of gospel union," further checks and reproofs were cautiously imposed on him, and his resentment flamed. "Under these trials so painful to the Ministry," McNemar wrote, "the artful sophist missed no opportunity of exciting the sympathy of all that he could influence: as if the Ministry were tyrannizing over him, & torturing him with all the cruelties of an inquisitorial judge, because, forsooth, they would not tacitly suffer him to convert a virtuous community of Gospel Believers into a new fangled association of infidels." To free the Society from "despotic sway," John, his brother, and a certain Ephraim McBride organized a group of "secret agents located in different parts of the church" and hoped to lead an insurrection. Eventually they were forced to give ground and leave, but "the anarchy & rebellion excited by their insidious labours . . . deeply affected the community in its most vital parts."

John Whitbey removed to New Harmony and from this jerry-built redoubt of rationalism published *The Beauties of Priestcraft*, an account oddly sympathetic with all ranges of Shaker life but that of its governance. John's brother Richesson became an intimate of Fanny Wright in the equally ephemeral abolitionist millennium at Nashoba. McNemar's assessment was that the business of these "speculative gentlemen" seemed rather to be to "amuse themselves with philosophical discussions & rise into popularity among simple people than to acquire the knowledge & experience the humbling effects of gospel truth." Thus, he said, the prediction of Saint Paul in a similar case was verified at Pleasant Hill, grievous wolves rose up not sparing the flock.

But out of the wolf came forth sweetness. John Whitbey's song "Beautiful Valley" outlasted in the Shakers' memories all injuries he did the faith. It survives in manuscripts from four societies and is still sung by the sisters at Sabbathday Lake. The song also pleased unbelievers. It found its way into a Free-Will Baptist hymnal printed in North Carolina. The factory girls at Lowell printed a version from oral tradition in their journal (see the B version printed below). Children in the Hudson River Valley took it up, and it may survive there even yet as a game song.

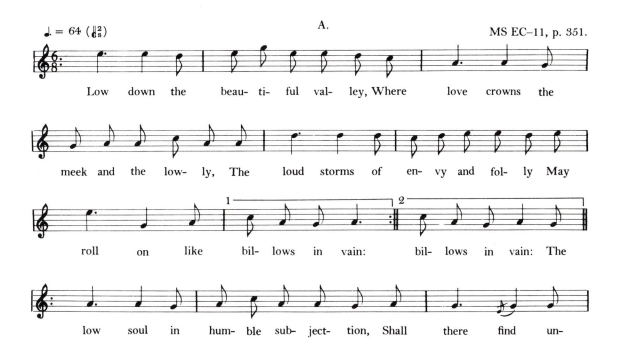

shak- en pro- tec- tion, While soft gales of cheer- ing re- flec- tion Their

minds soothe from sor- row and pain. The sor- row and pain.

B.

The Lowell Offering, 1 (1841), 345.

Lo down, down in yon beau- ti- ful val- ley, Where love crowns the

meek and the low- ly, Where rude storms of en- vy and fol- ly, May

roll on their bil- lows in vain, The lone soul, in hum- ble sub- jec- tion, May

there find un- shak- en pro- tec- tion, The soft gales of

cheer- ing re- flec- tion, The mind may soothe from sor- row and pain.

2 This lone vale is afar from contention,
 Where no soul may dream of dissension;
 No dark wiles of evil invention,
 Can find out this valley of peace;
 Lo there, there the Lord will deliver,
 And souls drink of that beautiful river,
 Which flows peace for ever and ever,
 And love and joy shall ever increase.

3 Ye lone sons of misfortune, come hither,
 Where joys bloom and never shall wither,
 Where faith binds all people together,
 In firm love to the sov'reign I Am:
 O there, there surrounded with glory,
 O Lord, we will tell the glad story,
 And shouting thy praise and bowing before thee,
 We'll sing Hallelujah to God and the Lamb!

Extra Song No. 6

LOVE IS LITTLE

In an age of reformers and prophets the Shakers bore their testimony with a difference. The heart of their witness is embodied in this simple song, "Love is Little." It was a mode of faith not sufficient for many another zealot of the day, including one Shaker apostate named Warder Cresson. He was "by nature a likely young man," Seth Wells said, "active & industrious—possesses considerable property—has a good education, & no small share of talents." His friends hoped the Shakers could "make a steady man of him."

After living a time at Watervliet, however, Warder secured the reluctant assent of the ministry to take a pamphlet he had written to be printed in Philadelphia. There he met a prophet newly come from England to warn America of impending judgments. Like a needle "within the atmosphere of a magnet" Warder was "instantly attracted & drawn into close contact." The two began to prophesy to "motley crowds of gaping auditors" in Philadelphia. Warder then advanced upon Lebanon "full of zeal & wildfire." Unable to convert the Believers, he and his prophet and "another congenial spirit" appointed a Sunday for preaching in front of the meetinghouse. It dawned in a violent December blizzard. Both the Shakers and the World prudently stayed at home, but the three marched together up and down the road proclaiming "to the utmost pitch of their voices" that within the year soldiers would barrack in the Shaker homes amid war, famine, pestilence and earthquakes.

As a Shaker, Seth Wells was no stranger to enthusiasm, but he pitied Warder for his error in allowing his spiritual imaginations to

> lift him far above the meek & lowly simplicity of the gospel; so that, like a weather-cock mounted on some lofty steeple, he is the sport of every breeze, from whatever quarter it comes, and thinks he is guided by *the wind of the spirit*, instead of *the power of the air*, and looks down on all below as insensible to "the high & heavenly breeze"— as ignorant of its course & direction, and unaffected by its power. No poor dung-hill fowl that treads the earth is subject to half the crosses, trials & afflictions that he is— for he always breasts the wind—and being perched on such an eminent station he is, by day & by night, continually subjected to clouds & tempests, snow, hail & rain, & all "the peltings of the pittiless storm." poor Weathercock!

(ɔ)   MS SU–15, p. 70.

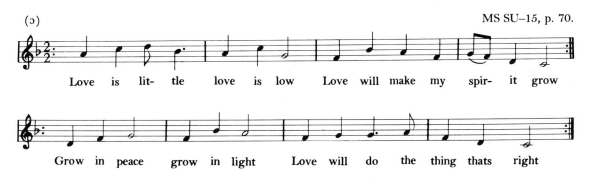

Love is lit- tle love is low   Love will make my   spir- it grow

Grow in peace   grow in light   Love will do   the thing thats   right

Extra Song No. 7

WHEN FIRST WE HEARD THE GOSPEL SOUND

This song originated at Lebanon about the year 1827, the time and the place Daniel Sizer first heard field and forest resound with the gospel proclamation. He arrived there on the twelfth of May in time for the Saturday evening service. It was a pleasant, moonlit evening, and the Church Family "felt a gift" to march down the road to the East Family, singing as it went. Halfway there the marchers met that family coming to greet them. After "a loving salutation," both groups went to the East Family yard and had a "pleasant meeting & feast of love" until nearly eleven.

Calvin Green noticed that Daniel Sizer kept alongside the group all the way, going and returning, "either in the road, or when that was too narrow, on the outside of the fence, so as to see & hear, all that went on." During the meeting at the East Family he climbed on top of a large stone to watch all "the operations of the Spirit." Observing him so "seriously awakened," the Believers "took much pains to instruct him," and Daniel received a burning conviction. After a second visit he opened his mind and set out in the Gospel. The Shakers had gained not only an excellent singer but a capable man who for many years would give leadership to the Upper Family at Canaan.

MS L–322, no. 24

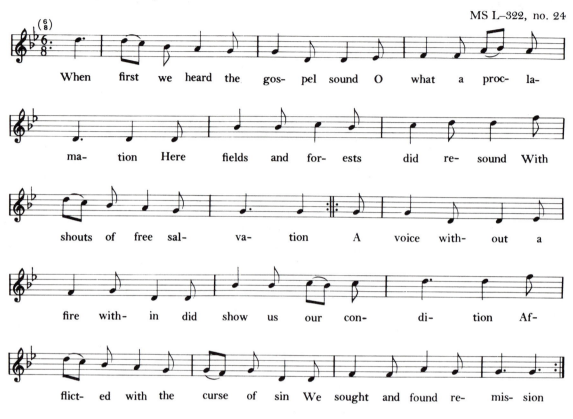

When first we heard the gos-pel sound O what a proc-la-ma-tion Here fields and for-ests did re-sound With shouts of free sal-va-tion A voice with-out a fire with-in did show us our con-di-tion Af-flict-ed with the curse of sin We sought and found re-mis-sion

Extra Song No. 8

THE HARVEST

Shaker manuscripts occasionally allude to the motioning of songs, but few provide descriptions detailed enough to give a clear picture of how a song was performed. A notable exception is the set of instructions sent along with a copy of "The Harvest" in a letter written in 1828 by Isaac N. Youngs. The song apparently had originated at Enfield, New Hampshire, only a short time earlier:

> This song is sung with motions, which I will try to discribe, thus: The general motion is a regular beat, with the back of the hands downwards: but on the 5th sylable *ga* the hands are carried out, as if to take hold under something; then on the syllable *ther* the hands are brot back, gently turning the ends of the fingers in, touching the back of the *fingers* together, & touching the ends thereof to the breast, on the word *in* (ie the 7th syllable). On the words, *Now to reap we will begin*, we make 3 motions like reaping; bending down, & taking the stroke where this ⌒ mark is made; likewise at the close of the song, minding to begin well to the right, so as to have a fair sweep, for a thro' in going to the left. On the word *seed*, we motion as if putting our right hand into the pail hung on the left arm, to get the seed, then on

the word *sown* bring the hand round with a proper motion to throw the seed.—
Now if you can understand me, you will do well.

♩. = 69 (𝄵²)   MS EC–11, p. 359.

Our sup- port we'll gath- er in; For the har- vest

time is come. Now to reap we will be- gin. Will you all now

help us on. Twas by Christ the seed was sown;

Now the har- vest does ap- pear; Now the crops are

ful- ly grown. Reap, O reap, get ev- er- y spear.

Extra Song No. 9

GREAT I LITTLE I

The first line of the following song recalls the alphabet jingle "Great A, little a, bouncing B,"
but the song is only one of many from the years around 1830 in which egoism is represented
by the capital I. Curious things happened as the singers tried to embody the symbol in a gesture
suitable for motioning. They seem first to have identified the I with a vertical wrinkle in the
forehead, which they in pantomine plucked off and trampled underfoot as they sang

> The devil in walking the earth to and fro,
> Has stamped the whole human race;
> This awful impression believers do know,
> Great I in the front of the face.

> Since Mother has taught me that this is the case,
> No more I'll be deceived with a lie,
> But now from my forehead I'll quickly erase
> The stamp of the devil's great I.

From this they slipped to the punning conception of the Great I as the organ of sight. Some
manuscripts, in fact, record the present song as beginning

> Great eye little eye great eye can see
> Little i is pretty i so little i will be. . . .

The song still speaks to the Shaker. On first hearing it in 1976, Sister Frances Carr exclaimed in pleasure, "Well, that says it all, doesn't it!"

Extra Song No. 10

THE WORLD I HAVE FORSAKEN

Two scribes at Harvard recorded this song about the year 1828, and both had trouble barring it. They sang the tune with rubato, a feature not accounted for in the rules of music they had studied. When the second half of this tune is sung in the Appalachians for "The Death of Queen Jane," the performance has the same trait. I suspect the Shaker song also contains a reminiscence of the seventeenth-century English song "A-Begging We Will Go."

Extra Song No. 11

I NEVER DID BELIEVE

This song dates from about 1829, and Isaac Youngs attributed it to Eldress Betsy Bates of Lebanon. A daughter of Elder Issachar, she was brought among the Shakers at the time of his conversion and proved as strong in faith and character as he. If one can judge by an unusually long and detailed account of her funeral in 1869, she was deeply beloved in the Society. The most vivid impression of her was written, however, by Mrs. Anne Royall, a penwoman who visited the Shakers about 1827. She arrived at the village with every sensibility ajar from the exertions of a walk from her lodgings in Lebanon Springs, a mile below. A Shaker lad relieved her of the burden of her reticule and led her to Eldress Betsy, who settled her in a parlor, brought refreshments, took her on a tour of the village, insisted upon laying a meal for her, and invited her to come again to services. Disarmed by such kindness, Mrs. Royall reciprocated with one of the few favorable accounts that had yet been written of the Shakers. "Miss Betsy," she stated, was a "tall and elegant figure, and very handsomely featured." She was a "female of good information; unaffected in her manners and conversation, affability and sweetness itself." Mrs. Royall's appreciation extended even to the services the next day. In the dances, she said, the Shakers' movements had "a solemnity and exactness attended with such inimitable grace" that the beholder was "ravished of his senses." She was equally moved by their kneeling in prayer "as solemn and silent as night." It was at such a moment in the service that Eldress Betsy might have sung her beautiful and reverential song.

Original tonic: D
♩ = 76 [♩ = 120 (2/4)]

From the singing of R. Mildred Barker.

I nev-er did be-lieve That I ev-er could be saved With-out giv-ing up all to God So I free-ly give the whole, My bod-y and my soul To the Lord God A-men.

Extra Song No. 12

LORD GIVE ME OF THY LIVING BREAD

Most Shaker prayer was unspoken. Before services the Believers sat in stillness in their retiring rooms for a half hour of prayer and meditation. They knelt together for silent prayer beside the table before and after each meal and beside their beds when they retired or rose. Prayer was felt so weighty that if at any hour of the day one knelt, others in the room knelt with him or kept silence. For this reason the singing of prayers developed rather late. Even in the 1830s prayer songs like this one and the two that follow were not very common. All three are preserved in but a single Lebanon manuscript. They are probably the private prayers of one composer.

Lord give me of Thy liv-ing bread On man-na may my soul be fed That heaven-ly man-na from a-bove The gifts of God and Moth-ers love Give me that liv-ing wa-ter too Re-fresh my soul with heaven-ly dew I want an ev-er-last-ing store That I may drink and thirst no more.

Extra Song No. 13

O LORD PROTECT THY CHOSEN FLOCK

At the close of evening meetings at Gloucester—and probably other societies as well—the people would often kneel together and sometimes sing a prayer song. Aurelia Mace says that until the late 1850s when anyone started a prayer song all would "put out their hands at right angles with the elbows, palms down." During a particularly moving song many would weep. As it ended, they would drop their hands to their sides, then "fold them very solemnly" and all rise together. The present prayer song would have been appropriate for such a moment, for its use of a plagal hexatonic scale has an effect peculiarly soulful.

O Lord pro-tect thy cho-sen flock And lead us to the ho-ly rock Where storm-y winds do cease to

blow And heaven- ly fruits in clus- ters grow O let us put our

trust in God He'll lead us to that safe a- bode Where love- ly

an- gels do u- nite In songs of prais- es day and night

Extra Song No. 14

AM I WORTHY

One of the singers who would have known this song when it was used at Harvard and Shirley in the early 1830s was Olive Hatch. She was born in 1774, married at eighteen, had a family, was "pleasantly situated as to outward circumstances, and enjoyed the things of time," but thought if she could find religion, it would increase her happiness. In 1813 she joined "the Calvinist church" in Spencer, Massachusetts, but soon learned from reading the seventh chapter of Romans that she must "give up *all* & live a *virgin life*, and become *pure* & *holy*, to be accepted of God." This belief prepared her to accept Shakerism when she later learned of it.

Olive felt she had been greatly rewarded for following Christ into celibacy. When she went blind in 1834 at the "beginning of a fit of sickness," she was in exchange "blessed with spiritual sight" in which she saw no darkness, but continual light, as of one eternal day. "I saw two large globes of light," she said, "passing swiftly around me. They appeared as large as the sun, & far brighter. I scarcely slept except a few moments at a time, for seven weeks, because of the heavenly beauties displayed before me." Later, spirits would bring her gems, and fruit, and "spiritual wine, new from the heavenly kingdom," which she could both taste and smell, and it many times cheered her spirit. Olive testified that she had "witnessed the glory of the latter day," and her soul was filled with love and gratitude to God and Holy Wisdom "for their loving kindness in opening the windows of heaven."

MS HD-18, no. 47.

Am I worth- y am I worth- y to ob- tain the

pre- cious pearl I will free- ly I will free- ly

I will free- ly give up all I will fol- low my dear Sav- ior

in his foot- steps I will tread for to such he

pro- mised sure- ly he would give them liv- ing bread

Extra Song No. 15

HELP ME O LORD

Three Lebanon manuscripts of the mid-1830s bar this prayer song correctly but give no time signature; the scribes had never heard of 5/4 measures. A later copy written at Canterbury shifts measure by measure from 2/4 to 3/4 time. The tune itself derives from the large family that serves such shape-note hymns as "Primrose" and "Consolation" and the ballad "The Bailiff's Daughter of Islington." In this tune family the second phrase typically climbs to a cadence on the fifth step of the scale, and the third phrase grows directly from it. The Shaker singer, however, bent the end of the second phrase toward a lower cadence, a structure more logical in the binary form used for Shaker Extra Songs.

MS L–14, p. [58].

Help me O Lord thy way to keep In truth and in sin-

cer- i- ty For what I sow that must I reap Through

time & in e- ter- ni- ty.

Extra Song No. 16

I WANT TO BE TRAVELING DOWN

Despite the reference to *traveling* in the opening line, we have the word of Russel Haskell that this piece was a standing song, not a march. He put it among songs learned at Enfield about 1830. Two Harvard manuscripts—our only other record of the song—place it two or three years earlier and name Canterbury as the source. A song rhythmically similar ("I want to be marching around, round") was composed at Union Village in the mid-1830s. No scribe satisfactorily solved the barring of either tune.

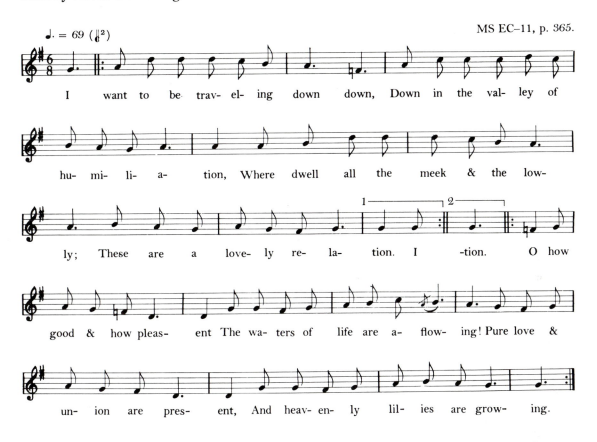

Extra Song No. 17

HOW GREAT IS THE PLEASURE

This song is preserved in but one manuscript, the work of an anonymous scribe at Lebanon in the 1830s. The composer may have been drawing upon familiar material. His text shares an opening couplet with "Music and Love," which Alfred Williams printed without tune in his *Folk-Songs of the Upper Thames*. P. W. Joyce's *Old Irish Folk Music and Songs* also holds an analogue, a loosely related melody with the suggestive title of "Single and Free."

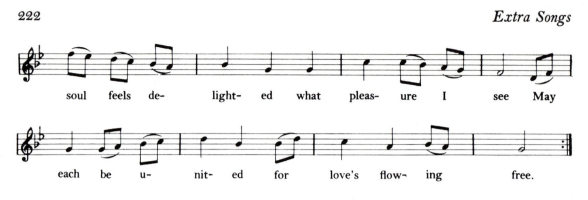

soul feels de- light- ed what pleas- ure I see May

each be u- nit- ed for love's flow- ing free.

Extra Song No. 18

MORE LIFE AND ZEAL

One Lebanon manuscript of the mid-1830s preserves this song. Its text would serve well for the Quick Dance, and the tempo and barring suggest that the scribe may have thought it one. But he has misbarred the melody, which is basically ternary, though irregular. It is an interesting tune, but not one the dancers could have negotiated with entire success.

($\frac{2}{4}$)   MS L–207, p. 321.

More life and zeal, More love and un- ion then good spir- its

will as- sem- ble and join us in com- mun- ion.

Extra Song No. 19

OUR FATHERS HANDS SO LIBERAL ARE

This song and the three that follow—as well as eight others in this collection—were recorded in a manuscript kept by John Wood at Lebanon. He seems to have lived in the Gathering Order there for several years in the mid-1830s, but probably defected. I judge that John had prior musical training and skill in fiddling, for he wrote in standard notation, setting many of his tunes unsingably high on the treble clef in the keys of A minor and C, D, and G major, and even using conventional appoggiaturas. A number of the songs—which may be his own, for few of them appear in other manuscripts—have melodic intervals less convenient for a singer than for a fiddler.

Original key
($\frac{6}{8}$)   MS L–129, p. 76.

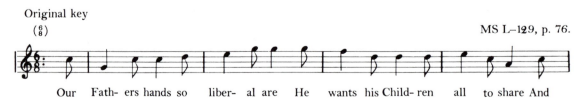

Our Fath- ers hands so liber- al are He wants his Child- ren all to share And

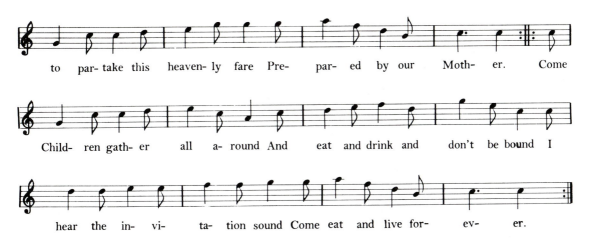

to par- take this heaven- ly fare Pre- par- ed by our Moth- er. Come

Child- ren gath- er all a- round And eat and drink and don't be bound I

hear the in- vi- ta- tion sound Come eat and live for- ev- er.

Extra Song No. 20

BEHOLD IN THE SPRING

For this piece the Shaker singer borrowed a theme from Isaac Watts's "How doth the little busy bee." But the Shaker bee is a distinct species. His real task was finding spiritual sweets, and his flight was sustained by such sentiments as the aged Daniel Moseley voiced in a Sabbath meeting at Lebanon in 1846:

> I can serve God with a hoe digging potatoes for my brethren & Sisters, or with an axe if I was able, or any other way. When I come to meeting, I feel to serve God with the whole of my ability, & I wish I possessed more ability than I do, for I am not able to fulfill the desire of my mind with my old broken down body; nor hardly begin. But I mean to make it do the best I am able, & that is but little. I tell you brethren & Sisters *Heaven is a lively place*; as lively as a humming bird's wings, & the nearer any Soul gets to it, the livelier they are. O I want to be agoing. Come let us have a song, I dont feel as tho I could wait a moment.

Original key
(6/8)

MS L–129, p. 143.

Be- hold in spring see ev- er- y thing A- live and cloth'd with

beau- ty Shall I a- lone an i- dle drone Be sloth- ful in my

du- ty. To gath- er hon- ey see the Bee Fly round from flow- er to

flow- er A good ex- am- ple there for me To well im- prove each hour.

Extra Song No. 21

WHAT JOY AND COMFORT

This melody from John Wood's manuscript has close relatives like "The Jolly Young Water-man" in the secular dance-tune repertory. But its family is far extended. Some of its lineaments are recognizable in two tunes in Patrick Joyce's *Old Irish Folk Music and Songs*, "My Darling Is on His Way Home" and "The Groves of Blackpool." But the latter is also clearly related to the Shaker hymn tune "The Heavenly Bridegroom and Bride," and this in turn is kin to tunes for other Shaker hymns, "Ezekiel's Vision" and "My Vineyard," and to that of the Gift Song "Step In & Be Healed." A variant more rhythmically subtle than any of these appears in another Gift Song, "Watch Ye." I suspect a kinship too with the tunes of the Extra Songs "We Have Cross'd the Red Sea" and "Protecting Chain"—these share at least the structural model, one in which the first, second, and fourth phrases are closely related and the third for variety ranges higher or lower than the others. A tune with this pattern might serve for secular dance, but in Shaker worship the customary figures made dance the one genre from which this traditional melody was excluded.

Original key   MS L–129, p. 177.

What joy and com- fort fills my soul Since I have cross'd the

deep And jor- dans floods be- hind me roll While I my pro- mise

keep. To fol- low on to know the Lord And gain that hap- py

shore Where An- gels sing in one ac- cord And sor- row is no more.

Extra Song No. 22

WE HAVE CROSS'D THE RED SEA

The escape of the Israelites from Egyptian bondage proved a story richly adaptive to American singers of spirituals. Shakers, unlike the slaves, associated Egypt with "its leeks & onions, and flesh pots . . . which ministered to a sexual nature." They were not awaiting the parting of the Red Sea waters, but viewed themselves as safe on the far bank, dancing. The present song, however, was not used for laboring. Haskell, who learned it from Lebanon about 1832, reliably classifies it with the standing songs. I rely too on his transcription—John Wood and the other scribes who recorded it at Lebanon did not so scrupulously note the Mixolydian tendencies in their singing.

♩. = 69 (♩²)   MS EC–11, p. 369.

We have cross'd the red sea; we're hap-py & free; We re-

joice on its beau-ti-ful banks: Our harps are a-string-ing, sweet

mus-ic is ring-ing, As for-ward we move in our ranks. We're

safe in the ark; we're not in the dark; We wel-come the heav-en-ly

dove. We've an em-blem of peace. May it ev-er in-crease, And be

ours in the man-sions of love.

Extra Song No. 23

TURN TO THE RIGHT

A turning gift frequently received notice in writings about the Shakers. As the apostate David Lamson described it, "This turning is not upon the toe, or heel, but by a continual stepping of one foot around the other, generally with the eyes closed." He had seen young sisters whirl round "at the rate of from forty to sixty turns in a minute" for three quarters of an hour without any appearance of dizziness. During a meeting one sister might begin to turn, and then another and another join in until five or six were engaged. Lamson charged that their adeptness was due less to supernatural power than to early training, but he failed to explain why Shakers should have thought the skill worth gaining. The answer, according to Alonzo Hollister, was "to signify willingness to turn out of our own ways." The gift might be executed either as "an operation of the spirit" or voluntarily. His words probably also explain how the following song would have been used at Lebanon in the late 1830s.

(ɔ) [♩ = 106 (♯³)]   MS L–207, p. 48.

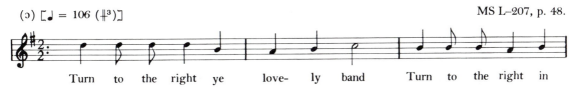

Turn to the right ye love-ly band   Turn to the right in

heart and hand   Lo   lo   rel   lo   lo   rel   lo   lo   lo

Lo   lo   rel   lo   lo   rel   lo   lo   lo   lo   lo   lo

Extra Song No. 24

HOW MY SOUL IS NOW DELIGHTED

An appropriate gloss upon this anonymous Lebanon song of the late 1830s is Daniel Sizer's comment upon his delight in his new Shaker home:

> The fruits that I discovered among this people were answerable to the ideas which I had formed of Christianity while quite young. Here I found a Society of people about six hundred in number living in a village having all things common, of one heart and of one soul, neither said any of them that ought of the things which he possessed was his own, loving each other, living together like brothers and sisters, none striving to be the greatest or the richest knowing that they who humbled themselves as a little child the same should be greatest in the kingdom of heaven, all fareing alike and dressing alike loving each other and living together as children of one family.

MS L–207, p. 220.

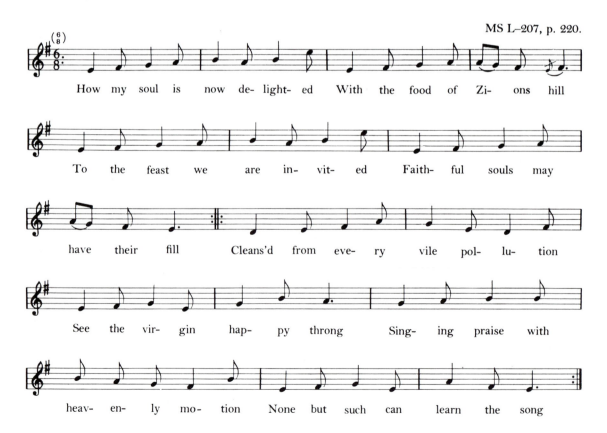

How my soul is now de- light- ed With the food of Zi- ons hill

To the feast we are in- vit- ed Faith- ful souls may

have their fill Cleans'd from eve- ry vile pol- lu- tion

See the vir- gin hap- py throng Sing- ing praise with

heav- en- ly mo- tion None but such can learn the song

Extra Song No. 25

PROTECTING CHAIN

"Believers are held together in union, by a golden chain," Mother Lucy Wright once declared; its links, "the gifts and orders of God." This saying was widely circulated in manuscript and often read, and its imagery gave rise to many a song. One it inspired was "O Ho the Pretty Chain." Another was "Protecting Chain," which originated in the short-lived village at Port Bay or Sodus, New York, in 1833, and was soon popular as far away as Maine and Kentucky. Reinforced by such songs, the image would also give rise to ceremonies like one witnessed by Elder Freegift Wells at Pleasant Hill in 1839, early in the Era of Spirit Manifestations.

Instruments announced, he said, that spirits had entered the meeting room with a golden chain to encircle the congregation. On their instruction, one of the two elders took a length of the spiritual chain and circled the brethren as they stood in their ranks facing the ministry. Coming up the center alley he handed the middle of the chain to the other elder and then retraced his steps with the remainder. An eldress was meanwhile performing similarly on the sisters' side of the room. When each had regained a place at the head of the room, the other eldress and elder were instructed to lock the ends of the chains together and put the keys in their pockets. "It will be perceived," wrote Elder Freegift, "that one of these chains surrounded the brethren twice, & the other the sisters twice & then were doubled at the upper end, & locked together by the Ministry on each side—This seems to be a striking Figure, to show, that the true & proper joining between Brethren & Sisters must be through, & in union with their Lead—as the connecting, or joining of the two Chains was committed exclusively to them."

MS EC–11, p. 371.

pearls of the sea; No gems of the moun- tain can with it com-

pare; And those who pos- sess it, how love- ly they are!

Extra Song No. 26

THE WILDERNESS RESTORED

This Shaker song, like many others, was shaped less by plan than by patterns of association. The tune quotes freely from an Irish song, "The Winter It Is Past." The text is a conflation of several Biblical passages and it progresses from antetype to type. The opening echoes Song of Sol. 2:13, "The fig tree putteth forth her green figs . . . Arise, my love, my fair one, and come away." These images suggested those of Isa. 35:1 and 6, "The wilderness and the solitary place shall be glad for them; and the desert shall rejoice, and blossom as the rose. . . . Then shall the lame man leap as an hart, and the tongue of the dumb sing." The singer felt this scene a prefiguration of 1 Cor. 15:55, "O death, where is thy sting? O grave, where is thy victory?"

His song pleased other Believers. The Union Village ministry, which had learned the piece from South Union, sang it at Watervliet and Lebanon during a visit east in 1840 and again in 1854 at Canterbury. Eleven Eastern scribes copied the song, and it was still sung in the West in the late 1850s.

O come, O come come a- way Where the fig tree for- ev- er is

bear- ing Where the flocks and the herds are so

pleas- ant and gay, And the des- ert a sweet smile is wear- ing

And the wil- der- ness re- stor- ed to her glo- ry The

tongue of the dumb sweet-ly sing-ing O grave! O grave, Where

is thy Vic- tor- y O death! Where is thy Sting

PART VII

Occasional Songs

Ballads commemorating a single event were rare among the Shaker songs; nearly as rare were songs that could be used only on specific recurrent occasions such as Christmas, funerals, or the arrival of visitors. I gather examples of them under the label "occasional songs" in order to introduce these minor genres without stressing them unduly—a Shaker would simply have spoken of "Christmas hymns," "funeral hymns," or "welcome songs," thinking of their differing uses and forms.

The seasonal songs of Old English tradition were quite absent from the Shakers' repertory. Their Puritan forefathers had long since abandoned festivals like May Day. Even the Harvest Hog slaughtered each fall at Canterbury in the early decades of the nineteenth century occasioned no song; he simply met the demands of the workmen for more ample provisions during the heavy labor of haying and harvesting.[1] Shaker manuscripts do record some Christmas hymns, but no English carols. The Shakers felt little need to celebrate the birth of Jesus. What they valued was not incarnation but rebirth into the spirit.

The Shakers did have a few seasonal observances of their own, but only Mother Ann's birthday seems to have been commemorated with special new songs. These seem indistinguishable from other Extra Songs and may have been as often sung in ordinary services. No songs at all survive for the footwashing service known at Shirley as early as 1825 and at Lebanon at late as 1845 and from 1828 practiced regularly at Canterbury for nearly a decade.[2]

Two other kinds of occasional songs were not uncommon. Manuscripts hold a fair number of funeral hymns. A few had years of use. Others, like those filling one entire North Union book, honor particular persons and were probably never sung again after their funerals.[3] Songs of welcome and farewell were fewer but much more frequently used. For years the Shaker custom was for hosts and visitors to salute one another in song. These greetings and funeral songs openly expressed, of course, the actual meaning of much Shaker singing: to strengthen the Believers in their bonds of love.

Occasional Song No. 1—Christmas

THE PRINCE OF PEACE IS COME

The words of this song imply that it may have been sung at Christmas. This would make the song unusual in the Shaker repertory. Not until 1876 did the Maine societies, for example, begin to observe Christmas with a decorated tree and gifts and Christmas carols. The song manuscripts hold a handful of hymns specifically composed for the season. In the earliest years—the time when this song was used—Believers were agreed that Christmas was not to be kept "after the manner of the world," but "had a labor" to know whether to observe the day at all, and whether to reckon it by the old- or new-style calendar. Mother Ann left others to discover the proper order. One good Believer, Hannah Hocknell, did not "feel satisfied" as to the "propriety" of observing the day, so she rose on Christmas morning intending to set about her business. As she dressed, "some unaccountable operation" repeatedly prevented her from putting on her shoes. Mother Ann then pointed out that this was "the most prominent sign recorded in the scripture of holy and sacred ground and purposes." As Hannah had intended to wash clothes and clean up the house, the sign meant that the "spiritual house ought first to be cleansed in a special manner" on Christmas.

Father Joseph built on this teaching in the 1790s, when he set Christmas as a "central time" for "confessing and putting away sins, and all wrongs from the camps of the Saints, and cleansing the spiritual house." His ordinance had the implication, later specifically stated in the Millennial Laws of 1845, that

> on Christmas day Believers should make perfect reconciliation, one with an other;
> and leave all grudges, hard feelings, and disaffections, one towards an other . . .
> and to forgive, as we would be forgiven; and nothing which is this day settled, or
> which has been settled previous to this, may hereafter be brought forward against
> an other.

(ɔ)   MS CB–25, p. 15.

The prince of peace is come O come join the heaven-ly train The arm-ies of the Lord re-joice the arm-ies of his name.

Occasional Song No. 2—Mother Ann's Birthday

COME BRETHREN LET US PLAY

Original keys   MS XM–5.

Come breth-ren let us play In the new and liv-ing way
Come sis-ter skip a-way We'll be free in all we say A good be-liev-er loves to dance A good be-liev-er loves to spring

Then   like   a   good   be-   liev-   er   sing   And   make   your   heaven-   ly   mus-   ic

ring   In   songs   of   love   and   un-   ion

In February 1824 those at Pleasant Hill felt a gift to celebrate Mother Ann's birthday, which was the last day of the month. In later years this observance was general in the Shaker communities, and the day was kept in much the same manner as Christmas. A distinctive feature in the first observance of the day at Pleasant Hill was the performance of a number of specially composed songs. Writing in her song manuscript on Mother Ann's birthday in 1860, Paulina Bryant set down nineteen songs she could remember from the service in 1824. Of these I transcribe the three most interesting.

"Come Brethren" may have been the work of Zechariah Burnette—a shape-note transcription of it survives from his hand. His family had entered Pleasant Hill in 1809, when Zechariah was eight, and he died there a faithful Believer in 1879. His brother Micajah was the chief architect at Pleasant Hill. Betsy Hutton was the composer of "A Rich Treasure." She had joined the Society in 1806 at the age of twelve and was commemorated when she died in 1862 as a "substantial pillar." A capable woman, she served as family deaconess and nurse. The third song, "Pretty Love," was by John Whitbey. His unhappy career has already been told. Ironically, his is the only song of the three to become widely popular with Believers.

Occasional Song No. 3—Mother Ann's Birthday

A RICH TREASURE

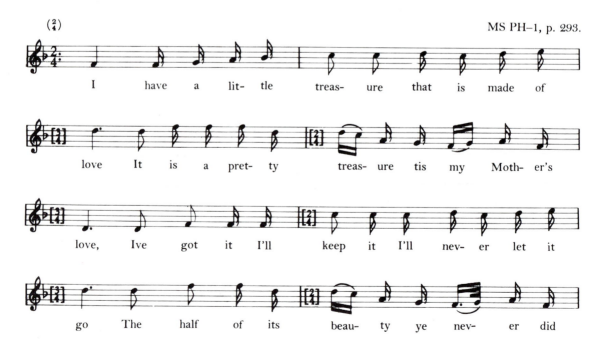

MS PH–1, p. 293.

I   have   a   lit-   tle   treas-   ure   that   is   made   of

love   It   is   a   pret-   ty   treas-   ure   tis   my   Moth-   er's

love,   Ive   got   it   I'll   keep   it   I'll   nev-   er   let   it

go   The   half   of   its   beau-   ty   ye   nev-   er   did

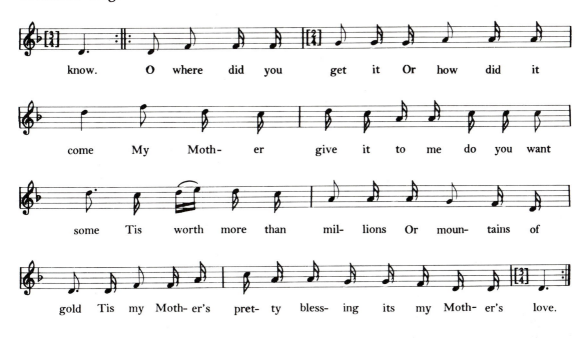

know. O where did you get it Or how did it

come My Moth- er give it to me do you want

some Tis worth more than mil- lions Or moun- tains of

gold Tis my Moth- er's pret- ty bless- ing its my Moth- er's love.

Occasional Song No. 4—Mother Ann's Birthday

PRETTY LOVE AND UNION

MS EC–11, p. 350.

Pret- ty love and un- ion, how I love thee! Pret- ty love and un- ion

thru me rolls. Pret- ty love & un- ion, I will have thee.

Pret- ty love and un- ion fills my soul. Stay with me, thou

love- ly treas- ure, Stay with me for- ev- er- more: Stay with me, that

I for- ev- er Pret- ty love and un- ion may a- dore.

Occasional Song No. 5—New Year

TO ALL THE GOOD CHILDREN, A HAPPY NEW YEAR

The tune for this dialogue hymn is a good variant of "The Cuckoo," a song widely popular in England and America. Even with this advantage, the Shaker piece had limited appeal. Russel Haskell learned it from Prudence Houston of South Union in July 1827, and seems the only scribe to have written it down.

2 Unto our good parents a happy new year.
  We love you, we bless you, without dread or
      fear.
  God's image and glory to us are made known;
  Thru our righteous parents they plainly are
      shown.

Occasional Song No. 6—Funeral

O MAY WE BE WILLING

The text of this song—composed, apparently, at Tyringham in 1838 for the funeral of some unnamed Believer—expresses the Shakers' characteristic attitude toward death. They willingly consigned dust to dust and neither wanted nor expected a resurrection of the body. For Believers, said Elder Henry Clough, the change at death amounted to no more than a move from one order to another in the Shaker community. The departing soul entered a higher order of the faith, and his still earth-bound friends strove to rejoice in his release.

Morbid preoccupation with death was not generally a Shaker failing, and leaders combatted "antichristian gloomy death religion" whenever they found it. Walking into a workshop one day Elder Henry Clough saw a book lying on the work bench and asked what it was. The eldest brother in the shop—an "honest-hearted" Believer, but one "subject to death like, sober, melancholly feelings"—answered that it was Hervey's *Meditations Among the Tombs* and that he thought it a very good book. "I think," said Elder Henry, "you had better put it in the fire.

I should think you were among the tombs enough." In Elder Henry's view cheerfulness "springing forth from justification in the gospel" should shine "thro' the cloud of nature" to "animate spiritual comforts" and "diffuse light and life."

Occasional Song No. 7—Funeral

OUR AGED SISTER

This melody shares cadences and other turns of phrase with the Appalachian fiddle tune "Shady Grove," though it is longer and more complex. Both probably come from Scotch-Irish tune stock, which was familiar to many of the western Shakers. The text was composed at Union Village on June 25, 1845, to honor Polly Abel. This hymn tells all we know about this sister. Probably she was another such a one as Lois Karl at Gloucester, who used to tell the young people she had early "made up her mind that as she had no beauty nor relations to recommend her she must be very good." Aurelia Mace says that "in truth, she did become a very good woman." She was "dearly beloved and she deserved all the love she got."

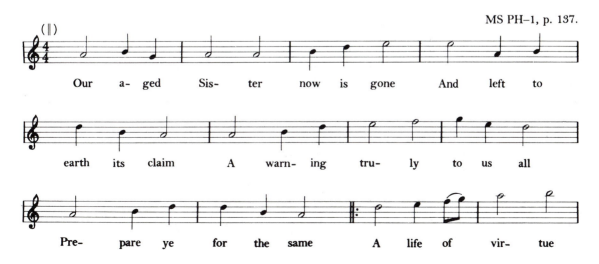

she has fill'd Was kind to young & old That faith she

dai- ly strove to live Her works have plain- ly told.

2 Her only aim was doing good
In spirit kind and free
She bowed submissive to her God
She said thy will be done
Mount Zion's Orders she did keep
In spirit and in truth
And now a rich reward will reap
Of heavenly love and truth.

3 How happy then must be the change
Our sister has pass'd thro'
Her spirit here no more remains
To earth she's bid adieu.
In mansions bright in realms above
She'll reap her just reward
In songs of praise and purest Love
Her voice will sweetly chord

4 Full forty years the path she trod
Unshaken in her faith
A Pillar in the House of God
She now is call'd to rest.
Altho' a loss with such to part
We must not now complain
But still united in one Heart
We bid a kind farewell.

Occasional Song No. 8—Welcome

GOOD BRETHREN FROM THE HOLY MOUNT

At Lebanon comings and goings were so frequent that by the 1830s only the ministry would be noticed with special songs, but to the smaller, more out-of-the-way societies visitors meant much and the elders saw that they were properly honored. At Gloucester, Elder Sister Betty Barnes would get Sarah Palmer to make up verses and Lavinia McIntyre to put them to music. The girls might have a fit of giggles in the clothes press as they tried to cudgel up inspiration, but they were "careful to keep it from Betty's ears, for she considered the subject too weighty to be turned into ridicule." Elder Otis Sawyer was equally "anxious" to have new songs with which to throw love over the guests by a "simple motion," they making "the motion of gathering it."

The custom of the Enfield Shakers must have been much the same. Haskell preserves a number of their welcome songs. The present one was prepared for Lebanon visitors when they came to Connecticut in April 1843. The prolific songstress Elsa Parsons worked it up, drawing apparently on a dim memory of an Irish tune, "The Song of the Blackbird."

♩ = 113 (‖³)   MS EC–11, p. 390.

Good breth- ren from the ho- ly mount, You're kind- ly wel- come

here. We're thank-ful for the priv-i- lege To meet our friends so

dear. We feel your love & bless- ing, And this we high- ly

prize. Tis tru-ly worth pos-sess- ing; It does our souls re- vive.

Fig. 26. Ritual Motions: Giving and Receiving Love
Tendering and gathering motions were used with songs of greeting and farewell or whenever appropriate to the song text.

Occasional Song No. 9—Farewell

MOST DEARLY BELOVED

In 1827 the South Union ministry bid farewell to Lebanon with this short hymn. The ceremony was probably similar to one with which they sped their own parting friends at South Union five years later. In a farewell meeting Benjamin Dunlavy "spoke a few minutes handsomely" and at the close led the singing of a farewell hymn. The visitors then replied by singing one of their own improvised as it were on the occasion for the purpose, they sang well, loud & forcible—passing back & forth waving their hands alternately to the Brn & Sisters; a pretty farewell—So we felt fully met.

MS EC–11, p. 284.

Most dear-ly be-lov-ed, and best of all friends, Good

Min-is-try, Eld-ers, whose love nev-er ends, And

kind lov-ing breth-ren and sis-ters, fare-

well; Your love and your kind-ness no mor-tal can tell.

2 We thank and we bless you for all your kind
        care,
    Still wishing an int'rest in your tender pray'r.
    So kindly so dearly so lovely farewell;
    So lovely so dearly so kindly farewell.

PART VIII

Anthems

The British subaltern E. T. Coke, who attended a Shaker service early in the 1830s, told of hearing "a strange composition, equally unintelligible and monotonous as an Indian chant at the feast of the Mohorum, or a Burman boat song as I have heard it on the Irawaddi, to which it bore no slight resemblance."[1] He called the piece a hymn, but must have been describing what the Shakers knew as an anthem. This was a genre less secure than others in the Shakers' own esteem, but for many years they customarily sang one anthem near the beginning of each worship service.

The name itself denotes a long piece with a prose text and through-composed melodic line. The model for these Shaker compositions was the anthem of the New England singing-school books of the late eighteenth century. Evidence that these were not unknown to the Shakers is found in a letter written by the aged Issachar Bates in 1835. He closes, he says,

> with the words of a farewell anthem, composed by a parting soul out of this world. The beginning of the anthem is this, "My friends I am going on a long and tedious journey never to return &c." The words and the sounds you will find below; and if you could sing them as I can, it would start a drop or two of tears.[2]

His Shaker friends may have taken the anthem to be original with Bates, but the good Elder must have known he was transcribing entire the leading voice of Daniel French's "Farewell Anthem," remembered from songbooks studied in his youth.

Prototypes such as this were models for the anthems introduced into Shaker public worship at Lebanon in 1812, but indigenous developments may have also contributed to the Shaker anthems. In 1810, in the aftermath of the Shakers' adoption of other forms of worded songs, they had tried singing "short anthems" composed of "words spoken by Mother Lucy in meeting and repeated by the assembly."[3]

Once the anthems had been given a formal place in Shaker worship they seem to have originated in two ways. Each corresponded to one of the two important decades of anthem-making, the first from 1812 to 1822 and the second from 1837 to 1847. An anecdote recorded by Aurelia Mace shows how anthems were created in the earlier of the periods. She says that one winter evening in the brethren's shop at Gloucester, Elder Oliver Holmes composed an anthem with a text beginning "These things saith the Son of God, who hath his eyes like unto a flame of fire." The young brethren gathered there with him to learn it by ear as a surprise for the sisters on the next Sabbath. Their secret was spilled by a little boy they sent to the kitchen for a pitcher of water. "They are making anthems out to the brethren's shop," he told the sisters, "and they have got eyes like flames of fire."[4]

The image that impressed him was Biblical, for the text of the anthem was a pastiche of verses from the first three chapters of Revelation. This book was a favorite with the early anthem-makers, as were Psalms, Isaiah, and Matthew. The musical settings were improvised by persons like Elder Oliver or—at Canterbury—Elijah Brown, who had but "slight knowledge of the rules of music" but conducted the singing in the Canterbury services. He "was credited" with a beautiful voice and a powerful musical memory. The model for his anthems may well have been the long anthem he memorized by ear while visiting Lebanon in 1809 and taught on his return home.[5] The strain of such efforts doubtless helped awaken the Shakers' desire to learn to write music. An anthem sent from Lebanon to Union Village in 1815 is in fact the first piece a Shaker is known to have "pricked."[6]

The term *anthem* also provided a ready-made label in the 1840s for a very different kind of song originating among another class of Believers. In this decade young persons fallen into a trance state often sang lengthy irregular songs. Their texts often echoed Biblical phrasing and the prophetic tone but were not scriptural. They might even contain passages in unknown tongues. The settings were "not formed by the practical knowledge of the Musical Rules, a humane System," but rhapsodic in structure, "as made known by the Angel of Love."[7] By these years musical scribes were plentiful and they made great efforts to record even anthems lasting a half an hour and exhibiting many vagaries of meter, mode, and text. Other Believers thought many of them worth the effort of memorizing.

Early or late, in creating their anthems the Shaker singers were at a disadvantage. They could draw on folk song for rhythmic patterns and phrasal formulas, but not for principles of extended structures. Since childhood they had known simple dance and song tunes, but no Shaker could have had a comparable experience with anthems. Few members had attended singing schools in the World and learned the anthems of the New England singing masters such as William Billings. Moreover, even the anthems of these composers have been criticized for wandering on the one hand into monotony and on the other into formlessness.[8] Shaker singers lacked even Billings' degree of awareness of forms like the rondo or the theme and variations. They also lacked resources for variety of texture, because the Shakers sang in unison. Shaker anthems consequently often seem, as Coke thought, rambling. In some few, however, a Shaker author, sensing the gratifications of both repetition and variety, has molded his material into a form achieving a pleasing balance.

Anthem No. 1

MOUNT ZION

The Shakers at Enfield, Connecticut, learned this anthem in 1819 as one composed by Issachar Bates while at Watervliet, Ohio. Elder Issachar's piece is only loosely representative of the early anthems. His text is unusual in being not an excerpt from the Scriptures, but a web of Biblical allusions. He had in mind certain lines scattered through Psalm 48:

Beautiful for situation, the joy of the whole earth, is mount Zion. . . . God is known in her palaces for a refuge. . . . Walk about Zion, and go round about her; tell the towers thereof. Mark ye well her bulwarks, consider her palaces. . . . For this God is our God for ever and ever: he will be our guide even unto death.

His text is furthermore unusual in that it begins in prose, slips midway into iambic feet, and closes with rhymed tetrameter couplets. Elder Issachar's musical setting for these words is also unusually coherent for an anthem. Whether because of his singing-school background or because he was naturally gifted in music, he unified his material through the use of a recurrent cadential formula. His handiwork pleased other Shakers. They copied and sang it for some fifty years. Henry C. Blinn thought highly enough of the piece to print it in 1852 in *A Sacred Repository of Anthems and Hymns.*

MS EC–11, p. 455.

Come, let us a- rise, and go up to the top of the mount Zi- on, and view her tow- ers; be- hold her might- y walls, and her bul- warks of ev- er- last- ing strength. Here we will ex- ult and sing, What hill or moun- tain is like thee, what hill or moun- tain is like thee, O thou ce- les- ti- al light! View from her bril- liant tops the hills & moun- tains round a- bout her, cov- er'd with de- so- la- tion. Re- turn, mine eyes, come home come home; once more ex-

plore this ho- ly hill. This is the hill of God's a- bode, this

♩ = 113 (‖³)

is the hill of God's a- bode, his ev- er- last- ing throne.

♩. = 56 (‖¹)

No nox- ious air can reach me here, No sick- ness, pain nor

death and fear. This is the hill I will a- dore; I'll

tar- ry here for- ev- er - more

Anthem No. 2

WITH PRECIOUS GIFTS

Russel Haskell included this short song in the anthem section of his "Record of Spiritual Songs," dating the piece about 1839. It is fairly characteristic of anthems produced during the period known as "Mother's Work." The song was not consciously composed, but "received" from the spirit of Mary Wood by someone in the Church Family at Enfield, Connecticut. Its text is prose, but not taken from Scripture. The melody is structurally free. This anthem is, however, somewhat more directly indebted to folk music than most of these pieces. Its opening phrase is that of one branch of "Barbara Allan" tunes, and the rest of the interesting melody flowers from it.

♩ = 96 (♯²)   MS EC–11, p. 491.

With pre- cious gifts you shall be blest, O my

tr

faith- ful child- ren; your souls shall find e- ter- nal

rest in Christ's an- gel- ic king- dom, your

souls shall   find e- ter- nal   rest in   Christ's an- gel-   ic king-

dom.   Lo   lo   lo   lo, here's bless- ings for   you.

Anthem No. 3

REVELATION

When the Era of Spirit Manifestations closed, Shaker anthems resumed their original form, becoming once again settings of scriptural passages. To make the present example in 1869, some singer at Canterbury in fact took words that had by 1814 served for one of the first Shaker anthems. The text itself, Rev. 14:1–4, was always central to the Shakers' understanding of their role in the millennium, as virgin followers of the Lamb. It had provided the rationale for their singing of wordless Solemn Songs in the 1780s. Their responsiveness to the text would keep the Canterbury anthem alive in oral tradition. In August 1974 it would be one of the songs chosen by the community at Sabbathday Lake for use in services commemorating the bicentennial of Mother Ann's arrival on American shores.

(‖) [♩ = 106 (‖³)]   GME–4, pp. [106–107].

I   looked   and   lo   a   lamb stood on   Mt.   Zi-   on   And

with   him   an   hun- dred   for-   ty   and   four   thou-   sand

hav-   ing   his   Fa-   ther's name   writ- ten   in   their   fore- heads

And   I   heard   a   voice   from   heav- en   as   the   voice of man- y

wa-   ters   As   the   voice   of   a   great   thun- der   And   I

heard   the   voice   of   harp- ers   harp- ing   with their harps

And they sang a new song they sang a new song be-

fore the throne of God They sang a new song which no

man could learn but the hun- dred and for- ty and four thou- sand

who were re- deemed from the earth These are the vir- gins

these are the vir- gins These are they who fol- low the Lamb

These are re- deemed from a- mong men the first

fruits un- to God and the Lamb they fol- low

Him whith- er- so- ev- er He go- eth

PART IX

Laboring Songs of the Middle Period

Between 1787 and 1797 the Shakers devised some seven forms of sacred dance. Two of these—the Holy Order and the Regular Step—remained their chief laboring manners for the next twenty years, during which time the Believers created but one new dance. They must have felt that the problem of finding a suitable mode of worship had been satisfactorily solved, and other matters now consumed their energy. The societies were quite poor, and their survival required close attention and heavy labor. The Believers had to clear lands and care for livestock and crops. They needed to build dwellings and barns and workshops. Times were also growing favorable once again for the winning of converts, and this required settled beliefs and a ready supply of scriptural and common-sense arguments for defending them. A number of the intellectual leaders now gave considerable time to writing apologies for the Faith. Such attention as could be spared for forms of worship they gave to the composition of the new worded songs. Not until the 1820s did the Believers renew their interest in the laboring manners. Then they began a second decade of innovations, creating the Round, Hollow Square, and Square Step dances and the Circular, Square, and Compound marches.

To say that six new exercises were created between 1822 and 1832 does not show precisely what happened, for in several ways most of these new manners were unlike those that originated in the 1790s. For one thing, the tunes for most of the new laboring manners of the 1820s were sung with texts. The use of words had first entered the laboring songs in 1811, when the Quick Dance was introduced, but the melodies for the Holy Order and Regular Step dances continued to be sung with vocables.

The Quick Dance had also introduced the circle into the dance figures. It was a form not well adapted to the first Shaker meetinghouses. These structures, built in the 1780s and 1790s on similar plans, measured only thirty-two feet by forty-two.[1] Part of the floor area was consumed by a small foyer and a stairwell at one end of the building and by seating reserved for visitors. The open floor encompassed about nine hundred square feet, not commodious for a congregation of one hundred fifty to two hundred fifty worshipers. The early dances were for good reason performed in close ranks and confined to narrow movements. The circular figure was not introduced until membership had ebbed. (The ministry's journal at Lebanon, for example, recorded a drop in the Church Family from two hundred thirty-three members in 1789 to only one hundred thirty in 1806.[2]) Even so, when circular laboring was begun in 1811, it was at first performed in two small circles, an economical use of space. When membership rose again in the second decade of the century, the largest Shaker communities were

Fig. 27. The Second Meetinghouse at Lebanon

In 1823, as the structure neared completion, the ministry wrote, "The house looks noble, but plain, though the work thus far is done neatly and very thorough; and it seems to meet the general approbation of believers who have seen it, and we hope it will be well pleasing to God; for surely it has been our greatest aim to build a house for his service, and such an one as he would own and bless."

Fig. 28. The Interior of the Second Meetinghouse at Lebanon

"Singing in it echoes," wrote Harvey L. Eades, "like the reverberations of a bugle among the mountains." The platform was a late addition.

prosperous enough to afford more spacious meetinghouses, and these must have been badly needed: the total membership at Lebanon by these years had climbed to more than five hundred. Around 1820 new halls were erected at Union Village, Pleasant Hill, and Lebanon, the latter having a dance floor sixty-three by seventy-eight feet.[3]

Beginning at the same time there was a flowering of expansive dance figures. Some, like the Hollow Square, were derived from the old patterns, but most employed the circle. They consisted basically of laborers progressing two or three abreast—men in one half of the circle and women in the other—around a vocal band standing in the center of the room. In variations, the inner and outer lines moved in opposite directions and stationary sections alternated with forward movement.

Another innovation in the 1820s had its origin in a different physical circumstance, the advancing years of the first converts. Many were now no longer able to unite as nimbly as they wished in the dance. Some of their number at Lebanon received in a vision the gift of marching. This form was within their capacities and the society as a whole gladly accepted it. The stationary sections of either a march or a dance demanded the use of the same shuffling step, but many marches had only continuous forward movement. There was also a marked distinction between a marching step and that used for dancing. The latter was a skip. In marching, the laborers merely paced, though with a "bounding, elastic step, quite different from that of the soldier of this world, who, marching to the sound of drum and fife, puts down his foot as if he wished it to stick forever."[4] Some variation was also allowed to the different age groups. One Kentucky visitor noted that at Lebanon the young Brethren "in a special manner marched as if they had springs to their knees & joints."[5] This zeal of the young was apparently approved; accounts by outsiders often contained notice of it. Thomas Hamilton told of seeing one boy who "signalized himself by a series of spirited saltations," and James S. Buckingham said that he watched some of the "more robust and enthusiastic" bound so high as to shake the floor on landing.[6] Some regional variations also developed. Easterners thought the Kentucky societies "stiff kneed in marching," and the Kentucky Shakers, who took quick, short steps, were surprised to see that the Lebanon brethren gave "spring to their step up & down" but "did not try to march so precise as we."[7] In the West the hands also timed the songs with a more "stiff precise up & down movement" than in the East. In the marches a few new hand movements were also added. Sometimes in the second section of a tune the hands were waved beside the head. Clapping was occasionally introduced at particular points, "at times so loud it makes a noise like pistols fired off."[8]

In all these new forms, however, the Shaker laboring remained distinct from secular folk dance. Key elements in the secular forms had no place in Shaker laboring. The Compound March might, like the running set, be composed of a sequence of figures, but their order was not determined by the whim of a caller. The Shakers planned and practiced their exercise in advance. Progression, the rotation of partners in secular dance, could have no place in Shaker worship. Whether in ranks or in circles, any advancing motion left unchanged both the position of the individual Shaker within a group and the relative positions of the male and female bodies of worshipers. The nearest approach to progression came when the outer and inner files of a circle were set going in opposite directions. This caused an individual to continuously alter his relation to each member of the other circle, but his position in his own circle was unchanged and the two bodies of laborers remained separate and distinct.

Another major divergence from the practices of secular folk dance entered Shaker exercises in the 1820s: the use of religious symbolism. In English tradition the dances associated with calendar festivals possibly employ vestiges of pagan symbolism, but these dances did not survive the Atlantic crossing. In America the ring shout of Blacks in the tidewater South and the sporadic dancing at revivals were performed as acts of worship but contained no specific symbolic message. Even among the earlier Shakers, dances appear not to have been explicitly symbolic. They did of course have religious import. They were felt as mortifying to lust or expressive of joy in salvation, and they mirrored the communal ideals of consecrated labor, unity, and chastity; but so far as written records show, the early Shakers did not make symbolic interpretations of elements in the dance.

In 1815, however, Mother Lucy Wright had suggested the use of gestures to accompany certain words in the song texts.[9] This "motioning" probably at first pantomimed the words, but the habit of interpreting movements must soon have spread to the conventional gestures, steps, and figures of the laboring exercises. The texts themselves reveal this adoption of symbolism. A typical Quick Dance song from 1811 proclaims simply that the dance rouses the religious feelings of the Believers:

> For dancing is a sweet employ;
> It fills the soul with heav'nly joy;
> It makes our love & union flow,
> While round and round and round we go.[10]

In contrast, a characteristic marching song from the early 1820s allegorizes the exercise:

> Come brethren & sisters, be thankful to God,
> That we have now enter'd this beautiful road,
> This little pathway in the wilderness found,
> Which truly does lead to the promised ground.
> Twas never beheld by the keen vulture's eye;
> The fierce roaring lion has never pass'd by;
> Nor has the young lion e'r traveld this way,
> Which leads to the mansions of eternal day.[11]

Further glossing of the symbolism is rarely found in early Shaker documents, but occasionally a visitor was interested enough to inquire and to record the answers. At Lebanon in 1827 Mrs. Anne Royall was told that the forceful steps of the brethren meant that they "tramp on the folly and riches of the world." The primary gesture used in laboring—beating time with the forearms parallel to the floor and hands turned palm downward—indicated, they told her, "shaking off the sins of the world."[12] How much further the development of such symbolism went in the 1820s and 1830s is not clear. Its flowering was not to come until the 1850s.

The physical movements of the march might suggest—and limit—the themes and symbols used in the texts, but they had a liberating effect upon the tunes. Since marches normally consisted of continuous forward movement, their melodies could be more various and free than those of the tightly patterned dances. The phrases of the marching song were not required to follow a saw-tooth contour. The tunes could begin with a low rather than a high strain. The sections might be of unequal length. The singers could expropriate ballad airs as easily as secular dance tunes.

The headnotes for the examples that follow will show that the marching songs in consequence exhibit many more ways of using traditional melodies. When taking a song tune for a march, the Shakers often kept it intact, although they would sing each half twice. In these cases the tune shows simply the kinds of melodic variation that occur in other variants of a song air. Believers sometimes, however, supplemented the original tune with a new one of the same length, repeating each entire tune. In contrast, when they borrowed from the fiddle or fife repertory, the Shaker singers normally retained only one strain of the secular tune. They extended it with some newly invented strain or perhaps with one from some other melody known to them. A song air, in short, tended to retain its identity virtually intact, while each strain of the dancing song was independent and needed only to combine with another strain appropriately higher or lower. Tunes that migrated between the two genres accordingly underwent contrasting forms of melodic variation in each. The fact poses maddening difficulties for the scholar trying to count or even establish criteria for "tune families." But for the nineteenth-century folk musician it opened the way to exuberant re-creation of traditional melodies.

The Quick Dance

The Quick Dance took two different forms. In both of them the singers stood along the side wall and the worshipers shuffled facing them during the second half of the tune. For the "promiscuous" form of the Quick Dance the brethren and sisters labored the first half of the tune without any particular order other than to keep within their own sides of the room. This suggests that the dance developed from the earlier Quick or Back Manner. The other form of the Quick Dance introduced a circular figure into Shaker laboring. The brethren spent the first half of the tune skipping leftward around a circle in their half of the room, while the sisters in their side skipped toward the right.[13]

From this figure the manner sometimes took the name Round Dance—this is what Haskell called it—but most Shakers used that term for a variation of the Quick Dance introduced about twelve years later. The Quick Dance itself lasted from 1811 into the 1870s, so the tunes were numerous. They normally show less regularity of phrase than tunes of the Holy Order and Regular Step families, since their turn sections were not bound by a twice-repeated dance figure. The songs were also lively. The 6/8 tunes—all of them 16 bars long—were sung in Shaker mode 7. Mode 3 was the tempo of the other tunes in 2/4 time (normally eight bars long, with one "beat of the foot" for each eighth note).

Unlike the earlier dancing songs, many Quick Tunes had words. Once the genre was well established, these song texts began to take a characteristic tone. They celebrated zeal and power, calling the Believer to wake up, leap, dance, and be alive. These songs were particularly appropriate, Aurelia Mace said, for use near the close of a meeting. Then the people would dance "each like a living spark, as David danced before the Ark," and then would come the gifts.[14]

Quick Dance No. 1

COME BRETHREN CAST YOUR ANGER OFF

Russel Haskell says that this was one of the first two songs used for the Quick Dance at Enfield, Connecticut. It was brought there by the ministry in 1811, but the text had been printed in 1807 in Richard McNemar's polemical volume, *The Kentucky Revival*. McNemar composed the song in reply to a letter from Barton W. Stone, founder of the Christian Church. His brother-in-arms while they were both dissident Presbyterian ministers, Stone was now horrified by McNemar's conversion to Shakerism. "Oh my Richard," he wrote, "shall I ever rejoice over you as a penitent prodigal?" McNemar's reply was

> Now, . . . if ever: I have just returned from feeding the swine, confessed my sins, been completely stripped, and clad with a suit completely new. The door has been opened into my Father's house, and I have entered, to go out no more. Now the family begins to be merry, and the elder son to wonder what it means—willing to get news from the meanest scullion. Don't you hear that it is MUSIC and DANCING? And is not the Father entreating you to come in? Then

Come brethren cast your anger off. . . .

Quick Dance No. 2

SINCE WE ARE UNITED

Samuel Parker of Harvard composed this song for the Quick Dance about 1813. According to autobiographical verses from his hand, he had farmed in Massachusetts before receiving the faith. He married at twenty-one and fathered six children in his twelve years of wedlock. The Harvard ministry did not record his death, so it is likely he fell back to the World.

Since we are u- nit- ed To vir- gins that are ho- ly, We're not con- dem'd to dance with them; But we can do it bold- ly. bold- ly. We have re-ceiv'd the Gos- pel, And keep it in pos- ses- sion. To dance and sing un- to our King, Be- longs to our pro- fes- sion. We -fes- sion.

Quick Dance No. 3

LEAP AND SKIP YE LITTLE BAND

This song originated at Lebanon during the early 1820s. Isaac Youngs wrote that this was a

> remarkable time for freedom and sociability, particularly on such occasions as in our meetings; it becomes all not to be straitned nor screwed up, but if any one feels to speak, or has any particular gift, he or she must be unembarrassed. . . . It is our faith that *"where the spirit of God is, there is freedom"* Our present Elder Br. is a remarkable man to disperse all superstition & bondage; and he has a peculiar gift to drive away darkness & heaviness & raise an assembly in life and cheerfulness. He abhors all grim; dull & bound up feelings. He has a particular gift also to change the sense of others from a scattered sense, and worldly mind, into union, & a gospel spirit; by little peculiar gifts, or expressions such as shaking, hating in some manner, or singing some little song or hymn adapted to the case. . . . He preaches simplicity & thankfulness as very worthy virtues. . . . He teaches us to labour for

Humility with chearfulness, fervency with wisdom, joy with thankfulness, love with purity, order without bondage and Godly fear without superstition.

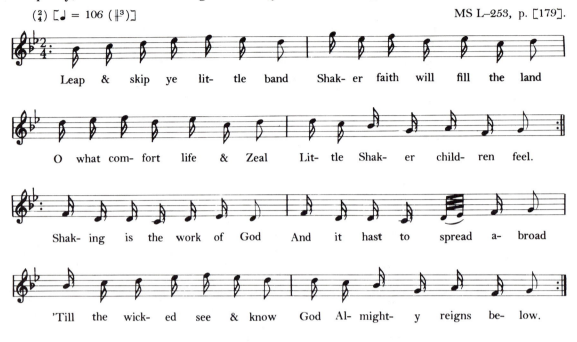

(²₄) [♩ = 106 (♯³)]   MS L–253, p. [179].

Leap & skip ye lit- tle band Shak- er faith will fill the land

O what com- fort life & Zeal Lit- tle Shak- er child- ren feel.

Shak- ing is the work of God And it hast to spread a- broad

'Till the wick- ed see & know God Al- might- y reigns be- low.

Quick Dance No. 4

COME LOVE COME LOVE

Eunice Freehart entered South Union in her thirteenth year and died there in 1887, "a faithful soul for eighty years." She received this little Quick Dance in 1831. The context of the gift must have been a scene like one that took place at Lebanon on July 4, 1827, in a time of revival. Elizabeth Lovegrove described it, saying,

> Now I cannot pen down the quarter part that we did in this good meeting, for my time and abilities are not sufficient. Elder Br. said this is the way; sing a little, dance a little, exhort a little preach a little, pray a little, and a good many littles would make a great deal; Jane requested to have a song of fredom sang, seeing it was independance, and freedom was declared, so we sung two songs on this occasion and went forth in the lovely way of freedom, rejoicing in the God of our Salvation. Charlotte administered a simple little gift of love & we all held out our hands to receive it, crying come love come love more love come. And it was our good fortune at this time to have our vessels right side up, so that we recieved a good measure, of this gosple Treasure, and I for one was so craving that I got my little dish filled to the brim; for I thought I never felt so free and loved my Brethren and Sisters so well in my life as I did at this time.

(²₄) [♩ = 106 (♯³)]   MS L–253, p. [31].

Come love come love Come sweet love and fill our souls

Come love come love Pre- cious love of Moth- er

Come sweet love & flow a- round And flow a- round & flow a- round

Come sweet love & flow a- round U- nite us all to- geth- er

Quick Dance No. 5

BY FREEDOM INVITED

A secular dance sometimes called "The Fairhaired Boy" serves this song. While the scribe who recorded the Shaker variant gave it a tempo marking too slow for the dance, the words of the song belie him, and I believe it to have been used for the Quick Dance or the Round Dance. Elder Issachar Bates made the song about the time he was recalled to the East from Watervliet, Ohio, in 1835. He was then seventy-seven. Until only a few years before, he "could dance and play in meeting about as spry as any of them," but the services in the Lebanon Church Family taxed his strength. The Thursday he arrived they assembled in the evening at eight and sang fifteen songs, laboring ten of them. On the next Saturday they labored twelve of eighteen songs. Meetings took up the greater part of Sunday. Elder Issachar jokingly wrote of "this purgatorial order," but approved the "many warm exhortations from every quarter" in the meetings. "All is freedom," he said, "—no bondage."

(⁶₄)   MS CB–36, pp. 124–125.

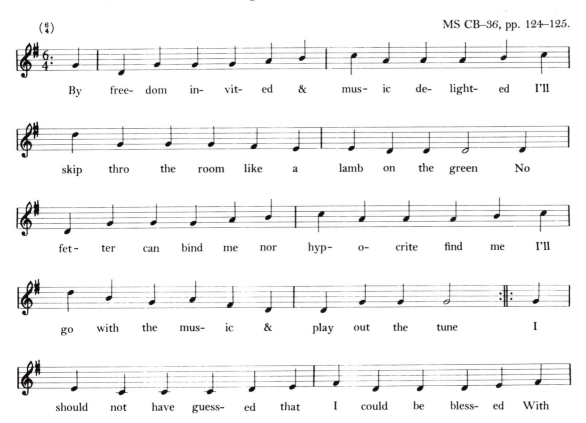

By free- dom in- vit- ed & mus- ic de- light- ed I'll

skip thro the room like a lamb on the green No

fet- ter can bind me nor hyp- o- crite find me I'll

go with the mus- ic & play out the tune I

should not have guess- ed that I could be bless- ed With

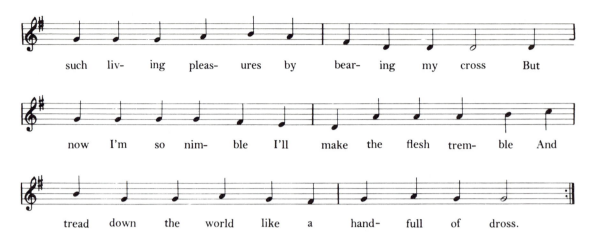

such liv- ing pleas- ures by bear- ing my cross But

now I'm so nim- ble I'll make the flesh trem- ble And

tread down the world like a hand- full of dross.

Quick Dance No. 6

COME LIFE SHAKER LIFE

In 1835, shortly after his return to Lebanon from the West, Elder Issachar Bates made this lively dancing song. His allusion was to the scriptural passage most often cited by Shakers in defense of their dances, 2 Sam. 6:14–16: "And David danced before the Lord with all his might. . . . And as the ark of the Lord came into the city of David, Michal Saul's daughter looked through a window, and saw king David leaping and dancing before the Lord; and she despised him in her heart." Other Shakers liked this song. It survives in a manuscript written at South Union and in oral tradition still in New Hampshire and Maine.

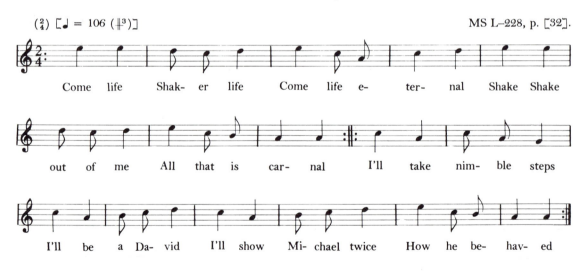

($\frac{2}{4}$) [♩ = 106 (♯³)]   MS L–228, p. [32].

Come life Shak- er life Come life e- ter- nal Shake Shake

out of me All that is car- nal I'll take nim- ble steps

I'll be a Da- vid I'll show Mi- chael twice How he be- hav- ed

Quick Dance No. 7

COME LOVE

Seven of the eight manuscripts preserving this song name an Ohio community as its source. But all these were written at Lebanon. The eighth songbook was compiled at South Union by Betsy Smith. She says in a note that she composed the text in 1835 and that "E McGuire" supplied the tune. This was probably Eveline McGuire, from whose hand some musical transcriptions survive. She may have fallen back to the World—South Union death lists do not contain her name—but Betsy was to serve forty-five years in the ministry there. She had entered the community at the age of ten and was twenty-two when she had the gift of this song.

Come love Moth- ers love O how I love to feel it
Flow- ing from the realms a- bove Liv- ing souls re- ceive it.
Love and un- ion free- ly flow- ing Love love so ho- ly
To the king- dom we'll be go- ing With the meek and low- ly.

Quick Dance No. 8

Molly Whyte of South Union sang this perky tune about the year 1834. She died in the faith in 1877, but the South Union church journal shows that her heavenly race was not run entirely within the bounds of the strait and narrow. "Molly was raised here," states one entry, "is now 32 years old & has supported a spirit contrary to the rules of our compact for such a series of years that a reformation is dispaired of, at all events until she ascertains more fully what is in the world." Accordingly, the ministry on September 11, 1839, directed two brethren to take Molly away in a carriage to "some respectable family." Molly persuaded the brethren to turn back, but finding it was "for no good that she desired to remain," the ministry sent her away again the next day. A year and a half later Molly desired to be "restored into union," and the ministry sent a two-horse wagon to fetch her, hoping she might be able "to act worthy of her privilege."

The ministry's decisions reflect both Shaker principle and considerable experience. Harmony was not attained in a Shaker village without constant effort. As O. C. Hampton saw it, any communitarian society inevitably contained a "super-added" degree of friction because of the number of people living close together. For Shakers, he felt, the situation was even more difficult than for secular communes:

> We, as Christians, were & are, obliged to receive all who profess to want to reform their lives, no odds how disagreeable they may be in their natural or acquired habits before they came amongst us. And therefore we have to make due preparation, to meet all these unamiable traits in those who join our Society, & discipline our minds in

patience and great heaps of charity toward such, until they can travel out of their
imperfections which all can do who remain faithful to the end of the conflict.

Quick Dance No. 9

TAKE THE LITTLE NARROW ROAD

This song is entered in one Harvard manuscript with the note "From Ohio 1836." It appears
in only two other collections, both of them written at Lebanon in the mid-1830s.

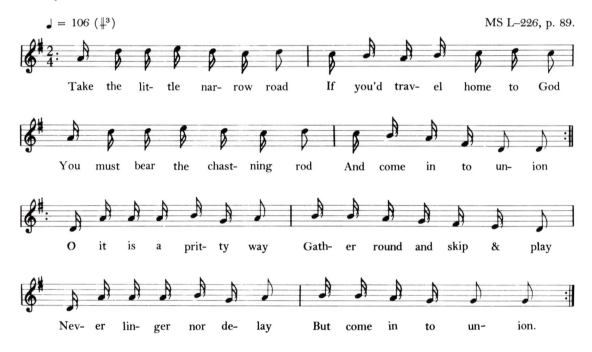

Quick Dance No. 10

Rhoda Blake, who had this Quick Dance in 1837, was the child of a Universalist couple from
Maine. Shortly after settling his family on a farm in the Berkshires, Rhoda's father died. Her
mother tried to support the children by home weaving, but Rhoda says the introduction of
power looms into the cotton mills in 1814 undercut her efforts. In 1819 she entered the Lebanon
society, taking her daughters Hannah and Rhoda, who was then eleven.

Before coming to Lebanon Rhoda had briefly attended a singing school. She had natural
talent and a resolve to understand the science of music. "Every scrap of paper with notes,"
she says, "I would seize as a choice bit to study." Her gift and zeal were noticed in the family,
but only one brother there could learn a tune from the notes or give any explanation of the

keys. An opportunity was sought for her to study with the singers at the Church Family. The ministry thought her too young—she was only fifteen—and instead appointed three older girls. When they came back from singing school, Rhoda borrowed their lessons and soon outstripped them all. She was to become one of the ablest scribes at Lebanon.

Quick Dance No. 11

HUMILITY

This song was transcribed at Lebanon about the year 1847. Clarissa Jacobs there was the only person to set it down.

Quick Dance No. 12

HERE IS LOVE LOVE LOVE

This is one of nine songs that William C. Bradford of Enfield, New Hampshire, wrote as a remembrance in a Lebanon manuscript in the summer of 1849. It also survives in one Canterbury songbook, where an additional whisp of text is provided in the second section of the tune.

Quick Dance No. 13

SOLDIER'S RESOLUTION

The spirit of Elder Benjamin Whitcher, who had died in 1837, sang this song in the Sabbath evening meeting at Canterbury on February 24, 1850. In performance this Quick Dance must have incorporated elements of the warring gift.

Who will rise who will rise Put the host of death to flight That now
lurk a- round your camp to sti- fle Zi- ons light
It is I it is I I'll u- nite in the war Let the
host of Sa- tan know 'tis the Lord I'm fight- ing for.

Quick Dance No. 14

I LOVE TO SEE A LIVING SOUL

Isaac Youngs received this tune in June 1852 in a letter from North Union. His correspondent was Jeremiah Ingalls, who was possibly also the author of the song. Brother Jeremiah may have had difficulty executing so sprightly a Quick Dance—he was fifty-five and "a very large man"—but he brought good credentials to the making of a melody. He was a son of Jeremiah Ingalls of Vermont, whose *Christian Harmony* songbook was the first to print the folk tunes current in the hymn singing of backwoods New England at the opening of the nineteenth century. The younger Jeremiah parted from his wife shortly before the birth of his second son. With his first, George Washington Ingalls, he entered the North Union society, where he lived until his death six years after sending Isaac Youngs this song. Both Jeremiah and George served as elders in the village.

I love to see a liv- ing soul, A- live in their de- vo- tion,

Quick- ened with the power of God, Free in eve- ry mo- tion. I

love to see them bow and bend, I love to see them turn- ing; Though

mor- ti- fy- ing con- des- cend, With them I'll be u- nit- ing.

Quick Dance No. 15

This dance tune was received at Lebanon on October 1, 1855, by Isaac Newton Youngs. Though few of the numerous songs ascribed to him have much distinction, his contributions to Shaker music were very great. It was his persistence and tact that induced Shaker musicians to unite in a single simple notational system. His manuscript and printed books of instruction were the chief sources from which the early Shaker scribes learned their rudiments of music. He himself also compiled many important collections of songs. And "Little Isaac" labored in many other ways for the cause of Zion: as tailor, teacher, joiner, clockmaker, mechanic, and scribe.

He was brought to the Shakers by his father in 1793, at the age of six months, after Isaac's mother had deserted her children and husband. (Although Isaac regarded her as grasping and unloving, the Shakers would in her old age pay for her support in Schenectady.) Having entered the Shaker community so young, Isaac never passed "any particular crisis, or turning point of conviction." His faith, he said, grew with his mind: "It grew with my growth, & strengthened with my strength." He never once meditated leaving the Faith; nevertheless, he had his struggles. Isaac says,

> My lost nature grew with manhood. My pride, selfwill, & passions increased with my body & mind. I had my own cross to bear, or suffer the goadings of Conscience. . . . I had my own choice to make. It was not suddenly made at any one time, it had to be seriously done over & over, continually setting out anew. . . .
>
> The pleasures of this world & my own will, were as a mysterious treasure hid in a box. An insatiable desire would harrass & prompt me to want to know what it was. I had not become bound with vicious habits, nor my passions inflamed by indulgence like an old sinner's, yet my ignorance of the effects of sin was as great a snare to me, as Adam & Eve's ignorance of the Tree of knowledge was to them.

In his last years Brother Isaac suffered from "a slow, wasting, nervous consumption," which caused depression and "such fearful forebodings as finally terminated in mental derangement." He needed to be constantly under watch. On the night of January 7, 1866, having heard of the burning of a building, he became possessed by the idea that the dwelling was on fire. Although he was so lame that it was believed he could not rise from his bed, in the two or three minutes when the brother watching him went to wake his relief, Isaac "jumped up from bed & precipitated himself out of the fourth story window onto the walk below;—he survived the incident about two hours, and then took flight to the spirit land." The ministry sorrowfully wrote, "No reflections are cast upon the poor demented & faithful Parent in Zion; but he is loved and blest forever and ever."

Quick Dance No. 16

WAKE UP THE SPIRIT CRIES

Preserved in a single Lebanon manuscript, with the note, "First Order Aug 13th 1863."

Quick Dance No. 17

I WANT MORE LOVE

Haskell alone preserved this song, entering it in one of his manuscripts about the year 1868.

The Round Dance

In this second form of circular dancing the vocal band stood in two rows in the center of the room (normally two brethren facing two others and three sisters the other three sisters). Around them the worshipers, two by two, formed a large circle. The men made up one half and the women the other. For the first section of the tune they skipped around the room, brethren beginning with the left foot and sisters with the right. In the last two beats of the section they turned toward the center, striking into the single shuffle for the remainder of the tune. Each section was sung twice.[15]

As in tunes for the Holy Order and Regular Step families, the turn section of the Round Dance melodies lies higher than that of the set. Round Dance tunes, however, have a distinguishing feature. Since forward movement occupied the whole of the first part of the dance and shuffling in place the entire second section, the tunes were not locked into a strict alternation of rising and falling phrases. Their turn sections may have three high phrases followed by a low one, while the set section reverses the pattern.

Except when the words of a Round Dance song describe the great turning wheel of the dance, the songs for this manner are indistinguishable from those for the Quick Dance. Most of the same tunes apparently served for both dances. Indeed the Round Dance is but an adaptation of the earlier Quick Dance. It simply substitutes a large circle for the two smaller ones of the earlier manner. The Round Dance in turn seems to merge into the Circular March. Aurelia Mace says that at Gloucester the laborers would "march" the turn section of the Round Dance tune and "shuffle" the set section.

An elder first proposed the Round Dance in a service at Lebanon one morning in 1822. "I have a feeling to try it," he said, "& *if we get beat, we can shake!*" Isaac Youngs thought it

> solemn & joyful to see the brethren & sisters advancing. O how happy they looked, how beautiful. Surely said I to myself, how mean are all earthly joys, how trifling are all the little trials which we have to pass thro in finding such spiritual comforts, such reviving glories which the gospel opens to our souls.[16]

Round Dance No. 1

THE GREAT WHEEL IS TURNING ROUND

Russel Haskell says this song came from the South Family at Enfield and places it with others dating from the years 1830 and 1831. The text alludes to the inner and outer rings of the Round Dance, as also to Ezekiel's vision of "a wheel in the middle of a wheel." The dancers were enacting that vision, for "the spirit of the living creature was in the wheels."

♩. = 180 (♭7)   MS EC–11, p. 52.

The   great   wheel   is   turn- ing round; The   lit- tle one's in

mo- tion; And all must come in- to this wheel, If

they do want a por- tion. With- in this wheel I'll

dance & play, And say I've got my por- tion: For

I do feel and plain- ly see I'm sail- ing in love's o- cean.

Round Dance No. 2

LIVING SOULS

Scribes recorded this song about as often in 6/8 time as in 2/4, but they are in general agreement that it originated in the First Order at Lebanon in 1853. The germ of the tune may lie in a Quick Dance that Rhoda Blake received there fifteen years earlier. Its opening bars are identical with the first two of the set section of her tune. "Living Souls" proved, however, far more popular. Hers seems to have been recorded only once. The later song survives in nine manuscripts and was known in at least the Lebanon, Groveland, and Harvard societies.

Liv- ing souls for heav- en bound there is no time to slum- ber

The Square Step

The Square Step, introduced in 1825 and practiced for some years, was based on the Regular Step and used the same tunes. In both manners the laborers stood in ranks facing the vocal band. They spent the latter half of a tune advancing three steps and retiring without turning or striking a shuffle. The first half of the Square Step was entirely new. The ranks stepped off a small square, at each corner making a quarter turn to the right and drumming the feet. The brethren started with the left foot, took three steps and drummed twice, then took two steps and drummed three times, alternating thus for the remaining two sides. The sisters meanwhile began with the right foot and made two steps and three pats, also alternating twos and threes. It required one turn of this section of the tune to complete the square. Both the turn and the set parts of the tune were sung twice. Alonzo Hollister called it "a beautiful & impressive exercise when performed by 200 people or more, in strait ranks."[17]

Square Step Tune No. 1

Richard Wilcox of Enfield, Connecticut, had this tune about 1835, his twentieth year. He lived on in the faith until his death in 1884.

MS EC–11, p. 121.

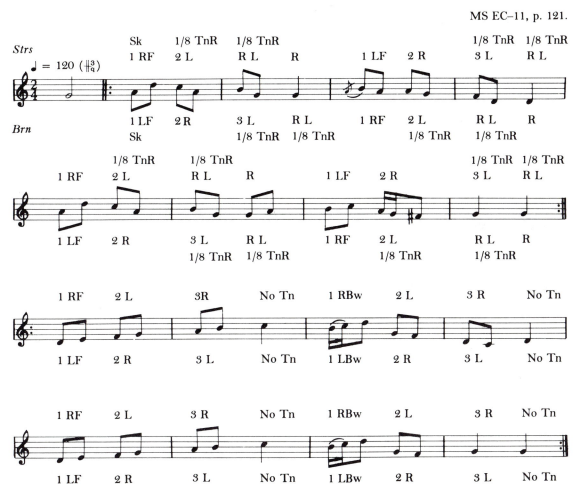

The Hollow Square

Tunes and figures from the Square Order Shuffle or Holy Order served for the Hollow Square, a dance learned in a vision at Harvard in 1825. As for the older dance, the singers stood midway along a side wall. Instead of turning toward them, the brethren faced the center of a hollow square in their half of the meeting room. One or more ranks of dancers lined each side of the square, with a small break at the corners. The sisters stood in a similar square on their side of the room:

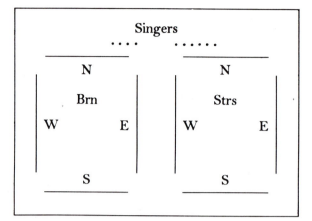

Diagram 1. The Hollow Square Dance

During the first phrase of the tune the east and west ranks would shuffle, while the north and south lines skipped forward toward each other three steps, turned and shuffled once, skipped three steps back, and again turned and shuffled. For the second phrase of the melody the east and west ranks advanced and retired in the same way while the other two shuffled in place. The laborers continued to alternate these actions throughout both parts of the tune. Each section was sung twice. A small variation sometimes introduced was the omission of the inside rank in each square. Sisters then formed the only east rank and faced brothers in the west rank across the length of the room.[18] From Harvard the dance was carried to Lebanon, Connecticut, and Canterbury. It seems to have lasted only a short time.

Hollow Square Tune No. 1

Haskell dates this tune 1828 and attributes it to Humphrey Smith of the Hancock society. This brother seems not to have died in the faith.

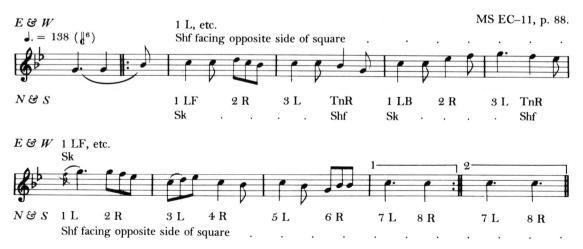

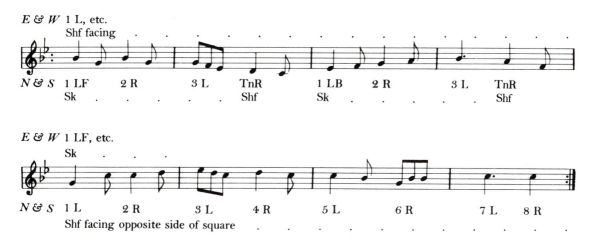

The Circular March

Shaker marches are more easily described than the dances. Although the marching tunes were composed of two strains, a single figure was usually performed during the whole tune and all its repetitions, and the footwork consisted simply of a step taken "as if the floor were elastic."[19] No tune was restricted to use with a particular march, except in the case of the Compound March of the 1830s and the later Slow March. All other marches could be performed to tunes similar to those used for the Regular Step or the Holy Order. In Haskell's transcriptions these are 2/4 tunes sung in Shaker mode 2 or 3, and 6/8 songs in mode 5. When marching tunes have texts, they almost always mention marching, traveling, walking or going. The songs were, in fact, also called Walking Tunes and Traveling Tunes.

By far the most common of the marches was the earliest, the Circular March, in which brethren made one-half the circle and sisters the other, going two or more abreast as the size of the room and the number of worshipers required. The vocal band stood in the middle of the circle, and the leading singer was encouraged to "keep the time with his foot, by stamping the floor" so the laborers could hear the beat and not drag behind the song.[20] From 1822 on, for eighty years or more, the marching of two or three songs in this manner often followed the opening hymn or anthem in the Shaker public worship.

Russel Haskell said the Circular March was "given for the aged more especially, and was seen in vision by some of the aged brethren at New Lebanon."[21] Whatever the original gift, Isaac Youngs' record of events at Lebanon shows that it underwent considerable refinement. The Believers there had already tried marching in 1817. Then on October 6, 1821, the Elder Brother had a gift for all to "walk together, so we walk in classes." On October 13, Youngs wrote "we walk in a circle, & the singers stand in the middle." Next, on October 14, as they walked they had the singers "turn with the rest, facing the leaders of the band." By October 21 the ministry had told the other families of this new manner of devotion, and persons came from them to see it.[22]

Fig. 29. A Form of the Circular March
From a second lithograph entitled "SHAKERS near LEBANON, their mode of Worship." Presumably the artist intended to show marchers circling the room while the vocal band performed in the center of the room.

Fig. 30. A Form of the Circular March
"The Shakers in Niskayuna" says the original caption of this magazine illustration, but the setting is the Lebanon meetinghouse. The artist appears to have blundered in placing the seated men in the foreground on the sisters' side of the hall.

Over the years several other variations were introduced into the Circular March. In 1827 Isaac Youngs suggested during a service that the inner file of laborers circle in the opposite direction from the outer one. This proved highly pleasing and was generally adopted. Sometimes the singers also formed a third circle in the center, heading the same way as the outer one.[23] In the year 1828 the laborers at Lebanon began another variation on the Circular March. The inner and outer circles marched in opposite directions and at one point on the floor each laborer turned from the outer circle into the inner, made one complete circuit, and wound back into the outer circle. From this it sometimes took the name Continuous Ring. How long or widely the Shakers practiced this form is not certain. Elder Henry Blinn entered a diagram of the manner into a Canterbury journal:

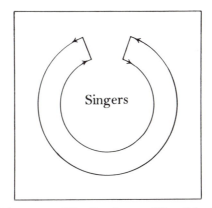

Diagram 2. The Continuous Ring March

He wrote that the New Hampshire ministry brought both this and the Changeable March back from Lebanon in 1828 and that for a few years the two were practiced "quite frequently," but "subsequently fell into disuse."[24] The only other clear reference to the Continuous Ring dates from Isaac Young's visit to Union Village in 1834. He saw there a continuous march in the form of a deep crescent.[25]

Variation could enter the footwork as well as the figures of the Circular March. A letter written from Watervliet, New York, in 1823 describes the use of shuffling during the second half of the tune. The laborers apparently halted and shuffled without facing toward the singers, and when the turn strain recommenced they again marched forward.[26] In a similar laboring manner that Aurelia Mace calls the "Celestial March" the worshipers at Gloucester would raise their hands at the beginning of the set section and turn around, then finish the set with a shuffle. Starting off in the march again on the turn section, they would clap their hands four times. "This," wrote Sister Aurelia, "was very beautiful and heavenly."[27]

Circular March No. 1

Most marching tunes served for both the Circular and Square Marches and for many other variations in the form. Occasionally, however—as in the present song—the text alludes to the circular figure. Such a song would have been restricted to use with the Circular March. Haskell recorded this example, placing it among the marches learned at Enfield about the year 1826.

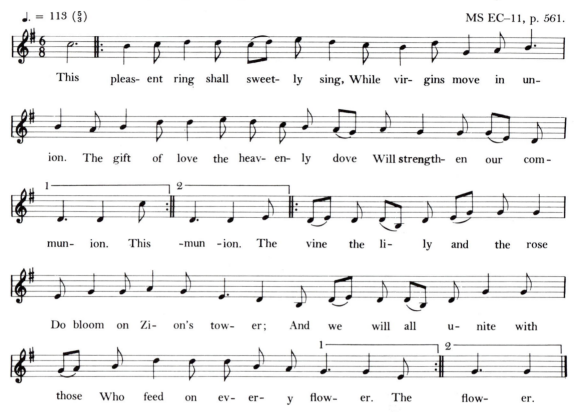

Circular March No. 2

A SWEET MARCH TO HEAVEN

This song started its journey from Union Village about the year 1836 and reached both Kentucky and Maine. Although only seven manuscripts hold it, the march must have been popular. It was still being entered into songbooks two decades later. One of these transcriptions shows that the tune was still undergoing change in oral tradition: the Lebanon singers had shifted its meter from 6/8 to 2/4 time.

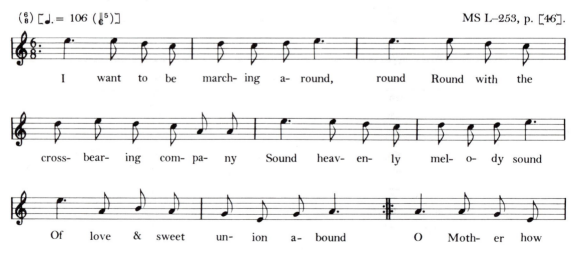

hap- py I feel I want to be ev- er re- joice- ing O fill me with

heav- en- ly Zeal To kill my old na- ture by cross- ing.

Circular March No. 3

A single manuscript from Enfield, New Hampshire, preserves this exultant march, dating it November 5, 1844.

♩. = 106 (𝄞⁵)   MS ENH–11, no. 326.

I love to see the wheels in mo- tion Love to see them

mov- ing round Love to hear the drums a- beat- ing Love to hear the

trum- pets sound.

The Square March

At the time they were devising the Circular March, the Shakers also marched "promiscuously." The brethren and sisters would march across their own sides of the meeting room without any particular arrangement, "some going east, while others were going west."[28] Haskell says that by 1826 this was improved at Enfield into a "regular method of marching . . . back & forth in strait ranks," called the Square March. Other societies had been marching in similar manners a little earlier. The Believers at Watervliet "went forth to worship God in a new manner" on November 4, 1821, "marching back & forth in a square body 8 brethren & 8 sisters at a time, 4 abreast & 4 deep: a beautiful gift."[29] In another march practiced at Watervliet in 1823, the worshipers formed into ranks with two or more brethren and as many sisters

THE DANCE

Fig. 31. A March
The original magazine caption ("The Dance") is erroneous. Lossing appears to be recording some form of Square March.

in front, and "as many deep as [was] consistent with the length of the meetingroom."[30] All would march solemnly forward and back. At each end of the room the laborers faced about and those in the rear led in going back.

In a related manner that would be practiced at Lebanon in 1847,[31] the laborers marched not as a square body but as files alternately facing north and south:

Diagram 3. One Form of the Square March

When the music began, the files passed each other, heading in opposite directions until they came to the north and south walls, where they turned back, passing again as they marched in the other direction. The Square March seems to have served as the basis for other elaborations too, the most complex of them being the Changeable March of the late 1820s.

The Changeable March

About 1828 someone at Lebanon or Watervliet blended features from the Square March and the Continuous Ring, forming a new manner of laboring. Elder Henry

Blinn called it the Changeable March, perhaps because the laborers as they progressed through its figure made frequent changes of direction. Another possible explanation of the name is that the figure of the march could itself be changed to accommodate a varying number of ranks of worshipers.

When the Changeable March was to be performed, the vocal band took its usual position in a line at the head of the meeting room. The brethren and sisters assembled in ranks on their halves of the floor. In the simplest form of this march, one described by Isaac Youngs of Lebanon, there were four ranks of each sex. Instead of facing the singers, the first and third ranks faced toward the center aisle of the meeting room and the second and fourth ranks toward the ends of the room. As the band struck up the march, the laborers advanced in their files, at the end of each row turning into the next one. As Diagram 4 (Form A) shows, the sisters were progressing toward the front of the room and the brethren toward the rear. The leading rank of each passed to the left of the main body to re-enter its rear rank.[32] D. A. Buckingham of Watervliet made two diagrams, labeled the Changeable Manner, in which the figure is altered to accommodate both six and eight ranks of laborers (see Diagram 4, Forms B and C).[33] At Canterbury Elder Henry Blinn drew off still another figure for use with eight ranks (see Diagram 4, Form D). Blinn says that the manner was highly popular for a few years, then fell into disuse.[34] Its figures must have prepared the way, however, for the complex marches of the early 1830s. It may also have served as the basis for a Changeable Shuffle practiced as a family manner at Enfield, Connecticut, in 1838. In this form, the laborers would presumably have shuffled in place during each return of the set section of the tune.[35]

The Compound March

In 1832 the young British officer E. T. Coke, who had watched the marching in a service at Lebanon, wrote, "I scarcely ever saw so difficult or so well-performed a field day. They had been evidently well drilled, or they could not have acquired such skill in manoeuvring." For the performance, fourteen singers gathered in the center of the room, and the rest of the worshipers formed a column five abreast. When the singers began, the column set forth and circled the room several times. It then halted, the inner files faced about, a brisker air was struck up, and the two columns moved off in opposite directions, making several more circuits of the room and halting to sing slow parts of the air. There followed, Coke said, "such a series of marching and counter-marching, slow step, quick step, and double quick step, advancing and retiring, form-ing open column and close column, perpendicular lines and oblique lines, that it was sufficient to puzzle and confound the clearest head of the lookers on."[36] He was witnes-sing a form of laboring that the Shakers generally called the Compound March.

Other visitors described scenes similar to the one Coke saw, and there are Shaker accounts as well. Isaac Youngs, while he was at Union Village on a visit in 1834, made notes on "some manners of marching new to us." One was the Encircled Square March.

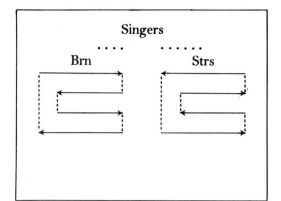

Form A—Youngs (Lebanon)

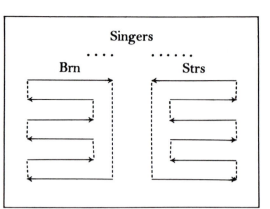

Form B—Buckingham (Watervliet)
[Conjectural reconstruction
of direction of movement]

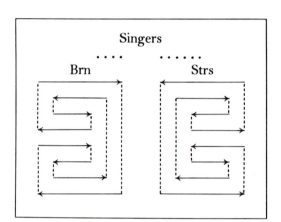

Form C—Buckingham (Watervliet)
[Conjectural reconstruction
of direction of movement]

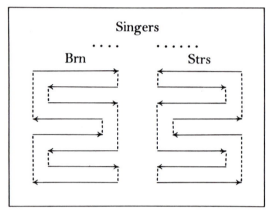

Form D—Blinn (Canterbury)
[Conjectural reconstruction
of the sisters' movements]

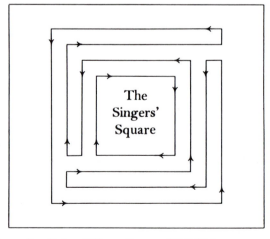

Form E—Union Village Papers (WLCMs, no. 347c)
[After an unlabeled, undated sheet; conjectural
reconstruction of direction of movement]

Diagram 4. The Changeable March

For this the main body of worshipers formed into squads four abreast and four deep. There were four such squads, each stationed on one corner of a large square of floor in the center of which stood the singers. When the exercise began, the squads followed one another as they marched from one corner to the next, made a quarter turn, and continued, each side of a squad leading in turn. Encircling this large square was a ring of other laborers who probably marched in the opposite direction from that taken by the squads:

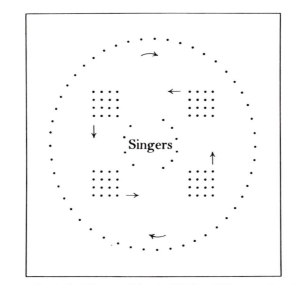

Diagram 5—Encircled Square March (Union Village—after Youngs)
[Conjectural reconstruction of the direction of movement]

Another march which Youngs witnessed at Union Village apparently bore an even closer resemblance to the Compound March. It was called a Kentucky March and consisted, he said, of "several forms a square a circle and a figure eight &c."[37]

These complex marches came into use around 1830 and seem to be a Shaker adaptation of the "sequence of 'changes'" that had been developed for the cotillion by secular dancing masters in the years after 1800. The ballroom dancers memorized each sequence and then danced through its changes "as though they were the verses of a song, with the 'figure' (or cotillion proper) taking the place of the chorus."[38] In the Shaker Compound Marches the marching alternated less strictly with standing songs and dances, but each march was necessarily choreographed in advance and practiced in private before its use in a service. For neither secular dance nor Shaker worship, however, did these formulas prove very satisfactory. The spontaneous calling of figures soon displaced the use of changes in square dancing, and after some five years' use the Compound Marches dropped from Shaker services. The Believer apparently found that their complexities stifled his spontaneous gifts.

Musically, the Compound Marches are composed of four or five distinct tunes strung together in a series. At the commencement of a new tune, the manner of laboring usually changes. As the following Compound March shows, the quality of the tunes varies. Several of the melodies in this example are commonplace, but the little Circular Quick Dance section is a gem. It apparently caught the ear of some Believers too, for at least one Lebanon manuscript from the end of the decade recorded it as a separate song.[39]

Compound March No. 1.

O come let us be march-ing; why should we de- lay? Our

time is too pre- cious to squan- der. Nev- er stop to cull

flow- ers that are by the way, Nor suf- fer our spir- its to

wan- der. For to rove af- ter flow- ers, we gath- er in thorns,

Which on- ly will serve to tor- ment us; And thus we're ex-

pos- ed to tem- pests & storms, With no sol- id good to con- tent

us. us. The way is plain; we'll not be slack; We don't re-

gard the weath- er. We'll move a- long, we'll not look back; We

all will go to- geth- er. And should af- flic- tion ev- er

call, We will be true to bear it. If an- y bless- ing

comes at all, Then we'll be sure to share it. it.

Shuffle

this:

♩. = 56 (⅓)

Stand, and sing this verse, facing in, and motioning:

O my gos- pel re- la- tion, how

love- ly you are! How sim- ple how pleas- ent in- deed you ap- pear!

No cross- es nor tri- als, how- ev- er sev- ere, Will cause our

spir- its to sev- er. All world- ly al- lure- ments how

light and how vain! Come ease or come pleas- ure, come sor- row or

pain, For one I'm de- termin'd with you to re- main For- ev-er and

Stand, and dance:

♩ = 113 (3/2)

ev- er and ev- er.

2 O how lovely is simplicity!
   It's the ornament of heaven.
   O how lovely is simplicity!
   It's the garment Mother's given.
   O lovely simplicity,
   O how pretty O how pretty!
   O lovely simplicity,
   O how pretty how pretty!

March No. 1

THE ROLLING DEEP

This song was fashioned from tested and proven folk-song formulas. Its melody is related to one popular in Scotland under the name "Drumdelgie," and its words echo the oath of constancy in the secular love song "My Love is like Some Blooming Red Rose." The song is a testimony for the Faith. For good reason then it struck a responsive chord among Believers. It is one of the oldest surviving in their oral tradition.

"The Rolling Deep" was received by Polly Lawrence in 1826, the year of her death. She was then only thirty-four, but had lived among the Shakers since being orphaned at the age of twelve. The Lebanon ministry, impressed by Polly's "benevolent, meek, quiet spirit" and by her executive ability, appointed her female lead for the new colony at Sodus, New York, but she died in her first year there. In the last meeting she attended, so large a crowd of people came that the Believers marched from the meetinghouse into the woods to hold the service. There they formed a circle, the visitors surrounding them, and sang and testified. As they marched back, Polly Lawrence led the singing of "The Rolling Deep." Many Shakers thought her voice excelled any they ever heard, and they said that on this day her singing was "uncommonly strong and melodious."

March No. 2

FAITHFUL SOLDIERS TRAVEL ON

Six scribes recorded this song, but only John Wood set down the syllables for the wordless section. Union Village seems to have been the place of origin, and the time perhaps as early as 1826.

Fol- low Moth- er   in   the   way   Lo rel lo   lo   lo rel lo

Lit- tle child- ren   skip and play   Lo rel lo   lo   lo   lo

March No. 3

A tune recorded by Sally Loomis at Harvard about 1826.

MS HD–20, p. 7.

March No. 4

Another in use at Harvard around 1826.

MS HD–20, p. 14.

March No. 5

These two related melodies were recorded in the 1820s. The origin of the first—which makes good use of the lovely possibilities of the Mixolydian mode—is uncertain. The second is attributed to Sarah Bates, the daughter of Elder Issachar. She was a girl of eleven when her father brought his family into the society at Watervliet, New York. In 1805 he went to the West as a missionary, and six years later Sarah removed to Lebanon, where she lived until 1881. She may possibly have seen her father when he returned from Ohio in 1835, but the only record of contact between them is a letter she sent him with the gift of a sweater:

New Lebanon May 20 1823—

Well Beloved Elder Issachar,

Thou art a friend known by this appallation with whom I was some acquainted a great many years ago, therefore my pen inclines, (moved by the heart,) to direct once more with the greatest obligations my never ceasing love and thankfulness to thee, for thy parental care to me. For thou wast always a kind parent to me. And I can truly say blameless before my eyes.

O that I could convey just one little stream from the fountain of grattitude I have ever felt to thee, for thy tender care and instruction to me when I was a child, and unable to help myself; for then thou wouldest know that thy labour was not all lost. Thou wast the one that first planted the truth of the everlasting gospel in my little vinyard, where I have toiled and laboured ever since. And I think after burning it over and over, and plowing and harrowing it so many years I have prospects of reaping some good fruit; if it is not blasted, (or blown off,) by the vain wind of imagination, (but this I must leave to prove by the fruits that I bring foarth,) to this scourge of the peace I always mean to set a double guard, and turn a deaf ear to the Devils lying polices which end in death. And go on my way rejoicing, making strait paths for my feet to walk in, clothing myself in that manner that I am willing to appear before God when I have done with time. . . . farewell

from little Sarah

March No. 6

Two manuscripts from Lebanon record this as a song originating in the Second Order there in 1827. Its first strain is yet another derived from "Gilderoy," the second related to that of Regular Step Tune No. 5.

March No. 7

When Sally Loomis compiled one songbook at Harvard in the late 1820s, she entered this march and the next with the attribution "E. B."—initials doubtless standing for Eunice Bathrick of that society. Many of the tunes by Eunice survive, and a number of manuscripts from her own hand. She also left an account of how she received her inspiration. "I have listened for hours," she wrote, "to delightful music, which seemd to flood the air high above my head. And tho' it seemed to be human voices, it sounded like chimes of bells, of different sizes & tones, but in perfect harmony." At other times when she "heard no audible voice" but simply felt her soul "filled with music which flowed forth in songs," she "sat at twilight" and sang "one new song after another till they seemingly numbered hundreds, all joined together like links in a chain."

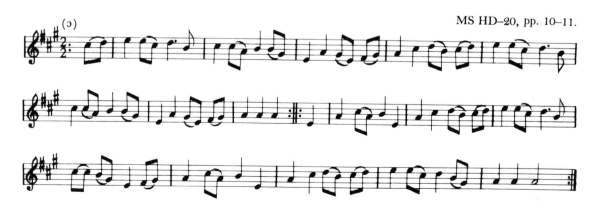

March No. 8

A second march by Eunice Bathrick recorded in Sally Loomis's manuscript.

MS HD–20, p. 17.

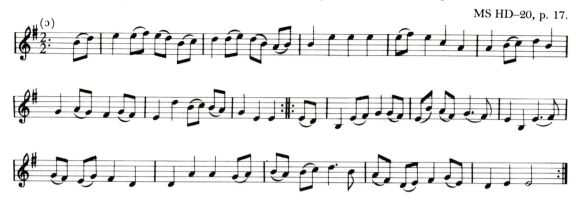

March No. 9

A march from Ohio learned at Harvard about 1828.

MS HD–15, p. [25].

March No. 10

A Canterbury tune from the late 1820s.

MS CB–35, p. [25].

March No. 11

Four manuscripts written around 1830 contain this song. One identifies it as a tune by Theodore Bates of Watervliet, New York. He was then a man of sixty-eight and may have been Elder Issachar's younger brother of the same name. Theodore, who headed the Watervliet broom industry, was credited by the Shakers with the invention of the flat broom.

MS XE–47, pp. [20–21].

March No. 12

This march is by James Wakefield of Gloucester and dates from about 1830. He was then a man of twenty-seven, a "very white, clean looking brother" with a "smooth, beautiful voice." Aurelia Mace recalled his singing in the first service she ever attended in the meetinghouse: "the music rolled from his lips in volumes." Song and setting overwhelmed her. "The blue wood work over head and the white ceiling between, the blue walls and white floor. All seemed wonderfull and the place was heaven to me."

MS ENH–2, p. [64].

March No. 13

This and the next seven marches are transcribed from a small manuscript of wordless laboring songs written by the year 1830. The collection is preserved at Sabbathday Lake. It may have been written there, although James Wakefield is the only early member known to have any acquaintance with the "rudiments of music." Otis Sawyer believed a songbook he himself began in 1842 to have been the first ever written at Gloucester, so this earlier manuscript may have been a gift from Harvard, Lebanon, or Canterbury.

MS XE–48, p. [10].

March No. 14

Most songs in the Sabbathday Lake manuscript appear in no other collection. This tune is an exception. A second songbook says it was one of four learned from the Poland Hill elders, who in turn had gotten it from Thomas Wright of Canterbury. He seems to have picked up at least its opening strain from a secular fife tune, "The Recruiting Sergeant."

MS XE–48, p. [74].

March No. 15

This song and the next two—all from the Sabbathday Lake manuscript—illustrate one way in which the Shakers remodeled older melodies. The second section of the common fife tune "The Girl I Left Behind Me" serves for the opening half of each tune, but in three different variations.

The Shaker tunesmiths completed their songs with new set strains. In all three cases these, in conformity with the Shaker dance-tune model, lie lower than the turn part of the melody.

MS XE–48, p. [77].

March No. 16

See the headnote for March no. 15.

MS XE–48, p. [79].

March No. 17

See the headnote for March no. 15.

MS XE–48, p. [80].

March No. 18

Another from the Sabbathday Lake manuscript.

MS XE–48, p. [88].

March No. 19

The irregularity in the third bar of this song from the Sabbathday Lake manuscript seems to have been intended, though it may have tripped any attentive marcher.

MS XE–48, p. [88].

March No. 20

The turn strain of this melody seems a modal variant of the second section of "My Love She's But a Lassie Yet," which circulated in American fiddle and fife collections. The Shaker tune originated at Harvard in 1830.

MS L–322, no. 52.

March No. 21

One of the five Shaker manuscripts preserving this song dates it "1830 about." Believers were still singing the song in the late 1840s, but by then for the Slow March. They credited the tune to Festus Miller of Hancock, but it has secular kin in "Gilderoy" and "The Bailiff's Daughter of Islington."

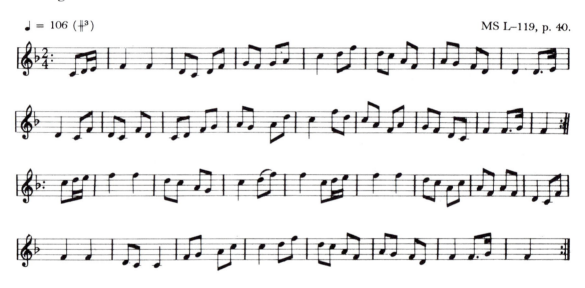

March No. 22

Elder Harvey L. Eades—the most prominent leader and musician in the South Union community—was never off Shaker land until he was twelve, when he went to Little Muddy River to help bring back two loads of posts. "O What a new world it was to me!" he exclaimed. Harvey had been born a Shaker at South Union shortly after the conversion of his parents. In 1831, when he made up this tune, he was twenty-four. The first real test of his faith had come only a year or two before. His account of it says that his mother's brother

> a well educated and wealthy man, a Judge and having the oversight of a College came
> to visit us, and said that he considered it wrong to keep so promising a young man . . .
> shut up in a Shaker Society, growing up in ignorance, and that if I would leave the
> People, he would send me to College and make of me a great man. He did not say
> this to me, but I heard it from others, and the idea of being educated was a great
> temptation to me, for I always carried my Grammar in my pocket, and studied it,

Fig. 32. Harvey L. Eades
1807–1892
South Union, Ky.

while I was driving my oxen. I thought to myself, Now if I accept my uncles invitation, this butcher's frock will be taken away, and I shall have a broadcloth coat, instead, and bid farewell to driving oxen in the mud, but best of all an opportunity to learn the languages. I did so much want an education! At last my uncle requested to see me at the Office. I did not dare to trust myself to go. I knew if I allowed him to flatter my vanity, and walk around the place with me, and perhaps hire a fine carriage, and drive round, that although at present I felt strong, I might be overcome. I therefore refused to see him. it was a great trial to my feelings, and I cried some then, as I do now at the reccollection. I wanted the education badly. I had considerable vanity, and wished to be as big as I could. I have had to have considerable many tumbles to make me humble and am not quite that now.

MS SU–25, p. [45].

March No. 23

A march from Lebanon recorded by Thomas Hammond at Harvard.

MS HD–15, p. 5.

March No. 24

Another song found in Thomas Hammond's manuscript and in the Sabbathday Lake tunebook.

MS HD–15, p. 11.

March No. 25

A third march from Brother Thomas's song collection. The opening half-phrase served two decades later as a building block in another march, "Treasures of the Gospel."

MS HD–15, p. 19.

March No. 26

The first half of this splendid melody has secular analogues in the Child-ballad tune "Jock the Leg and the Merry Merchant" and perhaps also "The Knight and the Shepherd's Daughter." The provenance of the Shaker manuscript that holds it is unclear.

MS XE–46, p. [19].

March No. 27

On February 11, 1830, Russel Haskell enclosed this tune in a letter to Harvard. A scribe there entered it in his songbook (keying it on A), but Haskell failed to recall the song when he began his "Record of Spiritual Songs." Despite his best efforts, his large collection is only a partial record of the Enfield repertory.

MS OCWR, iv.A.9, Feb. 11, 1830, p. [3].

March No. 28

A "Traveling Song" attributed to Thomas Wright, who came to Canterbury in 1808, when he was sixteen. His song dates from about 1830.

MS XE–46, p. [28].

March No. 29

Maria Price of South Union had this song around the year 1830, when she was in her early twenties. She was as gifted in singing as in getting songs. At the age of fifty-six she would even be released from the "Elder's Lot" in the North Family and moved to the Church Family to try to "bring up" its gift of singing.

MS SU–25, p. [53].

March No. 30

Elder Abraham Perkins recorded this song as one received in the Second Family at Enfield, New Hampshire, in 1832.

(ɔ)   MS ENH–2, p. [67].

March No. 31

THE MERRY EVENING

Three South Union manuscripts of the 1830s preserve this song and call it a "step tune." So irregular a melody, however, could have served only for the march. When a title heads a wordless song in the Shaker manuscripts, the tune is usually one remembered from the secular instrumental repertory, but I think this not the case with "The Merry Evening." Its author, James McNemar, was brought quite young to the Shakers by a family who would never have caroused with fiddlers. James was giving play to his own lively fancy in naming his tunes "Liberty," "Tranquility," "The Rapid Wave," "The Breeze from the Rose," and "The Merry Evening."

His high spirits were long remembered at Union Village. Susan Liddil sketched a typical scene in which he banters with a group of sisters bent on wheedling his help with a kitchen chore. Seeing him at the door "standing erect as ever he did in his early manhood," they "all feel a new spring of encouragement" and give out their "cunningly devised expressions that seem to come themselves, so impulsive, outspoken and witty are they, spiced up by mirthful rings of laughter." James shakes off their intrigues to get work out of him, saying, "You can't catch old birds with chaff." They in turn, under the "smart of their smitten pride," say James "has such a poor opinion of them that they are going to like Ithamar the best."

But it is likely he gave them a hand. One brother said of him,

> I have never seen that man in my life who had the strength or the skill to work with the ease and rapidity that James McNemar could. When he and I used to work together in the Cooper shop I often noticed that he never gave a stroke amiss and

what the rest of us would do for a day's work, James would knock off before dinner, and after dinner he would do another day's work and then go home with the rest of us as mirthful and teasing, and . . . fresh as a child from its play.

MS SU–8, p. [116].

March No. 32

THE BREEZE FROM THE ROSE

This second marching tune by James McNemar survives in only one manuscript and dates from perhaps as late as the mid-1850s. Susan Liddil left a sketch of his appearance in these years. "He is tall," she wrote, "has a muscular body. In his young manhood he had the blackest hair & beard, grey eyes & large features, & was said to be the strongest man in U. Village. His general weight is about two hundred pounds. He looks all the majesty and dignity of bearing that we imagine an emperor or king to have."

MS UV–21, p. [38].

March No. 33

WHILE NATURE LIES IN BURNING PAIN

When he sang of scorching old Nature, the Shaker voiced his craving for a full dominion not only over the passions but also over other frailties of his flesh and will. He tended to regard even bodily illness as evidence of spiritual failure and as a challenge to his faith. One spiritual autobiography copied by a scribe at Harvard, where the present song originated in 1836, illustrates the view. The account was written in the same year at Union Village by Elder James Smith. He told of being "taken with a severe cold" and feeling for a week "uncommonly stupid." One afternoon he fell to asking himself what he felt any care for. He discovered he could feel neither love for his brethren, nor desire for life, nor fear of death, nor even any concern for "the increase of the gospel." He would find his mind wandering "on forbidden ground"—"laboring with some turnback," or straying to the time, he said, "before I was a Believer, looking to see how much better I might have conducted to gain property than I did." He struggled to "get rid of those tormenting things" and to discover how he had lost his union, for he feared to die in this state.

His struggle lasted apparently for many days. One night, after he had a period of violent coughing, the "spirit of Mother" opened a dialogue with him. She reminded him that a year earlier she had inspired him with a gift to go out into the World to rescue some of the turnbacks, chiding him for having neither opened the gift to the ministry nor trusted that the spirit could carry out this work through him. The spirit then showed him three visions. The first was of his own soul, which "appeared about the size of a small pea, & looked like a small round ball of light." His heart sank at the sight of his insignificance, but the spirit then showed him the souls of many Believers, and all had small souls. "If your soul was no larger than a grain of mustard seed," said the spirit, "God could remove mountains with it. God never made a large soul."

The second vision was of "the *Man of Sin* in the Church." Challenged by the spirit, this being defended himself for putting away a childlike spirit now that he was in body and mind full grown. He complained of having been compelled to hear a great deal of preaching that had done him no good. He saw no value in following the rules, standing in appointed order in the meetings "& locking our fingers together, with our right thumbs & fingers uppermost" or "all stepping their right feet at once"—these rules he had complied with "merely out of courtesy." He also saw no reason to "apply to any other counsellor" to know whether he might stay away from meetings, and saw "no use in dancing, stamping & beating the floor" for another hour after doing a hard day's work. He also thought Believers worked too hard for their goods to squander them in acts of charity toward the ungrateful and undeserving poor. After this "great display and testimony" there seemed a silent judgment passed that this creature was "a murderer, a robber, a thief & a liar."

The third vision was of an "adorned soul." Elder James did not see it apart from its adorning, but "with *the adorning* it appeared about as large as a common person." Its "beauty, glory & shining brightness" were indescribable. They were not of the soul, but were the "power, wisdom, love & all the gifts & graces" of the spirit manifested in the soul. James said of these visions, "I believe that this exercise of mind was a gift of God—it felt so to me, and I mean to make a wise use of it. I shall labor hard to come down so low that the increase of the gospel may come into my soul."

Significantly, a turning point in both James's illness and his spiritual malaise had come in a burst of song. One night shortly before his colloquy with the spirit he had, he said,

a hard spell of coughing, and I got up & sat by the stove—A voice said to me, "Sing and praise God!" I answered, O Lord, how can I sing? I can hardly get my breath. The voice still said, "*Sing!*" I replied, I am nothing, and can do nothing: The Spirit said, "You are as large as a grasshopper, and it can sing." I then began to sing, and

a new song was given me, and I sung some time. I would then cough, & again sing—
and so it was, I sung & coughed alternately, till the cough subsided. I then laid
down & soon fell asleep, & rested well the remainder of the night.

MS XE–47, pp. [138–139].

While na- ture lies in burn- ing pain we'll clap our hands &

blow the flame And sing & dance on Zi- ons plain in

peace & Heaven- ly or- der We'll blow the trump as

we march round while vir- gins dance to the Heaven- ly sound Let

love & un- ion here a- bound thro' out Zions ho- ly bor- ders

March No. 34

WE ARE BOUND FOR SALVATION

Giles B. Avery recorded this march at Lebanon. He dated it 1836 and gave credit for the
song to Samuel Spooner, a brother who was to travel on in self-denial till his death twenty-
one years later at the age of seventy-five. Elder Giles's transcription is unusual for a Lebanon
manuscript; scribes there rarely indicated when the pitch of a note was variable in the course
of a tune.

MS L–14, p. [146].

We are bound for sal- va- tion We are bound to o- bey Trav- el

in a just re- la- tion In this great & glo- rious day Take the

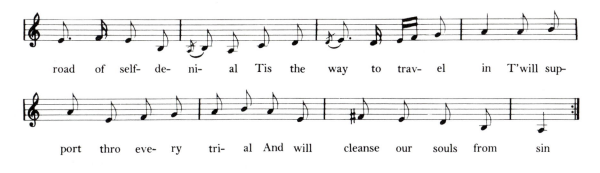

road of self- de- ni- al Tis the way to trav- el in T'will sup-

port thro eve- ry tri- al And will cleanse our souls from sin

March No. 35

In two Harvard manuscripts of the late 1830s this song bears the name of Eunice Bathrick. She was then about thirty years old and had lived in the society from the age of fifteen, when a spirit voice warned that if she wanted salvation she must "go & join the Shakers." The whole of her life was lived in frequent and familiar commerce with unseen presences. In her "autobiographic sketch" she wrote,

> I daily feel the presence of Angels & ministering spirits, & tho' I do not see them, I am confident they assist & give me strength, in whatever I am called to perform. I sometimes see peering over my shoulder, shadowy forms & faces, & when I turn to look at them, they vanish. Still I feel them near. I can recollect almost from infancy, a tawny visage peering over my shoulder, always bringing sunshine with him. Later in life I was told that this was my native guide who watched over me in my childhood.

(ɔ)   MS HD–15, pp. 6–7.

March No. 36

REJOICE AND BE YE THANKFUL

Two manuscripts written at Lebanon in the late 1830s preserve this song. Its text is a collection of Shaker commonplaces, but Believers felt them to be statements of a living fact. In workshop or union meeting, they daily exchanged tales of helpful spirits. Many of their stories that survive in manuscripts show a recurrent pattern: Once when feeling disquiet, the narrator had retreated to an empty room, where he saw a spirit. Usually it was that of a woman; she approached through a doorway, and she bore something emblematic about her. After speaking or performing an act she vanished. The narrator pondered the vision and found in it as many as three meanings: a comforting assurance of his acceptance, a prediction of good to come out of present trouble, and moral guidance.

One of the fullest of these narratives was set down by Calvin Green at Lebanon. On a day in 1826 he felt "a distressing warning as tho' some disaster was taking place." Soon the family elder was brought home so badly injured by a carriage accident that he looked unlikely to recover. This filled Calvin with "heavy tribulation" and anxiety about duties that might fall on him. Feeling much fatigued, he "entered a retired room" and lay down. Suddenly the door opened and a woman dressed in a "handsome green gown" came in. She held a year-old boy, also clad in a green gown. The child stretched its arms toward Calvin with an "ecstatic movement" and sprang towards him and clung about his neck, kissing his cheeks. Then both figures disappeared. Calvin "mused deeply" and had "impressively revealed" to him that the elder would fail and Calvin be called into his place. The woman was "a messenger clothed with Mother's lovely Spirit," and the child "a lovely little Spirit" that would minister to him as his "Guardian & helper." The child signified also that the family—a gathering order—would cling to Calvin, and the color green that its numbers would increase. The child was also an emblem of the character that Calvin ought to maintain. His vision was later fulfilled in fact, and he labored to fulfill it in character. The message and the aid, he said, called forth his "most grateful feelings." Elsewhere in this book I quote similar accounts by Jemima Blanchard, Richard McNemar, and Mary Hazard. Each story began as a memorate of an actual experience, but the occurrences themselves were shaped by and helped to shape the tales and visions of other Shakers.

$\left(\frac{3}{4}\right)$

MS L–334, p. [72].

Re- joice and be ye thank- ful Moth- er she will lead us

on If we will be true and faith- ful We shall

sure- ly have a crown Moth- er she will sure- ly

cloth us With a robe thats clean and pure She will

mark the way be- fore us And will guide us safe and sure

March No. 37

HEAVEN HEAVEN IS THE RESIDENCE

In secular tradition one 4/4 variant of this tune bears the name "Lady Campbell's Reel," though the immediate ancestor of the Shaker song may have been a jig. To judge from the text, however, Believers probably used the song for marching. It dates from 1838, when three scribes at Lebanon entered it in their books.

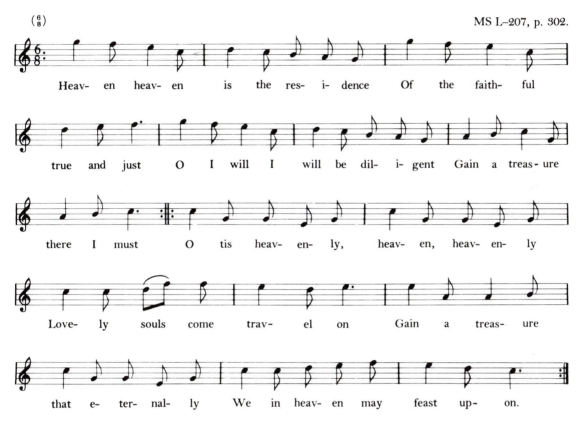

Heav- en heav- en is the res- i- dence Of the faith- ful true and just O I will I will be dil- i- gent Gain a treas-ure there I must O tis heav- en- ly, heav- en, heav- en- ly Love- ly souls come trav- el on Gain a treas- ure that e- ter- nal- ly We in heav- en may feast up- on.

March No. 38

This tune preserved in one South Union manuscript of the early 1840s has many cousins in the Southern fiddling tradition, where one strain or the other occurs in such tunes as "Cousin Sally Brown," "The Grey Eagle," "Piney Woods Gal," and "Solly's Little Favorite."

March No. 39

I WILL BE MARCHING ONWARD

Recorded about 1840 in one South Union manuscript.

March No. 40

COME ALL YE ZION TRAVELERS

One South Union manuscript preserves this song, ascribing it to "r. p." The song dates from about 1841.

March No. 41

This tune is dated July 1845 and attributed to "E. B." in the only manuscript holding it. Like Regular Step Tune no. 7 in the same manuscript, it is probably by Emily Babcock of Lebanon.

March No. 42

HAPPY HOME

This song originated at Harvard about the year 1845 and was widely known by Believers. Scribes from Maine to Kentucky set it down in their notebooks. In 1847 the Connecticut Shakers taught it to Adventists at a joint meeting. It was also one of four Shaker songs included in *The Pilgrim Songster*, a collection printed in Concord, New Hampshire, in 1853. But the Shakers borrowed as well as loaned; though cast into duple time and the major, their tune seems indebted to the Scottish song "Tom Bolynn."

March No. 43

LOVE O LOVE

John Robe, who received this song in 1846, had a cloudy origin and ending. Shaker records report his birth in 1818 on St. Croix. He was probably the "Molatto man" from the West Indies who arrived at Lebanon in 1839 after two years' correspondence with the Society. Rufus Bishop thought this seeker a "sensible young man, whether he will make a believer or not." Across the years, Shaker documents make only occasional mention of John Robe: now and then his authorship of a song; word of his remove in 1871 from the Gathering Order to the Church Family, where he was "introduced to the singing circle" in July; notice of a lecture he gave there on "Labor, Art, & Intellect" the following January—and of his apostasy later in the year at the age of fifty-four.

The following May he presented himself at the Watervliet society. I do not know what policy that society had toward apostates at the time. Sanctions against them were most severe in the early years, when many members were converts who had fought their way through personal crises to gospel ground and harrassment by the World was at its height. Later the Shaker reaction probably depended upon the apostate's reasons, upon whether he had gone so far as to sign the covenant, and upon the temperaments of both the apostate and the Lead. But even as late as the 1840s no "turnbacks" had ever at Union Village been "allowed another privilege though they appealed for the same in tears." When the spirit of Mother Ruth Farrington instructed that society through an instrument that some turnbacks were less bad than others and that the Lead might determine which could be readmitted, the aged brethren and sisters found the news "quite astounding." They had always believed "reuniting impossible in this life and even in the spirit world, to bear the humiliation of being always in the back rank." John Robe, in any case, did not end his days at Watervliet gathering lilies on Zion's banks. His name is not in the society's death lists, and the rest of his career is a blank.

♩. = 106 (♩⁵)   MS L–56, p. [124].

Love O love is sweet- ly flow- ing On its banks are lil- lies glow- ing These our Moth- er is be- stow- ing Love love heav- en- ly love. Come dear child- ren free- ly gath- er Learn to love and bless each oth- er This will bind our

hearts to- geth- er In love, love Heav- en- ly love.

March No. 44

Alonzo Hollister of Lebanon was eighteen when he received this march in 1848. He had come into the Society ten years earlier with his parents and from his ninth year held an "immovable conviction" that he could never "enjoy life, nor friendship, nor any other blessing while practicing carnal indulgence." Alonzo proved a supporter of the Faith until his death in 1911.

Brother Alonzo believed himself descended from an English "Lord of the manor" in Bristol, but his father was a "factory man" from Connecticut who moved about so often that he bequeathed his son chiefly "a roving disposition." This the Shakers curbed with a training strong in duty and discipline. As one of ten boys being raised in the Second Order at Lebanon he shared, he wrote,

> the care of the kitchen garden. The boys had to help plant potatoes & corn on the farm, also to hoe the crops after the plants came up, & to harvest them in the fall. They also had to help in haying & harvesting grain. Besides our regular work in the garden, we had to pick up the stones that had been turned up by the plow, on the new seeded fields that they might be mowed without striking the edge of the Scythe on a stone.
>
> Boys had to carry in the kitchen wood, nights & mornings & also to keep wood supplied to all the fires in the dwelling house, & the sisters shops, during cold weather. Each lad, had one, two, or three wood boxes to care for, during the winter. In the dwelling house, the boxes were larger & one box had to supply from three to five fires. A boy had to help the herdsman, morning & evening, & go for the cows & drive them again to pasture. In winter, to chop roots, feed the calves, pitch down hay, clean the stables, & such other chores as boys can do. At this, several took turns.
>
> One had to feed the hens & chicks evenings & mornings, & gather the eggs. These were our regular chores, besides many occasional ones, & the doing of errands.
>
> Boys were allowd a play day, in the forepart of Summer, to fish, or roam on the mountain—one ride each, after they were 10 years of age, to Pittsfield or Washington, 4 miles beyond, with the teams who went & returnd same day with lumber. & after 14 years of age, a ride with a team to Albany, & return the next day. It was also regarded as a holiday, to wander over the fields together, with Caretaker, Strawberrying—having our dinner with us—& returning so as to be in at supper time. Also, to get up at 3 O clock A. M. taking breakfast & dinner with us, & riding 10 or 12 miles to gather blackberries, Eating breakfast at the end of our journey before we began to work. The field of operation was deemd too rough for the Sisterhood, but not for boys—Riding home, the larger part of the way in the dark—after filling our vessels—& supping on the remnants from dinner. Boys were also allowd a day in the fall to scour the woods & fields for chestnuts or walnuts, all of which seemd like seasons of releasement. Sometimes a whole day would be spent riding— & others, boating on the pond.

Fig. 33. Alonzo G. Hollister
1830–1911
Lebanon, N. Y.

March No. 45

HEAVENLY HOME

One scribe at Union Village and another at Lebanon recorded this song about the year 1848. It had reached them from Pleasant Hill. Despite having two stanzas, the song was not regarded as a hymn, for both writers marked each half of the tune for repetition. Its tone, in any case, is that of a Gift Song for marching.

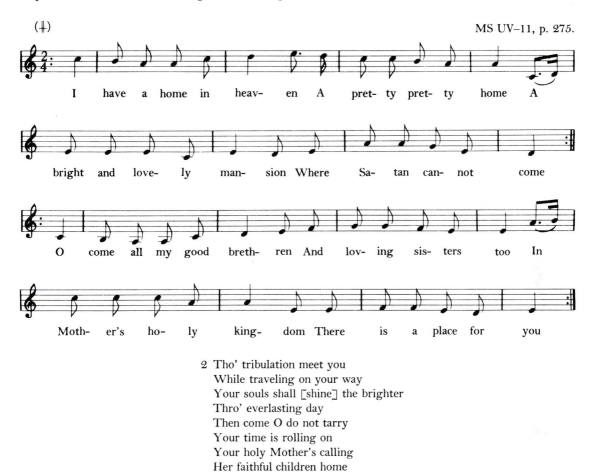

(♯)   MS UV–11, p. 275.

I have a home in heav- en A pret- ty pret- ty home A

bright and love- ly man- sion Where Sa- tan can- not come

O come all my good breth- ren And lov- ing sis- ters too In

Moth- er's ho- ly king- dom There is a place for you

2 Tho' tribulation meet you
   While traveling on your way
   Your souls shall [shine] the brighter
   Thro' everlasting day
   Then come O do not tarry
   Your time is rolling on
   Your holy Mother's calling
   Her faithful children home

March No. 46

PRESS ON

Russel Haskell left the only transcription of this song in a scratch book he wrote in 1849. I judge from the tempo and the text that the song was a march.

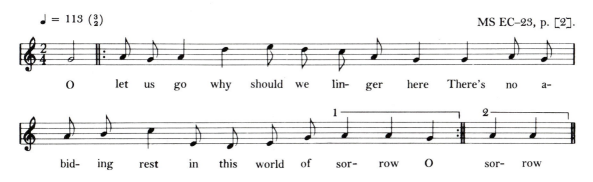

♩ = 113 (3/2)   MS EC–23, p. [2].

O let us go why should we lin- ger here There's no a-

bid- ing rest in this world of sor- row O sor- row

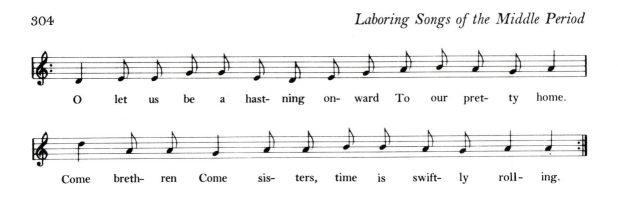

O let us be a hast-ning on-ward To our pret-ty home.

Come breth-ren Come sis-ters, time is swift-ly roll-ing.

March No. 47

FLYING INDIAN

This title occurs in secular fiddle-tune collections, but not with this melody. The tune does, however, have secular analogues. Its first strain resembles that of "Lop-Eared Mule." Except for their third phrases, "Flying Indian" and the Irish dance tune "The Spalpeen Fanach" are also near relatives. The Shaker tune was recorded at Whitewater, Ohio, about 1850.

♩ = 106 (♯³)   MS WO–8, p. 228.

March No. 48

HEAVEN BOUND

This march, the first half of which is related to "Zion's Soldier" in the shape-note tradition, dates from about 1852. Shaker manuscripts attribute the song to Elder John Martin. A native of Brown County, Ohio, he entered Union Village as a convert in 1823. He was then nineteen and was to give sixty years of service to the society, as a trustee and as an elder in several families at Union Village. From 1839 to 1859 he stood in the Western ministry, filling that place "with distinguished honor, to the great satisfaction of the people at large."

For heav- en I'm bound to go

I'll leave all earth- ly things be- low

March No. 49

ARMIES OF HEAVEN

This popular march branched into several traditions. It originated at Enfield, New Hampshire, about 1850 and reached Lebanon shortly afterwards. Four manuscripts written there at the time preserve the first form of the tune. Four more manuscripts of the late 1850s show that it was still in use in the community and that oral transmission was altering the tune. They record, for example, the opening five notes of the song a third higher than in the original, which I print. Meantime a letter from the East to Ohio must have contained a copy of the march written without a staff and without a clear indication of the rising and falling of the notes, for three Ohio scribes set down the first three and a half bars of the second strain an octave lower than the Easterners sang them. This cause of folk-song variation is peculiar to the Shaker notational system.

With the ar- mies of Heav- en, I will march on my way And in

praise to my Sav- iour, most sweet- ly I will play.

March No. 50

In making this song in 1852, Festus Miller of Hancock probably was stimulated by recollections of the fife tune "When Bidden to the Wake."

MS HN–7, p. [7].

March No. 51

Manuscripts do not classify this tune, but the anomalous length of its set strain precluded its use for any exercise but marching. In one Canterbury manuscript, the tune bears the note, "Elder John Martin's own song, sung by himself in the Chh. Cy Sep 1854." Elder John, then in his fiftieth year, was on a visit from Union Village.

MS WO–5, p. [31].

March No. 52

One manuscript containing this tune attributes it to Jeremiah Lowe, a brother who had entered the society at Watervliet, New York, in 1817, when he was nineteen. The tune dates from about the year 1852.

♩ = 128–160 (♯⁴)   MS WNY-18, p. 425.

March No. 53

LIVING SOULS LET'S BE MARCHING

A few scribes claim this march for Watervliet, New York, but most say it came from Tyringham in 1853. The song proved popular. Fifteen manuscripts from Lebanon, Watervliet, and Harvard hold it, and Brother Ricardo Belden of Enfield chose it for his only song in a taped interview in the 1950s. Perhaps Believers liked its one unusual feature, that the text weaves an allusion to the wise virgins (Matt. 25:1–13) into the commonplaces of the marching songs.

[♩ = 106 (♯³)]   MS WNY-27, p. [34].

Liv- ing souls lets be march- ing on our jour- ney to

heav- en, With our lamps trim'd & burn- ing with the

Oil of Truth, Let us join the heaven- ly

cho- rus And u- nite with our Par- ents, They will
lead us on to glo- ry In the path of right- eous- ness.

March No. 54

MY TREASURE IS IN ZION

This South Union song survives only in Eastern transcriptions made in the mid-1850s. The first half of the tune seems derived from that of the Irish ballad "Erin Far Away," but the Shaker singer invented a second strain to make it a proper marching song.

My treas- ure is in Zi- on my in- t'rest is here, I have
noth- ing to look back for, so on- ward I will steer; the
way is de- light- ful I love it more and more, As on- ward
I'm ad- vanc- ing to Ca- naan's hap- py shore.

March No. 55

MUSIC ON THE MOUNTAINS

On April 24, 1856, Israel Trotter of Union Village wrote to Isaac Youngs, enclosing this tune in his letter as a special memento. In his haste he misbarred much of the set strain.

(♯)   **MS OCWR, iv.A.73, April 24, 1856.**

March No. 56

PLEASANT WALK

Phidelio Collins of Hancock had this tune in 1857. He drew its first section from a fife tune, "The Cuba March," but capped it with a set strain far stronger than the one in the secular piece.

♩. = 106 (♭5)   MS L–279, p. [36].

March No. 57

In an Eastern manuscript of uncertain provenance this song bears a note reading "F. M.'s March 1858." The singer was probably Festus Miller of Hancock.

(♭)   MS XE–4, p. [44].

March No. 58

HOW BEAUTIFUL O ZION

On August 24, 1858, eight years after her death, Eldress Ruth Landon brought this fine marching song as a token for Benjamin Gates of the First Order at Lebanon. The instrument (identified only as "M. B."—probably Miranda Barber) had the book of Isaiah much upon her mind. The text of the song is woven from allusions to it: to such passages as "thou shalt call thy walls Salvation, and thy gates Praise" (60:18); "his name shall be called Wonderful, Counsellor, ... the Prince of Peace" (9:6); and "all they that despised thee shall bow themselves down at the soles of thy feet; and they shall call thee, The city of the Lord, The Zion of the Holy One of Israel" (60:14). For Miranda and others who sang it, the song must also have recalled the closing words of this chapter of Isaiah, "A little one shall become a thousand, and a small one a strong nation: I the Lord will hasten it in his time."

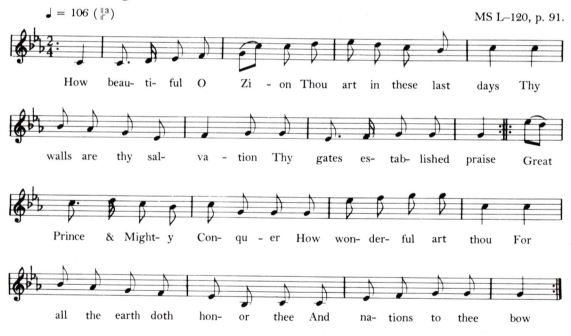

March No. 59

This "quick song" originated in the South Family at Canterbury about 1859. It bears some relation to the fiddle tune "Fire on the Mountains," as recorded in a nineteenth-century fiddle-tune manuscript.

MS XE–39, p. [13].

March No. 60

George Washington Curtiss, who received this song at Lebanon about the year 1859, was born in 1806 in Branford, Connecticut, in a house only a few rods from the harbor. The older brother of one of his friends was a ship captain who would often "notice" George, taking him on his knee, telling him of "the fine things that grew in the west Indies," and asking him if he did not want to go to sea. In 1815, when he was nine, George decided to run away as a cabin boy on the captain's vessel. The ship was to weigh anchor at midnight, and after he thought his parents were asleep, George slipped past his parents' open door and out of the house, carrying his shoes in his hand, and started for the wharf. Suddenly his mother called out for him to come back inside. "Had a bullet struck me," George wrote, "I could not have felt worse." The next day the ship was gone and George was sick with disappointment. His mother cured this with a sound dose of picra, a cathartic.

His parents had known his intentions and were very afraid they would lose him, "their youngest child & their favorite." As his mother had a brother, two sisters, and a nephew at Lebanon, they decided to take him to the Shakers for a year to get sea thoughts out of his mind. The effect was greater than they intended. When his father slipped away without saying good-by, George thought to himself, "If that is all my Father cares for me, to go away & leave me here, he may go, & I will try to find friends that I love as well as I do him." He soon developed a deep attachment to his aunt Hester. For Mother Lucy Wright, who gave him a pear from her basket and questioned him kindly when she met him in the road, he gained a love that he says "was the means of my early planting."

When his father returned for him a year later, George begged to be allowed to stay among the Shakers where he could "be good easier" and "go to Heaven." At first his father was stern, but then turned "very solemn" and "rose from his seat & rapidly walked the floor" with tears rolling down his cheeks. "Have I fought for Independence & liberty of Conscience, & here one of my own children pleading for that liberty! Can I stand between him & his Creator? God never gave me that right." At this, George said, "I felt a kind of glory within, for I had plead with all the earnestness I was able, that I might have a privilege to obey my Faith." His father departed, and George lived on in the faith until his death in 1873. He was "for several years the leading singer in the 2nd Order of the Church."

March No. 61

Manuscripts from Harvard, Canterbury, and Lebanon preserve this tune. Orren Haskins of the latter society had the song in May 1860. This brother was born at Savoy in the Berkshires in 1816 and came to the Shaker village when he was seven. His principal service was as a joiner and carpenter, and it was said that the record of his life would "pass the seat of judgment creditably."

March No. 62

THE SPRING DOVE

Harvey Eades learned this tune from Whitewater, Ohio, around 1858. The next marching song was recorded there five years later. Both open with a figure common in British and American dance tunes. The two songs derive, however, from an Irish air that P. W. Joyce calls "Sweet Cootehill Town" and describes as "usually sung at the little gatherings of friends on the evening before the departure of emigrants for America." The Shakers treated the melody as a two-strain laboring song, but retained the entire AABA song structure. Fiddle tunes that floated into their repertory, by contrast, rarely retained their original pairing of first and section strains.

March No. 63

See the headnote for March no. 62.

MS WO–11, p. [32].

March No. 64

Another marching song from Ohio, recorded in a Union Village manuscript about 1868. Like the two preceding tunes, this one has analogues in the fiddle-tune repertory—"Poll Ha'penny" in Francis O'Neill's *The Dance Music of Ireland* is closely related to it—but the melody probably derives ultimately from the ballad tune "The Jolly Beggar" or "The Gaberlunyie Man."

MS UV–1, p. 13.

March No. 65

I WANT TO GETHER DOWN

This song appears in one notebook written at Lebanon about 1866. No note tells its origin or use, but the song has a regularity of beat and a text that imply the marching exercises.

(‖)   MS L–275, p. [184].

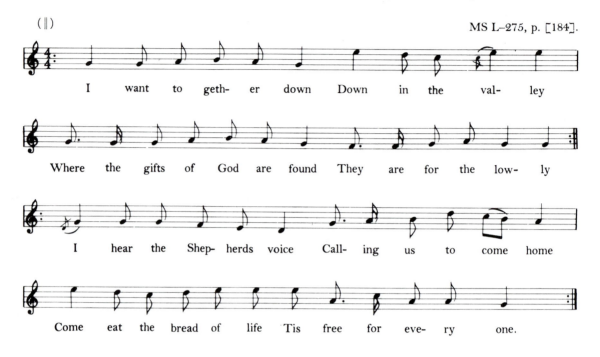

I want to geth- er down Down in the val- ley

Where the gifts of God are found They are for the low- ly

I hear the Shep- herds voice Call- ing us to come home

Come eat the bread of life 'Tis free for eve- ry one.

March No. 66

LOWLY VALE

This little march—received by Polly M. Rupe of Pleasant Hill in 1869 and still sung in Maine by Sister Mildred Barker—draws on typical Shaker images, the gentle breezes and lowly vale. Characteristically, this otherworldly song only implies by contrast the everyday toil and risks to which its country-bred singers were subject. Only a few years before she had this song, Polly went to harvest cherries and fell while attempting to fasten two ladders together in the top of the tree. She was "seriously, tho' not permanently crippled." Four years earlier William Runyon, the chief singer at Pleasant Hill, came near losing his life when a "furious bull" charged him one cold December morning and "felled him to the ground by a stroke with his horn, and ran over him, dangerously wounding & lacerating him; and he was only rescued . . . by the timely aid of John Thurman, who at the fearful risk of being himself gored into buzzard bait, beat back the beast with a bludgeon." Singers or not, the 350 members of the village kept busy in these years earning their livelihood. In 1856 they had the care of 35 horses, 85 milk cows, 186 other cattle, and 611 sheep. They raised—in addition to garden vegetables—3,358½ bushels of wheat and rye, 393 bushels of Irish potatoes, and 249 barrels of corn. This was only part of the brethren's assignment. Meantime, the sisterhood, among other chores, put up 9,432 jars of preserves, a total of 33,012 pounds. Reason enough to sing of a land of peace and delight.

(♯)

MS PH–6, p. [36].

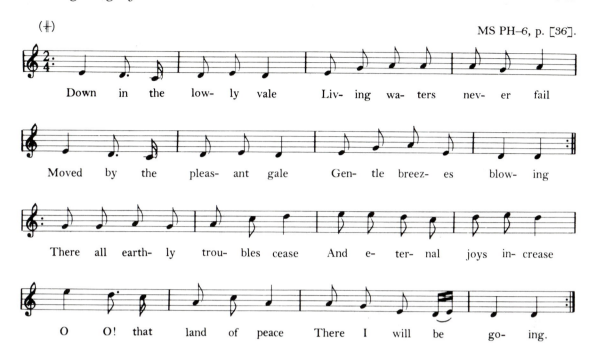

Down in the low-ly vale   Liv- ing wa- ters nev- er fail

Moved by the pleas- ant gale   Gen- tle breez- es blow- ing

There all earth- ly trou- bles cease   And e- ter- nal joys in- crease

O O! that land of peace   There I will be go- ing.

PART X

Gift Songs from Mother's Work

By this unusual name the Shakers referred to a period of renewed spiritual dedication that began in 1837 and lasted a full decade before tapering away. Its distinctive mark was that it was accomplished chiefly through spiritualist phenomena. While the seeds had been planted by Ann Lee—whose visions were recorded in *Testimonies of the Life and Character*—and had in some earlier seasons put forth a sprout, they were remarkably quickened by showers of the spirit in the 1840s and shot forth with many an extraordinary growth and bloom.

The record of the events of the period is quite full. Descriptions were left not only in letters and diaries, but also in "spiritual journals," detailed accounts of the meetings recorded at the direction of the ministry. Accounts were also set down in later years by Shakers with a historical bent. Apostates and visitors recorded their observations. All of these sources were drawn upon by Edward D. Andrews for a chapter of his *The People Called Shakers*. Here I shall present only as much summary as may be a necessary background and shall elaborate on topics that bear importantly on the songs of the era.

The chief facts of the period are easily given. On August 16, 1837, a group of girls in the children's order at Watervliet, New York, began to enter trances, telling later of journeys to heavenly mansions and of conversations with spirits. Excitement over these events sped not only throughout their own society, but to all other Shaker communities, and within about a year similar operations in all societies had affected many members. The next development occurred at the end of 1838, when spiritual beings began to appear to and in the persons of "instruments." First came early leaders, angels, and heavenly doves, then Mother Ann and Jesus, and eventually God Almighty and Holy Mother Wisdom. In 1840 early revelations of a childlike simplicity had passed and inspired writers began to serve as scribes for the delivery of prophetic books. In addition to spontaneous manifestations, persons in each society were appointed to serve as mediums at the need of the ministry. In 1842 spiritual directions were given for the preparation of feast grounds on holy hills for outdoor worship. Meetings had by this time become so extraordinary that the doors were closed to the World. By this time too "native spirits"—spirits of Indians and other pagan peoples—had begun to flock to the Shakers for spiritual instruction. In 1845 the public were readmitted to Shaker services. The native spirits departed in 1847, and the outdoor services at the feast grounds were discontinued by 1854. After the early 1850s there was only sporadic occurrence of happenings that had been common a decade earlier.

The effects of these phenomena upon Shaker song were quite powerful, and they touched it in almost every aspect. Mother's Work unlocked floods of new songs—no other period of Shaker song can compare with it in prodigality. It was not at all unusual when, during one evening meeting at Union Village in 1838, Richard McNemar's daughter Vincy after lying on the floor

> some length of time with her hands in motion, sung a beautiful new song, & before 10 Oclock she sung two more new songs. Soon after this she was taken to the Office being stiff, & helpless; after this she sung another new song, & by 11 Oclock she come too, so that she was able to go home.[1]

Matilda Southwick at Sodus had fifty new songs in one week. Isaac Youngs estimated in 1848 that in the preceding ten years there had been three hundred new anthems, "not far from one thousand little anthem like songs" for use in the "intervals between exercises & speaking," and 2,546 songs for exercise. Although this count of 3,850 songs includes some from other societies, it is primarily a tally of songs received at Lebanon alone. Brother Isaac felt that there were "enough to sing, without introducing a great many new ones for some time."[2]

He also reported that the greater number of these songs had been memorized and used in the society—an effort that had made this decade "a very laborious time for singers," requiring of them "much patience & perseverance." Their faithful labor was rewarded one evening at a singing meeting held for the purpose of learning new songs. Mother Ann manifested herself and

> said she must notice the singers tonight. Some of us thot the time taken to learn so many songs was lost time. Not so, said she; It is time well improved; & will not be lost. Some of you wonder why so many songs are given; many of you present will yet see the time that they will be needed. Many souls will yet receive faith from these pretty songs. . . . I love to have all of my songs noticed—every one of them. If you cannot improve them all, *keep* them; they will become of use to you. They are all sent to do good. . . . Be encouraged. I have many times been by your side while you were writing & noting these songs & seen how you did it. These are my words, & some of the songs are my own, & some are other good Spirits' songs.

Brother Isaac noted that this was "very encouraging to the singers." But at Lebanon the ministry was finally moved in 1848 to tell the singers it was thought best to have "some cessation of new songs bro't into meeting."[3]

The sheer plenitude of songs, however, was not the only cause of strain for the singers. Inspiration had other effects upon Shaker song. "A great portion of our songs given by inspiration," said Isaac, "are very difficult to time."[4] With scratchbooks in hand he and other scribes faithfully tried to capture changes of meter, tempo, and scale in songs that lasted as long as half an hour. These were not the only unaccustomed features in the songs—some were sung in unknown tongues, some had phrases sung to words spelled out rather than pronounced, some had "long groups of notes to one syllable." Sometimes phrases sung with vocables were introduced into a song, either at random or alternating with words of text. In short, both in musical form and in text these songs tended to be irregular and strange.

Habituated to traditional stanzaic structures and melodic patterns and provided as they were with a communal ethos and a body of simple Biblical and pastoral images for expressing it, the Shakers had never had difficulty producing coherent forms even in states of inspiration. Eunice Wyeth, for example, is described as receiving her songs visually, in the form of gold letters hanging from the ceiling of a dark room, yet in syntax, stanza form, and unity of development they are regular and clear. The inspired tunes of her niece Eunice Bathrick are equally crystalline. In the 1840s, however, a taste for rhapsodic form developed. I suspect one cause was that the vessels of inspiration in this period were not the leading singers, but generally—according to the observations of many Shakers—"such as were not considered natural singers."[5] One such was Sally Van Vike of the East Family at Lebanon, who had seventeen new songs given her in "Visions of the night by a good spirit" named Sister Rachel—one almost every night—yet she was a girl "uncommonly bashful, & but little gift in singing."[6] The average Gift Song is in consequence less aesthetically pleasing than the songs in other branches of the Shaker spiritual. This shift in the character of the singers, however, points toward the important function of songs in the decade of Mother's Work.

In Isaac Young's analysis, Mother's Work was a remedy for a decline in dedication that had gradually come upon the Shakers. The "first born"—those gathered by Ann Lee—and those who had become Believers during the ministry of Father Joseph Meacham were now of advanced age. Their faith had been tested and strengthened by the opposition of the World and the leanness of their material circumstances in the early years. But the "rising generation" of the 1830s was of a different stock. Many had not made for themselves a rough break with the World, but had been brought into the Society as orphans to be raised, or as children of converts, or if "lately gathered in," they had "embibed much of the spirit of the world." The "hearts of many became darkened & alienated." They were little interested in either "the inward work of God" or the "outward prosperity of God's people." Not surprisingly, the thirties seemed a cold time of religion: "the windows of heaven seemed fast closed, a thick curtain seemed drawn between heaven and earth." Some people fell away to the World, and not many "from without were added to the society."

These conditions were "a darkening influence" upon the aged, the ministry, and those of the young who were "honest hearted" and "kept on good gospel ground."[7] Since a Shaker community was a society of those who voluntarily entered into and supported a covenant, all rules and Holy Orders were but definitions of the shared values and guides to their specific applications in daily life. The only means of enforcement was the willing submission of each Believer. The only alternative was the expulsion of the heretical or recalcitrant member—a course that the Shakers were extremely loath to take. They acted instead on the hope of reformation of a troublesome member, and when there was a parting, it was generally the dissident who made the break. Any reformation of the Society had, therefore, to come from within the young Believers themselves. What is most interesting about the manifestations of Mother's Work is that they did originate in and continued to be found chiefly among just this class of Shakers. By means of the spiritualist phenomena of the era, large numbers of the youth were restored to order and the departure of the disaffected was hastened.

The stages by which this happened seem to have been, first, the arousing of awe and credence by behavior that Believer and doubter alike found inexplicable on any natural grounds. No doubt the young members were as impressed as Elder Rufus Bishop was when they watched Elleyett Gibbs fall into a trance that

> continued about 3 hours, & was very wonderful. She sung a number of beautiful songs, 2 of which seemed to be Father William's—She also sung some beautiful marches which she completely drummed with her fists on her knees, & at the same time with her feet on the floor as no mortal could do without supernatural power.[8]

Elder Rufus wrote that "The gift of Visions has had a powerful effect in removing doubts, and establishing the faith of such as were weak and wavering."[9]

After this preparation came other events even more awesome: the visitations of heavenly beings, culminating in those of Holy Mother Wisdom and God Almighty. These visits were announced in advance and were manifested in ceremonies of great solemnity. Through mediums the spirits admonished the erring and placed seals of approval upon the faithful.

The inclusion of Holy Mother Wisdom in the heavenly visitants deserves examination. Andrews writes, "This mysterious Being may have been a borrowing, in name at least, from older religions, a counterpart of the Sophia, Sophia-Sapientia, or Mater Dei of certain groups of Hellenic Jews and early Christians."[10] This is not convincing; the early Shakers were not encyclopedic in their knowledge of pagan and early Christian sects. But some of them were careful students of their Bibles, and it is to the Bible and to reason that authors of the treatises turned to justify their concept of the God-head. They cited Genesis: "God created man in his own image, in the image of God created he him; male and female created he them." On this basis they argued that

> it must appear evident that there exists in the Deity, the likeness of male and female, forming the unity of that creative and good principle from which proceeds the work of *Father and Mother*, manifested in *Power* to create, and *Wisdom* to bring forth into proper order, all the works of God. . . . But the manifestation of Father and Mother in the Deity, being spiritual, does not imply two *Persons*, but two *Incomprehensibles*, of one substance, from whom proceed all Divine power and life.[11]

For further clarification the Shakers turned to such passages as "Doth not Wisdom cry?—She crieth at the gates, at the entry of the city. . . . Unto you, O men, I call. . . . The Lord possessed me in the beginning of his way, before his works of old. I was set up from everlasting, from the beginning, or ever the earth was. . . . When he prepared the heavens, I was there. . . . I was daily his delight, rejoicing always before him" (Prov. 8:1–30).

A similar conception was present in the teachings of Mother Ann. When one early convert exclaimed to her, "Mother is my Savior," she replied, "you must be wise and careful how you speak—It is *Mother in* a Savior." But she also added "and a *Savior in* Mother."[12] Perhaps the two phrases actually conveyed the same meaning to the convert: for in both Godhead and vessel it was the feminine attribute that modified his understanding of Christianity. The imagination of an earlier generation of New

Englanders had been overawed by the conception of God as Sovereign Father. Masses of Americans of the early nineteenth century turned their imaginations from this aspect of Godhead to that of the sacrificed and redeeming Son. The Shaker experienced a yearning for Godhead as manifested in a tender and loving Mother. Mother's Work in the 1840s was a reassertion of the power of this symbol in Shaker life. It is the theme of hundreds of songs of the era.

A corollary of this commitment was that Shakers took with more than usual force the admonition of Christ "Except ye be converted, and become as little children, ye shall not enter into the kingdom of heaven" (Matt. 18:3). Just as the concept of Motherhood in the Godhead was experienced at its strongest in the 1840s, so was the ideal of achieving a childlike simplicity of spirit. This seems to have come in its fullest force after the visits of Holy Mother Wisdom. A typical scene was one in which "a band of the Angels of simplicity" came bestowing gifts of simplicity upon all who would gather them, "which made us act very simple and free."[13] Some of the Believers felt it extremely hard to accept this gift of childlike behavior. They found the exercises "revolting to the wisdom and pride of man"; the ministry believed that "to this end they are given, no doubt—to mortify and subdue the haughty pride of man."[14] Elder Henry Blinn understood the gifts in this way. "Through all this singular departure from the quiet, thoughtfulness of a Shaker life," he wrote, "a humble dependence upon the blessing of God was a lesson often inculcated by the spirit visitants."[15]

A second kind of gift rewarded the dutiful Believer, the presents brought by the spirits:

> robes, wreaths, satin slippers, handkerchiefs, gold chains, drinking-cups, pens, writing-desks, instruments of music, silver speaking trumpets, doves, singing-birds, lambs, baskets of fruit, flowers, leaves from different kinds of trees, with inscriptions of love thereon, and other things too numerous to mention.

Songs were an equally frequent form of spiritual gift, whether learned in a dream or trance from the singing of a spirit or seen with both words and music written upon some spiritual object or sung by an instrument while in a state of possession. Such spiritual origins of the gifts could be seen or heard only by the entranced persons, but the others "doubted not," said Elder Henry, "knowing them to be true and honest in their daily walk of life."[16] These phenomena seem to have been understood in different ways by members of the group. Some believed in the tangible reality of spiritual presents of doves and golden chains. Others took them to be symbolic and pondered them for meanings. In either case, as earlier gifts had admonished against failings, these new ones rewarded virtue. The effect of both was to gather the wandering minds into union.

Another phase of Mother's Work called the "taking in of the native spirits" commenced at Lebanon in 1842 and soon spread to other societies. Instruments for native spirits could be immediately recognized. Unlike those acting for beatified spirits, who whether "bowing, turning, walking the floor or standing in their places" always had their eyes closed, those who became instruments for the natives "did so with their eyes open, & only in manners & speech, appear different from ordinary."[17] Their behavior, however, was markedly un-Shakerlike. One journal keeper described the scene at a Sabbath meeting in 1843 as "inexpressible, to see so many persons possessed of Indian spirits acting out all the barbarian gestures, & speaking the Indian language with the utmost fluency."[18] Like the other instruments, "they are chiefly of the younger class, under 30, that act for the Indians."[19]

As the Shakers understood this phenomenon, one of its purposes was to "administer the gospel, & faith and conviction to those rude spirits, who could receive the gospel, by coming in contact with us, better than they could of the unbodied spirits."[20] It had precedent in the ministrations of Ann Lee, who had visions of herself with two powerful wings fanning away the gulfs of hell so that poor damned souls could come to God, and it had parallels in the overseas missions of other Christian sects of the era. There were, however, more immediate reasons why this phenomenon took place.

One reason was that it was regarded as even more mortifying to take in an Indian or Eskimo or Hottentot spirit and be compelled to perform uncouth actions than it was to execute some of the earlier gifts. Instruments felt it to be "somewhat crossing" to take the natives in, and many did so only as a duty, "to comply with the wishes of our heavenly Parents."[21]

Clearly the members of the ministry had been highly observant of all the spiritualist phenomena. They assumed as a matter of course that the devil would do all in his power to "bring some stain upon this work" since every inch that the Believers gained in it was "so much towards the down fall of his kingdom." He might work in two ways, either by causing some "young and inexperienced souls" to be inspired by "an evil spirit, & think it Mother, or some good spirit," or by "infusing into their minds a sense of their own superiority."[22] They believed they had detected some persons pretending to be inspired "on purpose to deceive . . . & then turn & take the advantage, & say it was all false!"[23] At North Union a sister who was an "appointed visionist" on one occasion shocked the Lead by "something . . . the mouthing of which entirely overreached the bounds of decency without bringing forward anything but nonsense." Three days later another visionist received Mother Ann's approval for removing the visionary powers of this sister.[24]

The mediums themselves were sometimes aware of flaws in their gifts. Eunice Bathrick, for one, said that while employed "as a writing medium" she had often had difficulty distinguishing between her own preconceived ideas and those of the spirit that was dictating, and even more troubling to her was the fact that she was sometimes later "made sensible" that two or more conflicting spirits had contributed to the communication. She believed that spirits who had not "ascended to the redemptive plane" differed in their opinions and that a strong-willed spirit would frequently interpose his own ideas into the communication of a weaker one. "This accounts," she says, "for much clashing of opinion & sentiment in communications thru mediums."[25]

But the Shakers' theories concerning spiritual possession went even further. It came to be accepted that as like gathers to like, so "a God-fearing soul or disciplined medium will not be likely to accept a coarse or vulgar spirit." Thus "taking in the spirits" was felt "to bring into action our own qualities, to exhibit our own characters."[26] To have one's own weakness thus exposed was not only a wholesome mortification, but also curative, for the malignant elements in the natures of the spirit and the medium by "divine law" produced "constant irritations, abrasions of comfort, . . . and unhappiness"—"the divine method to excite a desire in a soul to reforms of character and betterments of life." It was believed that "errors of a vitiated life, when a soul is made to see and feel them, become eventually a spiritual emetic and purgative which promotes desire for reform, and this condition clears the way for the access of good spirits."[27]

In all these manifestations the ministry had a difficult time. Its members wanted sincerely "to unite with every good gift & not to stand in the way of any genuine manifestation from the spirit world," but they knew it their duty to "properly hold the reins of government, for the general harmony & good of all." They were consequently hard put at times to "know how to exercise true wisdom," and they suffered "no small share of labor and tribulation." There was, however, "an important and cheering feature" throughout the whole period of Mother's Work, namely that there had been "a continual warning, thro' the Instruments themselves, to submit every gift to the visible *Lead*." Thus the ministry "was strengthened & assisted by those gifts" and at the same time acted "as a Center for the body to gather to."[28]

Though beginning in a period of restlessness among the youth and working itself out chiefly in members of that class of Believers, Mother's Work largely achieved the rededication of the youth that "honest-hearted Believers" had hoped for. There were, of course, costs. Some painful incidents occurred when an instrument overstepped or fabricated a gift. A number of persons who had had "beautiful gifts" of inspiration left the Society when one of these was checked. John Allen, for example, a prominent singer and instrument at Lebanon, felt "unreconciled" and apostasized when "the Ministry & Elders did not follow some inspired communications thro' him, & which we knew would be unprofitable."[29] Some members of intelligence and genuine spirituality like Hervey Elkins also withdrew in dismay. Earlier Hervey had been presented with a spiritual gift, a "Cup of Solemnity":

> I drank the contents, and felt for a season the salutary effects. During the revival I became sincerely converted. I, for a time, by reason of prejudice and distrust, resisted the effect of the impressions, which, at length, overwhelmed me in a flood of tears, shed for joy and gladness, as I more and more turned my thoughts to the Infinite. At last, a halo of heavenly glory seemed to surround me. I drank deep of the cup of the waters of life, and was lifted in mind and purpose from this world of sorrow and sin. I soared in thought to God and enjoyed Him in His attributes of purity and love. . . . Two years thus passed, in which my highest enjoyments and pleasures were an inward contemplation of the beauty, love, and holiness of God, and in the ecstatic impressions that I was in the hollow of His hand, and owned and blessed of Him.[30]

Such later gifts as those of the natives seemed to him not only often suspect in inspiration, but inferior in seriousness. Unable to reconcile himself to these developments within the Society, he withdrew. For those who remained, however, Mother's Work brought about a renewed sense of unity of purpose. One frequent act symbolized this: when a member entered a trance, either an elder "went to the Instrument" and held his hands, or "the Instrument to the Elder, as if for support or strength."[31]

In presenting Gift Songs from the period of Mother's Work I give thematic considerations precedence over those of genre or chronology, believing that such a use of song and headnote will help the reader more easily to understand the products of this revival. I use Gift Songs nos. 1 and 2 to provide a backdrop for the rest of the songs. They illustrate the general tenor of meetings during this era. Since a dominant trait of the revival was that it markedly heightened the Shakers' reliance on non-rational experience, I next show the background of this behavior in earlier Shaker thought and some of its consequences for relations between members of the Society and between the Shakers and the World (Songs 3 to 8). At this point I turn attention to the songs themselves, exploring first the states of mind in which members received songs (nos. 9 to 13), then the effects of inspiration upon the melodic form and the imagery of the Gift Song (nos. 14 to 25). The next long sequence provides information about the backgrounds of representative visionists and about their relation to the spirits. Songs 26 to 31 treat these topics in general terms. Then follows a group of eight songs (nos. 32 to 39) from native spirits and another set (nos. 40 to 44) given by the Shepherdess. This section builds toward another which is illustrative of the function of song in the highly dramatic rituals of the era—the Narrow Path, the Cleansing Gift, the visitations of Holy Mother Wisdom, and the services held at the feast grounds on the holy mounts (Songs 45 to 54). The last Gift Songs (nos. 55 to 58) show the dissemination of songs of this period from one community to another and the waning of the simple gifts.

Gift Song No. 1

O WHAT PRETTY SOULS

In the year before his death at the age of thirty-nine Elder Joshua Bennet received this song at Enfield, Connecticut. It came to him on Christmas Day, 1837, soon after the commencement of Mother's Work. Russel Haskell left an account of the background of Elder Joshua's gift:

> A meeting was held at the west family by the brethren and sisters there, and Eld. Brother Asa from the church, and the elders, brethren and sisters from the south family. The meeting commenced a little past two o'clock, P.M. And was attended with divine manifestations and great power of God, such as shaking, whirling, clapping of hands, speaking in an unknown tongue, kneeling with their faces to the floor, praying for God to forgive them of their dullness, yea, and begging the brethren and sisters to forgive; some rolling; some turning, down on the floor, while some had new songs given them, with some beautiful words, which were sung for an hour or more. The meeting continued over seven hours with the main body; in which time, some took opportunity to do their chores. Just before ten oclock, they began to disperse, and retire to bed. Joshua Bennet from the south tarried over night: he retired to bed, about eleven oclock, with Philip Burlingame, and had a spiritual view or visionary impression, as follows. He says that after lying in bed a few minutes, he saw the faithful brethren and sisters in one solid body, worshiping God with all their souls and bodies, and that it was the most beautiful worship he ever saw on earth. They were dancing in complete harmony, and singing the most melodious songs, without a jaring note among them. He then beheld a great company of angels

gathering around them untill they were completely surrounded. Then the angels began to sing new songs in a quick manner. The brethren and sisters were still, as to singing, for a few moments; then they would sing with them. The angels learnt them a number of songs, which were very beautiful. I then heard a voice, saying, Now is the time the angel is flying through the midst of Heaven, having the everlasting Gospel to preach to them that dwell on the earth. I then looked to the west, and saw many coming to obey the testimony of the Gospel, while some were coming from the north, east and south on the same errand. I then inquired within myself, What is the cause of their coming? And the spirit seemed to say, It is the Gospel sound that has gone forth from this body of saints.—From this view I had the following song given.

(c)   NYAP, Russel Haskell, "A Book of Visions," pp. 24–26.

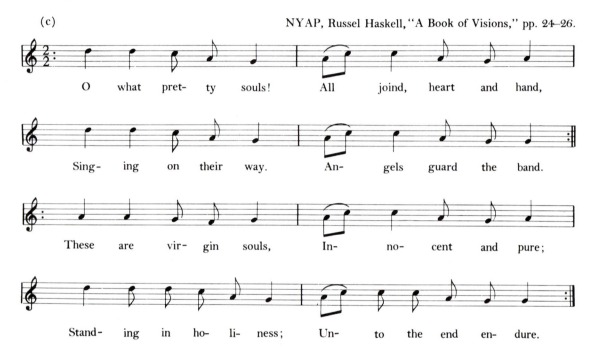

O what pret- ty souls! All joind, heart and hand,

Sing- ing on their way. An- gels guard the band.

These are vir- gin souls, In- no- cent and pure;

Stand- ing in ho- li- ness; Un- to the end en- dure.

Gift Song No. 2

BASKET OF TREASURES

News of the spiritual manifestations passed quickly from one society to another, and from Maine to Kentucky similar scenes occurred. "Mother's little Dove," who brought the song "Basket of Treasures" to Gloucester in 1846, probably descended in just such a meeting as that described in a Pleasant Hill journal in the same year:

Meeting commenced solemn, after singing a few songs with considerable power the Angel Love made his appearance through one of the inspired and said he had come in with wings loaded with heavenly treasures and wished us to shake off everything that would Obstruct a blessing; in which all united, then said he had come to unite with us in praise and thanksgiving to our Eternal Parents for the many rich blessings we had recieved, after labouring a few songs with considerable life and liberty, the Angel of Light made his appearance through another messenger and said he was showering from his wings balls of light and liberty for us to gather, he also brought a ball of our Heavenly Saviours love for E. Br. to burst for us to gather, of which we received in thankfulness, Mother Hannah came in, in company with many pretty Angels showering down heavenly fruits for all to gather and said she had filled the Youths baskets with roses for them to give to their aged brethren and sisters. Mother Hannah then gave to Eliza Gregory a bush fill'd with little white Doves for her to shak for all to gather in rememberance of our ever blessed Mother Ann whom she said was then beholding us, the Angel of Light, scatterd bright bands of love and union for us to bind each other to gather that we might be bound in cords of sweet union never to be broaken. So we continued to receive good during meeting

Our meeting Continued one hour lacking 5 minutes.

MS L–24, pp. 68–69.

Here's some pret- ty lit- tle bas- kets Fill'd with love, And man- y pre- cious treas- ures, Says Moth- er's lit- tle Dove. Here are jew- els and dia- monds, And man- y pret- ty rings, I have borne them to you on my sil- ver Wings. my sil- ver Wings. So good breth- ren and sis- ters I'm not bound, If you will re- ceive them, I will throw them round.

Gift Song No. 3

WOBEN MESA CRELANA

"What flows of the heavenly juice manifested by way of new songs!" Giles Avery wrote at Lebanon in March 1838. "Scarce a day passes without shedding many beautiful ones." Often these, he said, were "in language altogether uninteligible to us, save so far as we are able to understand their meaning by the feeling they carry with them." Ones in unknown tongues were also being received in other societies. At Enfield, New Hampshire, on the twenty-fifth of the same month "Woben mesa crelana" was "given and sung in a gift in the Chh's meeting." Thomas Hammond recorded it at Harvard, with a note saying, "I suppose the English is the translation":

> O Mother O Mother how blessed thou art
> I love thee sincerely sincere from my heart
> Thy gospel is blessed yea precious & pure
> I love it I'll keep it; twill forever endure.

Gift Song No. 4

O LORD MAKE ME PURE AND HOLY

Songs in unknown tongues were continuing to flow at Lebanon in 1839 when this song was received there. The fact did not entirely please all those who had to learn them. At a singing meeting in March of that year the spirit of Mother Ann took notice of their attitude. "Some of you," she said through an instrument, "wonder why there are so many sorts of words. But if it was not so, how would your Brethren that come to visit you"—meaning the spirits—"understand them? Many have not learned our language." For other singers, however, the very strangeness of the songs must have been impressive. Like the "heavenly emanations" that many saw, such as the "balls of light" with "brilliant print or writing inscribed on them, of a flame-like lustre," the inspired songs cured "doubts and fears." They left the caviler "without a possible way of accounting for what daily occurs, that is, on natural principles."

MS L–207, p. 240.

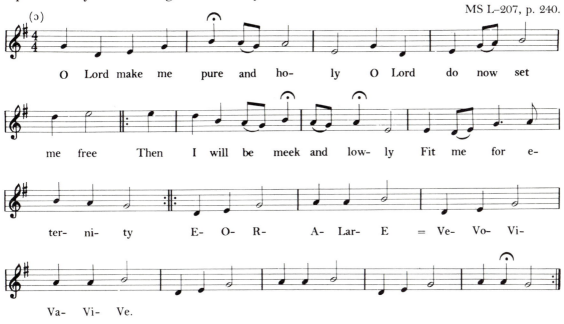

O Lord make me pure and ho- ly O Lord do now set

me free Then I will be meek and low- ly Fit me for e-

ter- ni- ty E- O- R- A- Lar- E = Ve- Vo- Vi-

Va- Vi- Ve.

Gift Song No. 5

HOW EXCELLENT IT IS

Shaker distrust of reason found its most extreme expression in such gifts of Mother's Work as the present song received at Watervliet in 1842. The more usual Shaker position, however, was that stated by Father Joseph Meacham. He taught that Believers had "a right to the improvements & inventions of man so far as is useful & necessary but not to vainglory or anything superfluous." The Church would therefore not encourage or teach more "than what is called common learning in the letter." Believers, he said, were "not called to excell or be like the world, but to excell them in order, union & peace, & in good works that are truly virtuous & useful to man in this life." It was because they saw Mother's Work as leading on to these higher virtues that even the more intellectual Shakers entered gladly into what Anna White would later defend as this "spiritual kindergarten."

♩ = 106 (♯³) MS WNY–28, p. 76.

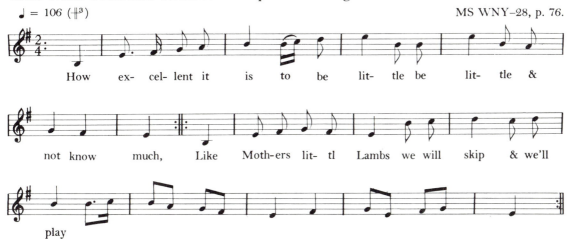

How ex- cel- lent it is to be lit- tle be lit- tle &

not know much, Like Moth-ers lit- tl Lambs we will skip & we'll

play

Gift Song No. 6

O THE BEAUTY OF ZION

In 1843 when this song was received at Union Village, such gifts were being liberally scattered, but not equally to all. Susan C. Liddil there had something of a gift of clairvoyance—though she feared it might be unreliable and found it drained her strength—but she regretted getting fewer songs than many other girls. Hers were so precious to Susan that she could remember distinctly the circumstances of each gift. The first she saw "like a little fold of tinted vapor and immediately sung it off words and tune together" to her caretaker and roommates. The second came "by impression" and she sang it too until the others had learned it. Many dedicated Believers, however, rarely had any gifts at all. John Lockwood of Groveland "loved them, & desired them, & labored & prayed earnestly" to receive them, but "could not feel them." This troubled him. "Well, John," an elder once said to him, "spiritual gifts are given to increase & strengthen Faith, & you have Faith enough without them." Nevertheless, from Shaker records certain patterns emerge. The gifts came to the common members rather than to the Lead, to the young much more frequently than to the middle-aged or the old, to the sisters more often than to the brothers. The most frequent recipients were girls in their teens.

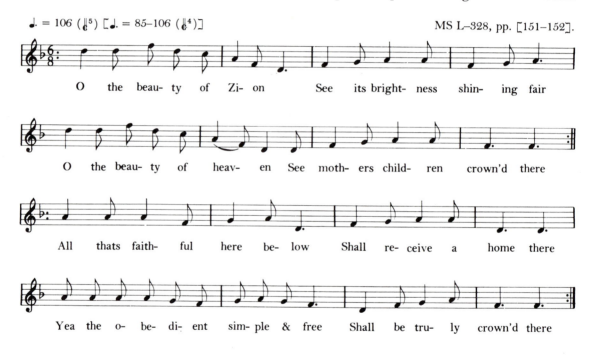

MS L–328, pp. [151–152].

O the beau- ty of Zi- on   See its bright- ness shin- ing fair

O the beau- ty of heav- en   See moth- ers child- ren crown'd there

All thats faith- ful here be- low   Shall re- ceive a home there

Yea the o- be- di- ent sim- ple & free   Shall be tru- ly crown'd there

Gift Song No. 7

PEACEFUL VALE

One Lebanon scribe entered this song in his manuscript with the note, "Sent to Elder Freegift & Co. while here,—From Ohio. It was given in a gift." The year was 1838. I have never seen any attribution more explicit, but Mrs. Hazel Spencer Phillips says the song was by Richard McNemar. If so, he received it on the eve of a painful rupture between himself and Elder Freegift. Two young troublemakers played no small part in the affair. Apparently sensing friction between the two men, a visionist named Margaret O'Brian became "inspired" at church meetings and publicly chastized Richard for his "proud spirit." One Randolf West was meantime forging scurrilous notes in Richard's hand and leaving them where Elder Freegift would find them. Their work launched Richard and several of his old associates into exceedingly troubled waters. Elder Freegift expelled them from the village. Richard, despite failing health, undertook a journey east to ask redress from the parent ministry, which restored him into union. The ministry sent him back to Union Village and cautioned all societies to guard against falsehood and pretence in the instruments. Margaret O'Brian thereupon withdrew from the Shakers, and after Richard's death in 1839, Randolf West confessed his forgeries, left the Society, and two years later killed himself. Richard and Freegift had meanwhile achieved a reconciliation, embracing and weeping during the church meeting as Richard declared, "Elder Freegift, I have always loved you. There never has been a moment when I entertained even the least ill-feeling toward you."

MS L-61, p. 73.

Here's my home my all and treas- ure, Down in Zi- ons peace- ful vale; Here in peace my days I'll meas- ure, While a qui- et sea I sail. What tho' world, and flesh be- set me, And my faith in ques- tion call; No such thing shall ev- er fret me, Here's my home my hope and all. O my home my pret- ty home, My pret- ty home's in heav- en; Where I lay my

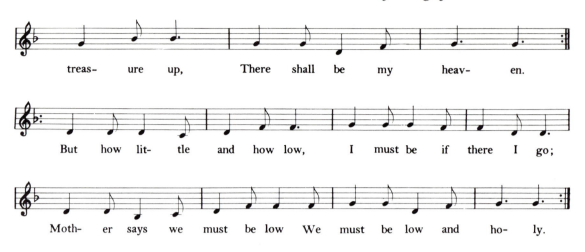

treas- ure up,   There   shall   be   my   heav-   en.

But   how   lit-   tle   and   how low,   I   must   be   if   there   I   go;

Moth-   er   says   we   must   be low   We   must   be   low   and   ho-   ly.

Gift Song No. 8

ZION'S VALLEY

This song originated at Enfield, New Hampshire, in 1840, and there is record of its being known within the year at Enfield, Connecticut, Lebanon, Watervliet, and South Union. Its popularity among Believers is not surprising. The song has a lovely tune, employs one of the Shakers' favorite images, and expresses their sense of separation from the World. The cleavage between Believers and the World is dramatized in an incident recorded in the journal kept by the ministry at Watervliet. On one weekend in 1839 twenty-seven men from the legislature came for a visit, with their five carriage drivers and "a load of worldlings from Schenectady." All spent the night and took supper, breakfast, and dinner—"a great burden . . . in this sickly time." The visit was in fact an inspection tour, and after the Sunday services the legislators visited individual Believers in their rooms, questioning especially the youth and children. The dignitaries, says the journalist,

> appeared wonderfully satisfied with what they had seen, heard & felt in our meetings & elsewhere, even to the shedding of tears. They saw & heard some of the wonderful works of God! But it is not likely they saw the Angels that stood behind them in the windows & spread a covering over them, nor the golden chains that our good Fathers, William & James stretched between them & the believers. But these, and many other wonderful things were seen by such believers as had their spiritual eyes open.

(ɔ) [♩ = 106 (‖³)]   MS L–207, p. 314.

In   Zi- ons   val- ley   does   a- bound   E- ter- nal   life   and

pow-   er   No sep- e- ra- tion   can   be   found   Here   in   this   low- ly

bow-   er   Ah,   where's   the   hon- ors   of   this   World   They're

doom'd to des- o- la- tion To ruin soon They

will be hurl'd But God is my sal- va- tion.

Gift Song No. 9

O COME SESENE MY LITTLE DOVE

Henry DeWitt dates this song December 16, 1838, and says it was one of three given to Mary Hazard "after we all had a little Dove sent to us by Mother & placed on the right shoulder so we might sing to them very handy." The song proves her sympathetic union with the general gift. On other occasions when her feelings were scattered a Gift Song might serve to gather them back into union. Late one afternoon she was "feeling quite bad and out of health" and retired alone to a garret. She sat by a window as it grew dark, knowing no one knew where she was or how she felt. After a while, she said, she "had an impression" to put her hand on her head to "see if there was anything for me." She found a little song, "Trumpet Comforter," written upon an olive leaf. Mother Ann brought it with words of comfort to refresh her, for

Fig. 34. The Interior of the Second Meetinghouse at Watervliet, N. Y.
In this architecture of the 1840s a barrier divides the visitors from the worshipers. Mother's Work had heightened the Believers' repudiation of the World.

she had seen Mary "sitting by a window, bearing a grave & solemn countenance, as if very weary and borne down with the burdens of this life."

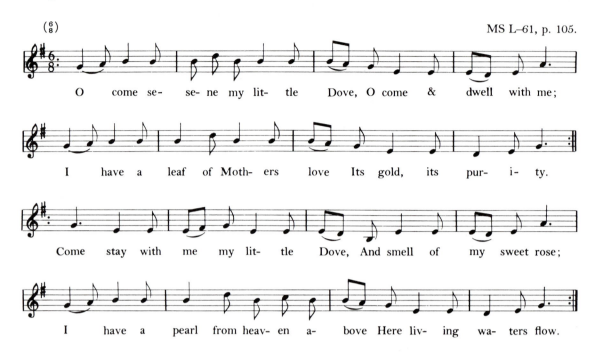

O come se- se- ne my lit- tle Dove, O come & dwell with me;

I have a leaf of Moth- ers love Its gold, its pur- i- ty.

Come stay with me my lit- tle Dove, And smell of my sweet rose;

I have a pearl from heav- en a- bove Here liv- ing wa- ters flow.

Gift Song No. 10

COME MY SOUL PRESS ON

One Lebanon manuscript attributes to "D. T." this song about pressing past Satan and his wily spirits. These enemies had seemed vividly real to the early Shakers. "Whenever I touched any one of you," exclaimed Father James at the close of a meeting, "I saw the evil Spirits come out of you in swarms." After one vision Mother Ann told of seeing some that looked like crows, but she said that no one who saw Satan himself would be able even to remain in his "earthly tabernacle." Satan was "a great body of darkness" and, like God, a "self-existent Being."

D. T. may have shared this conception, but by 1839, when he received this song, one writer in the West was arguing that the devil was no more real than darkness, which was merely a privative state. The writer accepted the existence of unlovely spirits in a rudimental stage of moral development, but did not think them seriously threatening. Most Believers were less intellectual than he, but shared at least his view that if a Believer stumbled in his travel the cause was his own weakness, not an external foe. Warring exercises, once intended to drive actual devils from the meeting room, were by 1839 probably understood by many to be purely emblematic rituals. After Believers had taken up spiritual swords, "thrusting, yelling, & barking" at the "enemy" during a warring gift at Pleasant Hill in that year, a visionist pointed the moral: "there had been unbelief enough drove out to sink a nation." Significantly, in all the hundreds of visions recorded in these years the devil is scarcely named. Songs that mention him are nearly as rare.

(ɔ)

MS L–334, p. [112].

Come my soul press on press on To ob- tain the gos- pel prize

Faith- less in- do- lence be gone In thy day my soul be wise

(2/4) Press on march on press on march on To ob- tain the

gos- pel prize E- vil spir- its with their wiles Haste to baf- fle

thy ca- reer Break through all dis- dain their smiles

Vic- tory's cer- tain nev- er fear Sa- tan is a van- quish'd foe

So's an e- vil na- ture too Press on march on press on

march on Faith with Love will bear thee thro.

Gift Song No. 11

I WILL FIGHT, FIGHT

This song was received by one "p. b." at South Union in 1842. The text implies its use in "warring," an exercise recurrent in Shaker worship from the earliest days until at least the late 1860s. The ritual was "calculated to manifest the war between Michael and his Angels, and the dragon and his Angels" described in the twelfth chapter of Revelation. The Believers warred "each and every one against HIM AND HERSELF EXCLUSIVELY," fighting "every evil and impurity" within them. The exercise was characterized by "many displays of strong muscular exercise, such as stamping, shaking, vociferating and shouting." O. C.

Hampton wrote that after "one of those meetings, the spirit was raised for the time being, above the rudimental influences of our common nature . . . nearer to the Throne of higher perfections."

MS SU–19, p. 5.

I will fight fight & nev- er slack un- til I o - ver-
come the en- e- my — I will fight fight & nev- er slack until I o- ver- come the en- e- my — I have got a lit- tle
sword which Moth- er Ann has give to me — I will fight fight
fight fight — fight & slay the en - e - my

Gift Song No. 12

HERE IS A PRETTY FEAST

Russel Haskell preserved this as a Tyringham song learned by the Enfield Shakers about 1843. From his hand we also have an account of a vision suggestively similar seen in Enfield in March of that year. At 9 o'clock on the "Sabbath forenoon" Rowland Wood suddenly found himself in the dark on a broad road, caught in the devil's net. He cut his way out of the net, but then found himself bound by a chain that wound five times about his body. For two days while his vision continued he lay in these bonds. On Tuesday morning, however, Father William rescued him and led him through the Garden of Eden to "a beautiful Mansion which was called a holy Mansion of rest." There, Rowland said,

> I went up 2 white steps into a large hall and then up stairs. Then Father William took me into a large room beautifully ornamented with Gold; the chairs and floor was pure gold, and the ceiling was white, over head it appeared to be gold, the curtains that hung up to the windows were white and were tinged with gold with 4 gold stars in the middle of them, which made them look very pretty indeed. In the center of this room was a table set with many kinds of fruit and wine. I was invited to partake which I did and felt refreshed. Under the table were many pretty Doves singing.

While the ethos that underlay both song and vision was shared by all the societies, the songs probably had a greater role in disseminating the imagery used to express it. Songs were more easily transmitted from village to village. Once learned, loved, and thought upon, they seeded the imagination of every Believer.

Here is a pret-ty feast that our bless-ed Moth-ers made It
is sweet love & un-ion and on it we will feed It's
for her faith-ful child-ren who al-ways watch and pray And
with their lamps a burn-ing do walk the nar-row way.

Gift Song No. 13

VERDANT VALLEY

This march originated at Harvard in 1847 and survives in a half-dozen manuscripts from Lebanon and Watervliet. Its text is a characteristically Shaker echo of Rev. 22:1–2, "And he shewed me a pure river of water of life, clear as crystal, proceeding out of the throne of God and of the Lamb. In the midst of the street of it, and on either side of the river, was there the tree of life, which bare twelve manner of fruits, and yielded her fruit every month: and the leaves of the tree were for the healing of the nations." But for Shakers such passages were not merely allegorical or prophetic scripture, but experienced realities. Eunice Bathrick of Harvard, for example, wrote that in the spring and summer of 1853 while going about her usual work or when standing before a window facing the south she sometimes had visions of the spirit land, a most beautiful landscape with "velvety lawns of lively green, sprinkled with star like flowers, which looked like eyes peering out from the closely shorn grass." Those gently sloping lawns, she said, "extended as far as the eye could see" and were surrounded by

beautiful fruit trees, some of gigantic size, & flowering shrubs. The fruit was exceeding fair to behold, & resembled oranges, while the leaves seemed gilded with gold, & sent forth prismatic hues. . . . There were also vines, full of rich clusters of transparent fruit, climbing to the tops of the trees, & their leaves had the same hues & gilding. At times a dense forest appeared in the distance, clothed in luxuriant foliage. Again a gently flowing river was seen whose banks were green to the waters edge.

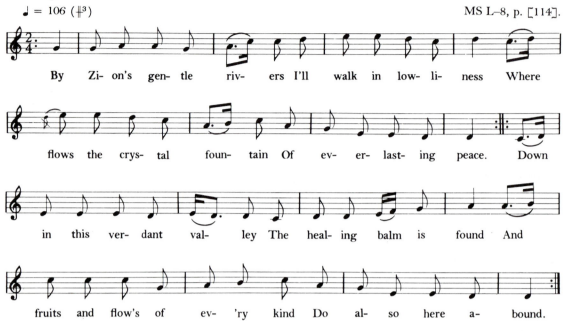

Gift Song No. 14

O LITTLE CHILDREN

Harvey L. Eades recorded this piece at South Union in 1840, and it shares melodic and stanzaic peculiarities with the earlier Pleasant Hill song "Pretty Love and Union." Both employ repetition in their texts and play with the same melodic figure. Their stanza structures echo those of the camp-meeting spirituals and their pentatonic tunes the most popular Appalachian form of "Black Jack Davy." They are examples of a group of songs by the Kentucky and Ohio Shakers that grew from Southern song rather than from the Northern traditions that dominated most of the Believers' song repertory.

Gift Song No. 15

SPIRITUAL DOVE

Henry DeWitt received this cheerful song at Lebanon on May 20, 1842. Its melody derives from "The Girl I Left Behind Me," but has a second strain lowered to conform to the Shaker dance-tune model. Henry must have heard the secular tune when quite young. His parents read a copy of *Testimonies of Christ's Second Appearing*, believed, and in 1813, when he was only eight, came down from Upper Canada with all their children to join the Society. Henry recorded his song in two of the handsome leather-bound notebooks which for years he supplied to the Lebanon singers.

O my pret- ty lit- tle Dove do stay with me O nev- er, nev- er

leave me For I will be faith- ful to keep a store, Of

heav- en- ly love to feed thee. feed thee.

Gift Song No. 16

CORDS OF LOVE

This melody seems to flow from some variant of "The Death of Queen Jane." Neither strain preserves the ballad tune intact, but echoes of it are recurrent. According to a note in one manuscript, "Br. William" brought the song while men from the Second Family of Canterbury were at the sugar camp on Saturday, June 19, 1847.

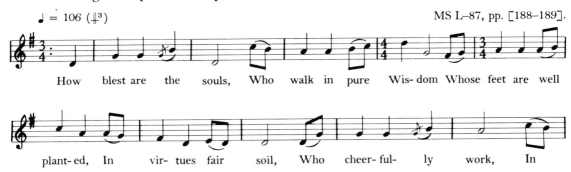

How blest are the souls, Who walk in pure Wis- dom Whose feet are well

plant- ed, In vir- tues fair soil, Who cheer- ful- ly work, In

Moth- ers pure gar-den And for her *Rich Bless- ings* do will- ing- ly toil. Such such shall dwell, In glo- ri- ous Man- sions, Yea soar in bright glo-ry a- bove, There, there, sing for- ev- er yea ev- er, and ev- er, En- cir- cled with cords, Of the pur- est love love.

Gift Song No. 17

I'LL BEAT MY DRUM AS I MARCH ALONG

The one manuscript that preserves this tune notes that Jane Sutton received it in December 1848. She was sixteen at the time, had lived at Pleasant Hill since she was two, and would later serve the society as a trustee and die in the faith in 1912.

Her fife-and-drum march makes use of "Yankee Doodle" cadences. Probably it was a Gift Song of one of the revolutionary forefathers like "Br. George Washington," who at a Pleasant Hill meeting several years earlier "made himself known through one of the inspired and said he had come in, with a beautiful band of Angels beating their drums for volunteers for Mother."

MS PH–7, p. 15.

I'll beat my drum as I march a- long I'll play on my fife sweet mu- sic   I'll

I'll blow my trump for free- dom too

I'll

Gift Song No. 18

LOW WITHIN THE VALE

The first four measures of this melody bear a marked resemblance to the opening half of a tune collected in Massachusetts with the ballad "The Two Brothers," but Eldress Paulina Bryant, who had this song about 1850, could hardly have known any of the music of the World. Her parents entered the Pleasant Hill community in 1810, when she was two. She lived her remaining seventy-six years in that society. The idioms of Anglo-American folksong formed for her as for other Shakers a native musical language.

MS PH–7, p. 173.

Low with- in the vale we lie   While

rag- ing storms are pass- ing by

Gift Song No. 19

WILLOW TREE

In *The Gift to be Simple* Edward D. Andrews printed this song from a transcription made by Mary Hazard at Lebanon about 1850. For contrast, I offer a variant closer to the form in which the song was received at the North Family there some seven years earlier. Each has its interesting touches, but Mary's is the more classic form. The years of singing had smoothed away every small awkwardness in the tune. The melody was possibly begotten by the opening phrase of the Child-ballad tune "The Mermaid." "Willow Tree," however, has no need to depend on high-born kin for its good name.

♩ = 106 (♯³)   MS L–260, p. 262.

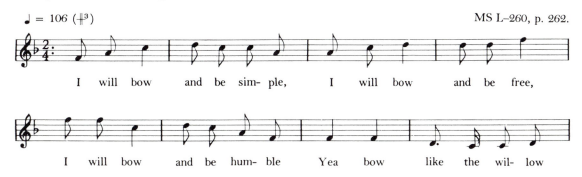

I will bow   and be sim- ple,   I will bow   and be free,

I will bow   and be hum- ble   Yea bow   like the wil- low

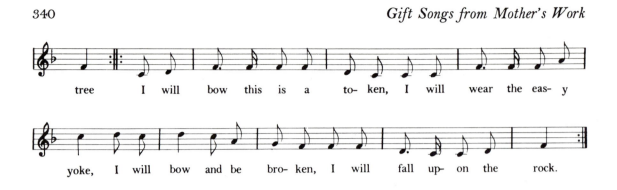

tree   I   will   bow   this   is   a   to- ken,   I   will   wear   the   eas- y

yoke,   I   will   bow   and   be   bro- ken,   I   will   fall   up- on   the   rock.

Gift Song No. 20

FALL ON THE ROCK

The second line of this little march implies that the song was a gift from a heavenly spirit, as does the alternation of text with "noted" phrases. The worldling's eye might find the lines cryptic. To a Shaker they would have been a clear call for humility. He would have remembered, for example, not only Christ's parable of the rock in Matt. 21:42–44 and Luke 20:17–18 but also Shaker discourses on the meaning of the verses. In 1845, the year when this song was received at Lebanon, Daniel Moseley spoke in one meeting there, saying,

> The work of Christ & Mother is a breaking up work. I repeat it, The work of Christ & Mother is a breaking up work—it is a humiliating work—Christ & Mother is the Rock of our Salvation. Blessed is that Soul that will fall on the Rock & be broken & not let the Rock fall on it & grind it to powder.

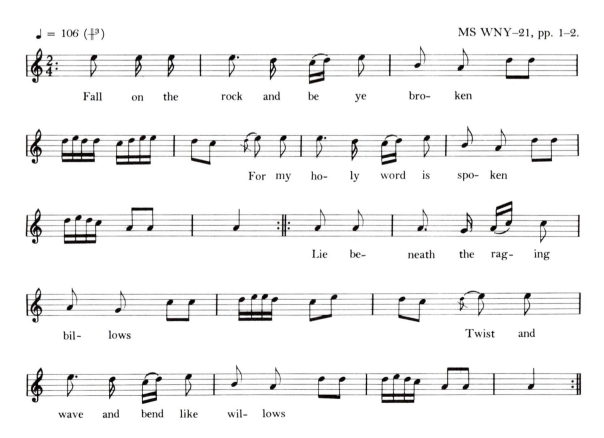

Fall   on   the   rock   and   be   ye   bro- ken

For   my   ho- ly   word   is   spo- ken

Lie   be-   neath   the   rag-   ing

bil- lows   Twist   and

wave   and   bend   like   wil- lows

Gift Song No. 21

O HERES A BEAUTIFUL SPREADING VINE

"Learned from a gold leafed vine given by Mother Ann," wrote the scribe who entered this song in a Lebanon manuscript. A Canterbury songbook also holds it—side by side with Gift Song no. 22—with word that the first was received at nearby Enfield in April 1849. The two songs are nearly identical in theme and image, yet not necessarily by the same Shaker. Particularly in the years of Mother's Work, scribes often recorded a string of similar songs by different members of a village. All were dipping their inspiration from the same spring.

O heres a beau-ti-ful spread-ing vine My lit-tle ones twill cov-er And all who will be tru-ly mine Must 'neath its branch-es hov-er And there no one shall make thee a-fraid Ye lit-tle chos-en num-ber For while you rest be-neath its shade I'll shield you from all dan-ger.

Gift Song No. 22

O HERES A LOVELY CREEPING VINE

Mother Lucy Wright often urged the protection afforded by the gospel. "If any of you should rise too high by reason of having great gifts of God," she wrote in 1806, "I desire you would labour to creep down the best way you can: for if you should fall it might hurt you." Doing the work, she felt, meant "coming down into the work of God, not rising above." Those who rise, "rise above their protection, & of consequence must suffer loss." By the 1820s this precept imbued Believers' use of vines in their song texts and gave the scriptural image a distinctively Shaker stamp.

[♩. = 106 (𝅘𝅥⁵)]

MS CB–8, p. 99.

O heres a love-ly creep-ing vine Its roots I have set deep And o'er these lit- tle ones of mine It shall for-ev- er creep And when the rough and rag- ing storms of trou- bles o'er you sweep Be- neath its shad- ow thou shalt rest It is a safe re- treat

Gift Song No. 23

I HAVE AN ASSORTMENT OF BEAUTIFUL FLOWERS

Only Russel Haskell preserves this Gift Song, but he says it was brought to Enfield in September 1851 from the "City of Peace"—Hancock. Its floral imagery suggests the gift drawings for which Polly Collins of that Society served as the instrument. Fourteen watercolors survive from her hand, the earliest dated January 1841, but all the rest executed between 1852 and '59. In all of them she draws trees hung with flowers of Union, Purity, Order, and Love, and bright borders or wreaths of pansies, strawberries, roses, lilies, and pinks. Polly's inspiration, like that of the singers, found its vehicle in traditional forms. Embroidery seems to provide the model for her motifs and the album quilt her favorite form, though she can vary it with great subtlety. Like this little Gift Song, her visions came as comforting rewards to the faithful. As the spirit of Mother Lucy told her on March 6, 1841, "there are beautiful flowers growing all around Mother's lovely vineyard, for those who are willing to labour therein."

♩. = 61 (𝅘𝅥¼)

MS EC–11, p. 132.

I have an as- sort- ment of beau- ti- ful flow- ers; And

Fig. 35. Floral gift drawing by Polly Collins, received at Hancock in Jan. 1853.

By Mother Dana this is given, But Polly Laurance aids in drawing.
'Tis July first, in fifty three, This little gift is sent to thee.

Submission.

Order.

Quiet -ness.

Arbor of Peace.

Fig. 36. Floral gift drawing by Polly Collins, received at Hancock in July 1853.

now of my choic- est take some. I dwell in Moth- er's

gar- den, a- mong her green bow- ers; And with her sweet

song- sters I've come. O here are some ros- es, O

here are some lil- ies, And here are some sweet pinks too.

Still on- ward with man- na & fruits I sup- ply you, O

♩ = 138 (⁴⁄₂)

with a great quan- ti- ty too. My Moth- er sent me with

them, With her love and her choic- est of gems.

Gift Song No. 24

HOLY SAVIOR'S LAMB

Elder Abraham Perkins of New Hampshire sang this song often on a trip to the New York societies in 1851, but never apparently in a complete form. Some scribes who recorded his singing omit the phrase with the *bah*'s. No scribe in New York set down the Quick Dance coda found in a manuscript written that year at Enfield, and none tells as much about the origin of the song as that manuscript does. "Taken," it says, "from the neck of a very pretty Lamb given by the Holy Savior. May, 1851."

Believers would have understood this lamb as an emblem, not a pet. They could delight in animals, as when Isaac Youngs thought the most interesting news he had to write South Union was how all the sheep and hens "gathered up" and even the feeding cattle "lifted their heads & tails, kicked up their heels & ran up" to watch a band of singing Believers march past, all the animals seeming "much surprised," "charmed," and "animated!" Believers, however, viewed animals as sharing in man's fallen nature. They thought that beasts were permitted to rebel against man; the Shaker was to bear with this and not "cruelize" them. On the other hand he was not to pet them, lest he catch their evil spirits. In the imagery of his songs he would use only the dove and the lamb, creatures that in scripture and convention symbolized meekness and simplicity. The Believer aspired to these qualities, and in his imagination the dove and the lamb embodied them so vividly that often they became emblems brought alive.

Gift Song No. 25

O SEE THE LOVELY ANGELS

Marcia Hastings of Canterbury entered this song in her manuscript with the annotation "Sister Mercy. Nov. 28 1840." It has several of the traits that the Shakers thought so peculiar in the songs of the early 1840s: "much spelling of the words," "many notes grouped to one syllable," and "many unknown words, mixed in with the common English." They felt, nevertheless, that such songs were "both Sollemn and Heavenly, beyond anything that Tongue or pen can describe." To hear them sung in the original gift, said Philemon Stewart, "is enough to cause ones Blood to chill."

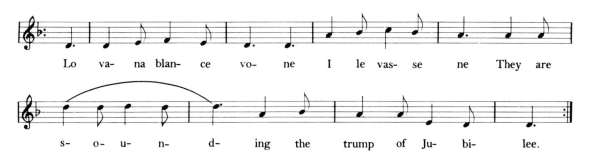

Lo va- na blan- ce vo- ne I le vas- se ne They are

s- o- u- n- d- ing the trump of Ju- bi- lee.

Gift Song No. 26

A SPIRITUAL VIEW

The single Pleasant Hill manuscript preserving this hymn dates it March 13, 1844, and attributes the tune to Lovina Price and the words to Sarah Pool. Both were lifelong Shakers, dying in the faith in their eighties. Little is recorded about Lovina. Sister Sarah was born in Kentucky in 1797 and entered Pleasant Hill at the age of eleven. In 1839 she was one of a group of seven brethren and thirteen sisters appointed to serve as "visionists," but she had already been gifted in that line "a considerable time." One journal reports that during a funeral in that year the spirit of the deceased sister "spoke to the assembly through Sarah Pool, made a confession of the unbelief which she had indulged only one week ago to-day—& warned the brethren & sisters against harboring such a spirit. She then sung a song to the brethren & sisters through Sarah—all of which was very striking indeed." This song seems not to survive. In her workaday life Sister Sarah served for many years as kitchen deaconess.

MS PH–2, pp. 46–47.

O what is pomp and splen- dor What is earth's

gold- en wealth With all her rich- est treas- ures

Per- tain- ing to the earth For like a fal- len

lil- ley Or as a blight- ed rose All earth- ly

things will fail you Your days on earth will close.

2 Then O beloved children
   While time with you doth last
   Prepare your souls a treasure
   That never will fade nor blast
   Gird on the cross and helmet
   With your bright sword in hand
   Determin'd on salvation
   And in Mount Zion stand

3 Then O beloved children
   Walk in the open light
   Nothing shall ever mar you
   Ye shall be cloth'd in white
   Ye shall be crown'd with glory
   And rest in peace and love
   With your Eternal Parents
   In beauteous realms above.

Gift Song No. 27

COME ON BRETHREN

German ancestry is implied by the surnames of many at Pleasant Hill—Claar, Lineback, Hooser, Rupe, and the author of the present song, Lucinda Shain (Schoen)—but I have been unable to demonstrate links between the melodic repertory of the Society and that of the "bush-meeting Dutch" or of Pennsylvania German secular folk music. Like William Hauser, the Funks and other Germans in the Southern uplands, the families of these Shakers seem to have given up German melody along with the language and to have adopted the largely British tune material prevailing in the region. Thus for "Lowly Vale" (March no. 66) Polly Rupe borrowed a pentatonic scale and cadential formula from Scotch-Irish melodic stock (probably directly from the Appalachian fiddle tune "Shady Grove").

Lucinda's background clarifies the social and psychological contexts of this process. She received her song—in a typical Shaker gift—on March 22, 1846, from "Br. Vincent Runyon and others of our deceased friends, who played it on their instruments of music." Vincent, a Believer of British and Huguenot stock, had died only five days before, at the age of fifty-six. Both he and Lucinda, who was then forty-four, had come to Pleasant Hill with their parents and siblings in its first wave of converts. Through most of Lucinda's life, Vincent's brother William was the dominant musician at Pleasant Hill. In the gift of singing he had no equal there. For more than fifty years his "shrill, melodious voice rang with clarion tones, through the consecrated halls & sacred sanctuaries of this holy hill, cheering the minds & thrilling the hearts of the pious worshipers & beholders."

Gift Song No. 28

BASKET OF FLOWERS

Rachel Merrill brought the Believers at Gloucester this bouquet of song and flowers in April, 1846. She had died only five years earlier. Rachel herself was one of the "first born," those accepting the faith in the first opening of the gospel. She was born in 1779 and would have been a young girl when her parents became converts and worked to establish the society at Gloucester. Manuscripts fail to record the name of the instrument through whom she delivered these tokens of her continuing attachment.

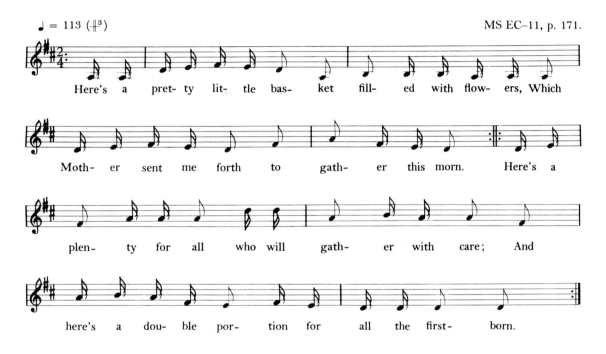

Here's a pret-ty lit-tle bas-ket fill-ed with flow-ers, Which

Moth-er sent me forth to gath-er this morn. Here's a

plen-ty for all who will gath-er with care; And

here's a dou-ble por-tion for all the first-born.

Gift Song No. 29

VALIENT WARRIOR

On Valentine's Day in 1851 the spirit of Elder Issachar Bates brought this Quick Tune as a "notice" to Louisa Youngs of Lebanon. One of many converts from Lower Canada, Louisa had come at the age of twelve, nine years earlier. She received the song with a message that Father William sent it with "his peculiar love & blessing and desired that she would be strong in the Lord." She did abide strong until her death in 1906.

De-part all thats e-vil go a-way from me I'll

be a val- ient war- rior I will be free   I will not be bound by

an- y foe for heaven I'm bound to heaven I'll go

Gift Song No. 30

THE ARMIES OF ISRAEL

The author of this song, like few others in Shaker history, was born into the society. Her parents, John and Nancy Lockwood, entered Lebanon in October 1815, and their daughter Hortency was born in the following March. She grew up "a good believer—was an intelligent, industrious & helpful sister. Unfortunately she overdid, bro't on a consumption & deceased at the age of near 37 years." Her song "The Armies of Israel" dates from the last years of her life. It was used as a Slow March, and according to one manuscript was "Learned of a little Bird, and given to Prudence [Morrell] by Hortency Lockwood May 5th 1851."

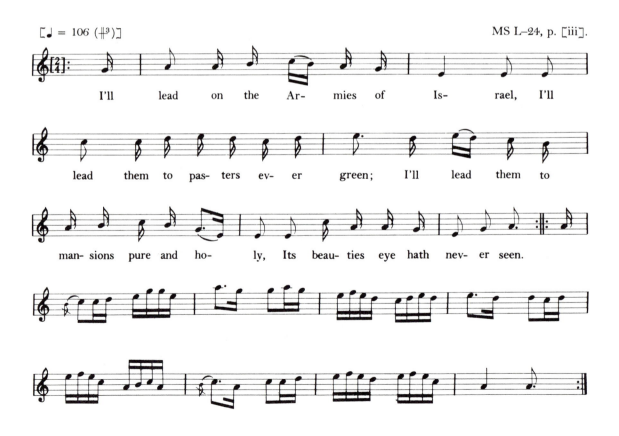

[♩ = 106 (♯³)]   MS L–24, p. [iii].

I'll lead on the Ar- mies of Is- rael, I'll

lead them to pas- ters ev- er green; I'll lead them to

man- sions pure and ho- ly, Its beau- ties eye hath nev- er seen.

Gift Song No. 31

THE RACE

At Enfield, Connecticut, in February 1847 a joint meeting was held by the Shakers and a body of Millerites. One Shaker journal reports, "The Adventists and Believers took turns, one lectured an hour, then the other side an hour, sometimes the Believers would sing and some-times they would sing. any shouted or said amen, who felt to." On this occasion there was little meeting of minds, but a number of disillusioned followers of William Miller did enter the various societies, bringing a few songs into the Shaker repertory. For a time the Shakers also got new songs like "The Race," which was "sung by a company of advent spirits" at Canter-bury on July 18, 1847. One manuscript directs that singers are to raise shouts of "Glory" and clap their hands before repeating the second strain.

♩ = 106 (♯³) MS GME–6, no. 413.

We have start- ed the race To the king- dom we're ad- vanc- ing

Let God be prais- ed with

mu- sic and with danc- ing

Hal- le- lu- ia to his name Hal- le- lu- ia to the Lamb Hal- le- lu- ia we will

sing to our blest Moth- er Ann While we safe- ly jour- ney home- ward to

free- dom's port We will raise man- y long and glor- ious shouts. shouts.

Gift Song No. 32

HE HAW TALLABO TALLABO

The apostate David Lamson saw an instrument named Sally Smith perform at Hancock a native dancing song doubtless much like this one received in 1847 at Enfield. She sang "in the Indian tongue" and at the same time imitated the Indian dance "with much vigor and spirit."

Lamson believed Sally herself worked up the "lively and theatrical" performance, for she was "a smart girl, a good singer, and a good dancer."

Few Shakers at the time had much knowledge of Indian culture. One Indian woman converted by Ann Lee was still alive at Groveland, and there had been others in the East—Hannah Adams, who died at Lebanon in 1814, and Winifer Denbo, who died at Canterbury in 1816. A few persons in the Western societies were well informed. John Slover, Sr., of South Union spent much of his youth as a captive and spoke three Indian languages. Others had made efforts to convert the Shawnees in the early years. But Slover died in 1813, and Shaker missionary efforts ended before the War of 1812. The instruments for the native spirits were born some years later.

When "crowds of Indian spirits" thronged the meetings in 1842 and "pressed for admittance," the ministry was predisposed to accept them. Both the theological writings and the *Testimonies* told of "bearing for the dead," and instruments had recently been warning that "hundreds & thousands" of "naked, hungry and needy" souls would come to the Shakers for salvation. Nevertheless, the Lead watched sharp. At Union Village when a Wyandott squaw took possession of Elizabeth West—an "ignorantly raised young thing" who it was presumed "never saw an Indian or knew anything of them"—the elders used a glossary in the Lewis and Clark journals to test her. The squaw could speak but little English, but "signed out" the meanings of words. When they pronounced *min shippa* (corn), she "instantly pointed to a little ear of pop-corn lying in her lap." Given the word *ma-ku-su* (an eagle), she answered by "kimboing her arms & commencing flying, then contracting her fingers in the form of an Eagles claws & pounced on a sisters arm just as the Eagle takes his pray." Such experiments convinced the elders of the authenticity of Elizabeth's gifts.

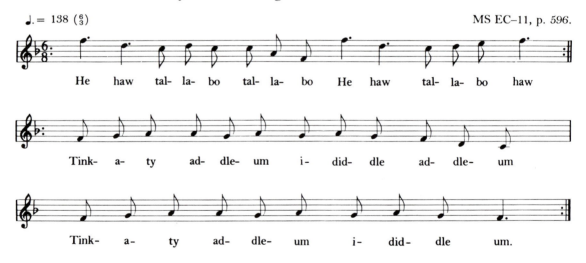

Gift Song No. 33

ME LOVE ME HILLS AND MOUNTAINS

Word went out from Lebanon late in 1842 concerning native spirits who had begun to visit the society. Soon instruments in other villages were also "taking in" the spirits. On January 6, 1843, the Indian chief Contoocook brought the song "Me love me hills and mountains" to the Believers at Enfield, New Hampshire. By March Samuel Hooser was rejoicing at Pleasant Hill about the news of the natives, although they had not yet manifested themselves in Kentucky. It was November before they visited North Union. For the next five years native manifestations were quite frequent and then began to be withdrawn. But native songs continued to be recorded sporadically for many years. Some were set down in an Alfred manuscript in 1875 and again in 1878. One Canaan manuscript holds many brought by natives during a revival in 1894.

The most vivid description of a visit from the natives is an entry in a Pleasant Hill journal for Sabbath, March 1, 1857. The writer reports:

> . . . among the various spirits that attended our meeting, their was an Indian Chief by the name of Red Hawk; he offered as an apology for his not attending meeting until it was half out, was that he had not confess'd all of his sins and that he had understood that no spirits was to attend this meeting only those who had confess'd all of their sins; so he had but just got through at that time he was verry glad to unite with us, he was verry anxious to lern how to dance our way, he appear'd to understand the Indian dance verry well; he would not go home for sometime after meeting was dismiss'd, he was all the time begging us to sing some of our prety songs, and lern him how to dance; finally by begging him with fare promises that we would sing for him this evening in our singing meeting he would go home, and done so; This same Chief has been here frequently before in his savage state; he was verry noisy and boisters with savage yells; today he was verry mild and gentle he says he has been dead 75 years and was kill'd in battle our meeting continued 2¼ hours; This evening at 5½ oclock all three of the familys attended singing meeting at the [Center Family] according to promis in company with a great many other spirits Red Hawk attended our meeting; the seats soon had to be taken out of the meeting room to give place for the spirits to sing and dance; of course broke up the singing meeting; the meeting has been represented by some of those that were there; to be one of the livelyest meetings they were ever in; Red Hawk alway takes possession of John Bunnel.

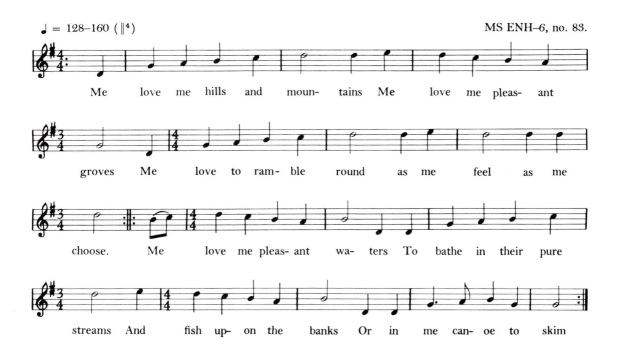

♩ = 128–160 (∥⁴)

MS ENH–6, no. 83.

Me love me hills and moun- tains Me love me pleas- ant

groves Me love to ram- ble round as me feel as me

choose. Me love me pleas- ant wa- ters To bathe in their pure

streams And fish up- on the banks Or in me can- oe to skim

Gift Song No. 34

IN ME CANOE

Russel Haskell, the only source for this song, recorded it with the note "From Mother Cassan Dana sung by a Native Spirit by the name of Abigal Gelhorn. Canterbury N. H." The song dates from 1848, probably from not long after the death of Eldress Cassandana Goodrich of Hancock on June 1 of that year.

Gift Song No. 35

ME CANNOT WEAR DE GREAT LONG FACE

"Sung by Native spirits February 28, 1848," says Russel Haskell, the one scribe who preserved this cheerful song. They apparently had some recollection of "Barbara Allan," for the first two phrases of the song bear strong resemblance to Bertrand Bronson's "Group C" of tunes for this ballad. The natives also Shakerized the tune by inventing a second strain out of the same material. For good measure, they added a Quick Dance coda.

pret- ty times's all o- ver Me want de joy to

fill me soul And love what be de mer- ry Come ho- ly

power and thro' me roll, Old bond- age me will bur- y Me

me will bur- y Now me hap- py feel Danc- ing in de whit- es zeal,

Me can step de tune com- plete De gos- pel shoes be on me feet. Woo ne wip a wa

Hal an e na hal an aw Woo ne wip a waw Hal- an e na haw haw.

Gift Song No. 36

NOGGIN OF LOVE

The Canterbury ministry was honored with the gift of this song while visiting the Holy Mount at Lebanon on September 2, 1847. A native spirit brought it, acting as a messenger for Mother Ann.

MS GME–3, no. 422.

I have a lit- tle nog- gin full of Love sweet Love Love

Moth- er sent me here with it To feed her sim- ple Doves.

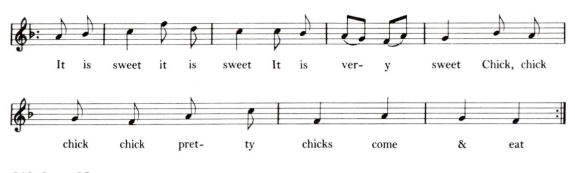

It is sweet it is sweet It is ver- y sweet Chick, chick

chick chick pret- ty chicks come & eat

Gift Song No. 37

HEAVY CROSS

The Southern white spiritual "To Die No More" has a melody like the second strain of this song, and both are variants of the ballad tune "The Three Crows." Outside Shaker tradition the shape-note song "Indian Convert" appears to be the only spiritual with a text in Indian pidgin English. This piece antedates the Shaker native songs and has survived them in living tradition. Christian Harmony singers in North Carolina and Alabama still perform it enthusiastically. From persons in the Shaker communities I have heard only one native song, Sister Mildred's "Me come very low." After the Era of Spirit Manifestations a Shaker like Anna White might take pride in the concern the Shakers had manifested for the souls of the natives, but few of the native songs were sufficiently devotional to have continuing appeal.

The visits of the natives exhibited one significant pattern: when the Indians first came they showed "some awkwardness & ignorance of the ways of white people," but they were "soon & easily tamed & brot into a degree of order & conformity" to Shaker customs. After one tribe had received gospel instruction, it withdrew and another came. Native songs like "He haw tallabo tallabo" and "Me love me hills and mountains" represent the early stage of a native visit, "Heavy Cross" a considerable travel in the gospel. The native who sang this song at Canterbury on June 17, 1847, must have been near the hour of departure.

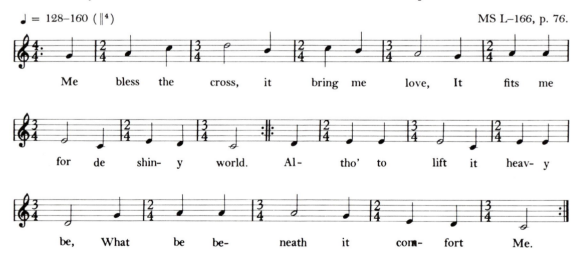

Me bless the cross, it bring me love, It fits me

for de shin- y world. Al- tho' to lift it heav- y

be, What be be- neath it com- fort Me.

Gift Song No. 38

I HAVE MOTHER'S LOVE IN STORE

This Quick Dance was "Sung by Jack" at Enfield, New Hampshire, about 1848. He was probably the "coloured spirit named Jack" who a year or so earlier had sung on the Holy Mount at Lebanon through Elder Abraham Perkins. How Jack may have danced is revealed in a comment written by Elder Henry Blinn of Canterbury in 1873. A band of fiddlers and dancers made up of black and white hands working for the Shakers serenaded him while he was visiting Pleasant Hill. One dance, he wrote, was performed to the music of a lone black who "beat the time with his hands by striking his body, exactly as the negro spirits did in our meeting room in 1843."

$\downarrow$ = 106 ($\sharp^3$)   MS EC–2, p. 83.

I have Moth- ers love in store And am dai- ly add- ing more Trol de dum da- dle da- dle da- dle dum de um Here's a great bounc- ing ball E- nough for each and all Trol de da- dle da- dle da- dle da- dle dum de um.

Gift Song No. 39

PRETTY HOME

A sizable number of blacks found a pretty home among the Shakers. In the East the most notable group was the out-family headed by Mother Rebecca Jackson in Philadelphia, but there was a scattering in the other societies. We know the names of a few of them: George and David Gennings ("among the first that believed"), Melinda Welch, and Mary Taylor at Lebanon, Sarah Mason at Shirley, and Phebe Lane at Watervliet. In the West the first Shaker missionaries often opened the gospel to "a Blessed assembly of people, white, yellow, & black," and the converts at Busro were in fact so mixed that Elder Issachar Bates feared they would prove ungovernable. South Union had members enough to form a black family under its own leaders. The names of at least a dozen black members are identified in the journals of Pleasant Hill, the home of the author of this song, Patsy Williamson.

Sister Patsy's experience was typical of that of the black Shakers at Pleasant Hill. She was born a slave in North Carolina. Her owners became Believers in 1809 in the first wave of Kentucky conversions, and Patsy with them. When they later "turned away," the Shakers purchased Patsy and "set her at liberty, that she might remain in the Society." She was then about eighteen, and Patsy "continued zealous in the cause, according to her understanding," until her death in 1860. Her song "Pretty Home" dates from the year 1849. Significantly, it shows no trace of black song style. Like other good Believers, Sister Patsy sought union with the general gift.

MS PH–7, p. 63.

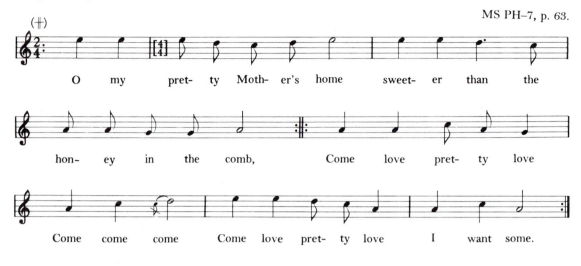

O my pret- ty Moth- er's home sweet- er than the

hon- ey in the comb, Come love pret- ty love

Come come come Come love pret- ty love I want some.

Gift Song No. 40

LITTLE LAMB

One of the spirits who often appeared through instruments during the period of Mother's Work was affectionately known as "the little shepherdess." She represented herself as having been "a keeper of sheep, in her earth home, and . . . as engaged in the same occupation since passing to the spirit-land." In the course of her visits the Shepherdess "became especially gifted in the ministration of a variety of beautiful songs." To Lebanon alone she brought 136 songs, and other societies got their share. Elder Henry Blinn reported that on one occasion the Shepherdess led a flock of sheep into the meeting room at Canterbury and "after making a spiritual exhibition of them" left some in the care of her "earth friends, with the assurance that the sheep would not make any special trouble." She must have made a similar present at Harvard when she gave the song "Little Lamb." It was one of sixty-two songs of the Shepherdess for which Joanna Randall was the instrument between November 1844 and the following January.

♩ = 106 (‖³)   MS HD–7, p. 74.

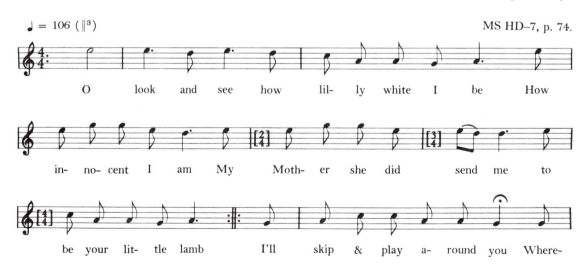

O look and see how lil- ly white I be How

in- no- cent I am My Moth- er she did send me to

be your lit- tle lamb I'll skip & play a- round you Where-

ev- er you do go For I de- light to com- fort Moth- er's

child- ren here be- low   child- ren here be- low

Gift Song No. 41

HERE TAKE THIS LOVELY FLOWER

A great many of the songs of the Shepherdess accompanied and described a spiritual gift. One Lebanon manuscript, for example, is composed of songs that came with such presents as "Mother Ann's Plumb Cake" for Elder Ebenezer Bishop, a "pretty little branch of Charity"

Fig. 37. Joanna Randall
1820–1902
Shirley, Mass.

Fig. 38. Mary Hazard
1811–1899
Lebanon, N. Y.

for Maria DeWitt, a "little cherry tree" for Eliza Sharp, a "bird of love" for Henriette Latham, "four thousand little honey bees" for Abraham Hendrickson, and for Johnson Shapley

"The Rose Bush"

O here is a bush of beautiful roses
sent from Holy Wisdom
And all may come and gather some,
They're Holy Mothers blessing,
Now place them on the top of your heads,
And if you'r true and faithful,
they will grow, flourish and spread,
And shelter you from all evil.

The Harvard song "Here Take This Lovely Flower," like "The Rose Bush," points out that the gift is a spiritual emblem. It was sent "From Mother Ann to Elmira Adams through her little Shepherdess June 6th 1847."

MS HD–2, pp. 103–104.

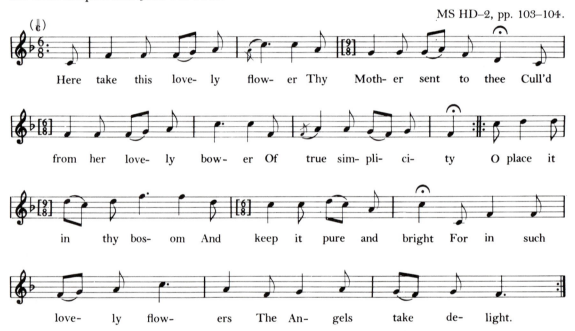

Here take this love-ly flow-er Thy Moth-er sent to thee Cull'd

from her love-ly bow-er Of true sim-pli-ci-ty O place it

in thy bos-om And keep it pure and bright For in such

love-ly flow-ers The An-gels take de-light.

Gift Song No. 42

DEEP LOVE

In the fall of 1849 the Shepherdess gave this song at Canterbury for Elder Ebenezer Bishop. One of the striking things about her appearances is that they occurred in many societies. She seems to have come first to Watervliet, New York, in 1841. As early as 1842 she had appeared at Canterbury, and there are records of songs given by her there as late as 1850. Dorothy Durgin was a frequent instrument for the Shepherdess in that society, and Philemon Stewart may have acted for her during his stay in Canterbury in the summer of 1841—he kept a note-book of her songs then, as he later did in 1842 and 1843 after his return to Lebanon. At Shirley Joanna Randall was her instrument frequently in 1844 and 1845, although other persons also received songs from the Shepherdess and continued to do so through 1847. Most of her visits were probably unrecorded.

During the period of Mother's Work, there were at each village visits from certain spirits who did not manifest themselves in other communities. The spirits who appeared in all the societies were those of the very highest order. The Shepherdess is the exception. It is significant that this spirit was that of a shepherdess, rather than a shepherd, and that she usually came as an emissary of Mother Ann or Holy Mother Wisdom. In the 1840s as in the 1780s holiness in its feminine manifestations was powerfully moving to the Shakers.

The song "Deep Love" shows the continuing power of this symbol. According to Eldress Marguerite Frost young Believers at Canterbury picked this song for a service in 1908 or 1912 to celebrate Mother Ann's birthday with "inward renewal." Eldress Marguerite herself tried to sing the song for me and twice broke off in tears, exclaiming, "I don't know if I can finish it. The song means so much to me!"

♩ = 128–160 (‖⁴)   MS CB–8, p. 130.

I love Moth- er I love her way I love her gos- pel pre- cepts to o- bey The King may have his throne And the mi- ser his gold The Mon- arch his pal- ace And the Prin- cess her home I cov- et none of theirs For I've the gos- pel call And a kind lov- ing Moth- er Which is bet- ter than them all.

Gift Song No. 43

THE SAVIOR'S WATCHWORD

Marcia Hastings entered this song in one of her manuscripts with the date May 6, 1849. It must have been received at Canterbury, a gift, to judge by the text, from the Shepherdess. The song appears in two other manuscripts, both of them from Alfred, and Sister Mildred Barker learned it there from oral tradition as a child. In the Canterbury copy the scale is pentatonic, and the song moves steadily along in duple time. One Alfred transcription has a hexatonic scale and breaks the duple rhythm once. Sister Mildred sings the piece in the Dorian mode and performs it with more rhythmic freedom. I present her version of the tune, as by far its most supple form.

Original tonic: B

From the singing of R. Mildred Barker.

Way down in the val- ley my lambs be ye found, Se-

cure from the tem- pest that now beats a- round 'Tis

low in the vale my bless- ings flow But on the bar- ren

moun- tains bleak and chil- ly winds do blow Be ye

strong though your tents are sur- round- ed with foes And

vile per- se- cu- tors rise up to op- pose Be ye strong

move as one and place your trust in me Re- mem-b'ring the

right- eous shall ne'er for- sak- en be.

Gift Song No. 44

THE NARROW PATH

On November 1, 1840, the spirit of Father William brought for each Believer at Lebanon a narrow path to walk, a path "as strait as straitness, no turning to the right nor left." He desired each one to devote ten minutes every day walking the path "until our heavenly parents should meet with us." The gift was probably performed individually and without music. Three days later Father James brought the following song "to walk the strait narrow path in." The gift was now improved in the services and taught to the other societies. The worshipers drew into ranks as if for the Holy Order—though they themselves did the singing—and marched very slowly, placing one foot directly in front of the other "so that the heel of one foot was placed to the toe of the other." The hands were allowed to fall by the side, "unless we were asked to read from spiritual books, in which case we held them before us." The books were entitled "Spiritual Reflections," and the whole exercise was performed "in solemn meditation, & in the fear of God."

♩. = 61 (2/7)   MS L–65, p. 31.

Pre- cept on pre- cept & line up- on line.

We'll walk in the path our

Moth- er has trod. Yea strait & clear strait-ness the pure way of God.

Gift Song No. 45

HEAVEN'S PURPOSE

One Canterbury manuscript is a treasury of the society's Gift Songs. It preserves "Heaven's Purpose" with a note that the song was "Given by a holy spirit for the two branches of the Church on Holy Ground. mon. morn. July 1 1844." The instrument was Dorothy Durgin, then a girl of nineteen who had lived ten years among the Shakers. The manuscript is rich in her songs, sixteen being ones she learned in a single dream.

"Heaven's Purpose" seems to have been inspired by a "cleansing gift" of which Elder Henry Blinn left an account:

A medium from Mt. Lebanon, N. Y., visited Canterbury, and organized a company of six Brethren and six Sisters as mediums to enter a spiritual work of special significance. The two leaders carried lighted lamps in their right hands, as a sign that the light must not be hid.

Every medium wore upon the right wrist, a strip of scarlet flannel, some two and one half inches wide, and attached to this a written inscription as follows;—"War hath been declared by the God of heaven, against all sin, and with the help of the saints on earth, it shall be slain."

This company marched through all the rooms in every building.

My can- dle is light- ed no more to be hid, Mine

eye is o- pen'd and none shall close the lid; For

I have pro- pos'd Je- ru- sa- lem to search, And

with my ho- ly bright- ness each heart to reach. With

my ho- ly work- men I'll pass thro' & thro' I'll

pull down the high while I build up the true. My

stand- ard is rais- ed, my law is the same, "Peace

peace for the faith- ful, but no oth- ers I claim."

Gift Song No. 46

THE ANCIENTS SONG OF MOURNING

The cleansing ceremonies directed at Canterbury by the medium from Lebanon lasted for two weeks:

At midnight, after the close of the third day, while the family was in silent slumber, a company of four Sisters passed through all the halls, and then through all of the Sisters' apartments, in the family dwelling. Their song was "The Midnight Cry."

Every sleeper, throughout the whole house, was aroused, and hastily prepared to join the ranks of the pioneers. On the next night at 2 a.m., a company of Brethren and Sisters, by previous arrangement, passed through the halls of the family dwelling, and again awakened all the inmates with their voice of song.

This midnight call had a strange effect upon most minds, by being so suddenly awakened from a deep sleep.

A similar scene took place in many societies, including Lebanon, where "The Ancients Song of Mourning" was received and sung in 1844.

We will walk with Moth-er & mourn We will walk with Moth-er & weep We will bow in sol-emn pray'r with her while Zi-ons child-ren sleep And through their sa-cred dwell-ings We will march and cry re-pent. In low hu-mil-i-a-tion Come low low & re-pent

Gift Song No. 47

WATCH YE

The Shepherdess brought this song in 1841 as a particular notice to Nancy Wells, a young sister at Watervliet, New York. It proved a favorite. Many musicians in other societies entered it in their notebooks, and twenty years later one enclosed a copy in a letter with the word that Elder Sister Rebecca Landon called it "a song that filled her soul." It was quite possibly sung in 1843 during one of the most unusual ceremonies ever enacted at Lebanon.

According to a ten-page account, Believers entered the meeting room at 7:30 on the evening of January 25 and found Philemon Stewart standing between the two doors dressed in a gray coat, drugget trousers, and blue jacket, and wearing "a red flannel pinner with a wide leathern belt tanned with the hair on, which was black." Before him on a small bench stood "a tin cylindrical box, covered with cloth and leather." He held "a small stick with a stuffed ball upon one end," with which he "beat upon the sounding box, or drum, almost constantly thro the meeting" at the close of every major statement or act.

In a line between the doors stood five sisters and five brethren holding burning lamps. They were instruments for most high angels and each wore a white handkerchief or pinner about the waist, except John Allen, who, acting for the Savior, wore white, black, and red.

Opening the meeting with Solemn Songs, the Elders took brightly burning lamps and passed through the assembly looking each squarely in the face. Some instruments then brought forth sheets of cloth four feet square, two white, one red, and one black. While they displayed these in the center of the room, the other instruments marched around with burning lamps, singing "a very solemn song of warning, to be ready for the coming of the Lord."

All were asked to write their names upon one of the sheets, and most chose the white. But the instruments for Holy Wisdom and the Holy Angel drew the black and red sheets nearly over the white ones, leaving only a narrow strip which their fingers crossed many times, "making, as it were, some connexion" between the white and the red. The white, they announced, "is truly the most pleasant, but the black and the red must be passed thro before the white is obtained." Nearly all those present then said they were willing to write their names upon the red and the black. The sheets were then borne about the room and waved before the assembly, while the instrument for the Holy Angel followed after, beating on his drum. The Holy Angel cried out, "tho clouds of darkness hover over Zion & blood to blood doth run, yet shall she never be entirely overcome."

$\downarrow = 106\ (\sharp^3)$ MS XM–3, Folder 3.

Watch ye watch ye & be read- y to meet me for lo I will come at noon day. Fear not fear ye not for with my hand I will lead you on & safe- ly I'll guide your lit- tle bark be- yond this vale of sor- row

Gift Song No. 48

ADDRESS TO HOLY MOTHER WISDOM

The solemnity of this vow to Holy Mother Wisdom can be appreciated only through accounts of her visits to the societies. At Lebanon she desired to meet first with the ministry, on the afternoon of Saturday, April 10, 1841. They gathered early and made ready for the event by washing their feet. At four o'clock the instrument, a girl named Miranda Barber, became "powerfully inspired" and was led in to them. Through her, Holy Mother Wisdom commended the Lead as "faithful & true" and promised that they should be "priests unto God forever." She rewarded the eldresses with "Robes of needlework, covered with flowers of 18 Colors" and each of the elders with "a Gold Breast-plate set with pearls & precious stones of 35 colors!" She also appointed a meeting with the church on the Sabbath "to set a mark on every person over 18 years of age, that when destroying Angels should be sent forth they might know who were vessels of mercy."

The following afternoon at one, both the First and Second Orders gathered in the meeting house. At the head of the meeting, directly before the ministry, seats were placed for "the appointed Mouth" and the four other instruments, who were "bearers & witnesses & seemed to be pretty much abstracted from the things of time." Two brethren and two sisters at a time were called up before the seat and through "her little Instrument Maranda" Holy Mother Wisdom offered each "whatever gifts such as recommendations, admonitions, warnings, encouragements &c as they justly deserved." Each addressed a vow to Holy Mother Wisdom and prayed for "wisdom, strength & power." She then set her own seal upon each and put round the heads of the brethren and sisters a gold band on which was written the name of the Almighty and the words, "Touch not mine Anointed."

This meeting lasted five hours and a quarter, and the ministry recorded that "it was such a meeting as we never saw before, and will no doubt be remembered through time, by all who were present." Memories of a similar ceremony at Canterbury must have remained vivid for the singer who had the following song there a decade later.

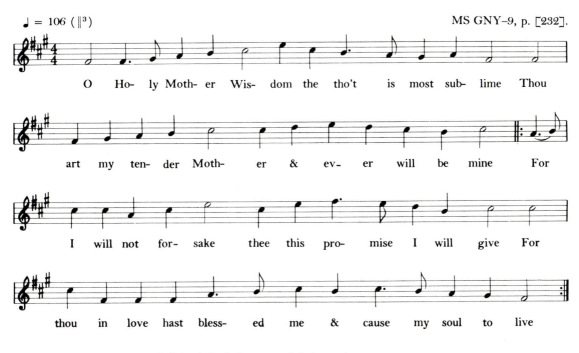

♩ = 106 (‖³)   MS GNY–9, p. [232].

O Ho- ly Moth- er Wis- dom the tho't is most sub- lime Thou
art my ten- der Moth- er & ev- er will be mine For
I will not for- sake thee this pro- mise I will give For
thou in love hast bless- ed me & cause my soul to live

2 O lend thy holy power & help me keep my vow
That I in resignation to thee may ever bow
That satain with his forces may tempt my soul
    in vain
And I thy child of pleasure forever may remain.

Gift Song No. 49

TREASURES OF THE GOSPEL

In 1844 a revelation at Lebanon directed that an outdoor place of worship be prepared on a high peak east of the village. This spot, named Holy Mount, was cleared and fenced, and provided with a piled rock altar, a shelter, and a small enclosure called the spiritual fountain, within which stood a tall inscribed stone. Soon in all the societies the instruments labored to discover the proper site for similar feast grounds. At Gloucester one was set off on top of the hill rising above the village on the west. There for more than ten years the society would go to hold meetings on beautiful days in the summer.

Aurelia Mace thought it a lovely sight to see the Believers marching four abreast up the lane, two brethren on the right and two sisters on the left, in their uniform of trimmed bonnets in light blue, their fringed mouse-colored shawls and white linen gloves. They sang as they marched and "Treasures of the Gospel" may well have been one of the songs; it was received at Canterbury in 1849 and was known in the Maine societies. On reaching the enclosure they would switch to a "bowing song," which was simply a slow march, and bow on the song while marching in. Then, said Sister Aurelia, "the very heavens came down, the meeting would be so spiritual. . . . Ancient spirits and prophets would often come, and bring messages, and a spiritual halo of light seemed to settle over the place.—and a power which none could resist."

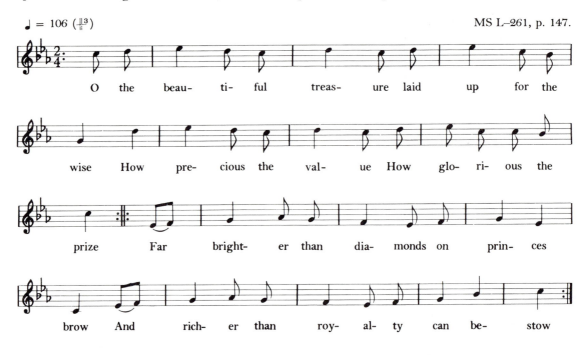

MS L–261, p. 147.

♩ = 106

O the beau- ti- ful treas- ure laid up for the
wise How pre- cious the val- ue How glo- ri- ous the
prize Far bright- er than dia- monds on prin- ces
brow And rich- er than roy- al- ty can be- stow

Gift Song No. 50

I'M ON MY WAY TO THE HOLY CITY

Several of the marks of the Gift Song are upon this piece: the wordless section, the word partially spelled. The journey motif that appears in its text had long been conventional for marches, but in November 1844, when the song was received at Enfield, New Hampshire, the villages were also enacting the same symbolism in their ascents to the feast grounds atop the holy hills. Anna White felt it particularly appropriate for the trip up the Holy Mount at Lebanon.

Fig. 39. Feast Grounds, the Holy Hill of Zion, Harvard, Mass. From a contemporary woodcut.

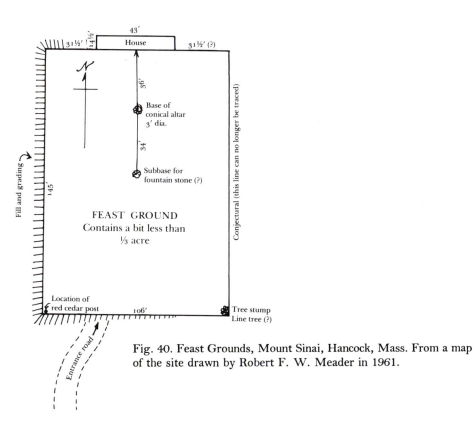

Fig. 40. Feast Grounds, Mount Sinai, Hancock, Mass. From a map of the site drawn by Robert F. W. Meader in 1961.

Twice a year, in the spring and in the autumn, she said, all the people would set forth

on the long climb, its rocks and cliffs, its stumbling places and its dark, forest depths, all typical of the hard, burdened, shadowed path through earth life, up the spiritual steeps of redemption. Hand might clasp hand, love's keen foresight remove some obstacles from the path, pleasant resting places be made . . . where a sweet rest, wide views of the glorious country of God be enjoyed and inspiring songs be sung;— songs and hosannahs and the beautiful watch-cry of the faith be shouted, "More Love!" Yet, each step of the way must be trodden by each one for himself. His own, her own, work of climbing must be done alone. But at the top,—the long, glad day of spiritual feasting and joy! What lessons were not taught the Believer, in its bright exercises, of spiritual requital for past toil? Here, on the summit, rose in spiritual sight, the spiritual temple of Mother Ann; its walls of purest marble, its adornments, gold and gems of celestial polishing; its windows open to celestial airs, its arches ringing to strains of celestial melody and echoing to words of celestial wisdom. Little children, free and happy, were led by their angel guardians, and were seen feasting on fruits, which, invisible to the eyes of others, were real and tangible to them.

♩ = 106 (♯3) MS ENH–11, no. 357.

I'm on my way to the ho- ly cit- y of the New je- ru- sa-
l- e- m Where I shall see our Moth- ers child- ren
Crowned with a roy- al di- a- dem

Gift Song No. 51

LIMBER WILLOW

One Pleasant Hill manuscript preserves this song and says it was learned at Union Village in 1851. The homogeneity of sentiment and expression throughout the societies during these years is shown by a comparison of "Limber Willow" with incidents in a service held at Pleasant Hill three years earlier. During the meeting Mother Ann's spirit had asked all to "leap out of bondage, stupidity, pride and every thing obstructing to the true spirit of simplicity and freedom." To aid them, she said,

> she had prepared and placed in the midst a holy fountain of pure Wine where of all might drink and become like the limber willow, and after makeing a pretty free use of it, she repeated again that all might drink and drink again untill they become limber, and could bow, bend and reel like the willow or a limber withe. After drinking again all seemed to be baptized into the spirit, and shewed their devoted feelings, zeal and simplicity there by.

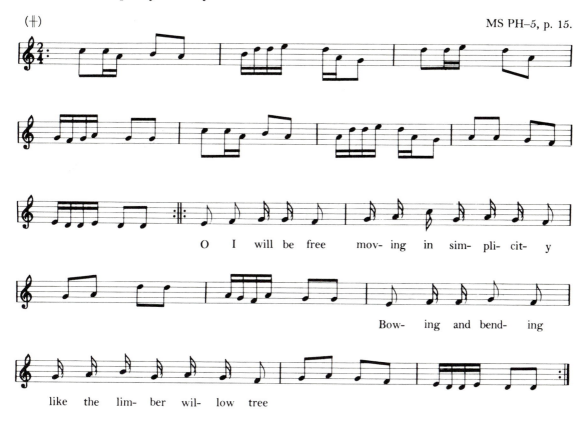

MS PH–5, p. 15.

O I will be free mov- ing in sim- pli- cit- y

Bow- ing and bend- ing

like the lim- ber wil- low tree

Gift Song No. 52

STEP IN & BE HEALED

The Holy Savior sang this song to Elisha Blakeman of Lebanon on November 20, 1851. It became a favorite, recorded in manuscripts from South Union to Canterbury. A variant of its pleasing tune had already served the hymn "Ezekiel's Vision." The text grew from John 5:3–4, describing the pool of Bethesda, where

> lay a great multitude of impotent folk, of blind, halt, withered, waiting for the moving of the water. For an angel went down at a certain season into the pool, and troubled the water: whosoever then first after the troubling of the water stepped in was made whole of whatsoever disease he had.

Calvin Green explained "this living pool" as "a type of the standing fountain of the elements or waters of everlasting life placed in the New Jerusalem." But Believers went beyond a typological reading of the scriptural passage. It touched them, and when they sang the song—probably at the fountain on the holy mount—not the first alone but all the sons and daughters must have stepped forward to find healing in the spiritual streams.

♩. = 61 (𝄵²)   MS L–60, p. 145.

An an- gel hath trou- bled the wa- ters Step in lit- tle ones and be healed Come come O my sons & my daugh- ters Come bathe in this beau- ti- ful stream. Tho maim- ed & halt deaf and blind you may be These wa- ters will heal you they will set you free; Sing glo- ry to Moth- er sing glo- ry a- gain Re- joice ye for- ev- er in my ho- ly name

Gift Song No. 53

SIMPLE GIFTS

This song gave a title to Edward D. Andrews' pioneering study of Shaker songs and a theme to Aaron Copland's ballet suite "Appalachian Spring." These men made it the most widely known of the Shaker spirituals. It also had popularity among the Shakers. More than fifteen manuscripts preserve the tune, and it survives in oral tradition.

The manuscripts identify the song as a Quick Dance, but give conflicting word of its origin. One written at Lebanon says that it was received from a Negro spirit at Canterbury. Andrews reports seeing it described as "composed by the Alfred Ministry June 28, 1848." I have been unable to find his authority, but several manuscripts do record the song from the singing of Elder Joseph Brackett and a company from Alfred, who visited a number of societies in the summer of 1848. In her youth at Hancock, Mrs. Olive H. Austin heard that it was Elder Joseph's own song. Eldress Caroline Helfrich there remembered seeing him sing it in a meeting room, turning about "with his coat tails a-flying."

Gift Song No. 54

VERDANT GROVES

The Alfred ministry brought this march its popularity among Believers. The song originated at Enfield, New Hampshire, in 1846, but appears not to have been widely known until Elder Joseph and his company took their tour in the summer of 1848. In July they sang it on the Mount of Olives, the feast ground at Enfield, Connecticut, and probably in other societies as well. Shortly after this time it was copied into some twenty-two manuscripts. Some of the scribes had learned it by ear, for the variants take four slightly different forms. The most common—though not predominant—form is that printed by Andrews. The present version is the one known at Pleasant Hill.

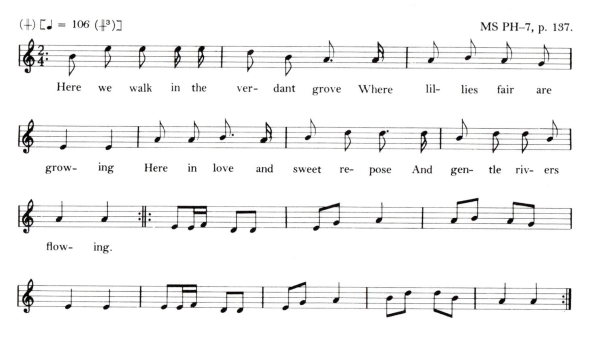

(♯) [♩ = 106 (♯³)]   MS PH–7, p. 137.

Here we walk in the ver- dant grove Where lil- lies fair are grow- ing Here in love and sweet re- pose And gen- tle riv- ers flow- ing.

Gift Song No. 55

THE SAVIOR'S CHEERING PROMISE

While on their tour in 1848, Elder Joseph Brackett and his company not only taught but also collected songs. One they obtained at Lebanon must have pleased them. At the holy fountain there on the evening of September 11 the Holy Savior's Angel sang "The Savior's Cheering Promise" as a special notice to the visitors. This was a Monday, so the company must have been guided up the Holy Mount to take a view of the feast grounds. Sarah Ann Lewis of Lebanon recorded the song in her manuscript at the time and was probably the instrument.

Left to her, the song would have been forgotten. But the Maine visitors entered it into their notebook too and liked it well enough to sing it upon their return home. In September of the next year the song came back to Isaac Youngs of Lebanon. He took it to have originated at Alfred or Gloucester, liked the song, and gave it currency in the society. Some people there afterwards understood it to have been received in the First Order in 1850. By that year it had traveled westward to Watervliet and on to Union Village and White Water in Ohio. By December 1851 it came to Pleasant Hill in a group of North Union songs, and the next year again from Union Village. The song also spread east from Lebanon. Haskell learned it at Enfield in the spring of 1852.

Scribes recorded it in twenty-two manuscripts that survive, and in seven different families of variants. These are distinguished, however, by only minor differences like a rebarring of the tune or the introduction of passing tones into one of the wider intervals. The song was no longer current at Alfred when Sister Mildred was gathering her repertory in the first decades of this century. Probably it was crowded from active use much earlier. The last manuscript copy of "The Savior's Cheering Promise" was written about 1855. Many Shaker songs of the era resemble it in the history of their diffusion, variation, and use.

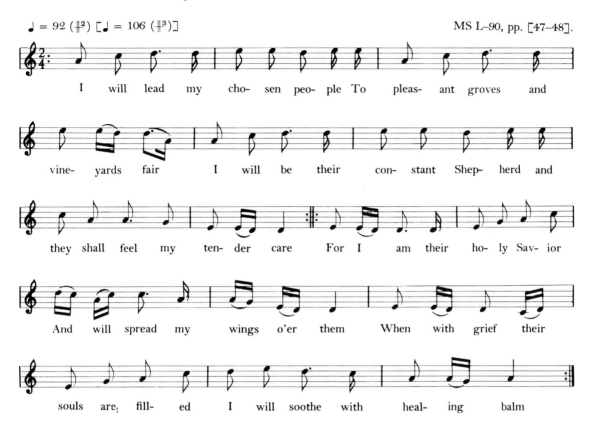

Gift Song No. 56

HERE ARE WATERS PURE AND SWEET

A fountain stood at the center of each feast ground. "There was never any water there," wrote Aurelia Mace, "except the water that could be seen by spiritual eyes," but the clairvoyant saw the fountain "rising through beautiful waves to the very heaven of heavens." Its sweet waters were recalled in song long after the closing of services at the feast grounds in the early 1850s. By 1858, when the present song was received at Union Village, the gifts themselves rarely flowed. Believers already felt that "the fountain may be there now, but this is a day of waiting."

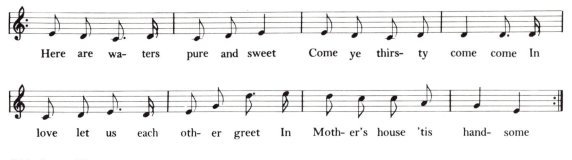

Here are wa- ters pure and sweet Come ye thirs- ty come come In

love let us each oth- er greet In Moth- er's house 'tis hand- some

Gift Song No. 57

LITTLE CHILDREN

Benjamin Dunlavy sent this marching song from Pleasant Hill to Daniel Boler at Lebanon in 1857. It proved popular in the East and survived in oral tradition at both Canterbury and Sabbathday Lake. Eldress Marguerite Frost never saw the song in written form and thought she must have picked it up in the young people's meetings when she was a girl. Her recollection was that they performed it as a Slow March with "no motions other than time marking." The sisters in Maine knew it simply as a song. Traditions in the two societies differed tellingly on another point. The Canterbury singers had come to regard the "noted" phrase as naive; they substituted for it the lines,

> Kindly bear the cross together,
> As ye journey onward.

The more traditional Maine communities retained the original "lo-lodle's." Singers there liked the song, and it never occurred to them to undertake improvements in the text.

Original tonic: E
♩ = 66 [♩ = 106 (♯³)]

From the singing of R. Mildred Barker.

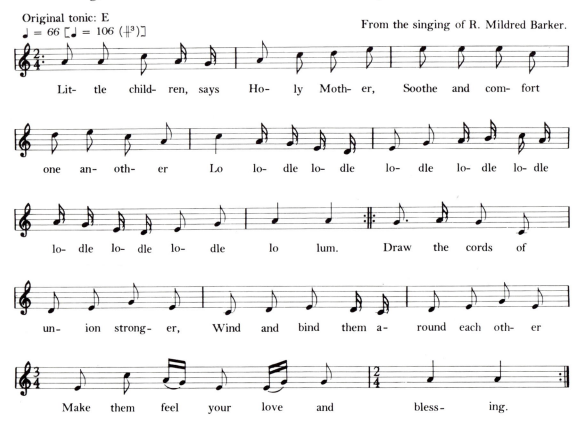

Lit- tle child- ren, says Ho- ly Moth- er, Soothe and com- fort

one an- oth- er Lo lo- dle lo- dle lo- dle lo- dle lo- dle

lo- dle lo- dle lo- dle lo lum. Draw the cords of

un- ion strong- er, Wind and bind them a- round each oth- er

Make them feel your love and bless- ing.

PART XI

Laboring Songs from the Era of Mother's Work

After the first years of the 1830s Shaker creativity in the laboring exercises entered a second period of dormancy from which it was awakened five years later by the revival known as Mother's Work. This movement stirred the creation of new dances and marches as it did of new songs. By November 1837, only three months after the beginning of the revival, young girls at Watervliet had visions in which they saw "the square check & several other manners practiced in the spiritual world."[1] Similar gifts were probably received in most of the societies. At Canterbury, according to the recollections of Elder Henry Blinn, the visionists introduced exercises called the Winding March, the Lively Line, the Changeable Dance, the Double Square, Mother's Star, the Cross and Diamond, Mother's Love, Elder Benjamin's Cross, the Finished Cross, the Lively Ring, the Moving Square, the Square and Compass, and the Celestial March. He says there were many more.[2]

Probably the instruments who received these new laboring manners were relatively few in number. At Watervliet it seems to have been principally Ann Maria Goff who saw the "disembodied spirits laboring." In one vision she beheld 344,000 spirits laboring in a new manner, which she later taught to her family: two abreast they formed three circles, the first and third turning to the left and the second to the right—"a beautiful sight."[3] After another trance she was able to recall a more unusual dance, which she demonstrated in union meetings, one requiring the worshipers to break down into checks, or groups of four persons, who danced facing each other. A short time later the spirit of Mother Lucy Wright instructed her that this new "check manner would do for active young people, but was not so well adapted for common practice, as all could not well unite in it." She then showed Ann Maria the Heavenly March, "one manner that all can learn." Mother Lucy directed that it be taught to the society.

This raised a problem. The elders "felt rather backward" about introducing a new manner of worship "without the union" of the ministry at Lebanon. They put the girl off. Mother Lucy appeared to Ann Maria a second time and gave her "strict charge" to tell the elders that they must learn and practice the Heavenly March. As the Lebanon ministry later reported the matter, this "brought the poor girl into great distress," which she "opened" to her elders. They too "felt straitened." The girl was only thirteen or fourteen. They wondered whether they could be "owned" in following the vision of a girl so young. Her anxiety over the matter was such that they had to introduce the march "for her releasement," but they also sent word to Lebanon, asking counsel. The ministry there felt the vision to be a genuine gift of God and caused the

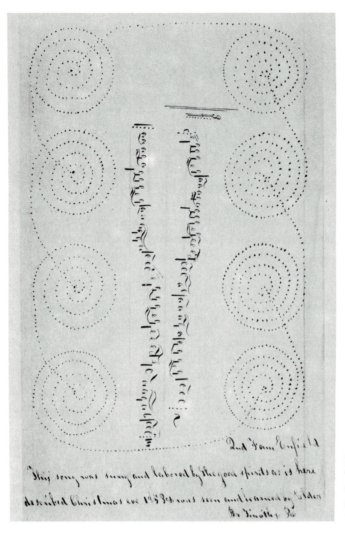

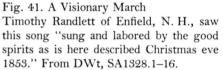

Fig. 41. A Visionary March
Timothy Randlett of Enfield, N. H., saw
this song "sung and labored by the good
spirits as is here described Christmas eve
1853." From DWt, SA1328.1–16.

march to be included in public worship. Several of the other new manners were practiced in family meetings, but not in public.[4]

The laboring manners brought forth in these years were innovative. They drew
upon elements of secular folk dance previously shunned in Shaker worship.[5] In both
the Square Check and the Heavenly March the worshipers executed figures in couples:
bowing to a partner, exchanging places, and performing an action in alternation with
another couple. The Native Dances broke even more radically with prevailing patterns
of Shaker worship. Instead of beholding the natives in visions, the inspired were led
to dance as the bodily instruments of the Indian spirits, who were not concerned to
provide a gift in which all could unite. Those Believers who were not themselves
possessed stood apart observing the solo dancers.

Such information as I could gather about these performances I present in the headnotes to native songs in the Gift Song section. I also place in that chapter certain other
exercises—such as the Narrow Path—which lie, like many rituals of the period, on
the outer borders of the dance. The remainder of the dances I describe in the pages
that follow, but I am able to reconstruct very few of them. Gift Songs of the era survive

by the thousands, but records of the dances are scanty. Novelty was succeeding novelty, and not one of these new forms remained for long in the repertory of Shaker laboring manners.

The Heavenly March

Of all the new laboring manners seen in visions by Ann Maria Goff and other girls in the Second Family at Watervliet, the Bowing Shuffle or Heavenly March found most favor with the society. On December 1, 1837, only a few weeks after the march had been received, an elder from Watervliet demonstrated it to the ministry at Lebanon. The Lead approved this gift and called in others to learn it.[6]

Russel Haskell and other writers left detailed accounts of how it was performed.[7] The singers gathered in the center of the meeting room. Around them the laborers, standing two by two, formed a large circle, brethren in one half and sisters in the other. During the first half of the tune all trotted around the circle as they did in the Round Dance, stepping off with the left foot. At the beginning of the set part of the tune, which was performed only once, all stopped in place, lifted up their hands with their palms toward their ears, and began with the left foot to step "as stepping upon the border of a small oval" from one rank into the other, each passing to the left side of his partner. Eight steps took a laborer around the oval and back to his original position, where on the last step he turned to face his partner. For the last quarter of the tune they shuffled facing one another, on every shuffle of the foot making a gathering motion before their breasts with their hands. They also nodded or bowed to each other at the beginning, middle, and end of this section. At Gloucester, if Aurelia Mace's account can be rightly understood, the laborers simply turned around in place instead of pacing the oval. Starting off in the march again on the turn section, "they would clap their hands four times." She thought the manner "very beautiful and heavenly."[8]

Heavenly March No. 1

THE JOYFUL SAINTS OF GOD

This is one of the few tunes known to have been sung for the Heavenly March. Daniel Sizer of Canaan had the song in 1838, when he had been a Believer for eleven years. According to his "testimony," he was born in Connecticut in 1804, and at the age of nine began to be exercised "concerning God, eternity, the Saviour, Heaven and Hell, and good and evil spirits." Discerning this, his grandmother, a "woman that feared God," taught him the scriptures. He "listened with delight and pleasure and in breathless silence" as she told and explained the Bible stories. Through her he became "an admirer and an ardent lover of Jesus Christ and his religion while very young."

Searching for a denominational home in his early manhood, he feared that "real Christianity was not to be found upon the earth." In practical virtue all churches seemed to him to "come short." By degrees his religious concerns wore off, but would at times revive, causing him "to sigh for a better state of things" both in himself and in the world. The turning point of his life was a reading of the Shaker book *A Summary View of the Millennial Church.*

Shortly afterwards he traveled to Lebanon to see the Shakers for himself. He arrived toward evening, nearly at the hour for family services. A supper was prepared for him, but he chose to forego it for the sake of the meeting. When the brethren and sisters assembled in their facing ranks and began to sing, he was struck, he says,

> with an inexpressible something that fill'd me with awe and solemnity. In their worship they appeared to me more like the inhabitants of heaven than of earth. The light that broke in upon my soul, the views that opened to my mental vision, the hope that swelled my bosom, the sensations of joy that I felt upon seeing the worship and hearing the testimony of this people I cannot discribe with pen or toungue.
>
> In about two months I finished settleing my business and returned to New Lebanon to take up my abode with the Shakers being then in the twenty third year of my age.

Heavenly March No. 2

WE WILL STEP THE HEAVENLY MARCH

About the year 1845 one scribe at Lebanon recorded this song. Its fragment of text suggests that the song came in a dream or vision of the Heavenly March, for which it may also have been used in Believers' worship.

MS L–207, p. 306.

We will step the heav-en-ly march and we will be u-nit-ed.

Heavenly March No. 3

I'VE SET MY FACE FOR ZION'S KINGDOM

The opening phrase of this tune resembles several in the shape-note tradition—"Christian Prospect," "Christian Hope," and "Who's Like Jesus"—and these are fashioned from the English morris-dance tune "Glorishears." The Shaker singer who reworked the tune stock to make this fine marching song was Betsy Spaulding of Pleasant Hill. The song dates from 1849, when she was twenty-four. She had come to the village at the age of eleven and would die there in 1904 after serving for thirty years as an eldress. A Shaker journal calls her "one of the most substantial sisters at that place."

MS PH–7, p. 54.

I've set my face for Zi-on's king-dom Ho-ly bright and glor-ious

Tho boister-ous winds may of-ten blow

To that bright home I'm bound to go

The Square Check

One of the dances learned in vision by Ann Maria Goff of Watervliet during the fall of 1837 was the Square Check. To perform it the brethren and sisters—doubtless keeping to their proper sides of the meeting room—gathered in groups of four. Those in

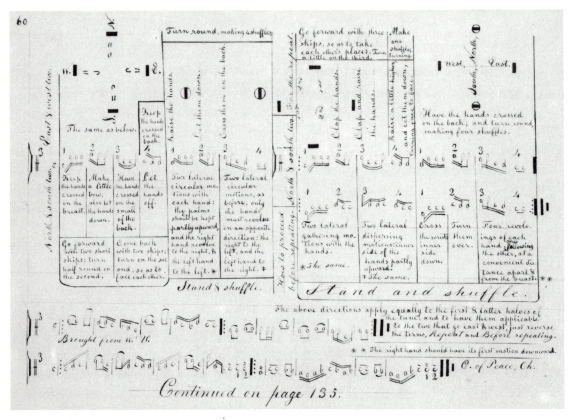

Continued on page 135.

Fig. 42. A Visionary Dance
Russel Haskell's directions for the performance of the Square Check, a dance learned from the angels by Ann Maria Goff of Watervliet in 1837.

each formed one "check" by placing themselves "as if standing one at each corner of a square." In the actions that followed, the brethren started each quarter of the tune with the left foot, the sisters with their right. In turning they took these same directions. When members of a check passed by one another, each went to his left. One crossed his hands and wrists often in this dance. The left hand was always placed next to the breast and the right wrist against the small of the back. As for footwork, each skip or shuffle contained "two beats of the foot." Haskell says the shuffling was the same as the "full single shuffle" but performed "without much bending of the knees, and with a little motion of the body, up and down, twice in each shuffle." A peculiarity of the dance was that during the first singing of the turn strain an introductory figure was performed. The turn was then sung two more times so that the first principal figure could be alternately executed by both the north–south and east–west pairs. The set was also repeated, with the couples reversing roles in the second singing. The dance was lively and contained figures unfamiliar in Shaker labor. As a consequence it was taught only to "the younger class" for use in private family worship: "none but the sprightly could do it."[9]

Square Check Tune No. 1

One of the three tunes taught by the Enfield ministry for the Square Check.

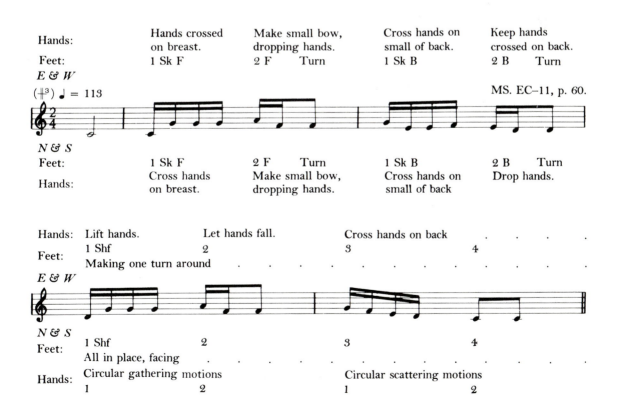

Hands: Clap the hands.   Clap and   Raise higher, and
                                                   raise hands.   let fall.

Feet: Sk F to take the other's place, going to left.   Make one Shf,
        1   2   3   turning face to face.

E & W

N & S

Feet: 1 Shf   2   3   4
         All in place, facing
Hands: Circular gathering motions   Circular scattering motions
         1   2   1   2

Hands: Hands crossed on the back
Feet: 1 Shf   2   3   4
         Making one turn around

E & W

N & S

Feet: 5 Shf   6   7   8
         All in place, facing
Hands: Cross wrists,   Turn them   Revolve hands around each other
         palms down.   over.   1   2   3   4

Hands: Clap the hands.   Clap and   Raise higher
                                                  raise the hands.   and let fall.

Feet: Sk F to take the other's place, going to left.   Make one Sh,
        1   2   3   turning face to face.
E & W

N & S

Feet: 1 Shf   2   3   4
         All in place, facing
Hands: Circular gathering motions.   Circular scattering motions.
         1   2   1   2

Hands: Hands crossed on the back
Feet: 1 Shf   2   3   4
         Making one turn around
E & W

N & S

Feet: 5 Shf   6   7   8
         All in place, facing
Hands: Cross wrists,   Turn them   Revolve hands around each other
         palms down.   over.   1   2   3   4

Antediluvian Square Shuffle

In 1843 an instrument at Watervliet, New York, announced a visit from an antediluvian couple, Anhileel the second son of Enoch, and "the woman his companion." They had come "to beg the love & blessing of God's people on Earth, that they might come into the work of Regeneration." During their brief stay Anhileel showed Believers how "Sons & Daughter's of God went forth to worship God" in his day.

As far as can be made out from the diagram of the dance recorded by D. A. Buckingham, probably himself the instrument, the labor was similar to the Square Order Shuffle in all respects except the figure in which the worshipers stood and the directions they faced. Presumably the laborers spent the first half of the tune alternately advancing and retreating three steps, turning around and striking a shuffle after each third step. This section was probably repeated, after which the dancers shuffled in place through one singing of the second half of the tune.

Brother Austin attempted to make the figure clear by means of a diagram, a wise precedent which I follow (see Diagrams 6 and 7, below). A *B* or an *S* marks the spot occupied by a brother or a sister. An arrow shows the direction in which each faced and, in fact, the track within which he performed the entire dance. He also diagrammed a "modern improvement" on the antediluvian manner. Showing the Shaker's aversion to gaps within the ranks, he found a way to transform the figure into a solid body of worshipers. Buckingham reports that by placing the worshipers "in the same order" one might enlarge the square "to any number desired."[10] No tunes are preserved for this dance, and there is no evidence that the society found either the Antediluvian Square Shuffle or Buckingham's modern improvement to be a significant advance over Shaker worship.

```
  .     .     .     .     .     .
            Singers

B→   B→   B→   S→   S→   S
↑                          ↓
B         B→               S
↑                          ↓
B         B→   S    S    S
↑              ↓    ↓    ↓
B    B    B   ←S           S
↑    ↑    ↑                ↓
B             ←S           S
↑                          ↓
B   ←B   ←B   ←S   ←S   ←S
```

Diagram 6. The Antediluvian Square Shuffle

```
  .     .     .     .     .     .
            Singers

B→   B→   B→   S→   S→   S
↑                          ↓
B    B→   B→   S→   S    S
↑    ↑              ↓    ↓
B    B    B→   S    S    S
↑    ↑    ↑     ↓    ↓    ↓
B    B    B   ←S    S    S
↑    ↑              ↓    ↓
B    B   ←B   ←S   ←S    S
↑                          ↓
B   ←B   ←B   ←S   ←S   ←S
```

Diagram 7. The Improved Antediluvian Square Shuffle

PART XII

Later Laboring Songs

Dances introduced during the Era of the Spirit Manifestations were the blooms of a short day in Shakerism. As it passed, they faded and were forgotten. But some of the tendencies they embodied continued important in Shaker life. The explicit symbolic content of Shaker rituals, for example, had markedly increased during the 1840s, and during the 1850s such rituals underwent further elaboration.

The difference between the ways the two decades employed symbolism reveals itself in interpretations given of the marches. Eldress Anna White explains that the marches up to the feast grounds on the Holy Mount in the 1840s were emblematic of the pilgrim soul's progress from the World to the Celestial City.[1] By contrast, in the 1850s a visitor attending services at Canterbury saw the brethren and sisters form themselves into a single file and march around the central body

> ultimately forming into four circles, with the singers as a common center. This was afterwards explained as symbolical of the four great "dispensations" as expounded in Shakerism. The first, from Adam to Abraham; the second, from Abraham to Jesus; the third, from Jesus to Mother Ann; and the fourth, the "millennial," which the Shakers claim they are now enjoying.[2]

At Lebanon in the same years Benson Lossing saw the worshipers sing a hymn as they stood in four concentric circles holding hands in token of their unity. He too was told that the encircling wheels represented the four dispensations, the "greater dispensation" including the others, and all of them "working to one end." The music of the vocal band in the center represented "*harmony* and *perfection* to which all tend and there is God."[3]

These rituals organized the entire body of worshipers to express doctrinal concepts. Their insistence on dramatizing the symbolism may derive from the Era of Spirit Manifestations, but the symbolic statement is no longer one of childlike simplicity. It represents the reemergence of an intellectualizing tendency that would gather force enough by the 1870s to largely overwhelm the folk traditions of the sect.

Another small but significant change in the laboring manner also hints of this trend. In 1842 the spirit of the Holy Savior "informed the Church" at Lebanon that "when they marched if they would hold the palms of their hands up . . . the Angels would bestow upon them the gifts of God."[4] Countless similar gifts were received and practiced for a single meeting or a month or two and then forgotten. But this change swept every Shaker community, it was taken up into both the march and the dance, and it persisted as long as the exercises themselves. Earlier, the downturned hands had been defined as meaning that the laborers shook off sin and evil magnetism. The acceptance of upturned palms as a symbol of openness to the Holy Spirit and its blessings implies a mellowing of attitudes. It suggests a readiness for the liberal phase of Shakerism that was soon to divert the progressive and meliorist strains in Shaker thought from self-purification to self-culture.

The same change was also manifested in a gradually increasing decorum in the Shaker worship. In earlier years the Shakers rejoiced in the effect their lively exercises produced on "wonder-struck worldlings." During the height of the spirit manifestations the doors of the meetinghouses had even to be closed to the World. Now the visitors would increasingly comment on the grace and stateliness of the Shaker exercises. The spontaneous gifts came less frequently, and the tempos of the laboring exercises began to grow slower.

In 1848 a new form called the Slow March or Solemn March was introduced. The name itself is indicative of the nature of this march. Its stately stepping and bowing made it easier for the aged than the livelier dances, but many of the young must also have thought it more refined. Over the next two decades the dances gradually fell into disuse. In 1874 a journal keeper at Union Village wrote that the worshipers had tried "to unite in the Step manner but it was very unsatisfactory." The trained dancers had "departed mostly," and "the handful of trained, and the uninitiated, made rather a poor performance."[5] In 1889 at Pleasant Hill visitors from Lebanon showed the Quick Dance to the young people, who had never seen it.[6] Marching persisted longer than dancing. By 1884 it had been several years since the worshipers at Canterbury had united in the Holy Order, the Regular Step, or the Quick Dance. Their exercise was limited to either a Quick, Common, or Slow March in the circle.[7] Except in the young people's meetings, all laboring had ceased by the first decade of the twentieth century, and in no society did even the marches continue much beyond 1930.[8] George E. Budinger, who was raised at North Union in the 1880s, recalled that even then the worshipers "just walked up and down" with their hands out, palms up. He saw no "twirling about." It was slow and dignified, he said: "they were in no hurry."[9]

The Quick March

In Shaker usage, tunes for most of the marching exercises were originally called simply "marches." As the years passed the performance of the march went unchanged except for an alteration in the manner of carrying the hands and the gradual displacement of all other forms by the Circular March. After the introduction of the Slow March in 1848, however, Believers often referred to the earlier songs as Quick Marches, and they gave this name also to new 6/8 tunes in Shaker mode 5 and to 2/4 tunes in mode 3. To call attention to this change of name, I present one example here, but the remainder of the Quick Marches dating from after 1848 will be found with other marching songs earlier in this volume.

Quick March No. 1

PILGRIM'S PATH

This march originated about 1857 at Alfred and in a very few years was a favorite throughout the East. It has a strong tune—one related to those of the shape-note hymn "Roby" and the Canterbury song "Deep Love"—but Believers also found great satisfaction in singing of themselves as pilgrims. The image is recurrent in their songs, as it is in those of several generations of other Americans. They intended more than simply an allusion to Bunyan. The image provided a definition of themselves peculiarly apt for people turning their backs on the worldly-wise and setting off into new Western lands, new livelihoods, new political and social orders, and new religious faiths.

Some like the Mummyjums gave themselves to a literal enactment of the symbol. This band of men, women, and children—who called themselves Pilgrims, but got their nickname from their rapid, mumbling ejaculations—straggled into the Shaker village at Lebanon on August 25, 1817. They were reported to have been "people of respectability and property" in Vermont and Canada, but had left all and were "led & directed by the spirit which influenced their leader," Isaac Bullard. Some were quite emaciated, for he kept them constantly fasting. The men wore long beards and all the company were dirty and lousy. They walked bent over, with a short staff in each hand, making odd gesticulations. The Shakers offered them food and lodging (the sexes to be in separate quarters). This the Pilgrims declined with great contempt, prophesying judgments upon Lebanon as they took their way on to the southwest.

Three years later a letter of apology came to Lebanon from one of this company, a woman named Fanny Ball. By her account, the Pilgrims had trekked westward preaching that "darkness has covered the land and gross darkness the people but God was now about to establish his kingdom on the earth." When they passed through Union Village, Bullard was thrown into confusion, and "the minds of the people began to scatter." They continued their pilgrimage, despite hardships that included an epidemic of smallpox, until they reached the wilds of Arkansas. Here all the Pilgrims were taken sick with ague and fever. Some died, and others went off. Bullard, too, fell ill and began to be "vary full of trouble." Eventually he called together the few he thought to have the "most light and understanding" and confessed his error and folly in opposing the Shakers. For Fanny "this was a vary serious time of reflection." Her family was scattered, her daughter ill and at the point of death, and she "in the wilderness disapointed" in one she had thought would lead her "in the way of truth and riteousness." With difficulty she gathered her family and took the path back to Union Village, where she became a Shaker. "I think all my tribulation," she wrote, "has served to unite my heart the more to my Mothers children."

($\frac{6}{8}$) [♩. = 106 (♩^{5})]

MS HD–38, pp. 13–14.

Fel- low pil- grims bound for heav- en With the staff of

truth in hand Yea the com- fort- er in sor- row

Which the Sav- ior said he'd send Tho the way be rough and crag- ged Moun- tains high and val- lies low Deep the riv- ers cur- rent rap- id Tis the pil- grims path we know.

The Slow March

The Slow March differed from others not in the figures the worshipers described on the floor (it was performed in both ranks and circles), but in the arm movements, the posture, and the tempo. Marchers alternately bowed and drew erect in time with the music. In each bow they gently swung their arms back past their sides. When they straightened they lifted their hands till their fingertips touched lightly together on their breasts.

Writing in the 1890s, both Henry Blinn and Aurelia Mace recalled the Slow March as an early form of laboring. Blinn thought it was introduced at Enfield, New Hampshire, in 1798, and Sister Aurelia wrote that the Believers at Gloucester had practiced it for eighty years. Their view is not supported by the accounts of early travelers or by older Shakers like Isaac Youngs and Russel Haskell. Haskell, in fact, bluntly stated that the Slow March was first practiced in Connecticut in 1848. In the West the exercise arrived even later. One letter says it was learned at Union Village in 1862, after being "in practice several years in the East."[10]

Slow March No. 1

HOW PLEASANT TO WALK IN THE LOWLY VALLEY

Many Shaker marching songs call for the faithful to hasten along toward the Heavenly City. A wilderness of toils and dangers encompasses the pilgrims about. But a second set of songs presents the march as a pleasant walk through delights attained. The struggle is past and the singers enjoy their reward in peaceful groves and vales. The number of such songs increases

Fig. 43. Marching Posture: "The regulation marching attitude; the forearms and hands were waved constantly up and down in perfect time with the music and the whole effect was most graceful"—Emily Williams, 1905.

Fig. 44. Marching Posture: "The lowly position of a 'bowing song,' intended to express the humility proper to an erring soul. While it was being sung the Shakers marched around, alternately bowing and standing erect in time with the music"—Emily Williams, 1905.

as the years pass. Like this example, which originated at Canaan in August 1861, they frequently served for the Slow March. No one was inclined to double-time past these delightful vistas.

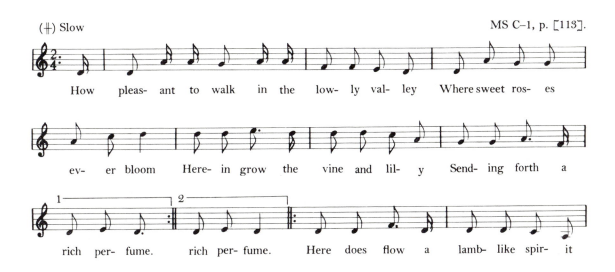

(♯) Slow

MS C–1, p. [113].

How pleas- ant to walk in the low- ly val- ley Where sweet ros- es

ev- er bloom Here- in grow the vine and lil- y Send- ing forth a

1. rich per- fume. 2. rich per- fume. Here does flow a lamb- like spir- it

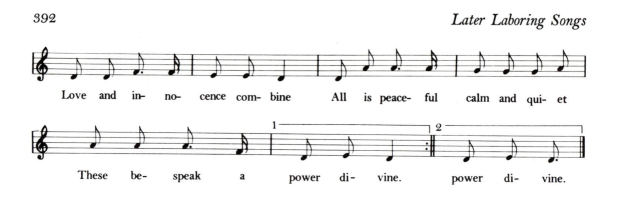

Love and in- no- cence com- bine   All is peace- ful   calm and qui- et

These be- speak   a   power di- vine.   power di- vine.

Slow March No. 2

FRUITS OF HUMILITY

This song originated at Union Village in 1852 and was soon known in all the societies. Twenty-five variants survive. The earliest were rhythmically strict, but by the time the present form became current at Shirley and Harvard late in the decade the song appears to have been dissociated from the marching exercises. The weakness of the tonal center of the original pentatonic tune had also tricked the singers into making a number of changes in the melodic intervals. An earlier Shaker variant of the melody was that used by Elder Issachar Bates for the ballad of his winter journey. The tune was later printed in shape-note hymnals as "The Wayfaring Stranger."

MS HD–14, pp. 16–17.

I'm   go- ing   down   to the   beau- ti- ful   val- ley   To

eat   of   its   fruits   &   its   vin- tage   so   sweet   'Tis

in   this   low   vale   a   crown   I'll   in- her- it   'Tis

there   my   re- demp- tion   will   be   com- plete   I'm

go- ing   down   where   the   low- ly   in   spir- it   Are

sound- ing   sweet   prais- es   to   God   ev- er- more   And

thro its pleas- ant groves & by its flow- ing foun- tains I'll

walk this love- ly re- gion o'er.

Slow March No. 3

I'LL SPEND AND BE SPENT

The phrase *travel from loss* was one of the most common—and most complex—in Shaker speech. It probably originated in Ann Lee's description of the suffering and travail in which she confessed her sins to God and cried to God continually to know if her confession had been accepted. By means of this sincere repentance, this work of regeneration, she had labored and travailed into her own spiritual rebirth. To these implications later Shakers added another: travel or progress toward perfect holiness, a spiritual journey to which they had dedicated themselves. In Shaker worship the word *travel* also alluded, of course, to the march, the emblematic exercise for which this beautiful song was received in 1858 by some unnamed member of the North Family at Shirley.

Original tonic: D♭

From the singing of R. Mildred Barker.

I'll spend and be spent in the cause of my God. My

all I free- ly re- sign. I will take up my cross and

trav- el from loss, and be faith- ful while here in

time. Though bil- lows may beat and waves o'er me roll Yet

true to my trust I will be, For God he is a- ble the

winds to con- trol And bear me o- ver the sea.

Slow March No. 4

A FULL BAPTISM

This song was received in February 1865 at the North Family of Lebanon by either Rhoda Offord or Anna White. A Maine manuscript calls it a "Bowing Song," and Eldress Marguerite Frost recalled that at Canterbury too it was "marched with a deep bending motion as going under waves." She emphasized, however, that the one who started such a song might instead fall to her knees, the others joining her, "bringing all to tears so deeply did they all want spiritual growth."

To a Shaker this full and spontaneous emotional awakening was the test of spirituality and the source of strength. Rhoda Blake, for example, was dissatisfied with merely striving to "keep the rules" and to be "true to my teaching, honest and upright in every thing." As she grew older she realized she could not find "more victory over the element of nature" without a "deeper baptism." She could kneel and "repeat a sensible prayer, which was a form of godliness, but the spirit was not there." She made a firm resolve to gain the gift of prayer and, weeping, sought the help of the elders. She also hoped for an "invisible spirit" to hear and answer her prayer. One day while she was "walking the floor in tribulation," she prayed for a song as a sign if she were heard. "It was not long," she wrote, "before I commenced singing and O how thankful I felt that the divine Love and Presence had found its way into my heart. It was gained by tribulation & sufferings of both soul and body. From this time onward I always had a peculiar gift to pray."

Slow March No. 5

GOSPEL KINDRED

By 1865, when Anna White had this "bowing song" at Lebanon, Shaker verse was increasingly favoring bald exposition over metaphor and symbol. But early and late, the Believers were always sensitive to symbolic nuances in behavior, especially as these bore upon gospel love and union. A story is told that when a sister was called away from one union meeting in 1818, another in the room rose, set the empty chair back, and moved her own to close the gap. Elder Rufus Bishop exclaimed, "I am glad to see you do that. The first Elders said where there was an empty chair standing between two, the evil spirits would get into it." In the 1880s the symbolic implications of one architectural change would be felt so strongly at Gloucester as to terminate the services in its meetinghouse. The century-old Church Family dwelling had been torn down to make room for a new one of brick that the designers gave but a single front door. In going to meetings, the brethren and sisters had formerly filed from the house by separate doors, crossing the road together, and entering the meetinghouse simultaneously. With only one door, the groups had to go separately. The males went first, and the females followed behind the smallest boys. "The beauty was all destroyed," wrote Sister Aurelia Mace, for the new arrangement overruled one of "the great Principles of the New Creation," the equality of the sexes. It was felt a hostile assertion of a "great 'He' spirit." No wonder, Aurelia said, that "by a Divine Controlling Power the Public meetings were suddenly stopped, and our very highly spiritual meetings in the Chapel of the Dwelling House were established in their stead."

Slow March No. 6

MY SOUL LOVES TO WALK IN THE VALLEY LOW

Eldress Marguerite Frost of Canterbury learned this gentle song in 1914, during a time when old songs were being renewed, and she sang it lovingly. She remembered that in performing it, "we simply walked around in a circle keeping step with the music, with no hand motions, stepping slow." She had never heard that the song was received by Serena Douglas at Gloucester in March 1871. Those at Gloucester who remember Sister Serena did not know the piece and were a little surprised to learn that she had ever had a gift of song.

The facts preserved of her life are few. She was born in Green or Lewiston, Maine, in 1853 and entered the Poland Hill Family in 1862 with her parents and younger sister. The family later moved to Gloucester, and when she died in 1924 the church journalist recorded that for more than twenty years she had "worked constantly in the Office kitchen carrying that burden faithfully." That she was felt a presence in the family is implied in his comment that "she is *one* more landmark removed." But the real record of Sister Serena is contained in his quiet phrase that she "lived the Shaker life"—and in her own song.

Original key

($\frac{2}{4}$) [♩ = 72 ($\frac{1}{2s}$)]

MS CB–13, p. 201.

My soul loves to walk in the val- ley low, Where the

beau- ti- ful fruits of the gos- pel grow, Where all dis- cord- ant

feel- ings flee, And the still small voice reigns tri- um- phant- ly

This is Wis- dom's vale where is joy and de- light Her

paths are peace and her bur- dens light And though heav- y winds and

tem- pests as- sail They can- not lay waste this beau- ti- ful vale.

PART XIII

Later Hymns and Extra Songs

After the Era of the Spirit Manifestations, Believers continued long to receive songs, but more frequently now by "divine impression" than from heavenly visitants. Hymns came rarely and were generally shorter. Dancing waned, and few tunes came for this form of laboring. Most of the new songs have only one stanza, and marches are not always distinguishable from standing songs. Manuscript annotations, for example, call "Glories Immortal" variously a Slow March and a "good extra song."[1] Probably many songs that had an even beat served both functions.

Mother's Work left one mark, however, on later Shaker spirituals. It prepared the singers to feel at ease with looser, more extended melodic structures. The gift for such songs seems to have been fairly general in the late 1850s and the 1860s. Examples survive from South Union, Hancock, Harvard, and Canterbury, but the most numerous and successful originated with the North Family at Lebanon or with Elder Otis Sawyer in Maine. They are among the most interesting of the Shaker melodies.

In the later period the texts of the songs also underwent a perceptible change, one reflecting a transformation gradually taking place in the Shaker services. In the earliest years Shaker worship had been almost wholly shaped by spontaneous gifts. After the gathering of the Church, these gifts were disciplined into group singing and laboring. At this time speaking seems to have been reserved for the Lead or for others specifically asked to offer a few words. The average member expressed himself through the general gift of song or laboring or in spontaneous physical exercises such as shaking or whirling. During the years of Mother's Work these manifestations turned verbal, though the speakers were merely instruments delivering messages from the spirits.

When these phenomena waned, they left the Society accustomed to spontaneous discourse from any member. During a service, for example, that Benson Lossing attended at Lebanon in 1853, the worshipers paused in their laboring to sing "a hymn in slow and plaintive strain" unlike anything that Lossing had ever heard, one "beautiful, impressive, and deeply solemn." As it died away "the clear musical voice of a female was heard from the external circle, telling in joyful cadence, how happy she felt as a member of that pure and holy community. To this many among the worshipers gave words of hearty concurrence." The spirit of the service then flowed on into other forms, as another sister broke into a song that sent the entire body of worshipers marching slowly in a single line around the central circle of singers.[2]

With the passing of the years more and more of the membership was unable, because of the infirmities of age, to unite in the laboring exercises. As a consequence, testifying gained increasing importance in the services. It offered an alternative means by which the sense of unity could be expressed. One by one each member would rise and offer some word of witness. If the spirit of the meeting grew livelier, those who "felt to" would break into songs and further testimonies. The songs themselves became in fact largely testimonial. The homely images once common in Shaker songs—the vine and the valley, the dove and the bending willow—faded from the songs. Eventually the songs became almost wholly discursive. Ecstatic prescience subsided into ethical resolves and declarations of faith.

Later Song No. 1

HEAVENLY LOVE AND HOLY FIRE

This song originated at South Union in September 1845. It survives only in a songbook written at Pleasant Hill, but the melody must have been drawn from common secular tune stock. Thomas Hammond at Harvard had recorded it as a wordless song (my B variant) just the year before. His tune is slightly more regular and probably served for the Holy Order dance.

Later Song No. 2

MOTHER'S TONGUE

Nearly ten manuscripts hold this song. Several date it November 6, 1845, and one ascribes it to D. A. Buckingham, the leading musician at Watervliet, New York. None gives a hint that singers ever performed it with motions, yet Sister Mildred Barker recalls a set used with the song. With palms turned upwards she gently beats time throughout the song, except when performing the following pantomine. When she sings the word *cross* she simultaneously gives a shake of the head, stamps her right foot, and makes a downward gesture to her right with both hands. On *crabbed* she repeats the actions, turning leftward. On *shun* and *ugly* she gestures again as she did for *cross*, but with greater emphasis. On the word *speak* she lays her right forefinger on her lower lip, keeping it there through the word *tongue*, then crosses her hands upon her bosom and bows slightly on *snugly*. In the Shakers' close-knit communities, every such reminder must have helped the members to adhere to the rule of speaking only with the tongues of angels.

With a New tongue I now will speak And keep the val- ley

low- ly I'll watch my thoughts & words this week And

have them pure and ho- ly. Old Cross and Crab- bed I will shun They

make one feel so ug- ly; I'd rath- er speak with Moth- ers

Tongue, And keep her Bless- ing snug- ly.

"With . . .

a New . . .

Cross . . .

Crabbed . . .

speak with Mother's Tongue . . .

keep her Blessing snugly."

Fig. 45. R. Mildred Barker Motioning "Mother's Tongue"

Later Song No. 3

MAKE ME LOWLY

The melody of this song received by Marcia Hastings in 1844 is closely related to that of "Thorny Desert," a shape-note piece published by William Walker eight years earlier, but she could hardly have known the Southern composition. She had come to Canterbury as a girl of fifteen in 1826. The tunes have a distant relative in the Union Village song "O the Beauty of Zion." All three no doubt derive from a secular source, probably a long-phrase ballad tune conforming to the AABA model. In "O the Beauty of Zion" the third phrase is lowered and the melody recast into the Shaker dance-tune pattern. The other two songs retain the original contour, but Sister Marcia deals more interestingly with it. Her variations on the A-phrase are inventive and subtle. The shape-note composer relied instead on repeat signs.

♩.= 71 (♩³) Slow—articulate

MS CB–15, p. 39.

Make me low- ly, keep me low- ly, May I nev- er, nev- er rise

'Bove the or- der God has placed me,— May I be both low and wise.

May I keep my eye di- rect- ed On the pil- lar of true light,

—God's a- noint- ed chos- en or- der,— This will guide my steps a- right.

Later Song No. 4

O HARDEN NOT THEIR HEARTS

For many years worldlings regularly attended Shaker services as an amusement, and apostates seemed never at a loss for a printer to publish their animadversions. It is remarkable then that we have record of few troups of apostates who took to the stage to profit from their knowledge of Shaker song and dance. In 1846 the Ministry of Enfield, New Hampshire, sent word of one band to Mount Lebanon:

> The Apostates from Canterbury, have joined together, and are exhibiting themselves for money, in Shaker attire: in dances, songs, speaking in unknown tongues &c. &c. They are now in Boston. James Otis, William Tripure, Russell Tallant, John Maloon, James Partridge, Lydia Grant, Lydia Chase, Julian Willard, Terrissa Bean, are among them we are told. How many more we do not know but we expect there are some from other Societies. We have seen their great *glaring* show Bills and enclose two slips from a Boston Paper to you.

Authenticity of performance they must certainly have had. Lydia Chase, who was billed as "the miraculous Shaker tetotum," had in fact served as an instrument for spiritual communications. One of Marcia Hastings' manuscripts attributes many songs to her. William Tripure had lived at Canterbury for twenty years and Russell Tallant for twelve. They are reported to have performed for seven or more consecutive weeks to "overflowing houses" at the American Museum in New York City. They also went on tour, and there was malice enough in their natures to send them riding through Union Village in July 1847 throwing out their handbills.

The reaction of the Enfield Ministry was to exclaim, "What blasphemy! and what Heave1

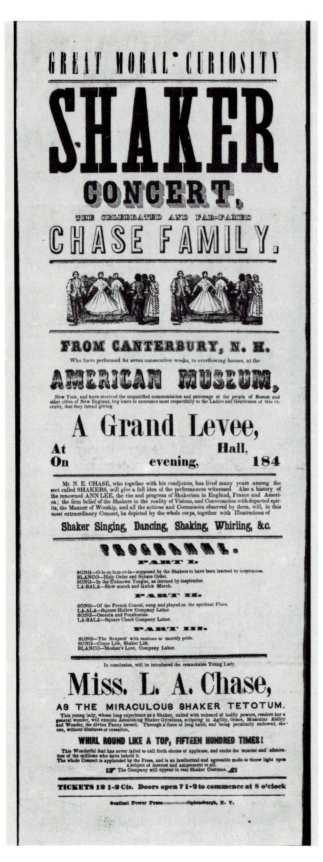

Fig. 46. A Playbill of the Canterbury Apostates

daring Rebels!" A gentler response was that of Marcia Hastings, who had known the apostates well. In 1845 she privately recorded the song which follows and wrote, "This song was breathed in deep anguish of soul, while contemplating the inevitable sad condition of souls who had been enlightened, & inspired with heavenly gifts, and turned away from the way of God, denied their faith & fallen from grace."

(‖)   MS CB–15, p. 41.

O hard-en not their hearts, let not their eyes be blind, Let them not turn a-gainst the work-ings of Thy hand. Their souls must writhe in an-guish, their tongues they'll gnaw for pain; — O save them kind Fa-ther, let them not curse Thy name.

2 They've heard Thy calling voice, Thy warnings
    they have known,
And oft have uttered forth predictions from Thy
    throne;
Shall these now be their daggers, for them to
    fall upon?
Restrain them, kind Father!—sufficient they have
    done.

Later Song No. 5

FAREWELL EARTHLY JOYS

Shakers knew of four bands of apostates who in 1847 had given theatrical performances of Shaker worship and "ministered to a bitter reprobate spirit, among many of the children of this world against Believers." One group from Maine got as far as Pittsfield, but "had to break up suddenly to escape riding on a Rail!!" Another set went to Washington, where their employer decamped with all the money. The band from Canterbury broke up at Buffalo—out of necessity, as two of the young women were seven months gone in pregnancy and could no longer gyrate as miraculous tetotums. They had not fulfilled their year's contract, so their manager exacted three hundred dollars in damages. "This left them," one Shaker elder heard, "nearly peniless, & several hundred miles from their homes and friends, in a cold season of the year! while their employer has gone into Canada with his booty, and left them to shirk for themselves: and we should think they might now have time for serious reflections." Perhaps they even came to share the Shaker view expressed by one Canterbury singer eight years later in the following song.

A.

♩ = 128–160 (♯4) [♩ = 106 (♯3)]   MS L–330, pp. [203–204].

Fare- well Earth- ly Joys, from my soul flee a- way I

cov- et some- thing high- er, That will not so soon de- cay

Some- thing that is last- ing, That for- ev- er will en-

dure A du- ra- ble treas- ure, ho- ly and

pure And by the cross I'll gain it And make it my

own By the cross I'll keep it and wear a Shin- ing Crown

This to me is com- fort This is re- al joy

Some- thing that is per- ma- nent the world can- not de- stroy

B.

Original tonic: D♭

From the singing of R. Mildred Barker.

Fare- well earth- ly joys, from my soul flee a- way; I cov- et some- thing high- er that will not so soon de- cay, Some- thing that is last- ing, that for- ev- er will en- dure, A du- ra- ble treas- ure ho- ly and pure. And by the cross I'll gain it and make it my own. By the cross I'll keep it, and wear a shin- ing crown. This to me is com- fort, this is re- al joy, Some- thing that is per- ma- nent the world can- not de- stroy.

Later Song No. 6

MIRIAM'S DANCE

The Shaker scribe who wrote down this composition prefaced it with Exod. 15:20—"And Miriam the prophetess, the Sister of Aaron, took a timbrel in her hand; & all the women went out after her, with timbrels & with dances." Had he scored the song for timbrels, the result would have been hardly less expected in a Shaker songbook. The musicians had made only three or four other experiments with harmony by 1847, the year when this song, and apparently the setting, originated at Canterbury. Both the ministry and the spirits had specifically cautioned against copying the World's manner of singing in parts. Isaac Youngs's *Short Abridgement of the Rules of Music* had abridged the science of harmony to a single sentence. Moreover, the song notebooks contained no staves, so that the scribe had to differentiate his three voices by writing the top line in red ink, the middle in black, and the lower in blue. His assigning the tune to the middle voice shows some awareness of practices current in the tunebooks of the country singing schools. But singing masters in that tradition would not have condemned the bass and treble to such monotonous lines. The setting would have killed any but so cheerful a tune.

MS WNY–18, no. 235.

With the tim- brel & song in the dance they went forth & a mer- ry mer- ry band were they. They had Ca- naan in view & their foes to sub- due While their voic- es

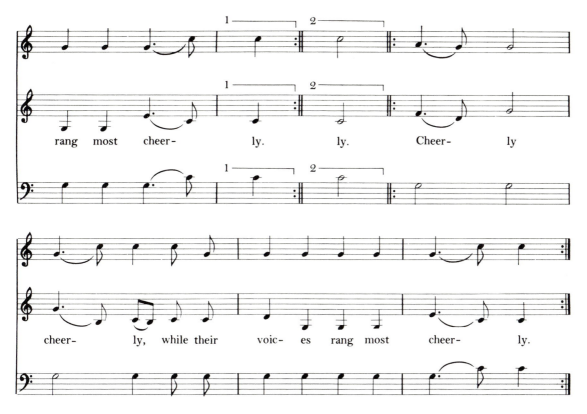

rang most cheer- ly. ly. Cheer- ly

cheer- ly, while their voic- es rang most cheer- ly.

2 We will sing to the Lord as we're journeying on
For a happy happy band are we;
And our foes we'll subdue while we've Heaven
    in view
   & we'll triumph gloriously—*Chorus* Gloriously
   &c.

3 In the dance we are free for all sin we forsake
& a lowly lowly band are we;
Here pure love does abound & true graces are
    found
So we'll skip quite merrily—*Chorus* Merrily &c.

Later Song No. 7

A LITTLE VOICE IS HEARD TO SAY

In March 1849 Lebanon received from Enfield, New Hampshire, a packet of songs that included this hymn. Its melody is related to that of the Irish song "Twas in the End of King
James's Street." Its text alludes to the still, small voice Elijah heard, to the broken heart
commended by the Psalmist, and to the rejoicing that greeted the prodigal son. All these are
woven into allusions to the Believers' worship and faith—a typically Shaker conflation of
sectarian stance, scripture, and folk melody.

♩ = 138 (‖⁴)   MS EC–11, p. 332.

A lit- tle voice is heard to say, Come fol- low me; this

is the way. My lit- tle flock I will con- vey, By lit- tle steps ad-

vanc- ing. Tis Moth- er bids her child- ren come, And

feeds them with the heav'n- ly crumb; The Fath- er greets them

wel- come home, With mus- ic & with danc- ing. danc- ing.

Later Song No. 8

FAREWELL EARTHLY GLORY

Elder Henry Blinn included this song in *A Sacred Repository of Anthems and Hymns,* one of the few Shaker publications to print tunes in letteral notation. Six manuscripts also record the song, one identifying the author as Elder Otis Sawyer of Gloucester. He had the song in 1849, when he was a man of thirty-five. At seven he had been brought from Portland to the Poland Hill Family, an early age for parting from earthly glory. Otis kept, however, one of the World's good tunes, that of "Pretty Saro," and used it for this song. His hymn copies the anapestic meter and rhymed couplets of the original text and even seems a reply to it. Both are songs of strangers far from home, but Elder Otis hardly condoned weeping in lone valleys for Saro's lily-white arms. Instead, he accepted at twenty-six the burdens of the ministry, the youngest person ever to fill that post in Maine. From then until his death in 1884, he served continuously in positions of responsibility, either in the ministry or as trustee and elder in the Church Family at Gloucester.

A Sacred Repository of Anthems and Hymns, p. 179.

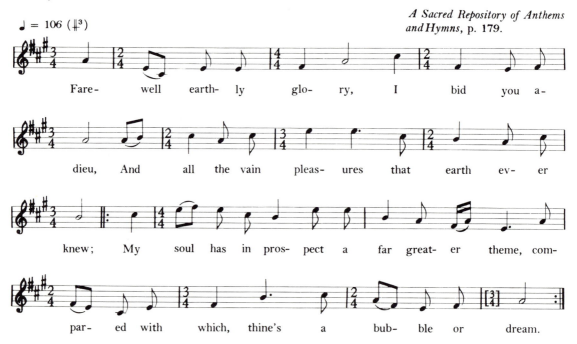

Fare- well earth- ly glo- ry, I bid you a-

dieu, And all the vain pleas- ures that earth ev- er

knew; My soul has in pros- pect a far great- er theme, com-

par- ed with which, thine's a bub- ble or dream.

2 Farewell, yea forever, thy pleasures, I find,
   Have nought in them real, a sting leave behind;
   When these I pursued, remorse, O how keen!
   Would pierce my poor soul, as no mortal can
      pen.

3 Your vain siren charms can no longer allure,
   Nor carnal delights, which my soul does abhor;
   I'll turn from your pleasure, so worthless and
      vain,
   And seek for those riches that ever remain.

4 In Zion are pleasures eternal and sure,
   For all who their robes keep unspotted and
      pure;
   My soul does possess them, O this shall be
      mine,—
   A conscience unspotted all others outshines.

Later Song No. 9

ETERNAL LIFE

The first half of this melody is a variant of the short-phrase ballad tune "The Braes of Yarrow." In keeping with Shaker preferences, the singer added and repeated material to make a second strain. The song dates from 1853. The singer was in the Gathering Order at Shirley and must not long since have bid his adieu to earthly strife and pleasure.

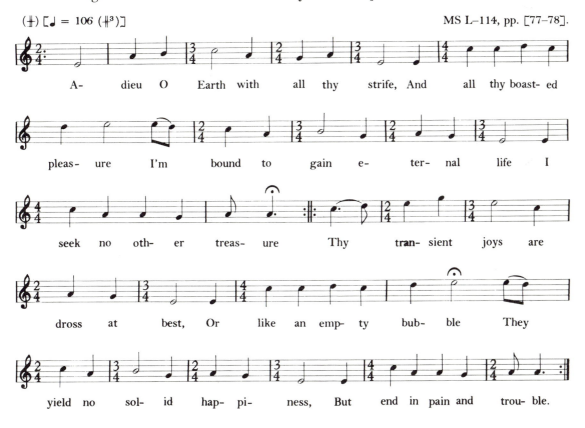

Later Song No. 10

FOOT PILGRIM'S SONG

"Learned by a weary, hungry, foot pilgrim on the road between Concord & Canterbury, June 23, 1851 Eld. A. Perkins," says a note in the one manuscript preserving this song. This note and the text of the song suggest that Elder Abraham arrived in Concord from a trip,

Fig. 47. Marcia E. Hastings
1811–1891
Canterbury, N. H.

Fig. 48. Abraham Perkins
1807–1900
Enfield, N. H.

only to find that the family had forgotten to send a wagon for him. He faced a ten-mile walk, and had vexation to subdue. It was thoroughly in character that he should find help in a song, for the words and tunes of "songs innumerable," he said, "have been engraven in my soul. How I received them, or whence they came, I am unable to explain."

In 1851 the good elder was a man of forty-four and had lived in the faith from the age of twenty. He came of parents "rigidly moral and much respected," his mother being a sister of a "one time member of the governor's council." At seventeen Abraham was a youth with ambition and a "fondness for festive society." He began the study of law in his brother's office, and on the death of his brother two years later "resolved to open a school" in Andover, New Hampshire. It was one of his pupils, a Shaker convert, who got around Abraham's naturally "mirthful disposition" and led him to the faith. After visiting the Shakers at Enfield, he asked his parents' permission to join the Society. They granted this wish, for at his birth the father had "promised before God that he would never oppose the religious convictions of his son Abraham."

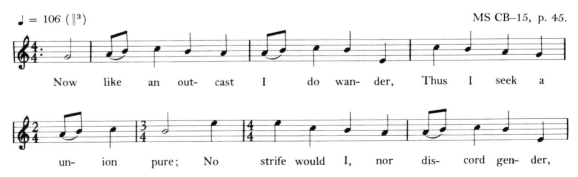

MS CB–15, p. 45.

Now like an out-cast I do wan-der, Thus I seek a
un- ion pure; No strife would I, nor dis- cord gen- der,

There- fore I all things en- dure. To live & walk in ap- pro- ba- tion Be- fore my God with con- science free, Is my de- sire, my con- so- la- tion, And gives my soul true lib- er- ty.

Later Song No. 11

MY VINEYARD

D. A. Buckingham of Watervliet recorded this song about the year 1850 and may have been its author. Both text and tune, however, were drawn from common stock. The melody had earlier served for the Shaker hymn "The Heavenly Bridegroom and Bride" and would in a few years be sung by Elder Joseph Wicker as a Solemn Song (my variant B). In shape-note hymnals it would appear under the title "American Star."

The text employs one of the images that, deeply rooted in Shaker yearnings and nourished by both Biblical associations and the experiences of workaday life, seem always to lift Shaker verse above its average level. They were often heard in daily prayer and exhortation. Perhaps the composer of "My Vineyard" had even been present in services such as Henry DeWitt described on a day when one of the Lebanon families had marched out to the orchards and "made a stand" to dance and sing among the trees:

> This was the 20 of May. Apple trees were all in the blow. . . . I never shall forget, as we were marching back, the upper side of the orchard, Garret K. [Lawrence] was invited to speak: he accepted the invitation; & took his text upon the apple tree. Spake of the branches being nourished by the root: from the blossoms on the limbs down to the root one must be nourished by the other according to its order:—So it was in our spiritual travel, the lesser must be bless'd by the better. . . . Speaking of pruning, he observed that it was known, fruit trees would not thrive well, if trimed while the sap was not flowing, but that fruit trees ought to be trimed while the sap was flowing, then the wound would heal over. Thus he said he had discerned the wisdom of God in not pruning him while in a dead and dry state; and he believed in such a time as this, when the gifts of God was flowing & souls were awake, it was the time, for souls to be pruned and to have evil branches cut off.

A.   MS WNY–14, pp. 276–277.

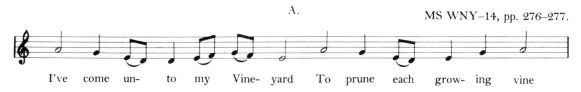

I've come un- to my Vine- yard To prune each grow- ing vine

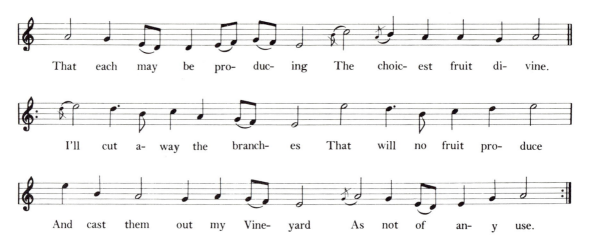

That each may be pro- duc- ing   The choic- est fruit di- vine.

I'll cut a- way the branch- es   That will no fruit pro- duce

And cast them out my Vine- yard   As not of an- y use.

2 This work I have commenced
   And some are cast away
   Of which the leaves were withered
   And fallen to decay.
   These chock'd the little branches
   And hindered their growth
   Disfigured the green foliage
   And sheltered the moth.

4 When all the wither'd branches
   Are sever'd from each vine
   And thrust without my Vineyard
   'Twill then in glory shine;
   How beautiful and lovely
   To me 'twill then appear
   And how it then will flourish
   With glorious clusters fair.

3 This work shall still continue
   While any branches die
   I'll prune & clear my Vineyard
   From what offends my eye.
   The clusters are all holy
   And precious in my sight
   Each living vine is lovely
   And gives me much delight.

5 My Father then can glory
   In such a lovely sight
   And Wisdom too can view it
   With joy & sweet delight
   The Bride & Groom can bless it
   And watch it with great care
   That no destructive insect
   Its precious fruit impair.

B.

MS WNY–51, p. [2].

Later Song No. 12

I AM THE TRUE VINE

This superior song originated at Gloucester in 1856 and should probably be credited to Elder Joseph Brackett. He was then fifty-nine. At the age of ten he took part, with his widowed

Fig. 49. Joseph Brackett
1797–1882
Gloucester, Me.

Fig. 50. Otis Sawyer
1815–1884
Gloucester, Me.

father, in the gathering of the short-lived society at Gorham, Maine. Both became stalwarts of the faith, and Joseph rose eventually to head the Maine ministry. He had "a remarkable and natural gift to sing by which he would often fill a whole assembly with the quickening power of God."

The insistent rhythm builds in this song toward the words "withered branches he'll shake off"—underscoring the fact that the text puts John 15:1–8 in the service of Shaker perfectionism. It is a theme consonant with Elder Joseph's life. Otis Sawyer said of him, "If he excelled in any one essential Christian grace more than another, it was his perfect consecration."

MS CB–43, p. 162.

I am the true vine which my Fath- er hath set In his love- ly king- dom fair Ev- ery branch found in me Which bring- eth forth fruit He purg- eth it with care. But the

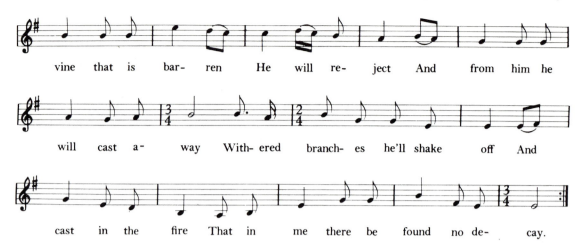

vine that is bar- ren He will re- ject And from him he

will cast a- way With- ered branch- es he'll shake off And

cast in the fire That in me there be found no de- cay.

Later Song No. 13

GOD'S WILL REVEALED

Meetings were no longer being held on the Holy Mounts when this song was received at Canterbury in 1856. Its imagery seems nevertheless to derive from those scenes: the throng of Believers young and old, the encircling forest trees, and at the center the inscribed fountain stone. Both the mountain ceremonies and this song celebrate the unifying power of divine law as revealed by the gospel parents through the anointed Lead.

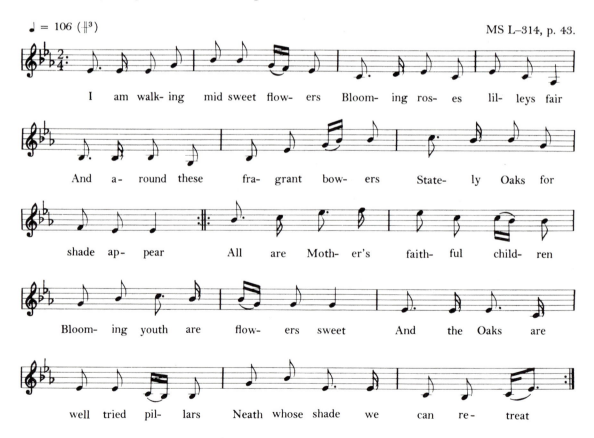

I am walk- ing mid sweet flow- ers Bloom- ing ros- es lil- leys fair

And a- round these fra- grant bow- ers State- ly Oaks for

shade ap- pear All are Moth- er's faith- ful child- ren

Bloom- ing youth are flow- ers sweet And the Oaks are

well tried pil- lars Neath whose shade we can re- treat

2 And, behold! here in the centre
Is the word of God reveal'd
On a tablet of white marble
Truth nor purity concealed
Line on line with precept fairly
Is portrayed in language plain
Not the law t'was given to Moses
But the word our lead proclaim

Later Song No. 14

PURITY

Alonzo Gilman, the composer of this prayer song, was a loyal Believer for many years before his death at Alfred in 1884. He served nine years as elder at the Poland Hill Family, but the appointment was unwise. His predecessor Philemon Stewart—once the leading instrument at Lebanon—had brought the family into "a very unsettled, broken, and destitute condition spiritually and temporally" and was recalled to New York in 1863 with "a severe, but very needful letter." The family's condition required a firm manager. Alonzo was well intentioned,

but by temperament a student rather than a leader. He himself realized this and eventually asked to be released and allowed to return to Alfred.

When he left Poland Hill, the family was so heavily in debt that it was forced to sell off timber to buy necessities. The handling of this crisis shows much about the governing of the Shaker villages. Elder Otis Sawyer of the Maine ministry went up to the family and convened meetings first with all the brethren and then with all the sisters. The problems of the family were fully discussed in the two sessions, and at the conclusion of each a unanimous decision was reached that the family should move down the road to Gloucester, leaving only a few persons behind as caretakers until the property could be sold. It was the "united opinion" of the sisters, however, that "if the brethren in that family would manage as well as the Sisters & be as enterprising, the family could sustain itself and pay their taxes." To this the ministry "responded in the affirmative."

Whatever Alonzo's weaknesses, he compensated Believers with this little song. It has been loved and sung in the Maine societies ever since he received it in 1851.

Later Song No. 15

MY SWEET HOME IN ZION

Elder Otis Sawyer's "My Sweet Home in Zion," a song dating from 1855, shows his predilection for extended melodic structures and the "minor key." Its words allude more directly than those of many Shaker songs to the struggle inherent in a sincere effort to live the Shaker life. All Believers were shocked when "false brethren" defected from the society, but those who headed families or villages suffered more from these incidents. They were often the focus of the dissident's resentment and felt themselves responsible for his salvation. Through the confessional system, they also bore the burden of being privy to any conflicts within the community and to the private troubles of individual members.

Elder Otis, as a gifted male raised from childhood within the society, also belonged to that class of Believers who had the hardest travel through "perils and deep waters" to reach gospel ground. Boys who were seriously affected by Shaker teachings, to judge from the situation of Calvin Green at Lebanon, won the approval of older Shakers, but at the cost of being resented and harrassed by more rebellious boys who wanted only to skirt as near the World as possible until they were old enough to leave the Shakers. As they came of age, young brethren like Otis, Isaac Youngs, or O. C. Hampton had a more painful struggle with the "propensities of nature" than those who entered the faith after undergoing a spiritual crisis in the outside world. If such experiences lay behind Elder Otis's song, the piece nevertheless spoke to many other Believers. It was widely copied by scribes in his day, and it remains a favorite of Sister Mildred Barker, from whose singing this transcription is made.

fords, All the pleas- ures this vain world can give, Nev- er could

pur- chase this treas- ure which I own. own. Al- though through deep

wa- ters and per- ils I pass, Al- though with false

breth- ren my lot may be cast, Faith in God is my

an- chor and truth is my shield On these I re- ly

when all else doth fail. fail.

Later Song No. 16

BEAUTIFUL CROWN

One "M. W." received this song at the South Family of Shirley about the year 1855. It was a gift for "the Elder Sister LBB." The song survives in five manuscripts from Harvard and Shirley and in one from Alfred.

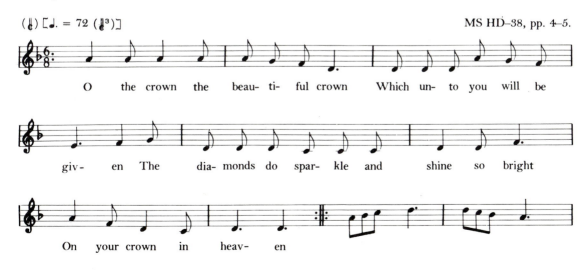

($\flat$) [♩. = 72 ($\flat$³)]

MS HD–38, pp. 4–5.

O the crown the beau- ti- ful crown Which un- to you will be

giv- en The dia- monds do spar- kle and shine so bright

On your crown in heav- en

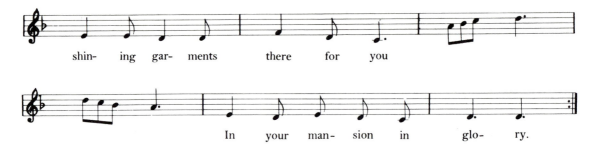

shin- ing gar- ments there for you

In your man- sion in glo- ry.

Later Song No. 17

CELESTIAL BEAUTIES

This song, which originated at the South Family of Lebanon in 1857, drew its dove image from Shaker tradition, but the rest of its diction from Victorian elegance. Its tune is related to "The Foggy Morning" in P. W. Joyce's *Old Irish Folk Music and Songs*, but the Shaker singer recast the traditional elements into a different structure and superimposed a rhythmic pattern probably derived from such hymns as Daniel Read's "Windham": ♩ ♩ ♩ ♩. To add a fillip of interest, the singer elided a beat from each phrase. The result is a fascinating mixture of influences—and an excellent tune.

MS GNY–13, p. 11.

Ce- les- tial beau- ties do un- fold With heaven- ly

mu- sic blend- ing Waft- ing gen- tly on its way The spir- it

to its rest- ing Wel- come notes of joy re- sound

Thro'- out the at- mos- phere of love Pur- est Ser- aphs

crown with bless- ing And with peace the gen- tle Dove.

Later Song No. 18

TREASURE SECURE

A song received in the First Order at Lebanon in 1861 and preserved in one manuscript written there and in one from Harvard. In text and tune the piece resembles songs by "m. b." of the same family, occurs in the same manuscript, and like some of them was sent over to Harvard as a token for Eldress Caroline. The writer at Lebanon fumbled badly in barring the tune. I present the transcription of the Harvard scribe, who avoided the errors by evading the problem.

MS HD–52, p. 99.

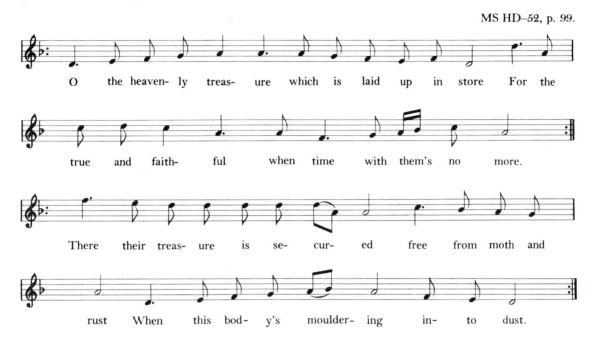

O the heaven-ly treas-ure which is laid up in store For the

true and faith- ful when time with them's no more.

There their treas- ure is se- cur- ed free from moth and

rust When this bod- y's moulder- ing in- to dust.

Later Song No. 19

A STILL SMALL VOICE

The anonymous manuscript preserving this song dates it January 28, 1861, and identifies the author as "m. b." The collection was written at Lebanon, and the initials must stand for Miranda Barber. This sister had come to the village from Middletown, Connecticut, in 1828 at the age of nine. When Harvey Eades of South Union visited the society in 1835, she was one of a half-dozen girls who wrote out a song for him in his notebook; Miranda's page shows her to be a skillful musician with a copybook hand. In the 1840s she briefly had prominence in the village as an instrument for Holy Mother Wisdom. Thereafter the record of her life is sketchy. A journal of the 1850s lists her as a basket maker. Later she served as a family deaconess. In the years around 1860 she received a number of lovely melodies. Miranda died in 1871 at the age of fifty-two. She left neither diary nor journal nor correspondence. Though she must have written song collections, Miranda, in her self-effacement, signed none of them.

MS L–167, p. 178.

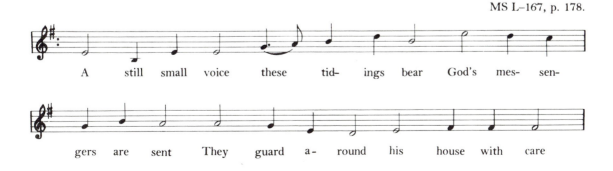

A still small voice these tid- ings bear God's mes- sen-

gers are sent They guard a- round his house with care

That Zi- on may re- pent. Come come up hith- er An- gels

say O leave the earth come come a- way.

Later Song No. 20

O WHAT BEAUTY EFFULGENT

The scribe who wrote "A Still Small Voice" in her manuscript entered this song on the same page with the note, "Received of Br. Alonzo Bounds [then three years dead] by m. b." The melody is a masterpiece of contour and pacing, but the text is stilted and abstract. It lacks the charm and vividness of the images that Miranda Barber executed in her spirit drawings of the 1840s. We have some twenty from her hand—three single-sheet drawings and part of a fourth, a set of fifteen emblems "copied from a book of prophetic signs written by the Prophet Isaiah," and a few representations of Holy Wisdom's Seal and her Rose of Approbation. While Miranda

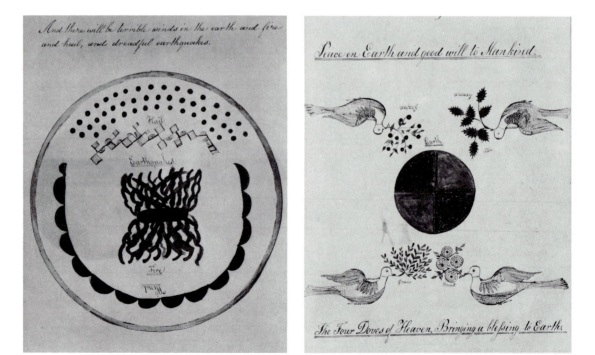

Fig. 51. Gift drawing by Miranda Barber: Winds, Fire, Hail, and Earthquakes.

Fig. 52. Gift drawing by Miranda Barber: The Four Doves of Heaven.

drew upon the stock of motifs favored by the Lebanon artists—the dove, harp, heart, rose, clock, crown, and candlestick—her range of designs extended beyond that of the others. She could draw angels, mansions, chariots, and the beasts of field and stream. She also devised symbols to represent fire, earthquake, hail, and the winds in the earth. Her drawings of the 1840s show a sensibility that could range from the childlike to the sternly prophetic. Perhaps one should not be surprised that in the 1860s it could encompass also the Shaker Victorian.

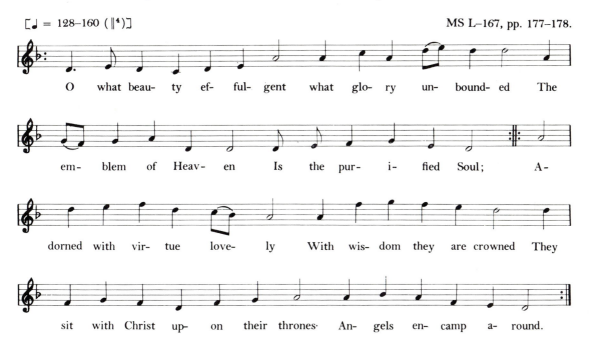

[♩ = 128–160 (‖⁴)]

MS L–167, pp. 177–178.

O what beau- ty ef- ful- gent what glo- ry un- bound- ed The

em- blem of Heav- en Is the pur- i- fied Soul; A-

dorned with vir- tue love- ly With wis- dom they are crowned They

sit with Christ up- on their thrones· An- gels en- camp a- round.

Later Song No. 21

HEAVENLY JOURNEY

In the late 1850s and the 1860s an unusual outflowing of songs took place in the North Family— or Gathering Order—of Lebanon. Nine songs in the following pages had their origin there, and it can be surmised from them that many singers shared the gift. One contributing factor was the strong leadership the family received in those years from Elder Frederick Evans and Eldress Mary Antoinette Doolittle.

Eldress Antoinette, a robust woman, set an example of meeting "the stern realities of life unflinchingly, and no circumstance could deter her when and wheresoever duty called." In temporal matters she taught prudence and the economical use of "the consecrated property held . . . in trust." As a spiritual leader she was described as

> Just and true in all her dealings with souls; discreet and cautious, lest she should 'hurt the oil and wine,' she held with loving embrace while chastening with her words, and after the rod would anoint with healing balm. But ah! to the designedly wicked and rebellious she was like a flaming herald of truth whose fire could not be quenched, until through baptism, confession and repentance, they became subjected and united to the gift of God.

Fig. 53. The North Family at Lebanon, N. Y.
Dwellinghouse and "office."

There is little evidence that Elder Frederick participated in the musical outpouring within the family—I have found only one song that bears his name—but many are attributed to Eldress Antoinette, including "Heavenly Journey," which dates from 1857.

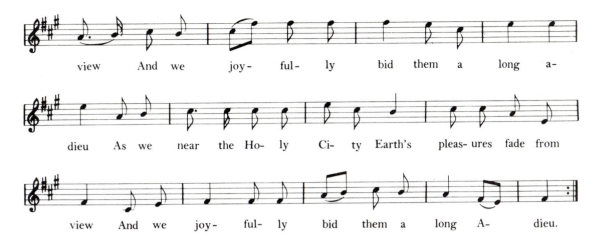

view And we joy- ful- ly bid them a long a-

dieu As we near the Ho- ly Ci- ty Earth's pleas- ures fade from

view And we joy- ful- ly bid them a long A- dieu.

Later Song No. 22

A CROWN OF GLORY

Eldress Mary Antoinette Doolittle left an account of how she came to set out on her own heavenly journey. She was raised, she said, a few miles below Lebanon but knew little of the Shakers until a chance meeting with some guilty-looking young women running away from the Society. One was leaving to marry a young man who soon followed them. They spoke well enough of the Shakers, but as Antoinette listened, "a strange sensation seemed to creep over" her and "something like a voice" said, "Why listen to them? Go to the Shakers, visit, see and learn for yourself who and what they are!" She obeyed this inner voice and within a few months wanted to enter the order. This deeply troubled her parents, for she was only fourteen.

One evening her father in the presence of the whole family reasoned with Antoinette until, she said, it "seemed as if it would break my heart." She could have borne severity better. Although he thought the Shakers deluded, he was not willing to compel obedience from a child of her age; but his advice was to remain at home till she was older. He said,

> Mary, if I thought you could go, and always remain, I would not try to hold you; but I have known many who have lived among the Shakers awhile and left them; and . . . they never seem happy after they leave . . . they are not company for themselves, or anybody else. Now if you go there and stay awhile, then return to me . . . I will still be your friend, and as long as I have a loaf of bread you shall share in it; but I could not feel towards you as I would have done had you accepted my advice. But the time has now come for you to make your choice.

Antoinette wept "bitter tears," but said, "Father, I will go!" A "death-like stillness" filled the room, for her mother's heart "was too full for utterance."

Her parents continued kind and gentle, but on the day Antoinette went away her mother took her hand, weeping, and said, "Mary, my daughter, I expect to see the time that you will tell me that you repent of having lived to see this day." Though it seemed her "heart would burst," Antoinette answered, "Perhaps you will; but I must go, and time will decide." It was all she could do to climb the hill to her Shaker friends and what—"under the good providence of God"—was to be her new home.

Eldress Antoinette said that in their later years her parents came to regard having given her the freedom to choose as "one of the crowning joys of their earth life." She was one of those who continued faithful to the end, and on her deathbed her last audible words were, "It is the gift of God." She recorded her sense of her vocation in 1859 in the song "A Crown of Glory."

Blessed, thrice blessed are the pure in heart, From such the blessing will never depart. They show forth the likeness of God's dear Son, As the heavenly course they joyfully run. Crowns of glory in the heavens await them, Angels of love draw near to sustain them, As robed in innocence they swiftly wing their way, To dwell in the light of an eternal day.

Later Song No. 23

BRILLIANT GEM

Like many other converts, Eldress Mary Antoinette Doolittle came to Shakerism because of her intuitive sympathy with the living example of the Believers. Indeed she seems not to have

Fig. 54. Mary Antoinette Doolittle
1810–1886
North Family, Lebanon, N. Y.

Fig. 55. Anna White
1831–1910
North Family, Lebanon, N. Y.
As a girl about the time of her conversion.

come to terms with most Shaker beliefs until after she had moved into the village. She had been raised a Calvinist and found the doctrines of atonement, election, reprobation, the Trinity, and a local Heaven and Hell "fastened" upon her mind, though she knew she had never reasoned herself into such beliefs. Her "soul sensibilities" had always been shocked when professing Christians asserted that "every breath they drew was sinful," that "soon as they drew the vital breath, the seeds of sin grew up for death," and that "the best prayer they ever uttered contained sin enough to damn their souls to all eternity."

After she came among the Shakers these beliefs caused conflict in her mind and she held arguments with the sisters, particularly about their concept of "Christian perfection." She thought it

> almost blasphemy to take the position that mortals could live free from sin; it was exalting self, instead of God. I called to my aid all the scripture that I could remember. . . . The sisters, in a kindly spirit, explained . . . [that] if to-day we lived up to our highest ideal of right and truth, we could do no more. As light increased, if obedient thereto, we might grow wiser and better every day. As an illustration of their position, they cited my mind to a hill of corn. When the blade first appeared, it might be perfect in that state; but it was not the ultimate. "First the blade, then the stalk, the ear, and the full corn in the ear."

Such a faith in attainable perfection underlies "Brilliant Gem," a song received by Anna White in 1859. She herself was then a young Believer under the care of Eldress Antoinette at the North Family.

[♩ = 128–160 (‖⁴‖)]   MS L–279, p. [158].

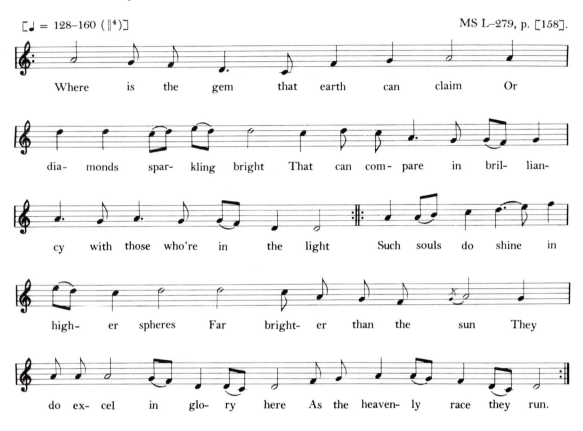

Where is the gem that earth can claim Or

dia- monds spar- kling bright That can com- pare in bril- lian-

cy with those who're in the light Such souls do shine in

high- er spheres Far bright- er than the sun They

do ex- cel in glo- ry here As the heaven- ly race they run.

Later Song No. 24

COME UP HITHER

In her diary on January 1, 1860, Anna White of the North Family at Lebanon wrote, "Had a song this morning beginning 'I hear a voice, &c.' The gift of songs is a beautiful gift, which I desire to prize greatly, & be more than thankful for the measure I have." The imagery of her song alludes to Prov. 8:1–21:

> Doth not wisdom cry? and understanding put forth her voice? She standeth in the
> top of high places. . . . Receive my instruction, and not silver; and knowledge rather
> than choice gold. For wisdom is better than rubies. . . . Riches and honour are with
> me; yea, durable riches and righteousness. . . . I lead in the way of righteousness, in
> the midst of the paths of judgment: That I may cause those that love me to inherit
> substance; and I will fill their treasures.

To Shaker theologians this passage and the verses that follow it provided grounds for defining a feminine aspect of the Godhead. Anna gave the lines another, but equally characteristic, interpretation. In her song Wisdom promises that the crown can be found in the low valley, and Anna herself had given up riches to gain it. According to Shaker tradition, this cousin of the architect Stanford White had forfeited an inheritance of $40,000 to follow her father into Shakerism. How completely she had absorbed Shaker traditions is proved by the purely traditional cast of her powerful Dorian tune.

I hear a voice say-ing come up hith-er See the treas-ure in store for the wise, Be-hold in the dis-tance in the low val-ley yon-der A crown and a beau-ti-ful prize; 'Tis worth more than rub-ies than gold or than sil-ver, Press on-ward my soul to ob-tain, If on Zi-on's moun-tain or in her low val-ley, I seek till this trea-sure I gain.

Later Song No. 25

BUSY BEE

Anna White received this song at Lebanon in the year 1860. The piece is one of the clearest illustrations of how Shakers remodeled older materials to make a song. The second half of the melody is a traditional tune that has been used with the ballad "Geordie." The first half is a free and appropriate extension of that tune. The text is indebted to print, not oral tradition. It echoes Isaac Watts's "How doth the little busy bee." Perhaps Anna also knew "Behold in the Spring," another Shaker improvisation on this theme, recorded at the North Family two decades earlier.

Like the lit-tle bus-y bee, I'll gath-er sweets con-tin-u-al-

ly from the life giv- ing love- ly flowers, which beau- ti-

fy fair Zi- on's bowers; No i- dle drone with- in her

hive, will ev- er pros- per ev- er thrive, then

seeds of in- dus- try I'll sow, that I may reap where- ere I go.

Later Song No. 26

DOWN LOW IN THE VALLEY

In April 1860 this song was received by Minerva Reynolds of the North Family at Lebanon. Four manuscripts record it, one written in her own hand. According to Shaker tradition Sister Minerva was "descended from the Mason family whose record in America began in the historic Mayflower." She came among the Shakers in young womanhood, bringing two children. Her psychic powers were strong, and she was often employed as a medium. In 1894, after many years as eldress in the Canaan family, she sought permission at the age of seventy-five to go to Florida with the mission to establish a Shaker community at Narcoosee. The effort failed, but for ten years there Sister Minerva "was a stronghold of power laboring with heart & hand in the work of a missionary pioneer."

♩ = 128–160 (♯⁴)   MS CB–39, p. [14].

Down low in the val- ley where An- gels do meet, The

voice of our Sav- ior we hear Say- ing come O! my

cho- sen ye lambs of my fold, To the foun- tain in

Zi- on draw near, While the wa- ters are trou- bled let

each one step in, For all may here wash & be

clean, Thro' the gift of re- pent- ance a balm will be

found, A bal- sam to heal eve- ry wound.

Fig. 56. Joshua Bussell
1816–1900
Alfred, Me.

Fig. 57. Minerva Reynolds
1819–1904
North Family, Lebanon, N. Y.

Later Song No. 27

STAND OFF YOU CARNAL NATURE

Henry Hollister of Lebanon had this song in 1859. Mrs. Olive H. Austin, who knew him after the last Lebanon Shakers moved over the mountain to join those at Hancock, recalls with what gusto he liked to sing in the services, and how raucously off-key because of his age and deafness. Henry was raised from childhood in the stringent principles of Shakerism and neither old age nor the withering of the Lebanon community could daunt his faith.

Many who entered the Shaker portals in hope of healing, however, were unwilling to follow the prescription given them. Richard Realf, for one, who had "gone thro' so much suffering" with John Brown, in "establishing freedom in Kansas," sought admission to Union Village in April 1860, six months after the Harper's Ferry raid. He was feeling "a terrible weariness" of the world and "wanted rest, not for his body but for his mind." The Shakers took him in and provided him instruction. Realf, they found, was a man of uncommon abilities, and they soon gave him the role of preaching in the public worship on Sundays, "to the great delight of both Believers and the world."

Oliver C. Hampton pronounced him "without doubt, the best speaker we ever had amongst us." Realf, however, after half a year withdrew from the Society, being "not quite ready to shoulder the whole cross, by which we are crucified to the world and the world to us." Elder Oliver regarded him warmly and regretted that "our dear friend Richard" had launched himself once more upon "the troubled Sea of the rudimental plane of existence." Though Realf "served with honor as a Major in the Civil war," he says, the man "afterwards became entangled in the meshes of a certain woman's wiles, and the parties being altogether unadapted to each other, in a few years Richard committed suicide."

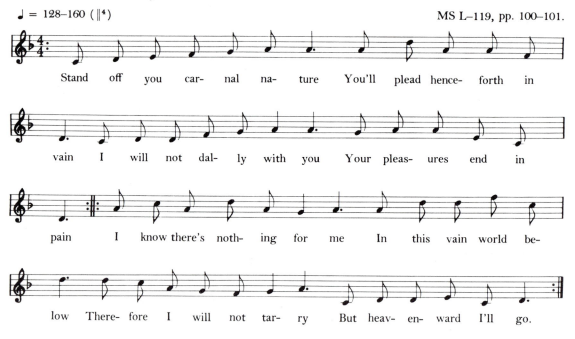

♩ = 128–160 (‖⁴)   MS L–119, pp. 100–101.

Stand off you car-nal na-ture You'll plead hence-forth in
vain I will not dal-ly with you Your pleas-ures end in
pain I know there's noth-ing for me In this vain world below There-fore I will not tar-ry But heav-en-ward I'll go.

Later Song No. 28

CARRIER DOVE

Eldress Betsy Smith of South Union learned this song "at the hour of 11 oclock Thursday night June 6, 1861." Except during the fervid years of Mother's Work, the sleeping hours were when most Gift Songs came. They shared to a degree the function of dreams. Both phenomena answered some disquietude of spirit, but each in its own way.

Dreams often asserted more of the conflict, as when Elder Harvey Eades had a horrific night vision that symbolized the Civil War through the combat of two huge, curly headed bulls. The sleek, tall Federal bull defeated the agile, gaunt, raw-boned Rebel bull, but only after a fierce struggle. Even his victory was shocking; he lunged at the Rebel, driving "one horn into his right Eye and the other back of the shoulder blade into his vitals." Probably war and rumors of war also lie behind Eldress Betsy's Gift Song, but the song offers reassurance for an only implied anxiety. It also states a moral imperative. Shakers believed that Gift Songs "admonished to the particular need or labor that the individual should be in at the time received." Eldress Betsy's song was thus asserting that a fuller consecration and a deeper trust would protect South Union from harm.

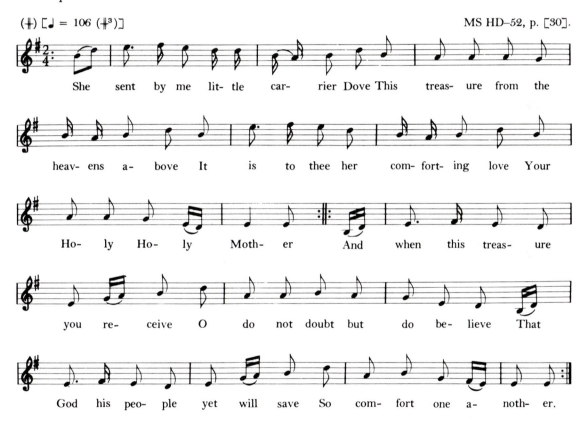

She sent by me lit- tle car- rier Dove This treas- ure from the heav- ens a- bove It is to thee her com- fort- ing love Your Ho- ly Ho- ly Moth- er And when this treas- ure you re- ceive O do not doubt but do be- lieve That God his peo- ple yet will save So com- fort one a- noth- er.

Later Song No. 29

WE ALL MAY SHOUT THE VICTORY

In the manuscript from which this militant march is transcribed it stands among songs learned in 1861 and bears the note "Harvard." The song is one of two "learned in a dream by Phebe Ann, 2nd Family." The Harvard membership lists, however, seem not to hold an eligible Phebe Ann. At Lebanon there was a Phebe Ann Reynolds. Phebe Ann Smith at Watervliet is another possibility—she was an active visionist, and we have evidence that her feelings were unsettled by the Civil War. In January of the following year, for example, she had "An open Vision of an Army of Spirits under command of Elder Issachar Bates, All of whom were Volunteers enlisted to fight for the safety of Zion, to the End of the Present War."

Her vision came in a Saturday evening service after the ministry had sung an "exceedingly heavenly" song inviting holy angels and spirits to join in the worship. Phebe Ann then saw a host in attendance, some of them "those valiant souls who went to the Western country and gathered many souls into Mother Anns pure Gospel." She counted fifty and saw many others in the rear:

> This beautiful and heavenly army with Elder Issachar at their head, were dressed in perfect uniform, indiscribably curious. It seemed as if made of a thousand golden wings: Each one united to the other by four shining pearls.
>
> These heavenly conquerers were not equipped with implements of carnal warfare; but they had palms of peace in their right hands, which contrasted with those most powerfully.—Their girdles were wreaths of Wisdom. To these were attached a musical instrument. Their feet were shod with thin red slippers, spangled with forbidden steel. Their crowns were set with love, for the souls of all mankind, as quivers full of arrows; and the finish was the overwhelming Power of God.

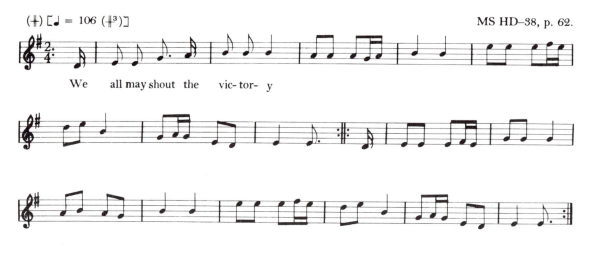

Later Song No. 30

WHAT THO' MY PATH

Aloof as the Shakers held themselves from the factions and contentions of the World, they could not remain exterior to a national crisis as severe as the Civil War. Although some of the younger brethren defected to the army, the Society continued to consecrate itself to purity of heart rather than to virtue militant. The war, however, brought the Shakers circumstances in which they had to choose between either opposing slavery or upholding pacifism and between a course of principle or one of prudence. That their fellow citizens were to treat them with leniency they had no reason to expect in such moments as when the Union Village ministry and elders gathered for a meeting on July 14, 1863. They had been asked by the citizens of nearby Lebanon to furnish teams to carry soldiers toward Camp Denison to counter a feared Rebel invasion of Ohio. Some Shakers believed that to refuse would provoke "extreme measures," including enforcement of orders for males to report for militia duty. In the Shaker council some argued that the Shakers must do all they conscientiously could to show support for the Union cause. They felt that "carrying soldiers along the highway was no more a crime than feeding the hungry soldiers or furnishing hospital stores," both of which the Shakers had already done. Being requested to give his views, Elder William Reynolds said,

> Am I called by my faith to appease the wrath and enmity of man by hiring him to be quiet, by the sacrifice of my Christian principles. This is a case that we have arrived at without any want of wisdom or indiscretion on our part, and I see no way how I can get around it without a sacrifice of my principles. I cannot myself conscienciously take a team and carry soldiers to the field of blood neither can I recommend it to my Brethren. If the world are stirred up by this to injure us for one I feel called upon to abide the consequences. The meeting adopted this view and concluded to not furnish any teams to carry soldiers.

Such a commitment explains why most of the Shaker spirituals of the Civil War years are like "What Tho' My Path"—a Canterbury song dating probably from 1861—in expressing only obliquely, if at all, feelings about the drastic events taking place outside the borders of Zion.

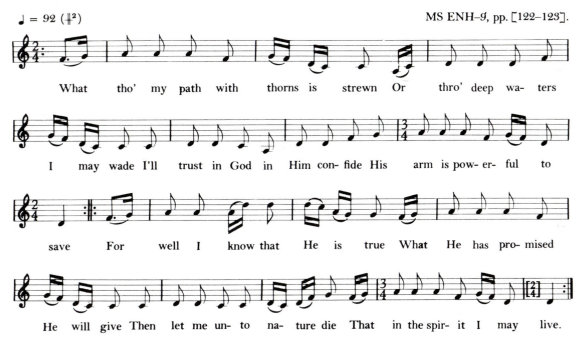

What tho' my path with thorns is strewn Or thro' deep wa- ters

I may wade I'll trust in God in Him con- fide His arm is pow- er- ful to

save For well I know that He is true What He has pro- mised

He will give Then let me un- to na- ture die That in the spir- it I may live.

Later Song No. 31

LORD TO THY ZION DRAW NEAR

The Shaker village at Alfred, Maine—where this prayer song was recorded on March 13, 1864—had no depredations to fear in the Civil War, but ties between even distant Shaker societies were strongly felt. They knew in Maine of the anxieties of their brethren in Kentucky, where the Shakers had cause to fear the marching and countermarching of the armies. In October 1862, for example, the Pleasant Hill journal recorded the arrival of a Confederate brigade. After encamping on Shaker land, the troops started for Harrodsburg and

> continued a moving mass the whole day. The advance was tolerably well furnished, but the main body were ragged, greasy and dirty, and some barefoot, and looked more like the bipeds of pandemonium, than the beings of this earth or the angels of

deliverance from Lincoln bondage.—Large crowds marched into our yards & surrounded our wells like the locusts of Egypt, and struggled with each other for the water as if perishing with thirst; and they thronged our kitchen doors and windows, begging for bread like hungry wolves. We nearly emptied our kitchens of their contents, and they tore the loaves and pies into fragments, and devoured them as eagerly as if they were starving. Some even threatened to shoot others if they did not divide with them. And then, when our stores were exhausted, we were obliged to drive them from our doors while they were begging for food. Heart rending scene! We dare not ring our bells, big nor little, at our meals for fear of a rush from this famishing multitude. The brethren and sisters were almost worn out with fatigue in their watchings and attentions to these pittiful objects. Notwithstanding such a motly crew, they abstained from any violence or depredations upon us or our possessions thus far, and appeared exceedingly grateful for the kindness bestowed upon them. They frequently pressed us to receive pay, but we declined . . . though it is believed we fed hundreds if not thousands. . . . In the evening orders came for the whole command to return to Lexington, and the wave recoiled and crowded like the rushing of waters. They drove the ordinance wagons into the East House yard to turn around. It was a strange and melancholy sight to see cannon for death & destruction within twenty paces of our dwelling house. . . . Notwithstanding such commotion they did not trespass much, they burnt some rails, used part of a hay stack and grabbled a few sweet potatoes. Quite an escape for such an occasion.—The officers apparently prevented all they could. An anxious and restless night ensued, disturbed by fearful apprehensions and the sound of horses traversing the streets.

MS GME–8, p. [44].

Lord to thy Zi- on now draw near And set thy An- gels round To guard thy her- it- age from harm While threaten- ing storms sur- round Though light'n- ings flash and thun- ders war The earth be rent in twain While fields of strife with blood run o'er Lord save the chos- en of thy name

Later Song No. 32

SUPPLICATION IN A NATION'S CALAMITY

One night in February 1862, according to a Shaker manuscript, this "prayer was sung three times over by a young sister" of the North Family at Lebanon "while asleep, & learned by another sister in company with her." A strange story, but one well attested by evidence in other song manuscripts. The singer was Cecelia Devyr. This interesting figure was born in Donegal, Ireland, about 1836. Her father was Thomas Ainge Devyr, a Chartist who, after trying to raise a guerilla force in Newcastle upon Tyne, was forced in 1840 to flee to America. Here he had a long career as a radical journalist. Devyr apparently gave Cecelia a rationalist upbringing, but she was already a spiritualist when she entered the Shaker Society in 1859.

The Civil War seems to have borne heavily upon her mind. Eldress Anna White wrote that Cecelia witnessed the assassination of President Lincoln "in the visions of the night" and quotes her account:

> The night after the announcement of the taking of Richmond, I dreamed that I was at a theatre, a splendid place, remarkable for its drapery of flags and brilliant lighting. At the back of the stage was a transparent curtain, on which negro faces were faintly traced. A man seemed to walk on the air out of one of the boxes; a flag flew after him, but he trampled on the end of it and disappeared. In a moment there was a wild

Fig. 58. Betsy Smith and Nancy E. Moore
1813–1897, and 1807–1889
South Union, Ky.

Fig. 59. Cecelia Devyr
1836–1912
North Family, Lebanon, N. Y.

commotion, such that the whole assembly swayed like people in anguish. I shared the intensity, but knew not the meaning. When I looked at the stage, four ropes were hanging from the ceiling, and distinctly through the tumult that prevailed was whispered, "For the great crime they are to be executed before the people, when the hour strikes." My terror at being compelled to witness so fearful a scene was just then relieved by the morning signal that awakens us from sleep in our quiet home. The dream, however, so burdened me that when it was related it made a deep impression on all who heard it. Eleven days after, the news of the assassination reached Mount Lebanon.

It is reported that Sister Cecelia's hymn "Supplication in a Nation's Calamity" was sung in all the Shaker societies at the time of Lincoln's funeral.

2 Lord, may the bands of the captive be broken,
  O! may this struggle bring true liberty,
  Teach man that love is a heaven born token
  And that the truth can alone make him free.

3 Guide Zion's Children in this trying hour,
  Keep us dependant on thy love & care,
  Down in the valley, we find thy true power,
  Lord, in thy mercy, O guard us still there.

Later Song No. 33

JUBILEE

In the Civil War years Shaker song writers shared the general enthusiasm for songs of Jubilee, the proclamation of "liberty throughout all the land unto all the inhabitants thereof" (Lev. 25:10). The Shaker, however—as the present hymn shows—celebrated the breaking of spiritual not political bands. Its rousing text was apparently the work of Elder Joshua Bussell of Alfred, the only person to record the song. Even he did not set down its equally stirring Irish tune. Sister Mildred Barker learned that as a child at Alfred from Eldress Harriet Coolbroth. She was taken with the piece because of "the whole feeling of what was going on—the gospel fire, and the vim." She liked songs "that had life in them!" Eldress Harriet did too. She was always telling the girls, "Sing up, sing up! Don't drag!"

Original tonic: A

♩ = 92

Text: MeSL, MS, f. t., "True Thankfulness," p. 64.
Tune: From the singing of R. Mildred Barker.

The gos-pel is ad-vanc-ing And free-dom is com-menc-ing With leap-ing and with danc-ing We'll hail the ju-bi-lee The fire is in-creas-ing The flame is nev-er ceas-ing I feel I am re-leas-ing, And now I will be free.

2 Now in the strength of union
Subdue the great apolyon
Believers in communion
Proclaim the jubilee
And while the trump is sounding
And antichrist confounding
Our love and zeal abounding
Determined to be free

3 With freedom I'm delighted
I will not feel affrighted
Come let us be united
And sound the jubilee
The bands of sin are breaking
The devel's kingdom shaking
And his foundation quaking
Because we will be free

4 And now each true believer
Will bind the old deceiver
And keep him bound forever
Throughout the jubilee
This work of tribulation
Is free from condemnation
And brings complete salvation
To all who will be free

5 The gospell fire is blazing
The world with wonder gazing
They say it is amazing
Is this your jubilee
But we will shout like thunder
And fill the world with wonder
We'll break our bands asunder
And then we will be free.

Later Song No. 34

BLEEDING LAMB

Two Canterbury manuscripts preserve this song, which was received in the Church Family there in March 1862. Both text and tune are remakings of available material. The Twenty-third Psalm is the ultimate source of the imagery, but the singer has shaded it toward peculiarly Shaker themes: humility, a cry for healing, and the conception of maternity in the Godhead. The melody is indebted to one used for the ballad "Waterloo," but is here tailored to fit a hymn stanza containing pentameter and dimeter lines and is cast into 3/2 measures with an insistent rhythmic figure: ♩♩♩♩. This pattern, though common in folk-derived hymn tunes printed in early shape-note songsters, did not greatly please the Shaker ear. It is rare in Shaker songs, and the scribes invariably record it in the incorrect 4/4 time.

♩ = 106 (♭³)   MS CB–16, p. 41.

A bleed-ing lamb would seek thy face, O Sav-ior kind;
Thy mer-cy and thy heal-ing grace I'd al-so find. Though
torn my fleece and deep my wounds, Thou canst re- store; ——
Thy mer-cy's great, thy love a- bounds,——These I im- plore.

2 And blessed Mother too, I seek Thy tender care;
   O take me, take me, frail and weak,
   And near despair.
   Thou wilt not cast me off, I know,
   Thou art too kind.
   I'll weep and creep, for I'm bro't low,
   Tis meet I should.

Later Song No. 35

COME TO ZION

One "p. b." of the North Family at Lebanon, according to a manuscript note, had this song in March 1864. In this year the only person with those initials living in the family was Paulina Bates. This sister, who had been a leading figure in the spirit manifestations at Watervliet two decades earlier, spent five years at Lebanon in the 1860s, serving in this Gathering Order, helping to call in the sin-sick souls.

In all the societies many who came soon found healing enough and turned back to the World. At Harvard, for example, Thomas Hammond calculated that 422 persons were gathered between 1791 and 1852, and of these, 191 after a shorter or longer stay left the Society. The chief social service performed by the Shakers was, in fact, to raise homeless or unwanted children and to offer either a haven or a healing respite to burdened and desperate minds.

♩ = 92 (♯²)   MS L–238, p. 18.

Come to Zi- on, come to Zi- on Sin- sick souls in sor- row bound

Lay your cares up- on the Al- tar Where true heal- ing may be found

Shout Al- le- lu- ia, Al- le- lu- ia, Praise re- sounds o'er land and sea

All who will may come and share The glo- ries of this Ju- bi- lee.

Later Song No. 36

I HAVE A SOUL TO BE SAVED OR LOST

Writers of fiction in the nineteenth century, like local village gossips, were pleased to imagine young Shakers eloping to marry. Hawthorne thought the theme affecting, as did William Dean Howells. In actuality, those who left the Shakers generally had far less romantic reasons. Many were orphans who had been raised by the Shakers and on coming of age chose not to enter into covenant. From the time of the cholera epidemic of 1834 onward, the Shakers freely admitted such wards and drew important converts from their number, but only about one in ten accepted the faith. Another class of persons leaving was that of the "winter Shakers," who made an insincere profession so as to be tided over hard times. These left without qualm or special inducement. The Shakers felt bound to extend charity to them, but were not unhappy to see them go. Of those who can be truly called apostates, most seem to have been of an unsettled temperament, given to speculation and unable to bear reproof or direction. John Whitbey and Warder Cresson seem to have had such a nature.

When a genuine Believer like John Deming was drawn out of union by physical passion, his chance for happiness in the World was not great. Stealing away from Lebanon one August night in 1821, John left on the floor by his bed this letter to his elders:

> As the awful period has come that I am forced by necessity to change my home, I
> tho't it would be unmanly to not give some reason why I do so. The truth is, that
> the vehement affection which I have to Minerva has undone me. I have had to struggle
> for life, but fondly hoped that some change would take place, which would save my
> credit—Her excessive kindness still increased my disease, and tho' not a word passed
> between us for years, yet, had it not been for my age, I should have known what it was
> in the outset, but I could not think her inclined to one of my age. But a letter which
> I found in my pocket last fall, opened to me the whole [truth]. It had no name to it,
> but I knew the hand, and warned her to do so no more: but being unwell, I went in
> to lay down, and she came in and sat on the bed and put her face to mine, and I flung
> my arm around her neck and kissed her! but nothing else took place at that time,
> neither have I ever gone any further since, but that has taken place a number of times

where we met. . . . I proposed to her to confess it, but she said if I did she would quit immediately, and then I knew there would be no mercy for me; I know the shock is dreadful, but what can I do?—to stay here & be a curse is more so. O brethren and sisters instead of being stumbled take warning by my fall! O God! O God! what shall I do?

A Shaker, then, would not have taken lightly the words of a song like "I have a soul to be saved or lost," which Russel Haskell recorded at Enfield in 1865.

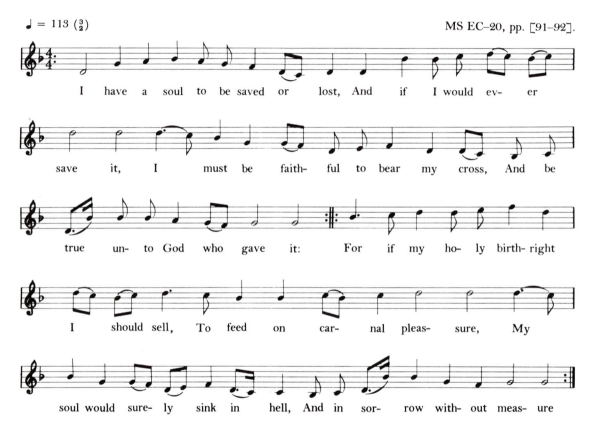

𝅘𝅥 = 113 (³⁄₂)   MS EC–20, pp. [91–92].

I have a soul to be saved or lost, And if I would ev- er

save it, I must be faith- ful to bear my cross, And be

true un- to God who gave it: For if my ho- ly birth- right

I should sell, To feed on car- nal pleas- sure, My

soul would sure- ly sink in hell, And in sor- row with- out meas- ure

Later Song No. 37

I KNOW HOW TO PRAY

I transcribe this Extra Song from performances by Sister Mildred Barker rather than from the manuscript of the composer, Elder Otis Sawyer of Gloucester. His barring was faulty and he wrote it in the Aeolian mode. Sister Mildred, who had the song from oral tradition, sings it as a Dorian tune, as Elder Otis himself probably did.

He composed the song in December 1867, finding his text in the *Testimonies*. The words were those of Father James, who was recalled as exclaiming as tears rolled from his eyes,

> O, how precious is the way of God to my thirsty soul!—I feel the love of God continually flowing into my soul, like rivers of living water;—it is sweeter in my mouth than honey in the honey-comb;—I know that God owns me as His son, and yet I

will pray to Him; I know how to pray; and I know how to be thankful for the gospel;
even my breath is continual prayer to God.

Original tonic: C

♩ = 66

From the singing of R. Mildred Barker.

This gos- pel how pre- cious to my thirst- y soul! O I

drink at the riv- er of life eve- ry day For

which I give thanks to my God I will pray. I know how to pray, I know

how to be thank- ful, For God he has blest me with

a bro- ken heart And true God- ly sor- row for sin.

Later Song No. 38

TO A FULLNESS

Manuscripts record this as a song that came from Enfield, New Hampshire, about the year 1868. The melody, however, was drawn from favorite tune stock. Only a few years earlier it had served for "Come to Zion." Eldress Marguerite Frost remembered the piece as a prayer song, one paced and accompanied with gentle motioning. In performing it she held her hands before her, palms up, beating time with an easy rolling shove that flowed down through her fingers at the bottom of each beat. This was varied by two other gestures. Her more frequent one was a bow, with the body half turned to right or left and both hands swung down past the knees on the side to which she bowed. The other motion was that of raising the hands to shoulder height, lifting and expanding them slightly on each beat. The timing of the motions is shown below by the symbols over the words they accompany. The rolling beat is indicated by ⌣, the bowing to the singer's right by ⭦ and to the left by ⭩, and the lifting of the hands by ↑. The motioning was graceful and flowing and was matched in Eldress Marguerite's singing by a sculpturing of the musical phrase intended to bring out the meaning of the words. The whole effect was one of meditativeness.

Original key

[♩ = 92 (♮²)]

Shaker Music, p. 41.

To a full- ness I will serve Thee, To a full- ness O my

God, For my soul this day re- joic- es In the

pow- er of thy word. 'Tis re- fin- ing Ŏ I

want it, Let the might- y deep break up, And I

will, I'll bear the wash- ing Till I'm ho- ly in thy sight.

Later Song No. 39

STAR OF PURITY

Composed in 1868, at the moment when the Shakers were on the verge of turning from their folk-song traditions, "Star of Purity" is one of the few older songs to survive this change in musical taste. In harmonized form it was printed in three of the late hymnals and continues to be used at both Canterbury and Sabbathday Lake. The fact that the melody is in the major was probably one of its attractions for later singers. The text of the song is also a superior expression of the most powerful aspiration of the Shaker.

The hymn was the work of two Union Village Shakers. Susannie M. Brady provided the tune, and the words were composed by Ezra T. Leggeth. The latter had grown up in the outside world and is reported to have "experienced Washington aristocracy" and worked as "first clerk or book keeper" in some large business establishment before he came to the Shakers at the age of forty. His experience was probably the reason he was delegated to go to Washington in 1870 to seek adjustment of the Shakers' income taxes. Post-war Washington was not his element. In one letter he wrote,

> I think if we manage to live thro' all the besetments & annoyances that assail us here we can easily make a fortune hereafter by sitting as models of patience on a monument. Washington is a queer place, you can buy everything you wish here with money, except honesty & piety. Here is poverty by the acre. And dazzling wealth & magnificence. We feel very much like a pair of eels waiting to be skinned alive.

Far different was his experience as a new arrival in the Shaker village. He said that "for months together it was continually with him like angel whisperings, and sometimes it was so impressive, he would have to take his pencil from his pocket and write a few verses by way of relief."

[♩. = 61 (♩²)]

MS GME–4, p. [76].

O bright- er than the morn- ing star Is the heart that's pure and free And the light that's ev - er glow- ing there The Star of Pu- ri- ty The sun shall wane the stars go down And reign of time be o'er But the liv- ing light in the heart that's pure Shall shine for- ev - er more

2 The gems within the ocean deep
And the wealth her caverns bear
Let the ocean and the caverns keep
In darkness hidden there.
But O Almighty Father send
Thine Angels from above
To kindle in my heart a fire
Of Purity and Love.

Later Song No. 40

EARNEST AND CAREFUL

This song offers a tempered resolve, not the doctrinal militancy of the early decades of the century or the simple gifts of the 1840s. It was composed by Joanna Trull of Canterbury in June 1866 and registers a change of mood felt in all the societies during the decade. At Union Village Oliver Hampton believed the Civil War had produced an "almost unperceivable spirit of apathy," a "decaying of spiritual zeal" among Believers. From the outside world they were also gaining fewer converts. After four months' experience as elder of the Gathering Order, Oliver felt a cloud drawing over his dream of attending the "high & glorious culmina-tion" of the Shaker dispensation. He saw that very few people could be "fished up" to become permanent members. They kept coming and going, coming and going, and Elder Oliver wondered when Zion would be "once more fill'd & adorn'd with bright & shining Lights." In this time of trial, he could only unwaveringly offer the prayer, "God's will be done."

Original final tone: F

♩ = 94 [♩ = 106 (♯³)]   From the singing of Marguerite Frost.

Ear- nest and care- ful, O my soul, Trav- el in self de-
ni- al. Free- ly and ful- ly give the whole, Wa- ver- ing not in
tri- al. Trust not an arm of flesh, for it fail- eth.
Cav- il not, for 'twill nev- er a- vail, But with thy life in thy
hand press on— On- ward and thou shalt pre- vail.

Later Song No. 41

I'LL COME INTO THE VALLEY

Eldress Marguerite Frost, who recalled this piece, knew nothing of its origin, but a manuscript identifies the author as one Mary E. Arnold of Enfield, New Hampshire. The song dates from the 1870s. By these years songs of vines and pretty gifts and the heaven-bound soldiers were fading from the Shaker repertory. Much more common were songs like this, a prayer for aid in bowing beneath cleansing waters. They are paralleled in some Shaker journals by introspection of a tone unrecorded by earlier Believers. Oliver Hampton, for example, wrote one July afternoon of his sense of "utter loneliness" as he entered the "awful sanctuary" of his memories. Between him and the "far off innocent days" of his youth a "fearful Hyatus" roared and seethed. Time, he said, had "trac'd in burning lines, upon my heart many an unutterable agony." Only after "long years of estrangement & disciplinning sorrow" had he "conquer'd a peace" with his fate and risen at last "into the regions of Peace perpetual —no more vulnerable." He had found man a "rude medley of errors crooks & contradictions." His own nature held "such painful antagonisms as cannot & never will be reconcil'd but by

the refining crucible of God's Divine Providence, awful and tremendous tho' it may—must be."
Still, he wrote, "I see my way out clearly—thro' a quiet & serene path of perfect resignation
& entire self abnegation—leaving all other considerations to the Divine Disposer of us all."

Original tonic.

♩ = 63

From the singing of Marguerite Frost.

I'll come in- to the val- ley And seek the strength I

need. A spir- it proud and haugh- ty Be- fore the truth shall

yield. O ho- ly an- gels aid me To bow 'neath Jor- dan's wave, And

wres- tle for that power Which a- lone the soul will save.

Later Song No. 42

GLORIES IMMORTAL

Someone in the Church Family at Canterbury originated this song in 1858, and it had great
popularity among Believers. Eldress Marguerite Frost remembered the song, and the family
at Sabbathday Lake sings it still. The song was a favorite at Lebanon too; half the twenty-eight
manuscripts preserving it were written in that society.

Perhaps the words of the song returned to Rhoda Blake at Lebanon in her old age. They
are suggestively similar to one vision she recorded. She had entered the village in 1819 and
had labored with consecration the whole of her adult life—taking full charge of the weaving
when she was twenty-one, moving on to serve many years as a deaconess, and then for a
decade to "fill the physician's lot." The waning of the society during her later years must have
troubled her deeply.

One night in September 1892 she awoke feeling the presence of an innumerable company
of spirits around her. In her account she says,

> I arose from my bed and stood by the window looking out to see what they were
> going to do—I could see nothing and returned to my bed. Then I saw a Cloud lifted
> up, from the Ark of God it was taken, and I was enveloped in the Cloud. All around
> and about me were shining myriads of spirits, sparkling like the stars on an August
> night, and they were beautiful indeed. While viewing the scene before me, I heard a
> gentle voice say, I will show you the work of God for ages and ages. It will never end,
> no more than the earth will cease to roll, for the Son and Daughter have laid the

Fig. 60. Rhoda Blake
1808–1895
Lebanon, N. Y.

Fig. 61. Serena Douglas
1853–1924
Gloucester, Me.

Fig. 62. Marguerite Frost
1892–1971
Canterbury, N. H.

Fig. 63. R. Mildred Barker
As a young sister at Alfred, Me.

foundation so deep, that no power can overthrow it. Then all the Armies of heaven cried aloud Amen!

Her hopes thus confirmed, Rhoda confidently added the words, "Even So it shall be."

♩. = 71 (♩³) MS L–21, p. [11].

The heav- ens are with us I know. [Rich] treas- ures like riv- ers do flow. I feel all that's earth- ly is pass- ing a- way And I'm tast- ing of glo- ries im- mor- tal. Bright An- gels a- round us do hov- er, With heal- ing our wounds they would cov- er, And they would waft, waft, waft our spir- its from toil and vex- a- tion to live in their un- ion for- ev- er.

Later Song No. 43

MOTHER HAS COME WITH HER BEAUTIFUL SONG

In one manuscript this song bears a spare note: "Paulina Springer. Alfred. Feb. 1887." Sister Mildred Barker, however, was told as a child that Paulina learned the song from a little bird. Such simple gifts had grown quite rare in the 1880s, but Paulina took part in Mother's Work and retained much of its spirit.

She was nearly ninety when Mildred came to Alfred, a girl of seven whose mother could not support all her children after the death of her husband. Paulina took a special liking to the new girl and asked that she be the one to help her with morning chores and errands. "It was my greatest delight to do it," says Sister Mildred, "because I thought she was just an angel." She served Paulina for two years, until her final illness. On her last morning Paulina wanted to say goodbye to all the children, so they filed past her bed. Mildred was last. As she lingered, Paulina took her hand, looked up, and said, "Mildred, I want you to promise me something." "I would have promised her anything in the world," Mildred says, "I didn't care *what* it was!" And Paulina asked, "Promise me you'll make a Shaker." Sister Mildred says, "It took me a great many years to fulfill that promise, and to come to the point where I knew what that promise meant. But it's always followed me as I've gone through life." After the children had left, Sister Paulina told those remaining in her room, "I'm not going to be here much longer. There's two angels standing over by the cupboard door, waiting for me."

Original tonic: F
♩ = 84

From the singing of R. Mildred Barker.

Mother has come with her beau-ti-ful song, Ho ho tal-la me ho. She's come to bless her child-ren dear Ho ho tal-la me ho, And Christ your Sav-ior will be near, Ho ho tal-la me ho.

Later Song No. 44

WE MUST BE MEEK

Over the years Shakers and former Shakers have often sung me songs that I did not remember seeing in the manuscripts but could find in subsequent searching. "We Must Be Meek," however, was not in any of the hundreds of songbooks I've read in the twelve years since Mrs. Olive H. Austin first sang it to me. All she could tell of the piece was that Eldress Sophia Helfrich and her sister Caroline frequently struck it up in services at Hancock.

The Helfrich sisters had come up from Enfield when it closed and had learned their repertory in the Connecticut society. Since Russel Haskell never recorded the song there, I believe it originated after his death in 1884. Both text and tune support the conjecture. Like many late songs, this one refers to Jesus, not Mother Ann, and in singing the tune, Mrs. Austin raised the seventh step, a hint that the composer may have been instructed in the use of leading tones in the minor scales. The song may be a late one, but it is worthy of the final place in a collection of Shaker folk spirituals. Its phrases have the arching contours of classic Anglo-American folk melody. Its theme is the central and unchanging aspiration in Shaker life.

Original tonic: B
♩ = 60

From the singing of Olive Hayden Austin.

We must be meek, We must be pure, Or God will

nev- er own us   own us   Low low low low, For

Je- sus saith we must be low.   low.

PART XIV

Epilogue

In Concord, New Hampshire, one Benjamin B. Davis interested himself in the Canterbury Shakers. He had known them from childhood, and whenever he saw young brethren or sisters visiting in the town he usually attached himself and shepherded them carefully till their departure. As he was a bachelor, some thought he had received the faith but lacked the strength to live it.

Davis was a "Professor of Music" and often lectured the Shakers on the decline of singing in their society. Though he warned them not to "imitate the fashions of the world," he wanted Shaker singers to attend a musical convention in Concord for "special discipline" under Professor L. O. Emerson of Boston. He also nagged at the Shakers for permission to give lessons at Canterbury. The ministry felt grateful for his interest in their "improvement" and in 1864, after much consultation, allowed him to teach in the village.

"When you sing as Shakers ought to sing," Davis told his class, "there is something in your music that thrills one, makes a man feel as tho' he wanted to bow his head, there is such a simple, earnest, religious feeling conveyed." But he also had a testimony "keen indeed" against what he called their "lazy, monotonous style of singing." He intensely disliked the Shakers' way of putting "slides, trills &c" into their music, calling these embellishments "pigs tails." The singers came to feel his lessons "weary seasons," and when a severe cold put an end to his visits they were quietly thankful. The immediate result of Davis's efforts was that the young people's desire for instrumental music "seemed at once to abate" and all became more interested to learn the old hymns and anthems. The Canterbury leaders wrote the Lebanon ministry that they hoped never again to forget its counsel against "employing the world to teach Believers how to sing praises."[1]

But this encounter with Davis had planted seeds. Having "our faults" pointed out so plainly by a stranger, they said, "confirmed us in the fact, that improvement was very necessary." By 1870 Canterbury had, on the advice of other music teachers, purchased a small organ from Boston, and Elder Henry C. Blinn was soon seeing the wisdom of using "round notes" in printing songs in the newly founded Shaker magazine.[2] In 1872 the Society secured the help of another teacher, Dr. Charles Guilmette, who had more impressive credentials. A Shaker account describes him as "a French Surgeon, physician & singing teacher & music teacher of great note," who had traveled fifteen years with a band of Italian singers and musicians in South America and could play "any and every kind of musical instrument." He had "often been paid $500, and $1000.⁰⁰ for an evenings services, in Boston, New York, Concord, &c &c." The Shakers called his views "very worthy of our observation." Dr. Guilmette, while commending the Shakers' "peculiar style and method of Church singing," gave them "many lessons in singing & elocution, and some on their Organ, gratis."[3]

By this time other societies were also undertaking to learn the science of music. Canterbury sent Nicholas Briggs to Lebanon in 1869 to give lessons, and in 1874 he would go out to teach at Union Village and South Union.[4] At Enfield, New Hampshire, a class was organized in 1873 that ranged in age from eight to sixty-seven. From Enfield, James G. Russell went the next year as a singing master to other New England societies. He found interest at Alfred and Gloucester "up to a good zealous degree," the brethren and sisters working early and late to gain time to attend two schools a day.[5]

This instruction more and more exposed the Shaker singers to musical influences from the World. The reformers taught, although without complete success, a genteel performance style. They drilled the singers in elocution, trying to eradicate regional pronunciations such as "rull" for *roll* or "pu-ah" for *pure*, and urged "twirling the ars—r's, equal any Irishman." They taught the "prolongation of sound on emphatical words" and the use of expressive accenting and dynamic contrasts. By 1874 the Union Village journal keeper noted that "the Eastern mode of accent, and swells is fast obtaining with our choir."[6] Of the Shaker singers I have heard, only those at Canterbury make any use of these interpretive devices. Eldress Marguerite Frost, for example, carefully though discreetly sculptured her phrases. Brother Ricardo Belden of Enfield, Connecticut, Sarah Collins of Lebanon, Mrs. Olive Austin of Hancock, and the Sabbathday Lake singers remained faithful to the less self-conscious folk-song style of performance. I suspect that the more artful renditions obtained chiefly with certain leading singers at Union Village, Lebanon, and Canterbury. No Shaker singer that I have heard affected vibrato or a covered tone.

The reformers had a greater effect on other musical practices of the Shakers. They got the societies to abandon the Shaker letteral notation for the "round-head" notes and to purchase for study such books as William B. Bradbury's *The Singing Bird, or Progressive Music Reader*, L. O. Emerson's *Singing School*, and Lowell Mason and George J. Webb's *Cantica Laudis*.[7] The musicians at each society also urged the purchase of an organ, "a simple instrument, of itself no more than a plow," which "if rightly managed would be of great advantage."[8] Most societies acquired one about 1874, and certainly the "Juvenile Saints" at Union Village were not alone in keeping the "Organ sounding morning & evening." Soon one brother at Union Village "drew a fine Bow over his Violin, accompanying the choir" in social meetings.[9] Canterbury formed an orchestra under the direction of "Professor Nevers" of Concord. Some of the sisters, including young Marguerite Frost, even learned to play the saxophone.[10] A vocal quartet composed of Canterbury sisters also performed Shaker selections in the outside world as well as at home. A visitor there in 1877 would hear young sisters singing "Ninety and Nine" and "Hold the Fort" from Moody and Sankey's gospel hymnals.[11] The first music I myself heard on a visit to Canterbury in 1960 was the "Meditation" from Massenet's *Thais* performed by Sisters Lillian Phelps and Aida Elam as a duet for organ and piano.

Acceptance of the World's fashions in music did not, however, put an end to the musical invention of the Shakers. Instead it inaugurated an active phase of composing, one recorded in song manuscripts and in a dozen hymnals printed between 1875 and 1908. For a time a few of the older melodies such as "To a Fulness" and "Star of Purity" were printed in the new books, but most of them were crowded out by more recent pieces.

A drastic change in the Shakers' taste in melodies shows itself in volumes like *Original Shaker Music*, compiled in the North family of Mount Lebanon in 1893. One can find in it an occasional borrowing from folk music. The new march "Onward Move Ye Valiant Souls," for example, uses the fiddle tune "Napoleon Crossing the Rhine," and the melody of "In Wisdom's Lovely Pleasant Ways" is related to that of the Southern spiritual "To Die No More" and of the ballads "The Three Ravens" and "Barbara Allan":[12]

Much more characteristic of the collection, however, are tunes like the following, ones showing a much slighter tincture of folk melodism:[13]

Mt. Lebanon, N.Y.

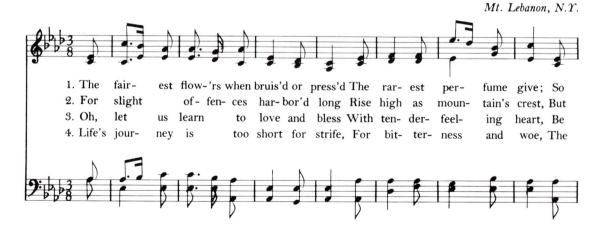

Like this example, all the pieces have simple four-part settings suitable for playing on a keyboard instrument. In consequence, harmony—once scarcely mentioned in Shaker musical treatises—now strongly influences the melodies. The early Shaker repertory had used gapped scales for a great many of its songs—nearly two-thirds of the early hymn tunes, for example—but in the new book the proportion has shrunk to only a fifth. As these are harmonized with the full diatonic major scale, the pentatonic is rare. Not a single one of the one hundred and twenty songs is in the Aeolian or Dorian mode. The contours of the phrases often respond directly to the chordal sequence in the accompaniment, and the tunes may even be little more than broken chords, convenient enough for the fingers but awkward for the voice. Early songs often opened with an upward leap of a fourth to the tonic, but the new melodies may leap a sixth to the mediant. Phrases now also close on the mediant, the subdominant, or the leading tone, cadence pitches rare in the older songs. A fourth of the pieces even show chromatic alteration of some tones. Other innovations are phrases of anomalous length and an occasional use of syncopation and dotted rhythms. In short, the new melodies show that their composers took for models the late-nineteenth-century parlor ballad and gospel hymn.

The Shakers did not step into these new paths without a backward glance. Canterbury singers led in this movement for musical reform, but even there Eldress Mary Wilson tried to revive some of the early songs during the years 1912 to 1915. She would place one on the bulletin board for young sisters to copy and learn for the vesper service; Marguerite Frost seems to have been one of the few who were much taken with them.[14] Some of the other societies were more conservative. At Hancock and Alfred the songs served as a bond between some of the children and the older Shakers. Sister Mildred Barker says it became a passion with her as a child to see how many songs she could learn, and she was "always pestering somebody" for one. Eldress Harriet Coolbroth was equally eager to teach them to her and would often invite Mildred into her room in the evening to learn one. Another from whom Mildred got many songs was Lucinda Taylor, then a sister in her mid-eighties. While at their work in the laundry, Mildred and other girls would call her into the ironing room and help her up onto one of the big ironing tables. Then, she says,

> we'd ask her to sing songs to us. She was kind of shy. She'd say, "Oh, you don't want me to sing to you." We'd say, "We do, we want to learn a song. So she'd teach us songs. And one of the songs I learned from her, which I specially remember, was the anthem "I looked and lo! a lamb stood on Mt. Zion." . . . Then we'd get her to show us some of the early dances which we never saw. And one special one which was most beautiful was "The Heavenly Father's March," which she could do. She was so graceful, and she had a voice just like a bird. A beautiful voice, even at that extreme age! So she really enjoyed the little singing periods as much as we did.[15]

The ministry in Maine also resisted for a time the purchase of a musical instrument. The societies there could ill afford either to buy them or to release members from their daily tasks to perfect themselves as players. "The *truth* is," the ministry wrote, that instruments "lead to *fashionable* life. The more musical instruments the less *manual labor*, more dress, &c &c. For us in Maine there is no way or hope, only, to *work* out our salvation."[16] But at Enfield, New Hampshire, the venerable elder of the Church Family was himself accounted the "most attentive and zealous schollar" in the music class.[17] At Union Village Elder O. C. Hampton, who championed the interests of the youth, strongly urged the musical innovations. One young brother there wrote, "That Instrumental Music must soon find its way into the House of God, is a sealed fact; it must come, priestcraft will not be able much longer to hold it in banishment; the popular voice will call it forth, and welcome it into the sanctuary."[18]

Many young Shakers now took some of the older beliefs and customs, as well as the older songs, a little less gravely. Miss Florence Phelps recalled, for example, that at Canterbury when she was growing up in the 1890s it amused the young sisters to hear some staunch old Believer speaking in strong language of "the fiery darts of the wicked" or "the beggarly elements of the World." Elder Abraham Perkins nearly sent the girls into a fit of giggles once when he walked into a union meeting and clapped a Connecticut brother on the shoulder, exclaiming, "Well, Brother George, what about purgation!" On another occasion an older sister came into one of the "young people's meetings" to teach them a dance. "Well," says Miss Phelps, "we got such a laugh out of it that they stopped it, and we never learned the dance."

The native songs provoked Miss Phelps's clearest assessments of the older traditions. She recalled hearing Sally Ceeley—then nearly ninety—sing such pieces as "Me will sing all the day, on me harp me will play" and "Me have come with the love from the Shiny Mudder's grove" and "Quee qui quickum quokum." Florence might notice Sally sitting outdoors scraping flag root and go to her saying, "I'll take care of you, Sally, while you're out here." Sally would quip, "You be my Mudder?" "Yea," Florence would answer, "I be your Mudder." These older Shakers, she remarked, "were very—they were very *simple*. They were simple, and you might say, *simply* lovely, *simply* kind." Miss Phelps thought their native songs "little homely things" and never felt as though they were "anything that ever got me any nearer to God." She "put them down as an expression for *that* time." Older Shakers too, she pointed out, though they referred to the songs reverentially, also felt they had "done their work" and put them away.[19]

One explanation for this change in Shaker musical taste is that it symbolizes a development common in the history of such sects, a movement away from exclusiveness and toward compromise with the larger world.[20] But one might even argue that the Believers' separation from the World had always been more a goal than an achievement. The states at times had subjected the brethren to military duty or tried to fine them for their noncompliance. Apostates sometimes dragged the Society into the law courts. Economic crises affected the sale of Shaker produce, and industrial advances displaced their handicrafts. On their part, the brethren watched the World's doings for ideas they could use to improve their farms, buying new breeds of cattle or the latest farm machinery. Shaker schools kept pace with those in the districts around them; as outside, the new generations were better educated than the old. After the Civil War, hot convictions were everywhere cooling into refined sentiments. Not even the Shakers could recover the spiritual fervor of the 1840s.

But the changes in Shakerism also had roots in the very nature of the faith. Because of its insistence upon celibacy, the survival of the Society depended upon recruitment of new members from the outside, a condition that intensified normal generational differences. Across the years one can, in fact, trace at least three phases in the conversions to Shakerism: (1) in the 1780s—if the *Testimonies* of 1827 are a fair picture— many converts were young adults who had since childhood been subject to "serious impressions" and had participated in a Free Will or New Light revival before learning of the Shakers; (2) in the early 1800s many were persons who had been brought into the Society as children of converted parents; and (3) after 1834, most were children taken in by the Society as wards. Those in the first group, having fought their way through a spiritual crisis, often became staunch Believers. The second group was bound to the Society by training and every tie of affection. Persons in the third group often proved less stable in the faith, and two of the major developments in Shaker history can be understood as contrasting ways of dealing with them. In the 1840s the Pentecostal phenomena of Mother's Work transformed many slack young members into committed Believers. In the 1870s a repetition of this work was impossible. The Society therefore accommodated itself to persons reluctant to commit themselves to some of its earlier sectarian ideals. The songs produced in the two phases reflect the contrasting solutions to a recurrent problem.

The two repertories of songs symbolize yet another aspect of Shakerism, its ready acceptance of all change. Central to Shaker beliefs was a trust that Divine Revelation unceasingly sheds an increasing light. When, therefore, young Shakers turned from

Fig. 64. Early and Late Building Styles at Enfield, Conn.
In the 1870s Shaker architecture, like the music, expressed an altered outlook.

the earlier folk spirituals to gospel song, they could argue their obedience to the same faith that earlier had led Believers to lay aside hymns and psalmody for Pentecostal folk song.

This paradox is but one of many in the history of the Shaker spiritual. Believers sang by ear and scarcely permitted a hymnal into the meetinghouse, yet they themselves preserved their oral tradition in voluminous transcriptions. Virtually no one was born a Shaker, and the membership was highly diverse—the converts came into the Society as children and as adults; they came educated and illiterate, native born and immigrant, New Englander and Southerner, Scotch-Irish and German, black and white and Indian— nevertheless, the Shakers developed a distinctive and remarkably unified song reper- tory. Many of their tunes were new and shaped to fit highly specific functions; they were at the same time firmly grounded in inherited melodic conventions. The United Society was one of the smaller religious bodies, but its songs far outnumber all the ballads and all the other spirituals known to have originated in American tradition.

Had they remained in the World as farmers, housewives, artisans, or tradesmen, most Shakers would have been merely bearers of older song traditions. Yet in lives that outsiders would regard as imprisoned in repetitive rituals, an authoritarian social order, toil and self-denial, those few persons whom Mother Ann and her teachings touched found a quickening of spirit that flowed forth into new songs. The Shakers themselves marveled at the gift. "And what makes it more striking," wrote an elder in 1820, "it is those who had never learned to sing at all—they could scarcely follow after those who were singers; Now they will sing as beautiful as I ever heard anyone; yea beautiful Anthems & Songs, all given when they are under the beautiful operations of the power of God."[21]

Distinctive as the Shaker spirituals were in their origins, numbers, themes, melodic forms, and ritual uses, they nevertheless shared a dominant trait of American folk song: they were a music profoundly social. Our native song has less often been the voice of the solitary singer of ballads or blues than of the ship's company or track-lining crew, the play-party circle or square-dance band, the singing school or shape-note convention, the camp-meeting throng or sectarian service. While Shaker spirituals usually originated in the most inward and private of the Believer's experiences—the Pentecostal gift—they too served almost exclusively for group singing. "I have reserved this anthem a long time for you," said the spirit of Mother Ann in bringing one song to Mary Hazard; "now you must not be covetous with it, but let the brethren & sisters share with you."[22] A special gift might even enjoin that to achieve a more perfect union all the Believers from Maine to Kentucky sing a particular song at the same hour.[23] Shaker aesthetic statements also rate the individual inspiration below the public value of song. Only those songs were "recommendable," Isaac Youngs had said, that were "given, as it were without the author's exertion of art" under "a heavenly sensation or spiritual impulse," but those songs were to be preferred which were "substantial, not given to great extreems, forcible, clear & plain"—in other words, "that which an assembly can best unite in."[24]

From the English Shakers the United Society had inherited a tradition of Pentecostal worship in which song tended to be individualized. As Valentine Rathbun described it, one Believer might

> begin to sing some odd tune, without words or rule; after a while another will strike in; and then another; and after a while they all fall in, and make a strange charm. . . . When they leave off singing, they drop off, one by one, as oddly as they come on.

At other times, he said, their singing was even less coordinated. They would be singing "each one his own tune; some without words, in an Indian tone, some sing jigg tunes, some tunes of their own making, in an unknown mutter, which they call new tongues." Song was thus of a piece with the rest of the early Shaker service. "In the best part of their worship," Rathbun declared, "every one acts for himself, and almost every one different from the other."[25]

American-born leaders would subordinate this Pentecostalism to new group rituals, forms "emblematical of the *one spirit* by which the people of God are led."[26] The subsequent history of Shaker song is the record of a creative interplay between these two traditions. The spirituals accordingly mirror also two underlying teachings: that salvation is only for the soul willing individually to strive for it, and that salvation is gained only by those who stand in united interest. "I have labored much upon it," said Mother Lucy Wright, echoing the views of Ann Lee, "& I do not know of any better way" than for each good Believer with a part in the vineyard of Christ to prune his own vine and keep it clean; "there is no possible way for one to do it for another, each one must pull up their own noxious weeds & plants that ought not to grow."[27] But she also followed Father Joseph Meacham's lead in declaring herself "more concerned about the union than almost anything else." In a key passage still read regularly in Shaker meetings she warned Believers that while a soul might easily enough be lost by itself, "You cannot go to Heaven alone."[28]

Notes on the Songs

The following entries give information of three kinds about the songs printed in this collection: (1) a list of other variants recorded in Shaker manuscripts and books; (2) melodic analogues found outside Shaker tradition; and (3) the sources of information in my headnotes. The song variants are presented in family groupings, those labeled with the Roman numeral ɪ being identical to the tune I print. Groups bearing higher numbers are progressively different. I print, however, any variants that are strikingly dissimilar.

Songs of the Gospel Parents

Mother Ann's Song no. 1—Variants: ɪ. NU–4, p. 16, written as a memento by Haskell in the 1850s, with the comment that "of late years" it was "sometimes sung much quicker & accompanied with marching."

Father William's Song no. 1—Variants: ɪ. GME–6, nos. 160 and 243; L–243, p. 219; L–244, p. [129]; XU–36, p. 22.

Father William's Song no. 2—Variants: ɪ. HD–48, pp. [i–ii]; XU–36, p. [9].

Father William's Song no. 3—Variants: ɪ. XE–47, no. 13; HD–48, p. [ii].

Father William's Song no. 4—Variants: ɪ. XU–36, p. [11].

Father James's Song no. 1—Variants: ɪ. L–330, pp. [134–135]. ɪɪ. HD–16, p. 67; XU–36, p. [13]. ɪɪɪ. GME–3, no. 242; GME–6, no. 230. ɪᴠ. NU–4, p. 82. ᴠ. SU–8, p. [85]; SU–14, p. 61. ᴠɪ. CB–25, p. 14. Cf. also CB–25, p. 16, and XE–47, p. 5.

Father James's Song no. 2—Variants: ɪ. EC–11, p. 10; HD–29, p. 30; HD–48, p. [1]; XE–47, p. [3]. ɪɪ. CB–25, p. [12]. ɪɪɪ. A–2, no. 91; GME–1, no. 116. Analogues: "Hind Etin" in Bronson, *Traditional Tunes*, ɪ, 333.

Father James's Song no. 3—Variants: ɪ. CB–25, p. 14, no. 32; (with text) EC–11, p. 3.

Solemn Songs

No. 2A—Variants: ɪɪ. HD–48, p. [1]; XE–47, no. 6; XU–36, p. [22]. ɪɪɪ. CB–25, p. 16, no. 50. Analogues: "Lady Isabel and the Elf Knight" in Bronson, *Traditional Tunes*, ɪ, 45, no. 9, and "The Famous Flower of Serving-Men" in ɪᴠ, 485–486, no. 6.1.

No. 2C—Variants: ɪ. A–2, no. 87; CB–25, p. 11, no. 6; XE–47, p. 7, no. 14. ɪɪ. CB–25, p. 14. Analogues: "Lame Dermot" in Joyce, *Old Irish Folk Music*, p. 374, no. 760.

No. 3—Analogues: "The Bailiff's Daughter of Islington" in Bronson, *Traditional Tunes*, ɪɪ, 520, no. 9.

No. 4—Variants: ɪ. GME–1, no. 113. ɪɪ. L–77, p. 40.

No. 5—Variants: ɪ. EC–11, p. 8; XU–36, p. [22].

No. 9—Analogues: "Hughie Grame" in Bronson, *Traditional Tunes*, ɪɪɪ, 180–181, nos. 2–4.

No. 10—Variants: ɪ. A–2, p. 44. Cf. also EC–11, pp. 8, 10.

No. 11—Analogues: "The Lover's Ghost" in Joyce, *Old Irish Folk Music*, p. 219, no. 408.

No. 12—Variants: ɪɪ. A–2, no. 86; GME–1, no. 111. Analogues: "Clerk Saunders" in Bronson, ɪɪ, 84, no. 3; "Diana" in Jackson, *Another Sheaf*, p. 106.

No. 15—Variants: II. GME–1, no. 120. Analogues: "Rejoice in Thy Youth" in Jackson, *Another Sheaf*, p. 29; "Separation" in Jackson, *Down-East*, p. 126.

No. 16B—Variants: I. CB–25, p. 13, no. 24. Analogues: "Johnie Cock" in Bronson, *Traditional Tunes*, III, 9, no. 13.

No. 18—Variants: I. CB–25, p. 16, no. 56.

Back Manner Tunes

No. 1B—Variants: I. XU–36, p. [16]. Analogues: "Year of Jubilee" in Jackson, *Down-East*, p. 231.

Holy Order Tunes

No. 3—Headnote: White and Taylor, *Shakerism*, p. 84.

No. 4B—Variants: I. HD–16, p. 70; XE–47, p. [114].

No. 5—Headnote: NYOC, Ac. 12,053, pp. 121, 137, 226.

No. 7—Variant: I. XE–40, no. 68.

No. 8—Variants: I. L–244, p. [67]; L–243, p. 105.

No. 9—Headnote: MeSL, Aurelia Mace, [Commonplace Book], entry for July 28, 1896, and MeSL, Letter, Sabbathday Lake, Jan. 24, 1905, Aurelia Mace to Mrs. Geo. M. Jackson.

No. 11—Variants: I. ENH–2, p. [54]; WNY–45, p. 204. Headnote: OCWR, VIII.B.249, p. 92.

Turning Shuffle Tunes

No. 4—Headnote: *Testimonies* (1827), p. 127.

No. 5—Analogue: "The Nightingale" in Sharp, *English Folk Songs from the Southern Appalachians*, II, 192–193.

No. 6—Variants: I. XE–47, p. [108]. II. EC–11, p. 68.

No. 7—Variants: I. HD–16, p. 69; XE–47, p. [109]. Headnote: OCWR, v.B.36, p. 40.

No. 8—Variant: I. XE–47, p. [107].

Regular Step Tunes

No. 2—Analogue: "Suidhidh sinn a bhàin gu socair" on Tangent TNGM–110: "Music from the Western Isles" (London, 1971). Glassites also used this "Galashiels" air.

No. 7—Headnote: Her musical memento is in SU–1, p. 45. Cf. OCWR, v.B.107.

No. 8—Headnote: WLCMs, no. 351d–5, p. 21.

No. 9—Variants: I. EC–10, p. [228]; HN–3, p. 68. Headnote: *The Manifesto*, June 1884.

Walking Manner Tunes

No. 3—Headnote: OCWR, VII.B.108, pp. 293–294.

Ballads

No. 1—Headnote: The New Light leaders alluded to in stanza three are Elijah Craig and John McGee. The Shaker missionaries appear in stanza nine. Some allusions are made clear by McNemar's *The Kentucky Revival* (Cincinnati, Ohio, 1807), pp. 3–4, 31–32. The ballad-text transcription follows McNemar's inconsistent punctuation of dialogue.

No. 2—Headnote: Hazel S. Phillips, *Richard the Shaker* (Lebanon, Ohio, 1972), passim. ODPL, W. J. Hamilton, "Richard McNemar, 1770–1839," 9 pp. McNemar's ballad is in OCWR, Letter, Watervliet, Ohio, Nov. 20, 1832, Richard McNemar to Rufus Bishop, and in OCWR, Turtle Creek [Union Village], Sept. 13, 1807, Richard McNemar.

No. 3—Variants: I. PH–1, pp. 21–23; UV–10, pp. 68–71. Headnote: OCWR, Letter, Watervliet, N. Y., July 10, 1821, Seth Y. Wells to Matthew [Houston], p. [2].

No. 4—Variants: II. SU–14, pp. 26–27. Analogues: "Jock o' Hazeldean" in Bronson, *Traditional Tunes*, IV, 401, no. 28, and "The Maid I Left Behind" in Emelyn E. Gardner and Geraldine J. Chickering, *Ballads and Songs of Southern Michigan* (Ann Arbor, 1939), p. 98. Headnote: WLCMs, no. 301, p. 95. "Humbling of Doctors & Divines" in KBGK, Shaker Record A, I, 40. "A Sketch of the Life and Experience of Issachar Bates," *The Shaker Quarterly*, 1 (Winter 1961), 160–161.

No. 5—Analogues: "Judgment" in Jackson, *Another Sheaf*, p. 147; "Poor Wayfaring Stranger" in Jackson, *Spiritual Folk-Songs*, p. 71; and George Petrie, *The Complete Collection of Irish Music* (London, 1905), p. 65, no. 265, and p. 308, no. 1222. Headnote: KBGK, Shaker Record A, I, entry for Jan. 16, 1809. WLCMs, no. 180, p. 11. NYOC, Ac. 12,051, vol. 2, p. 143. The song to which Elder Issachar alludes in stanza ten can be found in EC–11, p. 50.

No. 6—Headnote: OCWR, v.B.230, entries for the dates cited.

No. 7—Analogues: "The Famous Flower of Serving-Men" in Bronson, II, 533, no. 6, and "The Lowlands of Holland" in ibid., 424, no. 12. Also, "Clamanda" in Jackson, *Spiritual Folk-Songs*, p. 119. Headnote: OCWR, Letter, Union Village, Mar. 3, 1808, Mother's Children in the West to Beloved & Respected Parent. KLF, Mss/BA/.S527/4, entry for Jan. 4, 1854. Hooser was raised a Moravian. The brother he wrote was probably Martin, the father of the shape-note composer William Hauser, who in *The Olive Leaf* (Philadelphia, 1878) claims for his uncle Samuel the authorship of the revival spirituals "Old Ship of Zion" and "Shout Old Satan's Kingdom Down" (pp. 31, 354).

Hymns

No. 1—Variants: I. L–44, p. 225; L–136, p. 6; L–243, p. 235; XU–40, p. [13]. Analogues: "Spiritual Sailor" in Jackson, *Spiritual Folk-Songs*, pp. 154–155, where he lists many secular analogues.

No. 2—Variants: I. HD–19, pp. 70–73. II. L–136, p. 24. Analogues: "The Braes o Yarrow" in Bronson, *Traditional Tunes*, III, 324, no. 35.

No. 3—Variants: I. HD–8, p. 4; HD–22, p. 4; XU–40, p. [25]. Headnote: WLCMs, no. 343, p. 39; White and Taylor, *Shakerism*, p. 175; *Testimonies* (1827), pp. 136–138. The stone-carver Jonathan Worster was probably his great-uncle. Cf. also Henry S. Nourse, *History of the Town of Harvard, Massachusetts, 1732–1893* (Harvard, 1894).

No. 4—Headnote: NYOC, "Testimonies of Mother Sarah Kendal," p. [24].

No. 5—Alternate tunes: EC–11, pp. 215, 232. Analogues: "American Star" in Jackson, *Another Sheaf*, p. 92, and "The Groves of Blackpool" in Joyce, *Old Irish Music*, p. 268. Headnote: OCWR, Susan Liddil's annotated copy of *Millennial Praises*. WLCMs, no. 343a, pp. 47–51, and no. 344, p. 1.

No. 6—Analogues: "Will You Go" in Jackson, *Another Sheaf*, p. 200; "Gruel" in Caedmon TC–1144: *The Folk Songs of Britain*, vol. 3: "Jack of All Trades" (New York, 1961); "The Madrigal" in *The Fifer's Companion No. I, Containing Instructions for Playing the*

Fife, and a Collection of Music Consisting of Marches, Airs &c. (Salem, [1805]), p. 13, no. 31. Headnote: WLCMs, no. 338a, p. 139, in which I have silently added some punctuation for clarity.

No. 7—Variants: II. L–243, p. 232. III. L–136, p. 21. IV. PH–1, pp. 18–20. Analogues: "The President's March" in James Hulbert, *The Complete Fifer's Museum; or A Collection of Marches of all kinds, now in use in the Military line* (Northampton, Mass., [1817]), p. 21, not Philip Phile's tune of the same name.

No. 8—Variants: I. CB–25, p. 23; CB–34, p. 13. II. GNY–3, pp. 281–284. III. L–243, p. 228. IV. L–44, p. 230. V. EC–11, p. 248; XU–40, pp. [51–52]. The hymn also serves as a coda for the anthem "The Lamb." Headnote: WLCMs, no. 343, pp. 83–84, and Thomas Whittaker, "The Shakers and the Earthquakes," *The Shaker Quarterly*, 12 (Summer 1972), 77–80.

No. 9—Headnote: Anon., *The Select Songster or a Collection of Elegant Songs* (New Haven, 1786), p. 55; W. Chappell, *Popular Music of the Olden Time* (New York, 1965), II, 667. NYOC, Ac. 12,051, vol. 2, p. 147, copy of letter dated Feb. 25, 1837. John Woods, *Shakerism Unmasked* (Paris, Ky., 1826), p. 66. Letter from the Lebanon ministry, dated Feb. 25, 1828, in KBGK, Shaker Record A, vol. 2, p. 303, entry for Apr. 13, 1828. Only seven years earlier the "Millennial Laws" of 1821 had forbidden liquor on the Sabbath to all except those working in the kitchen or barn (*The Shaker Quarterly*, 7 [Summer 1967], 47). The Canterbury journal says that in the opening years of the nineteenth century brandy was added to apple cider to prevent its souring; each field worker was given a jug to take along to work. This was also the standard beverage on the dining tables of the community (NHCb, Henry C. Blinn, "A Historical Record of the Society of Believers in Canterbury, N. H.," II, 145).

No. 10—Variants: I. XU–40, p. [33]. Analogues: Cf. "Muirland Willie" in Alfred Moffat, *The Minstrelsy of Scotland*, 2nd ed. (London, n.d.), p. 150, and "Billie Boy" in Bronson, *Traditional Tunes*, I, 227, nos. 1 and 2. "Jockie to the Fair" in *Southern Folklore Quarterly*, 1 (1939), 9, and "The Mason's Daughter" in *Giles Gibbs, Jr., His Book for the Fife*, ed. Kate Van Winkle Keller (Hartford, Conn., 1974), p. 19. "Hope" in Jackson, *Another Sheaf*, p. 78.

No. 11—Headnote: WLCMs, no. 346a, pp. 323–325.

No. 12—Headnote: Letter, Union Village, May 11, 1812, David Darrow to Daniel Moseley and Peter Pease, in WLCMs, no. 245.

No. 13—Headnote: MeSL, "Biographic Memoir of the Life and Experience of Calvin Green," I, 127.

No. 14—Headnote: OCWR, Letters, South Union, May 1, 1814, Benjamin to Ministry in Lebanon, and March 6, 1814, Benjamin Youngs to Daniel Moseley. Cf. also, Blackwell P. Robinson, "Willie Jones of Halifax," *North Carolina Historical Review*, 18 (Jan. 1941), esp. p. 7. Charles Wylling Byrd (1770–1828) is discussed in KLxU, Film M–206, Reel 2: "Biographic Register, Being a part of the Church Record . . . Book C."

No. 15—Variants: I. EC–6, pp. 54–55; HD–10, pp. 17–19; HD–19, pp. 23–24. II. WO–4, pp. 68–70. Headnote: OCWR, Letter, Union Village, Mar. 22, 1824, Richard McNemar to Seth Y. Wells, p. 3.

No. 16—Variants: II. GNY–3, pp. 95–98; L–54, pp. 36–37; L–122, pp. 177–180; WO–4, p. 97. III. L–55, pp. 12–13; L–80, pp. 26–30; L–161, pp. 97–100; L–199, pp. 61–64; L–243, p. 247; L–342, pp. 50–53; XE–18, no. 48; XE–20, p. 168; XU–14, pp. 230–233. IV. CB–25, p. 225; GNY–2, pp. 186–187; HD–5, p. 6; L–136, p. 28; PH–1, p. 147; XM–4, Ac. 230590. Variants: "The Lowlands of Holland" in Bronson, *Traditional Tunes*, II, 419–424, esp. no. 12. Headnote: OCWR, Letter, Harvard, Jan. 21, 1830, Ministry to

Grove Wright, p. [2], and Lebanon, Nov. 21, 1825, Proctor Sampson to Joseph Tillinghast, p. [4]. Eunice Bathrick's comment is contained in her preface to HD–5, p. [xv].

No. 17—Analogues: The first half of Eunice Bathrick's tune has an analogue in that of Hymn no. 4 and of "The Bailiff's Daughter of Islington," Bronson, *Traditional Tunes*, II, 520, nos. 9 and 10, and in "Hiding Place" and "Consolation" in Jackson, *Down-East*, pp. 54, 146. For the second half of her tune, Eunice apparently elaborated new material out of the first section. Headnote: HD–5, pp. [ix–xviii] and PH–1, p. 114.

No. 18—Variants: II. HD–4, pp. [105–108]. III. XE–46, p. [48]. Headnote: HD–5, pp. [xiv–xviii].

No. 19—Variants: II. HD–6, pp. 275–279. Headnote: HD–5, p. [xviii].

No. 20—Variants: II. L–66, p. 115; L–253, pp. [60] and [116]. III. SU–25, p. [58]. Analogues: The cadences in the second half of the tune bear some kinship to those of Hymn no. 3 and Extra Song no. 7. Headnote: WLCMs, no. 348a, pp. 46–51. Stanza 2 is from HD–24, p. 175.

No. 21—Variants: I. L–228, p. [49]; L–262, p. [27]; OCWR, IV.B.19, p. 76. Analogues: "Barbara Allan" in Bronson, *Traditional Tunes*, II, 373, no. 148. Headnote: Susannah's testimony is on an uncatalogued loose leaf in NYAL. OCWR, Letter, Shirley, Feb. 22, 1847, Ministry to Rufus Bishop.

No. 22—Variants: II. L–54, pp. 59–61. Analogue: Gift Song no. 8 has a related tune in the major. Headnote: WLCMs, no. 353d, a hastily written draft, repunctuated here for clarity.

No. 23—Variants: I. L–80, pp. 160–162; L–131, pp. 77–78; XE–18, no. 132; XE–20, pp. 40–41. II. CB–36, p. 190; EC–2, p. 86; EC–6, pp. 21–23; EC–11, p. 327; HD–40, p. 89; L–15, pp. 216–217; L–330, pp. [286–288]; WNY–16, p. 211; WNY–37, pp. 41–42. Analogues: "The Grey Cock" in Bronson, *Traditional Tunes*, IV, 18–21, nos. 6, 7, 12. "Redemption" in Jackson, *Spiritual Folk Songs*, p. 40. Headnote: WLCMs, no. 338a, p. 188, slightly repunctuated.

No. 24—Variants: I. GNY–2, pp. 42–44; GNY–3, pp. 9–11; GNY–12, pp. 59–60; HD–10, pp. 24–26; L–80, pp. 17–19; L–122, pp. 180–182; L–136, p. 32; L–243, p. 244; XE–20, pp. 36–38. Headnote: MeSL, "Biographic Memoir of the Life and Experience of Calvin Green," I, 144; OCWR, VII.B.109, pp. 5–22.

No. 25—Variants: I. L–15, p. 148; L–78, pp. 130–131. Headnote: NYOC, Ac. 12,051, I, 120–123; WLCMs, no. 161, p. 230.

No. 26—Variants: I. L–131, pp. 195–197. II. XU–14, pp. 40–42. III. L–15, pp. 53–54. Analogue: "Innocent Sounds" in Jackson, *Down-East*, pp. 164–165. Headnote: NYPLMs, 58-M-140, vol. 2, entries for May 29, May 30, and June 5, 1839, and OCWR, VIII.B.24, entry for Dec. 15, 1839. Frederick Wicker was born in Lower Canada in 1795 and died at Watervliet in 1859.

No. 27—Variants: The tune alone is recorded with the title "The Gospel Trumpeters" in L–243, pp. 245. Analogue: "King Billy at the Boyne" on Folkways FW–3003: "The Orangemen of Ulster" (New York, 1961), and "A Soldier of the Legion" in Vanguard VRS–9158: "Almeda Riddle: Songs and Ballads of the Ozarks" (New York, n.d.). Headnote: Susan Liddil actually confused John with his cousin Robert Patterson and gave a detailed account of the latter's escape from Blue Lick in WLCMs, no. 344, p. 26. Cf. also a somewhat different version of the same story in *American Pioneer*, 2 (1843), 343–347. The Union Village journal entries are in WLCMs, no. 294, p. [1], and OCWR, V.B.231, p. 496. See also Charlotte R. Conover, *Concerning the Forefathers* (Dayton, O., 1902), *passim*.

No. 28—Variants: II. UV–24, p. 157. Headnote: OCWR, VI.B.37, pp. 166–167.

No. 29—Analogue: "Henry Martyn" in Bronson, *Traditional Tunes*, IV, 40–41, no. 38–41.

No. 30—Analogue: The jewel image is found in "Poor Sally Sat Weeping" in Frank Purslow, *The Constant Lovers* (London, 1972), p. 74. Cf. also, "My Parents Treated Me" and "The Sheffield Apprentice" in Sharp, *English Folk Songs from the Southern Appalachians*, II, 65, 67, and "Holy Son of God" and "Good Physician" in Jackson, *Spiritual Folk-Songs*, pp. 61–62, 158.

No. 31—Headnote: WLCMs, no. 50, p. 13, and OCWR, VI.B.30, pp. 234–235.

Extra Songs

No. 1—Variants: I. L–75, pp. 156–157; (wordless) XU–36, p. [26]. Analogues: "The Beacon" in *Shaker Music, Original Inspirational Hymns and Songs* (New York, 1884), p. 11; the second half is very close to that of "Jock the Leg and the Merry Merchant" in Bronson, *Traditional Tunes*, IV, 278, nos. 1–4. Headnote: OCWR, VII.B.89, pp. 32–49. Cf. also Sears, *Gleanings from Old Shaker Journals*, pp. 84–85, and OCWR, V.B.36, p. 35.

No. 2—Variant: II. XE–40, p. [52]. Headnote: Lydia Comstock died at Enfield, Conn., in 1822 at the age of forty-three. WLCMs, no. 343, pp. 197–198; I have repunctuated Susan Liddil's account slightly.

No. 3B—Variant: I. EC–25, p. 1. Headnote: OCWR, V.B.105, entry for Aug. 16, 1835.

No. 4—Headnote: OCWR, Letter, Enfield, N. H., June 8, 1854, Ministry to Beloved Ministry, p. [2].

No. 5A—Variants: I. L–56, p. 30; L–66, p. 47; L–187, p. 142; L–226, pp. 22–23; L–232, p. 6; L–253, p. [53]; UV–10, p. 23; and the singing of R. Mildred Barker of Sabbathday Lake. II. L–129, p. 62. III. PH–1, p. 246. IV. GME–12, p. 199. Non-Shaker printings of no. 5B include [A. C. Thomas], *Hymns of Zion, with Appropriate Music, Designed as an Aid to Devotion, in Families, Social Circles, and Meetings for Public Worship* (Philadelphia, 1839), p. 197; Silas W. Leonard and A. D. Fillmore, *The Christian Psalmist: A Collection of Tunes and Hymns for the Use of Worshipping Assemblies, Singing and Sunday Schools*, 18th ed. (Louisville, Ky., 1851), p. 24; *The Pilgrim Songster, A Choice Selection of Hymns, Designed for Tent, Conference and Prayer Meetings*, rev. ed. (Concord, N. H., 1853), p. 44; [text only], Rufus K. Hearn et al., *Zion's Hymns, for the Use of the Original Free-Will Baptist Church of North Carolina* (Falkland, N. C., 1854), p. 285; [different tune], William B. Bradbury, *Golden Shower* (New York, 1862), p. 14. Secular analogue: Constance V. Ring, S. P. Bayard, and Tristram P. Coffin, "Mid-Hudson Song and Verse," *Journal of American Folklore*, 66 (1953), 65, where other melodic analogues are cited. Headnote: WLCMs, no. 254, pp. 73–76, and John Whitbey, *The Beauties of Priestcraft* (New Harmony, Ind., 1828), passim.

No. 6—Headnote: OCWR, Letter, Lebanon, Apr. 17, 1832, Seth Y. Wells to Eleazar Wright. For Warder's spectacular career as an American eccentric subsequent to his rupture with the Shakers see Frank Fox, "Quaker, Shaker, Rabbi: Warder Cresson, The Story of a Philadelphia Mystic," *Pennsylvania Magazine of History and Biography*, 95 (1971), 147–194.

No. 7—Variant: II. L–129, p. 115. Headnote: OCWR, VI.B.30, p. 368. See also Sizer's own account in the headnote for Heavenly March no. 1.

No. 8—Variants: I. L–223, p. [39]; WLCMs, no. 347a, copy of Letter, Lebanon, July 29, 1828, Isaac N. Youngs to Andrew Houston of Union Village, p. [3]. Analogue: The second strain closely resembles the opening one of "Pleasures of Solitude" in David Hazeltine, *Instructor in Martial Music; Containing Rules and Directions for the Drum and Fife. With a Select Collection of Beats, Marches, Air's, &c.* (Exeter, N. H., n.d.), p. 30. Headnote: WLCMs, no. 347b.

No. 9—Variant: I. L–207, p. 43. Headnote: Peter and Iona Opie, *Oxford Dictionary of Nursery Rhymes* (London, 1951), p. 43. William J. Haskett, *Shakerism Unmasked* (Pittsfield, Mass., 1828), pp. 185–186.

No. 10—Variant: I. HD–18, no. 121. Analogue: The second half of the tune resembles "The Death of Queen Jane" in Bronson, *Traditional Tunes*, III, 146–147, nos. 4, 5, and 7.

No. 11—Variants: II. HD–18, p. [102]; L–223, p. 55. Headnote: Mrs. Anne Royall, *The Black Book; or a Continuation of Travels in the United States* (Washington, D. C., 1828), II, 45–52.

No. 12—Headnote: Theodore E. Johnson, ed., "The 'Millennial Laws' of 1821," *The Shaker Quarterly*, 7 (Summer 1967), esp. pp. 47, 48, and 55; and the "Millennial Laws" of 1845, reprinted in Andrews, *People*, pp. 263, 269, and 270. Also MeSL, Roxalana L. Grosvenor, "Elders," pp. 113–114.

No. 13—Headnote: MeSL, Aurelia Mace, [Commonplace Book], entry for Mar. 30, 1896.

No. 14—Headnote: OCWR, VII.B.89, pp. 99–107.

No. 15—Variants: I. CB–36, p. 193; L–228, p. [53]; L–262, p. [47]. Analogues: "The Bailiff's Daughter of Islington" in Bronson, *Traditional Tunes*, II, 519–522, nos. 7–16. "Primrose" and "Consolation" in Jackson, *Down-East*, pp. 146 and 172.

No. 16—Variants: II. XE–40, no. 18. III. HD–18, no. 69.

No. 17—Analogues: "Music and Love" in Alfred Williams, *Folk-Songs of the Upper Thames* (London, 1923), p. 306; and a round by Harrington in *The Musical Reporter*, no. 8 (Aug. 1841), pp. 382–383. "Single and Free" in Joyce, *Old Irish Folk Music*, p. 104, no. 213.

No. 19—Variant: I. HD–17, no. 1020.

No. 20—Variant: II. L–226, pp. 117–118. Headnote: OCWR, VII.B.108, p. 311.

No. 21—Analogues: "My Darling is on his Way Home" and "The Groves of Blackpool" in Joyce, *Old Irish Folk Music*, pp. 20 and 268.

No. 22—Variant: II. L–129, p. 177. Headnote: OCWR, SM506, p. [18].

No. 23—Variants: I. L–129, p. 85; L–226, p. 113. Analogues: The first half of the tune is a variant of the play-party song "Love Somebody"—cf. *The Frank C. Brown Collection of North Carolina Folklore*, V (Durham, N. C., 1962), 77, no. 107C. But the Shaker singer added a second section to make the tune complete. Headnote: David R. Lamson, *Two Years' Experience among the Shakers* (West Boylston, Mass., 1848), p. 54. OCWR, X.B.31, p. [172].

No. 24—Headnote: OCWR, VI.A.6, pp. 22ff.

No. 25—Variants: I. L–187, pp. 9–10; L–226, pp. 99–100, 141; L–323, pp. 185–186. II. GME–3, no. 624; L–207, p. 189; L–335, p. [20]. III. SU–8, p. 67; SU–14, p. 42; SU–15, p. 14. IV. CB–36, p. 109. V. CB–41, p. 217. Headnote: Frances A. Carr, ed., "Mother Lucy's Sayings Spoken at Different Times and under Various Circumstances," *The Shaker Quarterly*, 8 (Winter 1968), 106. OCWR, V.B.294, entry for Oct. 6, 1839.

No. 26—Variants: I. CB–17, p. 87. II. L–61, pp. 175–180; L–114, pp. 43–44; L–239, p. [230]. III. L–138, pp. [61–62]; L–229, pp. 210–211. IV. L–145, pp. 64–65; L–232, p. 15. V. WNY–18, p. 22. VI. EC–11, p. 396. VII. C–4, p. 67. Analogue: "The Winter It Is Past" in George Petrie, *The Petrie Collection of the Ancient Music of Ireland* (Dublin, 1855), p. 168.

Occasional Songs

Christmas—Headnote: Theodore Johnson discussed Shaker Christmas observances in three articles in *The Shaker Quarterly*, 4 (Winter 1964), 118–121; 7 (Winter 1967), 119–131; and 9 (Winter 1969), 141–147. For Hannah Hocknell's sign, see NYOC, Ac. 13,404, pp. 82–92. An account of more festive observances at North Union is given in Elmina Phillips, "Christmas Among the Shakers in the Olden Time" printed by J. P. MacLean in "The Society of Shakers. Rise, Progress and Extinction of the Society at Cleveland, O.," *Ohio Archaeological and Historical Quarterly*, 9 (July 1900), 82. She mentions the composition of special songs for the day and a sleigh ride by the choir to sing the new songs for each family in the village. Cf. also, the "Millennial Laws" of 1845 printed as an appendix to Andrews, *People*, esp. p. 265.

Mother Ann's Birthday Song no. 2—Variants: II. GME–12, pp. 15–16; XE–47, pp. [132–133].

Mother Ann's Birthday Song no. 3—Variants: II. L–66, p. 71; L–226, pp. 33–34; L–253, p. [77]. III. PH–1, pp. 285, 295. IV. XE–46, p. [40].

New Year's—Analogue: "The Cuckoo" in Sharp, *English Folk Songs from the Southern Appalachians*, II, 177.

Funeral Song no. 1—Variant: I. EC–11, p. 379. Headnote: NYOC, Ac. 13,404, pp. 64–65.

Funeral Song no. 2.—Analogue: "Shady Grove" in *The Songs of Doc Watson* (New York, 1971), p. 66. Headnote: MeSL, Aurelia Mace, [Commonplace Book], entry for May 29, 1896.

Welcome—Analogue: "The Song of the Blackbird" in Joyce, *Old Irish Folk Music*, p. 148, no. 316.

Farewell—Analogues: "The Rakes of Kinsale" in Joyce, *Old Irish Folk Music*, p. 112, no. 232. Headnote: KBGK, Shaker Record A, vol. 2, entry for Sept. 25, 1832.

Anthems

No. 1—Variants: II. CB–34, p. 52; CB–35, p. 1; Henry C. Blinn, *A Sacred Repository of Anthems and Hymns*, pp. 56–57; and additional manuscripts.

No. 2—Variant: I. EC–25, p. 18. Analogues: Bronson, *Traditional Tunes*, II, 376–387, nos. 153–186.

No. 3—Variants: I. ENH–12, pp. 52–53; L–102, pp. 112–113; L–148.1, pp. 294–296; L–297, pp. 172–174; and other manuscripts.

Quick Dances

No. 1—Variants: I. L–66, p. 13. II. EC–11, p. 15. Headnote: McNemar, *The Kentucky Revival*, p. 115.

No. 2—Headnote: The poem "New England was my native place" is in HD–27.

No. 3—Variants: I. L–56, p. [267]. II. EC–11, p. 43, a variant in 6/8 time. Headnote: WLCMs, no. 42, entry for Mar. 18, 1821.

No. 4—Variants: I. EC–11, p. 54; L–226, p. 81; SU–8, p. 48. II. L–14, p. [37]; L–228, p. [47]. Headnote: OCWR, v.B.94, entry for July 4, 1827. *The Manifesto*, 17 (Sept. 1887), 216.

No. 5—Variant: I. L–226, p. 147. Analogues: "The Fairhaired Boy" in Francis O'Neill, *The Dance Music of Ireland* (Dublin, n.d.), p. 41, and "The Old-Fashioned Bible" in Jackson, *Another Sheaf*, p. 82. Headnote: NYOC, Ac. 12,051, pp. 102, 127.

No. 6—Variants: I. L–14, p. [39]; L–262, p. [29]. II. EC–11, p. 55; L–226, pp. 84–85; L–253, p. [2]. III. SU–14, p. 68. IV. L–56, p. [272]; L–207, p. 25; L–313, p. 13.

No. 7—Variants: I. L–14, p. [109]; L–170, p. 120; L–228, p. [99]; L–262, p. [75]; L–313, p. 10; SU–8, p. 75. II. L–253, p. [2]. Headnote: Music written by Eveline McGuire can be found in OCWR, IX.A.3.

No. 8—Variant: I. SU–1, p. 304. Headnote: KBGK, Shaker Record B, entries for Sept. 11, 1839, and Jan. 11, 1841. WLCMs, no. 180, p. 139.

No. 9—Variants: I. HD–44, p. 39; L–313, p. 2.

No. 10—Headnote: WLCMs, no. 55, p. 41.

No. 12—Variant: I. CB–8, p. 114.

No. 13—Variant: I. EC–10, p. 149.

No. 14—Variants: I. GNY–9, p. 110; OCWR, Letter, North Union, June 16, 1852, Jeremiah Ingalls to Isaac N. Youngs, p. [4]. II. UV–17, pp. 244–245; UV–20, p. [188]; UV–24, p. 313. Headnote: OCWR, v.B.161, p. 126, and Charles Burleigh, *The Genealogy and History of the Ingalls Family in America* (Malden, Mass., 1903), p. 114.

No. 15—Headnote: OCWR, vi.B.36, pp. 292–310; OCWR, Letter, Watervliet, N. Y., Jan. 26, 1866, Giles Avery to Ministry, Pleasant Hill, on p. 117 of vii.B.235; OCWR, Letter, Lebanon, Jan. 30, 1830, Isaac N. Youngs to Nancy Farrell, Schenectady.

No. 16—I have rebarred the second half of the tune, which was sloppily written.

Round Dances

No. 1—Variants: I. L–129, p. 163. II. L–226, p. 119.

No. 2—Variants: II. GNY–14, p. 85; L–308, p. 4. III. L–224, p. 17. IV. L–79, p. [26]; L–119, p. 146; L–204, p. [282]; L–276, p. 25; L–330, p. [72].

Circular Marches

No. 2—Variants: I. GME–12, p. 21; L–66, p. [38]; L–226, p. 20; PH–1, p. 283. II. L–263, p. [232], a variant in 2/4 time.

Compound March

No. 1—Variants: I. L–168, p. 19ff., and other manuscripts.

Marches

No. 1—Variants: I. CB–13, p. 190; EC–11, p. 556; GME–12, p. [5]; HD–18, no. 1; L–66, p. 83; L–129, p. 37; L–253, p. [87]. Analogue: "Drumdelgie" on Caedmon TC–1144: "Jack of All Trades," vol. 3 of *The Folksongs of Britain* (New York, 1961), and "The Jolly Miller" in Peter Kennedy, *Folksongs of Britain and Ireland* (London, 1975), p. 514. Headnote: Both Eldress Marguerite Frost of Canterbury and the family at Sabbathday Lake sang the song for me in performances close in form to the manuscript versions. An account of Polly Lawrence is included in *Remains of Joseph A. H. Sampson* (Rochester, 1827), pp. 52–53.

No. 2—Variants: I. EC–11, p. 556; L–66, p. 29; L–226, p. 15; L–253, p. [35]. II. HD–18, no. 7. A variant of the tune in the major occurs in "Mother says be of good cheer" in L–207, p. 291.

No. 3—Variants: I. XE–46, p. [43]; XE–48, p. [86].

No. 5—Headnote: OCWR, Letter, Lebanon, May 20, 1823, Little Sarah to Issachar. The initial bar in Variant A represents my interpretation of the first note as a "gathering tone."

No. 6—Variants: I. L–187, p. [353]; L–282, p. 143.

No. 7—Headnote: OCWR, Alonzo G. Hollister, "Book of Lovely Vineyard," p. 56.

No. 11—Variants: I. HD–15, pp. 2, 12–13; HD–25, p. [41].

No. 12—Headnote: MeSL, Aurelia Mace, [Commonplace Book], entry for Sept. 18, 1896.

No. 14—Variants: II. XE–46, pp. [27] and [31]. Analogue: "The Recruiting Sergeant" in *The American Veteran Fifer*, facsimile ed. (Williamsburg, Va., n.d.), p. 8.

No. 15—Analogue: "The Girl I Left behind Me" in *The American Veteran Fifer*, p. 33.

No. 20—Analogue: "My Love She's But a Lassie Yet" in *The American Veteran Fifer*, p. 31.

No. 21—Variants: I. L–243, p. 220; L–244, p. [128]; XM–4, Ac. 230560. II. SU–14, p. 80. Analogues: "The Bailiff's Daughter of Islington" in Bronson, *Traditional Tunes*, II, 529, no. 34.

No. 22—Variants: I. SU–1, p. 301; SU–7, p. 72; SU–8, p. [134]; SU–15, p. 100. Headnote: KBGK, Shaker Record A, entry for June 10, 1819, and WLCMs, no. 61, p. 1.

No. 24—Variants: I. XE–48, p. [79].

No. 26—Analogues: "Jock the Leg and the Merry Merchant" in Bronson, *Traditional Tunes*, IV, 278, nos. 1–3, and "The Knight and the Shepherd's Daughter" in Bronson, II, 543, no. 17.

No. 27—Variant: I. HD–15, p. [26].

No. 29—Variant: II. SU–8, p. [111]. Headnote: *The Journal of Eldress Nancy*, ed. Mary Julia Neal (Nashville, Tenn., 1963), p. 127.

No. 31—Variants: I. SU–14, p. 78; SU–15, p. 99. Headnote: James McNemar's titled tunes are: "Liberty" and "Tranquility" in SU–14, p. 77, and "The Rapid Wave" in UV–21, p. [38]; others are printed in this collection. Biographical information comes from WLCMs, no. 344, p. 8, and no. 355, Folder C, p. 56.

No. 32—Headnote: WLCMs, no. 355, Folder C, p. 56, to which I have added punctuation.

No. 33—Variant: II. GME–12, p. 13. Headnote: WLCMs, no. 71, pp. 5–14.

No. 34—Variant: II. L–207, p. 70.

No. 35—Variant: I. XE–47, p. [22]. Headnote: OCWR, Alonzo G. Hollister, "Book of Lovely Vineyard," p. 56.

No. 36—Variant: I. L–207, p. 345. Headnote: MeSL, "Biographic Memoir of the Life and Experience of Calvin Green," III, 45.

No. 37—Variants: I. L–14, p. [310]; L–334, p. [32]. Analogue: "Lady Campbell's Reel" in NCCM, Early American Music Collection, vol. 72, p. 39.

No. 38—Analogues: "Cousin Sally Brown" and "The Grey Eagle" in Dorothea Joan Moser, "Instrumental Folk Music of the Southern Appalachians: A Study of Traditional Fiddle Tunes," M.A. thesis, University of North Carolina (Chapel Hill, 1963), pp. 95, 112–113; "Piney Woods Gal" in Thomas R. Carter, "Joe Caudill: Traditional Fiddler from Alleghany County, North Carolina," M.A. thesis, University of North Carolina (Chapel Hill, 1973), p. 92; and "Solly's Little Favorite" in Malvin N. Artley, "The West Virginia Country Fiddler: An Aspect of the Folk Music Tradition in the United States," D.F.A. dissertation, Chicago Musical College (Chicago, 1955), p. 24.

No. 42—Variants: I. PH–3, p. [185]; WO–3, p. 157. II. A–2, no. 31; EC–2, pp. 72–73; GME–6, no. 184; L–88, p. [268]; L–288, no. 109. Headnote: OCWR, v.B.15, pp. 10–11. The Shaker songs in *The Pilgrim Songster, A Choice Selection of Hymns, Designed for Tent, Conference, and Prayer Meetings, with an Appendix*, rev. ed. (Concord, N. H., 1853) are "Lo down in this beautiful valley" (p. 44), "I'm marching on" (p. 49), "The old Israelites knew" (p. 85), and "The people called Christians" (p. 97).

No. 43—Variants: I. A–3, pt. 2, no. 22; C–4, p. 192; EC–2, p. 190; L–24, pp. 34–35; L–127, p. 43; L–134, no. 159; L–181, p. [41]; L–204, p. 75; WNY–27, pp. [33–34]. Headnote: OCWR, v.B.70, entries for June 7, 1871, and Jan. 31, 1872; WLCMs, no. 336c, pp. 21–24.

No. 44—Variants: I. L–187, p. [351]. II. L–87, p. [207]; L–167, p. 140; L–244, p. [19]. Headnote: OCWR, x.B.31, pp. 157–161, 180.

No. 45—Variant: I. L–288, p. 103.

No. 47—Analogues: "Lop-Eared Mule" in Malvin N. Artley, "The West Virginia Country Fiddler: An Aspect of the Folk Music Tradition in the United States," D.F.A. dissertation, Chicago Musical College (Chicago, 1955), p. 50, and "The Spalpeen Fanach" in Francis O'Neill, *The Dance Music of Ireland* (Dublin, n.d.), p. 167.

No. 48—Variants: II. UV–24, p. 312. III. UV–17, p. 223; UV–20, p. [185]. IV. UV–2, p. 162. Analogue: "Zion's Soldier" in Jackson, *Spiritual Folk-Songs*, p. 72. Headnote: KLxU, Film, M–206, Reel 2: "Biographic Register, Being a part of the Church Record . . . Book C."

No. 49—Variants: I. L–144, p. 277; L–187, p. 316; L–210, p. [113]. II. ENH–3, p. [39]; L–39, p. [193]. III. L–261, p. 236. IV. UV–20, p. [144]; WO–9, p. 144. V. UV–11, p. 193. VI. L–25, pp. 102–103; L–105, p. 157; L–168, p. 149; L–274, p. 27.

No. 50—Variants: I. CB–43, p. 39; L–187, p. [353]; WNY–6, p. 30; XE–45, p. [45]. Analogue: "When Bidden to the Wake" in James Hulbert, *The Complete Fifer's Museum; or A Collection of Marches of all kinds, now in use in the Military line* (Northampton, Mass., [1817]), p. 14.

No. 51—Variants: I. CB–17, p. 91; SU–13, p. [94]; UV–17, p. 282.

No. 53—Variants: I. HD–6, p. 85; WNY–2, p. 10. II. L–75, p. 116; L–79, pp. [24–25]; L–214, p. [178]; L–307, p. 28; L–330, p. [69]. III. L–69, pp. 160–161; L–105, p. 91; L–224, p. [119]. IV. L–168, p. 50; L–308, p. 54; WNY–6, p. 96. V. WNY–44, p. [68]. Headnote: Brother Ricardo's interview was issued on a 10-inch 33⅓ rpm phonodisc, Shaker Village TV–25548: "14 Shaker Folk Songs," Side 1, "Introduction by Shaker Brother Ricardo Belden and Jerome Count, Director of Shaker Village Work Group."

No. 54—Variants: I. HN–3, p. 61; L–168, p. 127; XE–4, pp. [37–38]. II. HN–8, p. 101. Analogue: "Erin Far Away" in Helen Creighton, *Songs and Ballads from Nova Scotia* (N. Y., 1966), pp. 146–147.

No. 55—Variant: II. L–79, p. [260].

No. 56—Variants: I. XE–4, p. [24]. II. L–119, p. 18. Analogue: "The Cuba March" in *Giles Gibbs, Jr., His Book for the Fife*, ed. Kate Van Winkle Keller (Hartford, Conn., 1974), p. 29.

No. 58—Variants: II. EC–18, p. [223]; L–72, p. 4; L–105, p. 177; L–167, p. 79; L–168, p. 162; NU–3, p. [97]; WNY–2, p. 300.

No. 59—Analogue: "Fire on the Mountains" in NCCM, Early American Music Collection, vol. 73, p. 9.

No. 60—Headnote: OCWR, VII.B.109, pp. 59–70, and flyleaf of L–52.

No. 61—Variants: I. HD–49, pp. 153, 169; L–72, p. [33]; L–229, p. 17. Headnote: Obituary in *The Manifesto*, 22 (Dec. 1892), 289, and Lebanon church journals.

No. 62—Variant: I. UV–21, p. [133]. Analogues: "Sweet Cootehill Town" in Joyce, *Old Irish Folk Music*, pp. 191–192. Also similar openings in "Here's a Health to Our Leader" in Joyce, p. 88; "The Bailiff's Daughter of Islington" in Bronson, *Traditional Tunes*, II, 526, nos. 24–25.

No. 64—Analogues: "Poll Ha'penny" in Francis O'Neill, *The Dance Music of Ireland* (Dublin, n.d.), p. 169; "The Gaberlunyie-Man" in Bronson, *Traditional Tunes*, IV, 237, no. 29.

No. 66—Variants: I. GME–4, p. [101]; GME–13, p. 269. Headnote: KLxU, Film M–384, entries for July 14, 1863, and Dec. 8, 1859; KLF, Mss/BA/.S527/11, entry for Dec. 31, 1856.

Gift Songs

No. 1—Variants: I. EC–11, pp. 378, 591. Headnote: NYAP, "A Book of Visions and Divine Manifestations . . . wrote by Russel Haskell," pp. 24–26. Haskell classified the song as both a Standing Song and a March.

No. 2—Variants: I. L–8, p. [93]; L–67, pp. 79–80; WNY–18, p. 250. II. A–2, no. 253; GME–3, no. 258; GME–6, no. 226. Headnote: KLxU, Film M–206: "A Spiritual Journal," entry for Jan. 16, 1843.

No. 3—Variant: I. HD–18, p. [128]. Headnote: WLCMs, no. 53, p. 96.

No. 4—Headnote: OCWR, VIII.B.115, p. 167, and V.B.230, p. 142.

No. 5—Headnote: OCWR, Alonzo G. Hollister, "Extracts—Words of our Gospel Parents," p. [6], and White and Taylor, *Shakerism*, p. 235.

No. 6—Variants: I. L–31, pp. 145–146; L–323, pp. 125–126. II. L–27, p. [4]; L–37, p. 41; L–52, p. [333]; L–88, p. 86; L–191, p. [121]. Headnote: WLCMs, no. 336, p. 90, and OCWR, VII.B.109, p. 13.

No. 7—Variants: I. HD–18, pp. [142–143]; L–168, p. 16; L–227, p. 49; L–331, pp. 70–71. II. L–222, pp. 23–24; SU–17, p. 107. III. L–14, pp. [296–297]. Headnote: Hazel S. Phillips, *Richard the Shaker* (Lebanon, Ohio, 1972), pp. 112–116, and J. P. MacLean, *A Sketch of the Life and Labors of Richard McNemar* (Franklin, Ohio, 1905), chapter 8, pp. 56–58.

No. 8—Variants: I. L–256, p. [44]. II. C–4, p. 32; EC–11, p. 387; L–61, p. 169; L–65, p. 3; L–138, pp. [67–68]; L–145, pp. 83–84; L–184, pp. [56–57]; XU–31, pp. 154–155. III. WNY–43, pp. 242–243. Headnote: NYPLMs, 58-M-140, vol. 1, entry for Feb. 17, 1839.

No. 9—Headnote: DWt, L–74, pp. 26–32.

No. 10—Headnote: D. T. may have been David Turnbull, who died at Canaan in 1864, at the age of 81. Father James's statement is in OCWR, VII.B.108, p. 217. Mother Ann's vision is in *Testimonies* (1816), p. 231, and her definition of the devil in OCWR, VII.B.203, p. 145. The Western essay "Diabology" is in WLCMs, no. 331. The Pleasant Hill warring exercise is described in OCWR, V.B.294, entry for Feb. 3, 1839.

No. 11—Headnote: WLCMs, no. 180, pp. 25–27.

No. 12—Variant: I. EC–11, p. 390. Analogues: "One Day in My Rambles" in Joyce, *Old Irish Folk Music*, pp. 271–272, and "Van Diemen's Land" in Lionel Long and Graham Jenkin, *Favourite Australian Bush Songs* (Adelaide, 1964), p. 7. Headnote: WLCMs, no. 337b, p. 1.

No. 13—Variants: I. C–4, p. 274; L–178, p. [27]; L–187, p. 112; L–288, p. [186]. II. GME–3, no. 582; WNY–49, pp. 98–99; XU–43, p. 72. III. L–134, no. 174. Headnote: OCWR, Hollister, "Book of Lovely Vineyard," p. 56.

No. 14—Analogues: For general similarities see "Gone to Cripple Creek" (p. 358), "Porto Rico" (p. 359), and "Some Loves Coffee" (p. 383) in Sharp, *English Folk Songs from the Southern Appalachians*, vol. 2.

No. 15—Variant: I. L–56, p. 8. Analogue: "The Girl I Left Behind Me" in *The American Veteran Fifer*, facsimile ed. (Williamsburg, Va., n.d.), p. 33. Headnote: OCWR, V.B.97, "Preface," p. [1].

No. 16—Variants: I. L–9, pp. 7–8; L–39, p. 56; WNY–18, pp. 278–279; WNY–20, pp. [14–15]; XE–31, p. 172; XU–43, p. 202. II. GME–6, no. 446. Analogue: "The Death of Queen Jane" in Bronson, *Traditional Tunes*, III, 145, no. 2.

No. 17—Headnote: KLxU, Film M–206: "A spiritual Journal," p. 10.

No. 18—Analogues: "The Twa Brothers" in Bronson, *Traditional Tunes*, I, 390, no. 14; "Praise God" in Jackson, *Spiritual Folk-Songs*, p. 130.

No. 19—Variants: I. HD–48, pp. [24–25]; L–69, p. 108; WNY–18, p. 159. Analogue: "The Mermaid" in Bronson, *Traditional Tunes*, IV, 373, nos. 5–7.

No. 20—Variants: II. ENH–10, p. 261; HN–3, p. 8; HN–4, p. [80]; L–8, pp. [30–31]; L–91, p. 235; L–191, p. [xii]; L–220, p. 103; L–239, p. [213]; L–288, pp. [31–32]. Headnote: OCWR, VII.B.108, p. 307.

No. 21—Variant: i. L–24, p. 100.

No. 22—Variants: i. HD–11, p. 7; L–83, p. [125]. Headnote: OCWR, Letter, Canaan, Oct. 9, 1806, Mother Lucy Wright to Elder David, pp. [3–4] (formerly catalogued as BX9786/ L6W9).

No. 23—Variant: i. EC–10, p. 108. Analogue: "The Cumberland's Crew" on Library of Congress phonodisc, AAFS L–29: "Songs and Ballads of American History and of the Assassination of Presidents." Headnote: Nearly half of the Polly Collins drawings are reproduced in Andrews, *Visions of the Heavenly Sphere* (Charlottesville, Va., 1969); cf. plates iii, iv, v, and xi, and fig. 12. Nine additional drawings were apparently unknown to Andrews and to the compiler of the checklist in the volume. Six are in OCWR, viii.B.21, and the others in WLCMs, no. 135.

No. 24—Variants: i. ENH–5, pp. [22–23]. ii. L–32, p. 275; L–40, pp. [114–115]; L–144, pp. 345–346; L–187, p. 232; L–189, pp. 196–197. iii. GNY–9, p. 146; L–271, p. 114. iv. WNY–27, pp. 4, 6. Headnote: Isaac Youngs' account is from a letter describing the hallowing of Eleazer Grant's house, where Mother Ann had been attacked by a mob— OCWR, Letter, Lebanon, Nov. 2, 1845, Isaac N. Youngs to Harvey Eades of South Union, pp. 1–2. For Shaker attitudes toward animals, see *Testimonies* (1888), p. 219.

No. 25—Headnote: Isaac Youngs lists the peculiar traits of the Gift Songs in DWt, SA760, p. 159; Philemon Stewart's words are in WLCMs, no. 146, p. 160.

No. 26—Headnote: OCWR, v.B.294, entry for Aug. 24, 1839.

No. 27—Headnote: KLxU, Film M–384, entry for Jan. 13, 1865. Cf. Don Yoder, *Pennsylvania Spirituals* (Lancaster, 1961) and W. E. Boyer, A. F. Buffington, and Don Yoder, *Songs along the Mahantongo* (Hatboro, Pa., 1964). The survival of German tunes in Shaker manuscripts deserves, however, investigation by a specialist in German folksong. Two songs in German are attributed to Augustus Blase of Watervliet, N. Y.: "Sees a leeb und ine-Shaft" (MS L–214, p. [27]) and "O himmel, himmel" (Cook, p. 63).

No. 28—Variants: i. A–2, no. 201; EC–2, p. 43; GME–6, no. 98. Analogue: "The Miller" in Flora L. McDowell, *Folk Dances of Tennessee* (Delaware, Ohio, n.d.), p. 22.

No. 29—Variants: i. GNY–9, p. 2; L–24, p. [153]; L–56, p. [243]; L–118, p. 178; L–182, pp. [408–409]; L–204, p. 100; L–224, p. [57]; L–275, p. 15; L–308, p. 7; WNY–2, pp. 11, 39; XE–24, p. 124; XE–34, p. 61.

No. 30—Variants: i. EC–10, pp. 162–163; HN–2, p. [92]; L–24, p. [159]; L–39, p. [197]; L–67, p. 310; L–118, p. [207]; L–204, p. 121; L–210, p. [187]; L–214, p. 49; L–232, p. 2; XE–34, p. 65. ii. L–43, pp. 355–356. Headnote: MeSL, "Biographic Memoir of the Life and Experience of Calvin Green," i, 144.

No. 31—Variants: i. HD–34, p. [47]; HN–4, pp. [102–103]; L–8, pp. [104–105]; L–118, p. 136; L–178, pp. [16–17]. Analogue: Some resemblance to "When I Came to My Truelove's Window" in Joyce, *Old Irish Folk Music*, p. 85, No. 170. Headnote: OCWR, v.B.15, pp. [10]ff.

No. 32—Headnote: David R. Lamson, *Two Years' Experience among the Shakers* (West Boylston, Mass., 1848), p. 68. A song learned from Mother Ann "in the body" by the Indian woman at Groveland is recorded in L–61, p. 22. Winifer Denbo's life is told in NHCb, Henry C. Blinn, "A Historical Record of the Society of Believers in Canterbury, N. H.," ii, 170–171. John Slover's experience in captivity was taken from his own mouth and printed in *Narratives of a Late Expedition against the Indians; with An Account of the Barbarous Execution of Col. Crawford; and The Wonderful Escape of Dr. Knight and John Slover from Captivity, in 1782* (Philadelphia, 1773 [sic]), 38pp. The account of Elizabeth West is from OCWR, Letter, Union Village, Feb. 3, 1844, Jesse Legier to Beloved Elder Freegift, pp. [2–3].

No. 33—Headnote: Red Hawk's visit is recounted in KLF, Mss/BA/.S527/11, p. 174.

No. 35—Analogues: "Barbara Allan" in Bronson, *Traditional Tunes*, II, 361, nos. 110ff. Also "O God What Shall I Say" in Jackson, *Spiritual Folk Songs*, p. 215.

No. 36—Variants: I. EC–2, p. 78; GME–6, no. 427; L–271, pp. [55–56].

No. 37—Variants: I. L–8, p. [92]; L–84, p. [152]; L–87, p. 106; L–118, p. 163; L–135, p. 87; L–144, p. 85; L–184, p. [193]; L–220, p. 219; L–288, no. 150. Analogues: "The Three Ravens" in Bronson, *Traditional Tunes*, I, 314, no. 17, and "To Die No More" in Jackson, *White Spirituals*, p. 178. Headnote: "Indian Convert" is in William Walker, *The Christian Harmony*, ed. John Deason and O. A. Parris (n.p., 1968), p. 287. Sister Mildred sings "Me Come Very Low" in the second pressing of the phonodisc "Early Shaker Spirituals" (Sabbathday Lake, Me., 1970). Information about the native visits is quoted from OCWR, X.B.31, p. 173.

No. 38—Variant: I. CB–8, p. 127. Headnote: Elder Henry Blinn's account is in "A Journey to Kentucky in the Year 1873," *The Shaker Quarterly*, 5 (Winter 1965), 128.

No. 39—Headnote: The account of Patsy Williamson's life is in KLF, Pleasant Hill, Ky., Journal, entry for Aug. 28, 1860, and WLCMs, no. 27, entry for Aug. 28, 1860. Also WLCMs, no. 119, p. [4]. Cf. Gift Song no. 27. On George Gennings see OCWR, V.B.107, entry for July 18, 1846. Songs by the two Gennings can be found in MSS L–266 and XE–46.

No. 40—Headnote: Henry C. Blinn, *The Manifestation of Spiritualism among the Shakers* (East Canterbury, N. H., 1899), p. 46.

No. 41—Analogues: "The Willow Garden" or "Rose Connoley" in John and Alan Lomax, *Folk Song: U. S. A.* (New York, 1947), p. 302, and "The Garden Hymn" in Jackson, *Down-East*, pp. 166–167. Headnote: "The Rose Bush" is from L–113, p. 68.

No. 42—Variants: I. L–60, p. 18; L–70, p. [174]; L–90, pp. [106–107]; L–135, pp. 141–142. II. A–3, no. 38; EC–10, p. 14; GME–6, no. [759]; L–32, pp. 53–54; L–39, p. [138]; L–184, p. [146]; L–210, pp. [43–44]; L–263, p. [234]. Sister Mildred Barker sings the song on the phonodisc "Early Shaker Spirituals." Analogue: "Roby" in Jackson, *Spiritual Folk-Songs*, p. 161. Headnote: The *Testimonies* of 1827 prints Thankful Barce's vision of a heavenly shepherdess, a suggestive antecedent (p. 92).

No. 43—Variants: II. A–25, p. [1]; CB–8, p. 105; L–24, pp. 80–81; XM–1.

No. 44—Variant: I. L–61, p. 174. Headnote: NYOC, Ac. 6286, entry for 1840; OCWR, VIII.B.138, entry for Nov. 1, 1840; and NHCb, Henry C. Blinn, "A Historical Record of the Society of Believers in Canterbury, N. H.," I, 22. The text of the song is indebted to Isa. 28:10, 13. My decision to use this song was a late one; I am consequently unable to cite every variant I have seen.

No. 45—Headnote: Dorothy Durgin's sixteen dream songs are in CB–15, pp. 134ff; Henry C. Blinn, *The Manifestation of Spiritualism among the Shakers* (East Canterbury, N. H., 1899), pp. 49–50.

No. 46—Headnote: Blinn, *The Manifestation of Spiritualism among the Shakers*, p. 50.

No. 47—Variants: I. GME–6, no. 380; L–118, p. 38. II. WNY–35, pp. 41–42. Headnote: WLCMs, no. 53, pp. 147–157.

No. 48—Variants: I. GNY–8, p. 118; L–71, p. 269; L–114, pp. [79–80]; L–135, pp. 274–275; L–196, no. 143; L–199, p. 115; L–218, p. 156; L–295, pp. 183–184; L–330, pp. [84–85]. Headnote: NYPLMs, 58-M-140, vol. 2, entries for Apr. 10–11, 1841.

No. 49—Variants: I. A–3, no. 27; CB–8, p. 101; EC–22, p. [49]; GME–6, p. [375]; L–32, pp. 135–136; L–90, p. [90]; L–144, p. 245; L–187, p. 276. II. L–118, pp. [108–109]; L–224, p. [24]; L–263, p. [3]. III. L–186, p. [153]; L–204, p. 89. The song is printed in Andrews, *Gift*, p. 133, but with a cadence not corroborated by any manuscript I have seen. Headnote: MeSL, Aurelia Mace, [Commonplace Book], entry for Apr. 22, 1896.

No. 50—Variants: I. ENH–8, p. 47. Headnote: White and Taylor, *Shakerism*, pp. 230–232.

No. 51—Headnote: KLF, BA/.S527/6, p. 133.

No. 52—Variants: I. CB–15, p. 93; L–135, p. 226; L–189, pp. 180–181; L–214, p. [129]. II. HD–6, p. 61; L–166, p. 192; WNY–27, p. [16]; WO–11, p. [51]; XE–34, p. [82]; XU–43, p. 226. III. SU–12, p. [27]. Analogue: See Hymn no. 15. Headnote: Elisha Blakeman came to Lebanon from Sodus in 1834 and served in such roles as broom maker, joiner, printer, family deacon, and finally elder. He died in 1872 at the age of fifty-three. Figure 21 shows an instructional monochord he made in 1869. For Calvin Green's discussion of typology see WLCMs, no. 73, p. 8.

No. 53—Variants: I. C–4, p. 244; EC–11, p. 171; L–24, pp. 49–50; L–74, p. 37; L–84, p. [165]; L–87, pp. [204–205]; L–90, pp. [58–59]; L–130, p. 28; L–150, pp. 21–22; L–178, pp. [32–33]; L–220, pp. 302–303; L–263, p. [132]; L–288, pp. [240–242]; WNY–25, p. 120; XU–43, p. 14. Headnote: Mrs. Austin discussed the song during an interview in Clinton, Conn., in 1964.

No. 54—Variants: I. WO–5, p. [16]. II. L–32, p. 122; L–39, p. [178]; L–144, p. 235; L–210, p. [91]; L–225, no. 84. III. A–2, no. 260; GME–3, no. 291; GME–6, no. 259; GNY–9, p. 45; L–56, p. [129]; L–67, p. 243; L–90, p. [105]; L–91, p. 17; L–118, p. 180; L–186, p. [150]; L–204, p. 87; XE–45, p. [15]. IV. C–4, p. 240; EC–2, p. 42; L–84, p. [175]; L–263, p. [113]; XU–43, p. 15. Headnote: EC–2, p. 42, records the performance on the Mount of Olives.

No. 55—Variants: I. EC–10, pp. 111–112; EC–11, p. 98; EC–22, p. [49]; HN–2, p. [29]; HN–8, p. 53; XE–4, p. [22]. II. A–17, p. [35]; GME–6, p. [385]. III. L–75, p. 44; L–144, p. 237; L–261, p. 128; UV–20, p. [134]; WNY–27, p. [11]; WO–9, p. 127. IV. L–24, p. [121]; L–134, no. 185. V. PH–5, p. 35; PH–7, p. 213. VI. L–32, p. 119; WNY–31, p. 45. VII. WNY–44, p. 37.

No. 56—Variant: I. L–256, p. 158. Headnote: MeSL, Aurelia Mace, [Commonplace Book], entry for May 2, 1896.

No. 57—Variants: II. L–17, p. 226; L–25, pp. 92–93; L–101, p. [109]; L–120, p. 20; L–168, p. 147; L–279, p. [62]; WNY–19, no. 3. III. CB–41, p. 178; XE–39, p. [83]. Both Eldress Marguerite Frost at Canterbury and Sister Mildred Barker at Sabbathday Lake first sang the song for me in 1963.

Heavenly Marches

No. 1—Variants: I. EC–11, p. 59; L–222, pp. 62–63. II. L–270, p. 40; L–331, p. 60; L–335, p. [63]. Headnote: OCWR, VI.A.6.

No. 3—Variants: I. L–43, pp. 352–353; L–67, p. 238; L–134, no. 188. Analogues: "Christian Prospect" (p. 175), "Christian's Hope" (p. 176), in Jackson, *Spiritual Folk-Songs*, and "Who's Like Jesus" in Jackson, *Down-East*, p. 102. Headnote: KLxU, film M–206, reel 2, [Journal of Andrew D. Barrett], entry for Dec. 9, 1904.

Quick Marches

No. 1—Variants: I. CB–10, p. 170; EC–18, p. 99; HD–38, pp. 120–121; L–141, p. 168; XE–27, p. [85]. II. A–3, p. [160]; C–1, p. [27]; CB–17, p. 172; HD–49, pp. 96, 186; L–25, p. [157]; L–72, no. 84; L–229, p. 3; L–230, pp. [148–149]; L–279, p. [197];

L–341, p. [73]; XE–6, p. [32]. Analogues: "Roby" in Jackson, *Spiritual Folk-Songs*, p. 161; Gift Song no. 42. Headnote: NYPLMs, 58-M-140, vol. 7, pp. 51–52; OCWR, Letter, Union Village, Apr. 30, 1820, Fanny Ball to Beloved Elders Brothers and Sisters.

Slow Marches

No. 2—Variants: I. HD–37, p. [86]; HD–49, p. 84; SH–7, p. [170]. II. UV–11, pp. 254–255; XW–1, p. 87. III. L–32, pp. 330–331; L–189, p. 240; L–196, no. 98; L–214, pp. [149–150]; L–330, p. [51]; XU–14, p. [1]. IV. CB–17, p. 35; EC–19, pp. 58–59; L–141, p. 66; XE–4, pp. [6–7]. v. GNY–9, p. 119; HN–2, p. [120]; L–24, p. [xiv]; L–60, p. [211]; L–105, p. 60; L–204, p. 177; L–237, p. [68]; L–271, p. [203]; UV–10, p. 40. Analogues: See Ballad no. 5 and its secular relatives such as "The Wayfaring Stranger."

No. 3—Variants: II. HN–8, p. 161; L–286, p. 78; L–314, p. 66. III. L–141, p. 141; XE–17, p. [63]; XE–37, p. 168. IV. A–3, p. [64]; CB–41, p. 105. Headnote: Thomas Swain, "The Evolving Expressions of the Religious and Theological Experiences of a Community," Part II, *The Shaker Quarterly*, 12 (Summer 1972), p. 55; Virginia Weiss, "A Travel into Warfare: A Consideration of the Figures of the Heavenly Journey and the Internal Combat with Evil in the Shaker Experience," *The Shaker Quarterly*, 11 (Summer 1971), 47–80; and *Testimonies* (1888), p. 195.

No. 4—Variants: I. CB–37, p. 171; L–147, pp. 9–10; XW–1, p. 105; *The Musical Messenger: A Compilation of Hymns, Slow and Quick Marches, Etc., Used in Worship by Believers* (Union Village, Ohio, n.d.), p. 44; *Shaker Music* (Canterbury, N. H., 1875–1892), pp. 43–44, no. 58. II. L–19, p. 45. Both Eldress Marguerite Frost and Sister Mildred Barker sang the song. Analogue: "Huntington Castle" in a Newberry Library manuscript, Case/Ms/–VM/1450/M29, anon., [Manuscript of Dance Tunes], p. 19. Headnote: Letter, Canterbury, N. H., May 27, 1965, Eldress Marguerite Frost to Daniel Patterson, p. 3. WLCMs, no. 55, pp. 43–45.

No. 5—Variants: I. L–238, p. 69; WNY–20, p. [101]; WNY–26, p. 35. II. A–3, p. [181]; CB–37, p. 68; EC–12, p. 89; HD–14, pp. 91–92; SH–6, p. 24. III. L–19, p. 94. Headnote: The scribe consistently failed to dot the quarter notes. The story of the union meeting is from MeSL, Roxalana L. Grosvenor, "Elders," pp. 113–114. MeSL, Aurelia Mace, [Commonplace Book], entry for June 26–27, 1896.

No. 6—Variants: I. EC–13, p. 69; XE–43, pp. [33–34]. II. GME–4, p. [235]; GME–7, p. 6; L–121, p. [224]. Headnote: Letter, Canterbury, N. H., May 27, 1965, Eldress Marguerite Frost to Daniel Patterson, p. 3. MeSL, "New Gloucester Family Record, 1920—," p. 119.

Later Songs

No. 2—Variants: I. A–2, no. 27; GME–6, no. 273; L–43, pp. 58–59; L–113, pp. 191–192; L–135, p. 32; L–239, p. [202]; XU–35, p. [80]. Sister Mildred performs the song in Tom Davenport's film "The Shakers." Analogues: See Gift Song no. 6 and "Thorny Desert" in Jackson, *Another Sheaf*, p. 146.

No. 4—Headnote: OCWR, Letter, Enfield, N. H., Apr. 14, 1846, Ministry to Rufus Bishop, postscript. See also the "Postscript" to Andrews, *Gift*.

No. 5—Variants: II. A–11, p. [51]; HN–3, pp. 44–45; L–135, pp. 311–312; L–182, p. [370]; L–232, p. 18; L–246, p. 31; L–316, p. 19; XE–37, pp. 52–53. III. L–101, p. 19; L–308, pp. [159–160]. IV. A–3, p. [61]; L–179, pp. 140–141. v. L–117, p. 41; L–307, pp. 264–265; L–315, p. [340]. Headnote: OCWR, Letter, Lebanon, Mar. 18, 1847, Ministry to Groveland Ministry, pp. [2–3]. Hans Nathan cites a New York performance by a Lebanon apostate in 1835 and reproduces a depiction of a minstrel-show parody of Shaker dance (ca. 1840)—cf., *Dan Emmett and the Rise of Early Negro Minstrelsy* (Norman, Okla., 1962), pp. 94–95.

No. 6—Variant: I. CB–26, p. [177]. Headnote: The piece that precipitated the beginning of acceptance of harmony by the Shakers was D. A. Buckingham's anthem "The Harmony of Angels," which he received by inspiration in 1843 and sent out from Watervliet to the other societies in January 1844.

No. 7—Analogue: "Twas in the End of King James's Street" in Joyce, *Old Irish Folk Music*, p. 27. Headnote: Two additional stanzas of this hymn can be found in EC–21, p. [118]. Biblical allusions are to 1 Kings 19:12, Ps. 34:18, and Luke 15:24.

No. 8—Variants: I. A–2, no. 479; CB–26, pp. [218–219]; GME–6, no. 671; GME–16, no. 48; L–62, p. 53; XU–8, p. [59]. Analogue: "Pretty Saro" in Sharp, *English Folk Songs from the Southern Appalachians*, II, 10–12. Headnote: Additional biographical information about Elder Otis is given in Theodore E. Johnson, ed., "My Sweet Home in Zion," *The Shaker Quarterly*, 5 (Summer 1965), 60–62.

No. 9—Variants: I. GNY–9, p. [212]; L–196, no. 127. II. L–60, p. 274; L–135, p. 260; L–314, pp. 81–82. III. CB–43, p. 80; HN–8, p. 56; L–141, p. [9]; L–166, p. 207; XE–4, p. [9]. IV. EC–9, pp. 61–62; L–286, p. 33; WNY–19, no. 169. Analogue: "The Braes o Yarrow" in Bronson, *Traditional Tunes*, III, 320, no. 22.

No. 10—Headnote: *Autobiography of Elder Abraham Perkins and In Memoriam* (Concord, N. H., 1901), pp. 10–18.

No. 11—Analogues: See Hymn no. 5, and "American Star" in Jackson, *Another Sheaf*, p. 92, where he relates it to secular tunes like "Come under My Plaidie." Headnote: OCWR, v.B.97, p. [2], here slightly repunctuated.

No. 12—Variants: II. CB–17, p. 157; CB–40, p. [55]; L–69, pp. 206–207. Headnote: In the manuscript from which I take this song it is described as "Sung by Elder Joseph Brackett year 1856." Information about Elder Joseph is in R. Mildred Barker, "History of Union Branch, Gorham, Maine, 1784–1819," *The Shaker Quarterly*, 7 (Summer 1967), 72–73.

No. 13—Variants: I. CB–3, pp. 31–32; CB–17, p. 122; CB–28, p. [43]; L–116, p. 70; L–125, p. 49; L–182, pp. 310–312; L–279, p. [45]. Headnote: L–314 classifies the song as a "Standing Song" and most of the manuscripts indicate clearly that each section of the tune is to be repeated.

No. 14A—Variants: I. A–3, no. 6. II. CB–15, p. 72. The song can be heard on the phonodisc "Early Shaker Spirituals." Headnote: Information about Philemon's stewardship is recorded in NYPLMs, 58-M-140, vol. 4, entries for Apr. 16 and May 8, 1863. The account of Alonzo is based on Maine oral tradition, as reported by Sister Mildred Barker, and on MeSL, "A Record of Appointments," entry for May 8, 1872, and Aurelia Mace, [Commonplace Book], entry for June 6, 1884; "Church Journal," entry for Apr. 22, 1872.

No. 15—Variants: II. CB–43, p. 59; GNY–9, pp. [261–262]; L–135, p. 286; L–308, pp. [132–133]; L–314, p. 82; UV–3, p. 63; WNY–6, p. 69; WNY–19, no. 134; XW–1, p. 30. III. HN–8, p. 76; L–141, p. 78; XE–4, p. [25]; XE–37, p. 33. IV. HD–38, pp. 10–11; HD–49, p. 120; SH–7, p. 57. V. CB–17, p. 107. VI. L–182, pp. [249–250]. Headnote: MeSL, "Biographic Memoir of the Life and Experience of Calvin Green," chap. 4, para. 13.

No. 16—Variants: I. A–3, p. [44]; HD–36, p. 38; HD–49, p. [27]; SH–7, p. 10. II. HD–43, p. 137.

No. 17—Variant: II. L–182, pp. [380–381]. Analogue: "The Foggy Morning" in Joyce, *Old Irish Folk Music*, p. 254.

No. 18—Variant: I. L–167, p. 198.

No. 19—Headnote: See also the headnote for Gift Song no. 48; SU–1, pp. 42–44.

No. 20—Variants: I. C–3, p. 99; GME–13, p. 6; L–341, p. 170. II. L–314, p. 103; SH–6, p. [63]. Headnote: Miranda Barber's drawings consist of the following listed in Andrews, *Visions of the Heavenly Sphere* (Charlottesville, 1969), pl. VIII, fig. 3, p. 115 (Philadelphia Museum of Art, Accession no. 63-160-6), and pp. 119–122 (Western Reserve Historical Society, VIII.C.1). I believe she also executed the doves in fig. 9.

No. 21—Variants: II. A–3, p. [159]; CB–3, p. 192; CB–17, p. 159; CB–27, p. [3]; CB–41, p. 35; EC–19, p. [100]; EC–22, p. [186]; HD–38, p. 12; L–17, p. 148; L–119, pp. 53–54; L–168, p. 123; L–286, p. 26; WNY–2, p. 84; WNY–19, no. 197; XE–37, p. 61. Headnote: Quotation is from a memorial pamphlet entitled "Affectionately Inscribed to the Memory of Eldress Antoinette Doolittle, by her Loving and Devoted Gospel Friends" (Albany, 1887), pp. 5–6.

No. 22—Variants: II. A–3, pp. [60–61]; C–1, p. [1]; HD–11, pp. [168–169]; L–125, p. 52; SH–7, p. 146. Headnote: Information from a pamphlet, "Autobiography of Mary Antoinette Doolittle" (Mount Lebanon, N. Y., 1880), pp. 20, 28–31. When Lydia Wood cut her throat in November 1846, the ministry wrote that this was the fifth case of suicide among apostates from Watervliet—NYPLMs, 58-M-140, vol. 1, p. 282.

No. 23—Variants: I. CB–23, p. [31]; L–115, p. 55; L–120, p. 149; L–230, pp. [142–143]; L–256, p. 173; L–341, p. [66]. II. GME–13, p. [1]; L–117, pp. [232–233]; L–167, p. 129. III. HD–38, p. 67. IV. C–1, p. 16. Analogue: "Edward" in Bronson, *Traditional Tunes*, I, 244, no. 15. Headnote: "Autobiography of Mary Antoinette Doolittle," pp. 40–41.

No. 24—Variants: I. HD–49, p. 132; L–21, pp. [187–188]; L–99, p. [54]; L–116, p. 154; L–125, p. 71; L–167, pp. 136–137; L–286, p. 157; L–329, p. [163]; SU–4, p. 155; WO–6, p. [192]; OCWR, VIII.B.194, p. [6]. II. L–21, pp. [68–69]. III. CB–23, p. [15]; CB–39, p. [19]; CB–41, p. 213; ENH–9, p. [43]. Headnote: Anna White's diary is NYPLMs, 58-M-140, vol. 11. Her obituary appeared in the Pittsfield, Mass., *Journal*, Dec. 19, 1910.

No. 25—Variants: I. L–125, p. 80; WNY–20, p. 87. Analogues: "Geordie" in Bronson, *Traditional Tunes*, III, 273, no. 6; "Ester" in Jackson, *Spiritual Folk-Songs*, p. 46.

No. 26—Variants: I. C–1, p. [48]; HD–38, p. 52; L–99, pp. [68–69]; L–125, p. 84. Headnote: KLxU, film M–206, reel 2: [Journal of Andrew D. Barrett], p. 147.

No. 27—Variant: I. HN–3, p. 47. Headnote: WLCMs, no. 180, pp. 146–147.

No. 28—Variants: II. SU–12, p. [115]. III. HD–49, pp. 205–206; SH–7, p. 196. Headnote: Elder Harvey's dream is recounted in *The Journal of Eldress Nancy*, ed. Mary Julia Neal (Nashville, Tenn., 1963), p. 101. Cf. WLCMs, no. 336, p. 90.

No. 29—Variants: II. A–25, p. [14]; L–21, pp. [115–116]; L–83, p. [115]; L–168, p. 180; L–229, p. 100; L–286, p. 121; XE–6, p. [46]. Analogues: The tune seems to bear some relationship to "Good Physician" in Jackson, *Spiritual Folk-Songs*, p. 61, and to "On the Way to Canaan" in D. H. Mansfield, *The American Vocalist* (Boston, 1849), p. 235. Headnote: OCWR, VII.B.235, pp. 179–180.

No. 30—Analogues: "New Orleans" in Jackson, *Spiritual Folk-Songs*, p. 157. Headnote: WLCMs, no. 241, p. 9.

No. 31—Headnote: KLxU, film M–384, entry for Oct. 6, 1862.

No. 32—Variants: I. HD–38, p. [127]; HN–8, p. 160; L–49, pp. 171–172; SU–12, p. [194]. II. CB–16, p. 43; CB–37, p. 48; ENH–9, p. [84]; L–19, p. 110; WNY–24, unnumbered loose leaf; XE–4, p. [97]; XE–6, p. 43; XE–17, p. [64]. III. A–27, pp. [8–9]; L–163, pp. 47–48; L–201, p. [159]; L–229, pp. 190–191; L–273, pp. [143–144]; L–275, p. 167.

iv. HD–14, pp. 40–41; HD–52, p. [45]. v. C–1, p. [164]; CB–39, p. [265]; GNY–2, p. 173; HD–32, p. [122]; L–21, p. [183]; L–23, pp. 127–128; L–45, pp. 84, 224; L–71, p. 312; L–199, p. 172; L–342, pp. 104–105; SH–1, p. [16]; SH–2, p. [60]; WNY–2, p. 507; WO–2, pp. [121–122]; XE–37, p. 161. vi. L–149, pp. [109–111]; L–278, p. 13; SU–10, p. 117. Headnote: An account of Thomas Ainge Devyr is included in Ray Boston, *British Chartists in America, 1839–1900* (Totowa, N. J., 1971); Boston quotes Ira Harris's assessment of Devyr: "Too vain and presumptuous to act a subordinate part, he is too rash and indiscreet to be a leader" (p. 54). Cecelia's night vision is recounted in White and Taylor, *Shakerism*, p. 366.

No. 33—Analogue: A very close melodic analogue is "A Sheáin a mhic mo chomharsan" on the phonodisc Folkways FM–4002: "Songs of Aran: Gaelic Singing from the West of Ireland," ed. S. R. Cowell. Cf. also Petrie, nos. 1437 and 1438. Headnote: Sister Mildred Barker recalled this song in the course of a conversation with me in August 1973.

No. 34—Variant: i. CB–23, p. [180]. Analogue: "Waterloo" in Sharp, *English Folk Songs from the Southern Appalachians*, ii, 176. Cf. also Extra Song no. 15.

No. 35—Variants: i. L–123, p. 110; WNY–31, p. [113]. ii. EC–13, p. 90. Analogue: See Later Song no. 37. Headnote: Thomas Hammond's calculations are contained in HD–16, p. [ii].

No. 36—Headnote: Deming's letter is transcribed in WLCMs, no. 42, entry for Sept. 1, 1821. Four other apostates in 1846 had a similar reaction. Deacons went to Lebanon Springs to settle with them and found three shedding "a flood of tears when too late" and blaming the other, John Allen. He was "more braced for a time" but finally "bust forth almost in torrents." Mary Wicks said if "some one would dig a hole in the ground & bury her therein it would be a heaven to her!!!" (NYPLMs, 58–M–140, vol. 1, entry for Sept. 12, 1846). A good exploration of causes and consequences of Shaker apostasies is F. Gerald Ham, "Shakerism in the Old West," Ph.D. dissertation, University of Kentucky (Lexington, Ky., 1962), esp. pp. 168–205.

No. 37—Variant: i. GME–4, p. [10]. Headnote: *Testimonies* (1888), p. 288.

No. 38—Variants: i. CB–18, p. 82; WNY–47, p. [25]; XE–1, pp. 14–15. Analogue: See Later Song no. 35. A variant of the melody was used as early as 1811 for the hymn "Love" printed in *Millennial Praises*, pp. 134–136. Haskell preserved the form of the tune known at Enfield in EC–11, p. 227. Headnote: Eldress Marguerite sang and motioned this song for me at Canterbury in 1963. No film record was made of her performance of the song.

No. 39—Variants: i. A–3, p. [187]; CB–31, p. [40]; GNY–10, pp. [42–43]; HD–9, p. 67; HD–14, pp. 133–134; XE–4, p. [140]; *Shaker Music* (New York, 1884), p. 170; *A Collection of Hymns and Anthems* (East Canterbury, N. H., 1892), p. 85; *Shaker Hymnal by the Canterbury Shakers* (East Canterbury, N. H., 1908), p. 196. ii. EC–8, pp. 73–74; EC–12, p. 48; L–49, pp. 199–200; L–199, p. 201; SH–6, pp. [77–78]; UV–1, p. 50; XE–7, p. 5. iii. L–229, pp. 211–212. Headnote: WLCMs, no. 338a, p. 33 and pp. 150–151. OCWR, v.B.70, entry for Jan. 31, 1870.

No. 40—Variants: i. A–25, p. [18]; CB–18, p. 93; GME–4, p. [131]; L–154, pp. [121–122]. Headnote: WLCMs, no. 180, p. 154. NHCo, 289.8/U56uv/1870–1882, vol. 3, p. 10.

No. 41—Variant: i. GME–7, p. 134. Analogues: The third phrase is close to that of Solemn Song no. 15 and "Rejoice in Thy Youth" in Jackson, *Another Sheaf*, p. 29. Headnote: OCWR, v.B.247, entry for July 25, 1868.

No. 42—Variants: i. CB–13, p. 161; CB–17, p. 207; CB–27, pp. [78–79]; HN–8, p. 133; L–101, pp. [116–117]; L–105, pp. [186–187]; L–202, p. [72]; L–286, p. 93; L–308, pp. [196–197]; OCWR, Letter, Enfield, N. H., Sept. 19, 1858, Jasper S. Hurt to Isaac Youngs, p. [2]. ii. CB–28, p. [116]; L–9, p. [228]; L–17, p. 293; L–72, p. 268; L–116, pp. 24–25; L–256, p. 252; L–273, p. [50]; L–279, pp. [135–136]; L–314, p. 118; SU–10, p. 38. III. HN–3, p. 113; L–141, p. [25]; WO–10, p. [6]; XE–4, p. [74]; XE–37, p. 97; XE–45, p. [117]. Headnote: L–314, p. 118, calls the song a Slow March; L–202, p. [72], labels it a "good extra song." Rhoda Blake's vision is in WLCMs, no. 55, p. 73.

No. 43—Variants: I. A–23, p. [28]; A–28, p. [48]. Headnote: Sister Mildred wrote her recollections of Sister Paulina in a commentary on this song in *The Shaker Quarterly*, 4 (Winter 1964), 128–129. She also told about her in the phonodisc MO8P–3861 of *The Shaker Heritage*, ed. William Randle (Cleveland, Ohio, 1961), side 19, and also in interviews with Tom Davenport. These accounts differ slightly in their details; I follow the account as given to Tom Davenport, which accords best with accounts given me.

Checklist of Shaker Song Manuscripts

Musical publications by the Shakers are definitively surveyed in Mary B. Richmond's *Shaker Literature: A Bibliography* (Hanover, N. H., 1976), but the Shakers themselves printed only a small number of their early tunes. Nineteenth-century manuscripts hold most of the surviving songs. In the following checklist I provide a key to the symbols I have used in citing them. I aim, however, at more than a simple documentation of my sources. The listing holds every Shaker manuscript I have seen containing a significant amount of music—a total of 798 songbooks, exclusive of three found too late.

Mine is the second attempt at an extensive description of Shaker song manuscripts, the first being the "Collation of Manuscript Hymnals" printed in Harold E. Cook's *Shaker Music.* Cook's list will continue to prove useful. He included volumes containing only song texts, which I omit for lack of space, and he presented the holdings of each library as a unit. His work should, however, be used with caution. Cook's listings are incomplete, at least for the present holdings of the collections. At the Library of Congress he overlooked Russel Haskell's "A Record of Spiritual Songs" and five other manuscripts housed in the Music Division. He cited only three of the six tunebooks now in the University of Michigan Library and only seven of the nineteen in the Williams College Library. Several major depositories have also opened since 1946, when Cook did his work, most notably the library of the United Society of Shakers at Sabbathday Lake, that of the Shaker Museum Foundation, Inc., in Old Chatham, New York, and the Andrews Collection of the Henry Francis du Pont Winterthur Museum. Cook's checklist covers the holdings of nine libraries and three private owners: my own those of twenty-five public and thirteen private collections. I list 381 music manuscripts not in Cook's "Collation."

But my work will prove no more impervious to time than his. Cook describes three manuscripts shown him by Shakers at Lebanon and Hancock that have not found their way into the collections I have seen. Each year since I first began my study of Shaker songs I have discovered additional song manuscripts. I have also heard of private collections I could not track down and of one collector who has not permitted students to use his holdings.

Even working with the same materials, however, Cook and I differ in approach. Both of us give a physical description of each manuscript; this information is brief but sufficient for the identification of items in any collection hereafter dispersed. I have attempted, however, to design entries and an arrangement that will help later students find materials of value to their own projects. My descriptions tell how much music is to be found in a volume, what range of song types it holds, and when it was written. I arrange the entries by community of origin and author.

The number of Shakers who wrote music was large—much greater than the 168 persons I can positively identify as the authors of the collections in this checklist. In establishing the authorship of these manuscripts I have taken a very conservative course, relying chiefly on title-page information. Many of the songbooks have one or more names written on the end papers and flyleaves; I include these in my entries but do not consider them proof of authorship. I also refrain from attempting many attributions on the basis of handwriting. The penmanship of a large group of girls writing at Lebanon in the late 1830s and 1840s, for example, was astonishingly uniform, and I do not attempt to play my hunches. I venture my judgments only with the work of a few scribes like Russel Haskell, Isaac N. Youngs, and Thomas Hammond, Jr., with distinctive hands well known to me from signed documents.

The provenance of the manuscripts is usually a good deal easier to determine, particularly for ones written after the mid-1830s, when annotations became common. Tunes in a Lebanon songbook, for example, will bear notes such as "Hill Family," "Elder Sister Betsey B.," "A. W., North Family," "From Ohio," and "Brought from Canterbury." The collective weight of these annotations often establishes to a certainty the origin of the manuscript. Where I have doubt, I classify the volume under a looser heading such as "Provenance—Eastern" or "Provenance—Unknown."

At the beginning of my research I hypothesized that a distinctly local song tradition would have developed in each Shaker community. This proved, however, virtually impossible to document. The society at Enfield, Connecticut, did of course cleave to the Dorian mode for its "minor" tunes, and the Kentucky repertory was set somewhat apart by a tendency to employ repeated lines, pentatonic scales, and elements of certain tunes like "Black Jack Davy" popular in the region. But important factors minimized local variations. Most of the villages lay in Northern states, and the membership of even the New York and Ohio communities came largely from New England stock and had a shared song tradition. The Western colonies, which held a number of Southern converts, felt inferior to the Eastern societies and conformed to their practices as well as they could. When Elder Rufus Bishop and Isaac N. Youngs from Lebanon visited South Union in 1834, their "kind instructions" made the South Union Shakers feel "rough & awkward in almost every point—Stiff & careless." The Easterners, wrote the journal keeper at South Union, showed themselves "by all their deportment & conversation" greatly "in advance of all of us in the west. We are in the backwoods truly." It is not surprising that Harvey Eades undertook to copy upwards of five hundred tunes from Brother Isaac's song manuscript while the visitors tarried.[1] The Westerners, like other Shakers, also placed great value upon unity. The sharing of songs made Believers feel their oneness, so that they undertook to teach and learn songs when traveling, to send them in letters to distant societies, and to make presents of large song collections.

The chief obstacles to establishing differences between the repertories of the various societies lie, nevertheless, in two other circumstances. One is the difficulty of learning where a song originated. What I have accomplished in this line is the result of many years of searching for specific tunes. Only a computer could sift out the origin of each song in the manuscript record. The second difficulty, as Tables 5 and 6 show, is the unevenness of the coverage provided by the manuscripts. Believers at Lebanon wrote nearly half the songbooks that can be attributed to a community. By contrast, from Pleasant Hill and Union Village—societies which at their peak rivaled Lebanon in membership—we have barely thirty song manuscripts.

The parent society probably did have the largest number of active scribes, but it

TABLE 5. A COUNT OF SONG MANUSCRIPTS SURVIVING FROM EACH SHAKER SOCIETY

Community	Number of MSS	Community	Number of MSS
Alfred, Me.	28	Tyringham, Mass.	0
Canterbury, N. H.	46	Union Village, Ohio	26
Enfield, Conn.	25	Watervliet, N. Y.	53
Enfield, N. H.	13	Watervliet, Ohio	0
Gloucester, Me.	19	West Union, Ind.	0
(Sabbathday Lake)		Whitewater, Ohio	11
Groveland, N. Y.	14	Important Branch Families	
Hancock, Mass.	8	Canaan, N. Y.	10
Harvard, Mass.	58	Gorham, Me.	0
Lebanon, N. Y.	347	Philadelphia, Pa.	0
North Union, Ohio	4	Poland Hill, Me.	2
Pleasant Hill, Ky.	7	Savoy, Mass.	0
Shirley, Mass.	8	Provenance—Eastern	48
Sodus, N. Y.	0	Provenance—Western	2
South Union, Ky.	25	Provenance—Unknown	44
		Total:	798

was also more fortunate than most of the others in the preservation of its manuscripts. Through the foresight of Eldress M. Catherine Allen and of the bibliophile Wallace H. Cathcart, its library is preserved by the Western Reserve Historical Society. East and West, other Shaker custodians may have destroyed manuscripts out of a wish to protect them from profane eyes or discarded them as no longer of value.[2] At Alfred, Maine, an entire library was lost when the ministry's house burned in 1902.[3] Some of the smaller societies probably never kept manuscript transcriptions of their songs. Visiting Tyringham in 1846, for example, Elder Thomas Hammond, Jr., of Harvard found "no one there that understands the notes" except Elder Brother Albert Battles, who he says "understands something of it." The Tyringham songs that survive were recorded by outsiders like Elder Thomas, who "went into the house & went up stairs with Br. Niles & took down some songs" and wrote down others from the singing of "Hastings & Fanny."[4]

Although additional Shaker song manuscripts will come to light, the total surviving

TABLE 6. A COUNT OF SHAKER SONG MANU-
SCRIPTS BY DECADE OF COMMENCEMENT

Decade	Number of MSS
1820s	25
1830s	112
1840s	242
1850s	174
1860s	107
1870s	62
1880s	32
1890s	12
1900s	4
1910s	11
1920s	3
Uncertain dating	14
Total:	798

corpus must be far smaller than the number actually written by Shaker scribes. Those preserved give clear proof of this. The six from the hand of Thomas Hammond include the ninth and eleventh volumes of a numbered series. One of Russel Haskell's manuscripts is labeled "Book 3" and another "Book 4." Isaac Young's manuscripts include a "No 3" dating from 1834 to 1836 and a "Scratch Book No. 2" from 1839 to 1841. The remaining volumes of these series are lost. No music at all seems to survive from the hand of Abraham Whitney (1785–1882), who originated the Shaker letteral notation and corresponded for some years on musical matters with other scribes.

On many accounts then—some discussed above, others explained earlier in this book—the Shaker music manuscripts are an incomplete record of the Shaker song tradition. Such as they are, the manuscripts nevertheless hold an extraordinary collection of songs that others will wish to explore. My checklist offers the following information about them:

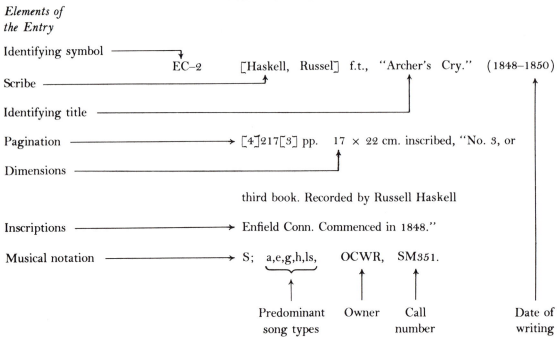

SAMPLE ENTRY

Each element of these entries requires explanation.

Identifying Symbol. The first letter derives from the name of the society. I add additional letters only if they are needed to distinguish one name from another beginning with the same letter. The numeral indicates the position of the manuscript in my alphabetical listing. I place those of known authorship first and gather all others under the abbreviation "Anon."

Scribe. I normally take this information from the title page. When I make the attribution on any other basis, I bracket the name—and follow the scribe's usual spelling of his name.

Date. Within parentheses I give the dates between which the manuscript appears to have been written. Only rarely does the scribe give this information. I usually infer it from dates mentioned in the book and from my knowledge of the dating of songs, the notational systems, and inks and paper.

Identifying title. For collections having no title page I give the opening line of text in the volume. This may be either the first song title (f.t.) or the first line of the first song (f.l.).

Pagination. In presenting this data I give the needs of the user precedence over conventional practice. I accordingly tell how many pages of music a manuscript holds and whether the songbook contains any list of contents. All bracketed numerals indicate pages that are either blank or filled with nonmusical writings. Free-standing numerals indicate pages mostly written with music. The abbreviation "cont" indicates that the pages preceding it hold some form of content analysis—this may be a list of titles or of first lines or of tunes. Usually it is an inconsistent mixture of the three. A change from free-standing to bracketed numbers and back shows that a stretch of blank pages interrupts the musical transcriptions.

Size. The dimensions of the volume are given in centimeters rounded to the nearest whole number, with height preceding width.

Inscriptions. At this point I enter all information bearing on the dating, authorship, and ownership of the volume. The jottings may be taken from the cover, the endpapers, the flyleaves, or pages of the manuscript.

Musical notation. The following symbols show the form of musical notation used in the manuscript:

> C—capital letteral notation
> E—Harvey Eades's linear letteral notation
> H—Russel Haskell's cursive letteral notation
> N—numeral
> P—patent or shape-note notation
> R—round-note or standard notation
> S—small letteral notation

Song types. Following a semicolon I enter a list of the genres of Shaker songs that predominate in the manuscript. The symbols, presented as minuscule letters, are as follows:

> a—anthems
> e—extra songs
> fp—songs of the first parents (Ann and William Lee, and James Whittaker)
> g—gift songs
> h—hymns
> ls—laboring songs (dances and marches, with and without words)
> ss—solemn songs

Present owner. The location symbols used in standard reference works such as the *Early American Imprints* are my model, but I have freely adapted them to meet my needs. The letters of each symbol thus stand for the state, the city, and the institution or private collector owning the manuscript:

CCA—Conn., Clinton, Mrs. Olive Hayden Austin
CHSL—Conn., Hartford, Connecticut State Library
CNHY—Conn., New Haven, Yale University (School of Music)
CWB—Conn., Watertown, Mr. and Mrs. R. W. Belfit
DWt—Del., Winterthur, Henry Francis du Pont Winterthur Museum
KBGK—Ky., Bowling Green, The Kentucky Library
KLF—Ky., Louisville, The Filson Club
KPH—Ky., Pleasant Hill, Shakertown at Pleasant Hill
MCB—Mass., Charlemont, Mrs. James H. Bissland
MeSl—Me., Sabbathday Lake, The United Society of Shakers
MHF—Mass., Harvard, The Fruitlands Museum
MiAU—Mich., Ann Arbor, The University of Michigan Library
MPBA—Mass., Pittsfield, The Berkshire Athenaeum
MPH—Mass., Pittsfield, Shaker Community, Inc. at Hancock
MWA—Mass., Worcester, The American Antiquarian Society
MWW—Mass., Williamstown, Williams College Library
NCA—N. C., Chapel Hill, Professor Raymond Adams
NHCb—N. H., Canterbury, Shaker Village
NHCbT—N. H., Canterbury, Mr. Charles S. Thompson
NHCo—N. H., Concord, New Hampshire Historical Society
NHLC—N. H., Lebanon, Mrs. Clarice Carr
NYAL—N. Y., Albany, The New York State Library
NYAM—N. Y., Albany, The New York State Museum
NYAP—N. Y. City, The American Society for Psychical Research
NYAS—N. Y., Albany, Mr. John E. Shea
NYBG—N. Y., Buffalo, The Buffalo and Erie County Public Library,
     Grosvenor Reference Division
NYHS—N. Y. City, The New-York Historical Society
NYLC—N. Y., New Lebanon, Mr. Jerome Count
NYLD—N. Y., Mount Lebanon, The Darrow School
NYNT—N. Y., North Chatham, Mr. Robert Temple
NYOC—N. Y., Old Chatham, The Shaker Museum
NYOCC—N. Y., Old Chatham, Mr. H. Phelps Clawson
NYPLM—N. Y. City, The New York Public Library, Music Division
NYPLMs—N. Y. City, The New York Public Library, Manuscript Division
OCoO—Ohio, Columbus, The Ohio State Museum
OCSH—Ohio, Cleveland, The Shaker Historical Society
OCWR—Ohio, Cleveland, The Western Reserve Historical Society
ODPL—Ohio, Dayton, The Dayton and Montgomery County Public Library
OLW—Ohio, Lebanon, The Warren County Historical Society
OOP—Ohio, Olmsted Falls, Mrs. Virginia M. Prahst
PLC—Pa., Lewisburg, Professor Harold E. Cook
PMA—Pa., Philadelphia, The Philadelphia Museum of Art
VaLD—Va., Lynchburg, Dr. Bailey F. Davis
WLCM—Washington, D. C., The Library of Congress, Music Division
WLCMs—Washington, D. C., The Library of Congress, Manuscript Division

Call number. The identifying numbers assigned by the various libraries may be accession numbers or ones taken from the Dewey decimal or Library of Congress systems. The smaller collections are generally not numbered.

ALFRED

A–1   Bussell, Joshua H. "A Book of Hymns For Zion's Children. . . . Written by Joshua H. Bussell begun July 6, 1847." (1847–1878) 85[73] pp. 16 × 10 cm. S; g,h. MeSL.

A–2   ———. f.t., "Pure Joys taken from Mother Ann's Hymn Book." (1845–1849) [2]212[4] pp. 21 × 17 cm. inscribed, "Eldress Harriett Coolbroth Alfred, Me" and "Joshua H. Bussell." S; a,e,g,h,ls. MeSL.

A–3   ———. f.t., "Truth will stand." (ca. 1848–1860?) [2]212[4] pp. 24 × 20 cm. S; a,e,g,h. MeSL.

A–4   Coolbroth, Harriet. f.l., "Holy Angels wilt thou help me." (1893–1895) [2]103[47] pp. 20 × 14 cm. inscribed, "Harriet Coolbroth 1893." S; e. MeSL.

A–5   Libby, Frank O. "Shaker Songs Frank O Libby Alfred Maine Inspirational." (1887–1892) [3]64[27] pp. 20 × 13 cm. inscribed, "Presented to Frank O. Libby by his Teacher Emeline Hart Oct 1889." S; e,h. MeSL.

A–6   Anon. f.t., "Call of the Spirit." (1875–1878) 150 pp. 20 × 14 cm. inscribed, "Eliza R. Smith Alfred Me, April 1875." S; e. MeSL.

A–7   ———. f.l., "Cry aloud spare not." (1875–1880) 260[8] pp. 18 × 12 cm. inscribed, "Mary Casey Alfred Maine." S; e. NYOC, Ac. 7993.

A–8   ———. f.l., "Dear Brethren and Sisters I love You." (1887–1889) [8]158[4] pp. 20 × 13 cm. inscribed, "This was Eliza J." and "Eliza R. Smith Jan. 1888." S; e. MeSL.

A–9   ———. f.t., "Encouraging Word to Zion's Children." (1860–1882) [8]73[119] pp. 13 × 11 cm. inscribed, "L. Taylor." S; a,e,h. MeSL.

A–10 ———. f.t., "Great I Am." (ca. 1880–1890s) [4]116[44] pp. 20 × 13 cm. inscribed, "Eld. Harriett Coolbroth Alfred, Maine." S; e. MeSL.

A–11 ———. f.t., "Guideing Star." (ca. 1877–1881) 170 pp. 17 × 10 cm. S; e,h. MeSL.

A–12 ———. f.t., "Holy Praises." (1857–1864) [2]75[49] pp. 22 × 18 cm. S; e,h. MeSL.

A–13 ———. f.l., "How it gladdens our hearts." (ca. 1869) [8]104[4] pp. 18 × 12 cm. inscribed, "Eliza R. Smith. March 14, 69, Alfred, Maine." S; e,g. MeSL.

A–14 ———. f.l., "I am thankful O how thankful." (1893–1899) [2]108 pp. 20 × 14 cm. inscribed, "Mary Ann Walker March 19th 1893." S; e. MeSL.

A–15 ———. f.l., "I love my gospel parents." (1891–1896) 191[11] pp. 20 × 13 cm. S; e. MeSL.

A–16 ———. f.l., "In a life of consecration." (1889–ca. 1893?) [2]216[2] pp. 20 × 14 cm. S; e. MeSL.

A–17 ———. f.l., "In showers and rich profusion." (1846–1849) [6]42[38] pp. 18 × 12 cm. S; e,ls. MeSL.

A–18 ———. f.l., "Not in vain." (1880–1883) 156[4] pp. 20 × 13 cm. S; e. MeSL.

A–19 ———. f.l., "O thou precious gospel by Mother." (1892–1895) [2]102[42] pp. 20 × 14 cm. S; e. MeSL.

A–20 ———. f.l., "O thou precious gospel by Mother." (1892–1895) [2]151[51] pp. 20 × 13 cm. S; e. MeSL.

A–21   ———. "O union pure union." (1892–1896) [2]188[8] pp. 20 × 14 cm. in-
            scribed, "E R S." S; e. MeSL.

A–22   ———. f.l., "Pour out thy spirit." (1879–1887) [2]140[2] pp. 19 × 13 cm.
            inscribed, "Paulina D. Smith Alfred Maine, Dec. 28, 1879" and "Harriet
            Choolbroth Alfred Maine." S; e. MeSL.

A–23   ———. f.t., "Preface." (1887–1889) [2]156 pp. 20 × 14 cm. inscribed, "Fannie
            C. Casey Jan. 1887." S; e,g,h. MPBA, V/289.8/Un3.3/vol. 8.

A–24   ———. f.l., "Pure love gospel love." (1887–1891) [2]216[3] pp. 20 × 14 cm.
            inscribed, "D. Haskell." S; e. MeSL.

A–25   ———. f.t., "The Saviors Watchword." (1862–1870?) [2]110 pp. (pages loose).
            25 × 20 cm. S; e,g,ls. MeSL.

A–26   ———. f.t., "Speak Gently." (1861–1881) [4]116[4] pp. 21 × 17 cm. inscribed,
            "Francella Blake's Book. Oct. 29th 1861." S; e,g,h. MeSL.

A–27   ———. f.t., "True Thankfulness." (1856–1886) [2]274[2] pp. 21 × 14 cm.
            S; a,e,h. MeSL.

A–28   ———. f.l., "We are marching thro' Zion." (1883–1887) [3]65[190] pp.
            18 × 12 cm. inscribed, "The Property of Lettie S Pender Alfred york County."
            S; e,h. MeSL.

CANAAN, NEW YORK

C–1   Clisbee, Betsey B. "A Collection of Spiritual Songs for Devotional Worship
            Transcribed by Betsey B. Clisbee. Canaan May 1859." (1859–1862) 228 pp.
            18 × 13 cm. S; e,h,ls. MPBA, V/289.8/C61.

C–2   Moore, Marriette. "Hymns of Believers Written by Marriette Moore Canaan
            May 17th 1868." (ca. 1868–1875) 163[17] pp. 18 × 11 cm. S; e,h. MHF.

C–3   Patterson, Mary Ann. "A Collection of Spiritual Songs used by Believers in
            Christ's Second Appearing. Mary Ann Patterson. Canaan N. Y. July 12th
            1846." (1846–1852) 378 pp. 17 × 11 cm. S; e. MHF.

C–4   Shaw, Levi. "A Selected Variety of Spiritual Songs. Used by Believers in their
            general Worship. Compiled by Levi Shaw. Canaan, N. Y., 1840." (1840–1848)
            311[15] pp. 19 × 13 cm. S; e,g,h,ls. MiAU, M/2131/.S4/S54.

C–5   Strever, Marritta. "A Collection of Inspirational Songs Selected and Transcribed
            By Marritta Strever." (1880–1884) [2]152[44] pp. 17 × 11 cm. S; e. OCWR,
            SM350.

C–6   ———. "Hymns of Beleivers. Copied by Marritta Strever Canaan Aug. 5th
            1869." (1869–1878) 192[4 cont] pp. 17 × 10 cm. S; a,e,h. NYPL, 66–M–13,
            vol. 67.

C–7   Anon. "Indian Songs. Given during the present manifestation of the native spirits
            gathered to the Shaker Order in Spirit Life." (1893–1894) [4]125[29] pp.
            18 × 11 cm. S; g. DWt, SA1106.

C–8   ———. f.l., "O let us live the angel life." (1880–1890) [3]228[11] pp.
            20 × 14 cm. S; e. DWt, SA1163.

C–9   ———. f.t., "On the beautiful hills of truth." (1873–1883) [2]246[4] pp.
            20 × 13 cm. S; e. DWt, SA1153.

C–10   ———. f.t., "Source of Light" (ca. 1875) [6]58[144] pp. 19 × 13 cm. S; h.
            OCWR, SM284.

CANTERBURY, NEW HAMPSHIRE

CB–1 Appleton, Margarett. f.t., "Shepherd of Israel." (1915–1916) [2]73[111] pp. 26 × 20 cm. cover, "Margarett Appleton." R; e, secular songs. NHCb.

CB–2 Blinn, Henry C. f.t., "Holy Call." (1847) [4]11[169 essays] pp. 18 × 11 cm. S; e. MeSL.

CB–3 ———. f.t., "The Holy Lamb of God." (1855–1857) [4]194[14 cont] pp. 19 × 12 cm. p. 1, "Henry C. Blinn. 1856." S; a,e,h. NYOC, Ac. 12,775.

CB–4 Chandler, Antoinette E. "Antoinette E. Chandler. Songs placed on board D #32." (1911–1915) [4]178[13 cont] 61[95] pp. 17 × 10 cm. R; e. NHCb.

CB–5 ———. f.t., "Song presented to Young People by Sr. Mary Ann Wilson." (1906–?) [6]143[47 cont] pp. 17 × 10 cm. inscribed, "A. E. Chandler." R; e. NHCb.

CB–6 Cochran, Alexander Y. "Alexander Y. Cochran. Chh Canterbury N. H." (1872–1874) 128[104] pp. 22 × 18 cm. R; e,h. NYOC, Ac. 12,768.

CB–7 Cook, Ella. f.l., "What the dew is to the flower." (1912–1915) 91[11] pp. 21 × 17 cm. cover, "Ella Cook." R; e. NHCb.

CB–8 Crooker, Sarah A. f.t., "Advent's March." (1847–1850) [4]188[14 cont] pp. 22 × 18 cm. inscribed, "Sarah A Crooker. Vol 1st 1848." S; e,g,h,ls. NYOC, Ac. 12,771.

CB–9 Evans, Jessie. f.t., "He Shall Feed His Flock." (1919) [4]26[242] pp. 22 × 14 cm. inscribed, "Jessie Evans." R; e, secular pieces. NHCb.

CB–10 Fairchilds, Calvin Miller. f.t., "Peaceful Habitation." (1860–1869) [4]222[4] pp. 20 × 14 cm. rear, "The foregoing songs were written by Calvin Miller Fairchilds who deceased December 6th 1869 aged 28 years." S; e,h. NYLC.

CB–11 Frost, Marguerite. f.l., "Away with all doubting." (1911–1915) [8 cont]198[4] pp. 21 × 17 cm. R; e. NHCb.

CB–12 ———. "Children's Songs. 1892. Volume I." (1892) [1]36[21] pp. 22 × 18 cm. R; e. NHCb.

CB–13 ———. "Shaker Songs from long ago. Placed on Board in D. 32 during 1912–1913–1914–1915." (1912–1915) 212[14 cont] pp. 22 × 14 cm. R; e,h. NHCb.

CB–14 Hastings, Marcia E. front cover, "Canterbury Chh. Songs. July 1840 to May 1842." (1839–1842) [8]154[2]76 pp. 22 × 19 cm. inscribed, "Songs received by inspiration in the Church, Canterbury, N. H., to be found in this part of the volume; those from other families and societies in the other part. All written by Marcia E. Hastings." S; a,e,g,h,ls. NYOC, Ac. 12,796.

CB–15 ———. front cover, "Canterbury Songs Chh. May 1842 to Nov. 1852." (1842–1852) [12]242[4]114[14 cont] pp. 21 × 17 cm. inscribed, "In this part are written songs received or originating in the Church on Holy Ground; Foreign songs may be found in the other part. M. E. H." S; a,g. PMA, 63–160–193.

CB–16 ———. "Sacred Hymns and Anthems For Divine Worship. Originating in different societies of Believers. AD. 1857 to 1864. To which are added many shorter pieces, to be sung to the March, and other wise. Canterbury, N. H." (1857–1864) [16 cont]182 pp. 19 × 12 cm. penciled on title page, "Written by M. E. Hastings." S; a,e,h. NYOC, Ac. 12,795.

CB–17 ———. "Sacred Songs for Divine Worship. Commenced Dec. 25, 1852; finished Jan. 1859. . . . Written chiefly by M. E. Hastings, Chh. Canterbury N.H." (1852–1859) [2]253[9] pp. 21 × 18 cm. S; e,g,ls. NYOC, Ac. 12,770.

CB–18   ———. "Songs of Devotion From the early part of 1864, To the close of 1868. Written by M. E. Hastings . . . Canterbury, N. H. May 27, 1875." (1875) [10 cont]164[2] pp. 20 × 14 cm. S; e,ls. NYOC, Ac. 12,764.

CB–19   Lindsay, Bertha. "Bertha Lindsay. Duets with Miriam Wall." (1924) [4]250 [14 cont] pp 21 × 14 cm. R; e, secular songs. NHCb.

CB–20   ———. cover, "The Shaker Chorus. Bertha." (1906) 58[6] pp. 25 × 20 cm. R; e, secular pieces. NHCb.

CB–21   ———. cover, "Trios. Bertha." (1920–1927) 50[58] pp. 27 × 20 cm. R; e. NHCb.

CB–22   Stackpole, Beatrice A. f.t., "Shepherd of Israel." (1929) 71[109] pp. 26 × 20 cm. cover, "Beatrice A. Stackpole." R; e, secular songs. NHCb.

CB–23   Stickney, Asenath C. "Asenath C. Stickney. May 6, 1860. Canterbury N H." (1860–1862) [4]178[4] pp. 20 × 14 cm. S; e. NYOC, Ac. 12,767.

CB–24   Weeks, Esther. "Choice Selections. Culled From Hymns Written by Esther Weeks at the request of Eld. Dorothea Cochran." (1912–1914) [2]94[12 cont] pp. 21 × 17 cm. cover, "Songs Blanche L. Gardner 1912." R; e. NHCb.

CB–25   Williams, Lucy. "A Book of Divine Anthems, Hymns, and Tunes without words sung by our first gospel Parents when on earth. Commenced by Lucy Williams, finished by M. E. Hastings. Church, Canterbury Shaker Village N. H." (1830–1861) [16]280 pp. 15 × 18 cm. C,S; a,fp,h,ss. NYOC, Ac. 12,777.

CB–26   ———. f.t., "Holy Habitation." (1820s–1850) [8]248 pp. 17 × 11 cm. inscribed, "Lucy Williams. Devotional Hymns. Some handsomely written, all neatly & economically. Music attached to most of them. 1824 to 1850. Some short songs in the midst." C,S; e,g,h. NYOC, Ac. 12,774.

CB–27   Anon. f.t., "The Best Love." (1857–1858) 88 pp. 20 × 16 cm. inscribed, "Eliza R. Smith Canterbury N. H. June 28, 1857." S; e,ls. MeSL.

CB–28   ———. f.t., "Call for Warriors." (1854–1859) [4]192[94] pp. 20 × 13 cm. S; e,h,ls. MeSL.

CB–29   ———. f.l., "Falling, falling like the fleecy snow-flakes." (1880s?) [14]26[188] pp. 18 × 28 cm. inscribed, "Marie King." R; e,h. MeSL.

CB–30   ———. f.l., ". . . the heart that loves to the uttermost." (1914–1915) 56 pp. 21 × 17 cm. R; e. NHCb.

CB–31   ———. f.l., "Here I am Lord Thou callest me." (1868–1869?) [3]63[86] pp. 20 × 17 cm. S; e. WLCM, M/2131/.S4E5.

CB–32   ———. f.l., "How Divinely bright & glorious." (1875–1879) [8]112 pp. 18 × 11 cm. S; e. NYOC, Ac. 12,814.

CB–33   ———. f.l., "I covet not earth's treasures." (1914–1915) 50[72] pp. 21 × 17 cm. R; e. NHCb.

CB–34   ———. f.t., "The Lamb." (1828–1835) [10]97[191] pp. 15 × 19 cm. inscribed, "Mary Ann Hill" and "EMP From R. A. S. 1931." C; a. MeSL.

CB–35   ———. f.t., "The Mount zion." (ca.1825) 32 pp. 22 × 27 cm. cover, "1815 One of the first written Music Books." C; a,h,ls. NYOC, Ac. 12,779.

CB–36   ———. f.t., "Musick." (1832–1854) [4]298 pp. 17 × 21 cm. inscribed, "Augustine W. Gordon" and "Susan Taylor Cty N H age 19 Born 1835." C,S; a,e,g,h,ls. NHCo, V289.8/S5275.

CB–37   ———. f.l., "O my God remember me." (1861–1863) 180 pp. 25 × 17 cm. inscribed, "Zieget 1957 From Sister Marguerite Frost." S; e,h. PMA, 63–160–203.

CB–38 ———. f.t., "Oh the Lord my God hath called me." (1911–1926) [6]131[33] pp. 17 × 10 cm. R; e. NHCb.

CB–39 ———. f.t., "Profession is vain." (1860–1862) [4]288[2] pp. 18 × 11 cm. S; e,h,ls. NYOCC.

CB–40 ———. f.t., "Renew'd Courage." (1856–1857) 88 pp. 20 × 16 cm. inscribed, "Eliza R. Smith Canterbury, N. H. 1856." S; e,ls. MeSL.

CB–41 ———. "Sacred and Divine Songs Selected and Written in the Second Family, Canterbury N. H." (1857–1861) [16 cont]286[5] pp. 29 × 23 cm. inscribed, "Arvilla Morrison Canterbury." S; e,g,h,ls. MeSL.

CB–42 ———. cover, "Sacred Hymns. Eldress Mary." (1912–1915) 72[48] pp. 21 × 18 cm. R; e. NHCb.

CB–43 ———. "A Sacred Repository of Songs and Anthems For Devotional Worship...." (1854–1857) [2]246[4 cont] pp. 21 × 17 cm. S; a,e,g,h,ls. MeSL.

CB–44 ———. f.t., "The Saviour's Voice." (ca. 1847–1866) [8]180[14 cont] pp. 21 × 13 cm. inscribed, "Martha Crooker. Canterbury N. H." S; h. NHCbT.

CB–45 ———. f.l., "Tho' but the sparrow's portion." (1880?) [5]68[127]2[10] pp. 18 × 27 cm. R; e,h. MeSL.

CB–46 ———. f.l., "Watching and praying." (1883–1889) [4]154[2] pp. 20 × 14 cm. inscribed, "Eliza R. Smith." S; e. MeSL.

ENFIELD, CONNECTICUT

EC–1 [Copley, J. W.] f.t., "The Invincible Band." (1856–ca. 1870) [22 cont] 102[116] pp. 19 × 13 cm. p. 22, "This book belongs to J. W. Copley and was begun by him On the 9th day of March 1856." S; h. OCWR, SM112.

EC–2 [Haskell, Russel.] f.t., "Archer's Cry." (1848–1850) [4]217[3] pp. 17 × 22 cm. inscribed, "No. 3, or third book. Recorded by Russell Haskell Enfield Conn. Commenced in 1848." S; a,e,g,h,ls. OCWR, SM351.

EC–3 ———. f.l., "Arise, and thresh, O children of Zion." (1847–1850) [4]57[107] pp. 23 × 14 cm. inscribed, "Lizzie Hebrank." S; a,e,h,ls. OCWR, SM356.

EC–4 ———. f.l., "Behold the lovely shining band of valiant volunteers." (1848) 32 pp. 19 × 16 cm. S; e. OCWR, SM237.

EC–5 ———. f.l., "Blessings for the faithful are descending freely." (1841–1842, 1898) [2]95[95] pp. 13 × 23 cm. S,R; a,e,g,ls. OCWR, SM355.

EC–6 ———. f.t., "Christ's Sufferings." (1850s) 67[18]16[26]60 pp. 19 × 13 cm. S; a,h. WLCM, M/2131/.S4E5.

EC–7 ———. f.t., "Firmness under Trials." (1855) [4]26[106] pp. 14 × 21 cm. S; e,h. NYPLMs, 66–M–13, vol. 118.

EC–8 ———. f.l., "Here I am Lord thou calledest me." (1868–1874) [2]201[41] pp. 17 × 21 cm. inscribed, "Commenced writing in this book, Sabbath, Oct. 4th, 1868." S,H; e,h,ls. WLCM, M/2131/.S4E5.

EC–9 ———. f.t., "Mansion of Peace." (1852–1865) [4]216[4] pp. 25 × 18 cm. inscribed, "Recorded by Russel Haskell of Enfield Conn Commenced 1852 No 4, or fourth book." S; e,h,ls. OCWR, SM330.

EC–10 ———. f.l., "O Holy Mother Wisdom Holy Wisdom." (1850–1859) [2]234 [36 cont] pp. 17 × 21 cm. S; e. DWt, SA1139.

EC–11 ———. "A Record of Spiritual Songs: Including the principal part of those which have been sung and retained either by individuals or by the Church at large, in this branch of the United Society, from the time of the first preaching of the gospel in this place, in 1781, until the year 1850: in XII Parts. Compiled by Leading Singers and Lovers of Heavenly Devotion in the Church . . . Enfield, Conn., 1845." (1845–1870s) [40]600 pp. 24 × 34 cm. S,H; a,e,fp,g,h,ls,ss. WLCM, M/2131/.S4E5.

EC–12 ———. f.l., "So boundless is the work." (1871) 136 pp. 19 × 12 cm. inscribed, "Scrap Book. These Songs were received in various Societies, mostly between the years 1862–68 copied by a member of Enfield Conn. a very good collection Only find two in book that have been printed. m. c. a." S,H; e. OCWR, SM345.

EC–13 ———. f.l., "Tho life's morn rose bright and cloudless." (1873–1875) [2]96 pp. 20 × 13 cm. H; e,h. NYLC.

EC–14 Lyman, Amelia. "Amelia Lyman's Book Commenced Nov. 18 1855." (1855) [5]129[2] pp. 21 × 14 cm. cover, "Enfield Conn." S; e,h. OCWR, SM231.

EC–15 Mumford, Harriet Jane. "Harriet Jane Mumford's Book Began Feb 18th 1860." [4]28[190] pp. 19 × 13 cm. S; misc. NYAM, no. 2283.

EC–16 Anon., f.t., "Gathering the Sheep." (1843) 13[31] pp. 29 × 24 cm. S; a. OCWR, SM271.

EC–17 ———. f.t., "Happy Change." (–?–) 28 pp. 21 × 17 cm. cover, "The property of Aaron Clapp." inscribed, "Miscellaneous Collection of Very Old Shaker Hyms & songs much used in Enfield Conn, seventy years since." S; e,h. OCWR, SM333.

EC–18 ———. f.l., "Lift up your heads ye righteous." (1849–1868) [4]240[2] pp. 17 × 21 cm. S; h. OCWR, SM209.

EC–19 ———. f.t., "Mother's voice." (1850–1856) [6]100[6] pp. 18 × 12 cm. S; e,h. DWt, SA1181.

EC–20 ———. f.l., "My soul does rejoice that I have been called." (1857–1873) [3]185[70] pp. 18 × 22 cm. S,H; a,e. OCWR, SM208.

EC–21 ———. f.t., "Our Days on Earth." (1835–1860) [6]236[22] pp. 18 × 13 cm. inscribed, "These hymns were copied by a Sister of Enfield Conn. They were given at various periods from 1835 to 1860." S; h. OCWR, SM82.

EC–22 ———. f.t., "Solemn Covenant." (1849–1856) [26]160[24] pp. 21 × 15 cm. S; a,e,h,ls. OCWR, SM156.

EC–23 ———. f.t., "A Song Rapped out at stratford Ct. by S. Y. W." (1849–1850?) 35[9] pp. 19 × 13 cm. S; e,g,ls. MeSL.

EC–24 ———. f.l., "These things, saith the son of God." (ca. 1822) 65[21] pp. 10 × 26 cm. inscribed, "Enfield, Conn. These anthems were written before the time of letteral notes & must be among the earliest made use of by Shakers." P; a. WLCM, M/2131/.S4E5.

EC–25 ———. [wordless tune dated "Jan 22 1838."] (1838–1841) [4]132[4] pp. 22 × 28 cm. S; a,e,g,h,ls. OCWR, SM272.

ENFIELD, NEW HAMPSHIRE

ENH–1 [Cummings, Rosetta.] "A Collection of Miscellaneous Songs, Benedictions, Valedictions, And School Songs Collected in the Church, Enfield N. H. . . . 1859." (1859–1870s) [1]129[20] pp. 14 × 15 cm. inscribed, "#241 H. C. B. Rosetta Cummings." Contains a three-page biography of Rosetta Cummings. S,R; e,h. NYOC, Ac. 12,762.

ENH–2   Perkins, Abraham. "A Collection of Noted Songs. Written by Abm. Perkins, Enfield 1832." (1832–1839) [2]86 pp. 12 × 20 cm. C,S; ls. MWW, 61/C68a.

ENH–3   [Randlett, Timothy.] "A present from Timothy Randlett to Mathew van Deuson April 25th 1852." (1851–1852) 70 pp. 15 × 9 cm. S; e,g. OCWR, SM123.

ENH–4   Russel, James G., "A Gradual Series of Lessons in the Science of Music. Exercises selected from a variety of Authors. Arranged for the School in Enfield N. H. by James G. Russel." (1868) 72[2] pp. 18 × 16 cm. inscribed, "Rosetta Cummings. Enfield N. H. Mar. 1868." S,R; exercises. OCWR, SM500.

ENH–5   Anon. "A Collection of Spiritual Songs. Received in the Church at Chosen Vale. Written for Brother Otis Sawyer . . . 1851." (1851) 30 pp. 17 × 10 cm. S; e,g,h,ls. MeSL.

ENH–6   ———. f.t., "Farewell Blessing of our Heavenly Parents." (1842–1843) [4]222[4] pp. 20 × 13 cm. p. [2], "Book commenced December 8th 1842." S; a,e,g. MWW, 61/H99/vol. 7.

ENH–7   ———. f.t., "The Harvest Day" (1850s) [4]47[53] pp. 16 × 10 cm. S; a,h. NHCbT.

ENH–8   ———. f.l., ". . . holy praises to your blest redeemer." (1844–1846) 269[8] pp. (many pages missing) 20 × 17 cm. S; e,g,h,ls. NHLC.

ENH–9   ———. f.t., "New Year's Reflection." (1860–1862) [3]191 pp. 18 × 17 cm. inscribed, "Mary Maria Basford." S; e,h. NYPLMs, 61–M–36, vol. 55.

ENH–10   ———. f.t., "Union Band." (1833–1844) [3]270[13 cont] pp. 17 × 13 cm. S; a,e,g,h. MHF.

ENH–11   ———. f.t., "A Valient Worrior." (1843–1845) [4]331[35 cont] pp. 20 × 17 cm. S; a,e,g,h,ls. NYBG, RBR/Shakers/M2.

ENH–12   ———. f.l., "Who shall stand on Zion's height." (1869–1870) [4]166[8] pp. 18 × 22 cm. inscribed, "Rosetta Cumings Enfield N H 1869." S; a,e. NYOC, Ac. 12,769.

ENH–13   ———. f.t., "Word of the Lord to Zion." (ca. 1880) [2]234 pp. 20 × 13 cm. S,R; e,h. NYOC, Ac. 12,763.

GLOUCESTER, MAINE

GME–1   Sawyer, Otis. "A Collection of Sacred and Divine Songs, most of which were received in vision by inspiration or revelation, and which have been sung 'with the spirit and the understanding also.' Book I. Commenced November 1842." (1842–1845) [6]148[2] pp. 22 × 17 cm. inscribed, "Otis Sawyer's Song Book The first of the kind ever written either at Alfred or New Gloucester." S; a,e,g,ls. MeSL.

GME–2   ———. "Otis Sawyer's Song Book. Commenced Aug 4th 1871." (1871–1876) [6]128[7]43[5] pp. 20 × 14 cm. S; e,h. MeSL.

GME–3   ———. f.t., "Soliloquy." (1844–1849) [4]459[9] pp. 21 × 17 cm. printed label, "Complete Library of Publications by the United Society. No. 70 For Special Reference Otis Sawyer. New Gloucester, Dec 1882." S; a,e,fp,g,h,ls,ss. MeSL.

GME–4   ———. f.t., "Wrestle for the Blessing." (1868–1871) [6]235[13] pp. 21 × 14 cm. last written leaf, "The Writer has recorded in this book Sixty little chants which the Angels and good spirits kindly breathed through his imperfect organs of vocal music, for which I here return my humblest thanks. Otis Sawyer." S; a,e,h. MeSL.

GME–5   Anon. f.l., "All crosses and trials I will bear." (1887–1891) 216[2] pp. 20 × 14 cm. S; e,h. MeSL.

GME–6   ———. f.t., "The Covenant of the Lord." (1844–1851) [6]471[7] pp. 21 × 17 cm. inscribed, "The Property of Aurelia G. Mace, West Gloucester. Dec. 30. 1888." S; a,e,fp,g,h,ls,ss. MeSL.

GME–7   ———. f.t., "Hail Glorious Morn." (1871–1888) [4]228[90 cont] pp. 29 × 24 cm. S; e,g,ls. MeSL.

GME–8   ———. f.t., "Heaven's Portals." (1860–1864) [6]74[152] pp. 20 × 13 cm. S; e,g,h,ls. MeSL.

GME–9   ———. f.t., "Heaven's Portals." (1865–1881) [6]61[146] pp. 20 × 14 cm. S; e,h. MeSL.

GME–10   ———. f.l., "I have something good I will tell you." (1859–1868) [4]76[160] pp. 21 × 18 cm. S; e,h. MeSL.

GME–11   ———. f.l., ". . . In thy deep water." (ca. 1874–1880) [6]188[4] pp. 20 × 13 cm. inscribed, "Annie June 17 1895. Sabbathday Lake, Maine." S; e. MeSL.

GME–12   ———. f.l., "March on march on." (ca. 1830) [8]212 pp. 8 × 16 cm. p. [viii], "Martha Thurlow's Song Book. Property of Aurelia G. Mace. West Gloucester, Maine. Dec. 30, 1900." and "E. M. P. 1932." C,S; e,h. MeSL.

GME–13   ———. f.t., "Peace Ye Raging Tempest." (1860–1870) [1]307[cont] pp. 21 × 18 cm. S; e. MeSL.

GME–14   ———. f.t., "A Prayer." (1892) [2]77[87] pp. 20 × 14 cm. S; e. MeSL.

GME–15   ———. f.t., "Prayer for Zion." (1861–1891) [4]254[2] pp. 17 × 12 cm. S; e. MeSL.

GME–16   ———. f.t., "A Short Roll." (1848–1888) [2]222 pp. 22 × 18 cm. inscribed, "Ada Cummings." S; g,h,ls. MeSL.

GME–17   ———. f.l., "Sow the seeds of purity." (after 1887) [2]24[34] pp. 20 × 17 cm. S; e. MeSL.

GME–18   ———. f.l., "Sow the seeds of purity." (1887–1891) [2]216 pp. 20 × 14 cm. inscribed, "Georgiana Blake. April 15th 1887. Gloucester Maine." S; e. MeSL.

GME–19   ———. f.t., "True Thankfulness." (ca. 1850?–1890) 200 pp. 20 × 13 cm. S; e. MeSL.

GROVELAND, NEW YORK

GNY–1   Cutler, Sarah. "Expressions of Praise In Songs and Anthems Written by Sarah Cutler." (1869–1872) [2]104[124] pp. 20 × 14 cm. rear, "Sarah Cutler Sonyea Livingston County." S; e. DWt, SA1150.

GNY–2   DeGraw, Emeline. "A Book of Divine Hymns Sung in our Sacred Worship. Written by Emeline DeGraw Groveland 1858." (1858–1864) [2]212[4] pp. 19 × 13 cm. S; h. MCB.

GNY–3   Dole, Laura. "A Choice Selection of Sacred Hymns Sung by Believers in Christ's Second Appearing By Laura Dole Groveland 1860." (1860) [14 cont]382 [8 cont] pp. 18 × 12 cm. S; h. OCWR, SM37.

GNY–4   ———. "A Collection of Millennial Hymns Adapted To the present order, of the Church . . . Laura Dole Groveland Apr 18th 1864." (1864) [6]34[182] pp. 19 × 13 cm. S; h. NYAL, CM10243(10).

GNY–5   Dole, Sophronia. "A Book of Sacred Songs. Suitable for divine worship. Collected and written with care, for the purpose of retaining them. Sophronia Dole. Groveland, Oct. 1846." (1846–1864) [14 cont]230(82–114 blank)[4] pp. 17 × 11 cm. S; a,e,g,h,ls. MCB.

GNY–6   Love, Ann Maria. "A Book of Divine Songs Composed by Members of this Society While Residing at Sodus Bay; and since their Removal to Groveland. (Those Originated at Sodus will have the Name attached.) By Ann Maria Love Groveland 1858." (1858–1864) [8]55[61] pp. 20 × 17 cm. S; e,g. OCWR, SM340.

GNY–7   ———. "A Collection of Various Songs, Composed by Ann Maria Love. Commenced in the 7th year of Her Age 1842 And by *Her* herein Transcribed in the 21st year of Her Age, In the Town of Groveland, Livingston Co. New York State, In the year 1855." (1849–1856) [2]62 pp. 21 × 16 cm. S; h. OCWR, SM423.

GNY–8   Thompson, Gabriel. "A Choice Collection of Sacred Holy & Divine Songs And Hymns Improved by the Believers in the solemn & Devotional Worship of God . . . Writtin by Gabriel Thompson. June 1st 1854." (1854–1860) [12 cont]171[129] pp. 17 × 11 cm. S; h. NYAL, CM10243(6).

GNY–9   ———. "A Choice Collection of Sacred Holy & Divine Songs. Improved by the Believers in Christ's Second Appearing . . . Transcribed by Gabriel Thompson March '52 A. D. Groveland, N. Y." (1852–1853) [6 cont]276 pp. 18 × 12 cm. S; e,g,h. OCWR, SM83.

GNY–10   Anon. f.l., "Illumed is our pathway." (1865–1876) [10]166[70] pp. 18 × 13 cm. inscribed, "Lydia Dole, Groveland." S; e. NYAL, CM10243(8).

GNY–11   ———. f.l., "Lovely Souls be awake." (1865–1878) [14]189[19 cont] pp. 18 × 12 cm. inscribed "Henry G. Cantrell." S; e,ls. MeSL.

GNY–12   ———. f.l., "O Lord of wisdom strength and power." (ca. 1847) [10 cont]106 pp. 18 × 12 cm. inscribed, "Justin Budine." S; h. OCWR, SM173.

GNY–13   ———. "Polly C. Lewis. New Lebanon, 1851. Alice Spooner Groveland, 1870." (1857–1860) [16 cont]33[367] pp. 20 × 13 cm. inscribed, "Louise Russell." S; e,h. NYAL, CM10243(5).

GNY–14   ———. f.t., "Truth an Anchor." (1852–1857) [4]97[49 cont] pp. 20 × 17 cm. S; e. OCWR, SM362.

HANCOCK, MASSACHUSETTS

HN–1   Augur, Mary Ann. "Mary Ann Augur's Book Written In the year 1859." (1859) [8]124[20] pp. 20 × 18 cm. S; a. OCWR, SM338.

HN–2   Anon. f.t., "All Glean with Care." (1850–1857) [2]191[31] pp. 20 × 13 cm. inscribed, "Malida Eldridge West Pittsfield." S; e,h,ls. CCA.

HN–3   ———. ". . . Book. West. Pittsfield Mass Written in 1859." (1859) [14]126[2] pp. 20 × 17 cm. S; e,h,ls. NYOC, Ac. 13,578.

HN–4   ———. f.t., "Funeral Hymn." (1844–1845) [8]107[3] pp. 18 × 12 cm. S; a,e,g,h,ls. DWt, SA1204.

HN–5   ———. [wordless tune, ascription, "G. T. H. Smith."] (by 1850) [4]85[21] pp. 15 × 24 cm. inscribed, "Mary Ransom." P; a,e,g,ls. WLCMs, no. 228.

HN–6   ———. f.l., "I wish you a happy New Year." (1867–1869) [8]112[62] pp. 20 × 14 cm. inscribed, "Emoretta Belden." S; e. DWt, SA1100.

HN–7   ———. [wordless tune, labeled "March."] (1850s–1870s) [2]130[2] pp.
            19 × 12 cm. inscribed, "Sarah E Smith March 21st 1850." S; e,ls. NYPLMs,
            65–M–93, vol. 70.

HN–8   ———. f.l., "O blessed Savior blessed Savior." (ca. 1850–1865) [12]200[2] pp.
            14 × 20 cm. S; h. DWt, SA1103.

HARVARD, MASSACHUSETTS

HD–1   Bathrick, Eunice. "A Collection of Hymns Adapted to the different ocasions or
            circumstances of Believers in Christs Second Appearing. 1850. Eunice Bathrick."
            (1850) [2]226 pp. 21 × 14 cm. S; h. MWW, 61/B32.

HD–2   ———. "A Collection of Songs Given by the Shepherdess through Different
            Instruments for Individuals dwelling in the Church & Second Family in Lovely
            Vinyard, Commencing in the year 1844, and Ending with the year 1847.
            Copied by Eunice Bathrick." (1844–1847) [12 cont]108 pp. 18 × 11 cm.
            S; e,g. MWW, 61/B32c.

HD–3   ———. "Hymns and Poems by Eunice Wyeth, Copied by Eunice Bathrick in
            1865." (1865) [6 cont]177[7 cont] pp. 23 × 13 cm. S; h. OCWR, SM11.

HD–4   ———. "Hymns & Poems Composed by Eunice Wythe of Harvard—Mass.
            Copied at Mt. Lebanon for Isaac N. Youngs." (–?–) [16]236[4] pp.
            18 × 11 cm. S; h. CNHY, Cupboard/Mx75/S4/En3.

HD–5   ———. "Hymns and Songs of Praise, Prayer and Thanksgiving By Eunice
            Wyeth. Copied by Eunice Bathrick in the Seventy-Second Year of her Age,
            1865." (1865) [20 cont]210 pp. 20 × 14 cm. S; h. OCWR, SM286.

HD–6   ———. "A Selection of some of the Sweet Songs of Zion, wherewith we praise
            the God of our Salvation. . . ." (1851–1863) [4]280 pp. 20 × 13 cm. note,
            p. 138, "The Following Hymns were composed by Eunice Wyeth; Copied
            by Eunice Bathrick in the year 1865." S; a,e,g,h. OCWR, SM77.

HD–7   ———. "Songs From the Shepherdess given thro Joanna Randall as Medium for
            the Elders Brethren and Sisters dwelling in Pleasant Garden 1844. Poems.
            Copied by Eunice Bathrick." (1844–1845) [10 cont]130 pp. 16 × 10 cm.
            S; e,g. MWW, 61/R15.

HD–8   Blanchard, Louisa B. f.t., "Wisdom." (1855) [6 cont]124 pp. 20 × 16 cm.
            inscribed, "Louisa B. Blanchard. Harvard. Mass. Commenced Jan 1st 1855.
            Finished July 10th 1855." S; a,h. OCWR, SM158.

HD–9   Chandler, Olive F. "Hymns Songs & Anthems Written For the Use of Zion's
            Children By Margaret McGooden Harvard Chh. 1851." (1860–1873)
            256[cont] pp. 21 × 13 cm. pasted on title page, "Written by Olive F. Chandler.
            Presented by Margaret McGooden to Olive F. Chandler as a keepsake just
            before she departed August 3d 1860." S; e,g,h. MHF.

HD–10   Clark, Lucy. "Lucy Clark's Book." (1828–1839) 304[4] pp. 19 × 12 cm. C,S;
            a,e,g,h. MWW, 61/H99/vol. 1.

HD–11   Foster, Maria. "A Collection of Songs Hymns & Anthems. Written by Maria
            Foster Harvard Church." (1850–?) [8 cont]237[33] pp. 19 × 13 cm. S;
            a,e,h. MHF.

HD–12   Hall, Betsy M. "A Collection of Various Kinds of songs given for the Use of
            Mother's Children Compiled and Written by Betsy M Hall Harvard Jany 5th
            1845." (1845–1870) [6 cont]69[88]23 pp. 21 × 18 cm. S; a,e,g,h. MHF.

HD–13 ————. f.l., "I will be more obedient." (1839–1852) [4]112[15]31[4] pp. 20 × 16 cm. label, "Betsey. Martha. Hall." S; a,e,g,ls. MHF.

HD–14 Hammond, Thomas. f.t., "Consecration—Give me thy heart." (1862–1869) [4]194[10 cont] pp. 18 × 11 cm. inscribed, "Thomas Hammond, Shaker Society Harvard Mass." S; e,h,ls. OCWR, SM18.

HD–15 ————. f.t., "Marches, Watervliet 2d Order." (ca. 1828–1835) [4]136 pp. 9 × 20 cm. C,S; a,e,ls. OCWR, SM270.

HD–16 ————. f.t., "Millennial Church." (1853) 296 pp. [An historical record of Harvard, with many songs scattered through it; preface signed by Thomas Hammond, July 2nd 1853.] MWA.

HD–17 ————. f.t., "961 'O my soul rejoice in love." (1834–1849) [4]100 pp. 22 × 18 cm. inscribed, "Book 9th Thomas Hammond Harvard." S; a,e. MHF.

HD–18 ————. f.l., "The rolling deep may overturn." (1826–1839) [4]215[3] pp. 10 × 20 cm. C,S; e,g,ls. MeSL.

HD–19 ————. f.t., "Victorious Love." (ca. 1828–1835) 166[4 cont] pp. 19 × 12 cm. inscribed, "Book 11th Thomas Hammond Harvard." C,S; a,e,h. OCWR, SM164.

HD–20 Loomis, Sally. [first song, wordless tune marked "Harvard."] (1825–1828) [2 cont]190[2 cont] pp. 15 × 24 cm. C; a,ls. OCWR, SM275.

HD–21 McGooden, Margaret. f.t., "Wisdom." (1855) [6 cont]222 pp. 20 × 13 cm. inscribed, "Harvard Mass. June 30, 1855" and "Br. Newcome Green. South Family." S; a,h. MHF.

HD–22 ————. f.t., "Wisdom." (1855) [6 cont]222 pp. 20 × 13 cm. inscribed, "Margaret McGooden Harvard. March 1855" and "Finished this book June 17th 1855." S; a,e,h. MHF.

HD–23 Orsment, Nancy. f.t., "Holy Mothers Cord of Love." (1851–1871) [4]252 [12 cont] pp. 21 × 14 cm. p. [iii], "Nancy Orsment Commenced writing this Book in 1851." S; e,h. OCWR, SM196.

HD–24 ————. "Nancy Orsments Book Commenced writing. 1845 South Family Harvard." (1845–1851) [4]195[9 cont] pp. 21 × 14 cm. S; h. OCWR, SM335.

HD–25 Tenny, Moses. "Moses Tenny's Note Book. Commenced Learning to Sing by note January 18th 1833. Harvard Mass." (1833–?) 44 pp. 16 × 20 cm. S; h,ls. MHF.

HD–26 Walker, Annie L. f.l., "The windows of heaven are open." (1878–1880) [4]186 [2] pp. 17 × 11 cm. inscribed, "Presented by Elder John Cloutman to Annie L. Walker Jan. 9th 1878 Commenced writing Feb. 17th." S; e. NYOC, Ac. 8895.

HD–27 Anon. f.t., "Angels Declaration." (1851) [9]3[94] pp. 17 × 21 cm. S; a,h. MWW, 61/H99b.

HD–28 ————. f.t., "The Angels Thanksgiving." (1843–1844) [4]287[1] pp. 20 × 13 cm. S; a,e,g. MWW, 61/H99/vol. 4.

HD–29 ————. f.t., "A Anthem Received from Isaac Watts. 1840." (1841–1856) [4]104[60] pp. 20 × 16 cm. S; a,e,g,h,ss. MWW, 61/H99/vol. 6.

HD–30 ————. f.t., "Beams of Glory." (1848–1861) [12]85[129] pp. 20 × 13 cm. S; e,h. OCWR, SM76.

HD–31 ————. f.t., "Beams of Glory." (1856–1871) [14]108[90] pp. 20 × 13 cm. S; e,h. OCWR, SM75.

HD–32   ———. f.t., "Beams of Glory." (1856–1868) [12 cont]198 pp. 20 × 13 cm. S; h. MHF.

HD–33   ———. f.t., "The Beauty of Zion." (ca. 1835–1854) [10 cont]142 pp. 12 × 19 cm. S; h. MWW, 61/H98/vol. 4.

HD–34   ———. f.t., "Blest Creator." (1840s–1860s) [10 cont]206 pp. 21 × 14 cm. inscribed, "Catherine Hall." S; e,g,h. MHF.

HD–35   ———. f.t., "City of Light." (1873–1886) 188 pp. 20 × 14 cm. S; h. OCWR, SM74.

HD–36   ———. "A Collection of Song's Anthem's & Hymn's For Mother's Children South Family Harvard Shaker's Mass. L. M. H." (1850s) 288[6] pp. 21 × 13 cm. S; e. MWW, 61/H98/vol. 3.

HD–37   ———. f.l., "Come Zion's children praise your king." (1830s) 150 pp. 21 × 12 cm. S; h. NYOC, Ac. 4132.

HD–38   ———. f.t., "Earthly Joys." (1855–1863) [8 cont]140 pp. 17 × 11 cm. S; e,h. NCA.

HD–39   ———. f.t., "Eternal Praises." (1843–1846) [14 cont]244[52] pp. 20 × 13 cm. S; a,e,g,h,ls. NYHS.

HD–40   ———. f.t., "Fellow Travellers." (1836–1842) [7 cont]196[1] pp. 19 × 12 cm. S; h. MWW, 61/H99/vol. 2.

HD–41   ———. f.l., "Give me the treasure that cannot be sold." (1870s–1887) 263[73] pp. 18 × 11 cm. S; h. OCWR, SM6.

HD–42   ———. f.t., "Harvest Reward." (?–1868) [6]106[14] pp. 21 × 13 cm. S; h. MHF.

HD–43   ———. f.t., "Hour of Prayer." (1855–1856) 194 pp. 21 × 14 cm. inscribed, "N L Fairbanks." S; e,h. MHF.

HD–44   ———. f.t., "A Hymn." (1843–1846) [16 cont]269[3] pp. 20 × 13 cm. S; a,h. OCWR, SM407.

HD–45   ———. f.t., "A Hymn of Praise." (1820s) 175[11 cont] pp. 20 × 12 cm. C; h. MHF.

HD–46   ———. f.t., "Hymn on Truth." (ca. 1834) 160[14 cont] pp. 18 × 19 cm. S; h. OCWR, SM165.

HD–47   ———. f.t., "Lines by W. L. for Mother's Birthday 1855." (1855–1879) [6]127[63] pp. 18 × 11 cm. S; e,h. NYOC, Ac. 4129.

HD–48   ———. f.l., "Now we're ready for our march." (1840–1844) 96 pp. 21 × 12 cm. [first leaf cropped from an older MS of solemn songs.] S; e. MHF.

HD–49   ———. f.l., "O Sing unto the Lord a new Song." (1854–1860) [12 cont]212 [8 cont] pp. 20 × 13 cm. S; e,h,ls. MHF.

HD–50   ———. f.l., "O what are the heavens telling." (1883–1885) [2]182[2] pp. 17 × 11 cm. S; e. MeSL.

HD–51   ———. f.t., "An offering of Thanksgiving & Praise." (1841–1842) 296 pp. 20 × 13 cm. S; a,e,g,ls. MWW, 61/H99/vol. 5.

HD–52   ———. f.l., "Only just across the river." (1860s–?) [28]216 pp. 20 × 13 cm. S; e,h. MHF.

HD–53   ———. f.t., "Paradise of God." (1834–1840s) [10]203[9] pp. 18 × 11 cm. inscribed, "W. A. Cunningham." S; a,h. MWW, 61/H99/vol. 3.

HD–54   ———. f.t., "A Poem." (ca. 1844) [4]90[50] pp. 15 × 10 cm. S; e,g. MWW, 61/H99li.

HD–55   ———. f.t., "Pure Love." (1839–1841) 286 pp. 14 × 18 cm. S; a,e,g,ls. MHF.

HD–56 ———. f.t., "Shining Band." (1841–1843) [7]118[21] pp. 22 × 17 cm. S; e,g,ls. MHF.

HD–57 ———. f.l., "A soft sweet voice from Zion stealing." (1879–1889) 82[94] pp. 20 × 13 cm. S; a,e,g,h. OCWR, SM160.

HD–58 ———. f.t., "Voyage of Mother Ann Lee." (1844–?) [2]33[131] pp. 16 × 14 cm. S; h. MHF.

LEBANON, NEW YORK

L–1 Allen, M. Catherine. "Inspirational Songs of Praise. Copied by M. Catherine Allen Mount Lebanon." (1889–1894) [20]83[78]39 pp. 18 × 28 cm. R; e,h. OCWR, SM273.

L–2 ———. f.l., "The Messiah has come Alleluiah we'll sing." (1861–1863) [2]98[2] pp. 20 × 14 cm. inscribed, "M. Catherine Allen Mount Lebanon N. Y. Begun in 1861, finished 1863. The greater part of the songs in this book originated in Mount Lebanon N. Y." S; e,h. OCWR, SM369.

L–3 Anderson, Martha J. "Sacred Songs." (1876–1880) [2]290 pp. 20 × 14 cm. inscribed, "Martha J. Anderson." S; e. MiAU, RBR/M/2131/.S4/1876.

L–4 ———. f.t., "Songs." (1867–1871) [2]210[8 cont] pp. 19 × 13 cm. S; e,h. MWW, 61/H99/vol. 8.

L–5 Anderson, William. "Wm Andersons' Book. December 1876." (1876–1878) [2]67[237] pp. 27 × 21 cm. R; e. NYOC, Ac. 7202.

L–6 Avery, Elizabeth R. "A Collection of Hymns, And Spiritual Songs. Improved in our general Worship, June 22, 1830. Elizabeth R. Avery." (1830–1888) [12 cont]172 pp. 15 × 10 cm. inscribed, "Louisa Crocker." S; a,e,g,h. OCWR, SM310.

L–7 ———. "A Collection of Spiritual Anthems; Given by Inspiration; As Rewards & Encouragements For Mother's faithful children . . . Written by Eliza Avery. Janry 11th 1840." (1840–1842) [6 cont]272 pp. 14 × 17 cm. penciled on title page, "and Rhoda Blake." S; a. OCWR, SM66.

L–8 ———. "A Collection of the Songs of Zion. Penned by Eliza R. Avery. 1842." (1843–1848) 187[7] pp. 17 × 11 cm. S; e,g. OCWR, SM136.

L–9 ———. "A Treasury of Heavenly Songs. Written by Elizabeth R Avery. 1848." (1848–1876) [2]266[88] pp. 18 × 11 cm. S; e,g,h,ls. OCWR, SM294.

L–10 Avery, Giles B. "Anthems Being a Collection of nearly all, given since the beginning, With the Tunes affixed. Collected, and Transcribed by Giles B. Avery." (1869?) [6 cont]156[64] pp. 14 × 21 cm. S; a. OCWR, SM55.

L–11 ———. "Anthems Given by Inspiration to the Children of Zion. Collected & Transcribed by Giles B. Avery." (1841–1843) [8 cont]228 pp. 14 × 13 cm. S; a. OCWR, SM59.

L–12 ———. "A collection of Anthems sent to Individuals as a Particular notice from the Spiritual World, also many others. All given by Inspiration. Commenced Jan. 8 1840." (1840–1841) [6 cont]128 pp. 17 × 13 cm. S; a,g. OCWR, SM260.

L–13 ———. "A Collection of Hymns, and Spiritual Songs, Improved in our general Worship. New Lebanon November 16 1828." (1828–1844) [10 cont]134 pp. 19 × 12 cm. penciled on title page, "Giles B. Avery"; flyleaf, "Hymbook No. 1 From 1828." S; e,h. OCWR, SM114.

L–14 ———. "A collection of Verses anthems & tunes &c &c of almost any description.

Written by Giles B. Avery." (ca. 1835–1836) 330 pp. 12 × 11 cm. S,P; e,g. OCWR, SM68.

L–15   ———. f.t., "Gospel Beauty." (1834–1837) [8 cont]248 pp. 17 × 12 cm. inscribed, "Giles B. Avery New Lebanon—N Y." and "Hyms used in the Church from 1830 to 1860." S; h,ls. OCWR, SM139.

L–16   ———. f.t., "March Tunes. A vision or dream of Mother Ann's Song. by Amos Hildreth." (1830?–1846) [6]151[141] pp. 8 × 21 cm. note pasted in rear, "Eld. Giles' Tune Book—Marches, quick dances, Round dance, Shuffling tunes, or Square Order. Slow marches & stand still songs—sung to one syllable, between lo & la. . . ." S,P; g,ls. WLCMs, no. 190.

L–17   ———. f.t., "Zion's Consolation." (1856) 297[1] pp. 17 × 12 cm. inscribed, "Transcribed by Elder Giles B. Avery before leaving 2nd Order to be one of the central Ministry of which he was a member for more than 30 years." S; h. OCWR, SM296.

L–18   Barrett, Andrew. f.l., "Arise arise be of good cheer." (1867–1868) [6]226 [20 cont] pp. 18 × 13 cm. S; e,g,ls. DWt, SA1149.

L–19   ———. "A Collection of Songs used in our General Worship . . . Commenced June 10, 1904 Andrew D Barrett." (1904) 134[110 cont] pp. 25 × 20 cm. S; e,h. OCWR, SM194.

L–20   ———. f.l., "Now forward Israel hasten." (1855–1856) 87[85] pp. 13 × 9 cm. inscribed, "These songs are Andrew Barrett's writing in his young manhood. Later Sister Rhoda Blake wrote the pencilings. After she past on, it came into my hands. A. H." S; e. OCWR, SM426.

L–21   Bates, Betsey. "A Collection of Extra Or Slow Songs, Sung by The Believers. To express emotions of prayer, praise And feelings of Devotion in the Worship of God. Eldress Betsey Bates. Commenced January 2nd 1859." (1859–1865) [8]208 pp. 18 × 13 cm. S; e,h. OCWR, SM289.

L–22   Bates, Elizaette. "A Collection of Anthems Adapted to the Worship of Believers in the Manifestation of Christ's Second Appearing." (ca. 1863) [22 cont]400 pp. 14 × 18 cm. inscribed, "This Book was written by Elizaette Bates." S; a. OCWR, SM257.

L–23   Bates, Sarah. "A Collection of Hymns and Extra Songs. Written in New Lebanon. By Sarah Bates. Begun in Novr 1850." (1850–1869) 180[106 cont] pp. 17 × 11 cm. S; e,g,h. OCWR, SM16.

L–24   ———. "A Collection of Marching Songs &c. Written by Sarah Bates New Lebanon 1849." (1849–1852) [4]190[2] pp. 17 × 11 cm. S; e,ls. OCWR, SM414.

L–25   ———. "A Collection of Marching Songs &c. Written by Sarah Bates New Lebanon 1858. Begun in January." (1858–1864) 241[75] pp. 17 × 11 cm. S; e. MPBA, V/289.8/Un3.3/vol. 18.

L–26   ———. f.t., "Holy Jubilee." (1839–1863) [8 cont]250 pp. 19 × 14 cm. inscribed, "Sarah Bates Church Family Mt. Lebanon. They have been gathered from different Societies and were given at various periods from 1814 to 1859." S; e,g. OCWR, SM247.

L–27   Bennett, Roby. "A Collection of Short Anthems & Marching tunes; Improved in the Sacred Worship, of the true followers of Christ. Began to be Written by R. Bt. at the close of 1843." (1843–1849) [18]161[17] pp. 17 × 11 cm. S; a,e,g,ls. OCWR, SM379.

L–28   ———. "A Collection of Spiritual Anthems Improved in Sacred Worship . . .

Transcribed by Roby Bennet. New Lebanon, N. Y. Beg' to be written March 14th 1840. Aged 42 Yrs." (1840–1846) [9 cont]255[4] pp. 16 × 16 cm. S; a,h. OCWR, SM183.

L–29   Bishop, James B. "The Infant Experience of James B. Bishop. Together With some Information, from other Authors, In Relation to our Blessed Mother, Ann Lee. Written By James B. Bishop. 1835." (1835) [4]14[6] pp. 13 × 10 cm. S; e,fp. OCWR, vi.A.6.

L–30   Blake, Hannah. "A Book Containing Songs of Praise, For the use of Mother's true Children, In Worshipful Devotion. New Lebanon Second Order, Hannah Blake, March 16th 1840." (1840–1842) [14 cont]144[4] pp. 14 × 17 cm. S; a,g. OCWR, SM431.

L–31   ———. "Holy & Divine Songs, Given for the Encouragement of Mother's Children on Earth. Transcribed By Hannah Blake. August 17th 1842." (1842–1845) [10]184[6] pp. 17 × 11 cm. S; e,g. OCWR, SM38.

L–32   ———. "In Songs of Adoration, Praise and Supplication, We unite our voices in the song That shall have no end; Selah! . . . Hannah Blake. April 1850." (1850–1853) [22 cont]372 pp. 13 × 14 cm. S; e. OCWR, SM61.

L–33   ———. "A Transcript of Beautiful Songs, Sent from the Abodes of the Redeemed In Heaven To the Saints On Earth, That they might Unite their Voices, in the Song That Shall have no End. Transcribed by Hannah Blake. Novbr 17th 1843." (1843–1847) 164 pp. 14 × 13 cm. S; a,g. OCWR, SM188.

L–34   Blake, Rhoda. "A Book of Anthems And songs; Improved by every Good believer. Written by Rhoda Blake." (ca. 1824–1840s) [4]49[43] pp. 9 × 19 cm. note on title page, "Begun perhaps in 1824 or 25 She was born Sept. 10th 1808, & became engaged to learn to write & read musical notes at the age of 15." P,R,S; a. OCWR, SM320.

L–35   ———. "A Collection of Anthems and Spiritual Songs Improved in the worship of believers . . . Began to be written January 1st 1840. Rhoda Blake." (1839–1843) [8 cont]288 pp. 17 × 11 cm. S; a,e,g. OCWR, SM218.

L–36   ———. "A Collection of Anthems, Given mostly by Inspiration; As rewards and encouragement, for Mother's true children; also for worship. . . . Transcribed by Rhoda Blake." (1842–1848) [9 cont]299 pp. 13 × 14 cm. S; a,h. OCWR, SM27.

L–37   ———. "A Collection of songs given Mostly By Inspiration. . . . Began to be written, May 28th 1843. Rhoda Blake." (1843–1845) [2]210 pp. 17 × 11 cm. S; e. OCWR, SM14.

L–38   ———. "A Collection of Spiritual Anthem's, Given mostly by Inspiration. Written by Rhoda Blake. March 1840." (1840–1846) [14 cont]364[4] pp. 16 × 20 cm. S; a,g. OCWR, SM325.

L–39   ———. "A Collection of Spiritual songs . . . Rhoda Blake. 1847." (1847–1852) [4]206 pp. 17 × 11 cm. S; e. OCWR, SM44.

L–40   ———. "A Collection of tunes Written Exclusively to Remember. The contents of this book are choice gems of the spirit; and Will ornament those who are Truly wise. R. B. Began to be written 1850." (1850–1857) 350 pp. 18 × 11 cm. S; a,e,g,h. OCWR, SM176.

L–41   Blow, Maria. "A Collection of Hymns, Many of Them Given by Immediate Inspiration Selected and Transcribed by Maria Blow 1847." (1847–1880s) [12 cont]344[4] pp. 17 × 11 cm. S; h. MiAU, BV/442/.B66.

L–42   Bowers, Grace. "Symphonies of Praise Copied by Grace Bowers Commencing

1883." (1883–1890) [4]152[2 cont] pp. 18 × 26 cm. R; e (piano settings). NYOC, Ac. 8801.

L–43   Brainard, DeWitt Clinton. ". . . Systematically arranged And Chirographically Compiled By DeWitt Clinton Brainard." (1849–1852) 427[25 cont] pp. 16 × 10 cm. S; e. MPH, 9775 Br.

L–44   Brown, John M. f.t., "Commemoration of the Birth of Christ." (1846–?) [4]244 pp. 15 × 10 cm. inscribed, "No. 2. John M. Brown New Lebanon N. F. August 30th 1846" and "Presented to Charles E. Greaves By J. M. B." S; h. NYOC, Ac. 13,480.

L–45   ———. "Millenial Praises, Containing A Collection of Gospel Hymns and Anthems. Transcribed by John M. Brown; commenced March 16th 1851. N. F., Holy Mount." (1851–1868) [4]269[193 cont] pp. 19 × 12 cm. S; h. MiAU, BV/442/.1851.

L–46   Burger, Martha Ann. "Spiritual Songs. Adapted to Believers Worship. Transcribed by. Martha Ann Burger. January 1875." (1875–?) 290 pp. 20 × 14 cm. S; e. PLC.

L–47   Burger, Sarah J. "A Collection of Spiritual Songs. Transcribed by Sarah J. Burger. January 1886." (1886–?) 20 × 13 cm. S; e. PLC.

L–48   Buzby, Ann. "A Collection of Hymns and Spiritual Songs Improved in the Worship of Believers New Lebanon September 26th 1832 Ann Buzby." (?–1832) 158[82] pp. 17 × 12 cm. S; h. MPH, 9775 Bu.

L–49   Crosman, Daniel. "Hymns & Anthems Written by Daniel Crosman. Commenced AD 1848." (1848–1876) [12 cont]254[94] pp. 17 × 11 cm. S; a,e,h. DWt, SA1134.

L–50   Curtiss, George W. "Anthems Mostly given by Inspiration, Designed for the worship of Believers, Written by George W. Curtiss. September 1841." (1841) 280 pp. 14 × 13 cm. S; a,g. OCWR, SM326.

L–51   ———. "A Collection of Hymns Improved in our sacred devotions. Written by George W. Curtiss began Mch 29th 1835." (1835–1846) [8 cont]87[153] pp. 21 × 13 cm. S; e,h. OCWR, SM277.

L–52   ———. f.t., "The rolling vi and the holy Cross." (1839–1843) 364 pp. 10 × 14 cm. inscribed, "This Book was owned or kept & written by George Curtiss for several years the leading singer in the 2nd Order of the Church." S; a,e,g,ls. OCWR, SM267.

L–53   ———. "A Song Book Anthems Such as are use In our Worship Wretten by George Curtiss Begone to be Wretten Jan. 12th 1840." (1840–1841) [16 cont]260 pp. 13 × 16 cm. S; a,g,h. OCWR, SM229.

L–54   DeWitt, Caty. "A Collection of Hymns and Spiritual Songs; Improved in our Worship—New Lebanon February 16th 1834 Caty DeWitt." (1834–1841) [6 cont]163[3 cont] pp. 17 × 11 cm. S; h. DWt, SA1112.

L–55   DeWitt, George. "George DeWitt. 1822." (ca. 1822) [6 cont]186[2 cont] pp. 17 × 10 cm. P,R; h. DWt, SA1109.

L–56   DeWitt, Henry. "A Choice Selection of Songs Of the best Quality Written by Henry DeWitt New Lebanon. Beginning Jany 1852." (1852) 148[20]44 pp. 13 × 11 cm. S; e,g. OCWR, SM28.

L–57   ———. "A Collection of Anthems Improved in our General Worship. Written and Pricked for the purpose of retaining them, By Henry DeWitt—AD— 1833." (1833) [2 cont]106[6] pp. 14 × 21 cm. S; a. OCWR, SM153.

L–58   ———. "A Collection of Anthems Improved in our General Worship: Written & pricked for the purpose of retaining them, by Henry DeWitt. Beginning Febr 8th 1840. New Lebanon Co Coy St. N. Y." (1840–1845) [11 cont] 303[2] pp. 15 × 13 cm. S; a. OCWR, SM56.

L–59   ———. "A Collection of Hymns, Improved in our Sacred Worship. Written by Henry DeWitt. New Lebanon—Columbia Coy—State N. Y." (1835–1851) [10 cont]184[2] pp. 18 × 12 cm. S; h. OCWR, SM295.

L–59.1   ———. "A Collection of Hymns Improved in our Sacred Worship. Written by Henry DeWitt. Beginning August 2nd 1852. New Lebanon Columbia Co. State N. Y. Peter H. Long's Hym Book Feb—1854." (1852–1862) [14]203[112] pp. 17 × 11 cm. S; h. NYAL, 355.

L–60   ———. "A Collection of Songs of various Kinds, Used for Singing, Extra Times in Meeting. Written by Henry DeWitt. Beginning September—1849." (1849–1854) 292 pp. 13 × 11 cm. S; e,g. OCWR, SM29.

L–61   ———. "A Collection of Songs of Various Kinds: Written and pricked for the purpose of Retaining them, by Henry DeWitt. New Lebanon Columbia Co. St. N. Y. Beginning AD 1837." (1837–1863) [26]302[292] pp. 20 × 12 cm. S; a,e,g,h,ls. DWt, SA1114.

L–62   Dixon, Mary. "A Collection of Hymns, Improved in the Sacred Worship of Believers in Christ's Second Appearing . . . Copied by Mary Dixon 1847." (1847–1870?) [14 cont]320[6] pp. 17 × 11 cm. S; h. DWt, SA1131.

L–63   Dow, Nancy. "Anthems of Joy And songs of thanksgiving Received from the bountiful stores of Heaven . . . Selected & Transcribed by Nancy Dow. September 7th 1842." (1842–1844) [12 cont]197[21] pp. 17 × 11 cm. S; a. OCWR, SM40.

L–64   Gates, Benjamin. "A Collection of songs of various kinds mostly received by Inspiration Written by Benjamin Gates Begining November 2nd 1839. Finished November 20th, 1840." (1839–1840) [10 cont]226 pp. 17 × 11 cm. S; a,e,g. NYOC, Ac. 12,322.

L–65   ———. "A Collection of Songs of various kinds. Mostly Received by Inspiration. Written by Benjamin Gates. Begining. December 15th 1840. Finished March 1st 1842." (1840–1842) [10 cont]366 pp. 16 × 10 cm. S; a,e,g,h. MPBA, V/289.8/Un3.3/vol. 17.

L–66   ———. "A Collection of Verses. Written & Pricked By Benjamin Gates. New Lebanon. 1836." (1836) [4]196 pp. 12 × 11 cm. S; e. OCWR, SM386.

L–67   Haskins, Orren N. "A Collection of Class and Extra Songs in general use In our Sacred Worship. Begun to be written 1848 By Orren N. Haskins." (1848–1851) [10 cont]332 pp. 17 × 11 cm. S; e. OCWR, SM13.

L–68   Hazard, Mary. "A Collection of Exercize Songs Written by Mary Hazard." (1867–1873) [4]98[112] pp. 18 × 12 cm. S; ls. NYOC, Ac. 8793.

L–69   ———. "A Collection of Extra Songs of Various Kinds Written and Pricked For the Purpose of Retaining them. by Mary Hazzard. Begining February 7th 1847." (1847–1856) [18]248[8] pp. 17 × 11 cm. S; e,fp,g,ls. DWt, SA1132.

L–70   ———. "A Collection of Extra Songs, Written by Mary Hazzard. Beginning February, 1845." (1845–1851) [14]240 pp. 17 × 11 cm. S; e,g. MPBA, V/289.8/Un3.3/vol. 12.

L–71   ———. "A Collection of Hymns, and Spiritual Songs; Composed by the

Millennial Church. Copied by Mary Hazard. New Lebanon, Febry 12th 1832."
(1832–1868) 326[6] pp. 20 × 12 cm. S; h. DWt, SA1111.

L–72 ———. "A Collection of Marches and Labouring Tunes Written by Mary Hazard
Beginning July 17th 1858." (1858–1867) [6]356[4] pp. 18 × 11 cm. S; e,ls.
DWt, SA1147.

L–73 ———. "A Collection of Songs of Various Kinds; Written & pricked for the
purpose of retaining them. by Mary Hazard. Beginning June 16th AD 1839."
(1837–1839) [12 cont]214[12 cont] pp. 14 × 14 cm. S; a,g,ls. DWt, SA1119.

L–74 ———. "Precious Crumbs of Heavenly Food and Celestial Ornaments Sent to
Mary Hazard, from her Everblessed Mother Ann, and other good Spirits."
(1839–1841) [8]66[2] pp. 13 × 11 cm. S; a,g. DWt, SA1085.

L–75 Hollister, Alonzo G. "Began & finisht by Alonzo G. Hollister. . . . Cannot conjecture the date only by dates of the songs." (1848–1856) [14]206[2] pp.
18 × 12 cm. S; e,g,h. DWt, SA1136.

L–76 ———. f.t., "Celestial Waters." (1848–1871) [12 cont]100[134] pp.
18 × 11 cm. S; h. DWt, SA1135.

L–77 ———. "A Collection of Pieces of various description for edification & encouragement Alonzo G. Hollister Mt. Lebanon commenced 1849." (1849–1852)
[6 cont]276[6 cont] pp. 19 × 13 cm. S; h. MPH, 9775 Ho.

L–78 ———. "January 1851. Hymn book No. 2nd." (1851) [16 cont]240[4] pp.
18 × 11 cm. on title page, "Written by A. G. Hollister." S; h. DWt, SA1140.

L–79 Hollister, Henry. "A Collection of Songs Written by Henry Hollister . . . May
1st 1853." (1853–1857) [6]224[2] pp. 13 × 14 cm. S; e,h,ls. DWt, SA1143.

L–80 Hollister, James. "Title Page Commenced 1849." (1849–1850) [15 cont]317 pp.
18 × 11 cm. rear, "Finished February 20th 1850 By James Hollister." S; h.
OCWR, SM179.

L–81 Hollister, Rhoda R. "A Book of Anthems Given by Inspiration to the Believers
in Christ's Second Appearing and used by them In their Sacred Worship.
Copied by Rhoda R. Hollister. New Lebanon. Commenced October 1st 1846."
(1846) [6]60[2] pp. 17 × 21 cm. S; a. OCWR, SM387.

L–82 Hollister, [–?–]. "Hollister's Hymn Book Written in the Fall of *1852*." (1852)
[7 cont]217 pp. 18 × 11 cm. S; h. OCWR, SM2.

L–83 Jacobs, Clarissa. "A Collection of Divine Praises, Selected and Transcribed, By
Clarissa Jacobs. Commencing, July 2nd 1858." (1858–1860) [2]180[14] pp.
18 × 11 cm. S; e. CWB.

L–84 ———. "A Collection of Sacred Songs. Used in our general worship Written
and Transcribed by Clarissa Jacobs. begining August 1847." (1847–1848)
[12 cont]246[4] pp. 18 × 12 cm. S; e,g,h. DWt, SA1130.

L–85 Jacobs, Lucy. "A Collection of Hymns From Various Authors Selected and
Transcribed By Lucy Jacobs. Oct. 1848." (1861–1865) [2]196[2] pp.
17 × 11 cm. S; e,g,h. DWt, SA1137.

L–86 Jones, Phebe Ann. "Phebe Ann Jones—Hymn Book 1837." (1837–1870)
[12 cont]83[149] pp. 18 × 11 cm. S; h. OCWR, SM207.

L–87 Lannuier, Augusta. "Beautiful, Heavenly and Sacred Are the Gifts which God in
his Wisdom Bestoweth upon his chosen People. Compiled by Augusta Lannuier.
Began to be written, May 4th 1846." (1846–1849) [4]286[2] pp. 13 × 14 cm.
S; e,g,h. OCWR, SM311.

L–88 ———. "Heavenly and Divine Songs. Receiv'd from the fountain of Everlasting

Goodness . . . Selected & Transcribed By Augusta Lannuier. January. 10th 1841." (1840–1846) [12 cont]300 pp. 13 × 13 cm. S; e,g. OCWR, SM67.

L–89   Lannuier, Elizabeth Terressa. "A Collection of Anthems and Spiritual songs Improved in Sacred Devotion. Selected and transcribed by Elizabeth Terressa Lannuier. Began to be written December 2nd 1839." (1839–1840) 254 pp. 10 × 13 cm. S; a,e,g. OCWR, SM318.

L–90   Lewis, Sarah Ann. "A Collection of Songs, of Various Kinds selected from the different Societies of Believers. August 16th 1849. Sarah Ann Lewis." (1849–1866) [16]91[77] pp. 12 × 11 cm. S; e. NYOC, Ac. 4444.

L–91   Lockwood, John. "Verse book No 3rd Gifts of the Spirit for Spiritual exercises. Commenced to be written here sometime in 1847." (1847–1851) [18 cont] 268 pp. 14 × 14 cm. inscribed, "I, John send this book a presant to the Beloved Ministry at Groveland . . . John" [another hand: "Lockwood"]. S; e. OCWR, SM24.

L–92   Long, Peter. f.t., "Crown of Life Eternal." (1835–1841) [4 cont]216 pp. 15 × 18 cm. p. [iv]: "This book was given to Alonzo [Hollister] when he was about 11 or 12 years of age by Elder Peter Long, who wrote the first part of it. A. began to write in it a year later—After writing it full, he gave it away because it was not writ nice enough to suit him. . . ." S; a,g. OCWR, SM150.

L–93   ———. f.t., "Vain World." (1830s–1850s) [12 cont]110[164] pp. 18 × 11 cm. p. [ii], "October 16 1856 I received this Book of Peter Long soon after He became one of the Elders. . . . This Book was half written before I received it Henry Youngs. Born January. 1st. 1788." S; h. CNHY, Cupboard/Mx75/S4/En 2.

L–94   Lovegrove, Elizabeth. "Elizabeth Lovegrove's Psalm or Hymn Book. AD 1830." (1830–1840) [6 cont]234 pp. 18 × 12 cm. S; e,g,h. OCWR, SM134.

L–95   Offord, Ann. "A Collection of Spiritual Songs. Containing Sentiments, Expressive of the feelings of those, who worship God, in the beauty of Holiness. Selected and Transcribed by Ann Offord. January 1st 1870." (1870–1873) [4]224[4] pp. 20 × 14 cm. S; e. DWt, SA1151.

L–96   Rayson, Eliza. "A Selection of Spiritual Songs Used in the Sacred Worship of Believers Transcribed By Eliza Rayson. Commenced March 4th 1867." (1867–1871) [4]346[2] pp. 18 × 12 cm. S; e. PLC.

L–97   Reed, Polly R. "A Collection of Songs, Or, Sacred Anthems, Mostly given by Inspiration. Written for Betsy Bates. Beginning November 29th 1840." (1840–1842) [12 cont]281[3] pp. 14 × 17 cm. penciled on title page, "By Eldress Polly R. Reed. Finished March 3rd 1842." S; a,g. NYAP.

L–98   ———. "A Small Record of Sacred and Divine Things, Received by Inspiration, Through Various Instruments, In the Church at New Lebanon. Copied July 22nd 1844. Polly Reed." (1844) 77[65] pp. 11 × 12 cm. S; a. NYOCC.

L–99   Reynolds, Minerva. "A Collection of Choice Songs, carefully Arranged and Transcribed by Minerva Reynolds, New Lebanon. October 11th, 1857." (1858–1862) [2]272 pp. 20 × 13 cm. S; e. OCWR, SM390.

L–100   Rude, Hiram. "The Book of Witnesses . . . Commenced by Hiram. Recommenced by Alonzo H. Nov. 1873." (1859–1865) 22[212, sermons] pp. 19 × 13 cm. S; e,h. OCWR, SM429.

L–101   Scriven, Ann Eliza. "Ann Eliza Scriven's Song Book: New Lebanon, Columbia Co. 1855. A Present from Ann Buckingham, Watervliet, November 1855." (1856–1872) [18]240[12] pp. 11 × 20 cm. S; e,g,ls. OCWR, SM34.

L–102   Sears, Adaline. "Anthems of Joy and Thanksgiving Praise and Adoration, Bro't
         unto us by Holy Messengers from the Fountain of Everlasting Goodness.
         Transcribed by Adaline Sears. June 11th 1846." (1841–1869) [3 cont]219 pp.
         17 × 12 cm. S; a,g,h. MPBA, V/289.8/Un3.3/vol. 14.

L–103   Sears, Florinda. "A Collection of Divine And Heavenly Songs. Improved in
         Sacred Worship. Written by Florinda Sears. New Lebanon. September 25th
         1847." (1847–1866) [12 cont]277[5] pp. 19 × 14 cm. S; a,g. OCWR,
         SM363.

L–104   Sears, Louisa. "A Collection of Anthems & divine Songs. Given from Heaven
         To the children of Zion . . . Selected & Transcribed by Louisa Sears. January
         1st 1844." (1844) [4 cont]176 pp. 17 × 11 cm. S; a,e,g,h. OCWR, SM46.

L–105   Sidle, Elizabeth. "A Selection of The Choicest & Most Mellodious Songs of Zion.
         Received in The Various Churches of Believers Both far & Near. and Herein
         Transcribed For the Purpose of Retaining them. Commenced March 25th
         18[ ] By Elizabeth Sidle." (1847–1859) [14]284 pp. 18 × 11 cm. S; e,g,ls.
         OCWR, SM250.

L–106   Sizer, Charles. "A Collection of Hymns, Improved in the Sacred Worship of
         Believers Selected and Transcribed by Charles Sizer. 1846." (ca. 1846–1857)
         [12]70[318] pp. 17 × 12 cm. S; h. OCWR, SM399.

L–106.1 ———. f.l., "Grant Lord that I may sit." (1870–1876) [4]200[4] pp. 18 × 11 cm.
         inscribed, "Commensed July 17th, 1870. Charles Sizer Esq." S; e,ls. MeSL.

L–107   ———. f.t., "Musical Trumpets." (1847–1851) [12]41[195] pp. 17 × 11 cm.
         title page, "Book of songs, Many from Union Village Copied by Charles Sizer.
         1847." S; a. OCWR, SM405.

L–108   Smith, Emily. "A Collection of Hymns and Spiritual Songs; Improved in Our
         Worship. Holy Mount February 5th 1854. Emily Smith's Book." (1854–1874)
         [12 cont]128[366] pp. 19 × 12 cm. S; e,h. CWB.

L–109   Smith, Phebe. "Anthems, and Songs of Praise and Thanksgiving. Given for the
         use of the Holy Church of God . . . Selected, and Written by Phebe Smith.
         May, 1843." (1843) [8 cont]221[93] pp. 13 × 14 cm. S; a. OCWR, SM62.

L–110   ———. "Anthems, of Praise, and Thanksgiving, Given for the use, of the,
         Holy Church of God. Selected, and Written, by, Phebe Smith Decbr. 1839."
         (1839–1842) [12 cont]208 pp. 13 × 14 cm. S; a,g. OCWR, SM105.

L–111   Stewart, Charles. "Hymns Used in the worship of Believers Written by Charles
         Stewart in the year 1823 & 56." (1856?) 65[25] pp. 19 × 12 cm. S; h,ls.
         OCWR, SM344.

L–112   Stewart, Philemon. "The forepart of this book contains many little Songs Given
         by the Shepherdess at Canterbury; While the writer was there, in the summer
         of 1842. The rest exercise tunes; Such as we use in our Class Demonstrations
         of Music. Sketched by P S from the years 42 and 46, and many others Occasion-
         ally." (1842–1846) [16 cont]268 pp. 17 × 11 cm. S; a,e,g. OCWR, SM297.

L–113   ———. "Many of the following Songs were received in spirit from the Shepherd-
         ess, Who was sent by Mother Ann. in 1843 and 4. The rest, extra songs of
         Praise; Sketched by the writer, P S. for the better improvement of his memory
         in Divine Songs. Written in the space, from 43 to 47. Holy Mount, NL.,
         1846!!" (1843–1847) [10 cont]230 pp. 17 × 11 cm. penciled on title page,
         "Philemon Stewart." S; e,g. OCWR, SM133.

L–114   ———. f.t., "Praises to the Lord." (1852–1859) [10 cont]272[4] pp.
         12 × 11 cm. inscribed, "Philemon Stewart's Song book—& mostly in his

hand writing. When not an Elder, he sang in the class." S; e,g. OCWR, SM107.

L–115   ———. f.t., "Saviours Invitation." (ca. 1859) 124 pp. 19 × 12 cm. rear, "This book was written by Philemon Stewart, & abused by foolish boys, who know not its value." S; e. NYNT.

L–116   Stone, Betsey. "Spiritual Songs Given to the Ransom'd of the Lord, in the New Jerusalem. Commenced Sep, 1858. by Betsey Stone...." (1858–1862) [16]298[4] pp. 14 × 13 cm. S; a,e,g,ls. NYOC, Ac. 13,464.

L–117   Thompson, Gabriel. "A Choice Collection of Sacred Holy & Divine Songs Improved by the Believers in Christs Second Appearing In the Solemn & Devotional Worship of God. Transcribed by Gabriel Thompson. May 13th 1855." (1855–1860) [6]269[25] pp. 18 × 11 cm. S; e. OCWR, SM375.

L–118   Traver, Mortimer. "A Collection of Songs Written by Mortimer Traver. Began September 5th 1844 New Lebanon Columbia Co, N. Y." (1844–1858) [2]252 pp. 17 × 11 cm. S; e. DWt, SA1126.

L–119   Vail, James P. f.l., "The Heaven's are op'ning." (ca. 1857) [24]304 pp. 20 × 14 cm. inscribed, "Writ by James Vail...." S; e,h,ls. CNHY, Cupboard/Mx75/S4/En 1.

L–120   ———. "Sacred Songs Vol 3rd Collected & Compiled by James P. Vail. AD— 1857 to 1862 inclusive." (1857–1862) [12]226 pp. 19 × 12 cm. S; e,h,ls. OCWR, SM200.

L–121   Van Hooten, Catherine. "In this book Will be found a collection of Beautiful Songs given by Inspiration selected and transcribed By Catherine Van Hooten Commenced 1864." (1864–1874) [6]231[41] pp. 20 × 14 cm. S; e,h. MeSL.

L–122   Van Hooten, Phebe. "A Collection of Spiritual Hymns From Various Authors Selected and Transcribed By Phebe Van Houten January 1st 1837." (1837–1849) [10 cont]234 pp. 17 × 10 cm. S; h. DWt, SA1113.

L–123   ———. "Millennial Praises, Containing A Collection of Spiritual Songs Adapted to the day of Christ's Second Appearing Given for the use of his people. Copied by Phebe Van Houten Mount Lebanon 1862." (1862–1865) [4]202[4] pp. 19 × 12 cm. S; e. NYPLMs, 58–M–140, vol. 21.

L–124   ———. f.l., "The time draweth nigh when God's powerful word." (1871–1878) [2]224 pp. 19 × 14 cm. inscribed, "From 1871–'78 Unless otherwise designated all the songs in this book were received in North Family Mt. Lebanon nearly all by very young Sisters. To page 47 copied by Sister Phebe Van Houten from 47th page on by Elvah Collins." S; e. OCWR, SM370.

L–125   White, Anna. "The song's of Zion. Copied by Anna White. 1858." (1858–1863) [6]256[6] pp. 20 × 13 cm. S; e,h. MiAU, M/2131/.S4/1858.

L–126   Wickersham, George M. "Believers' Hymns. compiled by George M. Wickersham. New Lebanon. 1846." (1846–1852) [4]100[284] pp. 17 × 11 cm. S; e,h. DWt, SA1127.

L–127   Wilkinson, Emily P. "Anthems of Joy and Thanksgiving Praise and Adoration Bro't unto us by Holy Messengers From the Fountains of Everlasting Goodness.... Compiled by Emily P. Wilkinson. June 11th 1846." (1846–1851) [6 cont]147 pp. 18 × 11 cm. second title page, p. 147, "A Collection of Short Songs. By Different Authors. For the Edification of Believers.... Compiled by Emily P. Wilkinson, June 11th 1846." [6 cont]145 pp. S; a,e,g. OCWR, SM90.

L–128   Wilson, Hannah. "A Collection of Gospel Anthems. Given to the followers of

Christ In his Second Appearing Selected and Transcribed by Hannah Wilson January 12th 1851." (1852–1874) [12 cont]87[65] pp. 18 × 13 cm. S; a. DWt, SA1188.

L–129   Wood, John. f.l., "Harmonious muse, delightful, good." (1830s) [4]184[12 cont] pp. 19 × 16 cm. R; e. OCWR, SM403.

L–130   Woodrow, Richard B. "Anthems Mostly given by Inspiration Used in Sacred Worship . . . Richard B. Woodrows. Began January 27th 42." (1842–1844) [4 cont]332 pp. 12 × 14 cm. S; a,g. OCWR, SM264.

L–131   ———. f.t., "Hour of Prayer." (1848) [12 cont]236 pp. 18 × 11 cm. last page, "Finished November 27, 1848. by Richard B. Woodrow." S; h. OCWR, SM168.

L–132   ———. f.t., "Jehovah's Warning." (1842–1845) [14 cont]170 pp. 17 × 11 cm. p. 170, "Finished March 2nd AD 1845 by R. B. W." S; e. DWt, SA1184.

L–133   Youngs, Isaac Newton. "A Collection of Anthems & Spiritual Songs; Improved in our General Worship. From the year 1813, to 1837. Transcribed and written in this Book, by Isaac N. Youngs: 1854." (1854) [6 cont]160 pp. 14 × 17 cm. S; a. OCoO, Ms. Coll. 119, Box 9, Item 2.

L–134   ———. "A Collection of Marching Songs For the Worship. Written by Isaac N. Youngs From 1838 to 1850." (ca. 1850) 212 pp. 13 × 11 cm. S; e,g. MPH, 9775 Yo.

L–135   ———. "A Collection of Spiritual Songs: Commonly called Extra Songs; Improved in our Sacred Worship. Written by Isaac N. Youngs. 1845 and onward." (1845–1860) [18 cont]330 pp. 11 × 14 cm. S; e,g. OCWR, SM70.

L–136   ———. f.t., "The following are tunes to certain hymns. . . ." (1834–1836) 45[11] pp. 10 × 19 cm. p. [1], "Book of songs, by Isaac N. Youngs" and cover, "No 3." R,S; h. OCWR, SM412.

L–137   ———. f.l., "Grant my prayer, O mighty Father." (1845–1859) [10]213 [17 cont] pp. 18 × 11 cm. pp. 168–169, "By Isaac N. Youngs. May 1859." S; h. OCWR, SM171.

L–138   ———. cover, "Scratch Book No. 2." (1839–1841) 23[85] pp. 17 × 11 cm. S; e,g. OCWR, SM45.

L–139   ———. f.t., "Trumpet of Peace." (1839–?) [4 cont]96 pp. 12 × 20 cm. S; a,g. CWB.

L–140   Anon. f.t., "Angel of Peace." (1840–1842) [10 cont]232 pp. 13 × 14 cm. S; a,g. MPBA, V/289.8/Un3.3/vol. 4.

L–141   ———. f.t., "The Angelic Train." (ca. 1853–1858) [4]188[4] pp. 20 × 13 cm. label inside cover, "Sarah B. Smith March 2nd 1853." S; e,g,h. DWt, SA1142.

L–142   ———. "Anthems Ancient & Modern Improved in General Worship. Writen 1856." (1856) [12 cont]174[108] pp. 14 × 13 cm. S; a. OCWR, SM57.

L–143   ———. f.l., "Arise Ye slumbring and awake." (1865–1871) 240 pp. 19 × 13 cm. S; e,ls. OCWR, SM115.

L–144   ———. f.t., "Be ye ready." (1845–1854) [14]349[11] pp. 18 × 11 cm. S; e,g. OCWR, SM177.

L–145   ———. f.t., "A Beautiful Home." (ca. 1840–1843) 24[cont]288[2] pp. 13 × 14 cm. S; e,g,ls. OCWR, SM20.

L–146   ———. f.l., "Beautiful upon the mountains." (1868–1880) [6]194 pp. 18 × 11 cm. S; e,h. DWt, SA1207.

L–147   ———. f.l., "Beauty full Gods habitation." (1867–1868) 148[102] pp.

20 × 13 cm. inscribed, "This collection between 1860 & 68 Mostly Mt. Lebanon." S; e. OCWR, SM79.

L–148 ———. f.t., "Beauty Union & Love." (ca. 1839–1841) [14 cont]520 pp. 22 × 13 cm. note, p. 519, "242 Anthems written in the Book." S; a. OCWR, SM195.

L–148.1 ———. f.t., "Beauty Union and Love." (?–1873) [10]314[18] pp. 11 × 20 cm. S; a. CHSL, 289.84/SH11coL/vol. 1.

L–149 ———. f.t., "Believer's Choice." (1850s–1860s) [10 cont]186[54] pp. 18 × 11 cm. S; e,h. OCWR, SM1.

L–150 ———. f.l., "Blessed Gospel Blessed Cause." (1867–1878) [2]155[51] pp. 21 × 17 cm. inscribed, "Isabella Graves." S; a. OCWR, SM360.

L–151 ———. f.t., "Blessed Promise." (1883–1888) [4]152[4 cont] pp. 26 × 18 cm. R; e,h. OCWR, SM421.

L–152 ———. f.t., "Blessings of Prayer." (1852–1858) [14 cont]47[257] pp. 17 × 11 cm. S; h. DWt, SA1141.

L–153 ———. f.t., "Blessings of the Righteous." (1864–1870) [4]104[110] pp. 17 × 12 cm. R,S; e,h. OCWR, SM137.

L–154 ———. f.l., "Bright spirits have come from their loved homes." (1864–1873) [10]199[5] pp. 17 × 12 cm. inscribed, "Andrew Fortier 1864." S; e. OCWR, SM135.

L–155 ———. f.t., "Brigt Joys." (ca. 1848–1859) [18]208[4] pp. 13 × 14 cm. S; e,h,ls. OCWR, SM21.

L–156 ———. f.t., "Call of Mother." (1838–1841) [12 cont]266[4] pp. 13 × 19 cm. inscribed, "Horace Haskins." S; a,g. OCWR, SM312.

L–157 ———. f.t., "The Call of Mother." (1838–1841) [16 cont]414[4] pp. 16 × 14 cm. S; a,g. OCWR, SM142.

L–158 ———. f.l., "Call the erring home." (1877–1881) [4]292 pp. 20 × 14 cm. S; e. DWt, SA1154.

L–159 ———. f.t., "Celestial Hope." (ca. 1839–1840, 1847) 252 pp. 17 × 11 cm. S; a,g,h. OCWR, SM43.

L–160 ———. f.t., "The Children of Light." (1839–1840) 187[105] pp. 19 × 12 cm. inscribed, "David Hawkins." P,S; h. OCWR, SM322.

L–161 ———. f.t., "Childrens Petition." (1849–1852) [12 cont]211[25] pp. 18 × 12 cm. S; h. OCWR, SM293.

L–162 ———. "A Collection of Anthems And Spiritual Songs, Improved in General Worship. New Lebanon April 5th 1840. Eliza Ann's Book." (1840–1844) [6 cont]238[2] pp. 17 × 11 cm. S; a,g. OCWR, SM181.

L–163 ———. "A Collection of Hymns Adapted to The Sacred Worship of Believers Commenced in the Year 1850." (1850–1864) [12]59[289] pp. 18 × 12 cm. S; h. OCWR, SM290.

L–164 ———. "A Collection of Hymns, and Spiritual Songs, Improved in our General worship. New Lebanon November the 27th 1830." (?–1848) [10 cont]130 pp. 19 × 12 cm. S; e,h. DWt, SA1110.

L–165 ———. "A Collection of Hymns, Improved by the Followers of Christ in his Second Appearing. . . ." (1833–1859) [8 cont]222[50] pp. 17 × 11 cm. inscribed, "Made for Edward Fowler; By Isaac N. Youngs, March 1833." S; e,g,h. MPBA, V/289.8/Un3.3/vol. 10.

L–166 ———. "A Collection of Songs, Adapted to the Worship of Believers In the

Second Apearing of Christ. Copied by different Individuals, Finished in 1854. New Lebanon." (1845–1854) [7 cont]251[6 cont] pp. 17 × 11 cm. S; e,g. MPBA, V/289.8/Un3.3/vol. 13.

L–167   ———. "A Collection of Songs and Anthems improved in Worship, by Believers in Christ's Second Appearing. Finished in 1870." (1857–1870) [24 cont]278 [18] pp. 17 × 11 cm. S; e. OCWR, SM307.

L–168   ———. "A Collection of Songs Improved [illegible] Worship Believers in the Second Appearing of Christ [illegible] New Lebanon 1st Order." (1841–1861) 216[22 cont] pp. 18 × 11 cm. S; e,g,ls. MPBA, V/289.8/Un3.3/vol. 16.

L–169   ———. "A Collection of Songs of Various Kinds Mostly Given by Inspiration Written & noted for the purpose of Retaining them. For, Betsy Bates New Lebanon. Chh Begun Novm 29th 1839. Finished October 11th, 1840." (1839–1840) [6 cont]220 pp. 13 × 13 cm. S; a,g. OCWR, SM189.

L–170   ———. "A Collection of Songs Variously used in Worship. Selected and transcribed. . . ." (1843–1845) [4]281[5] pp. 16 × 11 cm. S; e,g,ls. NYPLM, *MRA Collection.

L–171   ———. "A Collection of Spiritual Anthems—Given mostly by Inspiration. . . . Jany 1842." (1842–1848) [8 cont]200 pp. 14 × 13 cm. inscribed, "Mary E Oliphant." S; a,h. OCWR, SM227.

L–172   ———. "A Collection of Spiritual Hymns, From Various Authors. . . ." (1860–1867) [12]170[14] pp. 17 × 11 cm. S; h. OCWR, SM132.

L–173   ———. f.l., "Come home my soul." (1845–1867) [4]262[4] pp. 16 × 11 cm. S; e,ls. NYOC, Ac. 13,922.

L–174   ———. f.l., "Come pretty freedom dwell with me." (1866–1868) 222 pp. 21 × 18 cm. S; e. OCWR, SM422.

L–175   ———. f.l., "Come unto me ye weak." (1870s) [6]125[73] pp. 18 × 11 cm. S; e. NYOC, Ac. 14,383.

L–176   ———. f.t., "Crown of Life Eternal." (1837–1839) [6 cont]218[2] pp. 9 × 16 cm. rear, "Like Philemon Stewart's writing." S; a. OCWR, SM269.

L–177   ———. f.t., "Crown of Life Eternal." (1840–1842) [6 cont]232 pp. 16 × 11 cm. S; a,e,g,h. OCWR, SM50.

L–178   ———. f.l., "Do cultivate and norish the tender plant." (1847–1852) [3]215 pp. 14 × 14 cm. S; e,h. OCWR, SM226.

L–179   ———. f.t., p. 16, "Door of Hope." (1854–1859) 262 pp. 18 × 11 cm. inscribed, "Alice Hay." S; e,h,ls. OCWR, SM305.

L–180   ———. f.l., "Down by the side of the river of life." (1870s–1880s) 100[174] pp. 20 × 16 cm. S; e. DWt, SA1179.

L–181   ———. f.t., "Ensign of Freedom." (1845–1847) [14]72 pp. 17 × 10 cm. S; a,e,g. OCWR, SM124.

L–182   ———. f.t., "Ensign of Holiness." (1849–1858) [2]418 pp. 15 × 11 cm. inscribed, "Mary Dixon's Book." S; e,g. DWt, SA1138.

L–183   ———. f.t., "Extra Song. Key of C." (ca. 1875–1880) 120 pp. 19 × 12 cm. inscribed, "Clarissa Jacobs." R; e. CWB.

L–184   ———. f.t., "Extra Songs. Short Anthems &c." (1839–1850) [8]248[8] pp. 17 × 11 cm. S; a,e. OCWR, SM3.

L–185   ———. f.t., "A Faithful Child." (1839–1841) 164[cont] pp. 14 × 17 cm. S; a,g. OCWR, SM187.

L–186   ———. f.t., "Faithful Few." (1845–1854) [18 cont]226[4] pp. 13 × 11 cm. S; e,g,ls. OCWR, SM258.

L–187 ———. f.l., "Farewell unto this world." (1845–1865) [6]392[cont] pp. 18 × 12 cm. S; e,g,ls. DWt, SA1115.

L–188 ———. f.t., "First Founder." (1847–1857) [10]193[177] pp. 18 × 12 cm. S; h. NYAP.

L–189 ———. f.t., "First founders." (1850–1853) [12 cont]283[7 cont] pp. 13 × 14 cm. inscribed, "Presented to Emanuel M. Jones June 3rd 1863 by a friend." S; e,h. MPBA, V/289.8/Un3.3/vol. 6.

L–190 ———. f.l., "A flourish of trumpets." (1870–1873) [4]240 pp. 19 × 13 cm. S; e. DWt, SA1152.

L–191 ———. f.t., "Freedom & Simplicity." (1841–1845) [14]238[10] pp. 17 × 11 cm. S; e,g. OCWR, SM39.

L–192 ———. f.t., "Freedom's Reign." (1888–1894) [6 cont]141[15] pp. 18 × 26 cm. R; e. NYOC, Ac. 8807.

L–193 ———. f.t., "The funeral Hymn." (1848?) [10 cont]109[5] pp. 19 × 11 cm. inscribed, "Gideon Kibbee. Deceased—Mch. 1848," and "Alonzo G. Hollister Received Feb. 13.1870." S; h. OCWR, SM245.

L–194 ———. f.t., "Glad Tidings." (1855) [20 cont]278[2] pp. 18 × 11 cm. S; a. OCWR, SM175.

L–195 ———. f.t., "Glorious Pearl." (1839–1847) [16 cont]1[229] pp. 20 × 14 cm. S; a. OCWR, SM283.

L–196 ———. f.l., "Go away, go away every fleshly tie go away." (1849–1855) 261[45] pp. 18 × 11 cm. inscribed, "Songs in this book are compiled from various sources (different Societies) and were received between the years 1849—to 1859 Copied by a member of Church Family Mount Lebanon N. Y." S; a,e,g,h. OCWR, SM254.

L–197 ———. f.l., "Gods people I love." (1863–1870) [18 cont]204[20] pp. 18 × 12 cm. S; e,h. DWt, SA1192.

L–198 ———. f.t., "Good Faith." (1830s–1850s) [10 cont]174[54] pp. 13 × 20 cm. S; g,h. OCWR, SM12.

L–199 ———. f.t., "Gospel Blessings." (ca. 1862–1868?) [12 cont]226 pp. 17 × 13 cm. inscribed, "Henry Calver May 24th 1862." S; h. NYOC, Ac. 14,382.

L–200 ———. f.t., "The Gospel Scene." (1827–1839) [4 cont]77[19] pp. 15 × 24 cm. C,S; a. MWW, 61/H99a.

L–201 ———. f.t., "Gospel Trumpet." (1860–1862) [4]169[5] pp. 18 × 11 cm. inscribed, "Second F N.L." S; e. DWt, SA1148.

L–202 ———. f.l., "The gospel's my choice." (ca. 1862–1863) [2]94 pp. 17 × 12 cm. S; e. NYOC, Ac. 4445.

L–203 ———. f.t., "Grateful Praises." (1830s?) 28[212] pp. 13 × 22 cm. inscribed, "George Cutler, Esq with the compliments of 2nd Family Shakers Mt Lebanon N Y August 12/27." S; a. MPH, 9775 Gr.

L–204 ———. f.l., "Hail the sweet harmonious sound." (1850–1853) [4]282 pp. 13 × 10 cm. S; e,g,ls. OCWR, SM259.

L–205 ———. f.t., "Happy Anticipation." (1848–1856) [14 cont]301[11] pp. 18 × 12 cm. S; h. OCWR, SM180.

L–206 ———. f.t., "Happy new Year." (1847–1875) [10]310[4] pp. 19 × 13 cm. R,S; e. CWB.

L–207 ———. f.l., "Hark now the trumpet." (1830s–1860s) [4]350[38 cont] pp. 19 × 16 cm. S; e,g,h,ls. NYPLMs, 58–M–140, vol. 22.

L–208 ———. f.t., "The Harmony of Angels." (1843–1847) [18]117[165] pp. 14 × 13 cm. inscribed, "John C. Dalton, Mt. Lebanon" and "Wm. O. Goss, Mount Lebanon." S; a. DWt, SA1160.

L–209 ———. f.t., "Harvest Reward." (1868) [11]153[10] pp. 17 × 11 cm. S; e. OCWR, SM428.

L–210 ———. f.l., ". . . hath called me, To lay up a store." (1849–1852) 272 pp. 13 × 14 cm. S; a,e,g,ls. OCWR, SM60.

L–211 ———. f.t., "Heavenly Call to the Youth." (1839) [16 cont]216 pp. 11 × 13 cm. S; a,g. OCWR, SM316.

L–212 ———. f.l., ". . . heavenly hosts and wait a little." (1840–1847) [6]161[47] pp. 17 × 11 cm. inscribed, "Andrew Fortier March 1853." S; a,g,h. OCWR, SM91.

L–213 ———. f.t., "Heavenly Jerusalem." (1840–1844) [12]232 pp. 17 × 11 cm. S; a,g. MPBA, V/289.8/Un3.3/vol. 5.

L–214 ———. f.t., "Heavenly Joys." (1850–1855) 280 pp. 14 × 14 cm. S; e,g. OCWR, SM224.

L–215 ———. f.t., "The Holy Angels Warning." (1842–1872) [22]86[120] pp. 18 × 11 cm. inscribed, "Fred M. Rug, Mt. Lebanon, N. Y." S; a. DWt, SA1123.

L–216 ———. f.t., "Hour of Prayer." (1848–1860) [8 cont]239[95] pp. 18 × 11 cm. S; h. OCWR, SM167.

L–217 ———. f.l., "How peaceful and quiet." (1867–1870) [2]232[2] pp. 18 × 13 cm. inscribed, "CVH." S; e,ls. NYOC, Ac. 8794.

L–218 ———. "Hymns and Anthems." (1854–1859?) [16 cont]264 pp. 17 × 11 cm. inscribed, "Henry Clough June 24th. 1875. N. York." S; a,h. NYLD.

L–219 ———. "Hymns Improved in the Worship of Believers . . . Commenced Apl 17th 1837." (1837–1842) [12 cont]264 pp. 18 × 11 cm. S; a,e,g,h. OCWR, SM169.

L–220 ———. f.l., "I am coming I'm coming saith Jehovah." (1844–1848) [16 cont] 309[1] pp. 13 × 14 cm. S; e,g,h. OCWR, SM26.

L–221 ———. f.l., "I hear the Angels voices in gentle whispers say." (?–1859) [6]188 pp. 19 × 12 cm. S; e,g,ls. OCWR, SM302.

L–222 ———. f.l., "I know my Redeemer liveth." (1840s–1850s?) [6]23[23]154[302] pp. 20 × 14 cm. S; e,g,ls. OCWR, SM342.

L–222.1 ———. f.t., "I look to Thee." (1890–1893) [16]200[14] pp. 18 × 27 cm. R; h, secular pieces. NYAL, MK15304/Box 1/1038.

L–223 ———. f.l., "I love to feel little." (1827–1832) [2]69[1] pp. 10 × 13 cm. inscribed, "From Isaac Youngs to Alonzo Hollister 1864." R,S; e. OCWR, SM413.

L–224 ———. f.l., "I see the prize the lovely prize." (1851–1856) 262 pp. 13 × 11 cm. S; e,g,ls. OCWR, SM30.

L–225 ———. f.l., "I will stand I will stand." (1847–1857) 240[116] pp., scattered. 18 × 11 cm. S; e,g,ls. DWt, SA1186.

L–226 ———. f.l., "I'll take my gospel sword in hand." (1837) [35 cont]155 pp. 17 × 11 cm. S; e. OCWR, SM97.

L–227 ———. f.t., "In Love." (1835–1839) [8]186 pp. 17 × 10 cm. S; a,e,g,h. DWt, SA1120.

L–228 ———. f.l., "In the cross I've placed my faith." (ca. 1839?) [2]138 pp. 11 × 9 cm. inscribed, "Presented to Louisa M. Crocker by Eliza Avery." S; e,g. OCWR, SM33.

L–229 ———. f.l., "In the rough rugged path of progression." (1860–1869) [6]220 pp. 18 × 13 cm. S; e,ls. OCWR, SM120.

L–230 ———. f.l., "In the vale of Humility." (1855–1861) 196 pp. 18 × 11 cm. S; e,g. OCWR, SM131.

L–231 ———. f.l., "In Zion is my Home." (ca. 1863) [10]128[100 cont] pp. 18 × 12 cm. inscribed, "Helen A. Stone Feb 10th 1878." S; a. NYLD.

L–232 ———. f.t., "Invatation To Souls." (1859–1870) 130[188] pp., scattered. 17 × 11 cm. S; e,h. OCWR, SM86.

L–233 ———. f.l., "The joyful song of triumph." (1882–1890) [2]286[48] pp. 20 × 13 cm. R; e. DWt, SA1155.

L–234 ———. f.t., "Life from the Dead." (1840–1856) [6 cont]164[68] pp. 13 × 20 cm. S; a,g. OCWR, SM328.

L–235 ———. f.t., "Life In The Spirit." (1878–1880) [4]289[3] pp. 20 × 14 cm. S; e. DWt, SA1174.

L–236 ———. f.l., "Like the nightengale in spring to my Mother I will sing." (1844) [2]288 pp. 16 × 10 cm. S; e,g. OCWR, SM99.

L–237 ———. f.l., "Lo how beautiful is the way." (1850) [6]140[4] pp. 19 × 13 cm. S; e,ls. OCWR, SM348.

L–238 ———. f.l., "The Lord hath His way in the whirlwind and storm." (1863–1869) 358 pp. 18 × 12 cm. S; e. NYOC, Ac. 12,731.

L–239 ———. f.l., ". . . love forever, Nay nay I'll be simple." (1844–1846) 230 pp. 18 × 11 cm. inscribed, "Bound by Henry DeWitt for Edward Fowler, July 1844. New Lebanon." S; a,e,g,h,ls. OCWR, SM252.

L–240 ———. f.t., "Love is my Home." (1849–1854) [18 cont]329[13] pp. 18 × 12 cm. S; h. OCWR, SM291.

L–241 ———. f.t., "Lovely Treasures." (1850s) [12 cont]226[4] pp. 18 × 11 cm. S; h. OCWR, SM172.

L–242 ———. f.t., "A March." (1873–1885) [4]186 pp. 20 × 14 cm. S; e,h,ls. DWt, SA1171.

L–243 ———. f.t., "Marching Tunes Eleazer Stanley's 1820." (1840s–1863) [4]260[28] pp. 12 × 22 cm. S; ls. OCWR, SM314.

L–244 ———. f.t., "Marching Tunes. Eleazer Stanley's 1840." (1840–1858) 62[84], scattered writing. 12 × 22 cm. S; g,ls. OCWR, SM313.

L–245 ———. f.t., "Matin Hymn." (1860–1869) [18]80[88] pp. 17 × 11 cm. inscribed, "[name erased] Mt. Morris, Livingston Co, N.Y." S; e,h. OCWR, SM253.

L–246 ———. "A Miscellanious Collection of Spiritual Songs. Of Various Dates and Origin. First Order. New Lebanon." (1855–1859) [32]110[150] pp. 18 × 11 cm. S; e. DWt, SA1145.

L–247 ———. f.t., "Mother Ann's Invitation." (1841–1848) [8 cont]250[82] pp. 12 × 20 cm. S; a,h. OCWR, SM152.

L–248 ———. f.t., "Mother Ann's Words." (ca. 1857–1872) [12 cont]320 pp. 17 × 11 cm. S; h. NYOC, Ac. 12,732.

L–249 ———. f.t., "Mothers Babes." (1847–1854) [22]53[29]30[144] pp. 13 × 11 cm. S; e,g,h. OCWR, SM64.

L–250 ———. f.t., "Mothers Blessing." (1839–1849) [12 cont]190[84] pp. 14 × 17 cm. S; a,g. NYAP.

L–251 ———. f.t., "A Mother's Hand." (1844–1850) [10]80[164] pp. 14 × 18 cm. S; a,g,h. OCWR, SM23.

L–252   ———. f.t., "Mother's Trumpet." (1840–1841) [10]192 pp. 14 × 18 cm. S; a.
           MPBA, V/289.8/Un3.3/vol. 9.

L–253   ———. f.l., "Move on don't be bound." (before 1838) 200 pp. 12 × 11 cm.
           inscribed, "These songs mostly of Church Family. As nearly as we can discover
           by comparison with books which have some of this collection dated, this collec-
           tion covered the period between 1825 and 1837. It was compiled and transcribed
           by a member of the Chh. Family Mt. Lebanon N. Y." S; e. MPBA, V/289.8/
           Un3.3/vol. 2.

L–254   ———. "Musical Presents, from the Land of Souls." (1841–1861) 9[7] pp.
           20 × 12 cm. S; a,e,g. OCWR, SM366.

L–255   ———. f.t., "My Faith." (1903) [16]222[6] pp. 18 × 13 cm. S; e,h. MPH,
           9775 My.

L–256   ———. f.l., "My soul shall be no longer bound." (1860s) [4]278 pp. 18 × 12 cm.
           S; e,h,ls. OOP.

L–257   ———. f.t., "The New Years Gift 1821." (1830s) [2 cont]162 pp. 12 × 16 cm.
           S; a,g. OCWR, SM108.

L–258   ———. f.l., "O beautiful beautiful gospel." (–?–) [8]19[175] pp. 20 × 14 cm.
           S; e,h. DWt, SA1161.

L–259   ———. f.l., "O Brethren & Sisters how sacred the trust." (1869–1880)
           [2]78[120] pp. 20 × 14 cm. S; e. NYPLMs, 65–M–93, vol. 69.

L–260   ———. f.l., "O Brethren and Sisters." (1838–1843) [2]274 pp. 18 × 12 cm.
           S; e,g,ls. DWt, SA1116.

L–261   ———. f.l., "O come thou lovely Angel." (1848–1853) [24]352 pp. 18 × 11 cm.
           S; e,g,h. OCWR, SM306.

L–262   ———. f.l., "O here is growing here is growing the tree of life." (1835–1838)
           [2]190[8] pp. 14 × 10 cm. S; e,g. OCWR, SM190.

L–262.1   ———. "The Word of the Lord our God Almighty Jehovah." (1841–1852)
           [16]138[46] pp. 14 × 13 cm. S; g. MeSL.

L–263   ———. f.l., "O how pleasant and inviting." (1849–1851) 304 pp. 18 × 11 cm.
           S; e,ls. DWt, SA1105.

L–264   ———. f.l., "O love it is a heavenly treasure." (1837–1840) [10 cont]88[140] pp.
           11 × 12 cm. S; e,g,ls. OCWR, SM106.

L–265   ———. f.l., "O my blessed Mother has given unto me." (1840–1841) [14 cont]
           196 pp. 14 × 14 cm. S; e,g,h,ls. OCWR, SM222.

L–266   ———. f.l., "O my children my children." (ca. 1825–1828; ca. 1848–1850)
           76 pp. 7 × 10 cm. P,R,S; e,h. OCWR, SM396.

L–267   ———. f.l., "O precious youth be faithful." (1838–1845) [4]150[112] pp.
           16 × 10 cm. S; e,g. NYPLMs, 61–M–36, vol. 56.

L–268   ———. f.l., "O strenthen me my God I pray." (1868–1870) [6]123[19] pp.
           18 × 12 cm. inscribed, "Book No 4 M. A." S; e. OCWR, SM119.

L–269   ———. f.l., "O sweet purity." (1861–1867) [11 cont]223 pp. 18 × 12 cm.
           S; e. NYOC, Ac. 12,815.

L–270   ———. f.l., "O things eternal and sublime." (1837–1840) [8 cont]261[5] pp.
           11 × 10 cm. S; e,g. OCWR, SM192.

L–271   ———. f.l., "O Union thou cementing bond." (1848–1852) [2]256 pp.
           14 × 11 cm. S; e,g,ls. CCA.

L–272   ———. f.l., "O we will not waste." (1882–1895) [4]144[98] pp. 20 × 13 cm.
           S; e. DWt, SA1198.

L–273 ———. f.l., "Our Mother's gentle spirit's near." (1859–1862) [4]176[4] pp. 20 × 14 cm. S; e. NYOC, Ac. 8795.

L–274 ———. f.t., "A Parent Indeed." (1854–1860s) [10]33[253] pp. 13 × 11 cm. S; e. NYOC, Ac. 7224.

L–275 ———. f.t., "A Parting Blessing." (1857–1869) [4]281[99] pp. 18 × 12 cm. inscribed, "Martha Jane Brainard. Her book. 1859" and "Ida Thomas Mount Lebanon Columbia County, N. Y." S; e,g,ls. NYPLMs, 65–M–93, vol. 66.

L–276 ———. f.l., "The parting hour O has it come." (1850–1854) [2]47[223] pp. 13 × 11 cm. S; e. OCWR, SM103.

L–277 ———. f.t., "Path of Self-denial." (ca. 1839) [8 cont]194[24] pp. 18 × 12 cm. p. [viii], "Florence Howland." S; a,g,h. OCWR, SM178.

L–278 ———. f.l., "Peace peace the Angels resound." (1862) [8]86 pp. 17 × 12 cm. S; e. OCWR, SM427.

L–279 ———. f.t., "Pleasant Walk." (1857–1861) [16]232[8] pp. 19 × 12 cm. S; e. OCWR, SM372.

L–280 ———. f.t., "Pleasing Tho'ts." (1846–1853) [16]206[120] pp. 18 × 11 cm. S; h. DWt, SA1187.

L–281 ———. "A Present from Br. Robert Valentine Dec 3rd 1848 HYMNS . . . J. W. B. Proprietor." (1848–1854) 132[46] pp. 15 × 10 cm. S; e,h. WLCMs, no. 209.

L–282 ———. f.t., "The Purification of Zion." (1839) [10 cont]146[8] pp. 10 × 16 cm. P,R,S; a. OCWR, SM268.

L–283 ———. f.t., "The Request." (1850) [14]226[4] pp. 18 × 11 cm. S; h. OCWR, SM323.

L–284 ———. f.l., "Resurrected from the dead." (1874–1880) 95[45] pp. 18 × 11 cm. inscribed, "Songs in this book between 1874–80 All from Mt Lebanon & branch family at Canaan NY." S; e. OCWR, SM206.

L–285 ———. f.t., "Rules of Music." (1830s) 84[26] pp. 12 × 19 cm. S; e,g,h,ls. OCWR, SM505.

L–286 ———. f.t., "Savior's Precepts." (1857–1861) [2]284[2] pp. 18 × 12 cm. S; e. DWt, SA1146.

L–287 ———. f.t., "The Savior's Universal Prayer." (1845–1852) [14]259[1] pp. 17 × 11 cm. S; e,g,h. OCWR, SM89.

L–288 ———. f.t., "The Saviours Invitation." (1845–1848) [4]250[4] pp. 17 × 11 cm. inscribed, "Emma Woodworth 14 years old." S; e. OCWR, SM308.

L–289 ———. f.t., "The Saviour's Universal Prayer." (1849–1867) [6]199[139 cont] pp. 18 × 11 cm. S; h. OCWR, SM374.

L–290 ———. f.t., "The Saviour's Voice." (1845–1863) [16]131[149] pp. 13 × 14 cm. S; a,g. OCWR, SM104.

L–291 ———. "Sayings of Mother Ann." (1841–1844) [7 cont]161[76] pp. 21 × 13 cm. S; a,e,g,h. MHF.

L–292 ———. f.t., "Seal of True Redemption." (1840–1846) 234 pp. 13 × 20 cm. S; a,g. OCWR, SM251.

L–293 ———. f.t., "Searching Light." (1839–1859) [14]264[64] pp. 18 × 11 cm. S; h. OCWR, SM376.

L–294 ———. "A Selection of Hymns and Anthems Used in Worship. . . ." (1847–1868) [12 cont]183[203] pp. 13 × 14 cm. S; a,h. OCWR, SM191.

L–295 ———. f.t., "Selfdenial." (ca. 1835–1845?) [8 cont]206 pp. 17 × 12 cm.

inscribed, "Mary Ann Mantle's book . . ." and "These hymns were gathered from various Societies—By comparison with other collections they seem to have been given (written) during the years 1820 to 1851." S; e,g,h. MPBA, V/289.8/Un3.3/vol. 1.

L–296 ———. f.t., "Shining Silone." (1855–1870) [6]176[68] pp. 18 × 13 cm. S; a. NYAP.

L–297 ———. f.t., "Shining Silone." (ca. 1860–1874) [16 cont]214[2] pp. 18 × 12 cm. inscribed, "Mt. Lebanon N F A Fortier." S; a. MPBA, V/289.8/Un3.3/vol. 11.

L–298 ———. f.l., "Sing and be glad." (1869–1871) [4]114[2] pp. 20 × 14 cm. S; e. NYOC, Ac. 8797.

L–299 ———. f.t., "Solemn Trumpet." (1839–1840) [8 cont]250 pp. 14 × 14 cm. S; a,g,h. OCWR, SM228.

L–300 ———. f.t., "Song of Thanksgiving." (1855) [14 cont]274 pp. 18 × 11 cm. S; a. OCWR, SM174.

L–301 ———. f.t., "Song of Thanksgiving." (ca. 1858) [16]287[89] pp. 18 × 12 cm. S; a,g. OCWR, SM182.

L–302 ———. "Songs of Various Kinds &c Proper Scratch Book." (1838–1839) [14]316 pp. 17 × 11 cm. S; a,e,g. DWt, SA1117.

L–303 ———. f.t., "The Sound of Freedom." (1839–1842) [2]192[208 cont] pp. 20 × 12 cm. S; a,h. OCWR, SM417.

L–304 ———. f.l., "Sounds of the Alphabet." (1869) [4]86 pp. 9 × 19 cm. (instruction book) S; e. OCWR, SM256.

L–305 ———. f.t., "Speak Gently." (1875–1888) [3]52[65] pp. 20 × 16 cm. R,S; e. DWt, SA1197.

L–306 ———. f.t., "Stand to your Post." (1840s) 136[96] pp. 19 × 12 cm. inscribed, "Presented by John Brown to Alonzo Dec. 25. 1870 Alonzo G. Hollister." S; h. OCWR, SM402.

L–307 ———. f.t., "Sure Reward." (1852–1856) [18]298[4] pp. 18 × 11 cm. S; e. OCWR, SM292.

L–308 ———. f.l., "Sweet love and union, is a flowing all around." (1851–1858) [12]221[49] pp. 18 × 12 cm. S; e. OCWR, SM170.

L–309 ———. f.l., "Take courage, ye weary." (1866–1871) [16]156[38] pp. 17 × 12 cm. S; e. NYOC, Ac. 15,145.

L–310 ———. f.l., "There are the friends that love sincerely." (1860s?) [2]194 pp. 18 × 12 cm. S; a,e,h. OCWR, SM371.

L–311 ———. f.l., "There is joy in the gospel." (1871–1873) [4]195[5] pp. 20 × 14 cm. S; e. DWt, SA1195.

L–312 ———. "3rd book of psalms . . . Commenced November 1851." (1851–1853) [10 cont]278 pp. 18 × 11 cm. S; h. OCWR, SM7.

L–313 ———. f.l., "The time is come the Lord to fear." (1836–1839) [2]157[81] pp. 11 × 11 cm. S; e,g. NYOCC.

L–314 ———. f.l., "Travel on, travel on, O every good believer come." (1854–1870) [2]290 pp. 13 × 10 cm. S; e,h. OCWR, SM31.

L–315 ———. f.t., "True Heirs of Heaven." (ca. 1855–1857) [4]345[5] pp. 18 × 12 cm. S; g,h,ls. OCWR, SM378.

L–316 ———. f.t., "True Light." (1853–1865) [2]114[2] pp. 21 × 17 cm. S; e,ls. OCWR, SM232.

L–317 ———. f.t., "The True Spirit of Christ." (1840s) 58[182]36[86] pp. 17 × 11 cm. S; h. OCWR, SM220.

L–318   ———. f.l., ". . . va-des-ka-len-ka." (1840) 134[32] pp. 16 × 20 cm. S; a,g,h. OCWR, SM212.

L–319   ———. f.t., "A Vancenevone of Comfort." (1840–1849) [4 cont]232 pp. 20 × 14 cm. S; a,h. OCWR, SM71.

L–320   ———. f.l., "Vany, vany, we O vene vany." (1839) 114 pp. 17 × 11 cm. S; e,g. OCWR, SM404.

L–321   ———. "A Variety of Anthems and Spiritual Songs for Believers to improve in While in their Sacred Worship. Began 1842 New Lebanon Second Order." (1842–1844) [6 cont]242 pp. 14 × 14 cm. S; a,e,g,h,ls. OCWR, SM225.

L–322   ———. "Various Songs received in 1829 and 30 from different places. Some Harvard ones." (1829–1830) 39[5] pp. 21 × 18 cm. C,S; a,e,h,ls. OCWR, SM233.

L–323   ———. "Verse Book No. 2nd Spiritual gifts for Spiritual edification Commenced sometime in 1846." (1846) [28 cont]248 pp. 13 × 14 cm. S; e,g,ls. DWt, SA1185.

L–324   ———. f.t., "Voice from Heaven." (1844–1854) [10]109[143] pp. 14 × 18 cm. S; a,e,g,h. OCWR, SM22.

L–325   ———. f.t., "Voice of Father." (1840–1842) [4]234[4] pp. 17 × 11 cm. S; a,g. OCWR, SM138.

L–326   ———. f.t., "Voice of Mother." (1839–1849) [15 cont]119 pp. 14 × 13 cm. S; a,g. NYLD.

L–327   ———. f.l., "We are out in the sunshine." (ca. 1898–1903) 47[69] pp. 25 × 20 cm. R; e. CWB.

L–328   ———. f.l., "We have come says Mother Ann to prepare you for Heaven." (1840–1843) [12]172 pp. 17 × 11 cm. inscribed, "Martha Sherman." S; e,g. OCWR, SM211.

L–329   ———. f.t., "A Welcome for the Canterbury Ministry." (1840–1865) [6]12 [22]188 pp. 16 × 11 cm. S; e. OCWR, SM48.

L–330   ———. f.l., "What comfort does flow to the true overcomer." (1851–1865) [2]298 pp. 13 × 14 cm. S; e,ls. OCWR, SM151.

L–331   ———. f.l., "When we assemble here to worship God." (1837–?) 157[165] pp. 10 × 17 cm. inscribed, "Please return to Alonzo January 1st 1872." S; e,g. DWt, SA1169.

L–332   ———. f.t., "Wisdom's Blessing." (1842–1843) [6]174 pp. 14 × 13 cm. S; a,g. OCWR, SM223.

L–333   ———. f.t., "Wisdom's Roll." (1841–1857) [6 cont]202 pp. (confused paging) 17 × 11 cm. S; a,e,g,h,ls. OCWR, SM210.

L–334   ———. f.l., ". . . with pleasure soon we shall all be their." (1839–1840) 186 pp. 12 × 21 cm. S; a,e,g,ls. NYPLMs, 61–M–36, vol. 61.

L–335   ———. f.l., "With triumphant songs of gladness." (1833–1845) [18]170[64] pp. 11 × 11 cm. S; e,g. OCWR, SM69.

L–336   ———. f.t., "The Word of the Lord of Hosts." (1842–1865) [14]128[146] pp. 14 × 18 cm. S; a,g. OCWR, SM358.

L–337   ———. f.t., "Word of the Lord to Zion." (1854–1874) [2]130[148 cont] pp. 11 × 20 cm. S; a. DWt, SA1144.

L–338   ———. f.l., "Ye faithful Watchman." (1867) [6]16[74] pp. 17 × 12 cm. S; e. NYOC, Ac. 14,385.

L–339   ———. f.l., "Ye righteous souls." (1875–1885) [4]41[163] pp. 20 × 14 cm. S; e,h. DWt, SA1172.

L–340   ———. f.l., "Ye righteous souls be of good cheer." (1875) [8 cont]160[48] pp. 18 × 11 cm. inscribed, "Elder Daniel Boler's Book." S; h. OCWR, SM298.

L–341   ———. f.l., "Ye who've forsaken home & friends." (1858–1868) [4]238 pp. 19 × 13 cm. S; e,g. OCWR, SM81.

L–342   ———. f.t., "Zion the City of God." (ca. 1870) [16 cont]190[8] pp. 17 × 12 cm. inscribed, "Ann Maria Graves." S; h. OCWR, SM96.

NORTH UNION, OHIO

NU–1   Bennett, Rufus, and Walker, Lessette. "Funeral Hymns Selected by Rufus Bennett & Lessette Walker." (1850s–1870) [2]222[82 cont] pp. 10 × 20 cm. S; h. OCSH.

NU–2   McGill, Alma. "A Collection of Songs, Hymns, and Anthems, Selected & Written By Alma McGill. North Union, April 21st 1872." (1872–1878) 140[46] pp. 20 × 13 cm. S; a,h. OCSH.

NU–3   Anon. f.l., "Beat your wings ye mighty Seraphs." (1858–1860) [2]106[186] pp. 10 × 20 cm. S; e,ls. OCoO, MS Coll. 119, Box 9, Item 6.

NU–4   ———. f.t., "March." (1853–1860) [2]157[253 cont] pp. 16 × 20 cm. S; e,fp,ls. OCoO, MS Coll. 119, Box 9, Item 1.

PLEASANT HILL, KENTUCKY

PH–1   Bryant, Paulina. "A Hymn Book; Containing a collection of Ancient Hymns; Compos'd and sung, in the different societies, of believers, at various periods, prior to Mothers work, of inspiration. Compiled and Recorded by, Paulina Bryant. Executed at Pleasant Hill. Beginning June 1854." (1854–1861) 404[8 cont] pp. 32 × 21 cm. S; a,e,h. WLCMs, no. 361.

PH–2   Dunlavy, Benjamin. "Benjamin Dunlavy's Hymn Book Received June 1833. Bound by Jacob Claar, P. H. Ky." (1841–1847) 232[68 cont] pp. 11 × 18 cm. S; a,e,g,h,ls. OLW.

PH–3   Harris, Phebe. "Phebe Harris's Hymn Book Received April 1833 Bound by Jacob Claar Pleasant Hill Ky." (ca. 1833–1847) [2]240 pp. 9 × 17 cm. S; a,e,h. KLF, BA/.S527/34.

PH–4   Rupe, Polly M. "A Hymn Book Containing a collection of Sacred songs, Hymns, Anthems & Poems, mostly given by Divine Inspiration Compiled and Recorded, by Polly M. Rupe. Pleasant Hill, Mercer County, Ky. East House. Commenced in May 1846." (1846) 194[46] pp. 16 × 19 cm. S; a,h. OCWR, SM255.

PH–5   Anon. f.t., "Heavenly Invitation." (1851–?) 285[19 cont] pp. 20 × 13 cm. S; e,g,ls. KLF, BA/.S527/35.

PH–6   ———. f.t., "The Rolling Tide." (1868–1871) [6]153[57] pp. 14 × 19 cm. S; e,h,ls. KPH.

PH–7   ———. f.t., "Virgin Daughter." (1848–1852) [6]226[14 cont] pp. 16 × 19 cm. S,P; a. OCWR, SM381.

POLAND HILL, MAINE

PME–1   Trowbridge, Delia. f.t., "Gospel Treasure." (1854–1858) 254[28] pp. 24 × 20 cm. inscribed, "Delia Trobridges book, 1864 of songs and purity." S; e,g,h,ls. MeSL.

PME–2   ———. f.l., "When scenes of tribulation." (1852–?) [6]40[104] pp. (scattered writing) 20 × 18 cm. inscribed, "Delia A. Trowbridge. Poland. Maine. 1857." S; e,h. MeSL.

SHIRLEY, MASSACHUSETTS

SH–1   Prouty, Lorenzo. "Lorenzo Prouty. Shirley Village, Mass: January, 1862." (1862–1874) [14 cont]123[67] pp. 20 × 14 cm. S; h. OCWR, SM281.

SH–2   Randall, Joanna. f.t., "Safe Hiding Place." (1860s) [12]102[110] pp. 20 × 13 cm. inscribed, "Hymns Written by Joanna Randall." S; e,h. OCWR, SM80.

SH–3   Anon. "A Little Book Containing the Songs Given by the Shepherdess in the Church at Shirley Commencing Nov 3rd 1844." (1844) [2]92[98] pp. 15 × 10 cm. S; e,g. MWW, 61/H991.

SH–4   ———. f.t., "Living Shepherd." (1844–1884) 185[43 cont] pp. 20 × 13 cm. label, "Lorenzo D. Prouty, Shirley." S; h. OCWR, SM418.

SH–5   ———. f.t., "The Morning Dawn." (ca. 1877) 117[77] pp. 17 × 11 cm. S; e. OCWR, SM126.

SH–6   ———. f.l., "Praise the Lord Sing praises Unto his name." (1867–1868) 142 pp. 19 × 13 cm. inscribed, "Loella Whitney. 12." S; e,h,ls. OCWR, SM121.

SH–7   ———. f.t., "A Song of Prayer and Praise." (1854–1857) 226 pp. 20 × 13 cm. inscribed, "This book from Shirley Shakers September. 1908 Marrette F. Longley." S; a,e,h,ls. MHF.

SH–8   ———. f.l., "We will sustain the Structure." (1870s) 108[82] pp. 11 × 17 cm. printed label, "Lorenzo D. Prouty, Shirley." S; h. OCWR, SM4.

SOUTH UNION, KENTUCKY

SU–1   Eades, Harvey L. "A Collection of Hymns, Anthems & Tunes; Adapted to the Worship. By, The Singers at South Union, Ky. April 4th 1835. H. L. Eades." (1835–1850) [22 cont]338[16] pp. 23 × 13 cm. S,E; a,e,h,ls. NYAS.

SU–2   ———. "A Collection of Verses; By, The Singers at South Union, Ky. April 4th 1835. H. L. E." (1835–1852) [16]269[3] pp. 10 × 13 cm. S,P; e. NYLC.

SU–3   ———. "H L Ead's Music Book. Commenced on the 28th day of April 1875. Aged 68 yrs old today. Finished June 10th 1876." (1875–1876) 104[56] pp. 20 × 27 cm. R; e,h. KBGK, MSS 63/Box 5/F6.

SU–4   ———. "Hymn & Song Book Written by H. L. Eades Commencing May 9th 1858." (1858–1867) [2]252[36] pp. 26 × 19 cm. S; e,h,ls. OCWR, SM331.

SU–5   ———. f.l., "O Come to the fountain that cleanseth." (1880–1881) 71[123] pp. 20 × 26 cm. inscribed, "Commenced 1880 H. L. Eads." R,S; e,h,ls. KBGK, MSS 63/Box 5/F7.

SU–6   Houston, Prudence F. "A Collection of Hymns & Tunes; Prudence F. Houston South Union Jasper Valley Logan County Ky. March 4th 1833." (1833–1860) 122 pp. 20 × 13 cm. S; a,e,h. OCWR, SM242.

SU–7   Moore, Nancy Ely. "A Gradual Series of Lessons In the Science of Music; Copied by Nancy Ely Moore. South Union Ky., Feby 24th 1871." (1871) [5]122[3] pp. 19 × 16 cm. S; ls. OCWR, SM502.

SU–8   Smith, Betsy. "A Collection of Hymns, Anthems & Tunes; Adapted to the Worship—By Betsy Smith. Born 28th August 1813. South Union, 1st January, 1835." (1835–1867) [4]170[8] pp. 19 × 16 cm. S; a,e,h,ls. KBGK, Coke Collection [Bell and Howell Duopage 15551].

SU–9   Stout, Mercy. "Mercy Stout Her Book; South Union." (1843–1846) 154 pp.
          19 × 14 cm. S; a,e,h. OCWR, SM113.

SU–10   Anon. f.t., "Companions in the Gospel." (1862–1864?) [8 cont]172 pp.
          20 × 15 cm. inscribed, "Caroline Jaynes." S; e,h,ls. WLCMs, no. 218.

SU–11   ———. f.l., "Hark ye little flock the trumpet sounds." (1844–1853) [6]141[7]
          pp. 20 × 14 cm. inscribed, "Mary Edwardses Hymn Book." S; a,e,g,h,ls.
          KBGK, Coke Collection [Bell and Howell Duopage 15561].

SU–12   ———. f.t., "Hour of Prayer." (1850–1866) [4]179[3] pp. 12 × 14 cm. S;
          g,h,ls. KBGK, Coke Collection [Bell and Howell Duopage 15552].

SU–13   ———. "A Hymn Book Containing Several Plain Noted Songs; February 2nd
          1848. . . ." (1848–1854) [8]124 pp. 20 × 13 cm. S; e,g,ls. KBGK, Coke
          Collection [Bell and Howell Duopage 15558].

SU–14   ———. f.l., "I've quit that old relation." (ca. 1836–?) [16 cont]104 pp.
          20 × 17 cm. S; a,e,g,h. OCWR, SM198.

SU–15   ———. "Letter Music. A Collection of Hymns, Anthems & Tunes; Suitable for
          Believers Worship . . . South Union, Jasper Valley, Logan County, Kentucky.
          May 1st 1834." (1834) 106[28] pp. 20 × 18 cm. S; h. OCWR, SM197.

SU–16   ———. f.t., "Mother Anns Song of Praise." (1830s–1854) [4]170[4] pp.
          23 × 15 cm. S; a,g,h. OCWR, SM280.

SU–17   ———. f.l., "Now I am determin'd more faithful to be." (1842?) [14 cont]144 pp.
          19 × 12 cm. S; e,h. OCWR, SM162.

SU–18   ———. f.l., "O Lord remember me when I pray." (1868–1870) 117[9 cont] pp.
          20 × 16 cm. inscribed, "Eldress Mary Edwards' Book." S; e,h,ls. KBGK.
          MSS 63/Box 5/F3 [Bell and Howell Duopage 15556].

SU–19   ———. f.l., "O Mother help me help me to overcome." (1842) 146 pp.
          13 × 8 cm. S; e,g,h. OCWR, SM32.

SU–20   ———. f.l., "O Mother I am thankful." (1840–1849) [6]150 pp. 20 × 13 cm.
          S; a,e,g,h,ls. OCWR, SM111.

SU–21   ———. f.t., "The Present Time." (1843–1846) [4]143[3] pp. 19 × 13 cm.
          inscription, "Maria E. Price." S; a,g,h. VaLD.

SU–22   ———. f.t., "The Savior's Call." (1859–1866) [8]87[139] pp. 19 × 13 cm.
          S; h,ls. KBGK, Coke Collection [Bell and Howell Duopage 15553].

SU–23   ———. f.l., "A Semibreve is equal to two. . . ." (ca. 1845) 6[15]21 pp.
          16 × 20 cm. S; e,g,ls. KBGK, SC 177.

SU–24   ———. f.t., "Sure Refuge." (ca. 1870) 162[20] pp. 19 × 15 cm. S; e,h,ls.
          KBGK, MSS 63/Box 5/F2 [Bell and Howell Duopage 15555].

SU–25   ———. f.l., "The Virgin Spouse bigins to rouse." (1830s) 62[60] pp.
          11 × 21 cm. C,S; e,ls. OCWR, SM359.

UNION VILLAGE, OHIO

UV–1   Brady, Susannie M. "Millennial Praises Collected by Susannie M. Brady. 1868."
          (1868–1885) 242 pp. 22 × 14 cm. S; h. WLCMs, no. 220.

UV–2   ———. "The Vocalist; By Sussanna M. Brady, of Union Village, Ohio. O 1850."
          (1850–1851) [4]214 (confused paging) pp. 21 × 17 cm. S; a,e,h,ls. OLW.

UV–3   Burnham, Edwin. "Edwin Burnham's Hymn Book January 15th 1855." (1854–
          1862) 141[59 cont] pp. 18 × 11 cm. S; e,h,ls. WLCMs, no. 208.

UV–4   Eades, Harvey L. "H L Eades' Book. Commenced May 1852. And finished June

10th 1855. West Brick, Union Village Ohio." (1852–1855) 252 pp. 20 × 13 cm. S; e. KBGK [Bell and Howell Duopage 15559].

UV–5   Farr, Elizabeth. "Elizabeth Farr's Book March 9th 1878." (1878–1881) 122 pp. 22 × 14 cm. S; e. WLCMs, no. 223.

UV–6   Hampton, Charles D. "Inspired Anthems. Given on Gold Plates; August 30th 1846. Union Village, Ohio." (ca. 1847) 252[8 cont] pp. 21 × 18 cm. top of title page, "These Anthems were written by Charles D. Hampton, ("Gold Plates") about the year 1847, I think, Eliza Hunt while in meeting declared she saw (spiritually) gold plates presented to each of the Brethren & Sisters on these were written Anthems and the following are said to be the Anthems." S; a. WLCMs, no. 360.

UV–7   Hampton, Oliver C. f.t., "A Prayer." (1875) 104 pp. 21 × 18 cm. inscribed, "Hymn Book by O. C. Hampton." S; e,h. OCWR, SM392.

UV–8   Holland, Mary Ann. "Mary Ann Holland's Book, of Spiritual Songs; Commenced October 5th 1852." (1852–1862) 136[42]8[18] pp. 21 × 17 cm. S; e,h,ls. WLCMs, no. 215.

UV–9   Houston, Isaac N. "Hymn Book, The Property of Isaac N. Houston; Second Family, Union Village, Ohio, December 25th 1858." (1858–1861) [2]170 [10 cont] pp. 16 × 20 cm. S; e,h. WLCMs, no. 217.

UV–10   Liddil, Susan C. f.t., "A Balm of Love." (ca. 1852–1866) 170[324] pp. 20 × 14 cm. inscribed, "Susanna C. Liddel's Book." S; h. WLCMs, no. 183.

UV–11   McNemar, James. "James M'nemar's Book of Anthems, December 27, 1846." (1846–1854) [4]290 pp. 19 × 16 cm. S; a,e,h,ls. WLCMs, no. 206.

UV–12   McNemar, Vincy. "A Selection of hymns Composed After the year ending 42 Written mostly By Vincy McNemar Sketches From 1842 till 1856." (1842–1856) 124[10 cont] pp. 17 × 11 cm. S; h. WLCMs, no. 200.

UV–13   Redmon, Susannah. "A Collection of Hymns by Susannah Redmon. First Order Union Village November 4, 1844." (1844–1858) [4]206[30 cont] pp. 16 × 10 cm. S; a,e,h. OCWR, SM214.

UV–14   Risley, Lucina. "A Book of Anthems, & Spiritual Songs: Written by Lucina Risley. First Order, Union Village November 20th 1847." (1847–1848) 119[71] pp. 16 × 21 cm. S; a,e. OCWR, SM101.

UV–15   Rudy, Susanna. f.l., "O the precious love of Mother." (1854–1858) 140 pp. 16 × 13 cm. S; e,ls. PLC.

UV–16   Scott, Sylvia. "Sylvia Scott's Hymn Book; Containing a Selection of Hymns and Anthems; Adapted to the Worship of God, In Christ's Second Appearing. Union Village, June 1845." (ca. 1845) [6]144[10 cont] pp. 19 × 16 cm. S; a,e,h. WLCMs, no. 191.

UV–17   Thayer, Moses W. "A choice selection of Hymns Anthems And Spiritual songs. Adapted to the Use of believers Writen by Moses W. Thayer of Union Village Ohio 1. Order Aprile, 3, 1852." (1852) 282 pp. 10 × 15 cm. inscribed, "Sanford Russell's Book Written here the 30th of October 1852." S; a,e,h. OCWR, SM36.

UV–18   Anon. f.t., "The Angels Call." (1845–?) 84 pp. 20 × 16 cm. S; a,e,h. WLCMs, no. 205.

UV–19   ———. f.l., "Another week is gone." (1880s) [2]43[177] pp. 18 × 12 cm. S; e. DWt, SA1102.

UV–20   ———. ". . . Containing A choice selection of Hyms Anthems & spiritual songs used by the children of Zion . . . January 11th 1846." (1846–?) [4]196 pp. 17 × 20 cm. S; a,e,h. WLCMs, no. 207.

UV–21 ————. f.l., "Dear sister remember us when far away." (1856–1858?) 198 pp. 20 × 15 cm. inscribed, "Susanna M. Brady." S; e,h,ls. WLCMs, no. 216.

UV–22 ————. "A Funeral Hymn, Sacred to the memory of Brother Andrew C. Houston— Oct. 8th 1844." (1844) 9[31] pp. 16 × 10 cm. S; h. WLCMs, no. 202.

UV–23 ————. f.t., "Hymn 1st: Mother Anns birth." (1844–1861) [2]161[56 cont] pp. 16 × 10 cm. S; a,e,h,ls. KBGK, MSS 63/Box 5/F1 [Bell and Howell Duopage 15550].

UV–24 ————. f.l., "I am God's holy angel of Love." (1848–1851) 326[4 cont] pp. 16 × 21 cm. S; a,e,h,ls. WLCMs, no. 213.

UV–25 ————. f.t., "Request." (ca. 1862–1874) 300 pp. 20 × 15 cm. inscribed, "Wm N. Redmon." S; e,h. WLCMs, no. 221.

UV–26 ————. f.t., "Voice of the Angel of Mercy." (1857) [5 cont]143 pp. 18 × 11 cm. inscribed, "Phebe Wilcox." S; e,ls. DWt, SA1205.

WATERVLIET, NEW YORK

WNY–1 Anna, Angelina. "Angelina Anna's Book Watervliet Jany 6th 1834. Lydia Anna's Book. Presented to her by A A March 9th 1834." (1834) [4]34[14] pp. 19 × 12 cm. P; e. OCWR, SM346.

WNY–2 Ayers, Mary Ann. "Book No. 2 A Collection of Songs of Various Kinds Mostly Received by Inspiration. Written by Mary A. Ayers Wisdoms Lovely Vale March 14th 1853." (1853–1867) [6]294[20 cont] pp. 21 × 15 cm. S; e,h,ls. OCWR, SM341.

WNY–3 ————. "Mary Ann Ayers Book." (1875–1885) [2]289[7 cont] pp. 20 × 14 cm. S; e,h. DWt, SA1173.

WNY–4 ————. "Mary Ann Ayers's Hymn Book. Watervliet, Feb. 1849." (1849–1850) [4]138[8 cont] pp. 19 × 13 cm. S; a,e,h. OCWR, SM364.

WNY–5 Bates, Issachar, Jr. "Issacher Bates' Book. 1835." (1835–1854) 103[101] pp. 15 × 10 cm. S; a,e,h. OCWR, SM100.

WNY–6 Bates, Perline. "Perline Bates's Book. 1836." (1836) [6]74 pp. 19 × 12 cm. S; h. OCWR, SM303.

WNY–7 Blase, Augustus. "Book of Augustus Blase For Hymns and Anthems Written by him at the Second Family Watervliet. commencing 1840." (1840–1873?) 250[26 cont] pp. 17 × 11 cm. S; a,g,h. OCWR, SM144.

WNY–8 Bowie, Samantha. "Anthems of Praise. Samantha Bowie's Book. Watervliet Jany. 1st 1868." (1868) [10 cont]52[104] pp. 21 × 17 cm. S; a. OCWR, SM336.

WNY–9 Brackett, William Charles. f.t., "For Eldress Ruth Landon." (1843) [10 cont] 55[7] pp. 16 × 10 cm. note at end of contents, "Transcribed by WCB 1843." S; e,g. OCWR, SM52.

WNY–10 ————. "William. Charles. Brackett's Anthem Book. Watervliet Dec. 10th 1839." (1839–1842) [6 cont]164 pp. 20 × 15 cm. P,S; a,g. OCWR, SM73.

WNY–11 ————. "William. C. Bracketts. Hymn Book. Watervliet 7th 1829." (1829–1832) [6 cont]168[3 cont] pp. 19 × 13 cm. P; h. OCWR, SM248.

WNY–12 Buckingham, David Austin. "Anthems and Hymns for Public Worship . . . D. A. B. 1873." (1873) [6 cont]233[53] pp. 17 × 12 cm. penciled on title page, "Early Hymn book used at Mt. Lebanon N. Y." N; a. OCoO, MS Coll. 119, Box 9, Item 3.

WNY–13 ———. "D. A. Buckingham's Book. Divided into two parts; the first, containing a selection of Hymns, not calculated for common use; and the second, a variety of short Poetical Pieces . . . Watervliet. 1830." (1830) [2]48 pp. 19 × 13 cm. C,N,P; h. DWt, SA1168.

WNY–14 ———. "Gospel Adoration. Or A Collection of Gospel Hymns, adapted to the Worship of God in this latter Day of Christ's Second Appearing: Composed by, and for the use of Believers. Written by D. A. Buckingham. Watervliet. 1839." (1839) [15 cont]349[15 cont] pp. 19 × 12 cm. P,S; e. OCWR, SM288.

WNY–15 ———. "The Harmony of Angels." (1845) 13[1] pp. 11 × 20 cm. S; a,g. OCWR, SM9.

WNY–16 ———. "Love Union and Peace." (1837–?) 216[6 cont] pp. 19 × 13 cm. inscribed, "Written By D. A. B." S,P; h. OCWR, SM117.

WNY–17 ———. "Music Book Variety. D. A. Buckingham. 1873." (1873) [2]128 pp. 15 × 23 cm. P,R,S; e. OCWR, SM102.

WNY–18 ———. "Sacred Poems. Written by D. A. Buckingham." (1840–1852) 439[3] pp. 9 × 21 cm. S; a,e,g. OCWR, SM35.

WNY–19 ———. "A Selection of Choice Poems or Verses; Originating in the different Societies of Believers, and used in their Sacred Worship. Written by D. A. Buckingham. Watervliet, Mar. 9th 1853." (1853–1859) [4]320 pp. 11 × 18 cm. S; a,e,h,ls. OCWR, SM265.

WNY–20 Butler, Samuel S. f.l., "Im thankful for my Zion home." (1850s–1876) [8]344 pp. 18 × 16 cm. inscribed, "Bro Samuel S. Butler Hymn Book." S; a,e,h. OCWR, SM127.

WNY–21 Cramer, Rollin. f.l., "Fall on the rock and be ye broken." (1845–1847) [8 cont] 91[181] pp. 18 × 11 cm. inscribed, "This Collection of Sacred Songs was Compiled and Transcribed by Rollin Cramer of Watervliet N. Y. Songs received mostly during the years from 184[ ] to 1847. M. C. Allen." S; a,e,g,h. NYAL, 354.

WNY–22 Graves, Isabella. "Inspirational Songs, Transcribed by Isabella Graves. South Family Watervliet Feb. 1884." (1880s) 178[22 cont] pp. 21 × 18 cm. S; e,h. NYPLMs, 65–M–93, vol. 68.

WNY–23 Larkin, Eva Violet. f.l., "Come my soul to the fountain of life." (1880s) 50 pp. 19 × 12 cm. stamped on cover, "Eva Larkin." S; e. DWt, SA1177.

WNY–24 ———. "Inspirational Songs Copied By E. V. Larkin. 1895 For Elder Isaac Anstatt." (1895) [2]152[2] pp. 25 × 20 cm. S; e. DWt, SA1176.

WNY–25 ———. f.l., "Rise and shine for thy light has come." (1880–1882) [2]126 pp. 22 × 18 cm. cover label, "Inspirational Songs. No. 1. Eva Violet Larkin, 1880." R,S; e. DWt, SA1175.

WNY–26 Lomas, George Albert. "Geo. Albert's Song Book. June 1. 1867 Watervliet, N. Y." (1865–1870) [6]184[4] pp. 19 × 13 cm. S; e,ls. DWt, SA1170.

WNY–27 Lowe, Jeremiah. "A Choice Collection of Divine Songs Made Use of in our General Worship. Written by Jeremiah Lowe. Commencing August 10th 1851." (1851–1868) [2]112[240] pp. 21 × 15 cm. S; a,e,g,ls. OCWR, SM236.

WNY–28 ———. f.l., "O how pure is the way." (1840–1843) 82[4 cont] pp. 15 × 10 cm.

note in rear, "The End James Lowe or jeremiah Lowe." S; e,g,ls. OCWR, SM148.

WNY–29   ——. f.t., "The Precious Way." (1844–1849) 182 pp. 16 × 10 cm. front cover, "Jeremiah's Book, 1849." S; e,g,ls. OCWR, SM149.

WNY–30   Simons, Sarah. "Anthems Transcribed by Sarah Simons January 1841." (1840–1843) 192 pp. 16 × 15 cm. S; a. OCWR, SM98.

WNY–31   Anon. "A collection of Hymns and Anthems, mostly received by inspiration and suitable for Millennial worship. . . ." (1855–1865) 154[202] pp. 21 × 15 cm. inscribed, "Paulina Bates." S; a,e,h. OCWR, SM72.

WNY–31.1 "The Savior's Present to the North Family or Gathering Order." (1842) [11]3[8] pp. 17 × 11 cm. inscribed, "A present prepared by the Holy Savior, and blessed Mother Ann, for their needy and hungry children who reside in the gathering Order on the holy Mount. Delivered into the hands of the beloved Lead, in Wisdom's Valley, by Mother Ann, Revealed to the mortal writer by the holy Vialleen Angel from Mother's Mansion, April 5th, 1842." S; g. MeSL.

WNY–32   ——. f.t., "Come Sweet Conviction." (1869–1871) [2]96[4 cont] pp. 17 × 10 cm. inscribed, "Chancy Dibble." S; e,h,ls. OCWR, SM15.

WNY–33   ——. f.l., "Engaged for life in battle." (1883–1884) 104[74 cont] pp. 22 × 18 cm. inscribed, "No I Watervliet given by Eld. Anna Case." S; e,h. MeSL.

WNY–34   ——. f.t., "Fervent Devotion." (1841–1846) 114 pp. 16 × 10 cm. S; a,h. OCWR, SM146.

WNY–35   ——. f.t., "For Eldress Ruth." (1840s) [5]82[21 cont] pp. 13 × 8 cm. S; e,g. OCWR, SM262.

WNY–36   ——. f.t., "Humility." (1868–1870) [4]44[72] pp. 22 × 14 cm. S; e. DWt, SA1194.

WNY–37   ——. f.t., "Hymn First. Celestial Fountain." (1837–1853) [8 cont]258 pp. 20 × 13 cm. P; h. OCWR, SM246.

WNY–38   ——. f.t., "Immortal Scenes." (1842–?) [6]249[11 cont] pp. 18 × 12 cm. inscribed, "Book No 3." S; a. OCWR, SM377.

WNY–39   ——. f.t., "Jehovah's Promise to his People." (1840–?) [8 cont]44[72 cont] 112 pp. 18 × 11 cm. S; a. OCWR, SM141.

WNY–40   ——. f.t., "A March." (1839–1848) 155[61 cont] pp. 17 × 11 cm. inscribed, "Ann Maria Reynolds." S; a,e,h. OCWR, SM92.

WNY–41   ——. f.t., "Mother Ann's Closing Hymn." (1841–1846) [8]224[24] pp. 17 × 12 cm. S; g,h. OCWR, SM213.

WNY–42   ——. f.t., "A New Years Blessing." (1841–1844) [10 cont]192 pp. 10 × 17 cm. inscribed, "Henry White SOWV" and "Chancy Dibble." S; a. OCWR, SM329.

WNY–43   ——. f.l., "O how I love my faithful children." (1838–1842) 259[13 cont] pp. 17 × 10 cm. P,N; a,e,g. OCWR, SM140.

WNY–44   ——. f.t., "Part First. Marching Tunes and verse." (1854–1864) [4]152[4] pp. 18 × 13 cm. inscribed, "Chancy Dibble." S; e,g,h,ls. OCWR, SM304.

WNY–45   ——. f.l., "Prepare O my children prepare you a robe." (1842–1844) 270 pp. 18 × 12 cm. S; a,e,g,h,ls. OCWR, SM249.

WNY–46   ——. f.t., "The Purification of Zion." (1838–1840s) [6 cont]182 pp. 20 × 17 cm. S,P; a,g. OCWR, SM239.

WNY–47   ———. f.t., "Round Manner." (1866–1870) 160[80] pp. 17 × 11 cm. inscribed, "Chancy Dibble." S; e. OCWR, SM94.

WNY–48   ———. f.t., "Slow March." (1867–1870) 89[79] pp. 18 × 11 cm. inscribed, "Caroline Ulich Wisdoms Valley 1870" and "Isabella Graves." S; ls. OCWR, SM87.

WNY–49   ———. f.t., "Step Tunes." (1843–1867) [4]216[76] pp. 12 × 11 cm. S; a,e,g,ls. DWt, SA1125.

WNY–50   ———. f.l., "This strife on natures gloomy strand." (1870) [14]81[95] pp. 17 × 12 cm. S,R; e. DWt, SA1208.

WNY–51   ———. f.t., "Tunes not Originating in this Society. Copied in the year 1857." (1857–1866) 40 pp. 16 × 10 cm. S; g,ls,ss. OCWR, SM51.

WNY–52   ———. f.t., "Wisdoms Roll." (1839–1869) 72[70] pp. 20 × 17 cm. S,P; a. OCWR, SM243.

WHITEWATER, OHIO

WO–1   Ball, Stephen. "Stephen Ball His Book in union with his brethren and sisters." (1846–1847) 32[72]16[4] pp. 15 × 9 cm. S; e,g. ODPL.

WO–2   Frost, E. E. f.l., "I have adorned thee Jerusalem." (1854–1863?) 241[43 cont] pp. 13 × 11 cm. S; e,h. OCWR, SM63.

WO–3   Anon. f.t., "Coppied by Insp FOWWV. Mar 20 1847 An Anthem." (1847) 180 pp. 16 × 20 cm. inscribed, "Wesley S. King." S; a,e,h,ls. WLCMs, no. 210.

WO–4   ———. f.t., "The Harmony of Angels." (1847–1853) [2]307[225 cont] pp. 11 × 20 cm. S; a,h. CHSL, 289.84/Sh11coL/v. 2.

WO–5   ———. f.t., "Hymn from Isaiah—Chapter 35." (1852) [2]72[2] pp. 25 × 19 cm. inscribed, "Margaret Denning Book. It now belong to Hnnah Bryant." S; a,h. OCWR, SM193.

WO–6   ———. f.l., "I will be with my dear children." (1850s–1860s) [4]210 pp. 20 × 16 cm. S; e,h. OCWR, SM361.

WO–7   ———. f.t., "Mourners Comfort, U, V; 44." (ca. 1846) 222 pp. 21 × 18 cm. S; a,e,h,ls. OCoO, MS Coll. 119, Box 9, Item 10.

WO–8   ———. f.l., "My words shall be few and well seasoned with grace." (1848–1851) 272 pp. 16 × 21 cm. S; a,e,g,h,ls. OCWR, SM309.

WO–9   ———. "A Selection of Hymns and Pomes For the use of Believers White Water Village Ohio." (ca. 1842–1851) [4]153[45 cont] pp. 18 × 10 cm. inscribed, "Edwin H. Burnham's Hymn Book Bot at Cincinnati: November 27th 1841." S; e,h,ls. WLCMs, no. 198.

WO–10   ———. "This Book Belongs to Frederick Kromer From Germany . . . Now . . . of Watervliet—Near Dayton . . . in this year of our Lord Feb 10th 1859. . . ." (1859) 40 pp. 24 × 19 cm. rear cover, "Henry Edward Somerfield May 15. 1859." S; e. OCoO, MS Coll. 119, Box 9, Item 11.

WO–11   ———. f.l., "What a feast what a feast my soul does enjoy." (1863–1864) 172 pp. 20 × 16 cm. S; e,h. OCWR, SM278.

PROVENANCE, EASTERN

XE–1   Anon., f.t., "Angel Invitation." (1866–1875) [2]272[4] pp. 20 × 13 cm. S; e. DWt, SA1099.

XE–2   ———. f.t., "Angel of Peace." (1870s) 65[127 cont] pp. 21 × 14 cm. S; e,h. KBGK, Coke Collection [Bell and Howell Duopage 15562].

XE–3   ———. f.t., "The Angel Song." (1868?–1870s) [4]192 pp. 18 × 11 cm. S; e,h. NYHS.

XE–4   ———. f.t., "The Angelic Train." (1853–1868) 162[26] pp. 20 × 13 cm. S; a,e,h,ls. WLCMs, no. 219.

XE–5   ———. f.t., "Anthem." (after 1840) [2 cont]19[17] pp. 19 × 13 cm. S; a,e,h. DWt, SA1164.

XE–6   ———. f.l., "Arise O my soul." (1861–1862) [2]88[88] pp. 17 × 11 cm. S; e,g. NYOC, Ac. 12,766.

XE–7   ———. f.t., "Aspiration." (after 1868) 14[76] pp. 16 × 10 cm. S; h. NYOC, Ac. 14,386.

XE–8   ———. f.t., "Beams of Glory." (1854) [16]54[142] pp. 20 × 13 cm. S; h. OCWR, SM161.

XE–9   ———. f.t., "A Call to Zion." (1850) 75[157] pp. 19 × 13 cm. S; h. OCWR, SM201.

XE–10   ———. "Chaunt for The Worship of Believers in Society of Christ's Second Appearing . . . 1869." (1867–1868) [6]109[167] pp. 17 × 11 cm. S; e. NYOC, Ac. 13,577.

XE–11   ———. f.l., "Down in the lovely vac no ve." (1873–1882) [31]198[11] pp. 18 × 12 cm. S; e,h. OCWR, SM8.

XE–12   ———. f.t., "Eternal Glory." (1849–1854) [66]10[12]16[310] pp. 17 × 10 cm. S; a,e,h,ls. WLCMs, no. 103.

XE–13   ———. f.t., "Follow Me." (1869–1871) [2]60[84] pp. 17 × 11 cm. S; e,h. DWt, SA1190.

XE–14   ———. f.l., "For a robe thats pure and holy." (1871–1873) [2]82[146] pp. 19 × 13 cm. S; e. OCWR, SM367.

XE–15   ———. f.l., "From the heavenly shores I hear the sweet sound." (1870–1880) [4]109[37] pp. 20 × 14 cm. S; e. OCWR, SM282.

XE–16   ———. f.t., "Happy Land." (1850s?) 206[8 cont] pp. 16 × 11 cm. S; e,ls. NYAM, no. 2283.

XE–17   ———. f.t., "Heaven of True Rest." (1857–1863) [1]125 pp. 21 × 14 cm. S; e. DWt, SA1189.

XE–18   ———. f.t., "Holy Temple." (1848–1853) [8 cont]362 pp. 18 × 11 cm. S; h. MHF.

XE–19   ———. f.t., "The Honest Souls Reward." (1868–?) [10 cont]196 pp. 16 × 12 cm. S; h. NYOC, Ac. 14,384.

XE–20   ———. "Hymn Book Written in the Summer of 1852." (1852) [12 cont]216[4] pp. 18 × 11 cm. S; h. CHSL, 289.84/Sh11hy/1852.

XE–21   ———. f.l., "I will be an overcomer." (1870s?) 48 pp. 17 × 11 cm. S; e. NCA.

XE–22   ———. f.t., "Indian Songs." (1842–1843) [2]25[21] pp. 15 × 10 cm. S; g. OCWR, SM389.

XE–23   ———. f.l., "Lord we now appear before thee." (ca. 1830–1838) 64 pp. 12 × 19 cm. S; a,e. WLCM, M/2131/.S4M3.

XE–24   ———. f.t., "A Marching Song." (1850–1868) [2]192[10 cont] pp. 12 × 18 cm. S; e,ls. DWt, SA1133.

XE–25   ———. f.t., "Mount Lebanon/Anthem." (1870s) 175[5 cont] pp. 17 × 11 cm. S; a,e,h. OCWR, SM219.

XE–26 ———. f.l., "O come O come come away." (1855–1857?) [18]132 pp. 16 × 11 cm. S; e,ls. NYOC, Ac. 4128.

XE–27 ———. f.l., "O how bright how beautiful & glorious." (1863–1865) 132 pp. 19 × 13 cm. S; e,h. NYAM, no. 2283.

XE–28 ———. f.l., "Our moments are passing." (1875–1899) [2]102[88] pp. 19 × 12 cm. inscribed, "West Gloucester Maine." S; e. MeSL.

XE–29 ———. f.l., "Pour forth the testimony." (ca. 1889, 1909) 30[106] pp. 17 × 11 cm. S; e,h. OCWR, SM88.

XE–30 ———. f.t., "Precious Faith." (1850s) [4]106[110] pp. 19 × 13 cm. S; a,h. MiAU, BV/442/.18—

XE–31 ———. f.t., "Reflections on Mother Anns Birthday." (1840–1850) [10 cont] 193[63] pp. 17 × 11 cm. S; h. OCWR, SM93.

XE–32 ———. f.l., "Rejoice, rejoice all ye children." (1837–1867) [2]136[18] pp. 16 × 12 cm. P,S; a,e. OCWR, SM380.

XE–33 ———. f.t., "Rock of Ages." (1840s) 34[106] pp. 17 × 11 cm. S; h. OCWR, SM130.

XE–34 ———. f.t., "Soldier of Christ." (1846–1851) [4]140[4] pp. 12 × 20 cm. S; a,e,h,ls. OCWR, SM315.

XE–35 ———. "Songs and Hymns book." (1853) [4]130 pp. 15 × 10 cm. S; a,h. OCWR, SM353.

XE–36 ———. f.t., "Soul Trusting." (ca. 1881–1884) [4]87[11] pp. 17 × 10 cm. S; e. NCA.

XE–37 ———. f.t., "Strong Union." (ca. 1854–1862) [2]168[2] pp. 19 × 14 cm. S; e. MPBA, V/289.8/Un3.3/vol. 7.

XE–38 ———. f.l., "Tis not in station place or name." (1870s) [2]216[4] pp. 20 × 14 cm. S; e. OCWR, SM365.

XE–39 ———. f.t., "True Devotion." (ca. 1857–1896) 240 pp. 20 × 14 cm. S; e,h. MeSL.

XE–40 ———. "Various Songs received in 1827 and 1828 from different places Some of them belonging to Harvard." (ca. 1827–1828) 82[4] pp. 21 × 18 cm. C; a,e,h,ls. OCWR, SM234.

XE–41 ———. f.t., "Watchfullness." (1848–1860) [12 cont]277[3] pp. 20 × 12 cm. S; a,h. DWt, SA1178.

XE–42 ———. f.t., "We are Seen." (1843–1845) [10 cont]152[20] pp. 16 × 11 cm. S; e,h. DWt, SA1122.

XE–43 ———. f.l., "Where are thy joys." (1873–?) 57[181] pp. 20 × 14 cm. S; e. NYOC, Ac. 12,765.

XE–44 ———. f.t., "Word of the Lord to Zion." (1854–1906) [6]176[8 cont] pp. 20 × 14 cm. S; a,e,h. MeSL.

XE–45 ———. f.t., "Zions Children." (ca. 1852) [2]132 pp. 19 × 13 cm. S; e,h,ls. MeSL.

XE–46 ———. [wordless tune, ascription, "Amos Bishop."] (late 1820s) 64 pp. 13 × 16 cm. C,R; a,e,h,ls. OCWR, SM261.

XE–47 ———. [wordless tune, numbered, "4".] (late 1820s) 31[68]52[43] pp. 6 × 18 cm. C,S; e,fp,ls,ss. OCWR, SM321.

XE–48 ———. [wordless tune, no ascription.] (late 1820s) 17[55]25[35]5[11] pp. 9 × 15 cm. C; e,ls. MeSL.

PROVENANCE, WESTERN

XW–1   Anon., f.t., "Christmas Hymn." (ca. 1869) 166 pp. 13 × 21 cm. S; e,h,ls.
        WLCMs, no. 222.

XW–2   ———. f.l., "Peace peace peace be unto you." (1840s) [2]136[6] pp.
        10 × 17 cm. S; a,e,h,ls. OLW.

PROVENANCE, UNKNOWN

XU–1   ———. f.l., "Arrangements of exercises in Singing School." (ca. 1867)
        56[58] pp. 19 × 15 cm. inscribed, "Bettie Roberts 1867." S; e,h. OCWR,
        SM301.

XU–2   ———. f.l., "Behold I come quickly and my promise is sure." (1850–1870s)
        118 pp. 19 × 17 cm. S; e,h. NYLC.

XU–3   ———. "A Colection of Hymns and Spiritual Songs. Improved In our general
        Worship. For The edefication of Good Believers. September 1824." (1824–?)
        92 pp. 19 × 12 cm. R; h. OCWR, SM10.

XU–4   ———. f.l., "Come come heavenly love." (1840s) 62 pp. 16 × 19 cm. S; e,ls.
        OCWR, SM184.

XU–4.1 ———. f.l., "Come let us join heart and hand." (1858–1862) 293[89] pp.
        17 × 14 cm. S; e,h,ls. MeSL.

XU–5   ———. f.l., "Compete not with those who have means beyond your reach."
        (1870s) 22 pp. 18 × 21 cm. S; e. OCWR, SM203.

XU–6   ———. f.t., "Consideration of Time." (ca. 1865–1870) [4]130[14] pp.
        19 × 16 cm. inscribed, "Susannah Conway." S; e. DWt, SA1209.

XU–7   ———. f.t., "Contents." (ca. 1845–1867) [16 cont]137[163] pp. 18 × 11 cm.
        [except for table of contents, both texts and music are written in shorthand]
        S; h. DWt, SA1128.

XU–8   ———. f.t., "Fellow Travellers." (1849) 60 pp. 17 × 11 cm. inscribed, "Ger-
        trude Frances." S; h. MWW, 61/H99/vol. 9.

XU–9   ———. f.l., "A few Exercises in Dynamics." (1869) 16 pp. 21 × 14 cm. S; a,e.
        OCWR, SM230.

XU–10   ———. f.t., "Happy Land." (ca. 1856) [2]214[4] pp. 16 × 11 cm. S; e,ls.
        NYPLMs, 66–M–13, vol. 64.

XU–11   ———. f.t., "The Harmony of Angels." (ca. 1843) 246[12 cont] pp. 12 × 21 cm.
        S; a,e,g,h. WLCMs, no. 225.

XU–12   ———. "Hymns and Songs for the Boston meetings to be held Dec. 27th, 28th,
        & 29th 1869." (1869) 31[5] pp. 19 × 13 cm. S; e,h. DWt, SA1193.

XU–13   ———. f.l., "I call you O my children." (ca. 1852) [4]22[126] pp. 13 × 9 cm.
        inscribed, "Henery Peppers Book bought 1852." S; e. DWt, SA1098.

XU–14   ———. f.l., "I'm going down to the beautiful valley." (ca. 1852) [6]298[10 cont]
        pp. 18 × 11 cm. S; h. OCWR, SM205.

XU–15   ———. f.l., "In Jordan's waters we will bathe." (ca. 1877) [2]29[171] pp.
        20 × 14 cm. S; e. DWt, SA1162.

XU–16   ———. f.l., "In the heavens of glory." (ca. 1856–1860) [2]168 pp. 16 × 11 cm.
        inscribed, "Wed. July 2 1856 Norman Hayden came to this family to live
        From Lebanon." S; e,ls. NYPLMs, 66–M–13, vol. 63.

XU–17   ———. f.t., "The Lamb." (1825–1829) [9 cont]150[9] pp. 17 × 25 cm. C; a.
        OCWR, SM274.

XU–18 ————. f.t., "Lesson First." (1881–1884) 26 pp. 21 × 17 cm. S; e. OCoO, MS Coll. 119, Box 9, Item 9.

XU–19 ————. f.t., "The Little Flock." (1820s) [4]136 pp. 16 × 10 cm. R,S; h. OCWR, SM216.

XU–20 ————. f.l., "Love floats on the breeze." (ca. 1877–1893) [2]61[63] pp. 20 × 15 cm. S; e,h. WLCMs, no. 224.

XU–21 ————. f.t., "The Lovely Band." (ca. 1843–1847) 19[38] pp. 13 × 16 cm. P,S; e,g. OCWR, SM19.

XU–22 ————. f.t., "Millennial Morn." (ca. 1890) [14]16[44] pp. 18 × 28 cm. R; h. DWt, SA1165.

XU–23 ————. f.t., "My Home." (1862–1863) [4]33[113] pp. 20 × 13 cm. S; e,h. DWt, SA1191.

XU–24 ————. f.l., "O how bright how beautiful." (?–1865) 130 pp. 19 × 13 cm. S; e. NYPLMs, 66–M–13, vol. 65.

XU–25 ————. f.t., "O Where are Reapers." (ca. 1880s–1890s) [10]53[145] pp. 18 × 11 cm. S; e. NYOC, Ac. 8796.

XU–26 ————. f.t., "River of Love." (–?–) [4]224[16] pp. 22 × 14 cm. inscribed, "Louisa Willey, 1908." R; e. DWt, SA1199.

XU–27 ————. f.t., "Round Dance Songs." (1854–1861) [16]78 pp. 16 × 10 cm. S; e,ls. OCWR, SM406.

XU–28 ————. f.t., "Rules for Correct Singing." (–?–) 264 pp. 12 × 22 cm. R,S; a, exercises. MPH, 9775/A1Ru.

XU–29 ————. "Rules for Learning Music Copied in 1870." (1871) 64 pp. 24 × 20 cm. S; h. exercises. OCWR, SM501.

XU–30 ————. f.t., "Scenes of Glory." (1880s–1890s) [10]85[107] pp. 17 × 11 cm. S; e. NYOC, Ac. 8820.

XU–31 ————. f.t., "Serious Impressions." (ca. 1840) [8 cont]156 pp. 17 × 11 cm. S; e,g,h,ls. OCWR, SM17.

XU–32 ————. cover, "Shaker Music." (1880s?) [70]82 pp. 19 × 24 cm. R; h. OCWR, SM244.

XU–33 ————. f.t., "Shining Silone." (1847–1868) 76[54] pp. 21 × 17 cm. S; a. OCWR, SM235.

XU–34 ————. f.t., "Solemn Praise." (1869–1881) [6 cont]314[8 cont] pp. 22 × 13 cm. inscribed, "Effie Taylor book." S; a,e,h. OCWR, SM241.

XU–35 ————. f.t., "Songs & Anthems." (1845–1847) [4]120[4] pp. 16 × 10 cm. S; e,g,ls. NYHS.

XU–36 ————. f.t., "The Songs of Blessed Mother Ann." (1850s) 52 pp. 17 × 10 cm. S; e,fp,ls,ss. MeSL.

XU–37 ————. f.t., "*Songs* to be *Sung* at the *Boston Meeting* Dec. 28 29." (1869) 24 pp. 22 × 13 cm. S; a,e,h. OCWR, SM238.

XU–38 ————. f.l., "Sound sound the Tamborrine." (1872–1873) 50 pp. 20 × 17 cm. S; e,h. OCWR, SM300.

XU–39 ————. f.t., "Travelers Home." (1868–1871) 34[88] pp. 20 × 14 cm. S; h. OCWR, SM159.

XU–40 ————. f.t., "The Tree of Life." (early 1830s) [4]53[69] pp. 15 × 10 cm. S; h. OCWR, SM65.

XU–41 ————. f.t., "We are seen." (?–1852) [6]140[90] pp. 19 × 13 cm. inscribed, "The last hymn copied in this book was given in 1852. The others are mostly of much earlier date." S; h. OCWR, SM287.

XU–42   ———. f.l., "Whence comes this bright celestial light." (1850s) 166[24 cont] pp.
             21 × 15 cm. inscribed, "Mss Song Bk N. Union. O." [library hand?] S; e,h.
             OCWR, SM388.
XU–43   ———. f.l., "Who will bow and bend like the willow." (ca. 1847–1851) 314 pp.
             17 × 11 cm. S; e. WLCMs, no. 227.

PROVENANCE, MISCELLANEOUS
(Collections of songs on loose leaves written at various societies)

XM–1   MeSL, no call number.
XM–2   OCoO, MS Coll. 119, Box 9, Folder 2.
XM–3   OCWR, IX.A.1–5.
XM–4   WLCM, M/2131/S4S37.
XM–5   WLCMs, no. 349b.

Checklist of Additional Manuscripts Cited

CHCHS—*Conn., Hartford, Connecticut Historical Society*

MS Stack Albany Letter. 1785	Anon., Letter describing Shaker singing and dancing, Albany, July 24, 1785.

DWt—*Del., Winterthur, The Henry Francis du Pont Winterthur Museum, Andrews Shaker Collection*

SA144	"A Spiritual Journal Commenced June 1st 1841" [Lebanon, N. Y.].
SA760	"A Concise View of the Church of God and of Christ on Earth . . . New Lebanon 1856" [by Isaac N. Youngs].
SA799.1	"The first part of this Book is copied mostly from manuscripts found among the writings of Deacon Daniel Goodrich Senr after his decease."
SA1107	"David Slossons Presented to Benjamin Gates May 2, 1840."

ICHS—*Ill., Chicago, Chicago Historical Society*

—	[G. Flower Diary]

KBGK—*Ky., Bowling Green, The Kentucky Library*

—	"Shaker Record A: History of the South Union Shaker Colony from 1804 to 1836 Transcribed by Harvey L. Eades in 1870 from original journals and diaries."
—	"Shaker Record B: South Union, Ky., Oct. 1, 1836, to Dec. 31, 1852. Kept by Harvey L. Eades."
—	[Journal of a journey made in 1854 by four of the colony to the Eastern Shaker Settlements. Probably written by Eldress Betsy Smith of South Union.]

KLF—*Ky., Louisville, The Filson Club*

BA/.S527/4	"Family Journal, Kept by order of the Deaconesses of the East House . . . Pleasant Hill, Kentucky" [1843–1871].
BA/.S527/6	[Journal of Pleasant Hill church meetings, beginning 1846.]
BA/.S527/7	[Pleasant Hill journal, beginning July 1847.]
BA/.S527/11	"A Journal or Record of events kept By James T. Ballance . . . Pleasant Hill" [1854–1860].

KLxU—*Ky., Lexington, The University of Kentucky Library*

Film/M206/Reel 2	"Biographical Register, Being a part of the Church Record Kept by order of the Trustees, In three Books . . . Pleasant Hill, Kentucky 1845. Book C." [Original in the possession of the Mercer County Historical Society.]

Film/M206/Reel 2   [Journal kept by Andrew D. Barrett at Union Village, beginning 1902.]

Film/M206/Reel 2   "A spiritual Journal for the Year of our Lord one Thousand Eighteen hundred and forty three Commenced Jan 1st 1843" [Pleasant Hill].

Film/M–384   [Journal kept at Pleasant Hill, Jan. 1, 1856–March 1, 1871; original owned by Mrs. William Pettit of Lexington, Ky.]

MeSL—Me., Sabbathday Lake, The United Society of Shakers

—   "Biographic Memoir of the Life and Experience of Calvin Green. . . . This copy commenced Nov. 22, 1868," 3 vols.

—   "Church Journal" [kept by the ministry at Gloucester, Me.].

—   [Commonplace Book of Aurelia Mace, diary entry dated 1896.]

—   f.t., "The Golden Chariot" [including on pp. 62–66 a series of lessons entitled "Music," written about 1829 by James Wakefield].

    f.t., "Incidents related by Jemima Blanchard of her experience and Intercourse with Mother Ann and our first Parents. Written by Roxalana L. Grosvenor." [Cited as "Parents"]

—   f.t., "Incidents related by Jemima Blanchard, Of her experience and intercourse with Mother and the Elders. Written by Roxalana L. Grosvenor." [Cited as "Elders"]

—   Letter, Sabbathday Lake, Me., Jan. 24, 1905, Aurelia Mace to Mrs. Geo. M. Jackson.

—   [Letter Book of the ministry at Gloucester, Me., May 1872 to Jan. 1883.]

—   "A Record of Appointments" [kept by the ministry at Gloucester].

—   f.t., "True Thankfulness" [a collection of song texts compiled by Joshua Bussell, 1860s].

NCCM—N. C., Chapel Hill, University of North Carolina, Music Library

Early American Music Collection, vol. 72   [Anonymous, untitled collection of dance tunes.]

NCCF—N. C., Chapel Hill, University of North Carolina, Folklore Archives

—   "Daniel W. Patterson Collection."

NCDD—N. C., Durham, Duke University Library

Cab. 47/Harris, Henry St. George Papers, 1823–1887   Letter, William Harris to Margarete, New Lebanon Springs, Sept. 5, 1826.

NHCb—N. H., Canterbury, The Shaker Village

—   "Historical Notes having reference to the Believers in Enfield, N. H., by Elder Henry C. Blinn. Enfield, N. H.," 2 vols.

—   "A Historical Record of the Society of Believers in Canterbury, N. H., from the time of its organization in 1792 until the year one thousand, eight hundred and forty eight, by Henry C. Blinn," 2 vols.

NHCo—N. H., *Concord, The New Hampshire Historical Society*

289.8/U58uv/ 1870–82, v. 3   [Journal of the gathering order at Union Village, kept by Oliver C. Hampton.]

NYAL—*New York, Albany, The New York State Library*

324   "Sayings of Mother Ann, and The First Elders: Gathered from Different Individuals At Harvard & Shirley, Who were Eye & Ear Witnesses, Of The Divine Word & Power of God Revealed thro' Them, at Different Times and in Various Places."

358   "A Treatise on Music; agreeably to the Plan established and adopted at New Lebanon & Watervliet, N. Y. 1840" [Isaac N. Youngs and D. A. Buckingham].

CM 424–37   [Testimonies: "Testimony of Susannah Barrett," loose leaf dated Shirley, July 15, 1826.]

NYAP—*N. Y., New York, The American Society for Psychical Research*

—   "A Book of Visions and Divine Manifestations; The Writing of which was commenced in January, 1838: wrote by Russel Haskell. Enfield, Connecticut."

NYOC—*N. Y., Old Chatham, The Shaker Museum*

Ac. 6286   "Extracts from 'A Concise View of the Church of God and of Christ on Earth' . . . Compiled by Isaac N. Youngs . . ." [copy made by Marcia E. Hastings.]

Ac. 12,051   "A Sketch of the Life and Experience of Issachar Bates Sen. Transcribed from a Manuscript Copy belonging to the Church at Enfield, N.H. . . . February, 1860."

Ac. 12,053   [Journal of the missionary trip to the West in 1805.]

Ac. 12,743   [Autobiography of Elmira Allard, 1885.]

Ac. 12,752   "Rufus Bishop & Isaac Youngs, through the states of Ohio & Kentucky 1834. Journal, Volume 2nd."

Ac. 13,404   "Biography of Elder Henry Clough."

Ac. 17,917   Faith Clark, "Data on Seven Religious Marches of Shaker Worship Ritual" (typescript, 1964; based on interviews with Brother Ricardo Belden).

NYPLMs—*N. Y., The New York Public Library, Manuscript Division*

58–M–140, vol. 1   "A Daily Journal of Passing Events; Begun January the 1st 1830. By Rufus Bishop, in the 56th year of his age."

58–M–140, vol. 2   "A Daily Journal of passing events; begun May the 19th 1839, at Watervliet; By Rufus Bishop, in the 65th year of his age."

58–M–140, vol. 3   "A Journal or Register of passing events, Continued from former Volumes, kept by Rufus Bishop" [1850–1859].

58–M–140, vol. 4   "A Register of Incidents and Events Being a Continuation From other Records kept by the Ministry. Kept by Giles B. Avery. Commenced Oct. 20th 1859."

58–M–140, vol. 7   "Records Kept by Order of the Church" [by Isaac N. Youngs].

58–M–140, vol. 11   [Diary kept by Anna White from 1855 to 1873.]

—   Angell Matthewson (1769———), [Reminiscences in the form of a series of thirty-nine letters to his brother Jeffrey].

OCSH—O., Cleveland, *The Shaker Historical Society*

—   "Recollections of North Union Shaker Colony by George Engle Budinger" [transcription of a tape-recorded interview by Frank Myers and Harrison Collister, Nov. 23, 1962].

OCWR—O., Cleveland, *The Western Reserve Historical Society*

IV.A.9   Letter, Enfield, Conn., Feb. 10, 1834, Russel Haskell to Isaac N. Youngs.

IV.B.7   "Letter Book A" [Kept by the ministry at Lebanon, N. Y.].

IV.B.19–20 [Copies of letters sent and received by South Union, 1806–1887.]

IV.B.34   [Copies of miscellaneous correspondence made by Alonzo G. Hollister of Lebanon.]

IV.B.35   [Copies of miscellaneous correspondence, 1807–1864.]

IV.B.36   [Copies of miscellaneous correspondence, 1811–1841.]

V.B.10   [Diary kept by an unidentified Shaker at Enfield, Conn.]

V.B.15   "A record of spiritual things, meetings gifts presents moves and changes &c. Commencing January 1847" [by Anna Granger of Enfield, Conn.].

V.B.36   [Church journal kept at Harvard by Thomas Hammond, 1816–1872.]

V.B.46   "Daily Journal for the Ministry. Commencing November 9th 1840. Kept by Grove B. Blanchard."

V.B.70   "Domestic Journal" [kept at Lebanon, 1847–1855.]

V.B.93–94   "A Journal kept by Elizabeth Lovegrove, In time of the revival, in 1827," 2 vols.

V.B.97   [Journal kept at Lebanon by Henry DeWitt, 1827–1867.]

V.B.105   "A Journal or Day Book Written by Giles Avery" [Lebanon, 1834–1836].

V.B.106   "A Journal of Times, Rhymes, Work & Weather, Very much mixed up togather Commenced Feby 11th 1836 Kept by. Giles B. Avery" [Lebanon, 1836–1838].

V.B.107   "A Journal of Domestic Events and Transactions. . . . Commenced Feby 7th 1838. Kept by Giles B. Avery" [to 1847].

V.B.135   "Journal of meetings held in Church Order Mt. Lebanon N. Y. 1841."

v.B.152	"A Daily Journal Kept by Daniel Boler, On a western Tour thro Ohio & Kentucky; In Company with the Ministry from Holy Mount. Commencing June 7, 1852. New Lebanon, N. Y."
v.B.161	[Journal of a trip to the western societies by Hiram Rude and Hannah Ann Agnew, 1856.]
v.B.172	[Journal kept by Harriet Bullard of a visit to the Southern and Western societies in 1889.]
v.B.174	[Daily journal kept at Lebanon, with a "Yearly View of the Addition or Diminuation of numbers," pp. 151–159.]
v.B.230	"Records of the Church At Union Village Ohio," vol. 1 [1805–1861].
v.B.231	"Records of the Church At Union Village Ohio," vol. 2 [1861–1876].
v.B.241	[Journal kept at Union Village by Charles D. Hampton in 1839.]
v.B.247	[Journal kept at Union Village by Oliver C. Hampton, vol. 5, 1860–1874.]
v.B.279	"Records of the Church at Watervliet, N. Y.," vol. 1 [1788–1851].
v.B.294	"A Regular Journal of Events: Including Donations and Expenditures. Kept by Freegift Wells. Watervliet, March 1836."
vi.A.5	"Autobiographic Sketch of Eunice Bathrick" [Harvard].
vi.A.6	"Testimony of Daniel Sizer" [Lebanon].
vi.B.30	"Biographic Memoir of the Life and Experience of Calvin Green," vol. 2 [copy made by Alonzo G. Hollister at Lebanon].
vi.B.36	"Autobiography of the Saints or Stray Leaves from the Book of Life. Commenced April 19th 1868. Alonzo G. Hollister" [Lebanon].
vi.B.37	"Book of Immortality Autobiography of the Saints or Leaves from the Tree (Book) of Life. Volume 2nd—Commenced December 25th, or Christmas 1872 By Alonzo G. Hollister, Mount Lebanon. . . ."
vii.A.10	[Miscellaneous writings, including a biographical sketch of Elder Solomon King.]
vii.B.10	"Historical Notes having reference to The Believers in Enfield, N. H. By Henry C. Blinn. Enfield, N. H. (January, 1897)."
vii.B.17	[Miscellaneous writings beginning with "Circumstances respecting the Square House as related by Abel Jewet Johnathan Clark & others."]
vii.B.51	"This collection was Selected by James Palmer Vail" [Lebanon].
vii.B.89	"Anthems & Miscellaneous Writings. 1884: A Collection of Gospel Anthems . . . Selected and Transcribed By Sarah Woodrow. Canaan N. Y. June 1845. Given by Sarah to Alonzo—in 1884."
vii.B.107–110	"Alonzo G. Hollister. Mount Lebanon Book of Rememberance," vols. 3–5 [1867–1874].
vii.B.203	[Miscellaneous writings including "Extracts from sayings and writings of Father James & Father Joseph not found any where in print. Gathered from various sources by Elder Alonzo G. Hollister."]
vii.B.230	[Miscellaneous collection from South Union, f.l., "Gods blessing in sending the gospel to the West."]
vii.B.235	[Miscellaneous writings, including letters copied at South Union, 1823–1878.]
viii.A.73.Item 5	"The Visitation of the different Tribes of Native Spirits, &c. Together with a Night Vision or Dream, and The Faith, of the Writer briefly stated" [D. A. Buckingham of Watervliet, N. Y.].

VIII.B.21	[Miscellaneous spirit communications with drawings, including f.t., "From Mother Ann to Polly Collins. Nov. 9. 1840. A Roll."]
VIII.B.24	"Miscellany. Manuscript No. III" [Eunice Bathrick of Harvard.]
VIII.B.109	"A Preface, or Introduction to the Records of Sacred Communications, Given by Divine Inspiration, In the Church at New Lebanon" [Isaac N. Youngs].
VIII.B.115	[Miscellaneous song texts and writings, f.t., "Words of the Savior," with additions by Alonzo G. Hollister.]
VIII.B.138	[Journal of meetings at which inspired messages and communications were received, begun by Derobigne M. Bennett and continued by Isaac N. Youngs, Lebanon, 1840–1841.]
VIII.B.249	"A Spiritual Record, Comprised in Eight Volumes: A Record of Heavenly Gifts, Messages and Communications received from the Eternal and Spiritual World: Which were made known to us, through existing Members under Divine Inspiration, Church, Watervliet, Jan. 1. 1839" [D. A. Buckingham].
x.B.31	[Miscellaneous song texts and writings, f.t., "Mother Ann's Birth Day," with additions by Alonzo G. Hollister of Lebanon.]
XIII.7–7c	"Rufus Bishop's Scrap Book" [Lebanon.]
[BX9778/T5B7]	"Book of Lovely Vineyard. Given me at Harvard in 1890. A Miscellaneous Record. Alonzo G. Hollister—Finished May 28th 1897. Church—Mount Lebanon Columbia Co. N. Y." [Neither the librarian nor I have been able to find this manuscript since the re-classification of the Shaker collection in the early 1970s].
SM503	"The Patent Gamut or Scale of Music."
SM504	"A Musical Expositor: Being an index or key to the reading & writing of music according to the letter method. Enfield, Hartford county, Conn. 1831." [Russel Haskell].
SM506	[Miscellaneous collection, f.t., "A copy of a letter written to James Calver Mt. Lebanon."]
Letters	[For all unbound correspondence I give the place and date of writing, the author and recipient, or as much as possible of this information. The appropriate box and folder numbers can be found in Section IV of Kermit J. Pike, *A Guide To Shaker Manuscripts in The Library of The Western Reserve Historical Society* (Cleveland, 1974).]

ODPL—O., Dayton, The Dayton and Montgomery County Public Library

Personal Papers, Hamilton, W. J.	W. J. Hamilton, "Richard McNemar, 1770–1839."

WLCM—District of Columbia, Washington, The Library of Congress, Music Division

MT/7/.Y56	"The Rudiments of Music Displayed and explained. With a Sellected Variety of Lessons and Examples. By Isaac N. Youngs. New Lebanon—1833."

WLCMs—District of Columbia, Washington, The Library of Congress, Manuscript Division

Papers of the Shakers

No. 20	[Letters of Henry C. Blinn, Canterbury, 1874.]
No. 27	"Church Record Including Biographical Register of the Shaker Community at Pleasant Hill Mercer County, Kentucky, 1806–1879" [typescript].
No. 35	[Journal of a trip of the Kentucky ministry to Lebanon and other Eastern societies, June 9, 1869–Aug. 7, 1869.]
No. 42	"Narrative of Various Events. Beginning April 1815. By Isaac N. Youngs" [Lebanon].
No. 50	"Journal of a Memorable Journey From White-Water, Ohio. to New Lebanon. N. Y. Taken by Hannah R. Agnew when 16 years of age. In the Year 1836."
No. 53	"Historical Scetches or a Record of Remarkable events With Remarks & Illustrations Kept By Giles B. Avery. New Lebanon."
No. 55	"A Sketch of the life and experience of Rhoda Blake also a narrative of things which have taken place since 1808 . . . Began to be written in the year 1864, and copied in 1892. Rhoda Blake."
No. 61	[Commonplace book, f.t., "Testimony delivered by Elder Harvey Eades."]
No. 71	[Miscellaneous collection including James Smith's testimony in the form of a letter to Elder Freegift, dated "Square House Nov. 16th 1836."]
No. 73	"An Explanation of Certain Texts and figurs, Contained in the Scriptures; and important to be known by Believers in the Second appearance of Christ" [Calvin Green].
No. 78	"Biographic Memoir of the Life and Experience of Calvin Green . . . Written and Composed by Himself . . . First Order. New Lebanon. State of n. Y. America. Year of our Lord 1861," 3 vols. [copy made by Thomas J. Stroud in 1881].
No. 79	"A little Memorial Of Life and Experience From Birth to Old Age By Calvin Green . . . Written in the Church, First Order New Lebanon, New York. October 11th 1859."
No. 119	"A Journey by Issachar, John Dunlavy, Matthew Houston, Malcham Worley & James Hodge—Through Kentucky and the Wabash— 2.2: 5:1808."
No. 135	[Three gift drawings received by Polly Collins of Hancock.]
No. 143	"James S. Prescott—Journal" [North Union, 1846–1874].
No. 146	"A Monthly Journal of such transactions as is and may hereafter be considered of some importance to be kept . . . Commenced the 22nd of June 1830. By Philemon Stewart" [Lebanon].
No. 161	"A Sketch of the Life and Experiences of Issachar Bates, Sen" and "Here Commences the Journal kept by Samuel Swan McClelland Commencing Jany 1811, Ending March 1827" [Union Village].
No. 169	"A Journal kept by Naomi Ligier. Beginning October 13th 1840" [Union Village].

No. 180   "A History of the Principal Events of the Society of Believers, at Union Village Commencing in the Month of March 1805 Containing a Tolerably Explicit Account of Most of the Scenes of the Said Society Onward. Compiled both from Memory and the Several Journals Kept in the Society from the Beginning; by O. C. Hampton. Who Was a Member of Said Society Since 1822."

No. 193   "December the 21st 1823, Richard McNemars Book."

No. 232   "A Daily Journal" [Union Village, beginning May 31, 1806].

No. 241   [Journal of Union Village church meetings and miscellaneous materials, 1863–1874.]

No. 245   [Letterbook containing miscellaneous Union Village correspondence.]

No. 246   [Union Village, Ohio] "Letter Book, vol III. 1834.–5.6."

No. 254   [Commonplace books of Richard McNemar, vol. 2: "A Review of the Gospel. According to the Faith of the United Society Called Shakers. Designed for the use of Believers: . . . Pleasant Hill K. Y. August 1827."]

No. 291   [Union Village church record, Apr. 27, 1841–Mar. 23, 1844.]

No. 294   [Union Village journal, Oct. 9, 1874–Nov. 13, 1881.]

No. 301   [Commonplace book of Richard McNemar, beginning with p. 19, f.t., "An agreement of Parents respecting children."]

No. 331   "Diabology" [Lebanon, Calvin Green].

No. 336   [Autobiographical writing by Susan C. Liddil.]

No. 337a   [Miscellaneous writings, including "A Vision seen by Rowland Wood, Sabbath forenoon at 9 oclock March 5th 1843."]

No. 338a   [Autobiographical writings by Susan C. Liddil of Union Village.]

Nos. 339–344   [Historical notes on Union Village written by Susan C. Liddil], 6 vols.

Nos. 345–346   [Miscellaneous hymn texts.]

No. 347   [Miscellaneous letters, 1826–1863.]

No. 348   [Notes on the life of Richard McNemar, by Susan C. Liddil of Union Village.]

No. 351d–5   [Journal of church meetings at Union Village, Oct. 19, 1843–Mar. 10, 1844.]

No. 353   [Miscellaneous notes made by Susan C. Liddil of Union Village.]

No. 355   [Miscellaneous notes about Union Village made by Susan C. Liddil.]

SOUND RECORDINGS OF SHAKER SINGING

A. Long-playing Discs

"Early Shaker Spirituals: Sung by Sister R. Mildred Barker and Other Members of the United Society of Shakers, Sabbathday Lake, Maine," ed. Daniel W. Patterson. Somerville, Mass.: Rounder Records, 1976. (Rounder 0078)

[Forty-eight songs; the album differs substantially from two earlier forms of the recording issued by the United Society in 1967 and 1970.]

"14 Shaker Folk Songs," with an Introduction by Shaker Brother Ricardo Belden and Jerome Count. Mount Lebanon, N. Y.: Shaker Village Work Group, n.d. (Shaker Village TV–25548)

[One song performed by Brother Ricardo Belden in the course of an interview.]

The Shaker Heritage, ed. William Randle. Cleveland, Ohio: Western Reserve University Press, 1961.

[Side 14 of this set presents fifteen songs of the transitional era performed without accompaniment by the Sabbathday Lake singers. The combined singers of Canterbury and Sabbathday Lake perform later songs with instrumental support and lecture on the music in Sides 13, 15, and 16.]

B. MAGNETIC TAPE RECORDINGS

Binghamton, N. Y.—The State University of New York, Music Listening Library
"Roger L. Hall Collection"—1 reel.
[Recordings made at Canterbury, N. H., and Sabbathday Lake, Me., and transcribed in Roger L. Hall, "The Shaker Letteral System: A Practical Approach to Music Notation," M.A. thesis, State University of New York at Binghamton, 1972.]

Chapel Hill, N. C.—The University of North Carolina, Folk Music Archives
"Daniel W. Patterson Collection"—30 reels.
[Performances and interviews recorded between 1960 and 1974; informants include Sister R. Mildred Barker, Eldress Marguerite Frost, Eldress Bertha Lindsay, Mrs. Olive Hayden Austin, and Miss Florence Phelps.]
"Otto Jantz Collection"—1 reel.
[Dubbing of a tape copy of a wire recording made in 1950, for which Brother Ricardo Belden sang hymns from *Millennial Praises*.]
"Tom Davenport Collection"—45 reels.
[Chiefly interviews recorded in 1970–1972 at Canterbury, N. H., and Sabbathday Lake, Me., and partially used in the sound track of the film "The Shakers."]

Sabbathday Lake, Me.—The United Society of Shakers, Inc.
"The Shaker Library Collection"—40 reels.
[The recorded repertory and recollections of Sister R. Mildred Barker and other members of the Society.]

Shakertown at Pleasant Hill, Kentucky, Inc.
"Pleasant Hill Collection"—3 cassettes.
[Interview with Miss Florence Phelps and Mrs. Harriet Newman, recorded during a visit to Shakertown, Sept. 18, 1969.]

Winterthur, Del.—The Henry Francis du Pont Winterthur Museum
"The Edward Deming Andrews Shaker Collection"—1 reel (SA 1325).
[A dubbing of disc recordings of ten songs performed in 1937 by Sister Sarah Collins and an unidentified sister of Mount Lebanon, N. Y.]

Credits and Sources for the Illustrations

Courtesy of Professor Raymond Adams, Chapel Hill, North Carolina:
>   Fig. 15.
Courtesy of The Fruitlands Museum, Harvard, Mass.:
>   Figs. 8, 9, 22, 26, 43, 44 [a composite of these six photographs appeared in Emily Williams, "Spirituality as Expressed in Song," *The Connecticut Magazine*, 9 (Autumn 1905), 745–751]; 57.
Courtesy of The Andrews Memorial Shaker Collection, The Henry Francis du Pont Winterthur Museum Libraries, Winterthur, Del.:
>   Figs. 2 (SA253.1), 19 (SA1128), 20 (SA1116), 41 (SA35), 64 (SA340).
Courtesy of the Divisions of Manuscripts, Music, and Prints and Photographs, The Library of Congress, Washington, D. C.:
>   Figs. 17, 23, 27 (HABS, Photographer, William F. Winter, Jr.), 28 (HABS, Photographer, N. E. Baldwin), 34 (HABS, Photographer, E. J. Stein), 35, 36, 42, 53 (HABS, Photographer, N. E. Baldwin).
Courtesy of The Index of American Design, National Gallery of Art, Washington, D. C.:
>   Figs. 6 and 7 (Photographer, Noel Vicentini).
Courtesy of The New York Historical Society, New York City:
>   Figs. 29, 46.
Courtesy of The New York State Museum, Albany, N. Y.:
>   Fig. 59.
Courtesy of The Shaker Community, Inc., Hancock, Mass.:
>   Fig. 10 (Photographer, Elmer R. Pearson).
Courtesy of The Shaker Museum Foundation, Old Chatham, N. Y.:
>   Fig. 21 (Photographer, Pinto Photo Service, Kinderhook, N. Y.).
Courtesy of Mr. John E. Shea, Albany, N. Y.:
>   Fig. 16.
Courtesy of Mr. Charles Thompson, Canterbury, N. H.:
>   Fig. 62 (Photographer, Swenson of Concord).
Courtesy of The Shaker Library, The United Society of Shakers, Sabbathday Lake, Me., Inc.:
>   Figs. 45 (Photographer, John V. Goff), 49, 50, 56, 61, 63.
Courtesy of The Warren County Historical Museum, Lebanon, Ohio:
>   Fig. 25.
Courtesy of The Western Reserve Historical Society, Cleveland, Ohio:
>   Figs. 3, 4, 5, 12, 13, 14, 18, 24, 32, 33, 37, 38, 51, 52, 54, 58, 60.
Courtesy of The Shaker Collection, Williams College Library, Williamstown, Mass.:
>   Fig. 48.
Others:
>   Fig. 1: Adapted from James Logan, *Notes of a Journey through Canada, the United*

States of America, and the West Indies (Edinburgh, 1838), frontispiece.

Fig. 11: Scribal designs copied by Patricia O'Day, Chapel Hill, N. C.

Fig. 30: From "The Shakers in Niskayuna," *Frank Leslie's Popular Monthly*, 20 (Dec. 1885), 663–670.

Fig. 31: From [Benson Lossing], "The Shakers," *Harper's New Monthly Magazine*, 15 (1857), 169.

Fig. 39: From David Lamson, *Two Years among the Shakers* (West Boylston, 1848), frontispiece.

Fig. 40: After Robert F. W. Meader, "Zion Patefacta," *The Shaker Quarterly*, 2 (Spring 1962), [11], copied by Jan McInroy, Chapel Hill, N. C.

Fig. 55: From Leila S. Taylor, *A Memorial to Eldress Anna White, and Elder Daniel Offord* (Mount Lebanon, N. Y., 1912), p. 18 (copied by Elmer R. Pearson)

Diagrams 1–7: Prepared by Jan McInroy, Chapel Hill, N. C.

Notes to the Text

PREFACE

1 Edward D. Andrews, *The Gift to Be Simple: Songs, Dances and Rituals of the American Shakers* (New York, 1940); Phillips Barry, "Notes on the Songs and Music of the Shakers," *Bulletin of the Folk-Song Society of the Northeast*, 1 (1930), 5–7, and "Shaker Songs and Music," ibid., 4 (1932), 17–18; Clara E. Sears, *Gleanings from Old Shaker Journals* (Boston, 1916); and Harold E. Cook, "Shaker Music: A Manifestation of American Folk Culture," Ph.D. dissertation, Western Reserve University, 1946. Estella Weeks had also written several eccentric essays.

2 This manuscript in the Music Division of the Library of Congress is designated as "EC–11" in my checklist of Shaker song manuscripts.

3 Short of using a computer, I see no way to establish the number of surviving Shaker songs, but a tally of the ones printed in my collection throws some light on the question. The book holds 364 different Shaker melodies. Of these, 59 were recorded only in Haskell's great manuscript. His coverage, however, is strongest for the years before 1820 and rather weak after 1840. More than two-thirds of the songs in my collection—259 of them—do not appear in MS EC–11, and 175 of the songs survive in but a single manuscript. Clearly, much has been lost. Eighty-five of my songs are not found in manuscripts from the communities where they reportedly originated.

4 Knox (London, 1950); Whitworth (London, 1975); Noyes (Philadelphia, 1870); Nordhoff (New York, 1875); and Hinds, 2d ed. (Chicago, 1908). Some accounts, like Mark Holloway's *Heavens on Earth*, 2d ed. (New York, 1966) and Sydney E. Ahlstrom's *A Religious History of the American People* (New Haven, 1972), simply lack fresh insights. Some, like Elmer T. Clark's *The Small Sects in America*, rev. ed. (New York, 1949), are in addition unfriendly. Others like the account in D. D. Egbert and Stow Persons' *Socialism and American Life* (Princeton, 1952) manage in few words both to make factual errors and to spin an irrelevant theory. The best of these books—Arthur E. Bestor's *Backwoods Utopias* (Philadelphia, 1950)—shows thoughtful reading of primary sources, but draws some inferences contradicted by Shaker history.

5 Anna White and Leila S. Taylor, *Shakerism: Its Meaning and Message* (Columbus, Ohio, 1905).

6 Caroline Piercy, *The Valley of God's Pleasure* (New York, 1951), and Julia Neal, *By Their Fruits* (Chapel Hill, 1947).

7 Hannah Adams, *Views of Religion, In Two Parts*, 3rd ed. (Boston, 1801), pp. 113–115.

8 Henri Desroche, *Les Shakers américains, d'un néo-christianisme à un pré-socialisme?* (Paris, 1955); translated by John K. Savacool under the title *The American Shakers: From Neo-Christianity to Presocialism* (Amherst, 1971), pp. 292–293.

9 loc. cit., pp. 83–87.

10 John S. Dwight, "The Shakers at New Lebanon," *The Harbinger*, 5 (Aug. 14, 1847), 157.

11 F. Gerald Ham, "Shakerism in the Old West," Ph.D. dissertation, University of Kentucky, 1962; Robley E. Whitson, *Shaker Theological Sources: An Introductory Selection* (Bethlehem, Conn., 1969); Thomas Swain, "The Evolving Expressions of the Religious and Theological Experiences of a Community: A Comparative Study of the Shaker *Testimonies* . . .," *The Shaker Quarterly*, 12 (Spring 1972), 3–31, (Summer 1972), 43–67; and Theodore Johnson's introduction to "Rules and Orders for the Church of Christ's Second Appearing . . . 1860," *The Shaker Quarterly*, 11 (Winter 1971), 139–165.

12 Bryan Wilson, op. cit., pp. 205–206.

13 See Thomas Swain, op. cit.

14 Peter L. Berger, "Some Second Thoughts on Substantive versus Functional Definitions of Religion," *Journal for the Scientific Study of Religion*, 13 (1974), 129. In *New Heaven New Earth: A Study of Millenarian Activities* (Oxford, 1969) Kenelm Burridge formulates a kindred view, that millenarian movements adopt not only "new assumptions, a new redemptive process, a new politico-economic framework, a new mode of measuring the man" but also—in terms appropriate to the Shaker experience—"a new integrity, a new community" (p. 13).

15 See the opening of chapter two.

CHAPTER I

1 *The Christian Harmony; or, Songster's Companion* (Exeter, N. H., 1805), p. 71.

2 *White and Negro Spirituals* (Locust Valley, N. Y., 1943), p. 68.

3 Cf. Irving Lowens, *Music and Musicians in Early America* (New York, 1964), p. 139.

4 (Locust Valley, N. Y., 1953), p. 4.

5 Reginald Nettel, *Sing a Song of England: A Social History of Traditional Song* (London, 1954), pp. 10–12, and A. L. Lloyd, *Folk Song in England* (New York, 1967), pp. 131–132.

6 Percy Dearmer, R. Vaughan Williams, and Martin Shaw, *The Oxford Book of Carols* (London, 1928), pp. xiv–xv.

7 Cf. Lloyd, p. 130; Douglas Brice, *The Folk Carol of England* (London, 1967), p. 103 and *passim*; Frank Howes, *Folk Music of Britain—and Beyond* (London, 1967), p. 189; Elizabeth Poston, *The Penguin Book of Christmas Carols* (Harmondsworth, 1965), pp. 13–15; and Erik Routley, *The English Carol* (London, 1958),

pp. 122–124. In *An Introduction to English Folk Song* (London, 1973), pp. 56–61, Maud Karpeles refrains from speculations concerning the origin of the carol, and she recognizes the diversity of the songs to which this name is given. Her brief survey of English folk song makes no other mention of religious song. Her fellow collector Cecil Sharp quickly learned on his Appalachian tours to ask for "love songs" in order to avoid hearing "hymns instead of the secular songs and ballads which we wanted," and he "had but little truck" with members of the Holiness sect, "as their creed forbids the singing of secular songs" (*English Folk Songs from the Southern Appalachians* (London, 1932), I, xxiii and xxvi). Anne G. Gilchrist overcame distaste for "expressions of a sincere if uncouth religious emotion" sufficiently to publish "The Folk Element in Early Revival Hymns and Tunes," *Journal of the Folk-Song Society*, 8 (1928), 61–95.

8 Richard L. Greene, *The Early English Carols* (London, 1935), p. xxiii.

9 William Henry Husk in his *Songs of the Nativity* (London, [1868]), p. 181, reprints "The Twelve Days of Christmas" from a broadside entitled "An Old English Carol"; but Husk claims to be the first to include the song in a collection of carols and thinks it "can scarcely be said to fall within that description of composition, being rather fitted for use in playing the game of 'Forfeits,' to which purpose it was commonly applied in the metropolis upwards of forty years since." See also footnote 17, below.

10 Karpeles, pp. 56ff.

11 *The Ballad as Song* (Berkeley and Los Angeles, 1969), p. 104.

12 Ibid.

13 The classic statement of this view is that presented by Cecil Sharp in *English Folk-Song: Some Conclusions* (London, 1907), pp. 101–102.

14 *The Ballad Revival* (Chicago, 1961), p. 21; cf. p. 61.

15 Bronson, pp. 308–309.

16 *Traditional Tunes of the Child Ballads*, I (Princeton, 1959), 308.

17 The origins of various Christmas counting songs have occasioned much comment. The present concensus takes a "Puritan" composition dating from 1625 to be the prototype of those that entered English oral tradition—cf. Leah R. C. Yoffie, "Songs of the 'Twelve Numbers' and the Hebrew Chant of 'Echod Mi Yodea,'" *Southern Folklore Quarterly*, 62 (1949), esp. 393–403.

18 Lloyd, p. 129.

19 *The History of English Poetry* (London, 1781), III, 142–143.

20 The Child ballads I have listed doubtless have had a similar function, and for Catholics as well as Protestants. In singing "The Cruel Mother," for example, Mrs· Cecilia Kelly Costello commented that when her Irish father, "a very strict man," taught it to her, he took her between his legs, saying, "When you get married . . . and you have any children, moreso sons, don't you do what this woman's done what I'm going to sing to you" (Leader Record LEE–4054: "Cecilia Costello: Recordings from the Sound Archives of the BBC").

21 "Death and a Lady: Echoes of a Mortal Conversation in English and American Folk Song Tradition," M.A. thesis, University of North Carolina at Chapel Hill, 1966. Mrs. Barks discusses eighteen song texts. Those I quote here are from the following sources: Woodfall

Ebsworth, ed., *The Roxburghe Ballads* (Hartford, 1883), VIII, vii; Cecil Sharp, *Folksongs from Somerset* (London, 1911), p. 5; Olin Downes and Elie Siegmeister, *A Treasury of American Song*, 2d ed. (New York, 1943), p. 263; Prestige Record INT–DS 25001: "Georgia Sea Islands, Vol. 1" of *The Southern Journey Series*, ed. Alan Lomax; Folkways Record FA–2309: "Old Love Songs and Ballads," ed. John Cohen; and Elektra Records EKL–301/2: "Leadbelly: The Library of Congress Recordings," ed. Lawrence Cohn.

22 Nicholas Temperley, in "John Playford and the Metrical Psalms," *Journal of the American Musicological Society*, 25 (Spring 1972), 331–378, prints tables showing how few collections of psalm tunes held harmonic settings prior to the eighteenth century.

23 (London, 1686), pp. 100–101. "Southwell" tune is printed in this book both in its skeletal form and as it might be ornamented when sung. Temperley called attention to this book; a copy is in the Library of Congress.

24 Tangent Record TNGM–120: "Scottish Tradition 6: 'Gaelic Psalms from Lewis'" is an entire album of psalmody. Performances can also be heard on single bands of Ocora Record OCR–45: "Gaelic Music from Scotland," and Columbia Record KL–209: "World Library of Folk and Primitive Music, Vol. 6: 'Folk Songs from Scotland,'" ed. Alan Lomax.

25 "Gaelic Psalm-Singing on the Isle of Lewis," *St. Andrews Review*, 1 (Spring and Summer 1972), p. 57. Porter prints brief transcriptions of some of the ornamentation.

26 Jackson discusses this song style under the unfortunate name "surge song" in chapter 18 of *White and Negro Spirituals* and includes as an appendix musical transcriptions of examples of the style. William H. Tallmadge carries the exploration of the style further in "Dr. Watts and Mahalia Jackson—The Development, Decline, and Survival of a Folk Style in America," *Ethnomusicology*, 5 (Jan. 1961), 95–99. Good specimens of black performances in this style can be heard in Deacon Shinault's rendition of "I Cannot Live in Sin" on Blues Classic Record BLP–19: "Negro Religious Music, Vol. 3: 'Singing Preachers and Their Congregations,'" ed. Chris Strachwitz, and Deacon Harrison Smith's "That Awful Day Will Surely Come" on Savoy Record MG–14128: "Harrison Smith Presents the Old Time Prayer Meeting." Descriptions of early performances in the British Isles are quoted in the articles by Temperley and Porter and in the notes accompanying Tangent Record TNGM–120.

27 *The Grounds and Rules of Musick Explained; Or, An Introduction to the Art of Singing* (Boston, 1721), pp. 2, 4.

28 I do not believe it directly indebted to the most highly embellished solo song style of the British Isles, the archaic *sean-nós* of Ireland—for an analysis and transcription of this style, see Seóirse Bodley, "Technique and Structure in 'Sean-Nós' Singing," *Irish Folk Music Studies*, 1 (1972–1973), 44–53.

29 *Sea Songs and Shanties*, 6th ed. reprinted (Glasgow, 1948), p. 121.

30 In his early formulation of his views, "Folk Song Style," *American Anthropologist*, 61 (Dec. 1959), 937.

31 Walter, pp. 3–4.

32 In the preface to *The Psalms of David*, at any rate, Watts says, "I have formed my verse in the three most useful metres to which our psalm-tunes are fitted" *The Works*

of the Reverend and Learned Isaac Watts, ed. Jennings and Doddridge in 1753 (London, 1810), IV, 122.

33 Nelson F. Adams gives an admirably thorough survey of the eighteenth-century Methodist tunes in "The Musical Sources for John Wesley's Tune-Books; The Genealogy of 148 Tunes," S.M.D. dissertation, Union Theological Seminary, 1973, and reproduces the entire corpus in facsimile. Jackson discusses the influence of the American Lorenzo Dow on the English Primitive Methodists in chapter 7 of *White and Negro Spirituals*.

34 Robert H. Young, "The History of Baptist Hymnody in England from 1612 to 1800," D.M.A. dissertation, University of Southern California, 1959, p. 147.

35 From the subtitle of John Taylor's tract *A Swarme of Sectaries, and Schismatiques . . .* (London, 1641). James F. Hitchcock writes that "English radicalism presents a paradox, in that while it was preeminently a movement sprung from intellectual forebears . . . its membership seems to have been mostly the uneducated lower classes" and that "learned leadership does not seem to have maintained itself at the head of many groups" in his "Popular Religion in Elizabethan England," Ph.D. dissertation, Princeton University, 1965, pp. 207–208.

36 *The Ballad as Song*, p. 34. *The Gude and Godlie Ballatis*, which apparently were written as religious parodies of secular songs, antedate the Digger hymn by nearly a century but would not have been used in worship.

37 *Christian Songs; Written by Mr. John Glas, and Others*, 5th ed., corrected and much enlarged (Dundee, 1775), index.

38 *White and Negro Spirituals*, pp. 67–68, and *Airs Suitable for the Christian Songs* (Edinburgh, 1875), esp. "Gaelic Air," "Galashiels," and "The Gipsy Laddie." I am indebted to Mr. John A. Davidson for tracking down this and other printings of *Christian Songs*.

39 *Christian Songs in Two Parts*, 9th ed. (Edinburgh, 1805), pp. vii–viii.

40 The seventh edition of the Glassite hymnal was reprinted at Providence, Rhode Island, in 1787. A handful of its texts, with their traditional tunes, entered the general repertory of Northern spirituals. Richard Hulan has called my attention to the republication of several of these as late as 1849 in Amos S. Hayden's *The Sacred Melodeon* (as for example, "Boyd's" based on Glas's Song 31, and "Youngstown" and "Princeton" based on Glas's Song 76). Probably the nearest we can now get to the sounds of eighteenth-century American folk hymnody is the most conservative form of Primitive Baptist singing in the South—cf., the beautiful performances on Sovereign Grace Records 6058 and 6444: "Old Hymns Lined and Led by Elder Walter Evans, Sparta, North Carolina," issued by the Baptist Bible Hour of Cincinnati.

41 Quoted from John Smyth's "The Differences of the Church of the Separation" in Robert H. Young, p. 8, and Robert Barclay, *The Inner Life of the Religious Societies of the Commonwealth* (London, 1879), pp. 106–107.

42 Quoted in Young, pp. 12–13.

43 John L. Nickalls, ed., *The Journal of George Fox* (Cambridge, 1952), p. 164.

44 William C. Braithwaite, *The Beginnings of Quakerism* (London, 1923), p. 125.

45 Ibid., p. 252.

46 Quoted from George Fox and R. Hubberthorne, "Truth's Defence against the Refined Subtlety of the Serpent" (1658) in Barclay, p. 461n.

47 From Croese's *History of Quakerism* (1696) as quoted in Frederick J. Gillman, *The Evolution of the English Hymn* (London, 1927), p. 181. Gillman is troubled by this passage and warns that Croese "can be extravagant." I take it that in the words "collision, sound, and stretching of the voice, almost as the Spaniards" Croese is attempting to describe the high tessitura and the tendency toward embellishment already discussed as a characteristic of some British traditional singing and of Calvinist psalm singing.

48 Nickalls, p. 183.

49 [Benjamin S. Youngs and Calvin Green], *Testimony of Christ's Second Appearing*, 4th ed. (Albany, 1856), p. 617.

CHAPTER II

1 NCCF, Letter, Canterbury, May 25, 1965, Eldress Marguerite Frost to Daniel Patterson, p. 3.

2 In Shaker documents this community bears a number of names: New Lebanon, Lebanon, Mount Lebanon, and Holy Mount. To avoid confusion I hereafter refer to it simply as Lebanon. Similarly I use the name Gloucester for the village variously known as Gloucester, New Gloucester, West Gloucester, Chosen Land, and Sabbathday Lake.

3 [Benjamin S. Youngs and Calvin Green], *Testimony of Christ's Second Appearing*, 4th ed. (Albany, 1856), p. vi.

4 My headnotes to songs by these Shakers present their lives in more detail.

5 Seth Y. Wells, ed., *Testimonies Concerning the Character and Ministry of Mother Ann Lee and the First Witnesses of the Gospel* (Albany, 1827), p. 101.

6 Calvin Green and Seth Y. Wells, *A Summary View of the Millennial Church, or United Society of Believers* (Albany, 1823), p. 92.

7 Ibid., p. 93.

8 *Testimonies* (1827), p. 90.

CHAPTER III

1 NHCb, Henry C. Blinn, "A Historical Record of the Society of Believers in Canterbury, N. H., from the time of its organization in 1792 until the year one thousand, eight hundred and forty eight," II, 196.

2 DWt, SA760, pp. 347–348.

3 OCWR, Letter, Watervliet, N. Y, Nov. 12, 1834, D. Austin Buckingham to Russel [Haskell], p. 1.

4 OCWR, SM503, "The Patent Gamut or Scale of Music."

5 WLCM, MT 7/.Y56/case, "The Rudiments of Music Displayed and explained. With a Sellected Variety of Lessons and Examples. By Isaac N. Youngs. New Lebanon—1833." A "little gamut" written by Youngs about the year 1827 appears to have been lost, as does one drafted by Haskell in 1824.

6 *The Musical Reader; or Practical Lessons for the Voice*, rev. ed. (Utica, 1819).

7 John W. Callcott, *A Musical Grammar, in Four Parts*, First American, from the Last London Edition (Boston, n.d.).

8 MS EC–11, "Introduction," p. [ii], and OCWR, x.B.31, p. 165.

9 Callcott, p. 136.

10 "Rudiments," p. 38. [italics mine]

11 Ibid., p. 43.

12 Harold E. Cook, *Shaker Music: A Manifestation of American Folk Culture* (Lewisburg, Pa., 1973), pp. 135–136. Cook oddly states that Youngs disapproved of gapped scales, citing a letter in which Youngs criticizes James McNemar's musical transcriptions for omitting "three of the letters." Youngs, however, was not complaining about tetratonic scales. He says McNemar was using letters to stand for names of notes—i.e., *f* for faw, *s* for sol, *l* for law, and *m* for mee, the four solmization syllables used in the shape-note tunebooks of the day. Both Youngs and Haskell abandoned these names for others of their own devising. They gave a distinctive name to each of the seven degrees of the scale and fought against D. A. Buckingham's use of shape notes chiefly because of the ambiguity of the four-shape system he followed.

13 "Rudiments," p. 47.

14 Ibid., p. 49.

15 OCWR, Letter, Enfield, Conn., Feb. 10, 1834, Russel Haskell to Isaac N. Youngs, p. [6].

16 "Rudiments," p. 49. I share Norman Cazden's dissatisfaction with the use of church-mode terminology in folk-tune analysis (cf. his discussion in Edith Fowke, *Lumbering Songs from the Northern Woods* [Austin, Tex., 1970], p. 16), but until musicologists agree upon equally convenient terms, the rest of us have little choice but to continue to use the flawed ones.

17 OCWR, Letter, Enfield, Conn., Feb. 10, 1834, Russel Haskell to Isaac N. Youngs, p. [6], and Sept. 25, 1834, Russel Haskell to Austin Buckingham, p. 2.

18 In a few instances Haskell apparently chose A by mistake and inserted sharps before the F's to correct his error (MS EC–11, p. 8, third tune). In some cases, however, he apparently intentionally wrote a tune as Aeolian (MS EC–11, p. 12, sixth tune). Neither Haskell nor Youngs regarded the hexatonic or the pentatonic as distinctive forms of scales.

19 OCWR, Letter, Watervliet, N. Y., Nov. 12, 1834, D. A. Buckingham to Russel Haskell, p. 3.

20 MS UV–4, p. [202].

21 Isaac N. Youngs, *A Short Abridgement Of The Rules of Music. With Lessons For Exercise, and A few Observations, For new Beginners* (Lebanon, 1843), p. 17.

22 Ibid.

23 "Rudiments," p. 37.

24 The song "Children all do be good" is found in "Rudiments," p. 108, no. 42, and MS L–223, p. [15].

25 The one song Dorian in nineteenth-century manuscripts is "Where is the gem." Others sung by Sister Mildred in the Dorian mode are "Farewell, earthly joys," "Gospel kindred, how I love you," "I never did believe," "I'm thankful, I'm thankful that I'm a believer," "O blessed Savior," "The gospel is advancing," and "This gospel how precious to my thirsty soul." Her Aeolian tunes were "How pretty 'tis to see," "I love Mother, I love her way," "Love, love is the treasure I want to obtain," and "O how swift time is passing." Those with a variable sixth were "I'll spend and be spent" and "My home, my sweet home in Zion." The two I do not recall seeing in manuscripts are "How pretty 'tis to see" and "The gospel is advancing."

26 For example, "The joyful saints of God" in the present collection.

27 Her hexatonic "What a home I have in Zion" was Aeolian in the manuscript transcriptions and her hexatonic "Blessed, thrice blessed" was Dorian.

28 The hexatonic "Farewell, earthly joys" became Dorian in her singing, and other hexatonic tunes keyed on A in the manuscripts have the major sixth in her singing ("I will toil on to the end" or "O the gospel of Mother" or "Low down in the valley"). Sister Mildred also unconsciously alters "We must be meek" which she learned from a tape recording of the singing of Mrs. Olive H. Austin. Mrs. Austin sang the song as a hexatonic tune with minor third and major seventh; Sister Mildred lowers the seventh when she sings the song.

29 For example, "We have crossed the red sea" in this collection. Haskell in his *Expositor*, p. 73, discusses and illustrates the variable flatting of the seventh tone in the major.

30 "Rudiments," p. 85.

31 Both forms of distortion seem to mar the barring of, for example, "Tender Thought" on page 25 of Ananias Davisson's *Kentucky Harmony*, fifth ed. (Harrisonburg, Va., 1826). An example of a Shaker tune that some scribes set down without any barring and others wrote with alternating 3/4 and 2/4 measures is "O Holy Father" in this collection.

32 See for example "In vain we call on flesh and blood" and "The name of Herod signifies."

33 See for example "O may we be willing and be reconcil'd."

34 MS PH–2, pp. [23–24].

35 OCWR, Letter South Union, Apr. 22, 1833, Harvey Eades to Isaac N. Youngs, p. [1].

36 "Rudiments," pp. 143–152.

37 OCWR, IX.A.1, leaf written by Russel Haskell, f.t., "A Short Anthem," p. [2].

38 "Rudiments," pp. 63–64, and *A Short Abridgement*, p. 7.

39 "Rudiments," p. 114.

40 Ibid.

41 *Expositor*, p. 51.

42 Ibid., p. 45.

43 Ibid., pp. 45–46.

44 "Rudiments," p. 124.

45 *Expositor*, pp. 62–63.

46 WLCMs, no. 241, p. 247.

47 As for example, the singing of Sacred Harp conventions in the Deep South or the congregational singing of Primitive Baptists in North Carolina and Regular Baptists in Kentucky.

48 Shaker singing can be heard on Rounder Record 0078, "Early Shaker Spirituals," ed. Daniel W. Patterson (Somerville, Mass., 1976). The solo performances closely resemble those of Mrs. Carrie Grover of Gorham, Me., which can be heard on Library of Congress disc AAFS L–21. The renditions match the profile given by Alan Lomax for the European song-style family in his *Folk Song Style and Culture* (Washington, D. C., 1968), p. 101. Celibacy has not, however, caused Shaker singing to accentuate appreciably any of the features of song style that Lomax correlates with sexual repressiveness.

49 WLCMs, no. 42, entry for April 2, 1815.

50 Mary Dyer, *A Portraiture of Shakerism* (Concord, N. H., 1822), p. 279.

51 *Shakerism Unmasked; or the History of the Shakers* (Pittsfield, Mass., 1828), pp. 185–186.

52 *Extract from an Unpublished Manuscript on Shaker History, (by an eye witness.)* . . . (Boston, 1850), p. 19.

53 This song and Youngs' description of the motions to accompany it are presented as Extra Song no. 8.

54 This information is based upon interviews with Mrs. Austin in 1963 and 1974, with Sister Mildred and Eldress Marguerite over a number of years in the 1960s, and with Miss Florence Phelps in 1974. Miss Phelps demonstrates motioning in the brief film "Reminiscences" shot at Pleasant Hill by Alfred Shands of Louisville, Ky.

55 Mrs. Austin's song is not printed in this collection but can be found in MS L–31, p. 183.

56 WLCMs, no. 241, p. 156.

57 OCWR, SM506, p. [18].

58 NYOC, Ac. 12,743, p. 65.

59 WLCMs, no. 241, p. 8.

60 OCWR, viii.B.249, p. 50.

61 WLCMs, no. 241, pp. 8–9.

62 OCWR, Letter, Lebanon, N. Y., Aug. 6, 1830, Isaac N. Youngs to Andrew, p. [2].

63 J. S. Buckingham, Esq., *America, Historical, Statistic, and Descriptive* (New Haven, 1836), ii, 61.

64 From a letter written in 1812 by Abraham Chapline, quoted in "Nourse-Chapline Letters," *Kentucky Historical Society Register*, 31 (1933), 167.

65 NYOC, Ac. 12,051, vol. i, p. 19.

66 OCWR, Letter, Union Village, Feb. 28, 1808, Samuel to Calvin Green, p. [1].

67 MS L–200, note on the anthem "Destruction of Jerusalem," Oct. 1, 1839.

68 OCWR, Letter, Lebanon, Aug. 6, 1830, Isaac N. Youngs to Andrew, p. [2].

69 *Millennial Praises, Containing a Collection of Gospel Hymns, in Four Parts: Adapted to the Day of Christ's Second Appearing* (Hancock, 1813), p. iv.

70 OCWR, v.B.93, p. 21.

71 As for example, one entered into a manuscript with the note, "The foregoing song was seen by one of the young brethren at Holy Mount, as he opened a door presented plain to his view" (MS EC–18, p. [238]). In fig. 6 of *The Gift to be Simple* Andrews reproduces a drawing of a song seen "printed and pricked" upon a leaf; Cook prints another on page 109 of *Shaker Music*.

72 This information was given me by Eldress Bertha in an interview at Canterbury in August, 1974.

73 OCWR, Letter, Lebanon, Aug. 6, 1830, Isaac N. Youngs to Andrew, p. [2].

74 *Shaker Music*, chapter 5.

75 Ibid., p. 150.

76 For tabulations based on Haskell's manuscript I used the first one hundred tunes in each genre, or all of the tunes if Haskell provided fewer than a hundred from the genre.

77 *Down-East Spirituals and Others*, 2nd ed. (Locust Valley, N. Y., 1953), p. 9.

78 OCWR, viii.B.115, p. 168.

79 It is not surprising to learn from Haskell that in the earliest years "for a short season the young converts were led to sing, some of the time, such as they had been accustomed to sing, before they believed" (MS EC–11, p. 11). We know that in 1794 the newly gathered society at Gloucester opened its first meeting with "Behold the man three-score and ten," a hymn printed in at least three New England collections between 1790 and 1794 (MeSL, Aurelia Mace, [Commonplace Book], entry for Mar. 12, 1896). More commonly, however, the Shaker singers either avoided earlier hymns or adapted them, as they did Philip

Doddridge's "Ye hearts with youthful vigor warm" (see MS L–322, p. [8]). The hymns they consciously recorded from the singing of the World can be counted on one hand: "I've left my worldly honors and to glory I will go" and "O tell me no more of this world's vain store" in WLCMs, no. 193, pp. 9–10 and 14–15; "In the dark woods no Indian nigh," with the date June 8, 1836, in MS XM–2; and a set of Adventist pieces discussed below. I doubt that these were ever sung in Shaker services.

80 Cook found the following Shaker songs in the hymnals of other denominations: "A people called Christians," "Hail the day so long expected," "How joyful, how thankful, how loving I feel," and "The old Israelites knew," all of them texts printed in *Millennial Praises*. He also found a few others that the Shaker manuscripts establish as ones originating within the sect: "When the midnight cry begins," "The Patriarch," and "The gospel is lovely." (As printed in D. H. Mansfield's *The American Vocalist*, the last song is a garbled version of a tune known to Sister Mildred.) A few other Shaker songs were also taken up into non-Shaker books, most notably "Markham," an air attributed to Sarah Ann Markham of Pleasant Hill in William Hauser's *The Hesperian Harp*, "I'm marching on to my happy home," which entered the Adventist repertory, and "Low down the beautiful valley," a song widely printed.

81 MS EC–3, p. [158], a manuscript dating from about 1847. The text was printed without tune in Joseph Hillman's *The Revivalist*, rev. ed. (Albany, 1869), p. 265, under the title "Father in the Promised Land," and in at least nine other Northern books. The melody that Haskell recorded is a variant of that used for the sea chantey "Boney was a warrior."

82 MS SU–4, p. 114. Eades' transcription was made about 1859. The song is distantly related to "Hebrew Children," which Jackson reprints in *Spiritual Folk-Songs of Early America*, 2nd ed. (Locust Valley, N. Y., 1953), p. 201. In addition to the verses recorded with the tune, Eades set down the following stanzas for "The Promised Land":

2 I wonder whah's de weepin Mary
  'Way ober in de promisd land
      Chorus—O far ye all well &c

3 O by & by we'll go & see her
  Way ober in de promisd land
      Chorus—

4 I wonder whahs de good ole Steben
  Way ober in de promisd land
      Chorus—

5 Hes gone up to lib wid Jesus
  Way ober in de promisd land
      Chorus—

6 I wonder whahs de doutin Thomas
  Way ober in de promis land
      Chorus—

7 I wonder whahs de good ole Daniel
  Way ober in de promis land.
      Chorus—

83 Cook in *Shaker Music*, p. 43, lists five Adventist songs recorded without texts in MS L–243, p. 246: "The Glory of Zion," "Christ is Coming," "Hail Happy Day," "Lots Wife," and "Mariner's Hymn." He overlooked "King & Queen" on the same page of this manuscript. Texts were recorded along with some of these tunes in other manuscripts: MS L–13, p. 119, and OCWR, vii.B.51, pp. 9–14, etc. Another Adventist song, "When I was down in Egypt land," is preserved in MS HN–3, pp. 124–125.

CHAPTER IV

1 See George P. Jackson, *White Spirituals in the Southern Uplands* (Chapel Hill, 1933), pp. 320–322.
2 MS EC–11, p. [iv], and OCWR, iv.A.9, pp. [22–23].
3 The "View of the Length of Notes" is printed in Haskell's *A Musical Expositor* (New York, 1847), p. 17.
4 Haskell misdates the meeting as having occurred in September 1841 (MS EC–11, p. [iv]); Youngs recorded the results of this deliberation in a manuscript entitled "A Treatise on Music; agreeably to the Plan established and adopted at New Lebanon & Watervliet, N. Y. 1840" (NYAL, 358).
5 OCWR, Letter, Lebanon, Nov. 16, 1842, Isaac N. Youngs to Austin Buckingham, Watervliet, p. [1].
6 See MS EC–2, p. 111.
7 MS EC–11, p. 553.
8 See MSS HN–5 and L–34.
9 See MSS CB–36 and WNY–43.
10 Pp. 70–76 and 152–154.
11 Ibid., p. 76.
12 OCWR, Letter, South Union, Apr. 22, 1833, Harvey L. Eades to Isaac N. Youngs, pp. 1ff.
13 MS SU–15, p. 3.
14 This information is drawn together from a number of manuscripts and from the performances of two songs still sung with the vocables—these can be heard in the recording "Early Shaker Spirituals" issued by the community at Sabbathday Lake.
15 MS EC–11, pp. 109–110.

PART I

1 *Testimonies* (1816), p. 104, and *Testimonies* (1827), p. 177.
2 The total body of these songs is nowhere brought together. The Enfield tradition is preserved in Russel Haskell's major manuscript, EC–11, pp. 1–6, a collection of thirty-one songs. Another notable collection is MS XU–36, "The Songs of Blessed Mother Ann," a small, beautifully written manuscript compiled possibly at Lebanon. The songs remembered at Canterbury are found in MS CB–25, and those at the Maine societies in MS GME–3 and MS GME–6. The last two also hold songs known at Harvard; MS XE–47 probably also derives from the Harvard tradition. All told, a scattering of these songs can be found in twenty-five manuscripts.
3 Cf. MS XU–36, p. [20], and MS GME–6, no. 239.
4 *The Virginia Gazette*, Nov. 9, 1769, p. 1.
5 D. Hamilton Hurd, *The History of Essex County, Massachusetts* (Philadelphia, 1888), ii, 1167.
6 John Rogers, *The Biography of Elder Barton W. Stone, Written by Himself: With Additions and Reflections by Elder John Rogers* (Cincinnati, 1847), p. 40.

7 Examples of mouth music—also called "lilting," "chin music," and other names—can be heard on such phonodiscs as "Heather and Glen," ed. Alan Lomax (Tradition TLP–1047) and "The Lark in the Morning," ed. Diane Hamilton (Tradition TLP–1004). Elizabeth Greenleaf described Newfoundland mouth music in her *Ballads and Sea Songs of Newfoundland* (Cambridge, Mass., 1933), p. xxiii.
8 NYPLMs, Angell Matthewson, [Reminiscences in the form of a series of thirty-nine letters to his brother Jeffrey], Letter vii, p. 63.
9 F. B. Sanborn, "The Original Shaker Communities in New England," *The New-England Magazine*, n.s., 22 (1900), 305.
10 MS EC–11, p. 3.
11 Ibid., p. 2.
12 *Testimonies* (1816), pp. 208–209.
13 Ibid., p. 180.
14 MS EC–11, p. 6.
15 MeSL, Roxalana L. Grosvenor, "Elders," p. 35.
16 Ibid., p. 52.
17 *Testimonies* (1816), p. 48.
18 Cf., for example, articles in *The American Museum Or Universal Magazine*, 1 (Feb. 1787), 148–150, and 10 (Aug. 1791), 100–101, and Reuben Rathbone, *Reasons Offered for Leaving the Shakers* (Pittsfield, 1800), p. 27.
19 See Thomas Swain, "The Evolving Expressions of the Religious and Theological Experiences of a Community: A Comparative Study of the Shaker *Testimonies* Concerning the Sayings of Mother Ann Lee; An Exploration of The Development from Oral Traditions to Written Forms as Preserved in Four Documents," *Shaker Quarterly*, 12 (Spring 1972), 3–31; (Summer 1972), 43–67.
20 MeSL, Roxalana L. Grosvenor, "Parents," p. 58.
21 *Testimonies* (1816), p. 266.
22 DWt, SA799.1, p. 124.
23 *Testimonies* (1888), pp. 160–167. Swain's study, however, shows the caution with which the reader needs to approach each of the texts when addressing this question; see his pp. 58–62.
24 *Testimonies* (1816), pp. 226, 251.
25 MeSL, Roxalana L. Grosvenor, "Elders," p. 48.
26 *Testimonies* (1816), p. 206.
27 OCWR, vi.B.37, p. 68.
28 NYAL, "Sayings of Mother Ann, and The First Elders: Gathered from Different Individuals At Harvard & Shirley," pp. 101–103.
29 [Calvin Green and Seth Y. Wells], *A Summary View of the Millennial Church* (Albany, 1823), p. 41.
30 Ibid.
31 *Testimonies* (1816), p. 340.
32 *A Summary View*, p. 40.
33 *Testimonies* (1816), p. 330.
34 *Testimonies* (1816), p. 342.
35 MeSL, Roxalana L. Grosvenor, "Parents," p. 83.
36 OCWR, Letter, Enfield, Conn., Feb. 25, 1782, Father James to a brother in Hancock.
37 *A Summary View*, p. 43.
38 MeSL, Roxalana L. Grosvenor, "Elders," p. 35.
39 *Testimonies* (1816), p. 366.
40 "First Shaker Imprint," *Shaker Quarterly*, 2 (Winter 1962), 154–155.
41 *Testimonies* (1816), p. 372.
42 MeSL, Roxalana L. Grosvenor, "Parents," pp. 57–58.

43 *Testimonies* (1816), p. 328.

44 Ibid., pp. 276 and 367. Father Eleazer's song is "O do you know my loveyer."

PART II

1 DWt, SA799.1, pp. 119–120.

2 Timothy Dwight, *Travels in New-England and New York* (New Haven, 1822), III, 159.

3 *The Literary Diary of Ezra Stiles*, ed. Franklin B. Dexter (New York, 1901), III, 243.

4 DWt, SA799.1, pp. 125–126.

5 NYOC, Ac. 6286, p. 4.

6 The most detailed schedule of the meetings is given in a Pleasant Hill manuscript, KLF, BA/.S527/7, pp. [v–vi]. Another informative account from Lebanon is in OCWR, x.B.31, pp. 162–170.

7 One of the best accounts of a Shaker meeting—and an easily obtainable one—was written by Benson Lossing and published anonymously in *Harper's New Monthly Magazine*, 15 (1857), 168–169.

8 These manuscripts are listed in footnote 2 to "Songs of the Gospel Parents."

9 NHCb, Henry C. Blinn, "Historical Notes having reference to the Believers in Enfield, N. H.," I, 91.

10 MS XE–1, p. 17.

11 "A Sketch of the Life and Experience of Issachar Bates," *The Shaker Quarterly*, 1 (Fall 1961), 101–103, 113–114.

12 *Our Revolutionary Forefathers: The Letters of François, Marquis de Barbé-Marbois*, trans. and ed. Eugene Parker Chase (New York, 1929), pp. 181–182. Motif K607.3.2, "Sham-dead deceived into moving by absurd action," Stith Thompson, *Motif-Index of Folk-Literature*, rev. ed. (Bloomington, Ind., 1956). For Shaker tales quoted or summarized in the remainder of this book, I do not cite Thompson numbers. Except in the joke category, his indices do not well accommodate religious tales of Dissenting and Evangelical sects. The Protestant motifs and tale types are either wholly omitted or ill served by Thompson's too narrowly conceived descriptive labels. To identify a tale of faith healing, for example, one would have to choose between his V221, "Miraculous healing by saint" and the equally inappropriate D782.1, "Disenchantment by touch of holy man." His terms *angel, saint, ghost, revenant*, etc., are particularly irrelevant to the Shaker concept of *spirits*. E. W. Baughman's American indices add only Mormon materials. Both indices in fact profile the bias of tale collectors against Protestant sectarianism. As late as 1967 one collector could believe his compilation of stories to "well represent the full storehouse of American Negro folktales," although he had elicited from informants scarcely a tale of faith healing, conversion, visions, or remarkable providences. It took amateurs coming from another direction to gather the conversion tales published in *God Struck Me Dead*, ed. Clifton H. Johnson (Philadelphia, 1969). Like these black narratives, Shaker tales were of the highest importance to both teller and listener. Although generally memorates, the stories begot similar tales, for they induced and provided models for the experiences of others.

13 DWt, SA799.1, p. 102.

14 NYAL, "Sayings of Mother Ann, and The First Elders," p. 11, and MeSL, Roxalana L. Grosvenor, "Elders," p. 1.

15 WLCMs, no. 53, pp. 218–222.

16 *Testimonies* (1816), p. 243.

17 DWt, SA799.1, pp. 120–121.

18 Ibid., p. 122.

19 *Testimonies* (1816), p. 248.

20 OCWR, VII.B.203, pp. 39–40.

21 *Testimonies* (1816), p. 296.

22 DWt, SA799.1, pp. 102–103.

23 OCWR, Letter, Watervliet, N. Y., Nov. 10, 1821, Seth Y. Wells to Cornelius Camden Blatchley.

24 DWt, SA799.1, p. 123.

25 *Testimonies* (1816), p. 241. In an article "'Bearing for the Dead': A Shaker Belief and Its Impress on the Shaker Spiritual," *The Shaker Quarterly*, 8 (Winter 1968), 116–128, I quote several additional accounts of bearing for the dead not included in the *Testimonies* and pursue the topic further than in the present discussion.

26 *Testimonies* (1816), pp. 233–234, 238.

27 Ibid., p. 244.

28 Ibid., pp. 241–243.

29 NYOC, Ac. 13,404, pp. 83–84.

30 *The Letters of François, Marquis de Barbé-Marbois*, pp. 182–183.

31 MeSL, "Biographic Memoir of the Life and Experience of Calvin Green," I, chap. 5, paragraphs 6–10, 37–38.

32 NYPLMs, Angell Matthewson, [Reminiscences in the form of a series of thirty-nine letters to his brother Jeffrey], Letter VI, pp. [59–61].

33 *The Letters of François, Marquis de Barbé-Marbois*, p. 181.

34 MeSL, Roxalana L. Grosvenor, "Elders," p. 46.

35 Ibid., pp. 38–39.

36 CHCHS, Anon., Letter, Albany, July 24, 1785, p. 4.

37 MeSL, Roxalana L. Grosvenor, "Parents," p. 86.

38 If the *Testimonies* of 1827 offer an accurate picture, the converts were mostly too young to have inherited property or established themselves in the world, rather than persons raised in poverty. The book holds thirty-one testimonies; twenty-three of the writers came to the Shakers between the ages of fourteen and twenty-five. In a revealing statement one of them who had formerly worked as a domestic servant declares, "Though I was a poor girl, and of poor parentage, yet I have never seen any difference made on that account, but I have always fared as well among Believers as the daughters of the rich" (p. 59).

39 DWt, SA799.1, pp. 105–106.

40 OCWR, VII.B.203, p. 108.

41 NYOC, Ac. 12,051, pp. 27–29.

42 *The Shaker Quarterly*, 1 (Winter 1961), 146–148.

43 From "Personal Narrative" in Clarence H. Faust and Thomas H. Johnson, *Jonathan Edwards, Representative Selections, with Introduction, Bibliography, and Notes*, rev. ed. (New York, 1962), pp. 58–59.

44 OCWR, "Book of Lovely Vineyard, Given me at Harvard in 1890. A Miscellaneous Record. Alonzo G. Hollister—Finished May 28th 1897. Church—Mount Lebanon Columbia Co. N. Y.," pp. 50–55. A more polished and pale text of Eunice Bathrick's autobiographic sketch can be found in OCWR, VI.A.5.

45 *Testimonies* (1888), p. 206.

46 MeSL, Roxalana L. Grosvenor, "Elders," pp. 116–117.

47 MeSL, "Biographic Memoir of Calvin Green," chap. 10, paragraphs 11–12. Olive Fairbanks' song "How lovely are the faithful souls" can be heard in the recording "Early Shaker Spirituals" (Rounder Record 0078).

PART III

1 R. C. Galbraith, Jr., *The History of the Chillicothe Presbytery from the Organization in 1799–1889* (Chillicothe, Ohio, 1889), pp. 22–23.

2 Julian Ursyn Niemcewicz, *Under their Vine and Fig Tree: Travels through America in 1797–1799 . . .*, trans. and ed. Metchie J. E. Budka, in Collections of the New Jersey Historical Society at Newark, XIV (Elizabeth, N. J., 1965), p. 177.

3 Frederick Marryat, *Diary in America*, ed. Jules Zanger (Bloomington, Ind., 1960), p. 92.

4 Frederick von Raumer, *America and the American People*, trans. William W. Turner (New York, 1846), pp. 333–334.

5 OCWR, Letter, Watervliet, N. Y., May 5, 1823, Ministry to Union Village Ministry, p. 3.

6 The Connecticut State Library in Hartford preserves a Shaker broadside listing nineteen "Scripture Texts" in defense of dancing.

7 Benjamin S. Youngs, *Testimony of Christ's Second Appearing*, 4th ed. (Albany, N. Y., 1856), pp. 584–588.

8 *Shakerism Unmasked* (Paris, Ky., 1826), p. 18.

9 OCWR, x.B.31, p. 166.

10 WLCMs, no. 78, vol. 1, pp. 49–50.

11 *The Beauties of Priestcraft; or a Short Account of Shakerism* (New-Harmony, Ind., 1826), p. 16.

12 Youngs, p. 588.

13 *A Letter from Daniel Rathbun, of Richmond in the County of Berkshire, to James Whittacor . . .* (Springfield, Mass., 1785), p 116.

14 "A Sabbath with the Shakers," *The Knickerbocker, or New-York Monthly Magazine*, 11 (June 1838), 532–537.

15 OCWR, Letter, Watervliet, N. Y., May 5, 1823, Ministry to Union Village Ministry, p. 2.

16 OCWR, v.B.93, p. 17.

17 Cecil Sharp, *The Country Dance Book, Part I* (London, 1909), p. 10.

18 *World History of the Dance* (New York, 1965), p. 415.

19 Quoted in Andrews, *Gift*, p. 103; also in KLF, BA/.S527/6, pp. 94–95.

20 OCWR, x.B.31, p. 171.

21 Andrews, ibid.; MS EC–11, p. 59.

22 MeSL, Aurelia Mace, [Commonplace Book], entry for May 3–6, 1896.

23 MWA, Thomas Hammond, [Historical Record of the Shaker Church at Harvard, Massachusetts], p. 120.

24 OCWR, Letter, Watervliet, N. Y., ibid.

25 Russel Haskell assembled ninety-six Regular Step tunes and 188 Holy Order tunes for his compendious song collection, MS EC–11. He found only thirty-one for the Turning Shuffle, eleven for the Walking Manner, seven for the Drumming Manner, and four for the Skipping Manner.

26 *Hill Country Tunes* (Philadelphia, 1944).

27 A Holy Order tune from MS EC–11, p. 82.

28 My sample consisted of Haskell's first fifty tunes for each of these dances in MS EC–11, pp. 69–77 and 111–117.

29 William Chappell, *The Ballad Literature and Popular Music of the Olden Time* (New York, 1965), II, 732. As early as 1811 a variant of the tune was in use at Enfield as an Extra Song, with words that opened "More love, precious good Mother's love"—cf. MS EC–11, p. 342, and MS L–129, p. 32.

30 MS EC–11, p. 83.

31 Chappell, I, 293.

32 NYOC, Ac. 6286, p. 8.

33 My entire discussion of the Back Manner is heavily indebted to MS EC–11, p. 11.

34 WLCMs, no. 143, p. 140.

35 WLCMs, no. 241, p. 131.

36 The fullest accounts of the performance of the Holy Order are those of Isaac Youngs (NYOC, Ac. 6286, p. 8), and Alonzo Hollister (OCWR, x.B.31, pp. [171–172]). Other useful ones are WLCMs, no. 343, p. 185, and MeSL, Aurelia Mace, [Commonplace Book], entry for Apr. 6, 1896.

37 MS EC–11, p. 72.

38 WLCMs, no. 42, May 13, 1821.

39 OCWR, v.B.152, p. 29.

40 WLCMs, no. 42, Mar. 17, 1821.

41 MS L–328, p. 12.

42 Andrews reprints the text of the 1845 revision of the "Millennial Laws" in *People*, pp. 249–289. The relevant passage is pt. II, sec. II, paragraph 10.

43 MS EC–11, p. 70.

44 MS EC–11, pp. 62, 597–598.

45 WLCMs, no. 78, p. 49.

46 OCWR, v.B.174, pp. 151–159.

47 MS EC–11, pp. 63–68.

48 WLCMs, no. 78, p. 49.

49 The best accounts of the Regular Step (those in MS EC–11, p. 109, NYOC, Ac. 6286, p. 9, and OCWR, x.B.31, p. [172]) do not settle the matter; but see the Walking Manner for additional evidence.

50 NYOC, Ac. 6286, p. 9.

51 MS EC–11, pp. 69, 109–123.

52 Ibid., p. 114.

53 WLCMs, no. 232, p. 50.

54 MS EC–11, pp. 61–62, 597. Haskell alone describes this manner of dance.

55 OCWR, Letter, Enfield, Conn., Feb. 28, 1830, to Hancock, p. [2].

56 MS EC–11, pp. 109–110.

57 OCWR, VII.B.10, p. 31.

PART IV

1 MeSL, Roxalana L. Grosvenor, "Elders," pp. 34–35.

2 WLCMs, no. 245, Letter, Watervliet, Ohio, Jan. 19, 1860, William Redmon to Eliza Sharp.

3 ICHS, G. Flower Diary, vol. 2, entry for Oct. 6, 1816.

4 John B. Boles has a valuable discussion of the religious leaders' concern over the state of society and souls in Kentucky in the second chapter of his *The Great Revival, 1787–1805* (Lexington, Ky., 1972).

5 See Boles, chapter 7.

6 Even in founding their new communities as complete units, the Shakers were, for example, following a long-standing New England tradition. Southerners, by contrast, habitually settled new country as scattered, independent small farmers. The Shakers' potential converts in Kentucky and southern Ohio were largely of Southern stock and were products not only of the backwoods but also of Southern culture. Cf. Raymond D. Gastil, *Cultural Regions of the United States* (Seattle, 1975), pp. 76–79.

7 *New Songs, on Different Subjects, Composed by Issachar Bates* (Salem, N. Y., 1800), Song 6 and Song 1. Bates's poem on the death of Isaac Orcutt is a masterpiece of the genre; it eclipses even the celebrated effusions of Emeline Grangerford.

8 In addition to the examples printed in this book, Shaker ballads include Issachar Bates's "On the first day in the first month in eighteen hundred five," an account of his journey as one of three missionaries sent from Lebanon to the Kentucky Revival (see WLCMs, no. 345c). In 1809 Richard McNemar wrote a ballad entitled "Will a man rob God?" With more interest in didacticism than in narration he told how a "black-painted band" of "lucrative monsters" broke into Union Village one midnight demanding money. Mc-Nemar, who had been sleeping in an attic, so far forgot his pacifist beliefs as to hurl a chair down upon the robbers. The clatter caused a rout, for which McNemar gave due credit to the Almighty. He sang the ballad in church the next morning and published it in *A Selection of Hymns and Poems: for the Use of Believers* (Watervliet, Ohio, 1833), p. 170. Much later, in 1852, Elisha Blakeman of Lebanon composed a ballad entitled "An Awful Scene on Lake Erie," which describes an explosion on a steamboat carrying a small party of Believers. A recurrent use of the phrase "lowlands low" in this text suggests that Blakeman knew the English ballad "The Golden Vanity." A copy of his ballad is preserved in WLCMs, no. 161, pp. 234–239.

PART V

1 MS EC–11, p. 323.
2 NYOC, Ac. 6286, entries for 1805 and 1806.
3 OCWR, v.B.10, entries for July.
4 OCWR, Letter, Watervliet, N. Y., Oct. 17, 1810, Jethro to Elder Brother, p. 1.
5 WLCMs, no. 42, entry for June 1817, and for Sept. 3, 1820; no. 53, p. 14.
6 NYOC, Ac. 6286, entry for June 1817; OCWR, x.B.31, p. 163.
7 MeSL, "Biographic Memoir of the Life and Experience of Calvin Green," chap. 7, paragraphs 2 and 4.
8 Three sizable collections of tunes for the hymns in *Millennial Praises* can be found in MSS XU–40, L–136, and EC–11. The latter collection contains a number of attributions for both texts and tunes, especially for ones originating in the Eastern societies. Attributions of Western hymns were recorded chiefly by Susan Liddil—cf. WLCMs, no. 346. For John P. MacLean she also annotated a copy of *Millennial Praises*, now preserved at OCWR. Some other copies of the book contain a few attributions, most notably one at NYAP. I have compiled a list of attributions and of tune locations for a forthcoming issue of *The Shaker Quarterly*.
9 *Testimonies* (1888), p. 181.
10 MS L–317, pp. [274–276].
11 Folk-Legacy Recording FSA–2: "Joseph Abel Trivett."
12 WLCMs, no. 245, p. 5.
13 Bertrand H. Bronson, *The Ballad as Song* (Berkeley and Los Angeles, 1969), p. 138.
14 George P. Jackson, *Spiritual Folk-Songs of Early America* (Locust Valley, N. Y., 1953), pp. 111–112. He cites six additional printings of the piece. His version is in the key of F major; I transpose it to facilitate comparisons.
15 Bronson, *Traditional Tunes of the Child Ballads*, I (Princeton, 1959), 390 (Child 49, no. 14), I transpose the tune.
16 Cecil J. Sharp, *English Folk Songs from the Southern Appalachians* (London, 1932), II, 67.

17 Its text is from *Millennial Praises*, pp. 184–186. The tune is related to that of "Voyage to Canaan," and distantly to the "Lowlands of Holland" tune.
18 The piece was sung as early as 1807 but is not included in *Millennial Praises*. These subdivisions of the ballad-tune phrase were briefly discussed by Samuel P. Bayard in "Prolegomena to a Study of the Principal Melodic Families of Folk Song," reprinted in MacEdward Leach and Tristram P. Coffin, eds., *The Critics and the Ballad* (Carbondale, 1961), pp. 127–128.

PART VI

1 NYOC, Ac. 6286, entry for 1810.
2 MS EC–11, pp. 70, 341.
3 Eldress Gertrude Soule has described to me the pleasant exchanges of songs that took place during such tasks as ironing. Marcia Hastings' song is "O Harden Not Their Hearts" (Later Song no. 4).
4 See Hymn no. 21 (which is sometimes recorded with only one stanza and may originally have been an Extra Song) and Anthem no. 2, a Gift Song. Many other songs also develop from the "Barbara Allan" melody, as for example "With Precious Manna," MS WNY–35, p. 20. All these melodies develop from Bronson's Group D tunes for "Barbara Allan."
5 *English Folk Songs from the Southern Appalachians* (London, 1932), I, 233.
6 Bertrand Bronson reprints Sharp's tune, interpolating his view of the phrasing, in *Traditional Tunes of the Child Ballads*, III (Princeton, 1966), 215 (Child 200, no. 35). I feel that Bronson was justified in inserting the phrasing only in those cases where he could be guided by actual performances of a traditional singer. The point is significant. We base our understanding of folk-song stanzas more upon the conventions of printers than upon the habits of the ballad as song.
7 Carl Sandburg, *The American Songbag* (New York, 1927), p. 166. His tune was learned in Illinois and two of his stanzas are traced to a Kentucky version learned in the 1840s.
8 One use of the phrase occurs in "Little Lamb" (Gift Song no. 40), the other in an anthem, "The Lily White Rose," which can be found in MS L–332, pp. 18–22.
9 This textual conflation clearly did not result from *zersingen*. Oral transmission normally caused only minor changes of phrasing in Shaker songs. Alterations in the six-stanza hymn "The Humble Heart," to take a typical example, are limited to nine word substitutions: "it" (for "this"), "Thy" ("This"), "shock" ("stroke"), "features" ("feathers"), "are like" ("are of"), "my" ("their"), "love" ("dove"), "those" ("these"), and "does" ("shall").

PART VII

1 NHCb, Henry C. Blinn, "A Historical Record of the Society of Believers in Canterbury, N. H.," II, 146.
2 OCWR, Letter, Shirley, Nov. 12, 1825; DWt, SA760, p. 172; NHCb, Henry C. Blinn, op. cit., II, 218. In an account entitled "Christmas Among the Shakers in the Olden Time" Elmina Phillips described footwashing on Christmas Eve at North Union—see J. P. MacLean, "The Society of Shakers. Rise, Progress and Extinction

of the Society at Cleveland, O.," *Ohio Archaeological and Historical Quarterly*, 9 (July 1900), p. 82.

3 MS NU–1.

PART VIII

1 *A Subaltern's Furlough Descriptive of Scenes in Various Parts of the United States* (New York, 1833), I, 196.

2 WLCMs, no. 161, pp. 136–139.

3 NYOC, Ac. 6286, p. 11.

4 MeSL, Aurelia Mace, [Commonplace Book], entry for Mar. 27, 1896. The anthem to which she refers is entitled "The Faithful Witness." The music was recorded by Haskell in MS EC–11, p. 431ff. The anthem also appears in Henry C. Blinn's *A Sacred Repository of Anthems and Hymns*.

5 NHCb, Henry C. Blinn, "A Historical Record of the Society of Believers in Canterbury, N. H.," I, 130.

6 WLCMs, no. 42, entry for May 1815.

7 OCWR, Letter, Watervliet, N. Y., Jan. 24, 1844, D. A. Buckingham to Beloved Friends, p. [2]. The letter accompanies and explains an anthem entitled "The Harmony of Angels," in which a three-part harmonic setting is attempted—the first of its kind among the Shakers.

8 J. Murray Barbour, in his *The Church Music of William Billings* (East Lansing, 1960), pp. 133ff., summarizes critical comments made about Billings's anthems by Hamilton C. Macdougall and attempts to defend the compositions. The English models for the New England specimens have also been criticized by Ralph T. Daniel in *The Anthem in New England before 1800* (Evanston, 1966), p. 47, for treating each line of text independently "so that the result is a series of sections bearing little musical relationship to one another."

PART IX

1 Anna White and Leila S. Taylor, *Shakerism: Its Meaning and Message* (Columbus, Ohio, 1904), p. 92. The building of these meetinghouses is discussed by Robert Meader in "Reflections on Shaker Architecture," *The Shaker Quarterly*, 6 (Summer 1966), 38–40.

2 OCWR, v.B.174, p. 151.

3 This hall was completed in 1824; cf. Meader, p. 40. The Union Village building was completed in 1818 and had a floor sixty by forty-four feet, according to Mrs. Hazel S. Phillips, "Shaker Architecture, Warren County Ohio" (Oxford, Ohio, 1971), p. 10. These were then the only societies with over five hundred members. Pleasant Hill, which had nearly that number, built in 1820 a meetinghouse with interior dimensions, says Shakertown Curator James C. Thomas, of forty-two by fifty-nine feet. Enfield, Connecticut, which had about two hundred members, built a new meetinghouse in 1827. Enlargements were not made elsewhere until the late 1840s, when North Union and Watervliet, New York, also needed more space for their worshipers. The North Union dance floor measured fifty feet by fifty, according to J. P. MacLean ("The Society of Shakers. Rise, Progress and Extinction of the Society at Cleveland, O.," *Ohio Archaeological and Historical Publications*, 9 [1900], 48). These larger halls also allowed the laborers to take longer steps, a fact that particularly struck Thomas Hammond of Harvard while on a visit at Lebanon (see OCWR, v.B.36, p. 95).

4 OCWR, XIII, 7–7c, n. p., quoted from the *Berkshire American*, June 22, 1826.

5 KBGK, [Journal of a journey made in 1854], p. 22.

6 Thomas Hamilton, *Men and Manners in America*, 2d Am. ed. (Philadelphia, 1833), II, 150; James Silk Buckingham, *America, Historical, Statistic, and Descriptive* (New York, 1841), I, p. 61. In constructing their meetinghouses the Shakers were careful to allow for the stress of so many people bounding in rhythm. (Cf. OCWR, Letter, South Groton, Dec. 13, 1855, Lorenzo D. Grosvenor to Giles, pp. 1–4.)

7 KBGK, Shaker Record A, entry for Sept. 1, 1834.

8 KBGK, [Journal of a journey made in 1854], pp. 22, 28; and NCDD, Henry St. George Harris Papers, Letter, William Harris, New Lebanon Springs, Sept. 5, 1826, to Margarete, p. 2.

9 WLCMs, no. 42, entry for Apr. 2, 1815.

10 MS EC–11, p. 15.

11 Ibid., p. 551.

12 *The Black Book; or a Continuation of Travels in the United States* (Washington, D. C., 1828), II, 51. C. D. Arfwedson, who visited a Shaker meeting in the early 1830s, reports that a Shaker brother explained the circular figure as meaning "sin on earth, and our evolutions round it show our abhorrence, as well as the powerful effect of the Holy Ghost on us." Arfwedson was the most satirical of observers, and I am uncertain how far to trust his account. Cf., *The United States and Canada in 1832, 1833, and 1834* (London, 1834), I, 101–102.

13 The account of the dancing is pieced together from numerous descriptions, including WLCMs, nos. 241, p. 237, and 169, entry for May 22, 1842; MS EC–11, pp. 11, 15; and David R. Lamson, *Two Years' Experience among the Shakers* (West Boylston, Mass., 1848), pp. 54, 86–88. Cf. NYOC, Ac. 17,917, pp. 16–17.

14 MeSL, Aurelia Mace, [Commonplace Book], entry for Apr. 6, 1896.

15 The dance is reconstructed from accounts in MS EC–11, pp. 38–39; MeSL, Aurelia Mace, [Commonplace Book], entry for May 3, 1896; and OCWR, x.B.31, p. [166].

16 WLCMs, no. 42, entry for Apr. 14, 1822.

17 The dance is reconstructed from descriptions in MS EC–11, p. 119; NYOC, Ac. 6286, entry for 1825; and OCWR, x.B.31, p. 172.

18 Sources for the description of the dance are MS EC–11, p. 87, and NYOC, Ac. 6286, p. 13.

19 OCWR, IV.B.35, p. 86, a clipping from an unidentified newspaper. Amos Stewart's directions for marching warned against a disagreeable scuffing of the feet. All, he said, "should lift their feet clear from the floor, & set them down square" (WLCMs, no. 143, p. 140).

20 WLCMs, no. 143, p. 141. For other useful directions see NYOC, Ac. 17,917, pp. 11–12, 15.

21 MS EC–11, p. 547.

22 WLCMs, no. 42, entries for dates in 1821.

23 OCWR, v.B.93, p. 17.

24 NHCb, Henry C. Blinn, "A Historical Record of the Society of Believers in Canterbury, N. H.," II, 215 Cf. also NYOC, Ac. 6286, entry for 1828.

25 NYOC, Ac. 12,752, vol. II, p. 59.

26 OCWR, Letter, Watervliet, N. Y., May 5, 1823, Ministry to Union Village Ministry, p. [3].

27 MeSL, Aurelia Mace, [Commonplace Book], entry under date May 6, 1896. Blinn says that the New Hamp-

shire ministry introduced clapping in the marches on its return from Watervliet, N. Y., in 1831. (op. cit., p. 238.)

28 MS EC–11, p. 547.

29 OCWR, v.B.279, entry for Nov. 4, 1821.

30 OCWR, Letter, Watervliet, N. Y., May 5, 1823, Ministry to Union Village Ministry, pp. 2–3.

31 DWt, SA760, p. 171.

32 NYOC, Ac. 6286, entry for 1828.

33 OCWR, viii.A.73, Item 5, p. [15]. The diagrams occur without any accompanying explanation in a small volume of inspired communications written in 1843. It is possible that the manners were not used earlier than this date at Watervliet.

34 "A Historical Record of the Society of Believers in Enfield, N. H.," ii, 216.

35 OCWR, Letter, Enfield, N. H., Mar. 20, 1838, Ministry to Rufus Bishop at Lebanon, p. [3], describing a changeable shuffle learned by Jason Kidder the previous winter at Enfield, Conn.

36 *A Subaltern's Furlough . . . during the Summer and Autumn of 1832* (New York, 1833), i, 198–199.

37 NYOC, Ac. 12,752, vol. 2, p. 61.

38 S. Foster Damon, *The History of Square Dancing* (Barre, Mass., 1957), p. 24.

39 MS L–61, p. 6.

PART X

1 OCWR, v.B.294, p. 103.

2 OCWR, viii.B.115, pp. [11–12] and p. 167.

3 NYPLMs, 58-M-140, vol. 2, entry for Jan. 30, 1848.

MS SU–17, p. 136, copy of Letter, Lebanon, Sept. 1, 1840, Isaac N. Youngs to Harvey Eades, South Union. We have abundant evidence of the speedy recording and even learning of the new songs. Elder Rufus Bishop gives one instance in an account of a Saturday evening meeting at Lebanon, in which "there were some precious gifts from the heavenly world, among which I received a beautiful little Song from the Blessed Savior, brought by his little Dove, with a great store of his richest love & blessing for all the Ministry. The Song & words were given there & then, & sung in meeting. John Allen, the Instrument, & others, male & female went into the Porch & sung it by Elder Ebenezer's bed side [to comfort him in his illness], & Henry Dewit wrote the words & noted the tune in the Porch before we went to rest, which was nearly 11 O'clock. P. M."—NYPLMs, 58-M-140, vol. 2, entry for April 5, 1845.

5 NYPLMs, op. cit., entry for Jan. 30, 1848, and OCWR, op. cit.

6 OCWR, vii.B.230, p. [115], quoting Letter, Lebanon, Dec. 13, 1837, Ministry to South Union.

7 OCWR, viii.B.109, p. 10.

8 NYPLMs, 58-M-140, vol. 1, entry for Jan. 15, 1838.

9 OCWR, iv.B.36, p. 101, copy of Letter, Lebanon, Jan. 25, 1839, Rufus B. to Beloved Ministry. The Lead of course gave equal credence to most of the manifestations. An instrument for native spirits, for example, begged Elder Rufus to give his "Spiritual Lamp to lighten them out of darkness." He took the request seriously and confessed himself "some loth" to give up his lamp, but said, "as I did it in charity to lost souls, I hope to be considered & not left in darkness myself"—cf. NYPLMs, 58-M-140, vol. 2, entry for Feb. 2, 1845.

10 Andrews, *People*, p. 158.

11 *A Summary View of the Millennial Church, or United Society of Believers* (Albany, N. Y., 1823), p. 92; MeSL, "Biographic Memoir of . . . Calvin Green," chap. 7, paragraph 2; Calvin Green, "Biographical Account of the Life, Character, & Ministry of Father Joseph Meacham," *The Shaker Quarterly*, 10 (Summer 1970), 59–60.

12 NYAL, "Sayings of Mother Ann, and The First Elders," p. 98.

13 OCWR, v.B.46, entry for Aug. 17, 1842.

14 OCWR, v.B.230, p. 137, loose leaf.

15 Henry C. Blinn, *The Manifestation of Spiritualism among the Shakers, 1837–1847* (East Canterbury, N. H., 1899), p. 45.

16 Ibid., pp. 83–84.

17 OCWR, x.B.31, pp. 173–174.

18 WLCMs, no. 291, entry for Oct. 15, 1843.

19 NYPLMs, 58-M-140, vol. 7, entry for Aug. 29, 1842.

20 Ibid., entry for Nov. 9, 1842.

21 OCWR, x.B.31, p. 174.

22 OCWR, iv.B.35, p. 115, a copy of Letter, Hancock, June 20, 1838, Ministry to South Union, and ibid, p. 92, a copy of Letter, Union Village, Aug. 29, 1838, to South Union.

23 NYPLMs, op. cit., loc. cit.

24 OCWR, v.B.241, entry for May 4, 1839. When instruments at Enfield, N. H., similarly used "outrageous language" on one occasion, the interpretation of their behavior was that evil spirits had seized them—cf. NYPLMs, 58-M-140, vol. 7, entry for Jan. 27, 1845.

25 MS SH–4, pp. 165–166.

26 NYPLMs, op. cit., entry for Nov. 9, 1842.

27 Giles B. Avery, quoted in Blinn, pp. 69–70.

28 NYPLMs, op. cit., loc. cit.

29 NYPLMs, ibid., p. 273. Defections like that of John Allen, who absconded with three other members, also caused much "depression of spirit . . . and struggling thro' dark & gloomy prospects."—cf. DWt, SA760, p. 176.

30 Hervey Elkins, *Fifteen Years in the Senior Order of Shakers* (Hanover, N. H., 1853), p. 54.

31 OCWR, x.B.31, p. 173.

PART XI

1 OCWR, Letter, Lebanon, N. Y., Apr. 3, 1838, Seth, to Canterbury Ministry, p. [3].

2 Henry C. Blinn, *The Manifestations of Spiritualism among the Shakers* (East Canterbury, N. H., 1899), p. 31.

3 NYPLMs, 58-M-140, vol. 1, entry for Dec. 1837.

4 OCWR, Letter, Lebanon, N. Y., Apr. 3, 1838, Seth, to Canterbury Ministry, p. [3].

5 On seeing secular dancing in 1873 Elder Henry Blinn was struck by the parallels. He had arrived at Pleasant Hill, and the black and white hired men came up one evening to the Office to honor this Eastern visitor with fiddling and dancing. As they executed one dance in which "all four persons took part," Blinn thought its "movements" similar to one of the "visionary dances" that the children at Canterbury had learned thirty years earlier.—See "A Journey to Kentucky in the Year 1873," *The Shaker Quarterly*, 5 (Winter 1965), 128.

6 OCWR, v.B.97, p. 72.

7 MS EC–11, p. 58.

8 MeSL, Aurelia Mace, [Commonplace Book], entry for May 5, 1896.

9 This account is based upon MS EC–11, pp. 59–60, and OCWR, v.B.97, entry for Dec. 1, 1837.

10 OCWR, viii.A.73, Item 5, pp. 8–9.

PART XII

1 See the headnote for Gift Song no. 50.

2 Charles E. Robinson, *A Concise History of the United Society of Believers Called Shakers* (East Canterbury, N. H., 1893), p. 116.

3 "The Shakers," *Harper's New Monthly Magazine*, 15 (1857), 169, and Emory Holloway, "Walt Whitman's Visit to the Shakers," *Colophon*, pt. 13 (Spring 1930), p. [8], where the text of Lossing's field notes is printed under the erroneous impression that Whitman was the author.

4 DWt, SA144, entry for July 24, 1842.

5 WLCMs, no. 241, p. 448.

6 OCWR, v.B.172, entry for Pleasant Hill.

7 NHCb, Henry C. Blinn, "A Historical Record of the Society of Believers in Canterbury, N. H.," i, 39.

8 Eldress Marguerite Frost recalled 1913 as the last year when laboring was practiced at Canterbury (interview with author, July 1963); Aurelia Mace stated that at Gloucester the marches "were closed altogether" in 1903 (MeSL, [Commonplace Book], entry for Apr. 6, 1896); Sr. Mildred Barker remembers their use in the meetings of the young people at Alfred perhaps as late as 1930; Ezra J. Stewart, writing an article on "Sunday among the Shakers" for the Washington *National Tribune*, July 18, 1918, stated that at that time the march was still practiced—but this article does not make clear which community he was describing.

9 OCSH, "Recollections of North Union Shaker Colony" (tape-recorded interview, Nov. 23, 1962).

10 This account is based on MS EC–11, p. 547; MeSL, Aurelia Mace, [Commonplace Book], entry for May 6, 1896; Henry C. Blinn in OCWR, vii.B.10, p. 31; WLCMs, no. 20, pp. 6–7; and WLCMs, no. 241, p. 14. See also Faith Clark's useful directions in NYOC, Ac. 17,917, p. 14.

PART XIII

1 Cf. MSS L–314, p. 118, and L–202, p. [72].

2 "The Shakers," *Harper's New Monthly Magazine*, 15 (1857), 168–169.

PART XIV

1 OCWR, SM506, pp. [9–14].

2 Lillian Phelps, "Shaker Music: A Brief History" (Canterbury, N. H., n.d.), p. [1].

3 OCWR, Letter, Enfield, Conn., Sept. 11, 1872, to Ministry, Watervliet, N. Y., pp. 2–3.

4 OCWR, v.B.70, entry for Apr. 23, 1869; WLCMs, no. 241, pp. 410–415.

5 OCWR, iv.B.20, p. [70].

6 OCWR, SM506, passim, and WLCMs, no. 241, p. 421.

7 OCWR, v.B.70, entry for Apr. 6, 1874; MeSL, Letter, Gloucester, Feb. 21, 1873, to Ministry, Watervliet, N. Y., in "Letter Book, May 1872–Jan. 1883," p. 63; OCWR, SM506, pp. [1–5].

8 WLCMs, no. 241, pp. 410–412.

9 Ibid., pp. 313, 415.

10 Lillian Phelps, pp. [2] and [6].

11 A. B. Harris, "Among the Shakers," *The Granite Monthly*, 1 (Apr. 1877), 24; Anna White and Leila S. Taylor, *Shakerism, Its Meaning and Message*, p. 339.

12 Compare *Original Shaker Music Published by the North Family, of Mt. Lebanon, Col. Co., N. Y.* (New York, 1893), pp. 34–35, with S. P. Bayard, *Hill Country Tunes* (Philadelphia, 1941), no. 90, and *Original Shaker Music*, p. 47, with G. P. Jackson, *White Spirituals in the Southern Uplands* (Chapel Hill, 1933), p. 178.

13 "Forgiveness" in *Original Shaker Music*, p. 123.

14 On visits to Canterbury I was generally directed to Eldress Marguerite as the one sister with an interest in the older songs. Other sisters there had knowledge of some of the songs but preferred to sing the later repertory.

15 From an interview recorded by Tom Davenport at Sabbathday Lake on May 29, 1972, in the University of North Carolina Folk Music Archives.

16 MeSL, Letter, Gloucester, Feb. 21, 1873, to Ministry, Watervliet, N. Y., in "Letter Book, May 1872–Jan. 1883," p. 65.

17 OCWR, iv.B.20, p. 69.

18 WLCMs, no. 241, p. 313. The writer, William Redmon, complained, "we are worn out in the Tread Mill, of theology; we want something, innocent, more exacting and Intellectual" (p. 240).

19 From an interview with Miss Florence Phelps recorded by the author in Gloucester, Mass., Aug. 1974, in the University of North Carolina Folk Music Archives.

20 See Bryan Wilson's discussion of "Sect Development" in *Religious Sects: A Sociological Study* (New York, 1970), pp. 233ff.

21 OCWR, Letter, Pleasant Hill, Apr. 1, 1820, Elder Samuel Turner to Br. Calvin, in iv.B.34, p. 136.

22 MS L–75, p. 9.

23 WCLMs, no. 246, p. 359, and no. 53, p. 8.

24 OCWR, Letter, Lebanon, N. Y., Aug. 6, 1830, Isaac N. Youngs to Andrew, p. [3].

25 *An Account of the Matter, Form, and Manner of a New and Strange Religion . . .* (Providence, R. I., 1781), pp. 7, 12.

26 Benjamin S. Youngs, *Testimony of Christ's Second Appearing*, 4th ed. (Albany, N. Y., 1856), pp. 584–588.

27 OCWR, vii.B.17, pp. 27–28.

28 Frances A. Carr, ed., "Mother Lucy's Sayings Spoken at Different Times and under Various Circumstances," *The Shaker Quarterly*, 8 (Winter 1968), 105.

CHECKLIST OF SHAKER SONG MANUSCRIPTS

1 OCWR, Letter, South Union, Ky., Jan. 26, 1835, Harvey L. Eades to Isaac N. Youngs, p. [2]; KBGK, Shaker Record A, entry for Sept 1, 1834.

2 See Edward D. Andrews's discussion of Sister Alice Smith's attitude toward the gift drawings in *Visions of the Heavenly Sphere: A Study in Shaker Religious Art* (Charlottesville, 1969), p. [3]; for a history of the collection at OCWR, see Kermit J. Pike, "Shaker Manuscripts and How They Came to be Preserved," *Manuscripts*, 29 (Fall 1977), 226–236.

3 R. Mildred Barker, "A History of 'Holy Land'—Alfred, Maine," *The Shaker Quarterly*, 3 (Fall 1963), 90.

4 OCWR, v.B.36, pp. 50, 55.

Index of Persons and Subjects

Index of First Lines and Titles

Index of Non-Shaker Songs Cited

Library of Congress Cataloging in Publication Data

Patterson, Daniel Watkins.
    The Shaker spiritual.
    "Checklist of Shaker song manuscripts" : p. 479.
    "Checklist of additional manuscripts cited" : p. 529.
    Includes index.
    1. Shakers—Hymns—History and criticism. 2. Shakers
—Hymns. 3. Folk-songs, American—History and criticism.
4. Folk-songs, American. 5. Folk dancing—United
States. I. Title.
ML3178.S5P4   [M2131.S4]   783'.026'98   77-85557.
ISBN 0-691-09124-2